THE COLLECTED PAPERS OF
FRANCO MODIGLIANI

VOLUME 2

The Life Cycle Hypothesis of Saving

THE COLLECTED PAPERS OF FRANCO MODIGLIANI

Edited by Andrew Abel

The MIT Press

Cambridge, Massachusetts, and London, England

Second printing, 1986
Portrait of Franco Modigliani by Bachrach Photographers of Boston, Massachusetts.

See pages 523–524 for acknowledgments to publishers.

Printed and bound by Edwards Brothers, Inc.
in the United States of America

Library of Congress Cataloging in Publication Data

Modigliani, Franco.
The collected papers of Franco Modigliani.

Includes bibliographical references and indexes.
CONTENTS: v. 1. Essays in macroeconomics.—v. 2. The life cycle hypothesis of saving.—v. 3. Essays in the theory of finance. Stabilization policies. Essays in international finance. The role of expectations and plan in economic behavior. Miscellanea.
1. Economics—Addresses, essays, lectures. I. Abel, Andy.
HB171.M557 330 78-21041
ISBN 0-262-13150-1 (v.1)
ISBN 0-262-13151-X (v. 2)
ISBN 0-262-13152-8 (v. 3)

TO SERENA

CONTENTS

Volume 2 The Life Cycle Hypothesis of Saving

Preface ix

Introduction xi

Part I. Antecedent and Overview

1. "Fluctuations in the Saving-Income Ratio: A Problem in Economic Forecasting," *Studies in Income and Wealth*, vol. 11, pp. 371–402, 427–431. New York: National Bureau of Economic Research, 1949. Paper presented at Conference on Research in Income and Wealth. 3
2. "The Life Cycle Hypothesis of Saving Twenty Years Later," *Contemporary Issues in Economics*, edited by M. Parkin, pp. 2–36. Manchester University Press, 1975. 41

Part II. The Theory

3. "Utility Analysis and the Consumption Function: An Interpretation of Cross-Section Data," (with Richard Brumberg), *Post Keynesian Economics*, edited by Kenneth K. Kurihara, pp. 388–436. Rutgers University Press, 1954. 79
4. "Utility Analysis and Aggregate Consumption Functions: An Attempt at Integration," (with Richard Brumberg). MIT Press, 1979. 128
5. "Consumption Decisions Under Uncertainty," (with Jacques Drèze), *Journal of Economic Theory* 5 (December 1972): 308–335. 198

Part III. Empirical Verifications

6. "The 'Permanent Income' and the 'Life Cycle' Hypothesis of Saving Behavior: Comparison and Tests," (with Albert Ando), *Consumption and Saving*, vol. 2, pp. 74–108, 138–147. Wharton School of Finance and Commerce, University of Pennsylvania, 1960. 229

7. "The 'Life Cycle' Hypothesis of Saving: Aggregate Implications and Tests," (with Albert Ando), *American Economic Review* 53, part 1 (March 1963): 55–84. 275

8. "The Consumption Function in a Developing Economy and the Italian Experience," (with E. Tarantelli), *American Economic Review* 65 (December 1975): 825–842. 305

9. "The Life Cycle Hypothesis of Saving, the Demand for Wealth and the Supply of Capital," *Social Research* 33 (Summer 1966): 160–217. 323

10. "The Life Cycle Hypothesis of Saving and Intercountry Differences in the Saving Ratio," *Induction, Growth and Trade: Essays in Honour of Sir Roy Harrod,* edited by W. A. Eltis, M. FG. Scott, and J. N. Wolfe, pp. 197–225. Oxford: Clarendon Press, 1970. 382

Part IV. Policy Applications

11. "Long-run Implications of Alternative Fiscal Policies and the Burden of the National Debt," *Economic Journal* 71 (December 1961): 730–755. 415

12. "Monetary Policy and Consumption: Linkages via Interest Rate and Wealth Effects in the FMP Model," *Consumer Spending and Monetary Policy: The Linkages,* Conference Series No. 5, pp. 9–84. Federal Reserve Bank of Boston, June 1971. 442

Contents of Volumes 1 and 3 519

Acknowledgments 523

Name Index 525

PREFACE

The essays collected in these volumes represent a selection of my scientific contribution to economics published over a span of nearly four decades. The volumes do not include more popular writings in newspapers, magazines, and the like.

This collection has been on the drawing board for a good many years. But I kept postponing it on the grounds that there were one or more nearly finished papers whose inclusion in the collection seemed to me essential to elucidate my thinking. As it turned out, those essays took much longer than expected to reach publication. By the time they were ready, there were always some new, almost completed papers to take their place. I have finally been persuaded by many friends not to tarry any longer, especially since I have at long last come to realize that there is no such thing as "the final word."

I wish to express my gratitude to Andy Abel for undertaking the task of editing these volumes. He waded patiently through most of my writings, helped me in the final selection, and also meticulously looked out for needed corrections due to misprints or more serious errors. Such corrections are reported in the errata at the end of each essay. Fortunately, and to my pleasant surprise, Andy's zealous effort has yielded a surprisingly meager crop of errors. All the essays have been reprinted in their original form, with the single exception of an unpublished paper with Richard Brumberg, which appears in volume 2.

Throughout my career I have had the good fortune to be associated with stimulating colleagues. Many of these associations have blossomed into scientific collaborations, as evidenced by the substantial number of joint papers included in this selection. I wish to express my appreciation for permission to reprint these joint papers and extend my thanks to these coauthors for their contribution to these volumes: Albert Ando, Hossein Askari, the late Richard Brumberg, Kalman J. Cohen, J. Phillip Cooper, Jacques Drèze, Emile Grunberg, the late Franz Hohn, Dwight Jaffee, Peter Kenen, Giorgio La Malfa, Merton H. Miller, Tommaso Padoa-Schioppa, Lucas Papademos, Robert Rasche, Robert Shiller, Richard Sutch, Ezio Tarantelli, Stephen J. Turnovsky, H. Martin Weingartner.

My thanks go also to my secretary, Judy Mason, who not only helped with these volumes but patiently typed countless, almost illegible, drafts of many of the essays collected here.

Finally, I want to acknowledge my gratitude to my wife Serena, knowing that words can not adequately accomplish this task. Throughout the forty years of our married life she has given me the encouragement to aim for the stars while trying her best to see that my feet remained planted on the ground.

INTRODUCTION

I have chosen to arrange the papers collected in these three volumes by topic—except when a paper covers more than one topic. Under each topic the order is generally chronological. The major exceptions are the lead papers in volumes 1 and 2. In volume 1 the first paper is one of my most recent contributions, the Presidential Address to the American Economic Association in 1976. I feel that this essay serves as an overview of my present thinking on macroeconomics, the focus of my contribution to economics and of these volumes. Its numerous references to other papers contained in the volumes make it a useful guide to the entire collection.

The topical arrangement helps to bring into relief the basic theme that has dominated my scientific concern, namely that of sorting out the lasting contribution of the Keynesian revolution by (1) integrating the main building blocks of the *General Theory* with the more traditional and established methodology of economics that rest on the basic postulate of rational maximizing behavior on the part of economic agents; (2) testing and estimating the resulting structure by means of empirical data; and (3) applying the results to policy issues, including the issue raised by the monetarist counterrevolution as to whether there is a valid case for active policies.

The first line of endeavor has been pursued from my very first significant scientific contribution in 1944, which appears as the second essay in part I of volume 1. Its main purpose was to examine to what extent the novel results of the *General Theory,* including its explanation of ''equilibrium'' unemployment, could be traced to the unorthodox assumption of wage rigidity. My conclusion was that the ability of the model set out in the *General Theory* to explain the persistence of unemployment could be traced primarily to the assumption of wage rigidity. The one exception was the so-called liquidity trap, or "Keynesian case." It is logically of undeniable importance, although its empirical relevance appears now very limited, especially once the message of the Keynesian revolution served to innoculate the economy against the repetition of the Great Depression.

The same basic issue, as well as the analysis of the working of monetary and fiscal policies in a system with rigid wages (at least in the short run), was picked up some twenty years later in the third essay, a more polished and rigorous presentation benefiting from later developments, including valuable criticisms of the previous essay. This paper also attacked a new issue, namely how the working of the system is affected if the standard assumption of competitive money and credit markets is replaced by that of systematic credit rationing.

The conclusion of these two essays concerning the monetary mechanism is supported and illustrated in the last two papers of part I, but this time with the benefit of specific estimates of the relevant parameters. The estimates were the result of a lifelong concern with empirically modeling and testing the main behavioral equations of the Keynesian system, a concern that is evidenced by many of the essays collected in these volumes. This endeavor found a synthesis with the construction of the so-called FMP (Federal Reserve-MIT-University of Pennsylvania) Econometric Model of the United States in the second half of the 1960s, in collaboration with Albert Ando—an invaluable lifelong associate in this as well as numerous other undertakings—Frank deLeuw, and many others.

As is well known, the Keynesian system rests on four basic blocks: the consumption function, the investment function, the demand for and supply of money and other deposits, and the mechanisms determining wages and prices. The two essays in part II of volume 1 deal with the derivation and estimation of demand and supply functions for currency and deposits, based on the assumption of (expected) profit maximization on the part of banks and deposit holders, with proper allowances for U.S. institutional features and the cost of adjustment.

The original streamlined Keynesian model assumed that one interest rate controlled both the demand and supply of money and the rate of investment in various types of physical assets. In reality what is determined in the money market is a short-term nominal rate (or a family of closely interrelated short-term rates), whereas investment in physical assets, whose very nature is durability, must respond to long-term real yields of a maturity commensurate to the life of the asset. Furthermore, the yields also must generally reflect the uncertainty of the cash flow generated by physical assets in contrast with the contractual certainty of the return from loan instruments. The three essays in part III are devoted to modeling the relationship between short- and long-term nominal yields on loans. Earlier work had provided a definitive answer to the nature of that relation in a world of certainty; to wit, that the long-term rate depends, in a well-defined fashion, on the path of short-term rates over the life of the long-term instrument. The first essay in part III, written with Richard Sutch—one of the many outstanding graduate students with whom I have been blessed—proposes and tests an extension of this earlier model to a world of uncertainty, dealing with both the formation of expectations of future rates and the effect of their uncertainty. The second essay, also written with Richard Sutch, uses the same framework to test the then-fashionable view that the term structure could be readily and significantly manipulated through changes in the maturity structure of the national debt ("operation twist"); the results were negative. The third essay, the result of collaboration with another outstanding graduate student, Robert Shiller, extends the model to a world characterized by significant and uncertain inflation—an extension inspired by the experience of recent years. It also shows that the hypothesis about the formation of expectations embedded in the model is consistent with rational expectations.

The relationship between the bond yield and the return required to justify an investment in risky physical assets is developed in three essays, the results of a long and productive cooperation with Merton H. Miller. Because the issue examined and the method of attack fall somewhat outside traditional macroeconomics and lie close to the heart of the theory of corporate finance, the essays are grouped under the heading of "Essays in the Theory of Finance" in volume 3. Indeed, their greatest impact has been in the field of corporate finance—at least if one is to judge from the efforts devoted to refute them. The basic message that has caused all the furor is that (1) in a world of uncertainty, the maximization of profit criterion is ill defined and must be replaced by the maximization of market value and (2) with well-functioning markets (and neutral taxes) and rational investors, who can "undo" the corporate financial structure by holding positive or negative amounts of debt, the market value of the firm—debt plus equity—depends *only* on the income stream generated by its assets. It follows, in particular, that the value of a firm should not be affected by the share of debt in its financial structure or by what will be done with the returns—paid out as dividends or reinvested (profitably). In essence, it will be determined by the capitalization of the expected stream of returns before interest at the rate which differs from the sure loan rate by a risk factor reflecting the risk characteristics of that stream. From the viewpoint of macroeconomics, the main implication of the analysis is that there exists one further slip between monetary policy and the investment component of aggregate demand, namely the risk premium required by the market to induce it to hold equities (or directly physical assets) instead of bonds.

Part IV of volume 1 deals with another major critical building block, investment in physical capital, which the early Keynesians (if not Keynes himself) tended to regard as largely unpredictable and capricious. The essay reproduced in this part—the result of teamwork with three coauthors, Albert Ando, Robert Rasche, and Stephen Turnowsky—endeavors to derive an aggregate investment function from the classical postulates of maximization over the relevant horizon, allowing for both technological progress and the effect of (anticipated) inflation. The function relies on the twin assumptions of a putty-clay technology—whose implications for aggregate investment were developed earlier in a path-breaking contribution by Charles Bischoff—and of oligopolistic pricing behavior as elaborated in the essay, "New Developments on the Oligopoly Front," reproduced in part V. The resulting aggregate investment function appears to account quite well for the behavior of investment in the postwar U.S. economy.

The concluding part V of volume 1 contains my main published contributions to the analysis of the mechanism determining wages and prices. I must acknowledge that the models of wage determination proposed and tested in these papers—aside from the analysis of the dynamics of the flows through the labor market inspired by the work of Charles Holt—remain, in good part, in the old Keynesian tradition of empirical generalization and are not supported by a rigorous analysis based on maximizing behavior. But then I do not believe that anyone else has yet provided a convincing analysis satisfying this requirement while accounting for the distressing slowness with which wages and prices appear to respond to unutilized labor and plant capacity. Indeed, the modeling of wage behavior remains to this day the Achilles heel of macroeconomic analysis.

The remaining basic building block of the Keynesian system, the consumption or saving function, is the one to which I have unquestionably dedicated the greatest attention, and it in turn has provided me with the greatest reward. Volume 2 is entirely devoted to twelve essays dealing with this subject.

The second contribution offers a recent overview of the life cycle hypothesis of saving (LCH), the empirical support for it that has been built over the years, and some major implications of both an analytical type and a policy type, providing appropriate references to other papers collected in volume 2. It first reviews the foundations of the model, as laid out in the early 1950s, by relying on the classical postulates of utility maximization applied to a decision horizon consisting of the household's life cycle. It then shows that this framework, once supplemented by some plausible assumptions about the nature of tastes and combined with well-established regularities about the profile of the life cycle of earnings, can provide a unified explanation for many well-known, but sometimes puzzling, empirical regularities in saving behavior. These include such disparate phenomena as the short-run cyclical variability and the long-run stability of the saving ratio; the long-run tendency for the proportion of income saved by a family at any given level of real income to decline as an economy develops; the evidence that family net worth tends to rise with age through much of life but tends to fall beyond dome point; or the finding that black families tend to save more than white families at any given level of income. At the same time, the model has yielded a number of implications, sometimes counterintuitive, that were not known at the time the model was proposed and have since been largely confirmed. Among these implications one might cite the apparent lack of significant association of the aggregate (private) saving rate with the economic well being of the country as measured by per capita real income or with the retention policies of corporate enterprises, and the very striking association of the saving rate with the rate of growth of per capita income and the age structure of the population.

Part II of volume 2 covers the basic LCH theory. The first two essays, which are the result of collaboration with a young graduate student, Richard Brumberg, lay the foundation for what has become known as the Life Cycle Hypothesis. The first contribution is well known, but the second was never published, as Richard Brumberg's untimely death sapped my will to undertake the revisions and tightening that would no doubt have been required to make the paper acceptable to one of the standard professional journals. Much of the content of the second essay has since become known through other papers and even through some limited private circulation. But some portions are still novel, notably the analysis of the implications of the LCH for the working of the so-called Pigou effect. It is shown that this effect is transient rather than permanent, as is usually supposed, and that it can maintain full employment equilibrium through time only on condition of a constant rate of deflation. As I see it now, this result has one further interesting "general equilibrium" implication that I intend to pursue at some future time. Once the nominal interest rate has been reduced to its institutional minimum, a steady (and hence fully anticipated) rate of deflation implies a real rate of interest at least as high as the rate of price decline. Accordingly, while steady deflation would reduce the rate of saving, it would (at least under neo-classical assumptions) also reduce the rate of investment. To establish that the Pigou effect can maintain full-employment equilibrium, one must, therefore, consider whether and under what conditions steady deflation can be expected to reduce saving more than investment.

The third essay of part II, the result of a collaboration initiated with Jacques Drèze when he too was a graduate student, examines the implications of uncertainty for saving within the general framework of the life cycle. Among the many results reported, one that is of particular interest for macroeconomics is the derivation of the rather restrictive sufficient conditions that allow for the saving decision to be independent of portfolio composition decisions—an independence that is usually taken for granted in macroeconomic models.

Part III focuses on the empirical verification of LCH. The first essay is the abstract of a much longer monograph, written with Albert Ando, devoted to cross-sectional verification. It also deals with clarifying the relationship between the LCH and its contemporary, the Permanent Income Hypothesis of Milton Friedman, which shares with LCH the postulate of utility maximizing over time as well as the powerful intellectual influence of Margaret Reid's work and teachings. The second and third essays, coauthored respectively with Albert Ando and Ezio Tarantelli, are devoted primarily to time series tests, one for the United States and the other for a developing country like Italy. The second essay also explores the implications of LCH with respect to the short- and long-run propensity to consume out of labor and property income, respectively. It is shown that these propensities will in general be different, a result qualitatively consistent with Kaldor's model of two castes—parsimonious capitalists and spendthrift laborers. However, according to the LCH, the long-run propensity to consume out of property income could very well exceed that out of labor income and, in fact, could exceed unity. These quantitative implications, shown to be consistent with the empirical evidence, are altogether irreconcilable with the Kaldorian paradigm and the many applications thereof.

The fourth essay examines and tests the implications of LCH with respect to the short- and long-run relationship between wealth and income, including inferences about the effect of the national debt on the stock of private wealth and private tangible wealth developed in the first essay of part 4. Finally, the last essay applies the LCH to the explanation of intercountry differences in the long-run saving rate, confirming the insignificant role of per capita income and the dominant role of the rate of growth of per capita income predicted by the model.

The two contributions in part IV apply the LCH to policy issues. In the first essay, the conceptual framework is used to throw new light on the classical issue of the burden of the national debt. It implies that the burden can be attributed to the public debt "crowding out" productive private capital with a resulting loss of income. To a first approximation, this loss is commensurate with the future flow of debt service, although it might be somewhat smaller or larger, depending on a variety of circumstances such as tax laws and the responsiveness of the demand for wealth to the rate of interest. The second essay shows that the LCH implies a novel channel by which monetary policy affects consumption, namely through the market value of wealth responding to changes in the capitalization rate of property income induced by changes in market interest rates. Furthermore, simulation experiments with empirically estimated parameters suggest that this mechanism could play a major role in the working of monetary policy, since the response to consumption is not only appreciable but also fast relative to other channels. However, these results must be regarded as tentative until a number of remaining conceptual issues have been clarified.

Volume 3 includes the balance of my selected works in macroeconomics and closely related areas, as well as a selection of papers in other areas. The first three essays in part I—"The Theory of Finance"—were discussed earlier in the introduction. The remaining two contributions examine the impact of inflation on financial markets and investment decisions, with special reference to the disruptive effects of inflation on the mortgage and housing markets. They also explore the role and consequences of the introduction of indexed loan contracts and summarize some results of a larger monograph on "Mortgage Designs for an Inflationary Environment," written by a research team at the Massachusetts Institute of Technology.

Part II brings together a number of contributions in which the view of the macroeconomic system set forth in all the preceding essays is brought to bear on various issues of policy. The lead essay, coauthored with Giorgio LaMalfa, analyzes the first Italian endeavor at dealing with a nominal wage explosion in 1963–64 still in a world of fixed parities. The second essay criticizes the U.S. economic policy in 1973 and warns that the Federal Reserve's announced policy of adhering strictly to a no-more-than 6 percent growth rate of the money supply would lead to a serious contraction—as it did. The main relevance of the third contribution, coauthored with Lucas Papademos, is found not in the policy recommendations as such but in its analysis of the reasons for the sharp differences in policies prescribed by different schools for dealing with the great stagflation beginning in 1974–75. It attempts to sort out the role of different views of the monetary mechanism, different estimates of the relevant parameters in contrast with different valuations of the cost of tolerating inflation and unemployment, and different assessments of the risks of entrusting government with discretionary powers. It concludes that analytical differences play a minor role compared to value judgments and even political philosophy. In other words, contrary to the popular stereotype, economists do not really disagree on policy as economists—they disagree as men.

The last essay in part II, coauthored with an Italian colleague, Tommaso Padoa-Schioppa, was again inspired by the recent Italian experience. It examines the nearly hopeless task confronting stabilization authorities in an economy in which, with the help of 100 percent indexation, powerful unions are able to fix the real wage rate arbitrarily. In a closed, and even more clearly in an open, economy the authorities are confronted with a Phillips-curve type trade-off between permanent inflation and unemployment that is worse the higher the real wage, and which cannot be improved by conventional demand policies. It is shown, in particular, that the inflation does not significantly depend on the size of the government deficit (within limits) and that, in fact, an endeavor to reduce the deficit by measures such as raising indirect taxes or reducing government employment is likely to increase rather than decrease inflation. Other means of improving the trade-off are explored, with disappointingly meager results.

Part III of volume 3 brings together a number of essays in international economics. This is an area to which I first devoted major attention in the second half of the 1940s while working on the book *National Income and International Trade* in collaboration with Hans Neisser. This collaboration proved to be of great educational value to me.

The first of the essays in part III marks my return to international economics fifteen years later. This contribution, as well as the second essay, represents an endeavor—not very successful—to improve the tottering Bretton Woods system by attacking some of the major shortcomings of the day. The first paper, coauthored with Peter Kenen, was written at a time when the U.S. balance of payment deficit was the main source of international liquidity, and yet the rest of the world was deeply troubled by the size and persistence of that deficit. We proposed as a solution the creation of a new international fiat money—the Medium for International Transactions, or MIT. Its quantity was to be regulated by the agreed upon reserve targets of the participating countries, thus solving the troublesome problem of the potential instability in the demand for reserves. At the same time, the adjustment mechanism was to be improved by symmetrical penalties on the deviations of reserves from the target in either direction, and through more flexibility in changing parities. A mechanism was even suggested for stabilizing the purchasing power of the new money. An international money was later created—though with the much less colorful name of Special Drawing Rights (SDR)—but the other more novel suggestions had no visible impact.

The second essay, written with Hossein Askari, came five years later, by which time an even larger U.S. balance of payment deficit, compounded by a deteriorating current account balance, had brought the Bretton Woods System to the verge of collapse. Now the major difficulty was arising from the inability of the United States to devalue its currency relative to other currencies and from the threat of mass demands for conversion of foreign official dollar claims into gold or an equivalent. The two demands made on the United States—that it should make the dollar freely convertible while forsaking the right of changing parity unilaterally—were clearly inconsistent. The inconsistency would be resolved by the United States giving up control over its exchange rate, which would be entrusted to the other countries, but at the same time making the dollar inconvertible de jure. In addition, holders of dollar reserves would be given an option of exchange rate guarantees in terms of the SDR, which was to be turned into a stable purchasing power money by letting the rate of exchange between the dollar and the SDR vary inversely with an index of the purchasing power of the dollar. As it turned out, by the time the proposal came out in print, the Bretton Woods system had already received its death blow through the unilateral suspension of convertibility of the dollar.

The third essay takes issue with the then-popular view that fixed parities could be made consistent with full employment and freedom of capital movements even in the presence of price rigidities, provided fiscal policy was used to offset the gap between full-employment saving and the sum of investment at the world interest rates and whatever current account balance might result from the given exchange rate and domestic price level. The essay shows that, in fact, this approach is highly wasteful because it is inconsistent with capital flowing from countries with a potential surplus of saving to those with a potential deficit. In the absence of price flexibility, the flow can be achieved only via adjustment in exchange rates. The purported solution, instead of preserving freedom of capital movement so that capital would move, relied, in effect, on fiscal policy to control the movement of capital for the sake of preserving freedom of capital movement.

The next essay in part III, written in cooperation with Hossein Askari, endeavors to analyze the effectiveness of alternative exchange regimes, ranging from fixed parities through crawling pegs to free floating rates, in terms of the twin criteria of allowing long-term capital movements and minimizing the international transmission of internal disturbances. The analysis points to the crawling peg as the most promising solution, with floating rates as a second best.

The last essay is one sample of my many testimonies offered over the years to congressional committees. It was given in the spring of 1974, but is based on two articles written in January 1974 for the Italian newspaper, "Il Corriere della Sera," at the height of the oil crisis. It provides an analysis of the problems created for the world economy by the rise in the price of oil and how they should have been handled to minimize the negative consequences, which, I feel, still makes good reading.

From 1949 to 1952, I was in charge of a research project on "Expectations and Business Fluctuations" financed on a generous scale (for the time) by the Merrill Foundation for the Advancement of Financial Knowledge. Part IV of volume 3 contains two contributions that have come out of the project. Both deal with the role of expectations and plans in economic behavior and with the nature of the relevant expectation and planning horizon. Although limitations of space have made it possible to include only a token representation of the outcome of the project, I want to stress that the impact of that research on my professional development goes well beyond what one might infer from the relative allotment of space. For instance, as is pointed out in the first note of each of the joint papers with Richard Brumberg, the Life Cycle Model was partly inspired by the analysis, undertaken in the course of that project, of the role of inventories in permitting smoothing of the production schedule, with attendant cost advantages, in the face of variability—predictable and unpredictable—of sales. Another fallout from that project is reflected in my contribution to the book *Planning Production, Inventories, and Work Force,* coauthored with C. C. Holt, H. Simon and J. Muth.

The single essay in the concluding part V was written with Emil Grunberg while we were colleagues at the then-Carnegie Institute of Technology. It was originally conceived as a clever essay in methodology but has since acquired a new interest. The problem posed in the essay, whether it is possible to make correct public forecasts given that those whose behavior is forecasted respond to the forecast was answered by means of Brower's fixed point theorem. But that problem is formally the same as the one posed by the analysis of the working of an economic system in which agents form rational expectations in the Muthian sense. These expectations must be correct on the average after allowing for the fact that the future realization depends on these expectations.

PART I
Antecedent and Overview

Part V

Fluctuations in the Saving-Income Ratio: A Problem in Economic Forecasting

Franco Modigliani
Institute of World Affairs

This paper was prepared in connection with a research project of the Institute of World Affairs. The author is greatly indebted to Hans Neisser, whose criticisms were of invaluable aid. Thanks are also due Adolph Lowe for reading the manuscript and making helpful suggestions, and to the staff of the Institute of World Affairs for making the computations.

I The Problem

Considerable attention has been given in recent literature to the problem of forecasting the main components of national income, especially the level of savings at full employment in an early post-transitional year such as 1950. Almost invariably the method consists in projecting the relations between national income or gross national product and its components observed in the decades of the 'twenties and 'thirties (or only in 1929–40) to the much higher level of income expected for the post-transitional period. The aim of this paper is to show that because of the violent cyclical fluctuations that characterized the period of observation the results tend to be systematically biased. Some criticism on this score has already been voiced by other authors,[1] but no systematic attempt has apparently been made to formulate it precisely, to test its validity, and to indicate its quantitative implications for purposes of estimation and of forecasting.

We shall examine several relations among economic variables, show that there is evidence of a pronounced discrepancy between the cyclical, or short-run, and the secular, or long-run, form of these relations, and suggest methods of analysis by which it seems possible to estimate both. Although the results are tentative and leave many questions unanswered, it is hoped that the broad lines of approach suggested will be of some use in improving the reliability of our long-range as well as short-run forecasts.[2]

II Recent Estimates of the Consumption Function

Starting with the crucial question of forecasting savings from disposable income, a procedure for which several methods have

[1] See, for example, Hart, 'Model Building and Fiscal Policy', *American Economic Review*, Vol. 35, No. 4 (Sept. 1945), especially pp. 533–6; Colin Clark 'Postwar Savings in the U. S. A.', Institute of Statistics, Oxford, *Bulletin*, Vol. 7, No. 6 and 7 (May 19, 1945), pp. 97ff. A. H. Hansen gives an illuminating discussion of this problem in his *Fiscal Policy and Business Cycles* (Norton, 1941), Ch. 11.

[2] This study was completed before the publication of the revised estimates of national income and its components by the Department of Commerce in August 1947 ('National Income', *Survey of Current Business*, Supplement, July 1947). No attempt has been made to revise the quantitative results obtained for the United States, because the new estimates do not go sufficiently far back to allow for a satisfactory test of the hypothesis advanced in this paper. The implications of the revised estimates are commented upon in the Postscript, Section XIV. We merely point out here that although the revisions would affect some of the

been employed, we consider briefly those suggested by Mosak, Woytinsky, and especially Smithies.[3]

Mosak's method is most open to criticism. It consists in using the relation between consumption expenditure and disposable income in current prices observed during 1929–40 as a first approximation to the consumption function of the American economy.[4] Applying this relation to his forecast of disposable income in 1950, which, assuming 1940 rates of taxation, would amount to about 154 billion current dollars, Mosak obtains an estimate of individual savings of nearly $22 billion, some 14 percent of disposable income.

This approach has been severely criticized by Woytinsky who points out the logical difficulties involved in extrapolating a relation between undeflated dollar series. More generally, the relation between undeflated dollar series tends to be systematically biased, especially when the time series are for a period characterized by cyclical fluctuations as violent as those of 1929–40. Theoretical considerations as well as statistical evidence indicate that there is a marked tendency for prices to fluctuate together with physical quantities during a cycle. The cyclical covariation of prices in turn tends to cause a marked positive correlation between the dollar series, even if the 'true' relation between the series in real terms is slight or negative.

Hence, the relation between series in current prices, even if more pronounced than that between the corresponding deflated series (as it often is) is an unreliable tool of analysis; extrapolation of such a relation implies, among other things, extrapolating the cyclical relation between movements of real income and prices, a particularly unjustified procedure in *long-range* forecasting.

---

specific quantitative estimates given below for the United States, they do not in any way invalidate the substance of the argument.

[3] J. L. Mosak, 'Forecasting Postwar Demands: III', *Econometrica*, Vol. 13, No. 1 (Jan. 1945), pp. 25–53; W. S. Woytinsky, 'Relationship Between Consumers' Expenditures, Savings, and Disposable Income', *Review of Economic Statistics*, Vol. 28, No. 21 (Feb. 1946), pp. 1–12; Arthur Smithies, 'Forecasting Postwar Demand: I', *Econometrica*, Vol. 13, No. 1 (Jan. 1945), pp. 1–14.

[4] Mosak's paper indicates that he was aware of the oversimplification involved in his approach but felt that it would not affect his results unduly.

These remarks explain in part why Mosak's formula leads to untenable results when applied to estimates of disposable income and consumption for the years immediately preceding World War I, when prices were disproportionately lower than income as compared with 1929–40. Thus, for 1913 when, according to the latest estimates of the Department of Commerce, disposable income amounted to about $33 billion and savings to $3 billion, Mosak's formula gives a level of savings of −$2 billion! If this formula fails so completely when extrapolated only fifteen years back to a much lower level of income, we cannot put much confidence in the results of extrapolating it ten years forward to a much higher level.[5]

None of the objections leveled against Mosak's type of approach can be raised against the extrapolation of the equation used by Smithies:

II 1 $$C = 76.58 + .76Y + 1.15(t - 1922).$$

C denotes real consumption, Y real income per capita (both in 1929 dollars), and t time. In the first place, Smithies' equation is based on the relation between deflated series (the deflator being the cost of living index), and in the second, the period of observation includes the seven relatively stable years 1923–29.

Despite these differences in approach, when Smithies' formula is applied to forecasting the level of individual savings at full employment in 1950, the results are strikingly similar to Mosak's. Thus, for a disposable income of $154 billion in 1943 prices (corresponding to Smithies' assumption C with respect to the tax structure) he, too, estimates savings to be $21–22 billion, some 14 percent of disposable income.

These results deserve closer examination. Smithies' equation not only gives a very close fit for the period of observation, but also, contrary to Mosak's, appears to explain satisfactorily the

[5] Note that the relations between 1913 and the period of observation, on the one hand, and that between 1950 and the period of observation, on the other, are similar in many respects. Both years are separated from the period of observation by a major war with a marked price rise. Also, the level of income that may be expected to prevail in 1950 at full employment is likely to be nearly as much above the average income for the period of observation as the income prevailing in 1913 is below it.

relation between income and consumption prevailing in earlier decades. In Smithies' own words, "applying the above formula to changes in Kuznets' national income figures we obtain a close approximation to changes in his consumption figures".[6] This, in turn, raises an interesting question. As is well known, Kuznets' estimates indicate that the ratio of consumption to net national product has remained remarkably stable in the five decades 1879–88 to 1919–28, fluctuating between a minimum of 88 and a maximum of 89.2 percent, and showed no tendency to fall with the secular increase in income. Similarly, according to the Department of Commerce estimates, the average ratio of consumers' expenditures to disposable income in 1923–40 amounted to about 91 percent and remained consistently above 88 percent (except in 1923 when it was 87.4 percent). If Smithies' formula satisfactorily explains the relation between income and consumption prevailing in this period, why does application of the same formula, when extrapolated to 1950, yield a consumption-income ratio of only 86 percent?

To answer this question we must note that, according to Smithies' equation, the consumption-income ratio depends upon the rate at which income grows. From this equation we can, in fact, derive the following:

II 2 $$\frac{C_t}{Y_t} = \frac{(76.6 + 1.15t')}{Y_t} + .76; \; (t' \text{ denotes } t - 1922)$$

Equation II 2 shows that the ratio $\frac{C_t}{Y_t}$ will tend to rise, fall, or remain constant depending upon whether the fraction on the right side tends to rise, fall, or remain constant; and this, in turn, obviously depends upon the relation between the coefficient of t

[6] Smithies, *op. cit.*, p. 6. Kuznets' figures are those given in his 'Uses of National Income in Peace and War', National Bureau of Economic Research, *Occasional Paper 6*, March 1942, p. 31, Table 2, and p. 35, Table 6. These estimates were somewhat revised in Kuznets' later study, *National Income: A Summary of Findings* (National Bureau of Economic Research, 1946). Since this book was not published until after our study had been completed, the discussion in the rest of this section is based on the earlier estimates referred to by Smithies. Certain implications of the new estimates are, however, discussed in note 10.

and the actual rate of growth of income in time. In particular, the income-consumption ratio will tend to fluctuate around a constant level $\propto$, if

$$\frac{76.6 + 1.15t'}{Y_t} + .76 = \propto$$

that is, if Y grows at the specific rate given by the formula:

II 2a $$Y_t = \frac{76.6}{\propto - .76} + \frac{1.15t'}{\propto - .76}$$

In the five decades covered by Kuznets, the consumption-income ratio fluctuated around .89. If we substitute this figure for $\propto$ in formula II 2a, the coefficient of t is approximately 8.8. In other words, it appears that if income per capita is growing in the long run at the average rate of about $8.8 per year, *then, and only then,* will the consumption-income ratio computed from Smithies' equation tend to fluctuate around a constant long-run level of .89. The average growth of income per head in Kuznets' estimates happens to be precisely $8.5 per year. This, then, explains why Smithies' formula seems consistent with the constancy of the saving-income ratio exhibited by Kuznets' estimates. On the other hand, according to Smithies' forecast, disposable income at full employment in 1950 would amount to $1,060–1,070 per capita in 1929 prices, while the corresponding figure in 1940 was only $675. His forecast therefore implies an increase in real income per capita of nearly $40 per year from 1940 to 1950. With such an unprecedented rate of growth, Smithies' formula naturally leads to a saving-income ratio 20 to 30 percent higher than that implicit in Kuznets' historical estimates, and 40 and 60 percent higher than the ratio of saving to disposable income in the 'twenties and 'thirties, as estimated by the Department of Commerce.

We do not intend to discuss here whether the optimism of Smithies and of many other investigators in forecasting such a stupendous growth in the years to come is at all justified.[7] The

[7]It is true that by 1941 income per capita had already risen to about $775. Still, Smithies' forecast would imply an annual increase from 1941 to 1950 of some $30 per head. Inasmuch as in 1941 we were very close to full employment, this rise in income would have to be brought about almost exclusively by increases in

question that interests us here is whether, assuming the correctness of this forecast, we can put much confidence in the projection of Smithies' formula to a period when income is assumed to be rising at a rate about eight times as high as during the period of observation, and five times as high as during the period covered by Kuznets' data, to which this formula was applied. In other words, is the rise in the saving-income ratio (the fall in the consumption-income ratio) that follows from Smithies' formula for periods of rapid rise in income acceptable in the light of statistical experience?

Table 1 contains a partial answer. Although Smithies' formula gives a surprisingly good approximation to the actual total change in savings over the period as a whole, it fails rather badly in each subperiod in which the growth of income was markedly different from the critical rate of $8.8 per year (col. 4). The reason is not hard to find. As we have just seen, according to Smithies' formula the consumption-income ratio depends upon the rate at which income grows. Kuznets' estimates, on the other hand, show that the fluctuations in this ratio were not only very small but were essentially unrelated to the rate of growth of income. It must be noted in particular that in the last decade covered by Table 1, when per capita income rose at an annual rate of $16, or twice as high as the critical rate, Smithies' formula is biased distinctly upward, indicating an increase in savings 26 percent larger than the actual increase. How then can we apply this formula with confidence to a period in which income is supposed to grow at an even faster rate?

Since the publication of Smithies' paper, the Department of Commerce has made available revised estimates of disposable income and consumption for 1919–28[8]. If Smithies' method is applied to these revised data, the results are:

II 3 $$C = 71.7 + 78Y + .83(t - 1922)$$

---

productivity. (Also Smithies' forecast of disposable income includes a small amount of nonproduced income or net transfer payments; these, however, represent less than 2 percent of disposable income.)

[8] These estimates are reproduced in the Appendix Table, columns (1) and (2).

TABLE 1

Changes in Kuznets' Estimates of Savings compared with Changes computed by Smithies' Formula

Period	Changes in Av. Annual Savings (billions of current $)		% of Error $\frac{(3) - (2)}{(2)}$	Av. Annual Rate of Change in Real Income per Capita ($, 1929 prices)
	As given by Kuznets[a]	As est. by Smithies' formula[b]		
(1)	(2)	(3)	(4)	(5)
1879–1888 to 1889–1898	.42	−.08	−120	+3
1884–1893 to 1894–1903	.40	+.19	−52	+5.6
1889–1898 to 1899–1908	.84	+.83	−1	+8.8
1894–1903 to 1904–1913	1.17	1.08	−8	+8.1
1899–1908 to 1909–1918	1.83	1.29	−30	+6.1
1904–1913 to 1914–1923	3.57	2.83	−21	+8.7
1909–1918 to 1919–1928	3.63	4.58	+26	+16.1
1879–1888 to 1919–1928	6.72	6.62	−1	+8.5

[a] 'Uses of National Income in Peace and War', National Bureau of Economic Research, *Occasional Paper 6*, 1942, p. 31, Table 2, col. 2. Kuznets uses the term 'net capital formation' rather than 'savings'.

[b] The figures in this column were computed as follows: Kuznets' net national product (*ibid.*, col. 1) was deflated by using the price index implicit in his conversion of consumer outlay to 1929 prices (p. 35, Table 6), and divided by the average population for each decade (*Statistical Abstract of the United States, 1944–45*, p. 8). Substituting the resulting real income per capita series in Smithies' equation and giving to t the value corresponding to the middle of each decade, we obtain a series of computed changes in real consumption per capita.

At this point there were two possible lines of procedure. We could subtract Kuznets' changes in real consumption and Smithies' changes in real consumption from Kuznets' changes in real income, thereby obtaining a true and 'computed' series of changes in real savings per capita. This comparison, not given in the table since we are more interested in comparing changes in aggregate savings in current dollars than changes in real savings per capita, shows percentages of error considerably greater than those in the table, ranging from a maximum of 150 percent for the first period to a minimum of 21 and 18 percent for the third and fourth periods, respectively, and amounting to 73 percent for the last period.

The other possible procedure—the one followed—was to transform the series of 'computed' *changes* in 'real consumption per capita' into a series of 'computed' real consumption per capita, adjusting the constant term in Smithies' equation so that actual and computed series would agree in the last decade. This series was then converted into aggregate consumption at current prices by multiplying it by the price index and average decade population. Subtracting this series from Kuznets' series of net national product in current prices we obtain 'computed' average yearly savings in current prices for each decade. From this series we computed changes in savings (col. 3).

The multiple correlation coefficient, though somewhat lower than that originally obtained by Smithies, remains very high, .991.[9] What is significant, however, is the sizable fall in the coef-

[9] Smithies has informed us that the correct figure should be .996, rather than .97 as given in *op. cit.*, p. 6, note 2.

ficient of time—from 1.15 to .83. The new time trend of consumption is no longer in line with the rate of growth of Kuznets' national income; the new equation therefore gives a distinctly worse approximation even for the aggregate change in savings from the first to the last decade.[10]

To conclude: although Smithies' hypothesis is theoretically consistent, his contention that it explains past developments satisfactorily is not fully warranted. In fact, if we accept Smithies' hypothesis that consumption depends essentially on current income, plus a trend factor entirely independent of income, we must accept also the hypothesis that the apparent long-run stability of the saving-income ratio is essentially due to chance, that is, to the coincidence of the time trend of income with the 'independent' time trend of consumption. The latter hypothesis, however, is obviously not very satisfactory and, furthermore, does not stand up well under closer examination of the data.

This criticism leads us to formulate a counter-hypothesis: (a) the apparent long-run stability of the saving-income ratio in the course of the gradual secular expansion of income is not due to chance, but rather to a structural property of the system, a consistent phenomenon that can be extrapolated; (b) the tendency for saving to fluctuate together with and proportionately more than income, which according to the available evidence has been very pronounced in the interwar decades, is a cyclical phenomenon.

The hypothesis that the relation between savings, consumption, and income might be influenced by cyclical conditions has already been advanced by other authors and has recently been tested by Woytinsky. His approach, however, is not very convincing inasmuch as he segregated 1931–34 from 1923–40, and fitted separate equations to 1931–34 and to the remaining years (1923–30 and

[10] Kuznets' revised estimates in *National Income: A Summary of Findings* imply an upward revision of the ratio of net capital formation to income up to the decade 1914–23 (p. 53, Table 16). While we did not recompute our Table 1 on the basis of the revised estimates (given in full in Kuznets' *National Income since 1869*, National Bureau of Economic Research, 1946), there is reason to believe that Smithies' equation, especially after the revision of the time trend indicated in the text, would significantly underestimate savings in the early decades.

1935–40). This procedure seems to us too arbitrary and we see no reason therefore to place much confidence in the extrapolation of the various regression equations Woytinsky obtained for the 'more or less prosperous years' which indicate that the saving-income ratio tends to fall as income rises. The distinction between prosperity and depression is obviously quantitative, not qualitative, and can therefore be measured. This idea will be developed in the next section as we proceed to formulate our hypothesis more precisely, to demonstrate that it can be tested statistically, and to show that there is support for it.

III An Alternative Hypothesis Tested for the United States

First we formulate operational definitions of what we mean by 'cyclical' and 'secular' changes in income. By the secular movement of income we mean a movement that carries real income per capita above the highest level reached in any preceding year; by cyclical movement we mean any movement, whether upward or downward, that leaves real income per capita below the highest previous peak.[11] These definitions may be conveniently given in symbolic terms. Let Y_t denote real income per capita in the year t and Y_t° denote the highest real income per capita realized in any year preceding t; the change in income between the year t and the year $(t + 1)$ will be called cyclical, if both Y_t and $Y_{t+1} < Y_t^\circ = Y_{t+1}^\circ$; otherwise, it will be called secular. The quantity $\dfrac{Y_t - Y_t^\circ}{Y_t}$ will be referred to as the 'cyclical income index'. In terms of the above definitions and symbols, the hypothesis we offer states that the proportion of income saved will be positively related to, and largely explained by, the cyclical income index.

In Chart 1 the saving-income ratio is plotted against the cyclical income index for the twenty years 1921–40, both quantities com-

[11] This is in accordance with Marshall's use of 'secular', since an expansion in income above the highest previous peak must, in general, be due to the gradual secular improvement in technology and/or an increase in capital per worker.

CHART 1

Relation between the Saving-Income Ratio and the Cyclical Income Index $\left(\frac{Y_t - Y_t^{\circ}}{Y_t}\right)$
United States, 1921–1940

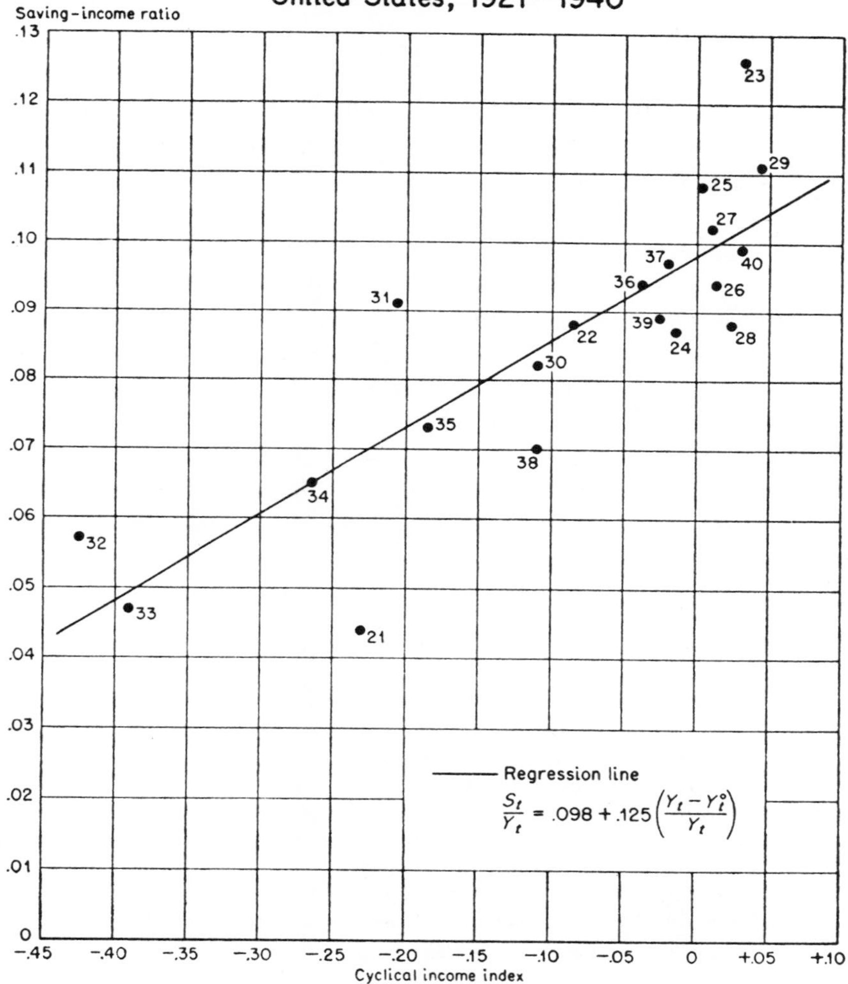

puted from the latest Department of Commerce estimates.[12] Evidently, between the two variables there is a marked direct

[12] For sources and methods of computation for these series, see Appendix references A and B.

relation which appears to be essentially linear. The coefficient of correlation is .84, definitely significant in view of the relatively large number of observations. The regression equation is:

III 1 $$S_t/Y_t = .098 + .125(Y_t - Y_t^{\circ})/Y_t$$

or

$$C_t/Y_t = .902 - .125(Y_t - Y_t^{\circ})/Y_t$$ [13]

According to this equation, if income were secularly constant savings would be about 10 percent of income, but if income rose r percent above or fell r percent below the previous peak, the ratio would change .125 (.01) r. (For instance, with a secular growth of 5 percent, the ratio would amount to approximately 10½ percent, while with a cyclical fall of 30 percent, it would amount to only about 6 percent.)

Our correlation coefficient cannot be compared directly with that obtained on Smithies' hypothesis, since the latter relates consumption to income, while in our equation it is the consumption-income ratio that is explained. To make a comparison, we must restate our hypothesis in terms similar to those of Smithies; this can be done by multiplying both sides of the equation III 1 by Y_t:

III 2 $$C_t = k\,Y_t - b(Y_t - Y_t^{\circ}) = (k-b)Y_t + b\,Y_t^{\circ}$$

This hypothesis can be tested by correlating consumption with Y_t and Y_t°. In making this test we shall also be answering one

[13] The analysis in the text refers exclusively to 1921–40, though the Department of Commerce has prepared estimates of disposable income and consumption as far back as 1909. It is, however, generally conceded that the margin of error in the estimates of savings for the period before 1919 is sufficiently wide to make the inclusion of these years inadvisable. Their inclusion would, we believe, reduce rather than increase the reliability of the regression equation for purposes of extrapolation. For the sake of comparison, we might add that with the inclusion of 1910–14 the correlation coefficient falls somewhat—from .84 to .77—and the regression equation changes only slightly:

$$S_t/Y_t = .094 + .114(Y_t - Y_t^{\circ})/Y_t$$

Finally, if we extrapolate our equation III 1 back to 1910-14 we get, in all cases, a distinctly better approximation to the Department of Commerce estimates of consumption than by extrapolating Smithies' equation II 3. Both equations underestimate the consumption-income ratio; in equation III 1, the underestimate ranges from zero to 3 percent.

important objection that can be raised against our initial approach: namely, that by using the saving–income ratio instead of saving itself as a dependent variable we are assuming *a priori* and without test that consumption is an homogeneous function of the independent variables. This assumption, however, should be tested by carrying out the correlation indicated by equation III 2, then examining whether the constant term in the resulting equation is sufficiently small to be consistent with the hypothesis that its true value is approximately zero. If we make the correlation the regression equation is:

III 3 $$C_t = 2(\pm 32) + .773Y_t + .125Y_t^\circ$$

The corresponding multiple correlation coefficient is .992,[14] practically the same as the coefficient, .993, obtained by applying Smithies' hypothesis to the revised Department of Commerce estimates for 1921–40.[15] Furthermore, the constant term in equation III 3 is evidently quite small and is statistically insignificant, being only a small fraction of its standard error, 32.

This last result is of particular interest from our point of view. The equations obtained by Mosak and Smithies (and by most other investigators as well) contain relatively large positive constants, implying that the marginal propensity to consume is less than the average and that changes in income tend to produce

[14] The simple and partial correlation coefficients are $r_{cy} = .988$; $r_{cy^\circ} = .15$; $r_{yy^\circ} = .07$; $r_{cy.y^\circ} = .992$; and $r_{cy^\circ.y} = .54$. The partial correlation $r_{cy^\circ.y}$ is not very high; nevertheless, in view of the large number of observations, it is statistically significant; in fact, by the usual test, its level of significance lies between 1 and 2 percent. Furthermore, the partial correlations are distinctly larger than the corresponding simple ones. Also, for the revised Smithies' equation, II 3, the partial correlation $r_{ct.y}$ is also only .59. If we use the ratio of the mean square successive difference to the variance of the residuals (hereinafter referred to as K) to test the randomness of the residuals in time, we get a value of 2.51. On a 5 percent level of significance, this value of K is not inconsistent with the hypothesis that the residuals are random. It is in this sense that we refer to K as insignificant in the discussion that follows. (See B. I. Hart and John von Neuman, 'Tabulation of the Probabilities for the Ratio of the Mean Square Successive Difference to the Variance', *Annals of Mathematical Statistics*, Vol. 13, pp. 207–14.) The appropriateness and efficiency of this test for our purpose is open to considerable doubt. Nonetheless, it appears to be as good a test as is available.

[15] The addition of the years 1921 and 1922 to the period originally used by Smithies (1923–40) raises Smithies' multiple correlation from .991 to .993.

less than proportional changes in consumption. On this basis both authors are led to conclude that the saving–income ratio is bound to increase whenever income rises (Mosak) or at least, whenever real income tends to rise at a sufficiently high average annual rate (Smithies).

Our results indicate instead that we must distinguish between (a) the short-run or cyclical marginal propensity to save, and (b) the long-run average and marginal propensity.

a) As long as income rises secularly, Y_t and Y_t° will rise together. Therefore, the saving–income ratio will depend not on income, but essentially on the rate of change in income. This can best be seen if we rewrite equation III 3 using the identity $S_t = Y_t - C_t$:

$$S_t = -2 + .102Y_t + .125(Y_t - Y_t^\circ)$$

Since the constant term is entirely negligible in comparison with the relevant values of Y, saving tends to represent approximately 10 percent of income plus some 12 percent of the increment of income. Because of the last term, the proportion of income saved will tend to vary somewhat in years of secular expansion, increasing as the rate of change in income accelerates.[16] But since the normal secular growth is in the order of 2 to 3 percent, we may conclude that the saving–income ratio will tend to fluctuate around a level of about $10\frac{1}{2}$ percent. This figure clearly measures also the proportion of any secular increment in income that will tend to be saved in the long run (that is, the long-run marginal propensity to save).

b) In the case of cyclical fluctuations in income, on the other

[16] Such a lag seems to explain, for instance, the high saving-income ratio for 1923 and 1929. It undoubtedly explains also, at least in part, the exceptionally high saving-income ratio for 1941, when, according to the Department of Commerce estimates, real income per capita increased 15 percent—three to four times more than the largest annual growth in the entire period of observation. If we extrapolate our equation to this year, we obtain a saving-income ratio that is higher than in any other year but still falls considerably short of the Department of Commerce figure, 15.9 percent. It is not unlikely that for exceptionally high secular rates of increase above the highest previous peak, the lag of consumption may be more pronounced (and possibly last longer) than indicated by our equation; this point will be briefly considered later. Extrapolation of Smithies' equation also fails to explain the behavior of consumption in 1941, since it gives the very same figure as our equations III 1 and 3.

hand, $Y_t°$ is fixed by definition. Hence, the relation between saving and income takes the form: $S_t = -(2 + .125Y_t°) + .23Y_t$. The cyclical marginal propensity to save is given by the coefficient of Y_t or .23, as compared with the secular marginal propensity of .10 to .11. Also, on account of the constant term, the saving–income ratio tends to fluctuate with income during each cycle, falling below the secular level as income declines and rising toward it again as income increases.[17]

IV The Common Sense of the Hypothesis

Is our hypothesis based on, or at least consistent with, realistic assumptions concerning economic behavior? Clearly, the confidence we can place in our results depends largely on the answer.

Our long-run hypothesis may at first appear entirely unrealistic. Casual observation, fully confirmed by all budget studies, reveals that the rich save more than the poor. However, both everyday experience and budget data relate to the behavior of different people at the same point of time, whereas our hypothesis concerns the behavior of aggregates in time. There is strong reason to suppose that as aggregate income increases, persons moving into progressively higher income brackets do not tend to acquire the saving habits characteristic of persons formerly in the income bracket; on the contrary, they may tend to save less. Indeed, it can easily be demonstrated that the hypothesis that they save as much would lead to rather absurd results.[18] Our tentative con-

[17] Our conclusions must, of course, be qualified to the degree that our estimates of the regression coefficients, especially that of $Y_t°$, are subject to error. What has been said, however, will help to make clear the full implications of our hypothesis and statistical results.

[18] All budget studies consistently show that the lowest group of income receivers as a whole tends to dissave a more or less substantial proportion of its income. Now, let us consider the 'break-even' income in the latest available budget study; then as we move back in time to lower and lower levels of aggregate income, we must expect to find a gradual increase in the proportion of income receivers who got less than this 'break-even' income. We should therefore be led to conclude that the proportion of income receivers who dissaved would also grow larger and larger as we move further back in time, a conclusion that can certainly not be considered very realistic. (The alternative would be to make even less realistic assumptions concerning changes in income distribution.)

clusion is, in fact, supported by a careful analysis of American budget material carried out by Dorothy S. Brady and Rose D. Friedman.[19] The reason persons in each income bracket tend to save less as aggregate income rises secularly, and the plausibility of our long-run hypothesis become apparent when one considers the nature of economic progress. Economic expansion is not characterized by the availability of increasing quantities of the same commodities, but rather by the continuous improvement of many old commodities and by the continuous appearance of entirely new ones. If consumers had no choice except to spend their increasing income on more and more of the very same commodities, then indeed it would not be surprising to find at least some relative increase in saving as income rises. Actually the increment in income accruing to each group of income receivers tends to be absorbed by the new commodities that gradually become available. If we compare the consumption of a family with a certain income in 1940 with that of a family with the same (real) income in 1870, we would expect to find that the additional spending of the 1940 family was absorbed by the purchase of commodities that did not exist in the earlier period. Thus, the hypothesis that the saving–income ratio tends to be relatively independent of the secular expansion of income (that is, in comparison with its cyclical behavior) is not unrealistic and also is not inconsistent with, but is supported by, budget data.

With respect to our cyclical hypothesis, there are numerous supporting factors. We confine ourselves here to considering briefly the three that seem to be quantitatively most important: (a) cyclical changes in the income distribution, (b) rigidity of acquired consumption habits, and (c) fluctuations in the level of unemployment.

a) There is some evidence that, at least for higher income brackets, the distribution of income tends to become less unequal as income contracts, and tends to resume its initial shape as income recovers. Though the quantitative importance of this phenomenon has not been firmly established, it is well known that agricultural income

[19] See 'Savings and Income Distribution', *Studies in Income and Wealth, Volume Ten*.

and profits in general tend to fluctuate proportionately more than other incomes during a cycle;[20] and there is good reason to suppose that profit earners or entrepreneurs, especially farm families, have, on the whole, a greater than average propensity to save.[21] We have, therefore, grounds for expecting that a cyclical fall in income will tend to be accompanied by a redistribution of income from groups having a greater propensity to save to groups with a smaller propensity to save, while a cyclical rise in income will have the opposite effect.[22]

b) A marked fall in income below an accustomed level, such as occurs during a cycle, creates strong pressure on acquired consumption habits. This pressure tends to be met by partly maintaining consumption at the expense of saving. That is, savings tend to bear the brunt of a cyclical change in income, falling proportionately more than consumption and income as income declines. Similarly, as income moves back toward the initial level, there is pressure to restore the initial relation between income and saving. In other words, the saving-income relation tends to retrace the same cyclical path in the opposite direction, saving rising relatively faster than consumption as income increases.[23]

It may be objected that if income remains below the highest previous level for a considerable time, there must be a tendency for consumers to become fully adjusted to the lower level by rearranging their expenditure pattern without waiting for income to recover. However, in the available estimates, there is no evidence of such an adjustment. In any case, such an adjustment is likely to be much less important than may appear at first glance, es-

[20] The proposition concerning the cyclical behavior of aggregate profits is tested in Section VIII.

[21] With regard to farm families, see Brady and Friedman, *loc. cit.*

[22] For a further theoretical discussion of this point, see, for instance, Michael Kalecki, *Essays in the Theory of Economic Fluctuations* (Farrar & Rinehart, 1939), pp. 42–74, especially p. 65, and pp. 116–49. Note that in his 'trendless economy' fluctuations in income coincide with what we have defined as cyclical fluctuations in income.

[23] This factor was especially stressed by James Duesenberry in a paper presented at a meeting of the Econometric Society in Atlantic City, N. J., in January 1947. Mr. Duesenberry independently developed and tested a hypothesis very similar to our equation III 1.

pecially in an expanding economy. First, income receivers are inclined to look upon a fall in income as temporary and therefore be less willing to make any further painful adjustments. Second, the individual does not consciously pattern his consumption habits on the period when his income was highest. Again, the point is that the secular expansion of income brings with it a continuous change in the types of commodities available and in the structure of expenditures. These commodities, as well as the habits of using them, obviously cannot disappear even when income falls to, or below, some previous level at which they did not exist. Finally, the quantitative importance of a gradual adjustment is further minimized by a third feature that characterizes the cycle.

c) As is well known, cyclical fluctuations in income are much more the result of changes in unemployment than of changes in the income of the employed.[24] The cyclical income index may therefore be expected to move in close harmony with the ratio of the unemployed to the total labor force. Now, if there is a long-run tendency for employed persons to consume a constant proportion of their income, any substantial fluctuation in the level of employment will cause consumption to fluctuate proportionately less than income, since though the unemployed produce no income, they necessarily maintain at least part of their consumption.[25] In other words, the level of savings corresponding to any given level of income tends to be lower (that is, the level of consumption tends to be higher), the greater the unemployment, since the savings of the employed are partly offset by the dissavings of the unemployed.

The above arguments explain why savings tend to fluctuate proportionately more than income as long as income fluctuates below its previous peak. But the same sort of consideration also explains why a similar relation holds when the cyclical income

[24] After the contraction of 1929, for instance, per capita income did not recover until 1940, but per capita income of employed persons had virtually recovered by 1935.

[25] This is not strictly true for disposable income, which includes transfer payments to the unemployed. See, further, Section V in which a statistical attempt to measure the influence of the specific factor of unemployment is discussed.

index is positive. As explained above, when this index is positive, it measures essentially the rate of growth in income, and if this rate is much higher than the normal secular rate determined by the rate of technological progress, the saving-income ratio too must tend to rise above its normal secular level. First, if the growth is larger than can be accounted for by technological progress, it must tend to be accompanied by a further fall in unemployment. Second, such a development is likely to be accompanied by features characteristic of boom years, such as abnormally high profits and raw material prices. Finally, our hypothesis states that eventually consumption will rise in proportion to income, but this adjustment may easily occur with some lag. It is theoretically conceivable that the relation between the saving-income ratio and the cyclical income index may not be the same quantitatively when the latter is positive and when it is negative. From the few observations at our disposal we cannot estimate separate relations, although there is some indication that the line of relation may be somewhat steeper for positive than for negative values of the cyclical income index.[26]

V Attempts at Refinements

Since the characteristic cyclical-secular pattern of saving is due to the joint action of several factors, should we not introduce these factors directly into the analysis instead of measuring them indirectly through the cyclical income index? There is no denying that the approach presented so far is greatly oversimplified. On the basis of theoretical considerations, one should introduce not only the specific factors mentioned in the preceding section but also other factors, some of general significance (for example, fluctuations in instalment credit, capital gains and losses, permanency of the highest previous income level), and some of special

[26] On this point see also note 16. The relation may not be linear. The difficulty of estimation is increased by the fact that the variance of the positive values of the cyclical income index must, because of its nature, be relatively small. Whereas there are no *a priori* limits to the negative values of the cyclical income index (since current income may theoretically fall to zero) the possibility of increases above the previous peak is generally limited by technological conditions.

significance for the United States in the period under consideration (for example, changes in income taxation and in the volume of transfer payments).

Any attempt to refine our approach, however, meets serious difficulties. For one thing, no estimates are available for some of the theoretically relevant variables; and those that are available are so crude as to make their value dubious for the purpose of refining the approach. Moreover, it is doubtful that the present estimates of consumption and saving are sufficiently accurate to justify a more refined approach involving a large number of independent variables, especially when we consider that the simple correlation between consumption and income is already in the order of .99. The most important consideration, however, is more technical. As we have argued, all the factors of greatest quantitative importance have a strong cyclical character and are highly intercorrelated among themselves and with the cyclical income index. Hence, even if we had the necessary statistical information, any attempt to measure the separate influence of each factor would lead at best to highly uncertain estimates. These *a priori* considerations are fully confirmed by certain attempts in this direction made during the course of this study.

One such attempt, which aimed at measuring the separate influence of unemployment, may be briefly described here both as an illustration of this point and for its intrinsic interest.

Total consumption may be considered to be made up of the consumption of the employed and of the unemployed. The first quantity (denoted below by C_E) may again be assumed to depend on the current and on the highest previous income: using E for the number employed, I for the aggregate income they earn (net of personal taxes), and $\frac{I_t^\circ}{E_t^\circ}$ for the highest previous income per employed person, we have:

$$\text{V 1} \qquad C_E = \left[\mathrm{a}\frac{I_t}{E_t} - \mathrm{b}\left(\frac{I_t}{E_t} - \frac{I_t^\circ}{E_t^\circ}\right)\right] E_t$$

$$= \mathrm{a}I_t - \mathrm{b}\left(\frac{I_t}{E_t} - \frac{I_t^\circ}{E_t^\circ}\right) E_t\,; \ (1 > \mathrm{a} > \mathrm{b} > 0)$$

Next, denoting by U the number unemployed, by C_U their consumption, and by TY the amount of transfer payments going to the unemployed, we may assume the following approximate relation:

$$\text{V 1a} \quad C_U = \left(\text{c} + \text{d}\frac{TY}{U}\right)U = \text{c}U + \text{d}TY; (\text{c} > 0, 0 < \text{d} < 1)$$

Adding V 1 and 1a, we have for total consumption, C:

$$\text{V 1b} \quad C = C_E + C_U = \text{a}I_t - \text{b}\left(\frac{I_t}{E_t} - \frac{I_t^{\circ}}{E_t^{\circ}}\right)E_t + \text{c}U + \text{d}TY$$

$$= \text{a}(I + TY) - \text{b}\left(\frac{I_t}{E_t} - \frac{I_t^{\circ}}{E_t^{\circ}}\right)E_t + \text{c}U + (\text{d} - \text{a})TY$$

Equation V 1b may conveniently be further transformed to express per capita consumption in terms of disposable income per capita and the proportion of unemployed workers. Denoting population by P, the labor force by L, and aggregate disposable income by $Y = I + TY$, and recalling that in the period of observation the labor force was practically a constant proportion of population (let us say, $L = \propto P$), we obtain:

$$\text{V 1c} \quad \frac{C}{P} = \text{a}\frac{Y}{P} - \propto \text{b}\left(\frac{I_t}{E_t} - \frac{I_t^{\circ}}{E_t^{\circ}}\right)\frac{E}{L} + \propto \text{c}\frac{U}{L} + (\text{d} - \text{a})\frac{TY}{P}$$

An attempt was made to test equation V 1c statistically for 1923–40, although information on employment and unemployment is far from satisfactory. The subscripts 1 through 5 refer to the variables of equation V 1c in the order in which they appear. If we first correlate per capita consumption with income per capita and the coefficient of unemployment, we obtain results very similar to those obtained for the hypothesis of equation III 2, namely, a multiple correlation of .992, a partial correlation $r_{14.2}$ of .62 (note, however, that we have lost two observations), and the following regression equation:

$$\text{V 2} \quad \frac{C}{P} = 8.6(\pm 26) + .88\frac{Y}{P} + 105\frac{U}{L}$$

It appears that the secular relation between consumption and income (that is, the relation that prevails when U/L is small and constant) is essentially the same as that obtained from equation III 3. The constant term is again quite small, and is insignificant when compared with its standard error (26); the secular propensity to consume (.88) is only slightly lower. Furthermore, this equation indicates that for a given level of income, consumption tended to increase 105 (real) dollars per unit change in the unemployment coefficient. (Since the labor force is about 40 percent of the population, this implies that aggregate consumption tended to increase $260 per unit increase in the number unemployed, a result not entirely unrealistic.)

Finally, if we assume a 'full employment' value for U/L of some 2 percent and extrapolate the equation for values of real income of between 900 and 1,000 real dollars (the only range we need consider for 1950), we again obtain a saving–income ratio of not quite 11 percent. The similarity of these results with those of equation III 3 are, of course, not surprising since, as we have argued, the quantity U/L and the quantity $(Y-Y^{\circ})$ are bound to be very closely related.

But if we now proceed to introduce the quantity $\left(\frac{I}{E}-\frac{I^{\circ}}{E^{\circ}}\right)\frac{E}{L}$ as a fourth variable, we get entirely unsatisfactory results. The net correlation between consumption and the coefficient of unemployment, $r_{14.23}$, falls to .2, and similarly, the net correlation $r_{13.24}$ is only $-.49$, whereas $r_{13.2}$ was $-.72$. Both partial correlations are now so low that the corresponding regression coefficients, which should measure the separate influence of the two variables, are entirely unreliable.[27]

It is to be hoped that as new and more reliable statistical information becomes available for a greater number of years, it

[27] In view of these results, it seems useless to add to the correlation the last variable of equation V 1c, namely, TY/P. In any event, the importance of this variable could not be large, since transfer payments represented at best a small fraction of income; furthermore, the weight of this variable in equation V 1c should be theoretically equal to the difference between the (long-run) marginal propensity to consume earned income and the marginal propensity to consume transfer payments.

will become possible to refine the analysis.[28] All we can say with relative confidence at present is that the *joint* effect of the various factors was to produce a cyclical marginal propensity to consume in the order of 75 percent as compared with a long-run average and marginal propensity of 89 to 90 percent.

The failure to reach reliable quantitative conclusions for the individual factors is probably not as serious as might appear. As we have argued, the intercorrelation between the theoretically relevant independent variables is a systematic phenomenon that may be expected to hold in the future. If so, the determination of the separate influence of each variable, though undoubtedly of theoretical interest, is not of crucial importance for forecasting. Pending further refinements, it appears that our simplified approach, despite its theoretical crudeness, may be extrapolated with relative confidence. These conclusions are fully supported by an analysis of Canadian and Swedish material.

VI The Hypothesis Tested for Sweden and Canada

The consumption-income relation in Canada for 1923–39 is shown in Chart 2.[29] Owing to the nature of the original estimates, the two series differ considerably from those used for the United States, not only in reliability but also in concept. The series graphed on the horizontal axis is deflated gross national product; the consumption estimate graphed on the vertical axis includes government expenditure but excludes expenditure on consumer durables except motor cars, for which a crude adjustment was

[28] One factor of special importance is instalment credit because it tends to offset, to some extent, the action of the three factors discussed in Section IV. As a result of the decline in the expenditure on durable goods as income falls cyclically, new instalment borrowing tends to decline, falling short of repayments on outstanding loans, which depend on purchases contracted for earlier. This tends to maintain saving as income declines. The opposite movement occurs when income is recovering, the increase in saving being partly offset by an increase in net instalment borrowing. Unfortunately, no adjustment could be made for this factor because good estimates of instalment credit are unavailable for the period before 1929. For 1929–40, if one subtracts from aggregate savings the net yearly change in instalment credit, the scatter of Chart 1 improves considerably.

[29] For the sources and derivation of the series on which Chart 2 is based, see Appendix reference C.

made. (Estimates of net national product seem somewhat less reliable than those of gross national product.) For lack of a better

CHART 2
Relation between Consumption and Gross National Product
Canada, 1923 – 1939

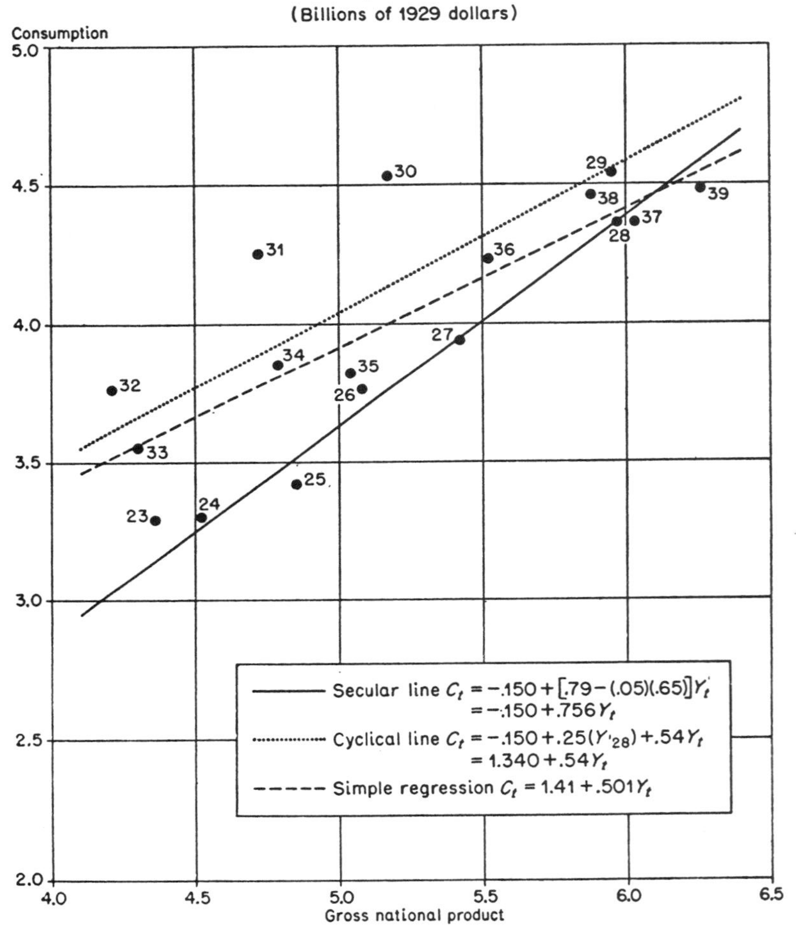

See Appendix reference C for sources and derivation of series.

deflator, the cost of living index was used to deflate both series. Obviously the two series thus obtained are theoretically not entirely satisfactory; nevertheless, they should be adequate to indicate whether generalizations can be made from the results for the United States.

The scatter of points follows closely the pattern indicated by our hypothesis: during the cyclical fluctuations in income from 1928–29 to 1937, consumption did not retrace the path it had followed during the expansion from 1923 to 1929, but remained consistently higher, fluctuating around a cyclical line distinctly flatter than the secular line. Furthermore, the configurations of the scatter suggest also a marked short lag of consumption behind income, a lag that did not appear in the case of the United States (see, however, Sec. XII).

All this is clearly brought out by correlation analysis. The simple correlation between consumption and income is only .77. The regression equation of consumption, C, on income, Y, (both expressed in billions of deflated dollars) is:

VI 1 $$C_t = 1.41 + .50Y_t$$

This would indicate a marginal propensity to consume of only about 50 percent. But when we introduce lagged income, Y_{t-1}, and the highest previous income, Y_t°, as additional variables, the correlation rises to .97 and the regression equation takes the form:

VI 1a $$C_t = .15 + .135Y_t + .405Y_{t-1} + .25Y_t^\circ$$[30]

From equation VI 1a we may easily compute both the cyclical and secular relation of income and consumption. To obtain the first we recall that, for cyclical changes in income, Y_t° is a constant, and we rewrite equation VI 1a:

VI 1a1 $$C_t = (-.15 + .25Y_t^\circ) + .54Y_t - .405(Y_t - Y_{t-1})$$

[30] Denoting the variables C_t, Y_t, Y_{t-1}, Y_t°, by the subscripts 1, 2, 3, and 4, the relevant simple and partial correlation coefficients are: $r_{12} = .77$; $r_{13} = .91$; $r_{14} = .65$; $r_{12.34} = .44$; $r_{13.24} = .79$; $r_{14.23} = .78$.

What is striking is the apparently negligible net influence of current income as measured by the net correlation $r_{12.34}$. Apparently, lagged income has a much greater influence in terms of both simple and net correlation. From a purely statistical point of view, current income could be neglected, since it does not raise the multiple correlation significantly. From the economic point of view, however, it is hardly conceivable that current consumption should not be influenced, at least in some degree, by current income. The variable Y_t is therefore included, although this diminishes the reliability of the individual regression coefficients. The value of the statistic K is 2.11, which is not significant (see note 14).

This shows that the cyclical marginal propensity to consume is indeed, on the average, only about .54; it is somewhat higher if income is falling, in which case $(Y_t - Y_{t-1})$ is negative, and somewhat lower if income is rising. To estimate the secular relation, on the other hand, we replace Y_t° by Y_{t-1}:

VI 1a2 $$C_t = -.15 + .79Y_t - .65(Y_t - Y_{t-1})$$

This indicates that even when the normal secular growth of income is allowed for, the secular marginal propensity is in the order of .75, which is 50 percent higher than the estimate based on the simple regression. Furthermore, the constant term in equation VI 1a, contrary to that of equation VI 1, is definitely small (the mean value of Y is 5.23) and does not differ significantly from zero, indicating again that the long-run average and marginal propensity to consume are almost the same. The secular relation between consumption and income, given by equation VI 1a2, is graphed as a solid line in Chart 2, assuming that income grows 5 percent a year (the average percentage growth for 1923–29). By comparing this line with the simple regression equation VI 1, graphed as a broken line in Chart 2, we can see how significant the difference between our approach and the usual one becomes when the relations are extrapolated to levels of income sizably higher than were realized in the period of observation.

According to these results, both cyclical and secular propensities to save are impressively higher than those obtained for the United States. The difference, however, appears to be largely explained by differences in definitions. When adjustment is made as closely as possible to United States Department of Commerce definitions, the secular marginal propensity to save in terms of national income may be estimated to be 11–12 percent.[31]

[31] Based on the estimates given, depreciation constitutes some 13 percent of net national income in years of secular expansion. If we accept this figure, and assume a normal secular growth of income of 3 to 5 percent, the marginal (and average) propensity to save would be 14 to 15 percent. From this figure we must still subtract expenditure on the relevant part of consumer durables. Expenditure on these goods in the United States may be roughly estimated to be 3–4 percent of net income (based on the estimates in 'Consumption Expenditure, 1929–1943', *Survey of Current Business*, June 1944, Table 2). The percentage need not be strictly applicable to Canada; it is nevertheless clear that with this final adjustment the net marginal propensity to save cannot be far from 11 to 12 percent.

It must, of course, be recognized that this brief analysis of Canadian experience is necessarily rather crude and that the quantitative results are tentative. In particular, the exceptionally marked lag of consumption behind income deserves further investigation. However, even our crude analysis shows rather convincingly that the discrepancy between the cyclical and secular relation of income and consumption is at least as pronounced in Canada as in the United States.

The data for the United States and Canada analyzed so far cover a period that is relatively short and entirely dominated by the cycle of the 'thirties. It is important to test our hypothesis over a longer interval. Probably the only country for which this can be done at present is Sweden, for which continuous estimates of national income and consumption are available from 1896 to 1934, though, again, they are conceptually somewhat different from those used for the United States.[32] These estimates, adjusted for changes in prices and population, are plotted in scatter diagram form in Chart 3 (omitting the war years 1914–18). The relation between the two variables appears to follow the pattern indicated by our hypothesis: when income falls below the previous peak there is a distinct tendency for consumption not to retrace the secular path, but to remain at a higher level, fluctuating about a line markedly less steep than the secular line. Indeed, the hypothesis of equation III 2 appears to fit the data remarkably well, as indicated by a multiple correlation coefficient of .997 and significant partial correlations for all variables.[33] The regression equation is:

VI 2 $\quad C_t = 61 + .85Y_t - .35(Y_t - Y_t^\circ) = 61 + .50Y_t + .35Y_t^\circ$

[32] The major conceptual difference is that the Swedish estimates include taxes and corporate savings in income, and government expenditures on goods and services in consumption. For sources and methods used in computing these series, see Appendix reference D. Estimates are available for 1935–39 also, but are not truly comparable with earlier years.

[33] The simple and partial correlation coefficients are:

SIMPLE CORRELATIONS	PARTIAL CORRELATIONS
$r_{cy} = .985$	$r_{cy.(y-y^\circ)} = .996$
$r_{c(y-y^\circ)} = -.26$	$r_{c(y-y^\circ).y} = -.88$
$r_{c(y-y^\circ)} = -.1$	

The value of K is 1.54, which is not significant (see note 14).

CHART 3
Relation between Income and Consumption
Sweden, 1896–1934 (1914–18 omitted)
(Kronor of 1910–13 purchasing power)

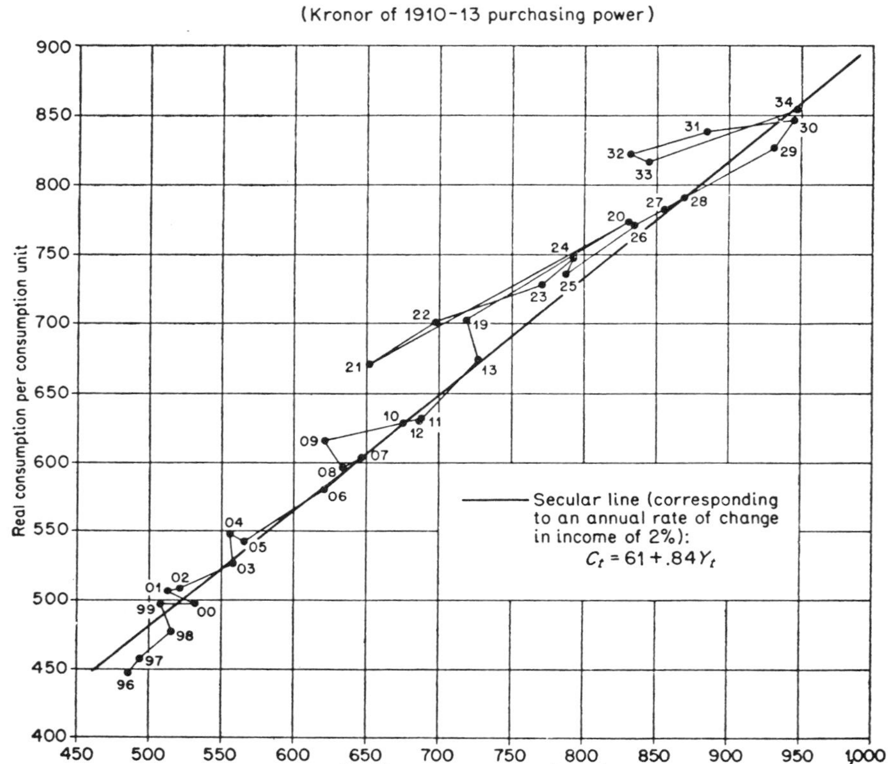

From this equation it appears that the long-run marginal propensity to consume is in the order of .85 or slightly less, depending on the secular growth of income, while the short-run marginal propensity is only .5.[34] The fact that the cyclical marginal propensity appears to be so much lower for Sweden than for the United States probably reflects the influence, in the course of the cycle, of cor-

[34] If we assume the normal secular growth of income to be some 2 percent per year (approximately the average growth in the past) we can replace Y_t° by $.98Y$, obtaining: $C_t = 61 + .50 + .98(.35)\ Y_t = 61 + .84Y_t$. This equation may be considered the long-run consumption function and is graphed as a solid line in Chart 3. It indicates a long-run marginal propensity to consume of about .84.

porate savings and dissavings, which are included in the Swedish income estimates (see Sec. XII). Similarly, the somewhat lower long-run marginal propensity obtained for Sweden (.84 to .85 as compared with .89 to .90 from the Department of Commerce series) cannot be taken as a certain indication of structural differences, since it too may reflect, in some degree, purely conceptual differences.

There is, however, one interesting difference between equations III 3 and VI 2 that can hardly be explained by differences in definition alone: equation VI 2 contains a constant term that is relatively large and significant in the statistical sense (the standard error of the constant is 9.6). Because of this constant term, equation VI 2 indicates that the long-run average propensity to consume does not coincide as closely with the long-run marginal propensity as it does in the United States; it tends instead to fall gradually as income rises, a fact that can be checked directly from the original data. This, however, in no way invalidates the substance of our argument. What is important is that the long-run marginal propensity to consume is distinctly higher and closer to the average than the short-run marginal propensity, so that the tendency for the saving-income ratio to rise with income is quantitatively rather small in the long run, and much smaller than during a cycle.[35] If we compare years characterized by similar secular growth of income at the beginning and at the end of the period covered by the Swedish series, we find that the consumption-income ratio varied only from about 92–93 to about 89–90 percent, though real income per consumption unit almost doubled.[36] During a single cycle, on the other hand, this ratio fluctuated as widely as +12 to −3 percent. Finally, if equation VI 2 should continue to hold, the long-run saving-income ratio would tend to rise at

[35] As already noted in connection with equation III 3, during the course of the cycle the constant term in equation VI 2 is $61 + .35Y_t^{\circ}$; in the long run, when Y_t° varies together with Y_t, the constant term is close to 61.

[36] According to our regression equation, the change in the consumption ratio corresponding to the actual change in income would be somewhat smaller, that is, from 94–95 to about 90 percent, because actual consumption in the first few years was somewhat less than our equation indicates. In this connection, see note 39.

an even slower rate (unless per capita income should rise at a much faster rate).[37]

The statistical material available for Canada and Sweden appears to confirm the validity of our hypothesis and the main conclusions that follow from it: the extrapolation of the simple regression equation of consumption on income is entirely misleading and seriously underestimates the future of consumption; and in the long run the saving-income ratio tends to fluctuate very slowly, if at all. It is entirely possible, as the Swedish material suggests, that this ratio might have a tendency to rise as income gradually rises from a very low level, *other things being equal*. Even this tendency, however, is probably weak in comparison with, and may be obscured by, the 'other things' that also change slowly in the long run—for example, the age structure of the population, degree of urbanization, income distribution.[38] Furthermore, our statistical results, as well as theoretical arguments beyond the scope of the present empirical investigation, suggest that once the saving-income ratio has reached a relatively high level, the tendency for a further rise, if present, would be particularly weak under normal peacetime conditions.

VII Implications for Forecasting

We may now briefly examine the implications of our results for purposes of extrapolation. As we have seen, the relation between income and consumption in the United States in the interwar pe-

[37] From the long-run consumption function in note 34, we see that the long-run consumption-income ratio is:

$$\frac{C}{Y} = \frac{61}{Y} + .84$$

For this expression to equal .87 (corresponding to a saving-income ratio of 13 percent) real income per consumption unit should exceed 2,000 kronor; it was about 950 in 1934. Similarly, it would take an income of over 3,000 kronor to bring the consumption-income ratio down to .86.

[38] Evidence of slight shifts in the saving-income ratio from decade to decade are to be found in Kuznets' estimates in *Uses of National Income in Peace and War*, as well as in the Swedish estimates. In view of the margin of error in the estimates, it is, of course, difficult to say how much significance can be attributed to these slight shifts.

riod may be explained approximately as well on Smithies' hypothesis as on our own. For the period of observation, the two hypotheses are equally tenable. But the difference between them becomes quite significant when one tries to make a long-range forecast for 1950. According to Smithies' hypothesis, the gradual upward drift in the short-run consumption-income schedule would depend on the passage of time alone and is therefore entirely unrelated to the growth of income; the relative stability of the saving–income ratio in the past reflects merely a coincidence between the trend of consumption and of income. But, according to our hypothesis, this gradual upward drift is directly related to the growth of income (through the factor Y_t°); it is not a mere coincidence but a systematic phenomenon that can be extrapolated.

The difference between the level of income prevailing in 1940 and the level that may be expected in 1950 at full employment is so large that the relation between Smithies' consumption trend and the secular rate of growth in income no longer holds. On the basis of Smithies' hypothesis we are therefore led to expect a much higher saving-income ratio than was ever realized in the period of observation. On the basis of our hypothesis the saving-income ratio in 1950 would not depend directly on the level of income but only on the cyclical position of that year. Assuming full employment and a normal rate of growth of income (let us say, 2 to 4 percent), equation III 2 or 3 would lead us to expect a saving-income ratio of 10 to $10\frac{1}{2}$ percent.[39] When disposable income is $154 billion, this implies a savings level of $16–17 billion; the forecast was $21–22 billion, or about 14 percent, according to Smithies and Mosak, and $10–11 billion, or about 7 percent, according to

[39] According to equation III 3, the saving-income ratio will not be entirely independent of the actual level of real income. From this equation we have, in fact:

$$\frac{S}{Y} = 1 - \frac{C}{Y} = 1 - \left[.898 - .125\left(\frac{Y_t - Y_t^\circ}{Y_t}\right) + \frac{2}{Y_t}\right] = .102 + .125\,r - \frac{2}{Y_t}$$

Here r denotes the assumed rate of growth of income. The value of the last term in the right side of the equation obviously depends on the assumed level of real income, Y_t. However, since real income per capita was nearly $700 in 1940, the value of this term is, in any event, extremely small. Different assumptions about Y_t (as long as they remain within realistic limits) will not affect the forecast of the saving-income ratio significantly.

Woytinsky.[40] One other approach to the problem of forecasting—that of V. Lewis Bassie, which appeared too late for us to compare his results thoroughly with ours—leads to estimates close to those of Smithies and Mosak.[41] But our examination of Bassie's method gives us no reason to modify our conclusions.

According to the latest estimates of the Department of Commerce, in the first quarter of 1946 disposable income and savings were running at a seasonally adjusted rate of some $140 billion and $19 billion, respectively,[42] indicating that the saving-income ratio had already fallen from the wartime peak of over 28 percent (reached in 1944) to 13½ percent. On the basis of our results a further significant decline may be expected by 1950. This decline will not necessarily proceed without interruption since in the first transitional and post-transitional years the relation between income and consumption is and will be affected by several exceptional circumstances, tending to produce opposite results, any of which may dominate temporarily. For example, shortages of com-

[40] Woytinsky's equations are extrapolated as follows: A disposable income of $154 billion in 1943 prices corresponds to about $130 billion in 1941 prices. Substituting this figure in the two equations considered most reliable by Woytinsky (*op. cit.*, equations 11 and 21a), we obtain $11 billion and $9.5 billion for savings.

[41] 'Consumers' Expenditures in War and Transition', *Review of Economic Statistics*, Vol. 28, No. 3 (Aug. 1946), pp. 117–30. Bassie's hypothesis yields the somewhat odd result that real consumption per capita depends not only on real income per capita but also on the size of the population. It is true that his equation fits the data remarkably well. But the income and consumption series he used are old Department of Commerce estimates, which differ from the current ones, especially for the prewar period. For the period after 1921, the difference between Bassie's and Smithies' hypothesis is not as great as may appear. The short-run marginal propensity to consume is again about .77, while the linear trend is replaced by the gradual increase in population.

The above consideration shows that in Bassie's, just as in Smithies' hypothesis, the upward drift of the consumption schedule is independent of the rate of increase in income. Hence, if we extrapolate Bassie's equation into a period in which income is expected to rise considerably faster than in the past, relative to population, we again get a distinctly higher saving-income ratio than in the period of observation. We are not in a position to compare directly Bassie's forecast of the saving-income ratio with the other forecasts discussed here, since Bassie's results are not given explicitly except in graphic form. If we use our standard test assumption of $154 billion at 1943 prices, Bassie's equation yields a saving-income ratio of about 13.5 percent.

[42] 'Income, Consumption and Savings', *Survey of Current Business*, May 1946, p. 5.

modities and acquired wartime saving habits will tend to keep consumption down, while the backlog of demand for consumer durable goods and the large volume of liquid assets will tend to raise it.[43] If experience after World War I is a criterion, it may be four years before a 'normal' relation is reestablished. In any event, the influence of the transitional phenomena will have largely petered out by 1950. We may therefore expect that the downward trend of the saving-income ratio, already manifest, will eventually prevail, even if a high level of employment is maintained.

Our forecast is, of course, subject to a margin of error that may be negligible relative to consumption but significant relative to saving. As stressed above, this is particularly true of a long-range forecast, such as the present. But even if we try to take into account factors that may in the long run affect the basic level of the saving-income ratio, we have much more reason to expect a downward than an upward shift.[44] It is therefore clear that if our hypothesis is fundamentally correct, as the various tests and arguments previously developed strongly suggest, a saving-income ratio of some 14 percent is entirely out of the question; indeed, even allowing for the margin of error, we should not expect the saving-income ratio to exceed significantly an upper limit of some 11 percent.[45]

[43] For a discussion of the problems of these transitional phenomena see Bassie, *op. cit.*

[44] In addition to the possible effect of accumulated wartime savings, which may lessen the inducement to save, several other long-term factors may be expected to work in the same direction. For an analysis of such factors, see, for instance, George Terborgh, *The Bogey of Economic Maturity* (Machinery and Allied Products Institute, Chicago, 1945), Ch. 4 and 12. A downward shift of the saving-income ratio would also be in line with the marked downward trend exhibited by the revised Kuznets' estimates.

[45] This statement must be qualified to the extent that real income in 1950 may exceed the highest previous income by much more than the 2 to 4 percent assumed in our forecast. In fact, according to equation III 2 or 3, the saving-income ratio will tend to be higher, the higher the rate of increase in income in the given year. Furthermore, the experience of 1941 suggests that in the case of exceptionally sudden increases in income, the saving-income ratio may rise even higher than indicated by our regression equations.

XIII Wider Implications

To sum up: this paper suggests that in studying past relations between national income and its components, attention should be given to the possible influence of the cyclical position of the economy. We found for each series analyzed a marked and significant difference between the cyclical or short-run and the secular relation. Extrapolating the secular relation under specific cyclical assumptions, we obtained estimates for the near future significantly different from other current forecasts. In particular, we found that the share of aggregate income accruing to profits (especially to corporate profits) and the saving–income ratio may be expected to be substantially lower than when estimated by the usual method. This conclusion is of special importance since it suggests that though the task of maintaining full employment may well be difficult in the near future, the dark pessimism of many current investigations is not fully justified. Our results encourage optimism also in that they show that income is probably less sensitive to fluctuations in the level of investments than is usually supposed. We have seen, in fact, that the behavior of savers, especially corporations, has tended to act, and may therefore be expected to act in the future, as a powerful stabilizer. While the maintenance of the secular expansion of income may be expected to require net investments of some 11 to 12 percent of income, a fall in investments may be expected to reduce real income not by 9 times, but only by 2 to 3 times.

The results of our investigation have certain broader implications of a methodological nature. The starting point of our whole approach is the recognition that the relation between economic variables need not be, and frequently is not, symmetric or reversible. The change in X_1 associated with a given change in X_2 may depend on the nature of the change in X_2. The reasons for this irreversibility are, of course, different for different relations. In the case of the consumption function, for example, it is partly due to the irreversibility of consumption habits. In the case of profits, it is probably due partly to the asymmetric behavior of overhead costs which are largely fixed as long as output fluctuates below capacity but become variable when capacity has to be increased. In the case of corporate dividends, it probably reflects the direct and indirect influence of the net surplus position, as Tinbergen suggested.

But these are obviously not the only cases of irreversibility. Many other instances can readily be found. A typical case, for example, is that associated with short- and long-run supply schedules in the Marshallian sense. The quantity supplied at any given price at point of time t will depend upon the existing capacity, say q_t°. As long as the price remains below a certain critical level (given by the long-run supply schedule) at which it pays to expand capacity, both price and output will move along a short-run supply schedule, say $q_t = f_t(p_t, q_t^\circ)$. But if the price remains for some time sufficiently high to induce an expansion of capacity to a new level, $q^\circ(t + \theta)$, the short-run supply schedule will itself shift upward (if quantity is measured on the vertical axis), and the quantity supplied at any given price will tend to be larger than before capacity was expanded.

To give one more example of irreversibility, the distribution of total employment by main branches of economic activity may be expected to be closely related, in a given country, to the level of real income. At the same time, theoretical considerations, which are confirmed by preliminary investigations carried out for the United States and for Sweden, suggest that the effect of a given change in income on the distribution of employment may be expected to differ substantially depending on whether the change in income is of a secular or of a cyclical nature. The irreversibility in this case is due not only to the rigidity of consumption habits, but also, and even more especially, to differences in the employment structure of different economic sectors. Sectors in which the self-employed play a larger role or, more generally, in which the ratio of employers to employees is relatively high (for example, trade, services, agriculture) will tend to be less affected by a cyclical fall in income (and therefore also by a cyclical rise in income) than sectors in which this ratio is relatively low (for example, manufacturing, mining, transportation). The effect of a secular rise in income, on the other hand, obviously bears no necessary relation to the ratio of employers to employees.[87] In general, therefore, cyclical and secular changes in income will have an asymmetric effect on the distribution of employment. In

[87] For instance, in trade and services a secular rise in income has been accompanied in the past by a relative increase in employment, but in agriculture the opposite has been true.

particular, it is entirely possible (and this seems to be true, for example, for the service industries) that a *cyclical rise* in income will be accompanied by a *fall* in the proportion of people employed in a given sector, whereas a *secular rise* in income will be accompanied by a *rise* in this proportion; or, what amounts to the same thing, that the proportion employed in a given sector will tend to rise both when income *falls* cyclically and when income *rises* secularly.

Many more examples of irreversible relations could be cited. Indeed, irreversibility may be expected to occur whenever economic expansion creates certain *new* obstacles; consequently, if a contraction takes place, the variables will follow a different path from the one they followed before obstacles had been created by the expansion. Rigidities of this type are likely to be quite widespread in our economic system.

Such irreversible relations have not always been sufficiently recognized in the past, or, if recognized, have not infrequently been explained by time trends. Indeed, in an expanding economy, the gradual shift of the short-run schedule along the long-run schedule may easily give the appearance of a time trend, especially if the expansion is fairly steady. But in many cases these apparent trends can and should be resolved into what they really are—systematic relations among economic variables. The establishment and estimation of these relations, whenever possible, amounts to replacing a trend factor, whose value depends only on the passage of time and that can be extrapolated only mechanically, with one whose value depends on the actual performance of the economic system. Our results indicate that this method of analysis, quite apart from its greater theoretical elegance, may be of great practical importance in problems of forecasting since it may enable us to improve our estimates of the short-run relation as well as our long-range forecasts. In fact, whenever the relation is irreversible, the observed values of the variable will lie on different short-run schedules. Hence the equation of relation obtained by simple correlation, or by any other method of estimation that does not properly take into account the irreversible nature of the relation, will describe neither the long- nor the short-run relation.

These considerations are especially important for those engaged in analyzing the American economy, since many statistical series are available only from 1929 or, at best, from the early 'twenties. The period from 1929 to 1941 consists essentially of a single cycle and even the longer period is entirely dominated by the violent cyclical fluctuations of the 'thirties; therefore, whenever the given relation is cyclically sensitive, estimates of the parameters based on this period of observation are in danger of being cyclically biased to a marked degree. The danger implicit in this situation is further increased by the fact that the war economy tended in many cases (for example, in the profit-income relation, the saving-income relation, the distribution of employment) to continue the cyclical relation of the 'thirties; in some cases this relation held until the very end of the war. This situation only heightens the illusion that the relation of 1929–41 can be safely extrapolated into the post-transitional period.

Errata

Page 376, equation II.3: "$C = 71.7 + 78Y + \cdots$" should read "$C_t = 71.7 + .78Y + \cdots$."

1

The life cycle hypothesis of saving twenty years later

Franco Modigliani

In deciding to devote this lecture to a survey of the life cycle hypothesis of saving—its intellectual origins, its relation to other models, its consistency with evidence, its implications for economic policy—I was swayed by two major considerations. First, it is just about twenty years ago that Richard Brumberg and I completed a draft of our two joint papers on the life cycle hypothesis (LCH); the first, dealing with cross-sectional implications, was published a year later in the volume *Post-Keynesian Economics*, edited by Kurihara [45], while the other, dealing with time series implications, was never published [46]. The second consideration is that it is here in England that Richard Brumberg met his premature death only two years later; this seems, to me, therefore, a fitting occasion and a fitting way of paying tribute to his memory.

1 Intellectual origins

To understand the circumstances that gave origin to our joint effort one must recall the nature of the approach to the analysis of consumption and saving behaviour which prevailed in the late '40's and early '50's. Under the impact of Keynes's well known and frankly empirical 'psychological law' [26] the analysis of saving behaviour was dominated by crude empiricism and tended to be cast in a static framework hard to believe today. And this despite the fact that several authors, notably Fisher [15], had already shown how one could develop, from the received theory of consumer's choice, a sound theory of saving (and dissaving) in the context of a dynamic model of resource allocation over time, and that Keynes himself had made, in the course of chapters 8 and 9 of the *General Theory*, numerous if not very systematic references to the role of income expectations, wealth and the function of saving in the reallocation of resources over time.

Saving had come to be regarded as merely one of the 'commodities' to which the consumer could allocate his income, and one was free to exercise one's ingenuity as to what might be the variables controlling its demand.

There was, however, universal consensus that saving was a 'superior' commodity, i.e. such that the amount acquired would rise with income, and fairly general agreement that it was in fact a 'luxury', the expenditure on which would rise proportionally faster than income. Since, in addition, saving had the peculiarity that it could be negative as well as positive, most economists seemed to have few qualms in accepting at face value the linear individual saving function with a sizable negative intercept that seemed to provide such a reasonable approximation to the description of cross-sectional or budget study data, even though such a function implied negative saving for income receivers below some critical level—the so-called break-even income.

The linear individual saving function, in turn, conveniently implied a linear aggregate saving function with negative intercept, and this implication appeared to receive support from the time series data which were then becoming available for the United States for the pre-war period from 1929 to 1941. These data appeared to confirm that the saving ratio was an increasing function of income, and that it would take negative values for a sufficiently low level of aggregate income. Yet it should have been apparent that a linear function with negative intercept could not possibly provide a satisfactory general description of the relation between saving and income, either at the cross-sectional or at the aggregate time series level.

At the aggregate level, when account is taken of the secular growth of income, the linear saving function implied negative saving for all years preceding the date at which income, in the course of its growth, first reached the break-even level. Now for the US these years would clearly include all those earlier than, say, the first decade of the current century, raising some interesting questions as to how the large stock of capital already then in existence could have been accumulated, let alone the question of how a country could dissave unless it had saved before.

Similarly, with reference to budget data, it should have been obvious that the average dissaving associated with low levels of current income could not possibly describe the behaviour of the permanently poor because in our society few are ever allowed to accumulate a significantly negative net worth. Hence the average dissaving must reflect the inclusion among the currently poor of transiently poor who had managed to save in the past and/or would save in the future. And this observation should have raised questions as to whether the high saving ratios in the high income brackets could not also be significantly affected by the high saving of transiently rich households.

The logical difficulties inherent in an aggregate saving function with a significant negative intercept were soon highlighted by Kuznets' findings [27] about the long-run stability of the saving–income ratio, or, at any rate, its lack of systematic association with real income, aggregate or *per capita*. These findings in turn, were reconciled with the evidence from budget studies in the path-breaking paper by Brady and Friedman [7]. They were able to show that the consumption function implied by family budget data at successive points of time appeared to shift upwards at the same time as mean income increased; and that, in fact, all these functions could be roughly collapsed into a single, time-invariant function if, in each year, family income was measured not in absolute terms but relative to the mean family income of that year. In essence, the proportion of income saved appeared to be an increasing function not of family income as such but rather of the relative standing of the family in relation to mean income. Therefore, provided only that the frequency distribution of relative income remained reasonably stable in time, it was possible to reconcile the dependence of the saving ratio on income, within each survey, with the stability of the aggregate saving ratio in the face of rising mean income.

These findings inspired the first significant modifications of the simple linear consumption, function, proposed independently by Duesenberry [12], and in a paper of mine [36], both appearing in 1949—though these modifications still fell within the empiricist tradition of the earlier period. Duesenberry, in particular, suggested that because of imitation effects the individual consumption–income ratio would depend on the relative rather than on the absolute income of the family. Furthermore, to reconcile the cyclical variability of the saving ratio with its long-run stability, he suggested that consumption was determined not only by current income but also by the highest income previously reached. In my own paper I also proposed and tested the proposition that consumption could be expressed as a homogeneous function of current and highest previous income—or, equivalently, the saving ratio as a linear and decreasing function of the ratio of the highest previous income $\mathring{Y}_t$ to current income $\mathring{Y}_t$. In my formulation, however, I was laying much less stress on the fact that people consciously anchored their consumption to the highest previous income than on the fact that, in an economy characterised by a stable long-run growth, the ratio $\mathring{Y}_t/Y_t$ could be taken as a good indicator of cyclical conditions. There were, in fact, many reasons for supposing that the saving ratio should fluctuate pro-cyclically. In particular, cyclical fluctuations of income would be accompanied by inverse fluctuation in the rate of unemployment, which in turn should be correlated with the ratio C/Y, since the unemployed could be expected to consume on a scale commensurate with that of the employed though not contributing to income. Cyclical fluctuations in saving might also be expected to result from pro-cyclical shifts in the share of income accruing to profits. It was left for T. M. Brown [8] to pursue the Duesenberry formulation to its logical implication by suggesting that the highest previous income should be replaced by the highest previous consumption. It should be noted, however, that the Duesenberry–Modigliani–Brown hypothesis could still not provide any explanation of the basic long-run level around which the saving ratio fluctuated cyclically. Similarly, Duesenberry's relative income hypothesis could not explain how 'relatively' poor people could go on on dissaving indefinitely.

Shortly after Duesenberry's book, however, some highly imaginative work of Margaret Reid (never published) [52] pointed to a totally different explanation for the association between the saving ratio and relative income, based on the notion that consumption was controlled by normal or 'permanent' income rather than by current income.

Thus the challenge that Brumberg and I faced as we began our co-operation around 1950 was that of building, from the received theory of consumer's choice over time *à la* Fisher, and a minimum set of plausible postulates, a unified model of consumption and saving behaviour capable of accounting for, and integrating, all the macro and micro evidence cited above and which could, in turn, lead to new, testable implications.

2 The basic model

(a) *Original formulation and relation to Friedman's 'permanent income' hypothesis*

Our first exciting discovery was the terribly simple one that, if one was prepared to dismiss the bequest motive as an important determinant of saving—at least, for the overwhelming mass of consumers—and if the frame of reference for the measurement of income and consumption was broadened from an arbitrary calendar unit, such as a year, to the lifetime itself, then one could immediately conclude that the average and marginal propensity to consume with respect to life income would be equal to each other and equal for all 'households' independently of life income; for, clearly, that propensity had to be one. It is for this reason that initially we stuck firmly to the assumption of no bequests, though we soon found that, at least in terms of aggregative implications, this assumption could be replaced by a much weaker and plausible one, stated below. In what follows we refer to the version of the model incorporating this weaker assumption as the 'generalised' form, and to the version in which planned bequests are ruled out as the 'elementary' form.

Clearly, even in the absence of bequests, one could expect saving in some phases of life to be matched by dissaving in others—or what Harrod [23] had suggestively labelled 'hump saving'. Total absence of saving could prevail only if the utility-maximising path of consumption happened to coincide exactly with that of income—an event to which one could confidently attach zero probability. But we promptly realised that the proposition about the coincidence of the average and marginal propensity to consume with respect to life resources could be readily extended to any sub-period of life by introducing the simple and plausible postulate that (for any given rate of interest) the preferred pattern of allocation of life resources to consumption in each sub-period of life is independent of the size of resources to be allocated. Technically this amounts to postulating that the (ordinal) utility function $U(C_1, C_2, \ldots, C_L)$—where C_t denotes real consumption at age t—is homothetic, i.e. homogeneous of any positive degree in all of its argument. This postulate implies, in fact, that C_t can be expressed as $C_t = kV_t$. Here V_t denotes life resources at age t, the sum of the present value of expected labour income (which Friedman was later to label human wealth) and of the market value of net assets (non-human wealth), and the proportionality factor k is independent of V_t, though it would generally depend on age, t (reflecting tastes), and on the real rate of interest (reflecting market opportunities).

The last result bears a close similarity to the implications of the other major model of saving behaviour anchored in the theory of consumer's choice, namely Friedman's 'permanent income' hypothesis [18], which has many affinities with the LCH. In Friedman's model, which followed by three years the publication of [45], current consumption reflects again the optimum allocation of total resources to the current period; but in his approximation the length of life is treated as infinite. Therefore his smooth rate of consumption (permanent consumption) is proportional to the maximum that can be consumed currently and for ever thereafter—that is, to the return on total capital, which he calls 'permanent' income. By contrast, the difference between current receipts and permanent income he labels 'transient income'. This terminology can be usefully applied also in the context of the LCH, but in this model 'permanent income', for a given age class, should be interpreted as measuring that portion of life income that normally accrues in that age bracket. That proportion, in turn, depends on the complex set of forces that shape the life profile of income, such as education, occupation, family size and other institutional factors.

(b) *Some later extensions to allow for uncertainty*

The LCH model was based on the assumption of subjective certainty about future labour income, rate of return on assets and length of life, and largely ignored, at least at the formal level, problems resulting from uncertainty about these variables. In recent years, however, a good deal of effort has been devoted to extend the analysis to encompass uncertainty, by combining the life cycle model with the expected utility theory of choice under uncertainty (see, for example, Leland [31], Samuelson [53], Merton [34, 35] Drèze and Modigliani [11], Hakansson [21]). In this analysis the consumer is assumed to choose current consumption and the allocation of his net worth between alternative assets (and liabilities) so as to maximise the *expected* utility of consumption over life. The future consumption associated with any given consumption and portfolio decision is, of course, a stoachastic variable because of the stochastic nature of the return on assets, and possibly of future labour income and length of life itself. Drèze and Modigliani [11] have analysed extensively the two-period case under very general assumptions. Other authors have extended the analysis to the multi-period case, although, to arrive at concrete results, they have generally been forced to make restrictive assumptions about the nature of the utility function. In particular the (cardinal) utility function has been assumed to be 'additive' (i.e.

$$U(C_1, \ldots, C_L) = \sum_{1}^{L} U(C_t)\,(1+\rho)^{-t}$$

or, in continuous form,

$$\int_0^L U\{C(t)\}\, e^{-\rho t}\, dt).$$

It is not possible to provide here a systematic review of these important developments. One result, however, deserves special note because of its obvious bearing on the remainder of this survey. The only additive cardinal utility function that satisfies the Modigliani–Brumberg homogeneity postulate is the power form $U(C)=AC^{\gamma}$ (including as a limiting case the logarithmic form), which implies a constant relative risk aversion $1-\gamma$ (with $\gamma<1$ to ensure risk aversion).

It has been shown (see, for example, Merton [35], Hakansson [21]) that with this utility function, and with standard assumptions about the stochastic nature of returns on assets, the basic Modigliani–Brumberg result, that the ratio of consumption at given age to life resources is independent of the level of resources, continues to hold (at least as long as income is not itself stochastic). The ratio does, however, depend not only on the sure rate but also on the parameters of the joint probability distribution of return on assets.

3 Some cross-sectional implications

Brumberg and I were thrilled to discover that, by combining our basic model with some information derived from experience and introspection about the nature of the typical life cycle of income and of tastes, one could readily derive a number of interesting implications, some of which were obviously consistent with the facts, though they threw new light on them, while others were novel and testable.

Concerning tastes, observation as well as introspection suggested that the preferred path of consumption was likely to be relatively stable over life (proper allowance being made for the effect of the life cycle of family size along the lines developed later in [43] and [39]). Similarly, it was clear that current income, as defined in the national income accounts and in budget studies, could be expected to exhibit substantial short-run variation of an accidental type as well as systematic variation over the life cycle, tending, in particular, to be well below average in the late years of life (the 'fact' of retirement). But this implied that the relation between a family's saving and its income, as measured over the relatively short span of time typically used in budget studies, would be largely determined by the extent to which current income was above or below average lifetime earnings (based on past income and expectations for the future). Families with current income well above life average could be expected to exhibit large current saving, while those with income well below average could be expected to report large dissavings.

Taking into account the positive correlation to be expected for the population as a whole between transient income and actual income (relative to mean income), one could infer the existence of a marked positive association between current measured income and the current saving ratio of the type observed in budget studies—despite the fact that the ratio of life consumption to life income was, by assumption, unrelated to the size of life income. Furthermore, by assuming a reasonable stability over time in the distribution of the transient component of income one could infer that the ratio of transient to permanent income, and hence the saving ratio in any given income bracket, would be an increasing and stable function of the ratio of income in that bracket to overall average income of the population. One could, therefore, predict and explain the Brady–Friedman results [7]. On the other hand, as was shown, for example, by Modigliani and Ando [44], the results obtained when families were classified not by current income but by some criterion correlated with permanent but not with transient income (such as city class or outlays on rent for tenants and value of house for home owners), indicated that the proposition 'that the proportion of income consumed is, on the average, independent of the level of total resources', which is central to Friedman's model as well as to the LCH model in its elementary no-bequest version, 'represents at least a good approximation, if we are concerned with a broad cross-section of the (urban) population' (p. 167). At the same time, for certain relatively high-income sub-groups of the population, notably self-employed and salaried professional people owning their home, the estimated elasticity of consumption with respect to income remained distinctly below unity, though much higher than the value obtained by the conventional current income classification. These results are consistent with the hypothesis that consumption depends on life resources but are otherwise not consistent with the pure Friedman or the elementary life cycle model, though they can still be reconciled with the generalized LCH model allowing for a bequest motive, along the lines sketched in section 4(a) below.

The model could similarly account for a number of other findings which had been misinterpreted or remained puzzling. For instance, it could account for the high marginal propensity to save in occupations with unstable income, such as farming, without implying a high average propensity, for which there was, in fact, no evidence. It could also account for the finding that, at any given level of income, black families in the US typically appeared to save more than white families (see Fisher and Brown [14]), on the ground that the average income for the population of black families was appreciably lower than that for white families.

These implications, it should be noted, could also be derived from Friedman's permanent income hypothesis, since his 'infinite life' approximation is quite satisfactory for the analysis of a wide class of problems focusing on short-run saving behaviour; for this class of problems the permanent income and the LCH model lead, in general, to analogous inferences. However, this approximation prevents Friedman from drawing systematic conclusions about the role of age, which instead follow readily from the LCH. One such conclusion, which is well supported by empirical evidence, is that net worth should tend to rise with age up to the prevailing age of retirement, and fall thereafter. Another obvious implication is that the ratio of consumption to 'permanent income' for different age brackets should be controlled by the relation between permanent income in that age bracket and lifetime income (both expressed as rates per unit of time), as well as by the relation of optimal consumption at that age to lifetime consumption, which is heavily influenced by the life cycle of family size. Other, and more subtle, implications were also drawn in [45], e.g. about the parameters of consumption functions estimated by relating consumption to income and net worth over different age classes. In particular, the marginal propensity to consume with respect to wealth should tend to rise with age, at least in the large, as the number of remaining years over which that wealth has to be allocated declines. On the other hand, the cross-sectional marginal propensity to consume with respect to labour income should have some tendency to fall with age, provided current income is a good measure of expected income.

Nothing was known about the actual behaviour of these propensities at the time of our paper, and, unfortunately, even at this time very few explicit tests have been carried out to my knowledge, in part, no doubt, because of the scarcity of comprehensive and reliable data on households' net worth. Some of the tests have not been too favourable (see, for example, M. R. Fisher [16] and Modigliani and Ando [43]), but there are also some fairly impressive favourable results. For instance, Landsberger [28], analysing the response of consumption to windfall increments in wealth (indemnifications received by Israeli citizens from the German government and certain other windfall receipts) found fairly impressive evidence that the response tended to be larger for older age groups. More recently Rasche [51] presented some results based on a re-elaboration of some American data on family consumption, income and wealth assembled by the Federal Reserve Board [49, 50]. Although his results must be regarded as tentative and will require further checking (see Modigliani [41]), they appear to provide strong evidence that the negative effect of wealth on saving tends to increase systematically with age.

4 Aggregative implications

(a) *Steady-state implications and tests*

These were first explored in the unpublished joint paper with Brumberg [46], and from the very beginning struck us as most promising and exciting.

The first obvious implication was that, since the over-life marginal and average propensity to consume coincided, the aggregate saving ratio could not but be independent of *per capita* income; nor could it be related to individual thriftiness, since, by assumption, the over-life propensity to consume was one for all households. We discovered that, despite this assumption, the model was quite consistent with a positive (or negative) aggregate rate of saving, but that this rate would depend primarily on the *rate of growth* of income.

In a stationary economy, with zero population and productivity growth, the saving ratio was bound to be zero, independently of the life cycle of the saving ratio for individual households, because the saving of those currently accumulating with a view to later dissaving in other phases of their life cycle would be precisely offset by those finding themselves in such phases. At the same time we found that, even assuming that the only basic source of 'hump saving' was the fact of retirement, a stationary society could be expected to hold a substantial and realistic volume of assets in relation to income. Specifically we found that the ratio of aggregate private wealth to aggregate private net-of-tax income would be of the same order of magnitude as the ratio of the adult life span to the length of the retirement period, or, say, in the neighbourhood of five.

We next established that income growth would lead to a positive saving ratio, and that, in steady state, the ratio would be constant and an increasing function of the rate of growth, whether the growth resulted from population growth or productivity growth (see Modigliani [38]). Population growth leads to positive saving by increasing the ratio of younger households, in their accumulation phase, to retired households, in their dissaving phase.[1] Similar conclusions tend to hold in the case of constant productivity growth, since such growth implies that each successive generation enjoys a lifetime income exceeding that of earlier generations by the rate of growth. Hence the saving of the younger generations would be keyed to providing for a rate of retired dissaving exceeding correspondingly the rate of dissaving of the generations currently retired. This mechanism was also independently discovered and lucidly explained by Bentzel [6].

In the unpublished paper with Brumberg [46] a number of numerical calculations were carried out to obtain a general idea of the quantitative impact of the rate of growth from each source on the saving ratio, implied by the model. These calculations were based on some conveniently simple assumptions about the life path of earning and consumption—including the assumption that consumption was planned at a constant rate through life, independently of the life cycle of family size, and that income expectations did not incorporate the continuation of past productivity growth. The results, reported in part in [38], suggested that population and productivity growth, within a realistic range, would lead to similar rates of saving. Furthermore the implied saving rate was of a very realistic size; e.g. for a rate of growth of 3–4 per cent, roughly the historical growth rate of the US, the saving ratio turned out to be in the range of 11–14 per cent, which was roughly consistent with long-run US saving rate. (The figures quoted were calculated on the assumption of zero rates of return on assets; the likely effect of r on the saving and wealth ratio will be discussed below.) Since that time Tobin [60] has made much more extensive calculations incorporating assumptions about the life cycle of income and of family size, and mortality rates based on US experience, and on this basis also concluded that 'it seems quite possible that life cycle saving can account for the United States capital stock' (p. 256).

It is interesting to note that Friedman's 'permanent income–permanent

[1] It must be recognised that population growth also increases the ratio of dependent children to labour force, and this *per se* is likely to have some depressing effect on the saving ratio. On the whole, however, the positive effect referred to in the text may be expected to dominate, at least within the empirically prevalent range of population growth—see Modigliani [39, section 5] and the last paragraph of this section.

life' model leads to quite different implications about the effect of growth on the saving ratio. He does not explicitly discuss the effect of population growth, but, as far as one can see, this should have no effect at all, since, with infinite life, there cannot be a systematic relation between saving and age. But he explicitly suggested that productivity growth should tend to *depress* the saving ratio on the ground that a rise in income 'expected to continue tends to raise permanent income relative to measured income and so to raise consumption relative to measured income' [18, p. 234]. It must be acknowledged that, to the extent that expectations of future labour income incorporate an extrapolation of past growth, the mechanism hypothesised by Friedman will be at work also in the LCH framework. But the resulting unfavourable effect of productivity growth on the saving ratio may be expected to be more than offset by the favourable effect resulting from the 'Bentzel' mechanism outlined above. This conclusion is again confirmed by the results obtained by Tobin [60] under the assumption that expected income growth was equal to past growth. It seems safe to conclude that the LCH implies a marked positive association between productivity growth and the saving ratio, at least under realistic assumptions, including the recognition that, in a private economy, it is nearly impossible for a household ever to accumulate a significantly negative net worth (cf. Modigliani [38], p. 170, n. 1).

The suggestive inferences about the positive association between the saving ratio and the rate of growth were untestable at the time they were derived, as data on aggregate income and saving were scanty and limited to the US and at most a handful of other industrial countries. Only fairly recently has information become available for many countries in quite different stages of development and exhibiting very different rates of productivity and population growth. Even casual observation suggests that this information supports the LCH model inference about the saving ratio being positively related to the rate of growth rather than to the level of real income. It is well known that the highest saving ratio is found in Japan, the country with the fastest rate of growth, but whose *per capita* income, until quite recently, was relatively low, at least among the industrial countries; similarly high saving ratios have prevailed in other countries with exceptionally high rates of growth, but not necessarily high *per capita* income—Italy, Finland, the Netherlands, Taiwan, Spain—while the countries with the highest *per capita* income, the United States, Sweden, Canada, France, Australia, New Zealand—which generally exhibited only middling rates of growth, have also exhibited middling saving ratios. These impressions have been confirmed by more systematic analysis of the data (cf. Modigliani [39] and the sources cited there, and Swamy [58]). This analysis has also confirmed the separate role of productivity growth and of the age composition of population, particularly between active and retired (cf. Modigliani [39], Leff [30]).[2] In steady state

[2] The analysis of Modigliani [39] has recently been replicated and fully confirmed by Florissi [17], using a sample of thirty-three countries largely overlapping with that of [39] but with some interesting additions such as Finland, Switzerland, Taiwan, and using in most cases a longer and more recent sample, generally 1958–67.

(but only in steady state) this composition is uniquely related to, and therefore its effect can be captured through, the rate of growth of population.[3]

(b) *The aggregate consumption function*

The other major concern of the unpublished paper [46] was the derivation of an aggregate consumption function. To this end we noted that, on the reasonable assumption that the average expected labour income of any age group, i, could be approximated by its average current income, up to a proportionality factor depending on i, the LCH implied that the aggregate consumption of each age group could be expressed as a linear function of its aggregate current labour income and of its aggregate net worth. But then aggregate consumption in any year t could be expressed as a linear function of aggregate labour income, say YL, and of aggregate private wealth, A,

$$C_t = \alpha_t YL_t + \delta_t A_t \tag{1}$$

In (1) the coefficient α_t is clearly a weighted average of each age group income coefficient, weighted by its share of aggregate labour income. It must therefore depend on those factors controlling the coefficients of each age group—tastes, the life cycle of family size, the rate of return on assets, the life profile of income, expected productivity growth—and on the factors determining the share of income going to each age group—population growth

[3] The results in [39] also provided some tentative evidence, for the sample as a whole, on the depressing effect on the saving rate of the proportion of population below working age (though still suggesting a positive association, in steady state, between the saving ratio and population growth, at least in the empirically relevant range). However, the depressing effect could not be confirmed within the two sub-samples of developed and less developed countries (though it receives strong, if indirect, confirmation from the replication reported by Florissi [17, table 2]). Leff's results seem to imply a much stronger negative effect for dependent children, and furthermore, both in [29] and in his rather convincing defence against his critics [2, 20] in [30], showed that the effect held within each sample, and was particularly strong for the sample of forty-seven underdeveloped countries. Indeed, his coefficient estimates for this sample and the tone of his conclusions suggest that this effect might be so strong as to imply a negative association between the saving ratio and population growth in steady state. Unfortunately, his coefficients are difficult to interpret because of his choice of a double logarithmic form (which is particularly questionable, since S/Y and g could be negative, as they were for a few of the countries included in the sample used in [39]). Furthermore, Gupta [20], in his criticism, showed that the effect seemed to be strong only for the more advanced of the less developed countries. In any event, within the LCH one could well conceive of population growth having a favourable effect on saving in the developed countries (which dominate the sample in [39]) and a less favourable one for countries at different level of development, even to the point of causing the saving rate to decline with population growth beyond some rate within the empirically relevant range. The differential impact could result from many factors, such as differences in the prevailing age of entering the labour force, in mortality experience, in the cost of children's education, etc. However, before accepting such a striking conclusion, Leff's results (which, among other things, are based on the saving ratio for one single year) as well as those of [39] will require further probing.

and again the life profile of income. Similarly the coefficient δ_t is an average of each age group asset coefficient weighted by its share of total wealth, and thus depends on the same factors. Hence, in steady state, including a constant rate of return on assets, r, both coefficients in (1) could be taken as time-independent.

As one might expect, in view of the steady-state results reported earlier, an equation of the form (1) with α, δ constant implies in turn that, with a constant rate of growth of income, ρ, both the saving–income and the wealth–income ratios remain constant in time. This conclusion had in fact already been reached by Ackley [1] with respect to the saving ratio for a consumption function in which YL was replaced by total income, Y. To establish that it holds equally for (1) we note that $Y = YL + rA$ and that, in steady state, unexpected capital gains can be ruled out, while expected gains must be included in r and thus in Y. Hence, in steady state, we must have

$$\Delta A = S = Y - C = \rho A$$

Making use of (1) to substitute for C, we deduce:

$$\frac{A}{YL} = \frac{1-\alpha}{\rho+\delta-r}; \qquad \frac{A}{Y} = \frac{1-\alpha}{\rho+\delta-\alpha r}; \qquad \frac{S}{Y} = \rho\frac{A}{Y} \tag{2}$$

We were also able to verify, with the help of numerical calculations, that the coefficients of (1) would not be very sensitive to variations in the rate of population or productivity growth, and hence in their sum, ρ, nor to short-run departures of income from its growth trend. The first result, together with (2), implies that, according to the LCH, the wealth ratio should tend to decline with the growth trend. It also confirms that the saving ratio is zero for zero growth and increases with ρ, though at a decreasing rate. The second result suggests that, for an economy fluctuating around a reasonably stable growth trend, the coefficients of (1) could be taken as constant—except possibly for the effect of variations in r, to which we shall come back presently.

These aggregative results were derived from the strictest version of the LCH. which assumes the absence of saving for the purpose of bequests. However, they can be generalized to the case where we replace that assumption by the much weaker, and eminently reasonable, one that bequest behaviour can be accounted for by a generalised relative income hypothesis. Specifically, we modify the homogeneity postulate to read: the preferred allocation of *life consumption* over a sub-period of life is independent of the size of *life consumption*. However, we allow for life consumption to fall short of life resources—which now include inherited wealth—because of bequests left, with the following assumptions:

1 The share of its resources that a household earmarks, on the average, for bequests is a (non-decreasing) function of the size of its resources *relative* to the average level of resources of its age group, and this function is stable in time.
2 The frequency distribution of the ratio of life resources to mean life resources for each age group is also stable in time.

Under these assumptions equation (1) will continue to hold in steady state with α and δ constant, though these coefficients will now depend also on the specific form of the bequest function. As a result, the implications (2) also remain valid, though the wealth–income ratio will now include in addition to the component generated by 'hump saving' another component related to bequests.[4] It might be noted, however, that the scanty information available suggests that, at least for the US, inherited wealth is a rather small fraction of total outstanding wealth, probably between $\frac{1}{10}$ and less than $\frac{1}{5}$.

As noted earlier, the coefficients α and δ should, in principle, depend also on r, and this was again confirmed by some numerical calculations, though in this case our results were less clearly-cut or easy to generalise. The difficulty

[4] The reason why (2) continues to hold is that, under assumptions 1 and 2, *if* per capita *income is stationary*, the life saving of each cohort tends to zero, just as in the case of no bequests. To verify this proposition we note first that, once we allow for bequests received (B_R) and left (B_L), the lifetime budget equation can be stated as

$$B_L = YL^* + B_R^* - C^*$$

where the starred symbols on the right-hand side denote respectively life labour income, bequest received and consumption, all capitalised to the end of life. By assumption 1, the average bequest left by a members of cohort T having total resources $V = YL^* + B_R^*$, takes the form

$$B_L(V, T) = Vf\left(\frac{V}{\bar{V}(T)}\right)$$

where $\bar{V}(T)$ is the mean value of V for cohort T. We would expect the function f to have the property $f, f' \simeq 0$ for $V/\bar{V}$ below some threshold value and to become positive thereafter (though subject to the condition $\delta B_L/\delta V < 1$).

Next let $\phi(V/\bar{V})$ denote the cumulated frequency distribution of relative resources, which by assumption 1 is time-independent. Then the average bequest left by cohort T can be expressed as

$$\bar{B}_L(T) = \bar{V}(T) \int_0^\infty \frac{V}{\bar{V}(T)} f\left(\frac{V}{\bar{V}(T)}\right) d\phi\left(\frac{V}{\bar{V}}\right) = \sigma\bar{V}(T) = \sigma[\bar{Y}L^*(T) + \bar{B}_R^*(T)]$$

The average life saving of cohort T is then

$$\bar{S}(T) = \bar{B}_L(T) - \bar{B}_R(T) = \sigma[\bar{Y}L^*(T) + \bar{B}_R^*(T)] - \bar{B}_R(T) = \sigma \bar{Y}L^*(T) - \bar{B}_R(T)(1 - \sigma^*)$$

where

$$\sigma^* \equiv \sigma \frac{\bar{B}_R(T)}{\bar{B}_R^*(T)}$$

may be taken to be less than one (to rule out the possibility of $\bar{S}(T)$ being positive even if $\bar{Y}L^*(T)$ is zero). Under this assumption $\bar{S}(T)$ is seen to be a decreasing function of $\bar{B}_R(T)$. But since bequests left by one cohort are received by later cohorts, it follows that as long as $\bar{S}(T)$ is positive, $\bar{B}_R$ will grow in time, and conversely for $\bar{S}(T)$ negative. Hence, if $\bar{Y}L^*(T)$ is a constant YL^*, $\bar{B}_R$ must tend to

$$\bar{B}_R = \frac{\sigma}{1 - \sigma^*} \bar{Y}L^*$$

for which $\bar{S}$ is zero. If instead $\bar{Y}L^*$ grows at a constant rate, $\bar{B}_R$ will also tend to grow at this rate, and since this holds also for 'hump' wealth, it will hold for total wealth.

is the familiar one that a rise in r (which should be interpreted here as the long-term, real rate of return, as variations in the short-term rate around a stable long-run level would have negligible effects), labour income constant, affects the life profile of consumption both through an income effect, tending to raise consumption at all ages, and a substitution effect tending to shift consumption away from the present and towards a later age. In the case of current consumption these two effects go against each other, and the net effect cannot be ascertained unless one is prepared to make specific assumptions about the nature of the utility function. Our numerical results were obtained for the limiting case in which the substitution effect was assumed to be zero (corner indifference curves or strict complementarity). As expected, they showed that an increase in r would, in steady state, lead to a fall in the wealth–income ratio, A/Y, and thus to a fall in the saving ratio, for any given rate of growth. In terms of the consumption function (1) we found that a rise in r tended to raise both α and δ. The effect on α was relatively minor, but on δ it was proportionately quite large. Specifically δ appeared to increase linearly with r, or $\delta(r)=\delta^*+\mu r$, with μ roughly unity (and δ^* around 0·08). Substituting this expression for δ in equations (2), it is readily verified that, for $\mu=1$, an increase in r leaves A/YL unchanged (it actually decreases it marginally because of the effect on α); but it reduces A/Y and thus S/Y.

These results of the unpublished paper have since led me to conjecture that the effect of r on the LCH consumption function might be approximated by rewriting (1) in the form

$$C_t=\alpha YL_t+(\delta^*+\mu r_t)\,A_t \tag{3}$$

However, the value of μ would not necessarily be 1 but would depend on the strength of the substitution effect between current and future consumption.[4a] If (3) holds, then the equation (2) can be rewritten as

$$\frac{A}{YL}=\frac{1-\alpha}{\rho+\delta^*+(\mu-1)\,r},\qquad \frac{A}{Y}=\frac{1-\alpha}{\rho+\delta^*+(\mu-\alpha)\,r},\qquad \frac{S}{Y}=\rho\frac{A}{Y} \tag{2}$$

A/Y and S/Y would thus rise or fall with r, depending on whether μ is smaller or larger than α.

Some simulations reported by Tobin and Dolde [61] assuming an iso-elastic additive utility function with an elasticity of 1·5 appear consistent with a value of μ close to zero (see table 3, simulation 13), which implies that S/Y is an increasing function of r. Another set of calculations reported by Tobin [60], assuming the same type of utility function but an elasticity of 1, implying greater substitution, shows a stronger positive responsiveness of S/Y to r, suggesting a negative value of μ. Unfortunately, there is no way to establish *a priori* just how strong the substitution effect might be in reality. Thus, while I hypothesise that equation (3) provides a reasonable approximation to the role of r in the aggregate consumption function, there is little one can say *a priori* about the value of μ except that it should not exceed unity.

[4a] See addendum p. 36.

Because of a hunch that the substitution effect is unlikely to be strong relative to the income effect, I would rather expect μ to be positive and not very different from α, which would imply that S/Y is roughly independent of r; however, in principle it could be a good deal lower, and even negative.

5 Tests of the aggregate consumption function

(a) *Tests in the absence of wealth data*

At the time our unpublished paper was completed an equation of the form (1) was untestable, as no information was available on aggregate private net worth. Accordingly, both in that paper and in Brumberg [89], some effort was devoted to deriving implications that could be tested in the absence of an explicit measure of wealth.

It will suffice to point out here that these implications can be shown to be quite similar to those of the major competing models. First let us recall that when Friedman was required to specify an operational aggregate measure of his permanent income, Y, he relied on the Koyck adaptive model, which implies that Y can be expressed as exponentially weighted distributed lag of past incomes. As is well known, this formulation in turn implies that the aggregate consumption function can be approximated by

$$C_t = aY_t + bC_{t-1} \tag{4}$$

This equation differs from the Brown version of the Duesenberry–Modigliani hypothesis only in that lagged consumption replaces the highest previous consumption. Since for most of the economies for which data are available—at least in the post-war period—consumption has hardly ever declined significantly, the implications of two models are for all practical purposes observationally undistinguishable. Consider next the LCH equation (3); if one assumes that $\mu \simeq \alpha$ or that r_t is roughly constant in the relevant period, then (3) can be reduced to

$$C_t = \alpha Y_t + \delta' A_t \tag{5}$$

with $\delta' = \delta^* + (\mu - \alpha)r$, a constant. If one is also prepared to assume that windfall capital gains can be neglected and hence $\Delta A = S = Y - C$, then, as shown by several authors (e.g. Spiro [55], Ball and Drake [4], Evans [13]), A can be eliminated from (5), and the result is an equation of the general form (4). The similarity between the three models is not really surprising, since in each of them the constant term of the elementary linear consumption function is replaced by a smoothly changing, trend-like variable; wealth, which can change but slowly through saving or dissaving, behaves pretty much like lagged consumption, highest previous consumption or highest previous income (cf. Modigliani [38], pp. 177–81). Thus the substantial aggregative time series evidence supporting the other models can also be construed as consistent with the LCH.[5] But this in no way implies that the LCH is equivalent, either in its long-run or in its short-run implications, to the other models. We have already shown, for example that it has distinctive implications about the relation between the long-run level of the saving ratio and the growth trend of income which cannot be derived from the Duesenberry–Modigliani–Brown model, and which are radically different from those implied by the 'permanent income' hypothesis. With respect to the short run, as we shall presently see, it makes a very substantial difference whether or not consumption truly depends on wealth, and thus whether wealth is an approximation to lagged consumption or whether instead the reverse is true. But before exploring this point it is well to review briefly the results of tests in which an explicit measure of wealth has been used.

(b) *Tests relying on wealth data*

The first step in that direction was the pioneering test of Hamburger, using US data [22]. He assumed that labour income could be taken as proportional to the current average wage rate, and, lacking an explicit measure of total private wealth, approximated it as the sum of net government indebtedness to the private sector, plus other property income capitalized at a constant rate. He obtained very encouraging results, including a very significant coefficient for his measure of wealth. But the first fully fledged test (Ando and Modigliani [3]) had to wait until Goldsmith's monumental work [19] produced estimates of private net worth at current market value for a number of benchmark years. In addition to a net worth series based on these estimates, the test used an explicit estimate of after-tax labour income based on employees' income and an imputed labour income for the self-employed. The hypothesis tested was thus of the form (1), or equivalently (3), with the implicit assumption that $\mu(r_t - \bar{r})$ was small and could be impounded in the error term. The

[5] A more direct test of (5) has been reported by Swamy [58], who fitted to time series data of personal saving for each of nineteen countries (as well as to the pooled data) an equation of the form:

$$S = b_1 \Delta Y + b_2 S_{-1}$$

This equation follows readily from (5) if one uses again the approximation $\Delta A = S_{-1}$, with $b_1 = 1 - \alpha$ and $b_2 = 1 - \delta'$. Since according to the LCH δ' is positive and its presumed order of magnitude is around 0·1, one should find $b_2 < 1$ and of the order of 0·9. Similarly, b_1 should be positive and of the order of 0·3. Unfortunately, neither b_1 nor b_2 is likely to yield reliable estimates of the true coefficients. In particular, b_1 will tend to be upward-biased because of the short-run variability of property income. As for b_2, it is likely to be subject to both upward and downward bias whose balance is uncertain. Thus errors of measurement in ΔA will cause an upward bias. On the other hand, errors of measurement in S will cause a downward bias unless they are highly serially correlated, in which case the bias will again be up. The estimates of b_2 obtained by Swamy are uniformly less than 1 (except for Japan—0·993) and, at least for the countries for which the fit is good (say $R^2 > 0{\cdot}6$) they scatter fairly closely around 0·9, while the estimates of b_1 are overwhelmingly above 0·3. Finally, the estimates for pooled data, $\delta' = 0{\cdot}17$ and $\alpha = 0{\cdot}74$, are not hard to reconcile with those suggested by the LCH, considering the likely margin of error of the estimates.

results were strikingly favourable not only in terms of fit but also in the order of magnitude of the coefficients. In particular the coefficient of A, an estimate of $\delta^* + \mu\bar{r}$, was around 0·08. In the same year Lydall [32] showed that an equation of the form (5) fitted quite well the very different saving behaviour of three countries: the US (1920–41), the UK (1948–50) and Australia (1949–62). However, in the case of Australia his coefficients do not agree too well with those suggested by the LCH, the wealth coefficient (0·24) being much too high and the income coefficients too low (0·22); but this could well reflect his rather crude estimate of net worth, computed by adding cumulated saving to a bench-mark year estimate (which, in the case of Australia, seems to be a pure guess).

The results for the UK were fully confirmed in a paper by R. H. Stone [56] published in 1966 and based on a very extensive analysis of data on consumption, wealth and income. The results of this study agree remarkably well with the US estimates reported above, and even more closely with those which were obtained in the late 1960's in the process of re-estimating a consumption function to be used in the FRB–MIT–Penn (FMP) econometric model of the US. It is convenient to review these results first and then compare them with Stone's.

Since the US model is a quarterly one, our first task was to put together, with the help of the Flow of Funds section of the Federal Reserve Bank, a quarterly estimate of net worth at market value. This series was used by Ando to estimate the aggregate consumption function presently in the model. For the purpose of this re-estimation, partly because of the difficulty of securing a meaningful breakdown of net-of-tax income between labour and property income, we used a variant of (1) based on (3) as follows. First rewrite (3) as:

$$C_t = \alpha(YL_t + r_t A_t) + [\delta^* + (\mu - \alpha)\, r_t]\, A_t$$

Note next that $r_t A_t$ may be thought of as the long-run expectation of the flow of profits out of current assets, call it P^p, the capitalisation of which at the long-term rate r determines the market value of wealth, $A_t = P^p_t / r_t$. Since YL represents similarly expected 'permanent' labour income, the sum $YL + r_t A_t$ is quite analogous to Friedman's permanent income, Y^p. We can thus rewrite the equation to be estimated as

$$C_t = \alpha Y^p_t + \delta' A_t + e_t \qquad (6)$$

where the coefficient δ' is an estimate of $\delta^* + (\mu - \alpha)\bar{r}$, and $e_t = (\mu - \alpha)(r_t - \bar{r}) A_t$ is an error term included in the overall error, and, hopefully, small and uncorrelated with the other independent variables (though possibly serially correlated). Y^p was approximated by a long distributed lag (twelve quarters) of real disposable income (which excludes undistributed corporate profits, though a case could be made for their inclusion). To allow for a gradual response to changes in wealth resulting from capital gains or losses, which are a major component of short-run movements in this variable, A_t was replaced by a four-quarter distributed lag. The estimated weights actually assign about half the total weight to the current quarter. The results were again very much consistent with the implications of the LCH, confirming the earlier result of the annual tests to 1959; in particular, the addition of A makes a highly significant contribution of the fit, it cuts substantially the serial correlation of the error term, and its coefficient, δ', is of the right order of magnitude—just over 0·05. (This coefficient is lower than the earlier estimate of 0·08 but understandably so, since it is an estimate of $\delta^* + (\mu - \alpha)\bar{r}$ rather than of $\delta^* + \mu\bar{r}$.) The estimate of α is 0·67.

These results can be compared with those reported by Stone [56] for the UK, relying on an equation very close in spirit to our (6). Using annual data, and an estimate of net worth obtained by adding cumulated saving to a bench-mark year, he obtained a value for δ' of 0·06 (with a t ratio around 6–7) and for α of 0·77 (see table 1, columns A(i) and C(i)) for the years 1949–64, in which, incidentally, the saving ratio had a strong rising trend. He also showed that these estimates were quite stable with respect to changes in the period of estimation.[6] These findings have been further confirmed in a forthcoming paper [57] kindly made available by Professor Stone, which extends the tests to 1970 and uses revised data for the period 1949–64. The only

[6] Stone did not start out from the LCH but directly postulated a consumption function in which C depended on 'permanent' income and wealth as in (6) but possibly also on transient income and on 'transient wealth'. On this basis he tested a number of variants—including a variant in which he broke Y^p into a labour and property income component. The estimates reported in the text are based on his version (i), which takes the specific form

$$C = aY + dA + \gamma C_{-1} \qquad \text{(i)}$$

One can readily show that this is a close approximation to our (6), on the assumption that Y^p can be approximated *à la* Friedman by the Koyck distributed lag,

$$Y_t^p = (1-\gamma) \sum_{\tau=0}^{\infty} \gamma^\tau Y_{t-\tau} = (1-\gamma)\ Y_t + \gamma Y_{t-1}^p$$

Then, from (6), one obtains

$$C - \gamma C_{-1} = \alpha(1-\gamma)\ Y + \delta' A - \gamma\delta' A_{-1}$$

or

$$C = aY + dA + \delta'\gamma\Delta A + \gamma C_{-1}; \qquad a = \alpha(1-\gamma), \qquad d = \delta'(1-\gamma) \qquad \text{(ii)}$$

which reduces to (i) by neglecting the second-order term $\delta'\gamma\Delta A$. Stone estimated (i) both in first difference form (A(i)) and in ratio form, deflated by Y (C(i)). His estimates were respectively 0·050 and 0·048 for d, 0·65 and 0·64 for a and 0·15 and 0·17 for γ, from which one derives the estimate of α and δ' given in the text. He also gives results for equation (ii) above. The coefficient of ΔA turned out to be negative (though insignificant), which greatly puzzled Stone. This result is probably due to bias in the estimate. Note in fact that, because of the method of estimating A, $\Delta A \equiv S_{-1}$; now (ii) can be rewritten as

$$S = Y - C = (1-a)\ Y - dA - \delta'\gamma S_{-1} - \gamma C_{-1} \qquad \text{(iii)}$$

If the error term is serially correlated, as is likely, the estimate of the coefficient of $\delta'\gamma$ will have a positive bias in (iii) and hence a negative one in (ii).

The results of Stone's other equations are also quite revealing but they are best reviewed in connection with the last section.

difference is that the estimate of α is now reduced to 0·72, appreciably closer to the US estimate (0·67).[7] See also addendum, p. 36.

A few as yet unpublished results are also available for some other countries. Singh and Kumar have been engaged in preparing estimates of private net worth in the post-war for four additional countries, Canada, the Netherlands, Germany and India, and have reported in [54] some preliminary tests of the LCH model, measuring income either by disposable income (as in equation (5)) or by compensation of employees before taxes (a somewhat dubious approximation—see section 8). For the first two countries the results are quite encouraging in terms of both fit and order of magnitude of the coefficients (for equation (5), for example, the estimates of δ are respectively around 0·052 and 0·068 and are highly significant). For the other two countries the results are, however, rather mixed. For India the wealth coefficient is on the small side and not very significant. Especially puzzling is the case of Germany, where the estimated coefficients are altogether of the wrong order of magnitude and sometimes even sign.[8]

Some promising results have also been obtained for Italy (Modigliani and Tarantelli [47]) in a test of equation (1), including a variable to allow for the effect of structural and cyclical unemployment. These results must be interpreted with caution, as they rely on a rather crude measure of labour income (cf. section 8) and of wealth, which is approximated by the financial assets of the private non-bank sector. Nonetheless the fit is quite good (the standard error being of the order of 1 per cent of consumption), and A makes a substantial contribution (t ratio around 4). However, the estimate of α, around 0·75, appears on the high side, while that of δ, between 0·08 and 0·09 depending on the method of estimation, is probably somewhat low when we allow for the fact that measured A tends to under-estimate total wealth substantially. These results are discussed further in section 8.

6 Implications of the LCH in a complete model

The question to be considered next is whether, and how far, the acceptance of the LCH function affects our understanding of the working of an economy, and in particular of stabilisation policies. The answer is definitely affirmative.

[7] These results are based on the definition of consumption including expenditure on durables, as in the original paper. With consumption defined to exclude durable purchases, the wealth coefficient is 0·07 and the income coefficient 0·61. Note that the definition used in the US estimate falls between the two, as it excludes durable expenditure but includes an estimated rental value of the stock of durables.

Some tests for the UK have also been reported by Deaton [10], relying on a version of the LCH modified to allow for uncertainty. Unfortunately, his proposed way of allowing for uncertainty appears rather *ad hoc*, and his parameter estimates are not readily interpretable in terms of the standard LCH.

[8] The estimates referred to in the text cannot be inferred from the results reported in [54], table AII.3, which relate to a test of the author's own version of the LCH. The authors have, however, kindly provided me with estimates of an equation of the form (5) (with both sides scaled by Y).

Consider first fiscal policy. It can be readily shown (cf. Modigliani [40], section II.1) that a consumption function (CF) of the type (3) implies that the multiplier effect of an autonomous increase in expenditure is indefinitely large if the marginal tax rate is zero. (The income response increases linearly in time at the rate $\delta(1-\alpha)$); if the marginal tax rate is τ the multiplier approaches $1/\tau$, which is independent of the parameter of the CF. At a more abstract level, the LCH has widespread implications for the family of issues revolving around the burden of the national debt (Modigliani [37].)

But the implications for monetary policy are even more significant, as the LCH implies a direct and rather speedy link between interest rates and consumption (cf., for example, Modigliani [40]). This is because a change in (real) interest rates affects the rate at which the market capitalises the earnings from assets and thus the market value of assets and finally consumption. In the FMP model we allow explicitly for the effect of long-term interest rates on the market value of corporate equities (being unable to measure explicitly the effect on such other components of wealth as land and residential structures). We estimate that the elasticity of corporate stock with respect to the (real) long-term interest rate (R) for given profit expectations is roughly one. Since the market value of stock (V) is roughly one-third of A and A is roughly five times C, the elasticity of consumption with respect to R comes to

$$\frac{dC}{dR}\cdot\frac{R}{C}=\left(\frac{\partial C}{\partial A}\cdot\frac{A}{C}\right)\cdot\left(\frac{\partial A}{\partial V}\cdot\frac{V}{A}\right)\cdot\left(\frac{\partial V}{\partial R}\cdot\frac{R}{V}\right)\simeq 0{\cdot}05\times 5\times 0{\cdot}3\times 1\simeq 0{\cdot}08$$

At first sight this looks like a relatively modest response as compared with that of other components of demand whose dependence on interest rates has been traditionally recognized. For instance, in the FMP model we estimate that the highest long-run elasticity is that of investment in equipment, which is close to one, and that of housing, over 0·5 (cf. Modigliani [42], section 4). But to assess the impact of a change in R on total output one must take into account the share of these different components in total output. Since the share of C is roughly ten times as large as that of investment in equipment, it appears that the total long-run direct impact on aggregate demand through these two components is not very different.

There is, however, another important difference to reckon with; namely that the full response of consumption is quite fast—one half within the first quarter, and the rest within a year—whereas the response of equipment is estimated to be rather slow, beginning only in the second quarter. It appears, therefore, that our estimates imply that the response of consumption, via the wealth effect, plays a major role in transmitting the initial impulse of monetary policy. This conclusion is confirmed by simulations reported in Modigliani [42]; we compared the response of aggregate output to a change in the money supply in the full model with the response of a system in which the effect of R on A was cut out by eliminating the link from R to the market value of stock. It is found that the effect for the full model is much faster and larger; in quarters 2–6 it is nearly twice as large, and the peak effect is reached in quarter 5 rather than in two to three years.

2

7 Further probing of the effect of capital gains

Some critics of the model have objected that the above results depend critically on the fact that according to the CF embedded in the model, which is of the form (6), consumption responds in the same way to capital gains as to any other source of change in wealth. Now while a coefficient of 0·05 for A may not be unreasonable, they suggest that capital gains in the stock market should have a smaller effect, at least initially, in part because they may be regarded as transient, and partly because stock ownership is heavily concentrated in the highest income brackets, which may have a lower propensity to consume (or, in LCH language, a higher propensity to leave bequests).

To assess the validity of this criticism Ando has recently carried out a series of tests in which (3) was re-estimated, breaking up A into two components: the market value of corporate stock, say AS, which is the only portion explicitly incorporating capital gains, and all the rest of wealth, say AO. The tests allowed for a separate distributed lag for each component. He found that a slight improvement in fit resulted from allowing the response to AS to be slower than that to AO; but he also found that, provided the distributed lag on AS was sufficiently long, the sum of coefficients of the two components was very nearly the same. For instance, with a four-quarter lag for AO and a twelve-quarter lag for AS, the coefficients summed up respectively to 0·064 and 0·061; and these estimates and the fit were but little affected by shortening or lengthening both lags somewhat. Furthermore the differences between the two sums are statistically quite insignificant, so that no loss of fit results by constraining them to have the same value. In our final estimate, which is incorporated in the latest version of the model, we have used this constraint, no lag for AO and an eight-quarter lag for AS. The sum of the weights for both components is 0·058. (The fact that the estimate is marginally higher than the original 0·052 largely reflects revisions of the data.) The structure of the weights implies that, when a capital gain first occurs, its effect on consumption is only some 30 per cent of the final effect; however, this effect rises gradually, the longer the capital gain lasts, to 50 per cent by the second quarter, two-thirds by the third quarter, and so on, until by the end of two years its effect is undistinguishable from that of any other component of wealth.

These results have been broadly supported by an alternative approach pursued by Bathia [5]. He explains consumption by a distributed lag of Y and of stock market capital gains (estimated by him) and finds that capital gains make a highly significant contribution (t ratio of 3·6). Furthermore the weights have a hump-shaped distribution which can be shown to be consistent with the shape of Ando's weights (though their sum appears somewhat smaller than might be inferred from Ando). On the whole these tests confirm the hypothesis of an important link from monetary policy through consumption via capital gains, though the results of the simulation in [40] cited earlier may overstate the speed of response.

The model also fails to recognise the possibility that a change in the long-term real interest rate may affect in the same direction the expectation of the long-term returns from existing capital, thus reducing the size of capital gain (i.e. the long-run elasticity of the market value of stock with respect to interest rates may be less than unity). This is a point which has been correctly emphasised by Tobin and Dolde [61] and taken into account in their simulations, but not yet in our model.

8 On the relation of LCH to the Kaldorian model

We may conclude this survey by noting the relation of the LCH to the remaining major model of saving behaviour that has attracted much attention, namely the Kaldorian hypothesis (KH) [24, 25]. As is well known, this hypothesis, especially in the version underlying Pasinetti's use of it [48], postulates that society is composed of two hereditary castes: the 'workers' earning their income from labour, and having a very low propensity to save, s_w, and the 'capitalists' earning only property income and whose propensity to save, s_p, is high. Thus the KH CF can be written as

$$C_t = (1 - s_w)\ YL_t + (1 - s_w)\ P_t \tag{7}$$

implying

$$\left(\frac{S}{Y}\right)_t = s_w + (s_p - s_w)\frac{P_t}{Y_t} \qquad s_p,\ s_w > 0 \tag{8}$$

Since, by assumption, s_w and s_p are not functions of YL or P, this model shares the property of the other models that the saving ratio is not a function of income. Its special feature is that S/Y depends instead on the functional distribution of income P/Y; or, more precisely, that S/Y and P/Y are functionally related to each other through (8). When combined with the assumption of an exogenous rate of growth, ρ, and a technologically given fixed capital output ratio k, it leads to the well known implication that the distribution of income, P/Y, and the rate of return on capital, r, depend on the relation between $s\rho$ and s_w. In the limiting case of $s_w = 0$ it is inversely proportional to s_p, $P/Y = \rho k/s_p$, which further implies $r = \rho/s_p$. Pasinetti [48], under some further assumptions, has generalised the latter results even to the case of $s_w \neq 0$.

By rewriting (3) in the form

$$C_t = \alpha YL_t + \delta^* A_t + \mu P_t^p \tag{9}$$

and comparing it with (7) it is apparent that there are some further important similarities between LCH and KH in that both models assert that C is a linear function of labour income and profits, and with different coefficients. The main differences are:

1 In terms of arguments in the CF. For LCH they are the expected rate of earnings from human effort, closely related to Friedman's human capital, and the expected long-run return from current private wealth, in addition

to the value of wealth itself. In KH the last variable does not appear and the first two variables supposedly denote 'wages' and 'profits' at current rates—or at any rate, no distinction is made between current measured values and long-run expectations.

2 In terms of interpretation. For KH the coefficients of YL and P are different because they are received by the members of different castes. In the LCH, on the other hand, every household typically earns both kinds of income during at least part of its life cycle, and the coefficient of P^p cannot be interpreted as a marginal propensity, but measures instead the strength of the substitution effect between current and future consumption. The LCH *per se* has little to say about the value of this coefficient or even about its sign.

Yet the LCH permits some inferences about the results that one might expect to find if one were to estimate the coefficients of equation (7). Consider first the quantity dC/dP^p, which measures the response of C to a change in expected property income, but which it would be ill advised to interpret as 'the marginal propensity to consume with respect to property income'. Differentiating (9) totally with respect to P^p, and remembering the relation $P^p - rA = 0$, one obtains

$$c_p = \frac{dC}{dP^p} = \mu + \frac{\delta^*}{r} E_{AP} \tag{10}$$

where E_{AP} is the elasticities of A with respect to P^p. Thus according to the LCH the response depends on the nature of the change in P^p; if it changes because of a change in A, r constant—which is presumably the most common source of change—then E_{AP} will be one and

$$c_p = \mu + \frac{\delta^*}{r}$$

But if it changes only because of a change in r, then E_{AP} is zero and

$$c_p = \mu$$

Now, as we have seen, the value of δ^* seems to be in the order of 0·06–0·08 and hence δ^*/r is certainly positive and of the order of unity—and could even be above 1. On the other hand, the value of μ is quite uncertain—it is unlikely to exceed unity, but it could be much smaller and even negative. Thus an increase in profit due to a change in A is sure to increase C and the derivative is likely to exceed α, and in fact could even exceed unity; but, if due to a change in r, it might well be less than α and it could even be negative.

These conclusions have very interesting implications concerning the value of the coefficient of P that one should expect to obtain if one were to regress C or S on YL and P, or equivalently S/Y on P/Y. A partial analysis of these implications was provided in Ando and Modigliani ([3], section III) for the case in which the observations are time series of aggregates for a specific country, and in Modigliani ([39], section 6(iii)) for the case in which the observations are time averages for a cross-section of countries. We propose to review these analyses, integrating them and outlining some extensions.

Consider first the case where the observations are from a cross-section of countries, as in Modigliani [39]. According to KH the association between S/Y and P/Y must be positive, as is apparent from (8). In the case of the LCH, on the other hand, one can deduce from (9)

$$C = \alpha Y^p + \delta^* A + (\mu - \alpha) P^p$$

and

$$s \equiv \frac{S}{Y} = \frac{Y-C}{Y} = (1-\alpha)\frac{Y^p}{Y} - \delta^* \frac{A}{Y} + (\alpha - \mu)\frac{P^p}{Y} + \frac{Y - Y^p}{Y}$$

By taking averages of all variables over a number of years we may expect Y^p/Y to approach unity and the average value of A/Y and P^p/Y, say $\bar{a}$ and $\bar{p}$, to approach the noise-free values A/Y^p and P^p/Y^p. Thus

$$\bar{s} = (1-\alpha) - \delta^* \bar{a} + (\alpha - \mu)\bar{p}$$

and therefore the slope of the cross-country relation between the saving ratio and the profit share is given by

$$\frac{d\bar{s}}{d\bar{p}} = -\delta^* \frac{d\bar{a}}{d\bar{p}} + (\alpha - \mu) = -\frac{\delta^*}{r}\frac{1}{1+E_{ra}} + \alpha - \mu \qquad \text{(10a)}$$

where E_{ra} is the elasticity of the long-run rate of return with respect to the wealth–income ratio. It is thus apparent that the sign of the slope depends on the prevailing cross-country elasticity of r with respect to a. One would generally expect r to fall with a, and thus $E_{ra} < 0$. (This would be true, in particular, if one identifies a with the capital–output ratio and assumes the same well behaved neoclassical production function for all countries.) If, then, $E_{ra} < -1$ (r is elastic with respect to a, or, in terms of the neoclassical model, the capital–output ratio is inelastic with respect to r), then the first term of (10a) is positive and hence $d\bar{s}/d\bar{p}$ is also likely to be positive, i.e. the saving ratio will rise with the profit share, as predicted also by KH. But if $E_{ra} > -1$, then the first term of (10a) is negative, and $d\bar{s}/d\bar{p}$ could very well be negative. In other words, according to the LCH the association between $\bar{s}$ and $\bar{p}$ could be of either sign.[9] By a similar reasoning one can establish that if s is regressed on ρ and p, the partial association between s and p could again have either sign under LCH, while it must still be positive for KH. It was shown in Modigliani [39], that, for the sample of thirty-three countries for which the information was available, both the simple and the partial association between s and p was in fact slightly negative, or at most zero;

[9] The common sense of this result may be clarified by observing that, under the LCH, s is an increasing function of ρ, a hypothesis which, as noted earlier, is well supported empirically. On the other hand, as we know from equation (2), A/Y is negatively associated with ρ. Hence the association between $p = ra$ and ρ depends precisely on the elasticity of r with respect to a. If the elasticity is less than one, p, like a, will fall with ρ and hence $\bar{s}$ and $\bar{p}$ will be negatively associated.

this result is consistent with LCH but inconsistent with KH. It was also pointed out that this result could not be regarded as altogether conclusive, because the only available measure for YL was wages and salaries, and for P the rest of income. This measure clearly understates YL and overstates P by including in the latter the income of the self-employed, a large portion of which is really labour income; the bias is particularly serious for less developed countries with a large sector of agriculture and under-employed self-employed. In an effort to reduce this bias the test was repeated for a sub-sample of nineteen more developed countries. For this sub-sample the simple association of s and p was strongly positive implying on a KH interpretation, a propensity to save out of labour income of roughly zero and out of P of 0·35. However, even for this sample the *partial* association of s and p was essentially zero, which again is consistent with LCH but not with KH. Even in this test the error-of-measurement problem may not have been entirely eliminated; however, it is presumably much reduced and hence the results are considerably more conclusive.

We can proceed now to the case where the observations are time series of aggregates for a given country. In this case, presumably, most of the observed variation in profits must come from variation in A (through saving and dissaving) rather than from variations in r. Hence E_{AP} must be close to one and c_p must be close to $\mu + \delta/r$, a number which, as noted earlier, is likely to be substantial and may well exceed unity. However c_p is the coefficient of P^p. On the other hand, in testing the Kaldorian model it has been cutomary to use current labour income and current profit. The difference is not too important in the case of YL because labour income is quite stable, hence expected income will tend to be roughly proportional to current YL. But the situation is entirely different in the case of P. As was pointed out by Ando and Modigliani [3], since P tends to fluctuate substantially in response to fluctuation in aggregate demand, P^p must be based on an average experience from the past (as well as other information). Hence $dC/dP = c_p dP^p/dP$ will be distinctly smaller than c_p, since dP^p/dP is certainly smaller than one and may be close to zero if P exhibits much short-run variation. Thus, independently of the relation of c_p to α, a regression of C on YL and P is most likely to yield a P coefficient much smaller than that of YL, especially since YL will tend to proxy in part for P^p. In the case of the United States, for example, Ando and Modigliani [3] obtained a coefficient for YL of 0·93 and a coefficient for P of but 0·07 (and totally insignificant); this was true even though A, in contrast to P, contributed very significantly to the explanation of C.

The line of enquiry developed in [3] has been replicated and pushed further in the forthcoming paper dealing with Italy cited earlier [47]. In that country there have been several tests of the Kaldorian model, which is hardly surprising considering the widespread allegiance of Italian economists to the English Cambridge school. These tests have typically consisted in correlating C with current wages and salaries as a measure of labour income, and the remainder of current income as a measure of P. The results, to everybody's satisfaction, have appeared extraordinarily favourable to the Kaldorian model. For example, in a regression of C on YL and P for the period 1952–70 the coefficients imply a marginal propensity to consume (m.p.c.) out of labour income of 1·04 to 1·06 (depending on the method of estimation) and out of property income of 0·23 to 0·33 (a little *too* good?). But the interpretation of this result is highly questionable. To being with, the use of wages and salaries as a measure of the labour income share is particularly objectionable because, over the period of fit, the labour share so defined tended to rise as a result of the continuing shift of the working population from self-employment to dependent labour which accompanied the process

Table 1.1 Estimates of parameters of consumption function Italy, 1952–70

		Coefficients of							
	Dependent	YL	P	$L(P)$		P^p	A		
Row	*variable*	α	c'_p	λ	c''_p	c_p	δ	*Constant*	*SE*
1	C	0·88	0·42						255
		[33]	[2·8]						
2	C	0·74					0·092		210
		[16]					[4·4]		
3	C	0·74	0·07				0·083		215
		[16]	[0·4]				[2·7]		
4	C	0·73	0·37	0·7	1·11	1·48			211
		[13]	[3]		[2·9]				
5	A		4·74	0·7	11·9	16·6		−9,370	2,650
			[3·0]		[5·9]			[5·1]	
6	C	0·64	0·13	0·8	1·21	·134	0·060		191
		[9·2]	[0·8]		[2·3]		[2·1]		

of development. At the beginning of the period there was a large number of the marginally self-employed with low income, as evidenced by the fact that the *per capita* income of the self-employed was but 10–20 per cent higher than that of employees. As the self-employed shifted to employee status the *per capita* income of the self-employed was lifted relative to that of employees, so that by 1969 it was some 50 per cent higher (still not very high in terms of a Kaldorian cast society of poor workers and reach capitalists!); thus the rise in the employees' share can hardly be taken as indicative of a fall in the share of property income.

The simplest device to make a correction for the shift out of self-employment is to assume that, to a first approximation, the self-employed income includes an imputed labour component equal to the *per capita* income of employees. One can then estimate total current 'labour' income YL by multiplying the *per capita* income of employees by total employment. Property income can be obtained by subtracting this estimate of labour income from total income. The resulting estimates of the two components are before personal taxes. Corresponding net-of-tax series were obtained by assuming that the incidence of taxes is the same for the two components, an assumption which is plausible in the case of Italy.

As can be seen from table 1.1, which reproduces the major relevant results from Modigliani and Tarantelli [47], reliance on these revised measures reduces the coefficient of labour income to 0·88 and raises the coefficient of P to 0·42 (see row 1)[10].

The implied m.p.c.'s being more plausible, but still widely apart, might be interpreted as providing more solid support for the Kaldorian 'two castes' model. On the other hand, according to LCH the low coefficient of P merely reflects the fact that P is a poor proxy for wealth and/or expected long-run profit, P^p, the truly relevant variables. This supposition receives some indirect support from the fact that the coefficient of P is not only low but also has a relatively low t ratio. Furthermore, as is apparent from table 1.1, line 2, which reports the results of the test of the LCH mentioned in section 5(b)

[10] These estimates as well as those reported hereafter in the text are those obtained when the equations were estimated in linear form, constraining the constant term to zero, as called for by the models. When this constraint was not imposed the constant term was almost uniformly insignificant and the coefficient estimates were hardly changed. In every case the variables were expressed in real terms, deflating current values by the cost of living index, and the equation estimated included as an additional variable the number of unemployed, on grounds developed in [3], and more extensively in [47]. The coefficients were also estimated in ratio form to reduce heteroscedasticity, using total income, Y, as the deflator, and the results are reported in table 1.2.

Table 1.2 Ratio estimates of parameters, Italy, 1952–70

		Coefficients of							
				$L(P)$					
	Dependent	YL	P			P^p	A		
Row	*variable*	α	c'_p	λ	c''_p	c_p	δ	*Constant*	*SE*
1*R*	C/Y	0·87	0·43 [2·3]						0·0123
2*R*	C/Y	0·77					0·078 [3·1]		0·0113
3*R*	C/Y	0·78	0·14 [0·6]				0·063 [1·8]		0·015
4*R*	C/Y	0·68	0·41	0·7	1·48	1·89			0·0086
5*R*	A/Y		6·2	0·7	10·3	16·5		−11,200 [7·3]	0·118
6*R*	C/Y	0·59	0·28 [1·6]	0·8	1·9 [3·7]	2·18	0·003 [1·1]		0·0085

above, replacing P with the available estimate of A, despite all its shortcomings, improves the fit substantially. These results are thus in line with those of Ando and Modigliani [3] for the US. But a more telling test reported in line 3 consists in adding the variable A to the Kaldorian model: the coefficient of P then falls from 0·42 to but 0·07 and is insignificantly different from zero, whereas the A coefficient falls only from 0·092 to 0·083 and is still quite insignificant. This result is consistent with the LCH interpretation that P, in the Kaldorian equation of line 1, is but a poor proxy for the relevant variable, A.

In an effort to probe further the validity of this inference we endeavoured to estimate directly the coefficient c_p of equation (10) by replacing both A and P with some plausible approximation to P^p. An operationally simple approximation is given by

$$C_t = \alpha' YL + c_p' P_t + c_p'' P_{t-1} + \lambda C_{t-1} \tag{11}$$

which implies that expected labour income is given by an exponentially distributed lag of past labour income, while permanent property income can be expressed as the sum of two such distributed lags, which allows for the possibility of a longer average lag. Equation (11) is found to fit the data much better than the simple Kaldorian equation (the standard error falls from 255 to 203) and yields the following estimates: $\alpha' = 0{\cdot}53$, $c_p' = 0{\cdot}22$, $c_p'' = 0{\cdot}43$, $\lambda = 0{\cdot}28$. These results confirm that the coefficient of current labour income, 0·53, is much larger than that of current profit, 0·22. However, the coefficient of 'expected' labour income, $\alpha = \alpha'/(1-\lambda) = 0{\cdot}82$, is lower than that of P^p, $c_p = (c_p' + c_p'')/(1-\lambda) = 0{\cdot}90$. If the coefficients are estimated in ratio form the results are even more striking: $\alpha = 0{\cdot}79$. $c_p = 1{\cdot}02$. Clearly, these results contradict KH dramatically—indeed, they are impossible to interpret in that framework. But they are fully consistent with LCH and in fact within the reasonable *a priori* range.[11]

To be sure, the hypothesis (11) is rather restrictive as to possible shapes of the distributed lag for the two components, though the result, implying a very rapid decay for the weights of past labour income, and weights rising at first, then decaying more slowly for P, are certainly consistent with what one might expect *a priori*. As an alternative we assumed that expected labour income could be identified with the current value, YL, especially since the possible effects of cyclical variations in employment are taken into account through the unemployment variable, and relied on the specification

$$C_t = \alpha YL + c_p' P + C_p'' L(P) \tag{12}$$

in which L is an exponentially distributed lag beginning with P_{-1}. The rate of decay, λ, was estimated by scanning over the range $0 < \lambda < 1$ for the value

[11] The approach of equation (11) was first pursued in a yet unpublished study by Bruno Sitzia. He also pursued some alternative methods of estimating c_p, all of which confirmed that this coefficient is as large as or larger than α. His valuable contribution as well as his advice in designing the tests reported here are gratefully acknowledged.

minimising the residual variance.[12] From the results reported in row 4 it appears that the distributed lag makes a substantial contribution to the explanation of C, roughly comparable to that made by A in row 3; the value of λ, 0·7, indicates a rather slow rate of decay, much as one would expect in view of the short-run variability of profits. The coefficient of current profit is again only half as large as that of labour income, but when we add to it the very high coefficient of lagged profits we arrive at an estimate of c_p not merely higher than α but well above unity. This is likely to be a shocking and unacceptable result for those who mistakenly try to interpret c_p as the m.p.c. out of property income. But it is perfectly sensible in the LCH framework, as it is apparent from (10).[13]

One can actually attempt a more direct test of the consistency of the above estimate of c_p with (10) and the estimate of δ in row 2, by exploring the relation between A and a measure of profit expectation. On the assumption that r is reasonably stable in the medium run, A should be proportional to P^p. Relying on the hypothesis underlying the test of row 4 that P^p can be approximated by a linear combination of P and a Koyck lag beginning with P_{-1}, we were led to test

$$A = \mu' P + \mu'' \alpha(P) + a \tag{13}$$

We allow for a constant term on the ground that what we measure is not true A, say $\hat{A}$, but a proxy A, financial wealth. We hypothesise that the relation of A to $\hat{A}$ can be approximated by

$$A = b\hat{A} + a = \frac{b}{r} P^p + a \qquad 0 < b < 1,\ a < 0$$

since in the process of development financial wealth is likely to rise proportionately faster than $\hat{A}$. The results obtained in estimating (13) are shown in row 5. The fit is surprisingly good considering the rough approximation to $\hat{A}$ $(R^2 = 0{\cdot}994)$, and the value of $\mu' + \mu''$, 16·5, an estimate of b times the capitalisation factor, is not unreasonable (though probably on the high side). This estimate, together with that of δ in row 2, suggests that the coefficient of P^p in row 4 should be around $(0{\cdot}092) \times (16{\cdot}5)$, or 1·5, which is quite consistent with the actual estimate.[14]

[12] As a check we estimated separate exponentially distributed lags for YL; whenever this procedure was tried the estimate of λ for this component turned out to be around 1, while the estimate of λ for the P component was basically unchanged.

[13] In a test of the Kaldorian hypothesis Tarantelli [59] shows that, even using an alternative measure of labour income which eliminates the bias in the conventional measure of the labour share, the estimated m.p.c. out of profits is *at least as high* as that out of wages and salaries, or even *higher*. He chose not to comment on this latter result (see [59], p. 133, n. 44) because such a comment would have implied a framework of the type suggested by (10), which is not compatible with the Kaldorian hypothesis.

[14] Since in the test of row 2 A denotes the value of assets at the end of the preceding year, the same is true in (13), and row 5. Nonetheless, the explanatory variables include *current* profits, P. This was done on the ground that the variable P appears

In the last row of the table we report the result of an attempt to estimate the coefficients of the LCH function in its more general form (9), which includes both A and P^p. Particular interest attaches here to the sign and size of the coefficient of P^p, an estimate of μ in (9) which reflects the strength of the substitution effect; we expect this coefficient to be positive and less than 1, though we cannot rule out a negative value.

It is seen that when P and $L(P)$ are added to the elementary version of the LCH in row 2, the coefficient of A remains significant and of reasonable size, but P^p also makes a fairly significant contribution. Its coefficient is positive and, in fact, somewhat larger than 1, which is above the *a priori* upper limit. We are inclined to attribute this excessively high estimate primarily to the fact that our approximation to $\hat{A}$ is very rough and hence P^p may partly act as a proxy for $\hat{A}$. If so, the coefficient of A is downward-biased, as suggested also by the estimate in row 2, while that of P^p is upward-biased. Another source of upward bias is that, in a system which is growing rapidly, a Koyck-distributed lag of past profits may tend to underestimate current profit expectations; this shortcoming, it should be noted, would bias upwards the coefficient of P^p also in rows 4 and 5.[15] On the whole, then, the results point to the conclusion that the coefficient μ of equation (9) is positive in the case of Italy, though its size cannot be estimated reliably, and that c_p is above one.

While these striking results for Italy have not yet been replicated, they receive some support from scattered evidence for other countries. First Stone in his 1966 paper [56] provides us with an explicit estimate of δ^* and μ of equation (9), though his results are based on some rather stringent assumptions which may limit their reliability for our purpose.[16] His estimate of α is 0·79, and that of μ is positive and in fact only moderately lower, 0·67; at the same time the separation of income into labour and property income does not affect the estimate of δ, which remains 0·06. It is readily apparent from these

[15] To get some feel for the possible size of this bias we relied on an alternative estimate of the quantity $(r_t A_t)$ of the form: $L(P/A) \times A$ where $L(P/A)$ is a Koyck-distributed lag of past values of the *ex post* observed rate of return P_t/A_t. This measure, of course, is also affected by the shortcomings of our measure of A. Use of this alternative yields an estimate of δ^* of 0·05, close to that of row 6, but a much smaller estimate of μ, 0·27. Unfortunately, the fit is also poorer, the standard error being 204 as compared with 191 in row 6. These results confirm that the estimate of μ in row 6 is upward-biased but that with presently available data it is impossible to measure it reliably.

[16] The most sensitive assumptions for our purpose are that (*a*) permanent labour income can be approximated by a Koyck lag of the wage and salary component of national income; (*b*) permanent property income P^p is a Koyck-distributed lag of the remaining components of income, and (*c*) the weights of the distributed lag are the same for the two components.

---

in row 4 and the estimate of c_p is the sum of the coefficients of profits including the current value P. The very significant contribution of current P to the explanation of earlier A can be readily accounted for on the hypothesis that P is a good proxy for profit expectations for the coming year held at the end of the previous year which are reflected in A.

estimates that, for any reasonable value of the rate of return, r, the quantity $0{\cdot}67+0{\cdot}06/r$ will exceed the estimated m.p.c. out of labour income of 0·79, and in fact will exceed unity. He also endeavoured to estimate the m.p.c. out of transient income, defined as current less 'permanent' income; and the results are again quite enlightening. In the case of labour income he obtains an estimate of 0·77, only slightly lower than the m.p.c. out of permanent income (0·79); but in the case of property income, as predicted by our model, the m.p.c. for transient income is negligible, less than 0·10. These results have again been confirmed by his later paper extending the analysis to 1970 [57]. In particular, when relying on the alternative measure of consumption excluding durables, the estimates of both α and μ are reduced as expected, but in addition the difference between them shrinks further to only about 0·10 (and with a very small t ratio).

Finally for the US, Weber [62], following a rather different method of estimation, but allowing explicitly for the effect of the interest rate, has concluded that the partial derivative of C with respect to r is positive, implying again a positive value of μ and hence, again, a value of c_p most probably above unity or at least above α.

9 Concluding remarks and agenda

From this historical survey of the origin of the LCH and of what has happened in the last twenty years in terms of both understanding fully and verifying its implications, I trust it is not presumptuous on my part to suggest that the LCH has proved a very fruitful hypothesis, capable of integrating a large variety of facts concerning individual and aggregate saving behaviour, on the foundations of the received theory of consumer's choice and a few plausible postulates.[17] Needless to say, it would be naive and presumptuous

[17] It was only after this paper had been completed that I became aware of the extensive and painstaking survey of recent developments in the formulation and tests of models of saving behaviour contained in the recently published book of Thomas Mayer [33]. It is, unfortunately, impossible at this point to comment extensively on the content of this book. Nonetheless, since at least some of the conclusions reached by Mayer concerning the LCH may seem somewhat at odds with my own evaluation summarised above, I should like to offer three observations which may help the reader in placing Mayer's analysis and conclusions in proper perspective: (*a*) Mayer's major concern is with testing the proposition that the individual household saving–income ratio is independent of the level of permanent income (or life resources): as we have noted repeatedly, evidence inconsistent with this proposition may cast doubt on the usefulness of the LCH hypothesis in its elementary form but is still perfectly consistent with the 'generalised' version, as Mayer explicitly acknowledges (p. 351); (*b*) the relevant implications of the generalised version are not easily amenable to cross-sectional tests, and, as far as one can see, Mayer's results do not generally bear directly on this version; (*c*) the aggregative implications can be tested only from a cross-section of countries or from time series data for individual countries. Mayer's survey in chapter 6 is conspicuously and admittedly skimpy in terms of the first type of tests, failing even to cite such references as [29, 39] and the controversy

to suppose that this model can dispose once and for ever of the whole area of saving behaviour. In the first place, it should be regarded as a basic framework which can be amended and improved upon for the purpose of analysing specific problems (especially at the level of individual behaviour), or different institutions (e.g. non-market economies or systems in which retirement provisions are largely handled through forms other than private accumulation). In addition there are a number of issues that require and deserve closer scrutiny, such as the effect of the rate of return on the CF, and the quantitative impact of monetary policy on consumption, via capital gains, when allowance is made for the Tobin effect of interest rates on expected returns as well as on the capitalisation of this return.

Thus a good deal remains to be done. Indeed, as I look at the work accomplished and that still to be done, I sometimes feel that my only regret is that I have but one life cycle to give to the life cycle hypothesis.

References

1 Ackley, C., 'The wealth–saving relationship', *Journal of Political Economy*, April 1951.

2 Adams, N. A., 'Dependency rates and savings rates: comment', *American Economic Review*, June 1971.

3 Ando, A., and Modigliani, F., 'The life cycle hypothesis of saving: aggregate implications and tests', *American Economic Review*, March 1963.

4 Ball, R. J., and Drake, P., 'The relationship between aggregate consumption and wealth', *International Economic Review*, January 1964.

5 Bathia, K. B., 'Stock market gains, aggregate consumption, and money supply', paper presented at the econometric society meetings, Toronto, December 1972 (mimeo.).

6 Bentzel, 'Nagra synpunkter pa sparandets dynamik', in *Festskrift Tillagnad Halvar Sundberg*, Uppsala Universitets Arsskrift 1959 : 9, Uppsala, 1959.

7 Brady, D. S., and Friedman, R. D., 'Savings and the income distribution', *Studies in Income and Wealth*, vol. x, pp. 247–65.

8 Brown, T. M., 'Habit persistence and lags in consumer behaviour', *Econometria*, vol. xx, July 1952, pp. 355–71.

9 Brumberg, R. E., 'An approximation to the aggregate saving function', *Economic Journal*, May 1956, pp. 66–72.

10 Deaton, A. S., 'Wealth effects on consumption in a modified life cycle model', *Review of Economic Studies*, October 1972.

---

generated by [29]. As for aggregate time series tests, those of tables 22 and 23 seem rather questionable (even though in table 22 the LCH form, row F, ranks first among those tested, a result that Mayer manages to dismiss on the puzzling ground that 'Tobin many years ago suggested the inclusion of a wealth term in the consumption function'). In any event, the effectiveness of the LCH and the importance of the wealth variable in explaining aggregate consumption in the post-war period have been amply documented for the US in the references cited, notably in [40], which appeared too late to be fully taken into account by Mayer (cf. [33], p. 234, n. 42]; for the UK, especially in [56] and [57], neither of which is explicitly cited by Mayer (the second understandably, since it appeared only after his book); and for Italy [47] and the Netherlands [54a].

11 Drèze, J. H., and Modigliani, F., 'Consumption decisions under uncertainty', *Journal of Economic Theory*, vol. v, 1972.
12 Duesenberry, J. S., *Income, Saving and the Theory of Consumer Behavior*, Harvard University Press, 1949.
13 Evans, M. K., 'The importance of wealth in the consumption function', *Journal of Political Economy*, August 1967.
14 Fisher, F., and Brown, R., 'Negro–white savings differentials and the Modigliani–Brumberg hypothesis', *Review of Economics and Statistics*, February 1958.
15 Fisher, I., *The Theory of Interest*, Macmillan, New York, 1930.
16 Fisher, M. R., 'Exploration in saving behaviour', *Bulletin of the Oxford University Institute of Economic Statistics*, 1957.
17 Florissi, C., 'Verifica empirica dell'ipotesi del "ciclo vitale" del reddito e del risparmio e applicazioni alla interpretazione dei livelli di risparmio in Italia e in Europa', *Rivista di Politica Economica*, March 1973.
18 Friedman, M., *A Theory of the Consumption Function*, Princeton University Press, 1957.
19 Goldsmith, R. W., *A Study of Saving in the United States*, Princeton University Press, 1956.
20 Gupta, K. L., 'Dependency rates and savings rates: comment', *American Economic Review*, June 1971.
21 Hakansson, N. H., 'Optimal investment and consumption strategies under risk for a class of utility functions', *Econometrica*, vol. xxxviii, No. 5, September 1970.
22 Hamburger, W., 'The relation of consumption to wealth and the wage rate', *Econometrica*, January 1955.
23 Harrod, R. F., *Towards a Dynamic Economics*, London, 1948.
24 Kaldor, N., *Essays in Value and Distribution*, London, 1960.
25 — *Essays in Economic Stability and Growth*, London, 1960.
26 Keynes, J. M., *The General Theory of Employment, Interest and Money*, London and New York, 1936.
27 Kuznets, S., *Uses of National Income in Peace and War*, National Bureau of Economic Research occasional paper No. 6, 1942.
28 Landsberger, M., 'The life cycle hypothesis: a reinterpretation and empirical test', *American Economic Review*, March 1970.
29 Leff, N., 'Dependency rates and saving rates', *American Economic Review*, December 1969.
30 — 'Dependency rates and saving rates: reply', *American Economic Review*, June 1971.
31 Leland, H. E., 'Dynamic portfolio theory', Ph.D. dissertation, Department of Economics, Harvard University, 1968.
32 Lydall, H. F., 'Saving and wealth', *Australian Economic Papers*, December 1963, pp. 228–50.
33 Mayer, T., *Permanent Income, Wealth and Consumption*, University of California Press, 1972.
34 Merton, R. C., 'Lifetime portfolio selection under uncertainty: the continuous-time case', *Review of Economics and Statistics*, August 1969, pp. 247–57.
35 — 'Optimum consumption and portfolio rules in a continuous-time model', *Journal of Economic Theory*, December 1971.
36 Modigliani, F., 'Fluctuations in the saving–income ratio: a problem in economic forecasting', *Studies in Income and Wealth*, vol. xi, national Bureau of Economic Research, London 1949.

37 — 'Long-run implication of alternative fiscal policies and the burden of the national debt', *Economic Journal*, December 1961, pp. 730–65.

38 — 'The life cycle hypothesis of saving, the demand for wealth and the supply of capital', *Social Research*, summer 1966.

39 — 'The life cycle hypothesis of saving and inter-country differences in the saving ratio', in *Induction, Growth and Trade, Essays in Honour of Sir Roy Harrod*, London 1970.

40 — 'Monetary policy and consumption: linkages via interest rate and wealth effects in the FMP model', *Consumer Spending and Monetary Policy: the Linkages*, Federal Researve Bank of Boston, Mass., 1971.

41 — 'Stock market and economy—discussion', *American Economic Review*, May 1972.

42 — 'The channels of monetary policy in the FMP econometric model of the United States', *Proceedings of* Conference on Model-building, London Graduate School of Business Studies, 1973 (forthcoming).

43 — 'Tests of the life cycle hypothesis of saving', *Bulletin of the Oxford University Institute of Statistics*, May 1957, pp. 99–124.

44 Modigliani, F., and Ando, A., 'The permanent income and the life cycle hypothesis of saving behavior: comparisons and tests', in *Proceedings of the Conference on Consumption and Saving*, vol. II, Philadelphia 1970.

45 Modigliani, F., and Brumberg, F., 'Utility analysis and the consumption function: an interpretation of cross-section data', in *Post-Keynesian Economics*, ed. K. Kurihara, New Brunswick, 1954.

46 — 'Utility analysis and aggregate consumption functions: an attempt at integration' (unpublished).

47 Modigliani, F., and Tarantelli, E., 'The consumption function in a developing economy and the Italian experience', Banca d'Italia, 'Modello econometrico dell'economia italiana', May 1974 (Multilith).

48 Pasinetti, L. L., 'Rate of profit and income distribution in relation to the rate of economic growth', *Review of Economic Studies*, vol. XXIX, 1962.

49 Projector, D. S., *Survey of Changes in Family Finance*, Board of Governors of the Federal Reserve System, Washington, D.C., 1968.

50 Projector, D. S., and Weiss, G. S., *Survey of Financial Characteristics*, Board of Governors of the Federal Reserve System, Washington, D.C., 1966.

51 Rasche, R. M., 'Impact of the stock market on private demand', *American Economic Review*, May 1972.

52 Reid, M. G., 'The relation of the within-group permanent component of income to the income elasticity of expenditures', preliminary draft.

53 Samuelson, P. A., 'Lifetime portfolio selection by dynamic stochastic programming', *Review of Economics and Statistics*, August 1969.

54 Singh, B., and Kumar, R. C., 'An empirical evaluation of the life cycle hypothesis', University of Toronto (mimeo.).

54a Somermeyer, W. H., and Bannink, R., *A Consumption Savings Model and its Applications*, North-Holland, Amsterdam and London, 1973.

55 Spiro, A., 'Wealth and the consumption function', *Journal of Political Economy*, August 1962.

56 Stone, R. H., 'Spending and saving in relation to income and wealth', *L'Industria*, No. 4, 1966.

57 — 'Personal spending and saving in post-war Britain', in *Economic Structure*

and Development: Essays in Honour of J. Tinbergen, ed. H. C. Bos, H. Linnemann and P. de Wolff, 1974.

58 Swamy, S., 'A dynamic, personal savings function and its long-run implications', *Review of Economics and Statistics*, vol. XLX, February 1968.

59 Tarantelli, E., 'Note sul consumo nella teoria economica e nuove linee di ricerca per l'esperienza italiana', *Rivista Internazionale di Scienze Sociali*, vol. LXXXI, 1973, fasc. I–II.

60 Tobin, J., 'Life cycle saving and balanced growth', in *Ten Economic Essays in the Tradition of Irving Fisher*, 1967.

61 Tobin, J., and Dolde, W. C., 'Wealth, liquidity and consumption', in *Consumer Spending and Monetary Policy: the Linkages*, Federal Reserve Bank of Boston, Mass., 1971.

62 Weber, W. R., 'The effect of interest rates on aggregate consumption', *American Economic Review*, September 1970.

Addenda

Page 15, note 4a. In Somermeyer and Bannink [54a], which came to my attention when this paper was already in page proof, a similar approximation is derived, starting from an additive logarithmic utility function; in this approximation also the coefficient of income becomes $\alpha_0+\alpha_1 r_t$ and they that both α_1 and μ should be negative. (See especially pp. 188-91.)

Page 20. Very similar results have been derived for the Netherlands for the period 1949–66 by Somermeyer and Bannink [54a], testing an equation of the form (5) (cf. table 7.7). Their estimate of δ' is around 0·06, while their estimate of α, 0·5 to 0·6, is somewhat on the low side, though this might be partly due to their use of *current* income.

Errata

Page 4, paragraph 2, line 14: "$\mathring{Y}_t$ to current income $\mathring{Y}_t$" should read "$\mathring{Y}_t$ to current income Y_t."

Page 10, line 5: "net-of-tax income" should read "net-of-tax yearly income."

Page 13, paragraph 4, line 2: the period after "LCH" should be a comma.

Page 14, footnote 4, 9 lines from the bottom: the equation in this line should read

$$``\sigma^* \equiv \sigma \frac{\bar{B}_R^*(T)}{\bar{B}_R(T)}."$$

Page 14, footnote 4, 4 lines from the bottom: "Hence, if $\overline{YL}^*(T)$ is a constant YL^*" should read "Hence, if $\overline{YL}^*(T)$ is a constant, $\overline{YL}^*$."

Page 16, paragraph 2, line 3: "Brumberg [89]" should read "Brumberg [9]."

Page 19: footnote 6, below (iii), should read "If the error term is serially correlated, as is likely, the estimate of the coefficient of S_{-1} will have a positive bias in (iii) and hence the coefficient of ΔA in (ii) will have a negative bias."

Page 23: equation 7 should read "$C_t = (1 - s_w)YL_t + (1 - s_p)P_t$."

Page 27, line 6: "To being with" should read "To begin with."

Page 27, table 1.1, line 6: ".134" should read "1.34."

Page 29, line 7: "quite insignificant" should read "quite significant."

Page 35, Addenda, line 4: "they that both" should read "they show that both."

PART II
The Theory

[CHAPTER FIFTEEN]

Utility Analysis and the Consumption Function: An Interpretation of Cross-Section Data[1]

Franco Modigliani[2] *and Richard Brumberg*

Introduction

OF JOHN MAYNARD KEYNES' many hypotheses, the one that has been subject to the most intensive empirical study is the relation between income and consumption. By now, his generalization is familiar to all:

> The fundamental psychological law, upon which we are entitled to depend with great confidence both *a priori* from our knowledge of human nature and from the detailed facts of experience, is that men are disposed, as a rule and on the average, to increase their consumption as their income increases, but not by as much as the increase in their income.[3]

The study of the consumption function has undoubtedly yielded some of the highest correlations as well as some of the most embarrassing forecasts in the history of economics. Yet the interest in the subject continues unabated since, if it were possible to establish the existence of a stable relation between consumption, income, and other relevant variables and to estimate its parameters, such a relation would represent an invaluable tool for economic policy and forecasting.

[1] We are indebted to several colleagues, and especially to Messrs. R. Cyert, of Carnegie Institute of Technology, and C. Christ, of the Johns Hopkins University, for reading the manuscript and making valuable suggestions.

[2] My contribution to this paper is a direct outgrowth of the research carried out as director of the project on "Expectations and Business Fluctuations" financed by a grant of the Merrill Foundation for the Advancement of Financial Knowledge. I should particularly like to call attention to the relation between consumption, assets, income expectations, and the life cycle of income as developed in this paper and the relation between production, inventories, sales expectations, and the seasonal cycle of sales as developed in my joint paper with O. H. Sauerlender, "The Use of Expectations and Plans of Firms for Short Term Forecasting," *Studies in Income and Wealth*, Vol. XVII, in course of publication.

[3] John Maynard Keynes, *The General Theory of Employment, Interest, and Money*, 1936, p. 96.

The work done in this area during the last few years has taken two directions.[4] One has consisted in extensive correlations of data on aggregate consumption, or saving, with income and a large collection of additional miscellaneous variables. The second direction has been the exploitation of cross-section data. Old material has been reworked and new information collected. The most elaborate of the new studies have been those of the Survey Research Center of the University of Michigan. As in the time series analysis, more and more variables have been included, or are proposed for inclusion, in order to discover stable relations.[5]

By now the amount of empirical facts that has been collected is truly impressive; if anything, we seem to be in imminent danger of being smothered under them. What is, however, still conspicuously missing is a general analytical framework which will link together these facts, reconcile the apparent contradictions, and provide a satisfactory bridge between cross-sectional findings and the findings of aggregative time series analysis.

It is our purpose to attempt to provide such an analytical framework through the use of the well-developed tools of marginal utility analysis. We have shown elsewhere[6] that the application of this instrument proves of great help in integrating and reconciling most of the known findings of aggregative time series analysis. In this paper, we shall attempt to show how the same model of individual behavior can be applied to the analysis of cross-section data. We hope to demonstrate that this model provides a consistent, if somewhat novel, interpretation of the existing data and suggests promising directions for further empirical work.

[4] For two excellent bibliographies in this field, see: G. H. Orcutt and A. D. Roy, "A Bibliography of the Consumption Function," University of Cambridge, Department of Applied Economics, mimeographed release, 1949; and *Bibliography on Income and Wealth, 1937-1947*, edited by Daniel Creamer, International Association for Research in Income and Wealth, 1952.

[5] For example, see Lawrence R. Klein, "Savings Concepts and Their Relation to Economic Policy: The Viewpoint of a User of Savings Statistics," paper delivered at the Conference on Savings, Inflation, and Economic Progress, University of Minnesota, 1952.

[6] Franco Modigliani and Richard Brumberg, "Utility Analysis and Aggregate Consumption Functions: An Attempt at Integration," a forthcoming study.

Part I: THEORETICAL FOUNDATIONS

I.1 Utility Analysis and the Motives for Saving

Our starting point will be the accepted theory of consumer's choice. The implications of this theory have been so incompletely recognized in the empirically-oriented literature of recent years, that it will be useful to retrace briefly the received doctrine.[7]

Consider the following variables:

- c_t consumption of the individual during the t-th year (or other specified interval) of his life, where t is measured from the beginning of the earning span;
- y_t income (other than interest) in the t-th year (for an individual of age t, y_t and c_t denote current income and consumption, while y_τ and c_τ, for $\tau > t$, denote expected income and planned consumption in the τ-th year):
- s_t saving in the t-th year;
- a_t assets at beginning of age period t;
- r the rate of interest;
- N the earning span;
- M the retirement span; and
- L the life span of economic significance in this context, that is, $N + M$.

It is assumed that the individual receives utility only from present and prospective consumption and from assets to be bequeathed. If we assume further that the price level of consumables is not expected to change appreciably over the balance of the life span, so that the volume of consumption is uniquely related to its value, then for an individual of age t, the utility function can be written as

$$U = U(c_t, c_{t+1}, \cdots c_L, a_{L+1}). \tag{1.1}$$

This function is to be maximized subject to the budget constraint, which, if the rate of interest, r, is not expected to change appreciably over the balance of the life span, can be expressed by means of the equation

[7] For an extensive application of marginal utility analysis to the theory of saving see the valuable contributions of Umberto Ricci, dating almost thirty years back: "L'offerta del Risparmio," Part I, *Giornale degli Economisti*, Feb. 1926, pp. 73-101; Part II, *ibid.*, March, 1926, pp. 117-147; and "Ancora Sull'Offerta del Risparmio," *ibid.*, Sept. 1927, pp. 481-504.

$$(1.2) \qquad a_t + \sum_{\tau=t}^{N} \frac{y_\tau}{(1+r)^{\tau+1-t}} = \frac{a_{L+1}}{(1+r)^{L+1-t}} + \sum_{\tau=t}^{L} \frac{c_\tau}{(1+r)^{\tau+1-t}}.^{8}$$

For the utility function (1.1) to be maximized, the quantities c_τ and a_{L+1} must be such as to satisfy the first order conditions:

$$(1.3) \qquad \begin{cases} \dfrac{\partial U}{\partial c_\tau} = \dfrac{\lambda}{(1+r)^{\tau+1-t}}; & \tau = t, t+1, \cdots, L \\ \dfrac{\partial U}{\partial a_{L+1}} = \dfrac{\lambda}{(1+r)^{L+1-t}} \end{cases}$$

where λ represents a Lagrange multiplier. The equation (1.3), together with (1.2), yields a system of $L - t + 3$ simultaneous equations to determine $L - t + 1$ $\bar{c}_\tau$'s, $\bar{a}_{L+1}$ and $\bar{\lambda}$, the barred symbols being used to characterize the maximizing value of the corresponding variable.

If current income, $y_t + ra_t$, is unequal to c_t, the individual will be currently saving (or dissaving); and similarly, if $y_\tau + ra_\tau$ is not equal to $\bar{c}_\tau$, the individual will be planning to save (or dissave) at age τ. The traditional model suggests that we may usefully distinguish two separate reasons for such inequalities to arise. We refer to these reasons as the "motives for saving." [9]

I The first of these motives is the desire to add to the estate for the benefit of one's heirs; it arises when $\bar{a}_{L+1}$ is greater than a_t. Under this condition $y_\tau + ra_\tau$ must exceed $\bar{c}_\tau$ for at least some $\tau \geqq t$.

II The second motive arises out of the fact that the pattern of current and prospective income receipts will generally not coincide with the preferred consumption, $\bar{c}_\tau$, for all $\tau \geqq t$. This clearly represents an independent motive in that it can account for positive (or negative) saving in any subinterval of the life span, even in the absence of the first motive.

It is precisely on this point that a really important lesson can be learned by taking a fresh look at the traditional theory of the household; according to this theory there need not be any close and simple relation between consumption in a given short period

[8] See, for instance, J. Mosak, *General Equilibrium Theory in International Trade*, Ch. VI, especially pp. 116-117.

[9] Cf. Keynes, *op. cit.*, p. 107.

and income in the same period. The rate of consumption in any given period is a facet of a plan which extends over the balance of the individual's life, while the income accruing within the same period is but one element which contributes to the shaping of such a plan. This lesson seems to have been largely lost in much of the empirically-oriented discussion of recent years, in the course of which an overwhelming stress has been placed on the role of current income, or of income during a short interval centering on the corresponding consumption interval, almost to the exclusion of any other variable.

Before proceeding further with the implications of our model, it is necessary to devote brief attention to one conceivably important element that we have neglected so far, namely, the phenomenon of uncertainty. No attempt will be made in this paper to introduce uncertainty in the analysis in a really rigorous fashion. The reason for this procedure is simple; we believe that for the purposes in which we are interested, a satisfactory theory can be developed without seriously coming to grips with this rather formidable problem. An examination of the considerations that support this conclusion, however, is best postponed until we have fully explored the implications of our model under certainty. We may simply note at this point that the presence of uncertainty might be expected to give rise to two additional motives for saving:

III The precautionary motive, *i.e.*, the desire to accumulate assets through saving to meet possible emergencies, whose occurrence, nature, and timing cannot be perfectly foreseen. Such emergencies might take the form of a temporary fall in income below the planned level or of temporary consumption requirements over and above the anticipated level. In both cases the achievement of the optimum consumption level might depend on the availability of previously acquired assets.

IV Finally, as a result of the presence of uncertainty, it is necessary, or at least cheaper, to have an equity in certain kinds of assets before an individual can receive services from them. These assets are consumers' durable goods. If there were no uncertainty, a person could borrow the whole sum necessary to purchase the assets (the debt cancelling the increase in real asset holdings), and pay off the loans as the assets are consumed. In the real world, however, the uncertainty as to the individual's ability to pay forces the individual to hold at least a partial equity in these assets.

While we have thus come to distinguish four separate motives for saving, we should not forget that any one asset in the individual's "portfolio" may, and usually will, satisfy more than one motive simultaneously. For example, the ownership of a house is a source of current services; it may be used to satisfy part of the consumption planned for after retirement; it may be bequeathed; and, finally, it is a source of funds in emergencies. It follows that any possession which can be turned into cash will serve at least one of the four motives and should accordingly be treated as an asset. These possessions include, in particular, equities in unconsumed durable goods.

Saving and dissaving can then usefully be defined as the positive, or negative, change in the net worth of an individual during a specified time period. Correspondingly, consumption will be defined as the expenditure on nondurable goods and services—adjusted for changes in consumers' inventories—plus current depreciations of direct-service-yielding durable goods.[10]

As we shall see, the fact that assets are capable of satisfying more than one motive simultaneously provides the foundation for our earlier statement that it should be possible to neglect the phenomenon of uncertainty without too serious consequences. But a fuller development of this point will have to wait until later.

I.2 Some Further Assumptions and Their Implications

The currently accepted theory of the household, even in the very general formulation used so far, has begun to broaden our view of saving behavior. It is, however, too general to be really useful in empirical research. If we are to derive from it some propositions specific enough to be amenable to at least indirect

[10] Quite recently, many others have advocated this definition. See, for instance, Kenneth Boulding, *A Reconstruction of Economics*, Ch. 8; Mary W. Smelker, "The Problem of Estimating Spending and Saving in Long-Range Projections," Conference on Research in Income and Wealth (preliminary), p. 35; Raymond W. Goldsmith, "Trends and Structural Changes in Saving in the 20th Century," Conference on Savings, Inflation, and Economic Progress, University of Minnesota, 1951; James N. Morgan, "The Structure of Aggregate Personal Saving," *Journal of Political Economy*, Dec. 1951; and William Hamburger, "Consumption and Wealth," unpublished Ph.D. dissertation, The University of Chicago, 1951.

empirical tests, it will be necessary to narrow it down by introducing some further assumptions about the nature of the utility function (see Assumption II below). For convenience of exposition, however, we shall also find it useful to introduce several additional assumptions whose only purpose is to simplify the problem by reducing it to its essentials. These assumptions will enable us to derive some very simple relations between saving, income, and other relevant variables, and it will appear that the implications of these relations are consistent with much of the available empirical evidence. While some of the simplifying assumptions we are about to introduce are obviously unrealistic, the reader should not be unduly disturbed by them. In the first place we have shown elsewhere[11] that most of these assumptions (except Assumption II) can be greatly relaxed or eliminated altogether, complicating the algebra but without significantly affecting the conclusions. In the second place, the question of just which aspects of reality are essential to the construction of a theory is primarily a pragmatic one. If the theory proves useful in explaining the essential features of the phenomena under consideration in spite of the simplifications assumed, then these simplifications are thereby justified.

It may be well to recall, first, that one simplifying assumption has already been made use of in developing our basic model of equation (I.1) to (I.3); this is the assumption that (on the average) the price level of consumables is not expected to change appreciably over time. The first of our remaining assumptions will consist in disregarding altogether what we have called the "estate motive." Specifically, we shall assume that the typical household, whose behavior is described by equations (I.1) to (I.3), does not inherit assets to any significant extent and in turn does not plan on leaving assets to its heirs. These conditions can be formally stated as:

Assumption I: $a_1 = 0, \qquad \bar{a}_{L+1} = 0.$[12]

[11] Modigliani and Brumberg, *op. cit.*

[12] The assumption $\bar{a}_{L+1} = 0$ might be stated more elegantly in terms of the following two:

$$\text{(a)}\ \frac{\partial U}{\partial a_{L+1}} = 0; \qquad \text{(b)}\ a_{L+1} \geqq 0.$$

The first of these equations specifies certain properties of the utility function U; the second states an institutional fact the individual must take into account in his planning, namely that our economic, legal, and ethical system is set up so as to make it rather difficult to get away without paying one's debts. The addition of these two equations to our previous system implies $\bar{a}_{L+1} = 0$.

Assumption I, together with equation (I.2), implies that our household, in addition to having no inherited assets at the beginning of its life, also does not receive any gift or inheritance at any other point of its life; it can only accumulate assets through its own saving.

From Assumption I and equation (I.2), it follows immediately that current and future planned consumption must be functions of current and expected (discounted) income plus initial assets, *i.e.*,

$$\bar{c}_\tau = f(v_t, t, \tau), \qquad \tau = t, t+1, \cdots, L;$$

where

$$v_t = \sum_{\tau=t}^{N} \frac{y_\tau}{(1+r)^{\tau+1-t}} + a_t,$$

and t denotes again the present age of the individual.[13]

Now what can be said about the nature of the function f? Or, to reformulate the question, suppose that, on the expectation that his total resources would amount to v_t, and with a given interest rate, our individual had decided to distribute his consumption according to the pattern represented by $\bar{c}_\tau$. Suppose further that, before carrying out his plan, he is led to expect that his resources will amount not to v_t but, say, to $v_t + \Delta v_t$. Should we then expect him to allocate the additional income to increase consumption in any specific period of his remaining life (*e.g.*, his early years, or his late years, or his middle years), relative to all other periods, or can we expect him to allocate it so as to increase all consumptions roughly in the same proportion?

We are inclined to feel that the second alternative is fairly reasonable; or, at any rate, we are unable to think of any systematic factor that would tend to favor any particular period relative to any other. And for this reason we are willing to assume that the second answer, even if it is not true for every individual, is true on the average.[14] This gives rise to our second assumption, the only one that is really fundamental for our entire construction, namely:

Assumption II: The utility function is such that the *proportion* of his total resources that an individual plans to devote to

[13] The fact that $a_1 = 0$ by Assumption I of course does not imply $a_t = 0$.

[14] The expression "on the average" here means that if we aggregate a large number of individuals chosen at random, their aggregate consumption will behave approximately as though each individual behaved in the postulated way.

consumption in any given year τ of his remaining life is determined only by his tastes and not by the size of his resources. Symbolically, this assumption can be represented by the following equation:

$$\text{(I.4)} \qquad \bar{c}_\tau = \gamma_\tau^t v_t, \qquad \tau = t, t+1, \cdots, L$$

where, for given t and τ the quantity γ_τ^t depends on the specific form of the function U and on the rate of interest r, but *is independent of "total resources," v_t.*

As a result of well-known properties of homogeneous functions, it can readily be shown that a sufficient condition for Assumption II to hold is that the utility function U be homogeneous (of any positive degree) in the variables $c_t, c_{t-1}, \cdots, c_L$.[15]

The remaining two assumptions are not essential to the argument, but are introduced for convenience of exposition.[16]

ASSUMPTION III: The interest rate is zero, *i.e.*, $r = 0$.

As a result of this assumption, the expression

$$v_t = \sum_{\tau=t}^{N} \frac{y_\tau}{(1+r)^{\tau+1-t}} + a_t$$

can be rewritten as $y_t + (N - t)y_t^e + a_t$, where

$$y_t^e = \left(\sum_{\tau=t+1}^{N} y_t\right) \Big/ \ (N-t),$$

represents the average income expected over the balance of the earning span.

[15] More generally, it is sufficient that the utility index be any monotonic increasing function of a function U homogeneous in $c_t, \ldots, c_L$. This assumption can also be stated in terms of properties of the indifference map relating consumption in different periods. The postulated map has the property that tangents to successive indifference curves through the points where such curves are pierced by any one arbitrary radius vector are parallel to each other.

It may also be worth noting that a simple form of the utility index U satisfying our assumption is the following:

$$U = \log U = \alpha_0 + \sum_{\tau=t}^{L} \alpha_\tau \log c_\tau$$

since U is clearly homogeneous in $c_t, \ldots, c_L$. The above expression in turn has the same form as the well-known Weber Law of psychophysics, if we regard U as a measure of the intensity of the sensation and c as the intensity of the stimulus. One may well speculate whether we have here something of deeper significance than a mere formal analogy.

[16] For a discussion of the effects of removing them, see Modigliani and Brumberg, *op. cit.* Also, see various footnotes below.

Equation (I.4) now reduces to:

$$(1.4') \qquad \bar{c}_\tau = \gamma_\tau^t[y_t + (N - t)y_t^e + a_t]$$

which implies

$$\sum_{\tau=t}^{L} c_\tau = [y_t + (N - t)y_t^e + a_t] \sum_{\tau=t}^{L} \gamma_\tau^t.$$

Furthermore, taking into account Assumption I ($\bar{a}_{L+1} = 0$) we also have

$$(\text{I.5}) \qquad \sum_{\tau=t}^{L} c_\tau = y_t + (N - t)y_t^e + a_t.$$

From (I.4′) and (I.5) it then follows that

$$(\text{I.6}) \qquad \sum_{\tau=t}^{L} \gamma_\tau^t = 1.$$

Assumption IV: All the γ_τ^t are equal; *i.e.*, our hypothetical prototype plans to consume his income at an even rate throughout the balance of his life.

Let γ_t denote the common values of the γ_τ^t for an individual of age t. From (I.6) we then have

$$(\text{I.7}) \qquad \sum_{\tau=t}^{L} \gamma_\tau^t = (L + 1 - t)\gamma_t = 1;$$

$$\text{or,} \qquad \gamma_\tau^t = \gamma_t = \frac{1}{L + 1 - t} \equiv \frac{1}{L_t},$$

where $L_t \equiv L + 1 - t$ denotes the remaining life span at age t.

Part II: IMPLICATIONS OF THE THEORY AND THE EMPIRICAL EVIDENCE

II.1 The Individual Consumption Function and the Cross-section Consumption-Income Relation

Substituting for γ_τ^t in equations (I.4′) the value given by (I.7), we establish immediately the individual consumption function, *i.e.*, the relation between *current* consumption and the factors determining it:

$$(\text{II.1}) \qquad c = c(y, y^e, a, t) = \frac{1}{L_t} y + \frac{(N - t)}{L_t} y^e + \frac{1}{L_t} a;$$

where the undated variables are understood to relate to the current period.[17] According to equation (II.1), current consumption is a linear and homogeneous function of current income, expected average income, and initial assets, with coefficients depending on the age of the household.

The corresponding expression for saving is

$$\text{(II.2)} \qquad s = y - c = \frac{L - t}{L_t} y - \frac{N - t}{L_t} y^e - \frac{1}{L_t} a.$$

In principle, equations (II.1) and (II.2) could be directly tested; but they cannot easily be checked against existing published data because, to our knowledge, data providing joint information on age, assets (which here means *net worth and not just liquid assets*), and average expected income, do not exist.[18] We must, therefore, see whether we can derive from our model some further implications of a type suitable for at least indirect testing in terms of the available data. Since most of these data give us information about the relation between consumption in a given short interval and income over the same interval (or some small neighborhood thereof) we must seek what implications can be deduced as to the relations between these variables.

If the marginal propensity to consume is defined literally as the increment in the current consumption of the household accompanying an increment in its current income, divided by the increment in income, keeping other things constant, then, according to equation (II.1), this quantity would be $\frac{\partial c}{\partial y} = \frac{1}{L_t}$, which is independent of income but dependent on age. The consumption function (II.1) would be represented by a straight line with the above slope and an intercept $\frac{(N - t)y^e + a}{L_t}$; and, since this intercept can be assumed positive,[19] the proportion of income saved should tend to rise with income.

[17] For an individual of age $t > N$, by assumption, $y = y^e = 0$ and only the last term on the right-hand side of (II.1) remains.

[18] The valuable work in progress at the Survey Research Center of the University of Michigan gives hope that the variety of data required for such a test may sometime become available. Clearly, the problem of measuring average expected future income may prove a serious challenge. On this point, however, see text below and the Appendix.

[19] Obviously, both y^e and a will generally be nonnegative.

In order to get some feeling as to the quantitative implications of our results, let us say that the earning span, N, is of the order of 40 years, the retirement span, M, 10 years, and therefore the total active life span, L, of the order of 50 years. These figures are not supposed to be anything more than a very rough guess and their only purpose is to give us some notion of the magnitudes involved. On the basis of these figures, the marginal propensity to consume would lie somewhere between a minimum of 1/50, or 2 per cent, and a maximum of 1/11, or 9 per cent, depending on age.

These figures seem unreasonably small. This is because the above definition of the marginal propensity to consume is clearly not a very reasonable one. A change in the current income of the household will generally tend to be accompanied by a change in its expected income, y^e, so that there is little sense in including ye among the things that are supposed to be constant as y changes. Note, however, that the same objection does not apply to a, for a denotes initial assets and, for a given household, assets at the beginning of the current period necessarily represent a constant.

Once we recognize that y^e is generally a function of y, the marginal propensity to consume at age t may be defined as

$$\text{(II.3)} \qquad \frac{dc}{dy} = \frac{1}{L_t} + \frac{N - t}{L_t}\frac{dy^e}{dy}.$$

Since $\frac{dy^e}{dy}$ would generally tend to lie between 0 and 1,[20] the marginal propensity to consume would fall for different individuals between a minimum of 1/50 and a maximum of 4/5, depending both on age and on the value of $\frac{dy}{dy}$.

Unfortunately, the empirical validity of these statements cannot be tested from observations of actual individual behavior. The reason is that consumption and income can only have a *single* value for a *given individual at a given age*. To be sure, we might be able to observe the behavior of an individual whose income had changed in time; but, even if we could control the value of y^e, we could not keep constant his age nor probably his initial assets (*i.e.*, assets at the beginning of each consumption period). The only way we could possibly check these conclusions is by observing the behavior of (average) consumption of *different*

[20] See below, Section 3, especially footnote 39.

households at different income levels, *i.e.*, by observing the "cross-section" average and marginal rate of consumption with respect to income.[21]

Suppose we make these observations and, for the sake of simplicity, suppose further that all the households we examine have approximately the same age and in every case $y = y^e$. Should we then expect the marginal rate of consumption to be $\frac{N - t + 1}{L_t}$, as equation (II.3) would seem to imply? The answer is no; the individual marginal propensity to consume cannot be simply identified with the cross-section marginal rate of consumption. Turning back to equation (II.1), we can easily see that (if all individuals behave according to this equation) the cross-section marginal rate of consumption should be

$$\text{(II.4)} \qquad \frac{d'c}{d'y} = \frac{N + 1 - t}{L_t} + \frac{1}{L_t}\frac{d'a}{d'y},$$

where the differential operator d' is used to denote cross-section differentials. Although $\frac{da}{dy}$ must be zero for an individual, there is no reason why the cross-section rate of change, $\frac{d'a}{d'y}$, should also be zero. Quite the contrary. Our model leads us to expect a very definite relation between the (average) net worth of households at a given income level and the income level itself, which relation we now proceed to explore.

II.2 The Equilibrium Income-Asset-Age Relation and the Consumption-Income Relation in a Stationary and Nonstationary Cross Section

To see clearly the implications of our model it will be useful to examine at first the nature of the cross-section relation between consumption and income in a special case which we shall call a

[21] We speak here advisedly of average and marginal rate of consumption, rather than of "cross-section marginal propensity to consume," for, as will become clear, the use of the latter term is likely only to encourage a serious and already too frequent type of confusion. The word "propensity" denotes a psychological disposition and should refer to the way in which a *given* individual reacts to different stimuli, and not to the way in which *different* individuals react to different stimuli. The differential reaction of different individuals in relation to different stimuli may give us information about the individual propensity, but it is not, in itself, a propensity.

cross section of "stationary" households. A household will be said to be in stationary position if it satisfies the following two conditions: (a) at the beginning of its active life it expects a constant income throughout its earning span; and (b) at every point of its life cycle it finds that its original expectations are completely fulfilled in the sense that its past and current income are as originally expected and its expectations for the future also coincide with its original expectations.[22] From equations (I.4) and (I.7) (since by assumption $y_1^e = y_1$ and $a_1 = 0$) we see that for such a household the consumption plan at age 1, which we denote by $\bar{c}_\tau^1$, must be

$$(\text{II.5}') \qquad \bar{c}_\tau^1 = \frac{N}{L} y_1, \qquad \tau = 1, 2, \cdots, L;$$

and the saving plan

$$(\text{II.5}'') \qquad \bar{s}_\tau^1 = \begin{cases} \dfrac{M}{L} y_1, & \tau = 1, 2, \cdots, N \\ -\dfrac{N}{L} y_1, & \tau = N+1, N+2, \cdots, L. \end{cases}$$

Finally, the asset plan, which is the sum of planned savings, must be

$$(\text{II.5}''') \qquad \bar{a}_\tau^1 = \begin{cases} \dfrac{(\tau-1)M}{L} y_1, & \tau = 1, 2, \cdots, N \\ \dfrac{N(L+1-\tau)}{L} y_1, & \tau = N+1, N+2, \cdots, L. \end{cases}$$

We will make use of equation (II.5‴) to define the notion of "stationary equilibrium" assets. We say that initial asset holdings at age t, a_t, are in equilibrium relative to any given level of income, y, if

$$(\text{II.6}) \qquad a_t = a(y,t) = \begin{cases} \dfrac{(t-1)M}{L} y, & t = 1, 2, \cdots, N \\ \dfrac{N(L+1-t)}{L} y, & t = N+1, N+2, \cdots, L. \end{cases}$$

Now it can readily be shown that for households fulfilling the stationary conditions and behaving according to equation (II.1),

[22] For a generalization of the notion of stationary household, see below footnote 25.

assets, at any age, will coincide precisely with those planned at age 1.[23] But, by definition, for a household of age $t \leqq N$ in stationary position, current income, y, equals y_1; it follows that its assets at the beginning of the current period must be

$$a = \bar{a}_t^1 = a(y_1, t) = a(y,t) = \frac{(t-1)M}{L} y, \qquad t \leqq N \tag{II.8}$$

which exhibits explicitly the relation between current initial assets, income, and age. Substituting from (II.8) into (II.1) and (II.2) and remembering that, by assumption, income expectations coincide with current income, we find for any age $t \leqq N$,

$$c = \frac{N}{L} y, \qquad s = \frac{M}{L} y; \tag{II.9}$$

i.e., for households fulfilling the stationary conditions and within the earning span, current consumption and saving are proportional to the current income.[24]

[23] This proposition may be established by mathematical induction. Suppose that the proposition holds for t, *i.e.*, that

$$a_t = \bar{a}_t^1 = \frac{(t-1)M}{L} y_1; \tag{II.7}$$

then, since by assumption

$$y_t = y_t^e = y_1, \qquad t \leqq N - 1,$$

we have, from (II.2),

$$s_t = \frac{M}{L} y_1$$

and

$$a_{t+1} = a_t + s_t = \frac{(t-1)M}{L} y_1 + \frac{M}{L} y_1 = \frac{tM}{L} y_1 = \bar{a}_{t+1}^1.$$

Thus, if equation (II.7) holds for t it holds also for $t + 1$. But equation (11.7) holds for $t = 1$, since

$$a_1 = 0 = \frac{(L-1)M}{L} y_1 = \bar{a}_1^1.$$

Hence, equation (II.7) holds for all $t \leqq N$. By similar reasoning, it can be shown that it holds also for $N + 1 \leqq t \leqq L$.

[24] While this result implies that, at zero income, consumption itself would have to be zero, it should be remembered that, under our stationary assumptions, the current level of income coincides with the level received in the past and expected in the future. A household whose income is permanently zero could hardly survive as a separate unit. Or, to put it differently, a household, within its earning span, whose current income is zero or negative cannot possibly be in stationary equilibrium.

At first sight this conclusion may appear to have little empirical meaning, since the notion of a stationary household is a theoretical limiting concept with little operational content. But our result need not be interpreted literally. Clearly our model has the following very significant implication: if we take a cross section of households within their earning span, which are reasonably well adjusted to the current level of income (in the sense, that, for each household, current income is close to the level the household has received in the past and it expects to receive in the future), then we should find that the proportion of income saved is substantially the same at all levels of income.[25] Even this more general conclusion is not easy to test from available data. Yet we shall be able to show presently that some rather striking evidence in support of this implication of our model is provided by certain recent studies.

From the result just established it follows directly that, if our sample consisted primarily of households in stationary position, then the cross-section rate of change of consumption with respect to income, $\frac{d'c}{d'y}$, is entirely different from the individual marginal propensity to consume defined by equation (II.3). According to equation (II.9) the cross-section rate of change must be $\frac{N}{L}$, a result which can also be derived from equation (II.4), by observing that, for stationary households, equation (II.8) holds so that, for

[25] It can be shown that if we eliminate Assumption III, our model still implies that, for a stationary cross section, the proportion of income saved is independent of income; however, this proportion will tend to rise with age, up to retirement. The conclusion that the proportion of income saved is independent of income, given age, also continues to hold if we relax our Assumption IV and assume only that there exists a typical pattern of allocation of resources to current and future consumption which does not necessarily involve a constant planned rate of consumption over time. Finally this conclusion also remains valid if we recognize the existence of a typical life pattern of income and redefine a stationary household as one who expects its income not to be constant over time but rather to follow the normal life pattern, and whose expectations are continuously fulfilled in the sense stated in part (b) of the original definition in the text. Just what effects these two relaxations would have on the relation between the proportion of income saved and age depends, of course, on the specific shape of the pattern of allocation of resources to consumption over the life cycle and on the shape of the life pattern of income. Note, however, that since the line of relation between saving and income *for each* age group is supposed, in any event, to go through the origin, even if we fail to stratify by age, the regression of consumption on income should tend to be linear (though not homoscedastic) and a regression line fitted to the data should tend to go approximately through the origin.

given age t, $\frac{d'a}{d'y} = \frac{(t-1)M}{L_t}$. Note, in particular, that (a) the individual marginal propensity varies with age, whereas the cross-section rate of change is independent of the age composition of the sample (provided all households are within the earning span); and (b) the slope of the cross-section line could not even be expected to represent some average of the marginal propensities at various ages. Indeed, even under unity elasticity of expectations, the marginal propensity at any age (except age 1) is less than N/L.[26]

In general, however, a random sample would not consist entirely, or even primarily, of households in stationary position. Let us therefore proceed to the more general case and see what we can learn from our model about the behavior of households who are not in stationary equilibrium.

Making use of the definition of $a(y,t)$ given in (II.6), the individual saving function (II.2) can be rewritten in the following useful form:

$$\text{(II.2')} \quad s = \frac{M}{L} y^e + \frac{L-t}{L_t}(y - y^e) - \frac{1}{L_t}[a - a(y^e,t)]$$
$$= \frac{M}{L} y + \frac{N(L-t) - M}{LL_t}(y - y^e) - \frac{1}{L_t}[a - a(y^e,t)].$$

The quantity $(y - y^e)$, representing the excess of current income over the average level expected in the future, may be called the "nonpermanent component of income"[27] (which may be positive or negative). Similarly, the quantity $[a - a(y^e,t)]$, representing the difference between actual initial assets and the volume of assets which would be carried by an individual fully adjusted to the "permanent" component of income y^e, may be called the "imbalance in initial assets" or also "excess assets" relative to the permanent component of income.

[26] As we have seen, under the assumption $y^e = y$ $\left(\text{and therefore } \frac{dy^e}{dy} = 1\right)$ the individual marginal propensity to consume is $\frac{N - t + 1}{L_t}$, which reaches a maximum for $t = 1$, the maximum being $\frac{N}{L}$.

[27] Cf. M. Friedman and S. Kuznets, *Income from Independent Professional Practice*, pp. 325 ff.

The first form of equation (II.2′) states the proposition that saving is equal to: (1) a constant fraction of the permanent component of income (independent of both age and income) which fraction is precisely the stationary equilibrium saving ratio; plus (2) a fraction of the nonpermanent component of income [this fraction is independent of income but depends on age and is larger, in fact much larger, than the fraction under (1)]; minus (3) a fraction, depending only on age, of excess assets. A similar interpretation can be given to the second form of (II.2′).

Equation (II.2′) is useful for examining the behavior of an individual, who, after having been in stationary equilibrium up to age $t - 1$, experiences an unexpected increase in income at age t so that $y_t > y^e_{t-1} = y_{t-1}$. Here we must distinguish two possibilities. Suppose, first, the increase is viewed as being strictly temporary so that $y^e_t = y^e_{t-1} = y_{t-1}$. In this case $a_t = a(y^e_t, t)$.[28] There is no imbalance in assets and, therefore, the third term is zero. But the second term will be positive since a share of current income, amounting to $y_t - y_{t-1}$, represents a nonpermanent component. Because our individual will be saving an abnormally large share of this portion of his income, his saving ratio will rise above the normal figure $\frac{M}{L}$. This ratio will in fact be higher, the higher the share of current income which is nonpermanent, or, which is equivalent in this case, the higher the percentage increase in income.[29] Let us next suppose that the current increase in income causes him to raise his expectations; and consider the limiting case where $y^e_t = y_t$, *i.e.*, the elasticity of expectations is unity.

In this case the transitory component is, of course, zero; but now the third term becomes positive, reflecting an insufficiency of assets relative to the new and higher income expectation. Accordingly, the saving ratio rises again above the normal level $\frac{M}{L}$ by an extent which is greater the greater the percentage increase in income. Moreover, as we might expect, the fact that expectations have followed income causes the increase in the

[28] Since the individual was in stationary equilibrium up to the end of period $t - 1$, we must have $a_t = a(y_{t-1}, t)$ and, by assumption, $y_{t-1} = y^e_t$.

[29] From the last equality in equation (II.2′) and with $y^e_t = y_{t-1}$, we derive immediately

$$\frac{s_t}{y_t} = \frac{M}{L} + \frac{N(L - t) - M}{LL_t}\left(\frac{y_t - y_{t-1}}{y_t}\right).$$

saving ratio to be somewhat smaller than in the previous case.[30]

Our model implies, then, that a household whose current income unexpectedly rises above the previous "accustomed" level (where the term "accustomed" refers to the average expected income to which the household was adjusted), will save a proportion of its income larger than it was saving before the change and also larger than is presently saved by the permanent inhabitants of the income bracket into which the household now enters. The statement, of course, holds in reverse for a fall in income.[31]

II.3 A Reinterpretation of the Cross-section Relation Between Consumption and Income

The propositions we have just established are not easy to test directly with existing data, since such data do not usually provide information on the "accustomed" level but, at best, only on the level of income during a previous short period. However, even this type of information should be useful, at least for an indirect test of our conclusions. For, suppose we divide all the households into three groups: (*1*) those whose income has increased in the current year; (*2*) those whose income is approximately unchanged; and (*3*) those whose income has fallen. Then, unless most of the income changes just happen to be such as to return the recipients to an accustomed level from which they had earlier departed,[32] group (*1*) should contain a greater proportion of people whose income is above the accustomed level than group (*2*) and, a fortiori, than group (*3*). Hence, according to our model, the households in group (*1*) whose income has risen should save, on the average, a larger proportion of income than those in group (*2*), which in turn should save a larger proportion than those in group (*3*). It is well known that this proposition is overwhelmingly

[30] From equation (II.2′), with $y_t^e = y_{t-1}$ and since $a_t = \frac{(t-1)M}{L} y_{t-1}$, we derive,

$$\frac{s_t}{y_t} = \frac{M}{L} + \frac{(t-1)M}{LL_t}\left(\frac{y_t - y_{t-1}}{y_t}\right).$$

It is easily verified that the right-hand side of this expression is necessarily smaller than the corresponding expression given in the preceding note.

[31] This conclusion fails to hold only if the elasticity of expectations is substantially greater than unity.

[32] More precisely, unless there is a very strong correlation between the current change in income, $y - y_{-1}$, on the one hand, and the difference between the previous "accustomed" level and the previous year income, $y_{-1}^e - y_{-1}$, on the other.

supported by empirical evidence.[33] Even where some apparent exceptions have been reported, these have occurred largely because of the inclusion in expenditure of current outlays for durable goods which we do not include in consumption as far as they result in an increase in net worth.[34]

We will readily recognize that the proposition we have just derived is far from novel; but notice that our model suggests an explanation that is quite different from the one usually advanced. According to the usual explanation, which is already to be found in the *General Theory* (p. 97), consumer expenditure habits are sticky and only adjust with a lag to the changed circumstances; in the meantime, savings, which are considered as a passive residual, absorb a large share of the changed income. In our model, on the other hand, savings tend to go up either because the new level of income is regarded as (partly or wholly) transitory or, to the extent that it is regarded as permanent, because the initial asset holdings are now out of line with the revised outlook. If the outlook has improved, assets are too low to enable the household to live for the rest of its expected life on a scale commensurate with the new level of income; if the income outlook has deteriorated, then, in order for the household to achieve the optimum consumption plan consistent with the new outlook, it is not necessary to add to assets at the same rate as before, and perhaps even an immediate drawing-down of assets to support consumption may be called for.

We feel that this alternative interpretation has merits. While not denying that the conventional explanation in terms of habit persistence may have some validity, we feel that it has been made to bear too heavy a weight. We all know that there are hundreds of things that we would be eager to buy, or do, "if only we could afford them," and nearly as many places where we could "cut corners" if it were really necessary. Therefore, as long as we are dealing with moderate variations in income (variations whose possibility we had already envisaged at least in our day-dreams),

[33] See, for instance, G. Katona and J. Fisher, "Postwar Changes in the Income of Identical Consumer Units," *Studies in Income and Wealth*, Vol. XIII, pp. 62-122; G. Katona, "Effect of Income Changes on the Rate of Saving," *The Review of Economics and Statistics*, May, 1949, pp. 95-103; W. W. Cochrane, "Family Budgets—a Moving Picture," *loc. cit.*, Aug., 1947, pp. 189-198; R. P. Mack, "The Direction of Change in Income and the Consumption Function," *loc. cit.*, Nov., 1948, pp. 239-258.

[34] Katona and Fisher, *ibid.*, especially Section D, pp. 97-101; and G. Katona, *ibid.*

there is not likely to be any significant lag in the adjustment of total expenditure. Of course, there may be significant lags (and leads) in certain types of expenditures: moving to a more exclusive neighborhood may take years to be realized, but meanwhile that dreamed-of vacation trip may come off at once.[35]

Our discussion of the effect of income changes enables us to proceed to an analysis of the cross-section relation between current consumption and current income that we should expect to find, and actually do find, in a random sample which does not consist primarily of households in stationary position.

As is well known, budget studies typically show that the proportion of income saved, far from being constant, tends to rise from a very low or even negative figure at low levels of income to a large positive figure in the highest brackets. These findings are by no means inconsistent with our earlier results concerning the saving-income relation for a stationary cross section. Quite the contrary; the observed relation is precisely what we should expect on the basis of our model when we remember that, in the type of economies to which these budget data mostly refer, individual incomes are subject to short-term fluctuations, so that current income generally will tend to differ more or less markedly from the previous accustomed level and from current income expectations. Such fluctuations may vary in intensity according to time, place, occupation, and other characteristics of the sample covered, but they will never be entirely absent and frequently will be substantial.

[35] It is, in principle, possible to design an experiment to test which of the two hypotheses represents a better explanation of the observed behavior. One possible test might be as follows. Select the set of households whose income has changed unexpectedly in the given year T, and who expect the change to be permanent. Consider next the subset whose income in the immediately following years remains at the new level and whose expectations are therefore fulfilled. If the traditional explanation is the correct one, then by the year $T + 1$ saving should revert to the average level prevailing for all households who have been for two or more years in the income brackets into which our households have moved. On the other hand, if our hypothesis is correct, the saving of our subset of households should, in the years following T, continue to remain higher, on the average, than the saving of the households who have been *permanent* inhabitants of the relevant brackets. Furthermore, under our model, the difference between the saving of the new and the original inhabitants should tend to remain greater the more advanced the age of the household in the year T. Needless to say, the data for such a test are not available at this time and the case for our explanation must rest for the moment on the evidence that supports our model as a whole. The purpose of describing a possible experiment is to emphasize the fact that the two alternative hypotheses have implications that are, in principle, observationally distinguishable. Some of these implications are, in fact, of immediate relevance for aggregative time series analysis.

The very same reasoning we have used in the discussion of the effect of income changes leads to the conclusion that, in the presence of short-term fluctuations, the highest income brackets may be expected to contain the largest proportion of households whose current income is above the accustomed level and whose saving is, therefore, abnormally large. Conversely, the lowest income brackets may be expected to contain the largest proportion of people whose current income is below the accustomed level and whose saving is, therefore, abnormally low. As a result of the presence of these groups, which are not fully adjusted to the current level of income, in the lowest brackets the proportion of income saved will be lower, and in the highest brackets it will be higher than the normal figure (M/L in our model) which we should expect to be saved by the permanent inhabitants of these respective brackets. Thus, the proportion of income saved will tend to rise with income, and the cross-section relation between consumption and income will tend to be represented by a line obtained by rotating the stationary line clockwise around a fixed point whose x and y coordinates coincide approximately with the average value of income and consumption respectively.

While the general line of argument developed above is not new,[36] it may be useful to clarify it by means of a graphical illustration developed in Figures 1 and 2. We will start out by analyzing a cross section of households all belonging to a single age group within the earning span, and will examine first the consumption-income relation; once we have established this relation, the saving-income relation can easily be derived from it.

Our consumption function (II.1) can be rewritten in a form analogous to the saving function (II.2′), namely:

$$\text{(II.1}'\text{)} \qquad c = \frac{N}{L} y^e + \frac{1}{L_t}(y - y^e) + \frac{1}{L_t}[a - a(y^e,t)]$$

$$= \frac{N}{L}\left\{y^e + \frac{L}{NL_t}(y - {}^e) + \hbar \frac{L}{NL_t}[a - a(y^e,t)]\right\}$$

In the construction of our figures, we shall find it convenient to have a symbol to represent the expression in braces; let us denote it by $p = p(y,y^e,t,a)$. This expression may be regarded as

[36] See, for instance, the brilliant paper of William Vickrey, "Resource Distribution Patterns and the Classification of Families," *Studies in Income and Wealth*, Vol. X, pp. 260-329; Ruth P. Mack, *op. cit.*, and the contributions of Margaret G. Reid quoted in the next section.

the stationary equivalent income of the current set of values y, y^e, t and a, for the household, in the sense that, if the household were fully adjusted to a level of income $p = p(y,y^e,t,a)$, then it would behave in the same way as it currently does. Let us further denote by the symbol $\bar{x}(y)$ the average value of any variable x for all the members of a given income bracket, y. Then the proportion of income consumed by the aggregate of all households whose current income is y is, clearly, $\bar{c}(y)/y$. Our problem is, therefore, that of establishing the relation between $\bar{c}(y)$ and y. But, according to (II.1′), $\bar{c}(y)$ is proportional to $\bar{p}(y)$ whose be-

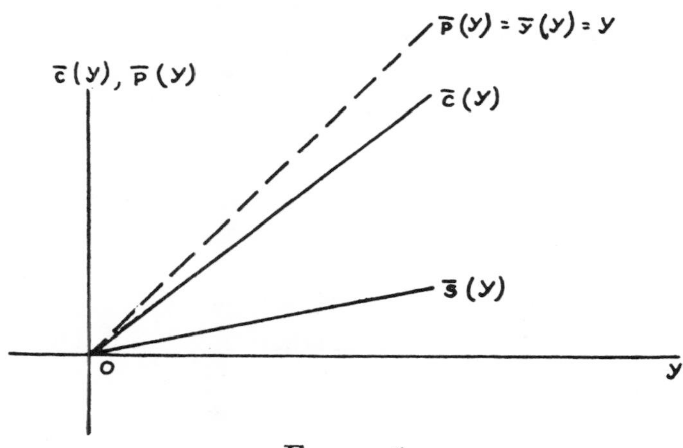

FIGURE 1

havior, in turn, as we see, depends on that of $\bar{y}^e(y)$ and $\bar{a}(y)$. We must therefore fix our attention on the behavior of these last two quantities.

In the case of a *stationary* cross section, illustrated in Figure 1, we know that for *every* household, $y^e = y$ and also $a = a(y^e,t)$. It follows that, for *every* household, $p = y$, and therefore the average value of p in any income bracket y, $\bar{p}(y)$, is also equal to y, *i.e.*, $\bar{p}(y) = y$. Thus, the cross-section relation between $\bar{p}(y)$ and y is represented by a line of slope one through the origin—the dashed line of our Figure 1. The consumption-income relation is now obtained by multiplying each ordinate of this line by the constant N/L, with the result represented by the upper solid line. Because the $\bar{p}(y)$ line goes through the origin, so does the consumption-income relation, $\bar{c}(y)$, and the elasticity of consumption with respect to income is unity. These same propositions hold equally for the saving-income relation, $\bar{s}(y)$ (lower solid line of Figure 1), obtained by subtracting $\bar{c}(y)$ from y. This merely illustrates a result established in the preceding section.

Let us consider now what we may expect to happen if income is subject to short-term fluctuations, a case illustrated in Figure 2.

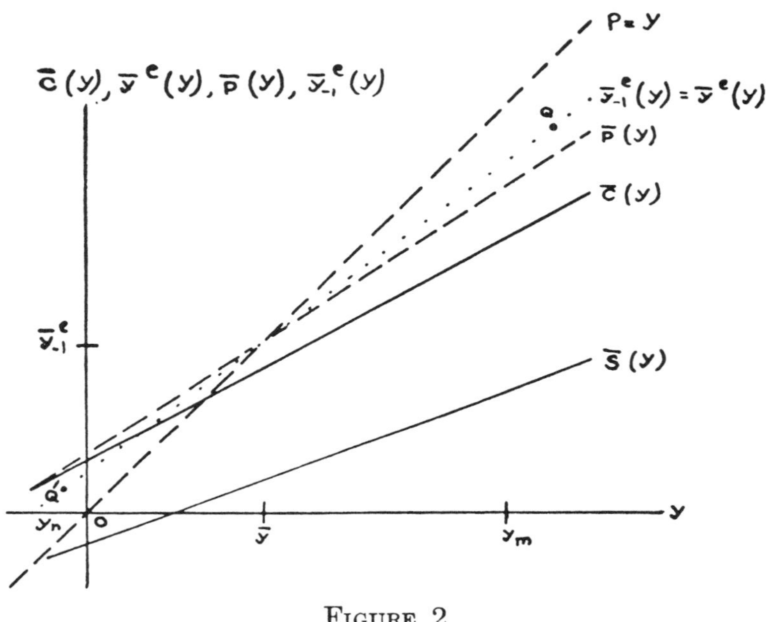

FIGURE 2

We may assume for expository convenience that on the average these fluctuations cancel out so that average current income, $\bar{y}$, is the same as the average future income expected in the year before by the sample as a whole, $\bar{y}^e_{-1}$. But, because of the presence of short-term variations, this equality will not hold for individual households; for some households current income will be higher than y^e_{-1}, while for others it will be lower. As a result of these fluctuations, as we have already argued, in the highest income brackets there will be a predominance of households whose current income is above y^e_{-1}. This, in turn, means that in these brackets the average value of $y^e_{-1}, \bar{y}^e_{-1}(y)$, will be less than y itself;[37] in terms

[37] The specific "technical" assumption underlying the entire discussion can be formulated thus:

(II.10) $$y_i = y^e_{-1i} + \epsilon_i$$

where the subscript i denotes the i-th household and the random term ϵ is assumed

of our graph, $\bar{y}^e_{-1}(y)$ will fall below the dashed line, which represents the line of slope one through the origin. For instance, corresponding to the highest income bracket shown, $y_m, \bar{y}^e_{-1}(\bar{y}_m)$ may be represented by a point such as q in our graph. Conversely, in the lowest income bracket shown, y_n, there will tend to be a preponderance of people whose current income is below y^e_{-1}, and therefore the average value of y^e_{-1} in this bracket, $\bar{y}^e_{-1}(y_n)$ will be greater than y_n and above the dashed line, as shown by the point q', in the figure. Extending this reasoning to all values of y, we conclude that the relation between $\bar{y}^e_{-1}(y)$ and y will tend to be represented by a curve having the following essential properties: (a) it will intercept the dashed line in the neighborhood of a point with abscissa $\bar{y}$; and (b) to the right of this point, it will fall progressively below the dashed line, while to the left of it, it will stand increasingly above this line. In our graph this relation is represented by the dotted straight line joining the points q' and q; in general, the relation need not be a linear one, although the assumption of linearity may not be altogether unrealistic. What is essential, however, is that the $\bar{y}^e_{-1}(y)$ curve may be expected to have everywhere a slope smaller than unity and to exhibit a positive intercept; and that its slope will tend to be smaller, and its intercept larger, the greater the short-term variability of income.

From the behavior of $\bar{y}^e_{-1}(y)$, we can now readily derive that of $\bar{y}^e(y)$, which is the quantity we are really interested in. The latter variable is related to $\bar{y}^e_{-1}(y)$ and to y itself through the elasticity of income expectations. The elasticity of expectations relevant to our analysis can be defined as the percentage change in income expectation over the two years in question, $\dfrac{y^e - y^e_{-1}}{y^e_{-1}}$,

to have zero mean and to be independent of y_{-1}. From (II.10), making use of a well-known proposition of correlation theory, we deduce

(II.10′) $$\bar{y}^e_{-1}(y) = \alpha + \beta y; \qquad \beta = r^2_{yy^e_{-1}}, \quad \alpha = \bar{y}^e_{-1} - \beta\bar{y}$$

Clearly, β is necessarily less than one and α is necessarily positive (since, by assumption, $\bar{y}^e_{-1} = \bar{y}$). A more general and realistic stochastic assumption than the one just formulated would be the following:

$$y_i = ky^e_{-1i}(1 + \epsilon_i^*),$$

ϵ' having the same properties as ϵ in (II.10). Since this assumption would complicate the analysis considerably (*e.g.*, it would destroy the linearity of (II.10′)) without affecting the essence of our argument, it has seemed preferable to base our discussion in this paper on equation (II.10).

divided by the corresponding percentage difference between current income and the previous year's expectation, $\frac{y - y^e_{-1}}{y^e_{-1}}$.

If we denote this elasticity by the symbol E, we have

$$(\text{II.11}) \qquad E = \frac{y^e - y^e_{-1}}{y - y^e_{-1}},^{38}$$

which in turn implies:

$$(\text{II.11}') \qquad y^e = y^e_{-1} + E(y - y^e_{-1}) = (1 - E)y^e_{-1} + Ey;$$

i.e., the current income expectation is a weighted average of the previous expectation and current income, with weights depending on the elasticity of expectation. If E is close to zero, current income will have little influence in reshaping expectations and y^e will be close to y^e_{-1}; if, at the other extreme, E is close to unity then current expectations will be determined primarily by the recent behavior of income. From (II.11′) we readily deduce the relation between $\bar{y}^e(y)$ and $\bar{y}^e_{-1}(y)$, namely:

$$(\text{II.12}) \qquad \bar{y}^e(y) = \bar{y}^e_{-1}(y) + E[y - \bar{y}^e_{-1}(y)].^{39}$$

[38] This definition is not altogether satisfactory for an individual household since y may have been expected to be different from y^e_{-1} (which is the average income expected over the entire balance of the earning span); in this case the fact that y differs from y^e_{-1} need not generate any revision of expectations, *i.e.*, y^e may be equal to y^e_{-1}. As an alternative definition that would give more adequate recognition to the causal relation between the behavior of current income and changes in expectations, we may suggest the following:

$$E = \frac{y^e - y^e_{-1}}{y^e_{-1}} \Big/ \frac{y - y^{e(t)}_{t-1}}{y^{e(t)}_{t-1}},$$

where $y^{e(t)}_{t-1}$ denotes the income expected in the previous year for the current year. However, when we aggregate a large number of households, it is not unreasonable to expect that, on the average $y^{e(t)}_{t-1} = y^e_{-1}$, in which case our alternative definition leads back to equation (II.11) in the text.

[39] In deriving (II.12) from (II.11), we are implicitly assuming that the average value of E is approximately the same at all levels of income, an assumption that does not seem unreasonable for the specific stochastic model with which we are presently dealing. A more general formulation of (II.12), which may be especially useful in establishing a connection between cross-section and aggregative time-series analysis, might be as follows:

$$(\text{II.12}') \qquad \bar{y}^e(y) = \bar{y}^e_{-1}(y) + E_1[y - \bar{y}^e_{-1}(y)] + E_2(\bar{y} - \bar{y}^e_{-1}),$$

which states that individual expectations depend not only on the behavior of individual income but also on that of average income for the entire community, $\bar{y}$. This hypothesis is supported by the consideration that changes in aggregate income may well represent a more reliable indicator for the future than just a change in individual

Equation (II.12) admits of a very simple graphical interpretation. Suppose, first, that E is zero: then $\bar{y}^e(y)$ coincides with $\bar{y}^e_{-1}(y)$, the dotted line of Figure 2. Next, suppose E is positive but less than one; then, for any value of y, $\bar{y}^e(y)$, if it were drawn, would lie between y and $\bar{y}^e_{-1}(y)$, *i.e.*, between the dashed and the dotted line and precisely E per cent of the way from the dotted to the dashed line. Finally, if E is greater than one, or less than zero, then $\bar{y}^e(y)$ will fall outside the band marked off by our two lines. The last two cases, however, may be regarded as extremely unlikely, when one remembers that y^e and y_{-1} are defined as expectations about the average level of income over the entire balance of the earning span.[40] In our graph we have assumed a zero value for E so that $\bar{y}^e(y)$ coincides with $\bar{y}^e_{-1}(y)$; this assumption has been chosen not because we think it is realistic but only because it eliminates the necessity of showing a separate curve in our figure. In general, we should rather expect E to be positive but less than one, so that the $\bar{y}^e(y)$ curve would fall between the dotted and the dashed line. *The slope and intercept of this curve will thus depend on the degree of short-term variability of income* [which determines the shape of $\bar{y}^e_{-1}(y)$] *and on the elasticity of expectations.* But note that where short-run fluctuations play a

---

income. It follows from (II.12′) that the elasticity of expectation for the community as a whole is

$$\frac{\bar{y}^e - \bar{y}^e_{-1}}{\bar{y} - \bar{y}^e_{-1}} = E_1 + E_2,$$

an expression that could be close to unity even if, as seems likely, E_1 is much smaller than one. On the other hand, it can be easily verified that if (II.12′) holds, with $E_2 \neq 0$, the elasticity of expectation as defined by (II.11) will generally change from income bracket to income bracket unless $\bar{y} = \bar{y}^e_{-1}$, an equality which has been explicitly assumed for the purposes of our discussion in the text and which makes (II.12′) identical with (II.12).

[40] Such cases are of course not impossible for an individual household; all we claim is that they are unlikely for the average of all households falling in a given income bracket. (See, however, footnote 38.)

There is, of course, no opportunity to test the above statement from available data, since no attempt has yet been made, to our knowledge, to secure information on y^e and y^e_{-1}. Data such as those collected by the Survey Research Center on income expectations for the following year, and presented, for example, in G. Katona, *Psychological Analysis of Economic Behavior*, p. 120, have only a rather remote connection with our concepts. In terms of our notation, these data refer to y_{iT}, y_{iT-1}, and $y_{iT}^{e(T+1)}$, where T denotes the calendar year of the survey. If one is willing to make the rather risky assumption that $y_{iT}^{e(T+1)} = y^e_{iT}$, and the even more risky one that $y_{iT-1} = y^e_{iT-1}$, then it can be inferred from Katona's tabulations that the proportion of households with E greater than one has been somewhat under 20 per cent, and fairly stable, in the surveys for which data are presented.

large role, as might be the case, say, for a sample of farmers, the elasticity of expectations may, itself, be expected to be small on the average, since current income will contain little new reliable information on the basis of which to reshape the previous expectation about average future income, y^e_{-1}. Hence, a large short-term variability of income will tend to depress the slope, and raise the intercept, of $\bar{y}^e(y)$ for two reasons: (1) because it pulls the $\bar{y}^e(y)$ closer to $\bar{y}^e_{-1}(y)$, and (2) because it diminishes the slope of $\bar{y}^e_{-1}(y)$.

We have thus exhibited the behavior of the first component of $\bar{p}(y)$. As we see from (II.1′), the second component is very simple to handle; it represents again a fraction, $\frac{L}{NL_t}$, of the difference between y and $\bar{y}^e(y)$, *i.e.*, of the distance from the dotted to the dashed line. Furthermore, for any reasonable assumption about the values of L and N, this fraction is quite small within the earning span. Thus, the sum of the first two terms of $\bar{p}(y)$ could be represented by a new line falling somewhere between the dashed and the dotted line but very close to the latter. Since it would be so close, this new line is not shown separately in our figure and we will assume that the line $\overline{q'q}$ represents already the sum of the first two components.

We may now proceed to the last component of $\bar{p}(y)$ which measures the (average) unbalance in assets at each current income level. A repetition of the familiar reasoning suggests once more that in the highest income brackets there should tend to be an abnormally large proportion of households whose current income expectation is higher than it had been in the past and for whom, accordingly, current assets are low relative to the current expectation y^e; and that the opposite should be true in the lowest income brackets. Hence, the last term will again be negative for sufficiently large values of y and positive for sufficiently small values. The zero point is again likely to occur for a value of y close to $\bar{y}$, although its location may vary depending on the previous history of the economy (especially the history of the last t years).[41] In any event $\bar{p}(y)$, which is obtained by

[41] The average gap between initial assets, a, and the stationary equilibrium value,

$$a(y^e,t) = \frac{(t-1)M}{L} y^e,$$

at any given level of income, can be derived from the stochastic assumption intro-

adding this last term to the previous two, will tend to have a slope everywhere smaller than our dotted line and a larger intercept; its graph may therefore look something like the dashed-dotted line of Figure 2.

We are now ready to exhibit the consumption-income relation $\bar{c}(y)$, which is obtained simply by multiplying the ordinates of $\bar{p}(y)$ by the constant, N/L. The result is represented by the upper solid line. As we intended to show, it is a line much flatter than the stationary cross-section line of Figure 1 (from which it can be obtained by rotation around its point $(\bar{y},\bar{y}^e)$) and it exhibits the large positive intercept characteristic of budget data. In other words, in the presence of short-term fluctuations in income, the proportion of income consumed will tend to fall with income and the elasticity of consumption with respect to

duced in footnote 36, with the addition of an analogous stochastic assumption as to the relation between a and y^e_{-1}, namely

(II.13) $$y^e_{-1i} = \lambda x_i + \omega_i,$$

where $$x_i \equiv a_i \bigg/ \frac{(t-1)M}{L}, \qquad E(\omega_i) = 0, \quad E(\omega_i x_i) = 0.$$

x_i may be regarded as a function of the income expectations held by the household during all previous years of its active life.

From (II.13), we derive

(II.14) $$\bar{x}(y^e_{-1}) = \mu + \nu y^e_{-1}; \qquad \nu = r^2 x_{y^e_{-1}}/\lambda, \quad \mu = \bar{x} - \nu \bar{y}^e_{-1}.$$

Since in a growing economy $\lambda = \bar{y}^e_{-1}/\bar{x}_i$ may be expected to be at least as high as unity, we must have $0 \leqq \nu \leqq 1$, $\mu \geqq 0$. From (II.14) and the definition of x_i, we obtain

$$\bar{a}(y) = \frac{(t-1)M}{L}\bar{x}(y) = \frac{(t-1)M}{L}[\mu + \nu \bar{y}^e_{-1}(y)].$$

Finally, taking into consideration the definition of $a(y^e,t)$, and using equation (II.12), we derive

$$E\{[a - a(y^e,t)]|y\} = \bar{a}(y) - \frac{(t-1)M}{L}\bar{y}^e(y)$$

$$= \frac{(t-1)M}{L}[\mu + (\nu - 1 + E)\bar{y}^e_{-1}(y) - Ey],$$

which can be expressed entirely in terms of y by making use of equation (II.10′). The above expression must fall as income rises, as stated in the text, since its derivative with respect to y is proportional to $-[E(1-\beta) + \beta(1-\nu)]$, which is necessarily negative (provided $E > 0$, which is assumed). In fact, we can establish that

$$E\{[a - a(y^e,t)]|y\} \gtreqless 0$$

as $$y \lesseqgtr \bar{y}\left[1 - \frac{\lambda - 1}{\lambda[E(1-\beta+\beta(1-\nu)]}\right],$$

which shows explicitly the level of income at which the average gap between a and $a(y^e,t)$ is zero.

income will be less than one. Another important result we have established is that the elasticity of consumption with respect to income should depend, according to our theory, on three major factors which are capable of variation in different samples. This elasticity depends, inversely, on (a) the degree of short-term variability of income; (b) the magnitude of variations over time in the permanent component of income that give rise to unbalances in the relation between assets holdings and the permanent component itself; and (c) directly, on the elasticity of income expectations.[42] Given the magnitude of these three factors, the elasticity should depend also on the age of the households in the sample since, as we see from equation (II.1′), the coefficient of the second and third components of p vary with age. This point, however, will receive proper attention in the next section.

In our discussion so far we have been concerned with a cross section of households within the earning span. The effect of the inclusion of retired households in the sample can readily be established. According to our model, these households should have, on the average, levels of consumption not very different from the over-all average,[43] while, at the same time, earning incomes well below average (in our present simplified version, no income at all). The inclusion of these households, therefore, will have the effect of raising still further the $\bar{c}(y)$ curves for low levels of y, thereby increasing its general tilting and possibly making it convex to the income axis.[44]

[42] We have seen that a high elasticity of expectations tends to pull $\bar{y}^e(y)$ closer to the 45-degree line; at the same time, however, it will tend to flatten the $\bar{p}(y)$ curve relative to the $\bar{y}^e(y)$ curve, for, if assets are approximately adjusted to y^e_{-1}, then the larger the gap between y^e and y_{-1}, the larger will tend to be the unbalance in assets. Since, however, the second effect does not quite offset the first (see the discussion of Section II.2, especially page 20), a high value of E will, on the whole, increase the slope and reduce the intercept of $\bar{p}(y)$ and thus of $\bar{c}(y)$.

[43] They may, in fact, have an average consumption level below the over-all average for two reasons: (a) because it seems likely that the level of consumption planned for after retirement will, on the whole, tend to be smaller than the average level during the earning span; (b) because of the secular rise in income per capita which characterizes most of the economies for which we have budget data. See, on this point, Modigliani and Brumberg, *op. cit.*

[44] Our statements about retired households find strong support in the data on the size distribution of income by age, reported by Janet A. Fisher, in "Income, Spending, and Saving Patterns of Consumer Units in Different Age Groups," *Studies in Income and Wealth*, Vol. XV, especially Tables 1 and 2, pp. 81 and 82. Actually, these tables are likely to overestimate the income (used in our sense) of elderly people, since income, there, is defined to include such items as pensions and retirement pay (p. 81, footnote 6). These inclusions also reduce the usefulness of the information on saving

Summing up, the typical findings of budget studies as to the relation between consumption, saving, and income in a given year, or some other short interval of time, are precisely what they should be according to our model. But, as we see, the interpretation of these findings that follows from our model is radically different from the one generally accepted. According to the usual interpretation, these findings show that the proportion of income saved rises with the economic status of the household. According to our model, on the other hand, they only show that households whose income is above the level to which they are adjusted save an abnormally large proportion and those whose income is below this level save an abnormally low proportion, or even dissave.

To be sure, up to this point, we have done little more than to show that the findings of budget data are consistent with either interpretation. It may be objected that this demonstration is an insufficient ground for discarding the old and widely accepted explanation for our new and radically different one. It would seem that, to support our claims, we should be able to produce some crucial tests, the result of which will enable us to discriminate between the two competing explanations. We believe that the remarkable piece of research recently reported on by Margaret G. Reid, discussed in the next section, comes as close to providing such a test as seems feasible with the kind of data that are presently available.[45]

---

and dissaving by age groups presented in Table 11 (p. 93). Even with the upward-biased definition of income, the proportion of positive savers is smaller in the age group 65 and over than in any other group except the group 18 to 24. For this latter group, of course, the figures are seriously affected by the inclusion of durable goods purchases in consumption. Presumably, had our definitions of income and saving been adopted, the relative scarcity of savers and predominance of dissavers in the elderly group would be much more pronounced.

[45] These results were first reported in a brief communication presented at the Conference on Saving, Inflation and Economic Progress, University of Minnesota, in May, 1952. The authors have also had the opportunity to consult a preliminary draft on "The Relation of the Within-Group Permanent Component of Income to the Income Elasticity of Expenditures," and have had the benefit of extensive discussion and consultations with Miss Reid. The hypothesis tested in the above-mentioned paper had already been partly anticipated in Reid's earlier contribution, "Effect of Income Concept upon Expenditure Curves of Farm Families," *Studies in Income and Wealth*, Vol. XV, especially pp. 133-139.

II.4 Some Evidence on the Constancy of the Saving Ratio for a Stationary Cross Section

In order to understand the foundations of Reid's highly ingenious techniques and the meaning of her results, we must turn back to our Figures 1 and 2, and to the reasoning underlying their construction. Suppose that, somehow, we had been able to locate a sample of households, within their earning span, each of which fulfilled completely our stationary specifications. For *every* member of this sample, because of the complete absence of short-term income fluctuations, we would have the chain of equalities $y = y^e = y^e_{-1} = y_{-1}$ so that the correlation between current and previous income, $r_{yy_{-1}}$, would be unity. Furthermore, if our theory is correct, the elasticity of consumption with respect to current income, η_{cy}, would also be unity. Moreover, this conclusion would continue to hold if the above chain of equalities were replaced by "proportionality," *i.e.*, $y = \frac{y^e}{k_1} = \frac{y^e_{-1}}{k_2} = \frac{y_{-1}}{k_3}$. In this case, all the households are out of stationary equilibrium but, so to speak, by the same proportion; this would affect the slope of the $\bar{c}(y)$ curve of Figure 1, but not its intercept, so that the consumption-income elasticity would remain unity.[46]

Now, since information on the permanent component of income and the degree of adjustment to it is not available, it is impossible to locate a sample fulfilling exactly our specifications. On the other hand, it may not be impossible to find one for which short-term

[46] If the equalities are replaced by proportionality, the correlation $r_{yy_{-1}}$ remains unity. Furthermore, replacing in (II.1) y^e by $k_1 y$, and a by

$$\frac{(t-1)M}{L}\nu y^e_{-1} = \frac{(t-1)M\nu k_2}{L}y,$$

(since by assumption, up to the beginning of the current year the assets of every household are proportional to the stationary equilibrium value, ν being the proportionality factor and having the same meaning as in note 41), we obtain

$$c = \frac{L + L(N-t)k_1 + M(t-1)\nu k_2}{LL_t}y,$$

so that, for any given age t, the consumption-income relation is still a straight line through the origin and therefore η_{cy} is still unity. Since, however, the slope varies with age, if we fail to stratify by age, we may find that the computed value of η_{cy} is not exactly one, even for a stationary cross section. On the other hand, it can be verified, from the above expression, that the variation in slope with age is likely to be rather small so that, in fact, η_{cy} should be quite close to unity, unless k_2 and ν are substantially different from unity, an unlikely case except in deep depression or at the peak of a boom.

fluctuations are of relatively minor importance and current income is relatively close to the level to which the household is adjusted. These conditions might be satisfied, for instance, by a sample of government employees or of college professors. For such a sample we would expect to find a correlation between current and previous income, $r_{yy_{-1}}$, close to unity and, *if our model is correct*, an elasticity of consumption with respect to income, η_{cy}, close to unity. At the other extreme, for a group of households for which random short-term fluctuations play a dominant role, say, a sample of farmers over a wide geographical region, we would have a low value of $r_{yy_{-1}}$ and, as we know from the analysis of Figure 2, a low elasticity of consumption with respect to income. This implication of our model clearly forms the basis for a crucial experiment; this experiment has not been carried out as such, although we look forward to its being performed in the near future by anyone having the resources and interest. Meanwhile, Reid's method is very similar to the comparison we have just proposed. The discussion that has led us to the formulation of our crucial experiment suggests that the correlation between current and previous income can be taken as indirect, approximate measure of the degree to which the current income of each household is close to the level to which the household is adjusted (or to a constant multiple of this level—see previous paragraph). In the first place, this correlation is a very good direct measure of strictly short-term fluctuations which, as we have seen, control the relation between $\bar{y}^e(y)$ and y. Secondly, it seems reasonable to expect that the gap between $\bar{p}(y)$ and $\bar{y}^e(y)$ will, itself, tend to be smaller the smaller the short-run variability of income; for, when incomes are basically stable, there should also be less opportunity for significant discrepancies between the permanent component of income and assets to develop. Thus, when the correlation between current and previous income is high, $\bar{p}(y)$ itself should tend to be close to y. The $\bar{p}(y)$ and $\bar{c}(y)$ curves should, therefore, be similar to those of Figure 1, and the elasticity of consumption with respect to income should be close to unity. Conversely, when the correlation between current and previous income is small, evidencing the presence of pronounced short-term fluctuations, the $\bar{y}^e(y)$, $\bar{p}(y)$, and $\bar{c}(y)$ curves should be similar to those shown in Figure 2, and the elasticity of consumption with respect to income should be well below unity.

Hence, if we take several samples of households and, for each of these samples, we compute (a) the correlation between current and previous income, $r_{yy_{-1}}$ and (b) the elasticity of consumption with respect to income, we should find a clear positive rank correlation between the two above-mentioned statistics and, furthermore, η_{cy} should approach unity as $r_{yy_{-1}}$ approaches unity. In essence, this is precisely the test Reid has carried out and her results clearly confirm our inference. The fact that for none of her groups $r_{yy_{-1}}$ is, or could be expected to be, as high as unity prevents η_{cy} from ever reaching the theoretical stationary value of unity; but her data do show that, in the few cases where r comes close to one, η_{cy} is also impressively close to unity. According to Reid's results η_{cy} ranges from a value as low as .1 for r in the order of .2 to values as high as .8 for the highest values of r, which are in the order of .8.[47]

The above discussion is, of course, not intended as an exhaustive account of Reid's techniques and many valuable results; for this purpose the reader is referred to her forthcoming publications. Nevertheless, the brief sketch presented should be sufficient to indicate why her results seem to us to represent as impressive a confirmation of one important implication of our theory, at the micro-economic level, as one may hope to find at this time.

In addition to the test just described, there are several other, partly older, findings that support our model and acquire new meaning in the light of it.

According to our model the typical findings of budget studies as to the relation between consumption and income are basically due to the fact that, in the presence of short-term fluctuations, income over a short interval is a poor and *seriously biased* measure of the accustomed level. In the previous test the extent of this bias was measured by the correlation $r_{yy_{-1}}$; the higher the correlation, the smaller the bias and, therefore, the higher the elasticity of consumption with respect to income. Margaret Reid and a few others have suggested and tested alternative methods of getting a more reliable index of the accustomed level than current income and, invariably, it is found that when consumption is related to such a measure, the elasticity of consumption with

[47] The figures just quoted are in part approximate since Reid has not used the statistic $r_{yy_{-1}}$ but, instead, one closely related to it. Although we do not have specific information on the age composition of the samples, we understand that retired households, if any, represent a negligible proportion of the samples.

respect to it rises markedly above the consumption-current income elasticity, and comes close, frequently remarkably close, to unity.[48]

Another set of results that supports our model is that reported in the classical contribution of Dorothy S. Brady and Rose D. Friedman, "Savings and the Income Distribution." [49] As is well known, their major finding is that the saving ratio appears to bear a much more stable relation to the position of the income recipient in the income distribution than to the absolute level of income itself. In other words, the proportion of income saved in a *given decile* varies much less over time and space than the proportion of income saved at a *given level of income*. It is not difficult to see that these results are what one would expect if our model is correct. As should be clear from the reasoning we have followed in developing our Figure 2, the relative frequency of households in a given income bracket whose income is below or above their accustomed level, depends, not on the absolute level of income, but, rather, on the position of the income bracket relative to the average income. For example, in a given

[48] See, for instance, Josephine H. Staab, "Income-Expenditure Relations of Farm Families Using Three Bases of Classification," Ph.D. dissertation, The University of Chicago, 1952; Reid, *op. cit.* (several new experiments are also reported in Reid's preliminary draft quoted above); Vickrey, *op. cit.* In essence Vickrey's point is that consumption is more reliable than current income as a measure of the permanent component of income (p. 273) and he suggests, accordingly, that the individual marginal propensity to consume (with respect to the permanent component) can be estimated more reliably by relating consumption (per equivalent adult), c, to $\bar{y}(c)$ than by relating $\bar{c}(y)$ to y, as has been usually done. It can be shown that Vickrey's suggestions receive a good deal of support from our model (with the addition of the stochastic assumptions introduced in various footnotes above) in that the relation between c and $\bar{y}(c)$ should be very similar to that between c and our quantity p. In particular, c should be nearly proportional to $\bar{y}(c)$, a conclusion that Vickrey himself did not reach but which is well supported by his own tabulations. A double logarithmic plot of c against $\bar{y}(c)$, based on his data, reveals an extremely close linear relationship with a slope remarkably close to unity. (We have estimated this slope, by graphical methods, at .97.) On the other hand, using the conventional plot, $\bar{c}(y)$ against y, the slope for the same data can be estimated at somewhat below .85, and, in addition, the scatter around the line of relationship is distinctly wider than for the first mentioned plot.

In the contribution under discussion Vickrey has also been very much concerned with the influence of the size composition of the household on saving behavior. This is a point which, because of limitations of space, we have been forced to neglect in the present paper. We will merely indicate, at this point, that our central hypothesis (that the essential purpose of saving is the smoothing of the major and minor variations that occur in the income stream in the course of the life cycle) provides a framework within which the influence of family size can be readily analyzed. We hope to develop this point in later contributions.

[49] *Studies in Income and Wealth*, Vol. X, pp. 247-265.

income bracket, say \$10,000, we should expect to find a large proportion of people whose accustomed level is less than \$10,000 if, say, the average income is \$2,000 and the level \$10,000 is in the top decile; while, in this same bracket, we should expect to find a small proportion of people whose accustomed level is below \$10,000 if the community average income were, say, \$50,000 so that the \$10,000 bracket is in the lowest income decile. More generally, it can be shown that provided, as seems likely, there is a fairly stable relation between average income in a given decile and the over-all average income, then the saving ratio, in a given decile, would depend primarily on the (relative) short-term variability of income.[50] Thus, if we compare, over time or space, groups for which the (relative) variability of income is not very different, the proportion of income saved in any given decile should be roughly the same for every group. As an example, we can compare the behavior of nonfarm families in different regions and at different points in time (see Brady and Friedman, Charts 1 through 4) and we find our inference confirmed. Furthermore, within a group, the greater the variability in income, the greater

[50] Making use of equations (II.10′), (II.12) and the expression for $\bar{a}(y)$ derived in note 41, our cross-section income-consumption relation can be reduced to the form

$$\bar{c}(y) = A + By = A^*\bar{y} + By,$$

where A^* and B depend on the coefficients E, α, β, λ, μ, ν we have introduced earlier, and on age. These coefficients, in turn, depend primarily on the variability of income as measured by $r_{yy^e_{-1}}$ and $r_z y^e_{-1}$, and, probably to a lesser extent, on the long-term trend of income (which affects λ, μ and ν) and on the cyclical position of the economy (which affects α and β and possibly E). Hence, if we have various samples of households for each of which the variability of income is approximately the same, the coefficients A^* and B should also be approximately the same for each sample, especially if the samples in question do not differ too markedly with respect to age, composition and the cyclical position of total income. Denoting by $\bar{c}_i$ and $\bar{y}_i$ the average value of consumption and income for all households falling in the i-th quantile of a given sample, we must have

$$\bar{c}_i = A^*\bar{y} + B\bar{y}_i.$$

If, furthermore, for each of the samples compared $\bar{y}_i/\bar{y}$ is approximately constant, so that we can write $\bar{y}_i = k_i\bar{y}$, we obtain

$$\bar{c}_i/\bar{y}_i = \overline{(c/y)}_i = \frac{A^*}{k_i} + B,$$

i.e., the proportion of income consumed in a given quantile, i, should be approximately the same for all samples compared, as stated in the text. We may add that, if we replace our simple stochastic assumption (II.10) by the more realistic one suggested at the end of note 37, the conclusion stated in the text would still stand, although the relation between $\overline{(c/y)}_i$ and i would be more complex than indicated by the right-hand side of the above equation.

should be the variation in the saving ratio as between the lower and the upper deciles. This inference, too, is supported by comparison of nonfarm and farm groups (compare Chart 2 with Chart 5).

It will be recognized that our theory offers an explanation for the Brady-Friedman findings that is fundamentally different from the social-psychological explanation that has been advanced heretofore.[51] Although our current interpretation is much simpler and integrates these findings with many others without recourse to additional postulates, we do not wish to deny that the earlier explanation may have some validity.

One more finding of some significance has to do with the relation between the elasticity of consumption with respect to income on the one hand and age on the other, to which reference has been made earlier. It can be shown that the slope of $\bar{c}(y)$ should tend to fall, and its intercept to rise, with age, unless, on the average, the elasticity of income expectations is extremely low, say, in the neighborhood of zero.[52] Since such a low average elasticity of expectations is rather unlikely to prevail, especially in a basically growing economy, we should generally expect the elasticity of consumption with respect to income to fall with age. This conclusion finds empirical support in the findings reported by Janet Fisher.[53] Our theory provides a common-sense explanation for her empirical finding. The increase in expected income, y^e, which accompanies the change in current income, produces a relatively larger increase in the anticipated total resources of a younger than of an older household, if E is above the minimal value, because of the greater number of years over which the

[51] For example, see James Duesenberry, *Income, Saving and the Theory of Consumer Behavior.*

[52] Making use of equations (II.10′), (II.12) and of the expression for $\bar{a}(y)$ of note 41, it can be verified that

$$\frac{\partial^2 \bar{c}(y)}{\partial y \, \partial t} < 0,$$

i.e., the slope of the cross-section consumption-income relation falls with age, provided

$$E > \frac{1}{M+1} - \frac{M\beta(1-\nu)}{(M+1)(1-\beta)}.$$

A very similar condition on E must be satisfied in order for the constant term to rise with age. Since $1/(M+1)$ should be in the order of 0.1, and β and ν are typically smaller than unity, the right-hand side of the above inequality cannot significantly exceed zero and is, in fact, likely to be negative.

[53] *Op. cit.*, p. 90 and p. 99.

higher level of income will be received. To give a specific illustration, suppose that $E = 1$, and that y, and therefore also y^e, increase by one unit. For a household of age $N - 1$, which has only one year to go before retirement, total resources, v_{N-1}, increase by only two units, and these two units have to be spread over the remaining two years of earning and M years of retirement. Therefore consumption rises by only $\frac{2}{M+1}$. At the other extreme, if the household had age 1, its total anticipated resources rise by N units, to be spread over $N + M$ years. Hence, current consumption rises by $\frac{N}{N+M}$ units. By a similar reasoning, one can conclude that the depressing effect on current consumption of the unbalance in assets that has been created by the change in income is greater the older the household, because of the smaller number of years available to the household to redress the unbalance.

In conclusion then, there is already ample evidence, and from widely different sources, which is consistent with the most distinctive implications we have derived so far from our theory and which is not equally consistent or, at any rate, readily explainable in terms of any other single set of hypotheses that, to our knowledge, has been advanced so far.

II.5 Individual Saving, Assets, and Age

In recent years a good deal of attention has been devoted to the influence of assets on consumption, and attempts have been made at estimating the cross-section relation between these variables on the expectation that the parameters obtained would yield information on the time-series relation. Our theory has something to contribute as to the pitfalls of such an attempt. To begin with, it suggests that the relevant concept of assets is *net worth;* unfortunately, most of the recent empirical work has concentrated instead on liquid assets, a variable which, according to our model, bears no definite relation to consumption, except perhaps as a very imperfect proxy for net worth.

But even if information on net worth were available, knowledge of the variation in consumption as between different households having different asset holdings, would give very little (and that little would be biased) information as to how a household would react if its assets were increased unexpectedly by a given amount, say, by an anonymous gift of the usual benevolent millionaire or, to take a more fashionable example, by an unexpected fall in the price level of consumables. This failing occurs because the observed asset holdings do not just happen to be there; instead, they reflect the life plan of the individual, which in turn depends on income and income expectations.

To interpret the positive correlation between assets and consumption as implying that people consume more *because* they have more assets would be only slightly less inaccurate than the inverse inference that people have higher assets because they consume more. The point is that both consumption and assets are greatly affected by the other variables: income, income expectations,[54] and age.

It may be objected that we are destroying a straw man; anyone studying the effect of assets would have sense enough to control the effect of, say, income. This may well be true, yet we feel that the above paragraph contains a useful lesson as to the relation between assets and consumption plans that one may too easily forget. For instance, the statement which has been repeated *ad nauseam* that in the early postwar years people bought durable goods lavishly *because* they had such large holdings of liquid assets (which may even find some apparent confirmation in survey results) might well stand a good deal of re-examination along the lines indicated above.

But our model tells us that it is not enough to control income or even income expectations. As it is brought out clearly by our analysis of the stationary case, assets depend also on age (see equation II.8); and this implication of our model is one for which scattered supporting empirical information is available.[55] Further-

[54] There is ample evidence of a very pronounced correlation between assets and income, at least as far as liquid assets are concerned. See, for example, Lawrence Klein, "Assets, Debts, and Economic Behavior," *Studies in Income and Wealth*, Vol. XIV, Table 1, p. 209; and Fisher, *op. cit.*, Table 6, p. 86.

[55] Gustave Cassel, *The Theory of Social Economy*, 1932 ed., p. 244; Horst Mendershausen and Raymond W. Goldsmith, "Measuring Estate Tax Wealth," *Studies in Income and Wealth*, Vol. XIV, Table 4, p. 140; and Fisher, *loc. cit.* The most systematic information we have found on this subject is that presented by Janet Fisher, although, unfortunately, her most interesting tabulations relate to liquid assets only. For this reason we will not attempt an extensive comparison of her findings with our theory. We may point out, however, that in terms of liquid assets, her data agree remarkably well with our theory in several respects. For example, a comparison of the mean income ratio (Table 1, p. 81) with the mean ratio of liquid asset holdings (Table 4, p. 84) by age groups, reveals that the ratio of assets per spending unit to

more, as we have seen, our hypothetical household goes on consuming a constant fraction of income (equation II.9) even though its assets continue to rise, and reach their peak just before retirement; the rise in assets relative to income does not depress saving because it is part and parcel of the life plan. In other words, higher assets do not necessarily affect saving; they do so only if, on account of unexpected variations, assets turn out to be out of line with income and age: it is only an excess (or shortage) of assets that affects the saving ratio (see equation II.2′).[56]

Finally, we can see from our equation (II.1) that the cross-section marginal rate of change of consumption (or saving) with respect to asset holdings (income and income expectations constant) could not yield a reliable estimate of the marginal propensity to consume with respect to assets. The reason is simple. From (II.1), it follows that this marginal propensity is

$$\frac{\partial c}{\partial a} = -\frac{\partial s}{\partial a} = \frac{1}{L_t}. \tag{II.15}$$

This expression is independent of assets and income but depends on age. We cannot, therefore, properly speak of *the* marginal propensity to consume with respect to assets, as this quantity will vary substantially from age group to age group, tending to increase with age.

Let us finally remember that, in order to compute the individual marginal propensity from cross-section data, it is also not sufficient to control age by introducing this variable linearly in a linear regression of consumption on income and assets,[57] for,

---

income per spending unit rises steadily with age. For the age group 45-64, which is her oldest group wherein active households presumably predominate, this ratio is nearly three times as large as for her youngest group, 18-24. For the age group 65-and-over, wherein, presumably, retired people predominate, the ratio nearly doubles again. This very high ratio is precisely what should be expected from our model where assets are drawn down slowly but income falls much faster with retirement. In terms of assets, rather than of the income/asset ratio, the peak should be reached just before retirement. Confirmation of this inference is found in the tabulations of Table 5 (p. 85).

Also suggestive of this relation is the complaint by Lawrence Klein, "Assets, Debts, and Economic Behavior," that: "There is some indication that the influence of age on savings may be obscured by a significant positive correlation between (L/Y) and a" (where Y = income, L = liquid assets, and a = age of the spending-unit head in years)."

[56] All this has, of course, some significant implications about the "Pigou effect" which are developed in Modigliani and Brumberg, *op. cit.*

[57] Cf. Klein, *ibid.*, pp. 220 ff.

according to our model, age does not enter in a linear fashion. The only way of estimating the marginal propensity at various ages and, in the process, test equation (II.15) is to carry out a full stratification by age groups (or some equivalent procedure). It is to be hoped that data for such a test may sometime be available.[58]

II.6 Uncertainty, Saving, and the Composition of Assets

The analysis of the previous sections is helpful in providing a justification for our earlier contention that the phenomenon of uncertainty can be neglected without seriously affecting the usefulness of the analysis.

As we have seen, even under the assumption of certainty there are sufficient incentives for the household to accumulate assets at a rapid rate during the early years of its life. Since the assets thus accumulated can be used to acquire durable goods and are also available as a general reserve against emergency, it would appear that the last two motives (p. 392), which are the result of uncertainty, need not affect significantly the saving behavior.[59]

To be sure, though assets can satisfy several purposes, their efficiency will not be the same in this respect. For instance, those assets which are best suited to satisfy the fourth motive are frequently not very well suited to satisfy the third. Accordingly, variations in the relative urgency of our four motives as between different individuals, and at various points of the life cycle for the same individual, will be reflected in the composition of the balance-sheet. This composition will also be affected by the current and prospective total resources, by the nature of the available alternatives, and, last but not least, by "social" pressures. Cautious individuals will hold relatively more liquid assets. Individuals with large means will tend to hold more durable goods. Examples of social pressure on the type of assets held are

[58] More generally, the essential implication of our theory that should be tested is that the (average) relation between consumption and net worth, given income and income expectations, is linear and with a slope which tends to grow with the age of the household. The specific value of the slope given by (II.15) depends on Assumptions III and IV which are convenient for exposition but are not essential to the theory.

[59] In the very early years these motives might possibly lead to a somewhat faster rate of accumulation than might occur otherwise. On the other hand, in his early years, an individual may feel less of a need for precautionary assets since, being a better risk, he will be in a better position to borrow, and may also be able to rely, for emergencies, on his relatives.

also not far to seek; witness the scramble for common stock during the 'twenties and the adoption of television after the Second World War.[60]

As to the effect of the life cycle on the composition of the "portfolio," one might expect that during the period of family formation people will put most of their savings into durables. Automobiles, refrigerators, stoves, and other appliances are felt to be essential to the establishment of an American household. After the initial purchase of durables, although depreciated goods are to be replaced and some additional goods are to be bought, savings flow into other kinds of assets. Various liquid assets may be acquired. The acquisition of a house, which requires (except for the recent G.I. housing) a prior large stock of cash, can be expected to occur throughout the life span. These generalizations are borne out by the existing data.[61]

In conclusion, uncertainty as well as many other factors must be recognized as being of great importance if one is interested in developing a satisfactory theory of the composition of the "portfolio" or, which is equivalent, of the rate of addition to the specific assets. They do not seem to be essential, however, for the development of a useful theory of the factors controlling the over-all rate of saving. Needless to say, the final justification of this statement must rest on whether or not our theory proves helpful in explaining facts which are presently known or will be revealed by further empirical work. The results so far are encouraging.

II.7 Summary

On the basis of the received theory of consumer's choice, plus one major assumption as to the properties of the utility function, we have been able to derive a simple model of individual saving behavior which is capable of accounting for the most significant

[60] Cf. Boulding, *op. cit.*, Ch. 3 and Ch. 5 for a novel approach to the choice of asset combinations. See also J. Marshack, "Money and the Theory of Assets," *Econometrica*, Oct. 1938, pp. 311-325.

Because durable goods generally seem more vulnerable to social pressure than the forms of saving that make up the ordinary (*e.g.*, Department of Commerce) definition, it is easy to see why they have been thought of as consumption. Keynes enforced the definition only by his interest in the modes of saving not necessarily matched by investment. However, the idea of ostentatious durables typifying "conspicuous consumption" preceded the *General Theory* by many years.

[61] See: Dorothy S. Brady, "An Analysis of Saving on the Basis of Consumer Expenditure Data," *Saving and Capital Market Study*, Section 3, R. W. Goldsmith, Director, preliminary; and Fisher, *op. cit.*, Tables 4, 5, and 6, pp. 85-89.

findings of many cross-section studies. Inasmuch as this model has been shown elsewhere to be equally consistent with the major findings of time-series analysis, we seem to be near the ultimate goal of a unified, and yet simple, theory of the consumption function.

The results of our labor basically confirm the propositions put forward by Keynes in *The General Theory*. At the same time, we take some satisfaction in having been able to tie this aspect of his analysis into the mainstream of economic theory by replacing his mysterious psychological law with the principle that men are disposed, as a rule and on the average, to be forward-looking animals.[62] We depart from Keynes, however, on his contention of "a greater *proportion* of income being saved as real income increases" (p. 97, italics his). We claim instead that the *proportion of income saved is essentially independent of income;* and that systematic deviations of the saving ratio from the normal level are largely accounted for by the fact that short-term fluctuations of income around the basic earning capacity of the household, as well as gradual changes in this earning capacity, may cause accumulated savings to get out of line with current income and age. The common sense of our claim rests largely on two propositions: (a) that the major purpose of saving is to provide a cushion against the major variations in income that typically occur during the life cycle of the household as well as against less systematic short-term fluctuations in income and needs; (b) that the provisions the household would wish to make, and can afford to make, for retirement as well as for emergencies, must be basically proportional, on the average, to its basic earning capacity, while the number of years over which these provisions can be made is largely independent of income levels. We have shown that our claim is strongly supported by budget data when these data are properly analyzed.

In *The General Theory*, Keynes did not put much emphasis on the proposition quoted above. But in the literature that followed, the assumption that the proportion of income saved must rise with income has frequently been regarded as one of the essential aspects of his theory and, as such, it has played an important role

[62] Our conclusions are also in complete agreement with B. Ohlin's brief but illuminating remarks and criticism of Keynes developed in "Some Notes on the Stockholm Theory of Savings and Investment," reprinted in *Readings in Business Cycle Theory;* see especially pp. 98-100.

in Keynesian analysis and its applications to economic policy and forecasting.

The task of developing the policy implications of our analysis falls outside the scope of this paper. We may, nonetheless, point out, as an example, that our new understanding of the determinants of saving behavior casts some doubts on the effectiveness of a policy of income redistribution for the purpose of reducing the average propensity to save.

Finally, we hope our study has proved useful in pointing out the many pitfalls inherent in inferences derived from cross-section data without the guidance of a clear theoretical framework. For instance, we must take a dim view of the attempts that have been made at deriving the time-series average and marginal propensity to save from the cross-section relation between saving and income. *The individual marginal propensity cannot, generally, be identified with the cross-section rate of change;* in fact, as we have seen, these two parameters need not bear any definite and stable relation to one another. We have further shown elsewhere[63] that the individual marginal propensity to save bears, in turn, a very complex relation to the time-series marginal propensity and hardly any relation at all to the time-series average propensity.

Needless to say, many implications of our theory remain to be tested. In fact, it is a merit of our hypothesis that it leads to many deductions that are subject to empirical tests and therefore to contradiction. We would be the first to be surprised if all the implications of the theory turned out to be supported by future tests. We are confident, however, that a sufficient number will find confirmation to show that we have succeeded in isolating a major determinant of a very complex phenomenon.

Appendix

Some Suggestions for the Adaptation of our Model to Quantitative Tests and Some Further Empirical Evidence

Of the many cross-section studies of saving behavior in recent years, the one that comes closest to testing the hypothesis represented by our equations (II.1) and (II.2) is the extensive quantitative analysis reported by Lawrence R. Klein in "Assets, Debts and Economic Behavior," *op. cit.* (see especially pp. 220-227 and

[63] Modigliani and Brumberg, *op. cit.*

the brief but illuminating comment of A. Hart, *ibid.*, p. 228). In this appendix we shall attempt to provide a brief systematic comparison of his quantitative findings with the quantitative implications of our theory.

We have already pointed out the many shortcomings of his analysis for the purpose of testing our theory, both in terms of definitions of variables and of the form of the equation finally tested. Because of these shortcomings, the result of our comparison can have at best only a symptomatic value. In fact, the major justification for what follows is its possible usefulness in indicating the type of adaptations that might be required for the purpose of carrying out statistical tests of our model.

Making use of the identity $N - t \equiv \frac{N(L-t)}{L} - \frac{Mt}{L}$, our equation (II.2) can be altered to the form

$$\text{(A.1)} \qquad s_i = \frac{L - t_i}{L_i} y_i - \frac{N(L - t_i)}{LL_i} y_i^e - \frac{a_i}{L_i} + \frac{M}{LL_i} t_i y_i^e,$$

where the subscript i denotes the i-th household, and L_i is an abbreviation for $L + 1 - t_i$.

Unfortunately, the variable y_i^e is usually unknown. Some information on it might be gathered by appropriate questions analogous to the question on short-term income expectations which has already been asked in the past. Klein himself, however, has not made use of this possible source of information in the study in progress. We must, therefore, find some way of relating y_i^e to the variables actually used by Klein, which are also those most commonly available.

It is clear that y^e must bear a fairly close and reasonably stable relation to current income, y. In fact, at various points in the text we have suggested that the relation between these two variables may be expressed by the equation

$$\text{(A.2)} \qquad \begin{cases} y^e = (1 - E)y_{-1}^e + Ey + A + U \\ \quad\;\, = (1 - E)(\alpha + \beta y) + Ey + U', \end{cases}$$

where A is a constant for a given sample (though subject to variation over time); E is the elasticity of income expectations defined by equation (II.11); U and $U' = (1 - E)\epsilon' + U$ are random errors; α, β are defined by equations (II.10′); and ϵ' is the random component of that equation.

If we also have information on previous year's income, y_{-1}, we can clearly exploit this information to get a better estimate of y^e_{-1}, and (A.2) then takes the form

$$y^e = \alpha^* + \beta_1 y + \beta_2 y_{-1} + U^*. \tag{A.3}$$

The coefficients of this equation, as well as the random component U^*, depend again on the short-term variability of income as measured by the correlation $r_{yy_{-1}}$, on the variance of U and on the elasticity of expectations E. It is not worth-while, however, to derive here this relation explicitly.

Substituting for y^e from (A.3) into (A.1), and rearranging terms (and neglecting the error term which is proportional to U^*) we get:

$$\text{(A.4)} \quad \begin{cases} s_i = -\dfrac{(N-t_i)\alpha^*}{L_i} + \dfrac{(L-t_i)(L-N\beta_1)-L(N-t_i)\beta_2}{LL_i} y_i \\ \qquad -\dfrac{a_i}{L_i} + \dfrac{(N-t_i)\beta_2}{L_i}(y_i - y_{-1i}) + \dfrac{M\beta_1}{LL_i} t_i y_i. \end{cases}$$

Finally, dividing through by y_i and making use of the identity $L \equiv M + N$, we obtain the result[64]

$$\text{(A.5)} \quad \begin{cases} \dfrac{s_i}{y_i} = \dfrac{(L_i-1)(L-N\beta_1)-L(L_i-M-1)\beta_2}{LL_i} \\ \qquad -\dfrac{(L_i-M-1)\alpha^*}{L_i}\dfrac{1}{y_i} - \dfrac{1}{L_i}\dfrac{a_i}{y_i} \\ \qquad + \dfrac{(N-t_i)\beta_2}{L_i}(y_i-y_{-1i})/y_i + \dfrac{M\beta_1}{LL_i} t_i. \end{cases}$$

If the quantity L_i were a constant, this equation would be identical in form with the equation Klein proposed to test;[65] although, in the actual statistical test he has found it convenient to approximate the first two terms by an expression of the form $\lambda + \mu \log y_i$, and the variable $\dfrac{y_i - y_{-1i}}{y_i}$ by $\dfrac{y_i - y_{-1i}}{y_{-1i}}$.

[64] The division by y_i creates certain statistical problems in connection with the random term; this difficulty can be handled by an appropriate modification of equation (A.2) or (A.3) which need not be discussed here since it would greatly complicate the presentation without basically affecting the conclusions.

[65] p. 220.

If we now look at Klein's results, we can take courage from the fact that all his coefficients have at least the sign required by our model; namely, a positive sign for income, income change, and age (t in our notation, a in Klein's) and negative for assets $\left(\frac{a}{y} \text{ in our notation, } \frac{L}{Y} \text{ in Klein's}\right)$. This result is of some significance, especially in the case of the age variable. According to our model, the positive sign of this coefficient reflects the fact that within the earning span, for a given level of income and assets, the older the household the smaller will tend to be its resources per remaining year of life, and therefore the smaller the consumption (*i.e.*, the higher the saving).

It would be interesting to compare the size of Klein's coefficients with the values implied by our model. At this point, however, we must remember that the analogy between Klein's equation and our equation (A.5) is more formal than real; for Klein treats his coefficients as if they were constant, whereas, according to our model, they are all functions of age since they all involve the quantity L_i. Consideration of the sensitivity of the coefficients of our equation to variations in t suggests that the error involved in treating them as constants might be quite serious. We must further remember that the specific value of the coefficients in (A.5) is based on Assumptions III and IV. As we have repeatedly indicated, these Assumptions are introduced for expository convenience but are not an essential part of our model. With the elimination of Assumption III and the relaxation of IV, along the lines suggested in footnote 25, the form of our equations and the sign of the coefficients are unchanged, but the value of these coefficients is not necessarily that given in equation (A.5), nor is it possible to deduce these values entirely on a priori grounds, except within broad limits.

We might, nonetheless, attempt a comparison, for whatever it is worth, by replacing the variable t_i in the expression L_i by a constant, say, by its average value in Klein's sample. Unfortunately, this average is not published, but we should not go far wrong by putting it at between 15 and 25 and computing a range for each coefficient using these two values." We must also take a guess at the value of β_1 and β_2. These quantities, it will be noted, are not observable. On the basis of an analysis of factors controlling these coefficients we suggest, however, that a value in the order of .5 to .6 for β_1 and of .2 and .3 for β_2, is not likely to be far from the mark. Using our standard assumption as to the value of L and N, we then get the following comparison:

Coefficient of	*Klein's estimates*[66]	*Our Model (linear approximation)*
Assets / Income	−.21; −.25 (.02) (.03)	−.04 to −.03
Income change	.03; .07 (.05) (.06)	.1 to .2
Age	.0013; .0055 (.0022) (.0024)	.003 to .0045

The age coefficient falls squarely within the range of Klein's results and nothing further need be said about it. The coefficient of income change estimated from the sample is lower than we should have expected, although, at least in one case, the difference from our estimate is well within the range of the standard error.[67] In the case of assets, however, the statistical coefficient is clearly far too great. A large part of this disparity is due, we suggest, to the fact that Klein's variable L represents liquid assets whereas our variable a represents net worth, which is clearly, on the average, several times as large as liquid assets. Hence, if liquid assets holdings are a reasonably good index of total net worth, Klein's coefficient would have to be a large multiple of ours.[68] While it is doubtful that this multiple could be as large as 6 or 7, there seems little doubt that this correction would cut the excess of Klein's coefficient over the theoretical value very substantially, probably to well within one half.[69]

[66] Figures in parentheses represent the standard errors. The two figures in this column represent the parameters of the equation for "Home Owners" and "Renters," respectively (*op. cit.*, p. 221). Since the completion of this Appendix, Mr. Klein has kindly informed us that the average age for the two samples combined is 46 years; this implies an average age, since entering the labor force, in the order of 20 to 25 years, which is within the assumed range.

[67] We suspect that expressing income change in terms of y_{-1} instead of y may also contribute to the discrepancy.

[68] If this explanation is correct, it would also follow that Klein's coefficient greatly overestimates the effect on consumption of an increase in assets due, say, to an unanticipated fall in the price level of consumables. In any event, as already pointed out, the relation between the cross section and the time-series marginal propensity is a complex one. In the companion paper quoted earlier, we have shown that the time-series marginal propensity to consume with respect to net worth should be in the order of 0.1.

[69] There is also reason to believe that failure to take into account properly the age variable may lead to an appreciable upward bias in the asset coefficient if the cross section includes retired people. Since we do not know whether Klein's sample does have a significant representation of retired households we cannot say whether this explanation is relevant.

Unfortunately, no definite statement can be made about the coefficient of income and the constant term on account of the logarithmic transformation introduced by Klein. However, approximate computations we have made suggest that these coefficients are in line with our theory in the case of his first equation and somewhat too large (in absolute terms) for the second.

It would thus appear that, at least in terms of orders of magnitude, Klein's findings agree with the implications of our model. We hasten to repeat that the comparison has very limited significance and its results must be taken with a good deal of salt; yet Klein's estimates, just as the many other empirical data we have been able to locate, would seem to warrant the feeling that we are on the right track.

Errata

Page 402: last equation in footnote 23 should read

$$``a_1 = 0 = \frac{(1 - 1)M}{L} y_1 = \bar{a}_1^1."$$

Page 409: second line of equation (II.1′) should read

$$``\frac{N}{L}\left\{y^e + \frac{L}{NL_t}(y - y^e) + \frac{L}{NL_t}[a - a(y^e, t)]\right\}."$$

Page 412: the four "*q*s" (line 4, line 9, and two on line 16) should be upper case.

Page 415, paragraph 2, second line from bottom: "line $\overline{q'q}$" should read "line $\overline{Q'Q}$."

Page 416, first line of footnote: "footnote 36" should read "footnote 37."

Page 416: last equation in footnote should read "$y \lesseqqgtr \bar{y}\left[1 - \frac{\lambda - 1}{\lambda[E(1 - \beta) + \beta(1 - \nu)]}\right]$."

Page 417, footnote 42, line 6: "especially page 20" should read "especially page 405."

UTILITY ANALYSIS AND AGGREGATE CONSUMPTION FUNCTIONS: AN ATTEMPT AT INTEGRATION

Franco Modigliani*
Carnegie Institute of Technology

and

Richard Brumberg
Johns Hopkins University

PART 1 Microeconomic Foundations

1.1 Introduction

This paper is an attempt to establish a link between the vast body of literature that has grown around the Keynesian consumption function on the one hand and the theory of consumer's choice on the other.[1,2] In order to appreciate the significance of such an attempt, a few introductory remarks on some benchmarks in the study of the consumption function may prove useful. (For the student in need of bibliography, Orcutt and Roy's work and the recently published *Bibliography on Income and Wealth, 1937–1947* can provide an excellent survey of the field.)[3,4]

Both the cross-section studies and annual time series collected during the prewar period seemed to confirm Keynes's hypothesis. A regularity in the aggregate consumption-income relationship was discernible, and, as Keynes had supposed, the saving-income ratio appeared to increase with income.[5,6] Cross-section data seemed to support these conclusions.

It was only natural, then, that when economists began to forecast postwar conditions they should turn to prewar relationships.[7] With the data at hand, it was a reasonable type of crystal gazing. Extrapolating their regressions, they tended to predict a level of saving so high, in relation to income, as to raise serious questions about the ability of private investments to absorb the saving potential at levels of economic activity anywhere close to full employment.

*My contribution to this paper is a direct outgrowth of the research carried out as director of the project on "Expectations and Business Fluctuations" financed by a grant of the Merrill Foundation for the Advancement of Financial Knowledge. I should particularly like to call attention to the relationships among consumption, assets, income expectations, and the life cycle of income as developed in this paper, and the relationships among production, inventories, sales expectations, and the seasonal cycle of sales as developed in my joint paper with O. H. Sauerlender, "The Use of Expectations and Plans of Firms for Short Term Forecasting," *Studies in Income and Wealth,* vol. XVII. in course of publication.

Even before the facts had had an opportunity to disprove the gloomy predictions of the "dismal science," a reaction had begun against this oversimplified approach. Alternative formulations and additional variables appeared throughout the journals.[8]

Prior to this debate, Simon Kuznets's historical estimates led him to conclude that, secularly, savings had not tended to increase proportionately more than income but rather that the proportion of income saved was not clearly related to the absolute level of income.[9] This contradiction of Keynes's hypothesis led to a variety of rationalizations, none of which were fully convincing.[10]

Another direction has been the exploitation of cross-section data. Old material has been reworked and new information collected. As in the time series analysis, more and more variables have been included, or are proposed for inclusion, in these cross-section studies in order to arrive at stable relations.[11]

With a few exceptions, the postwar studies on consumption and saving habits have been at an empirical level of analysis. A person thinks of a new variable, dredges up the data, computes, and announces a new high correlation. Perhaps this statement is too much of a caricature, but few would maintain that it is altogether inexact. Among the exceptions are the work of James Duesenberry, James Tobin, William Hamburger, Margaret Reid, many unrecorded comments of Dorothy Brady, and, at the conceptual level, the pioneering contribution of Tibor De Scitovszky.[12–16] The present writers owe a great debt to these authors, especially Reid and Scitovszky, and hope that this paper successfully integrates their major ideas.

The work of the last few years has taken two directions. One, mentioned above, is the addition of new variables in the time series analysis. For example, James Duesenberry and Franco Modigliani included the highest past income.[17,18] A recent variant of this modification has been the substitution of highest past consumption for highest past income.[19] Others have added such disparate variables as liquid assets and lagged income,[20] lagged consumption,[21] assets in general,[22] time,[23] population,[24] changes in income,[25] and an index of farm prices.[26]

In conclusion to this introduction, it may be said that, at the date of this writing (1952), the analysis of the consumption function has degenerated into a morass of seemingly contradictory, or at least disconnected, results, with each new empirical finding adding less to our understanding than to the existing confusion. Further empirical analysis is not likely to advance us very far until the economic theorist has been able to provide a conceptual framework to give coherence to past findings and guidance for the collection of more "facts."

It is our purpose to attempt to provide such an analytical framework on the solid foundations of the received theory of consumer's choice.[27] In a companion paper we have shown that from this theory it is possible to derive a model of individual behavior that yields a consistent interpretation of known cross-section findings and paves the way for further tests.[28] In this paper we shall attempt a similar task with respect to aggregative time-series data. We shall start by indicating how our model of individual behavior is derived from marginal utility analysis and then proceed to construct an aggregative consumption function by the algebraic summation of the individual consumption functions. We shall show that this function is consistent with the empirical findings reported by many authors and is susceptible to further tests as the required data become available. Finally, our model will be used to throw some light on the dynamics of the "Pigou effect."

1.2 Utility Analysis of Microeconomic Consumption Decisions

Since our starting point is the received theory of consumer's choice, we shall review this theory briefly.[29] Consider the following variables:

- s_t saving of the individual or, more precisely, the change (positive or negative) in his net worth during the tth year of his life, where t is measured from the beginning of the earning span;
- c_t consumption of nondurable goods and services plus current depreciation of direct-service yielding durable goods in the tth year;
- y_t income, other than from assets, in the tth year (for an individual of age t, y_t and c_t denote current income and consumption, while y_τ and c_τ, for $\tau > t$, denote expected income and planned consumption at age τ);
- a_t net worth (also referred to as assets) at the beginning of age t;
- r the rate of interest;
- N the earning span;
- M the retirement span; and
- L the life span of economic significance in this context, that is, $N + M$.

It is assumed that the individual receives utility only from present and prospective consumption and from assets to be bequeathed, and that prices and interest rates are not expected to change. Accordingly, for an individual of age t, the utility function can be written as

$$U = U(c_t, c_{t+1}, \ldots, c_L, a_{L+1}) \tag{1.1}$$

and the budget constraints

$$a_t + \sum_{\tau=t}^{N} \frac{y_\tau}{(1 + r)^{\tau+1-t}} = \frac{a_{L+1}}{(1 + r)^{L+1-t}} + \sum_{\tau=t}^{L} \frac{c_\tau}{(1 + r)^{\tau+1-t}}. \tag{1.2}$$ [30]

The left-hand side of the expression may be called the "total resources" at age t and will be denoted by v_t.

Maximizing (1.1) subject to (1.2), we obtain the first order maximum conditions:

$$
(1.3) \quad \begin{cases} \dfrac{\partial U}{\partial c_\tau} - \dfrac{\lambda}{(1+r)^{\tau+1-t}} = 0, & \tau = t, t+1, \cdots, L, \\ \dfrac{\partial U}{\partial a_{L+1}} - \dfrac{\lambda}{(1+r)^{L+1-t}} = 0 \end{cases}
$$

where λ denotes a Lagrange multiplier.

The equations in (1.3) together with equation (1.2) represent a system of $L - t + 3$ simultaneous equations to determine $L - t + 1$ c s, $\bar{a}_{L+1}$, and $\bar{\lambda}$, the barred symbols denoting the maximizing value of the corresponding variable.

If current income, $y_t + ra_t$, is unequal to $\bar{c}_t$, the individual will currently be saving (or dissaving). We may usefully distinguish two reasons why such inequalities would tend to arise, and these reasons we label the "motives for saving."[31]

I. The first of these motives is the desire to add to the estate that is to be bequeathed to one's heirs. It arises when $\bar{a}_{L+1}$ is greater than a_t; under these conditions $y_\tau + ra_\tau$ must exceed $\bar{c}_\tau$ for at least some value of τ.

II. The second and quite independent motive arises out of the fact that the pattern of income receipts will generally fail to match the pattern of consumption, which maximizes the utility function. In fact, according to the above model there need not be any close and simple relationship between consumption in a given short period and income in the same period. The rate of consumption in any given period is a facet of a plan extending over the balance of the expected life. The income accruing within the same period is but one element that contributes to the shaping of such a plan, and not a very important one if the period in question is relatively short.

If we are to proceed beyond these useful but broad generalizations, it will be necessary to introduce some restrictive assumptions about the nature of the utility function (see Assumption II following). At the outset, we will also add several other assumptions for expository convenience that will later be removed or greatly relaxed.[32]

Assumption I

$$
a_1 = 0, \qquad \bar{a}_{L+1} = 0;
$$

that is, no assets are inherited and the uility function is such that the optimum plan includes no bequests.

Assumption II The utility function is homogeneous (of any positive degree) in $c_t, c_{t+1}, \ldots, c_L$.[33]

As a result of well-known properties of homogeneous functions, these two assumptions imply that the solution of the system of equations (1.2) and (1.3) is of the form:

(1.4) $$c_\tau = \gamma_\tau^t \left[\sum_{\tau=t}^{N} \frac{y_\tau}{(1+r)^{\tau+1-t}} + a_t \right] = \gamma_\tau^t v_t, \qquad \tau = t, t+1, \cdots, L,$$

where γ_τ^t depends only on the specific form of the function U, the rate of interest r, and the present age of the individual (hence the superscript t), *but not on total resources,* v_t. By "the individual consumption function" we shall generally mean, hereafter, the current-consumption function at age t, which according to (1.4) is

$$c_t = \gamma_\tau^t v_t.$$

The remaining two assumptions are the most unrealistic and will be the first to be removed.

ASSUMPTION III The interest rate is zero; that is, $r = 0$. As a result of this assumption, the expression

$$v_t = \sum_{\tau=t}^{N} \frac{y_\tau}{(1+r)^{\tau+1-t}} + a_t$$

can be rewritten as $y_t + (N-t)\, y_t^e + a_t$, where

(1.5) $$y_t^e = \left(\sum_{\tau=t+1}^{N} y_\tau \right) \Big/ (N-t)$$

represents the average income expected over the balance of the earning span. Also, taking into account Assumption I, equation (1.2) reduces to

$$v_t = \sum_{\tau=t}^{L} c_\tau.$$

But from (1.4) we have

$$\sum_{\tau=t}^{L} c_\tau = \sum_{\tau=t}^{L} \gamma_\tau^t v_t = v_t \sum_{\tau=t}^{L} \gamma_\tau^t,$$

whence

(1.6) $$\sum_{\tau=t}^{L} \gamma_\tau^t = 1.$$

ASSUMPTION IV All the γ_τ^t are equal for a given t; that is, our hypothetical prototype plans to consume his income at an even rate throughout the balance of his life.

Let γ_t denote the common value of the γ_τ^t. From (1.6) we then have

(1.7) $$\sum_{\tau=t}^{L} \gamma_\tau^t = (L+1-t)\gamma_t = 1 \quad \text{or} \quad \gamma_t^t = \gamma_t = \frac{1}{L_t} = \gamma_\tau^t,$$
$$\tau = t+1, \cdots, L,$$

where $L_t \equiv L + 1 - t$ denotes the remaining life span at age t.

Substituting for y_t^l in equation (1.4) the value given by (1.7), we obtain immediately the individual consumption function (at age t) implied by our assumptions:

$$c_t = \frac{y_t + (N - t)y_t^e + a_t}{L_t} \quad (1.8)$$[34]

According to equation (1.8), current consumption is a linear and homogeneous function of current income, average expected income, and initial assets, with coefficients depending on the age of the household.

The corresponding expression for saving is

$$s_t = \frac{L_t - t}{L_t} y_t - \frac{N - t}{L_t} y_t^e - \frac{a_t}{L_t}. \quad (1.9)$$

PART 2 The Aggregate Functions

2.1 The Aggregate Consumption Function and the Behavior of Saving in a Steady-State Economy

We have now developed all the microeconomic tools we need for the moment, and we are ready to proceed to an analysis of the aggregate saving function.[35] For this purpose we require the following additional notation:

T calendar year or period (used also as a superscript to date a variable);
n_t number of households in age group t;
$\mathcal{N}$ total number of households; and

$\mathcal{N}_1 = \sum_{t=1}^{N} n_t$ number of households in the earning span.

A capital letter denotes the aggregate value of the same variable as its corresponding lower-case letter; for example, Y^T represents aggregate income in the year T. A lower-case letter with a subscript denotes, as in part 1, a variable for a household of the age indicated by the subscript; for example, c_t represents consumption of the household at age t. A lower-case letter with a subscript and a superscript denotes the average value of the variable for the age group, indicated by the subscript, in the calendar period of the superscript; for example, a_t^T represents average net worth of the age group t in the year T. Average income, other than income from assets, per household in the earning span will be denoted by $y^T = Y^T/\mathcal{N}_1^T$.

The variable "expected income" refers, at any given age, to any one of a number of future years. To distinguish between these years, we define

$y_{t\tau}$ the income expected for age τ by a household whose current age is t; and
$y_{t\tau}^T$ the average income expected at age τ by the age group t in the year T.

Making use of this notation, we now state Assumption V, which will be helpful in our derivation of the aggregate consumption function but will be relaxed at a later point.

ASSUMPTION V

(Va) For every T, $y_t^T = y^T$, $t = 1, \cdots, N$; that is, every age group within the earning span has the same average income in any given year T.

(Vb) For every T, $y_{t\tau}^T = y^{eT}$, $\tau = t + 1, \cdots, N$, and $t = 1, \cdots, N - 1$; that is, in a given year T, the average income expected by any age group t for any later year τ, within the earning span, is the same and we denote its value by y^{eT}.

(Vc) Every household has the same (expected and actual) total life and earning spans, L and N. (Note that this assumption implies $y_t^T = 0$ for $t = N + 1, \cdots, L$.)

Finally, we define the aggregate expected income in the year T, denoted by Y^{eT}, as the sum at T of the average yearly incomes expected over the earning span by each household; we can, therefore, write

$$Y^{eT} = \sum_{t=1}^{N} n_t^T \left(\sum_{\tau=t+1}^{N} y_{t\tau}^T \right) \Big/ (N - t).$$

From Assumption Vb and Vc, it follows that the average of the future yearly incomes expected by each age group y_t^{eT} is equal to the average income expected for any later year by every earning group y^{eT}. We may write, therefore,

$$Y^{eT} = \sum_{t=1}^{N} n_t^T \, y^{eT} = \mathcal{N}_1 \, y^{eT}.$$

Furthermore, from Assumption Va and Vc, we have

$$Y^T = \sum_{t=1}^{N} n_t^T \, y_t^T = y^T \sum_{t=1}^{N} n_t^T = \mathcal{N}_1^T \, y^T.$$

We may now develop the aggregate consumption function. According to equation (1.8), consumption for a household of age t is a linear function of the variables y_t, y_t^e, and a_t. It follows that the average consumption of the age group t in the year T must be the same linear function of the average values of income, expected income, and initial assets for this age group; that is,

$$c_t^T = \frac{1}{L_t} y_t^T + \frac{N - t}{L_t} y_t^{eT} + \frac{a_t^T}{L_t}. \tag{2.1}$$

Using Assumption Vb, we have

$$c_t^T = \frac{1}{L_t} y^T + \frac{N-t}{L_t} y^{eT} + \frac{a_t^T}{L_t}. \tag{2.2}$$

Summing over all age groups, the aggregate consumption function is

$$C^T = \sum_{t=1}^{L} n_t^T c_t^T = \sum_{t=1}^{N} \frac{n_t^T}{L_t} y^T + \sum_{t=1}^{N} \frac{n_t^T(N-t)}{L_t} y^{eT} + \sum_{t=1}^{L} \frac{n_t^T a_t^T}{L_t}$$

$$= \sum_{t=1}^{N} \frac{n_t^T}{\mathcal{N}_1^T L_t} Y^T + \sum_{t=1}^{N} \frac{n_t^T(N-t)}{\mathcal{N}_1^T L_t} Y^{eT} + \sum_{t=1}^{L} \frac{n_t^T a_t^T}{L_t}$$

or,

$$C^T = \alpha^T Y^T + \beta^T Y^{eT} + \mathscr{A}^T, \tag{2.3}$$

where

$$\alpha^T = \sum_{t=1}^{N} \frac{n_t^T}{\mathcal{N}_1^T L_t}, \quad \beta^T = \sum_{t=1}^{N} \frac{n_t^T(N-t)}{\mathcal{N}_1^T L_t}, \quad \text{and} \quad \mathscr{A}^T = \sum_{t=1}^{L} \frac{n_t^T a_t^T}{L_t}. \tag{2.4}$$

The aggregate saving function is, therefore,

$$S^T = Y^T - C^T = (1 - \alpha^T)Y^T - \beta^T Y^{eT} - \mathscr{A}^T. \tag{2.5}$$

Thus, our microeconomic model, with the addition of Assumption V, implies that aggregate consumption (and saving) in any year T is a linear and homogeneous function of current income, currently expected income, and the weighted sum of the net worth of each age group at the beginning of the year. This weighted sum, denoted by $\mathscr{A}^T$, will be called the "asset aggregate" for brevity and should not be confused with total assets,

$$A^T = \sum_{t=1}^{L} n_t^T a_t^T .$$

We also note that the weights assigned to the assets of each age group in the expression $\mathscr{A}^T$ depend only on the length of the total life span L. The coefficients of the income variables α and β depend on L and N and also on the age distribution of the active population,

$$\frac{n_t^T}{\mathcal{N}_1^T}, \qquad t = 1, \cdots, N.$$

In principle, equations (2.3) and (2.5) could be tested directly against empirical data. Unfortunately, despite the recent great additions to our historical information, the data on Y^{eT} and A^T required for such a direct test are not available at this time. The gap is particularly serious and wide in the case of assets. To our best knowledge, the information is scanty even for aggregate private net worth, not to mention its distribution by age groups.[36]

The only avenue open to us, therefore, is to derive from our model implications of a type that can be tested against the available evidence, which relates almost exclusively to consumption expenditure and (ex post) income. We shall show that most of the aggregate consumption functions that have been fitted to the data in recent years, and, in particular, those that have proved most fruitful in accounting for the behavior of consumption, can be considered as reasonable approximations to our equation (2.3). In the process of establishing this result we shall also uncover ways in which our model can be put to use for purposes of economic policy and forecasting, even in the absence of information bearing directly on aggregate assets and their distribution by age groups.

We shall find it convenient to begin by examining what our model has to tell us about the behavior of saving in an economy wherein both population and income are stationary. An economy will be said to be ''income-stationary'' in the year T if (1) all living age groups have received, and have expected to receive, over every year of their earning span the same average income and (2) this income is the same as the average income currently received and expected by every age group now in the earning span. Let us denote by $\bar{y}$ this common ''stationary'' level of average income in the year T.

We can establish the following relationship between $\bar{y}$ and the average consumption, saving, and assets of the age group t:

$$c_t^T = c(\bar{y}, t) = \frac{N}{L}\bar{y}, \qquad t = 1, \cdots, L, \tag{2.6a}$$

$$s_t^T = s(\bar{y}, t) = \begin{cases} \bar{y} - \dfrac{N}{L}\bar{y} = \dfrac{M}{L}\bar{y}, & t = 1, \cdots, N, \\ -\dfrac{N}{L}\bar{y}, & t = N+1, \cdots, L, \end{cases} \tag{2.6b}$$

$$a_t^T = a(\bar{y}, t) = \begin{cases} \dfrac{(t-1)M}{L}\bar{y}, & t = 1, \cdots, N, \\ \dfrac{NL_t}{L}\bar{y}, & t = N+1, \cdots, L. \end{cases} \tag{2.6c}$$

Our equations (2.6a, b, c) can be derived sequentially by following one ''generation'' through its life cycle and noting that, in our income-stationary economy, the life history of average consumption (saving, assets) of one generation is an exact replica of the cross-section relation between average consumption (saving, assets) and age. Alternatively, the validity of these equations can be established by mathematical induction. Suppose that equation (2.6c) holds for some t such that $1 \leq t \leq N-1$; then from equation (2.1), since $y_t^T = \bar{y} = y_t^{eT}$ and, by hypothesis, $a_t^T = [(t-1)M/L]\,\bar{y}$, we derive

$$c_t^T = \frac{(1+N-t)\bar{y}}{L_t} + \frac{[(t-1)M/L]\bar{y}}{L_t} = \frac{N}{L}\bar{y} = c(\bar{y}, t)$$

and

$$s_t^T = \frac{M}{L}\bar{y} = s(\bar{y}, t).$$

Thus, if (2.6c) holds for t, then (2.6a) and (2.6b) also hold for t. Furthermore, we have

$$a_{t+1}^{T+1} = a_t^T + s_t^T = \frac{(t-1)M}{L}\bar{y} + \frac{M}{L}\bar{y} = \frac{tM}{L}\bar{y} = a(\bar{y}, t+1).$$

Since $a(\bar{y}, t+1)$ depends only on age and not on calendar time, it follows that this expression must also be equal to the average assets of the age group $t+1$ in the year T, a_{t+1}^T. Therefore, $a_{t+1}^T = a(\bar{y}, t+1)$, so that if (2.6c) holds for t, it also holds for $t+1$. Moreover, according to (2.6c), $a_1^T = a(\bar{y}, 1) = (1-1)M/L = 0$, which we know to be true by Assumption IV; thus (2.6c) holds for $t = 1$. By similar reasoning, it can be shown that the equations also hold for $N \leq t \leq L$.

We next observe that our definition of an income-stationary economy, together with Assumption V, implies that $\bar{y} = y^T$ for every age group present. We deduce, therefore, that in such an economy the following relations hold between the average consumption, saving, and assets of every group and the overall average income, y^T, obtained by replacing $\bar{y}$ with y^T in the equations (2.6):

(2.7a) $$c_t^T = c(y^T, t),$$

(2.7b) $$s_t^T = s(y^T, t),$$

(2.7c) $$a_t^T = a(y^T, t).$$

The common sense of the stationary income relations is easily grasped by looking back at equation (2.1). Consumption depends on income, income expectations, and initial assets. But accumulated assets depend on previous income and income expectations. In a stationary economy, because of the assumed connection between past and current income and income expectations, the value of assets is uniquely related to current income, as shown by equation (2.7c). Hence, consumption and saving can themselves be expressed entirely in terms of current income.

On the basis of the relations we have just established, we shall hereafter say that the consumption of the age group t is in stationary equilibrium relative to total income in the year T if and only if $c_t^T = c(y^T, t)$, and similarly for saving and assets. Our model implies that in an income-stationary economy the ratio of average saving and consumption to average income, for every age group within the earning span, is M/L and N/L, respectively, which are constant, independent of both average income and age.[37]

By means of the equations (2.7a, b, c), we can now readily exhibit total consumption and saving in a stationary economy. We have

$$C^T = \sum_{t=1}^{L} n_t^T c_t^T = \sum_{t=1}^{L} n_t^T \frac{N}{L} y^T = \frac{N}{L} y^T \sum_{t=1}^{L} n_t^T.$$

But with a constant population, Assumption Vc implies $n_t^T = n$, a constant, for $t = 1, \cdots, L$. Furthermore, since we are not interested in aggregate consumption and income but only in their relation, we may, without loss of generality, assume $n = 1$. Hence,

$$C^T = \frac{N}{L} L\, y^T = N\, y^T = \mathcal{N}_1^T\, y^T = Y^T$$

and

$$S^T = Y^T - C^T = 0.$$

As in all well-behaved stationary economies, there is no net saving; the saving of households in the earning span is exactly offset by the dissaving of retired households.

This conclusion is illustrated by a simple numerical example in the first column of table 1. In this column the successive blocks of four rows show the behavior in period T of the age group that first entered active life in the period indicated on the far left. This age group, which we conveniently assume has a single member, we call the "generation of" the indicated period. To keep the table within manageable proportions each "period" consists of one decade; we also assume that each household earns during four decades and is, or expects to be, retired during its fifth and last decade. Accordingly, the generation of decade $T - 4$, shown first in the table, has zero income since it has reached retirement in decade T. For every other generation we assume an income, current and expected, of 20 units per decade, which is also the previous income of the retired generation. Consumption, saving, and initial assets are computed according to (2.6a, b, c). Aggregate saving, shown at the bottom of the table, is zero because the dissaving of the oldest generation, now about to disappear, just offsets the saving of the four younger generations. Note that in this economy the aggregate amount of assets is quite substantial, amounting to one half of decadal income, or five times yearly income, and that these assets are largely concentrated in the hands of the older generations.[38] These assets, of course, continuously change hands, passing from the oldest to the younger generations, while their total amount remains constant.

Table 1 Saving in a Stationery Economy with Stable and Falling Prices*

Generation of Decade		Stationary economy: Constant prices, Decade T (1)	Stationary economy: Prices fall 50% in decade T, Decade T (2)	Stationary economy: Prices fall 50% in decade T, Decade $T+1$ (3)	Growing economy: Constant prices, Decade T (4)	Growing economy: Prices fall 50% in decade T, Decade T (5)	Growing economy: Prices fall 50% in decade T, Decade $T+1$ (6)
	Income	0	0		0	0	
	Consumption	16	32		97⅔	195⅓	
$T-4$	Saving	−16	−32		−97⅔	−195⅓	
	Initial Assets	16	32		97⅔	195⅓	
	Income	20	20	0	320	320	0
	Consumption	16	22	22	195⅓	230⅔	230⅔
$T-3$	Saving	4	−2	−22	124⅔	89⅓	−230⅔
	Initial Assets	12	24	22	70⅔	141⅓	230⅔
	Income	20	20	20	320	320	640
	Consumption	16	18⅔	18⅔	230⅔	248	408
$T-2$	Saving	4	1⅓	1⅓	89⅓	72	232
	Initial Assets	8	16	17⅓	52	104	176
	Income	20	20	20	320	320	640
	Consumption	16	17	17	248	256	469⅓
$T-1$	Saving	4	3	3	72	64	170⅔
	Initial Assets	4	8	11	32	64	128
	Income	20	20	20	320	320	640
	Consumption	16	16	16	256	256	496
T	Saving	4	4	4	64	64	144
	Initial Assets	0	0	4	0	0	64
	Income			20			640
	Consumption			16			512
$T+1$	Saving			4			128
	Initial Assets			0			0
	Income (per decade)	80	80	80	1280	1280	2560
Aggregate	Consumption (per decade)	80	105⅔	89⅔	1027⅔	1185	2116
	Saving (per decade)	0	−25⅔	−9⅔	252⅓	94	444
	Initial assets	40	80	54⅓	252⅓	504⅔	598⅔
	Saving ratio	0	−.321	−.121	.197	.073	.173

*All variables are measured in terms of their purchasing power at prices of the year $T-1$.

Let us consider next the behavior of saving in a steadily growing economy in which the increase in income results from a constantly improving technology with a stationary population. In such an economy, each earning age group receives, in any given year, a higher income than in the previous year. Let us make the reasonable assumption that every age group expects the newly reached level of income to be maintained in the future. Then, if income is growing at the constant compound rate of $(\rho - 1)$ per year, saving will be a constant fraction of income (see Appendix 1),

$$s^T = \frac{M}{L} k_1 (M, N, \rho) Y^T,$$

where

$$k_1(M, N, \rho) = 1 - \frac{1 - \rho^{-M}}{M(\rho - 1)} + \frac{1}{N}\sum_{t=1}^{N-1} \frac{t}{L - t} [1 - \rho^{-(L-t)}]. \tag{2.8}$$

Formula (2.8) is illustrated by an arithmetic example in table 2, which is constructed along the same lines as table 1. In the first eight rows we follow the generation of decade T through its life cycle ending in decade $T + 4$. The history of this generation is spelled out in some detail to help explain the figures entered for the remaining generations. For numerical convenience, we assume that income grows at the forbidding rate of 100% per decade, so that in each successive decade up to retirement current income (row 2) is twice as large as in the previous decade. Since in every decade each age group expects to be able to maintain the higher income just reached, total expected income at the beginning of each decade (row 3) is equal to current income times the number of decades before retirement. Assets at the beginning of the period (row 4) represent the sum of previous savings or, also, end assets of the previous period (row 8 of previous column). Because of Assumption IV, current consumption (row 6) is obtained by allocating evenly over the remaining decades of life (row 1) the total resources anticipated at the beginning of the period (row 5), total resources being the sum of current income, expected income, and initial assets. The figures for the remaining generations are obtained in the same way; in any decade income is, by hypothesis, the same for all generations except the retired one (Assumption V).

In the columns headed $T + 4$ through $T + 6$, we have a complete cross section of a balanced population with the same number of households (one in our table) in each age group. Summing up income, consumption, and saving over the five living generations, we get the aggregates shown at the bottom of the table. It is seen that there exists in such a dynamic community a very substantial amount of saving, and it is due to two causes: (1) the generations within their earning spans save more than the equilibrium rate given by equation (2.7b) because their assets are continuously short of the equilibrium level for their current, revised expectations;[39] and (2) the retired generations dissave less than they would if they were

Table 2 Saving in a Growing Economy

Generation of Decade		Behavior in calendar decade						
		T	$T+1$	$T+2$	$T+3$	$T+4$	$T+5$	$T+6$
T	1) Remaining decades of life	5	4	3	2	1		
	2) Income, y	20	40	80	160	0		
	3) Total expected income	60	80	80	0	0		
	4) Initial assets, a	0	4	13	35⅓	97⅔		
	5) Total resources, (2) + (3) + (4)	80	124	173	195⅓	97⅔		
	6) Consumption, c	16	31	57⅔	97⅔	97⅔		
	7) Saving, s	4	9	22⅓	62⅓	−97⅔		
	8) End assets	4	13	35⅓	97⅔	0		
$T+1$	2) Income		40	80	160	320	0	
	6) Consumption		32	62	115⅓	195⅓	195⅓	
	7) Saving		8	18	44⅔	124⅔	−195⅓	
	4) Assets		0	8	26	70⅔	195⅓	
$T+2$	2) Income			80	160	320	640	0
	6) Consumptior			64	124	230⅔	390⅔	390⅔
	7) Saving			16	36	89⅓	249⅓	−390⅔
	4) Assets			0	16	52	141⅓	390⅔
$T+3$	2) Income				160	320	640	1280
	6) Consumption				128	248	461⅓	781⅓
	7) Saving				32	72	178⅔	498⅔
	4) Assets				0	32	104	282⅔
$T+4$	2) Income					320	640	1280
	6) Consumption					256	496	922⅔
	7) Saving					64	144	357⅓
	4) Assets					0	64	208
$T+5$	2) Income						640	1280
	6) Consumption						512	992
	7) Saving						128	288
	4) Assets						0	128
$T+6$	2) Income							1280
	6) Consumption							1024
	7) Saving							256
	4) Assets							0
Aggregate	Income					1280	2560	5120
	Consumption					1027⅔	2055⅓	4110⅔
	Saving					252⅓	504⅔	1009⅓
	Initial assets					252⅓	504⅔	1009⅓
	Saving ratio					.197	.197	.197
	Asset/Yearly income ratio					1.97	1.97	1.97

basing their consumption on assets accumulated at the current high level of income. It further appears that from decade to decade aggregate saving increases in the same proportion as income, so that the saving ratio remains constant, as indicated by our formula (2.10). In our example, this ratio amounts to just below 20%, a figure much higher than seems to prevail in the communities about which we have statistical information. This is, of course, due to our convenient but highly unrealistic assumption of a growth of 100% per decade.

The saving ratio implied by our model under more realistic assumptions can be found by evaluating $k_1(M, N, \rho)$. This task is rather tedious for sensible values of N and M, say in the order of 40 and 10, respectively, and for growth rates in the order of 2 to 4% per year. Fortunately, it is possible to fall back on a fairly simple and quite accurate approximation of k_1.[40] Using this approximation, we find that for the above values of M and N, and $\rho = 1.02$ (a growth of 2% per year), the saving ratio would be just below 8%; for $\rho = 1.04$ it would rise to about 14%. These results are not altogether unrealistic.

Besides technological improvements, however, much of the historical growth in aggregate income in western countries has been the result of population growth. To see what our model has to tell us about the effect of population growth, let us first consider the case in which income grows exclusively for this reason, but otherwise the economy is income-stationary. Because of the latter assumption, equation (2.7b) holds for each age group and

$$S^T = \sum_{t=1}^{L} n_t^T s_t^T = \frac{M}{L} \sum_{t=1}^{N} n_t^T y^T - \frac{N}{L} \sum_{t=N+1}^{L} n_t^T y^T$$
$$= \frac{M}{L}\left(1 - \frac{N}{M}\left[\left(\sum_{t=N+1}^{L} n_t^T\right) \Big/ \left(\sum_{t=1}^{N} n_t^T\right)\right]\right) Y^T.$$

Now suppose population grows at the rate of $(\mu - 1)$ per year; in view of our Assumption Vc, we can then write

$$n_t^T = n_1^0 \mu^{(T+1-t)}, \qquad t = 1, \cdots, L. \tag{2.9}$$

Substituting in the above expression and carrying out the indicated summation, we obtain

$$\frac{S^T}{Y^T} = \frac{M}{L}\left(1 - \frac{N}{M}\frac{1 - \mu^{-M}}{\mu^N - 1}\right) = \frac{M}{L} k_2(M, N, \mu). \tag{2.10}$$

The saving ratio is again a constant independent of Y and T, just as in the case of productivity growth. Furthermore, it turns out that $k_2(M, N, x) \simeq k_1(M, N, x)$ for values of x in the range relevant here, say $1 \leq x \leq 1.05$. It is easy to verify, for instance, that for $\mu = 1.02$, (2.10) yields a saving ratio just below 8%, and for $\mu = 1.04$, a ratio of 13%.

Thus, our model of individual behavior is seen to imply that in the long run the proportion of aggregate income saved depends not on the level of income as such but, rather, on the rate of growth of income; furthermore, for a given growth this proportion is very nearly the same whether the growth results from an expanding population, increasing productivity, or both.[41]

These results are very encouraging in light of the well-known findings of Simon Kuznets. His decadal data indicate that real income has been growing rather steadily for the six decades ending with 1929, at the rate of some 4% per year. According to our model, as developed so far, such a growth would generate a saving ratio of 13 to 14%. From Kuznets's estimates, we find that the ratio of net capital formation to net national product (which is probably the closest approximation to our concept that one may readily derive from his data) has fluctuated within the range of 11.4 to 14.6%, with no apparent tendency to rise with the increase in income.[42] It should be pointed out, however, that Kuznets's figures just quoted are based on definitions somewhat different from those underlying our model, and, as we shall see later, the saving ratio implied by the model is somewhat reduced when the existence of a nonzero interest rate is taken into account.[43]

Raymond Goldsmith, who includes durables in saving, has found similar secular results in his as yet unpublished findings. He reports, in particular, that the "secular rate of growth of saving has been so similar to that of national income that the ratio of saving to income has not shown a perceptible trend over at least the last sixty years."[44]

Finally, Kuznets's estimates exhibit a marked fall in the saving ratio for the decade 1929–1938. This drop is, however, a strictly cyclical phenomenon that is readily explained by our model, as we shall see in the next section.

One further implication of our model is that with a steady growth not only the saving-income but also the asset-income ratio would remain constant. (See, for example, the last row of table 2.) As shown in part 3, the asset ratio is given by the formula

$$\frac{A^T}{Y^T} = \frac{S^T/Y^T}{\rho - 1}, \qquad \rho > 1,$$

where $(\rho - 1)$ denotes the rate of growth regardless of cause. For example, with a productivity growth of 2%, the asset-income ratio would be about 4.0; with a 4% growth, about 3.5. This stability as well as the order of magnitude of the ratio finds some support in the wealth estimates recently published by Goldsmith.[45]

2.2 The Short-Run Consumption Function and the Cyclical Behavior of the Saving Ratio

So far, we have shown that our model is consistent with the long-run stability of the saving ratio. We know, however, that in the short run the proportion of income saved has been far from stable and has clearly tended to change with income. We shall now show that this phenomenon is fully accounted for by our model.

The consumption function at a given point of time T is represented by equation (2.3). Of the three aggregative variables appearing in this equation, the first two, Y^T and Y^{eT}, are indeed variables in the year T; but the third, $\mathscr{A}^T$, must be regarded as constant since it depends on assets accumulated before the beginning of the year T, that is, on the previous history of the economic system, which no event in the year T can possibly modify. Hence, in any year T, equation (2.3) is represented by a plane in the three-dimensional space defined by C^T, Y^T, and Y^{eT}, with intercept on the C^T-axis equal to $\mathscr{A}^T$.

The marginal propensity to consume and save may then be defined as

$$\frac{dC^T}{dY^T} = \alpha^T + \beta^T \frac{dY^{eT}}{dY^T} = 1 - \frac{dS^T}{dY^T}.$$

The quantity dY^{eT}/dY^T will hereafter be called the "coefficient of income expectations," and the marginal propensity to consume, corresponding to a unit coefficient $\alpha^T + \beta^T$, will be called the "normal" marginal propensity.

As we know, at any particular time T, α^T and β^T depend only on M, N, and the age distribution of the population. If population is growing at rate $(\mu - 1)$ per year, then from equations (2.4) and (2.9) we derive

$$\alpha^T = \frac{\mu - 1}{1 - \mu^{-N}} \sum_{t=1}^{N} \frac{\mu^{-t}}{L_t} = \alpha(L, N, \mu),$$

(2.11)

$$\beta^T = \frac{\mu - 1}{1 - \mu^{-N}} \sum_{t=1}^{N} \frac{(N - t)\mu^{-t}}{L_t} = \beta(L, N, \mu).$$

In this situation the quantities α and β are independent of time, as evidenced by the fact that the variable T no longer appears in the right-hand side of (2.11). For $\mu = 1$ (stationary population), and with our standard assumption about L and N, it is found that $\alpha(50, 40, 1) \approx 0.04$; $\alpha(50, 40, \mu)$, which we shall generally abbreviate to $\alpha(\mu)$, varies only slightly for values of μ in the relevant range, say between 1.0 and 1.03. Similarly, $\beta(50, 40, 1)$ is in the order of 0.57; $\beta(50, 40, \mu)$, though it increases with μ, is within some 5% of the above figure for μ in the relevant range.[46] Hence, the aggregate marginal propensity to consume would be in the order of 0.61 to 0.64 if the coefficient of expectations were unity. However, it might rise somewhat above this figure if the coefficient were above unity; at the other extreme, it might fall to a figure close to zero if the coefficient were close to zero, or negative. Consequently, the Keynesian (short-run) multiplier, measuring the impact effect on income of a change in investments (or more precisely, in "offsets to saving") would tend to be (in the absence of taxes) in the order of 2.5 to 3.0—although much smaller values would be possible on occasion.[47]

Having analyzed the slope of the consumption function, we may proceed to examine its intercept, $\mathscr{A}^T$, for which purpose we can conveniently utilize the results of the previous section.

Let us first derive the value of $\mathscr{A}^T$ for a stationary economy. Denote by $\bar{Y}$ the stationary level of income that prevailed up to the end of the year $T - 1$. It follows from the previous section, remembering Assumption V, that if $Y^T = y^{eT} = \bar{Y}$, then aggregate saving in the year T will be zero. Therefore, using (2.5),

$$S^T = (1 - \alpha)Y^T - \beta Y^{eT} - \mathscr{A}^T = (1 - \alpha)\bar{Y} - \beta\bar{Y} - \mathscr{A}^T = 0,$$

so that

$$\mathscr{A}^T = (1 - \alpha - \beta)\bar{Y}. \tag{2.12}$$

In other words, in a stationary economy the asset aggregate at the beginning of each year is a fraction, $1 - \alpha - \beta$, of the level of income that prevailed up to the end of the previous year.

We shall make use of equation (2.12) to define the "equilibrium level of the asset aggregate," $\mathscr{A}(Y)$, relative to any given level of aggregate income Y as

$$\mathscr{A}(Y) \equiv [1 - \alpha(1) - \beta(1)]Y. \tag{2.13}$$

Using this definition, our consumption and saving functions can usefully be rewritten as follows:

$$\begin{aligned} C^T &= Y^{eT} + \alpha(Y^T - Y^{eT}) + [\mathscr{A}^T - \mathscr{A}(Y^{eT})] \\ &= Y^T - (1 - \alpha)(Y^T - Y^{eT}) + [\mathscr{A}^T - \mathscr{A}(Y^{eT})]; \end{aligned} \tag{2.3a}$$

$$S^T = (1 - \alpha)(Y^T - Y^{eT}) - [\mathscr{A}^T - \mathscr{A}(Y^{eT})]. \tag{2.5a}$$

The quantity $Y^T - Y^{eT}$, representing the excess of current income over the average level expected for the future, may be labeled the "nonpermanent" component of income (which may be positive or negative). The quantity $\mathscr{A}^T - \mathscr{A}(Y^{eT})$, representing the difference between the actual level of the (initial) asset aggregate and the level that would prevail in a community fully adjusted to the permanent level of income, can be labeled the "unbalance in the asset aggregate." Equation (2.5a) then states that saving (or dissaving) occurs either because current income contains a nonpermanent component and/or because assets are not in balance with current income expectations. Note that the fraction saved out of the nonpermanent component of income is very close to unity. By the same token, a purely transitory fall in income would change consumption only slightly.

Substituting in equation (2.5a) the value of $\mathscr{A}^T$ given by (2.12) and rearranging terms, we obtain the short-run consumption function for the long-run stationary economy:

$$S^T = (1 - \alpha - \beta)(Y^T - \bar{Y}) + \beta(Y^T - Y^{eT}). \tag{2.14}$$

This result is illustrated in figure 1, which shows two limiting possibilities for income expectations. The solid line, $S^T S^T$, represents the saving function with $Y^{eT} = Y^T$ (unit coefficient of expectations). It has a slope of $1 - \alpha(1) - \beta(1)$, which has been shown to be approximately 0.4, and it intercepts the income-axis at $Y = \bar{Y}$. The dashed line, $S^{T'} S^{T'}$, shows the same function for $Y^{eT} = Y^{T-1} = \bar{Y}$ (zero coefficient of expectations). The intercept on the income-axis is the same as before, but the slope is $1 - \alpha(1)$, which we have seen is close to unity.

As long as income remains at the stationary level $\bar{Y}$, the saving function for any later year would continue to coincide with those shown in figure 1. But note that the only point on these functions we would be able to observe would be the point with coordinates $(\bar{Y}, 0)$. A departure from this level in the year T, however, would generate saving (or dissaving), whose amount in absolute terms, and relative to income, would be an increasing function of income. For instance, a rise in income from $\bar{Y}$ to a higher level Y_1 in the year T would raise saving (assuming $Y^{eT} = Y^T$) to a new level S_1^T. This rise would reflect the fact that households in their earning span would step up their saving, while the retired household could not offset this by increasing their rate of dissaving, which would be based on the previous level of income $\bar{Y}$.[48]

Before proceeding to a dynamic economy, let us consider briefly what would happen if income were to settle at the new level Y_1 (and assuming, for simplicity, $Y^{eT+j} = Y^{T+j} = Y_1$). An answer to this question could be provided by making use of our formal apparatus; this exertion, however, is unnecessary, for the broad

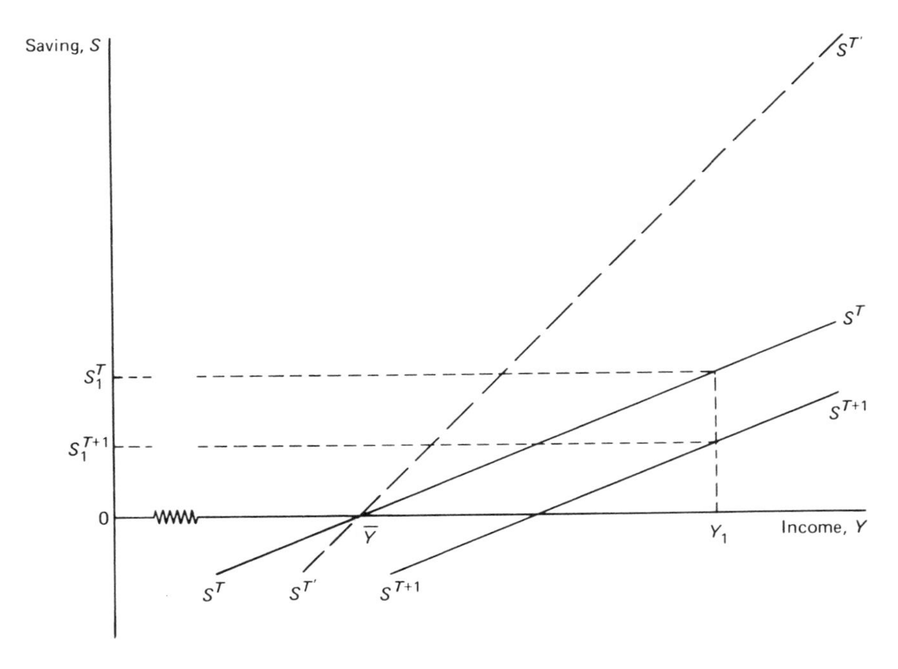

outline of what would happen is clear enough from our figure. Because of positive savings in the year T, the asset aggregate would increase so that $\mathscr{A}^{T+1} > \mathscr{A}^T$. As a result, in the year $T + 1$ the saving function would shift downward and would be represented by a line, $S^{T+1}S^{T+1}$, parallel to S^TS^T but intercepting the Y-axis somewhere between $\bar{Y}$ and Y_1. We would again find positive saving, although at a somewhat smaller rate. In the year $T + 2$, therefore, the saving function would once more exhibit a parallel shift to the right. This process would repeat year after year until, gradually, the saving function would intercept the income-axis at the point Y_1. Saving would become zero, and since the function would, ipso facto, stop shifting, saving and the saving function would remain at this level indefinitely, or until a fresh shift in income occurred.[49]

We shall now derive the value of $\mathscr{A}^T$ for a steadily growing economy in which growth is due only to increasing productivity. We saw in the previous section that if, through the year $T - 1$, income (and income expectations) grew at the annual rate $(\rho - 1)$, and if this growth continued in the year T so that $Y^T = \rho Y^{T-1} = Y^{eT}$, then saving in the year T would represent a fraction, $(M/L)k_1(\rho)$, of current income, ρY^{T-1}. Making use of equation (2.5) we have, therefore,

$$S^T = (1 - \alpha)\rho Y^{T-1} - \beta\rho Y^{T-1} - \mathscr{A}^T = \frac{M}{L} k_1(\rho)\rho Y^{T-1},$$

whence

$$\mathscr{A}^T = [1 - \alpha - \beta - \frac{M}{L} k_1(\rho)]\rho Y^{T-1}. \tag{2.15}$$

Substituting this value of $\mathscr{A}$ in equation (2.5a), we get our saving function for the year T:

$$\begin{aligned} S^T &= (1 - \alpha)(Y^T - Y^{eT}) \\ &\quad - \{[1 - \alpha - \beta - \frac{M}{L}k_1(\rho)]\rho Y^{T-1} - (1 - \alpha - \beta)Y^{eT}\} \\ &= (1 - \alpha - \beta)(Y^T - \rho Y^{T-1}) \\ &\quad + \beta(Y^T - Y^{eT}) + \frac{M}{L}k_1(\rho)\rho Y^{T-1}. \end{aligned} \tag{2.16}$$

In order to analyze this result, let us suppose first that $Y^T = Y^{eT}$ so that the middle term drops out. Since the quantity Y^{T-1} is a constant as of the year T, we see that our saving function in (2.16) represents a straight line parallel to the solid line of figure 1 (both have slope $1 - \alpha - \beta$) and goes through a point whose Y- and S-coordinates are ρY^{T-1} and $(M/L)k_1(\rho)\rho Y^{T-1}$, respectively.

The graphical presentation of figure 2 may be helpful in visualizing this result. The dotted line, $S(\rho)S(\rho)$, going through the origin and running through the entire figure, is the line $S = (M/L)k_1(\rho)Y$, which will be recognized as the secular line of the relationship between saving and income for an economy growing at the

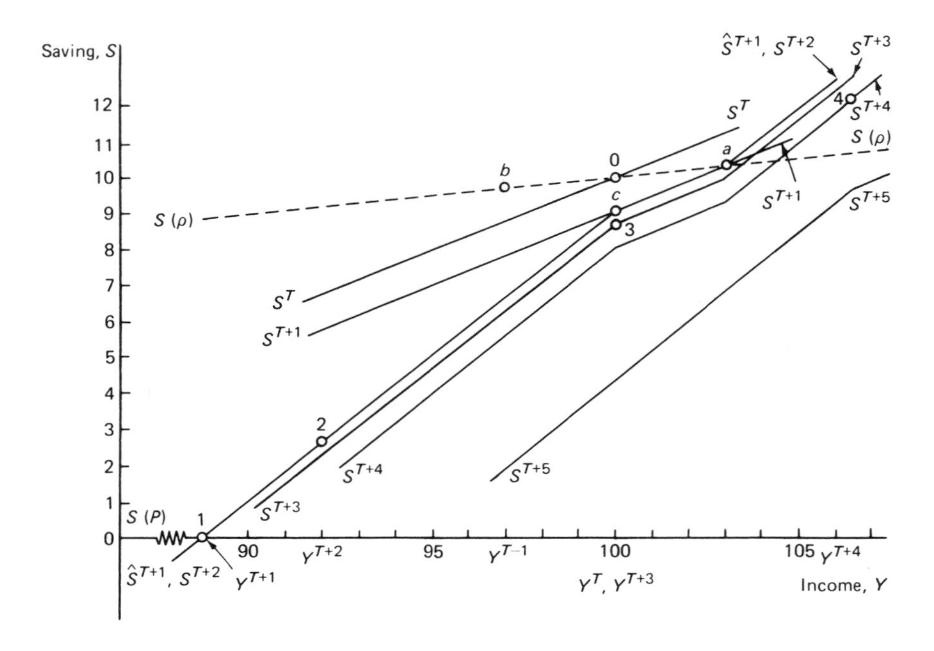

rate $(\rho - 1)$ per year (see equation (2.8)). Our figure is based on a growth of approximately 3% per year and the slope of the line is taken as 0.1, which is approximately the value of $(M/L)k_1(1.03)$, according to our standard assumptions about M and L. For Y^{T-1} we assume a value of 97 so that $\rho Y^{T-1} \approx 100$. Our saving function for year T is then represented by the solid line $S^T S^T$, with a slope of 0.4 and intercepting the long-run line at the point (100, 10). Suppose income in the year T were actually 100, then the only point we would observe on our function would be the point (100, 10), labeled 0 in our figure. The net saving of 10 accumulated in the year T would cause $\mathscr{A}^{T+1}$ to exceed $\mathscr{A}^T$. This would shift our saving function for the year $T + 1$ to the position indicated by the line $S^{T+1} S^{T+1}$, which is parallel to the line $S^T S^T$ and intersects the long-run line at a point a (103, 10.3). Similarly, the saving function for the year $T - 1$ (not drawn) would be represented by another parallel line intersecting the secular line at the point b (97, 9.7), which also would constitute the only point on the function actually observed. In brief, if income rose at the constant rate $\rho - 1$, only points such as b, 0, and a falling along $S(\rho)S(\rho)$ would be observed. An unwary observer confronted with this scatter of points might easily be misled into thinking that the slope of the flat secular line traced by these points represents the Keynesian marginal propensity to save, $\partial S/\partial Y$. Such an inference would be an error. The slope of the line joining any two observations in our figure is

$$\frac{\Delta S}{\Delta T} \Big/ \frac{\Delta Y}{\Delta T} \approx \frac{\partial S}{\partial Y} + \frac{\partial S}{\partial A} \left(\frac{\Delta A}{\Delta T} \Big/ \frac{\Delta Y}{\Delta T} \right).$$

This bears no stable relation to the marginal propensity to save (the slope of the short-run functions), which is the first term on the right-hand side and measures the change in saving per unit change in income at any one point of time.

Let us now suppose that, after following its trend up to the year T, income stopped growing so that $Y^{T+1} = Y^T$. We have already argued that the saving function for the year $T + 1$ is represented by the line $S^{T+1}S^{T+1}$. Hence, the observation for the year $T + 1$ must be the point marked c in our figure, falling on the $S^{T+1} S^{T+1}$ line immediately below point 0. The mere fact that income has ceased to rise causes saving and the saving ratio to fall below their secular levels, although the fall is relatively small (in our numerical example the ratio falls from 10/100 to 9.1/100).[50]

The conclusion that a mere cessation of growth in income might cause some reduction in saving is, of course, not new. The presence of lagged income in the consumption function would be sufficient to bring this about, and several authors have suggested that such a lagged variable should be introduced to account for a supposed phenomenon of habit persistence or lags in adjustment.[51] But note that, according to our model, the reason for the fall is really quite different; the model reflects the fact that our hypothetical economy has come one step closer to the time when it will have reached the monotony of the stationary state with zero saving.[52] As a matter of fact, if income were to remain at the level of the year T, saving would fall again in the year $T + 2$ and in the following years. Meanwhile, the saving function would continue to shift to the right until (after $L - 1$ years) it would come to intersect the Y-axis at point $(Y^T, 0)$, at which time stationary equilibrium would be reached. This conclusion has interesting implications when viewed against the background of the "stagnation" debate, which raged some years ago and is, perhaps, not yet finished.[53]

What would happen if in the year $T + 1$, instead of merely failing to rise, income were to fall very substantially, say to the level marked Y^{T+1} on the income-axis? In order to analyze this case we must reexamine one assumption that we have maintained so far, namely, the assumption of a unit coefficient of expectations.

As long as income remains equal to or higher than the previous peak, and provided that the rise above it is not altogether out of line with previous experience, this assumption appears reasonable, at least as an approximation. If, however, in a normally expanding economy, income falls below the previous peak, it is doubtful that this decline would lead to an equal downward revision of expectations about average future income. We should rather expect that for values of $Y^{T+1} < Y^T$, the quantity $Y^{T+1} - Y^{eT+1}$ would become negative[54] and, therefore, the saving function for the year $T + 1$ would fall below the line $S^{T+1} S^{T+1}$. If, for such values of Y^{T+1}, the coefficient of income expectations were as low as zero, the slope of the saving function would become $1 - \alpha$. Since a coefficient of zero is probably too extreme an assumption, we suggest that to the left of point c on the line $S^{T+1} S^{T+1}$ the saving function will have a slope somewhere between $1 - \alpha -$

$\beta = 0.4$ and $1 - \alpha = 0.96$. By the same token, one might expect that for abnormally large increases in income, say for $Y^{T+1} > \rho Y^T$, income expectations would fail to keep up with current income. Hence, to the right of point a on the line $S^{T+1}S^{T+1}$ (whose Y-coordinate is ρY^T) the saving function would again become steeper. When we take these considerations into account, our saving function for period $T + 1$ (and for all earlier periods) might look somewhat like the broken line $\hat{S}^{T+1}$, c, a, $\hat{S}^{T+1}$. For the sake of illustration, the slope of the two extreme segments has been taken as constant and equal to 0.8, although these segments need not have the same slope or, for that matter, be straight lines. The only thing that our reasoning enables us to say with some confidence is that the short-run function is likely to look somewhat like an integral sign, probably with a strong curvature in the neighborhood of the points where the slope changes in our figure.[55]

We now see that, with the assumed level of income, the observation for the year $T + 1$ would correspond to the point 1, and saving would be zero. But because of zero saving, $\mathcal{A}^{T+2}$ will be approximately equal to $\mathcal{A}^{T+1}$,[56] and the saving function for period $T + 2$ will roughly coincide with that for period $T + 1$.

By now the rest of the story can be told briefly. If income were to fall further, saving would become negative and the function would shift backward. If income were to recover weakly, say to the level marked Y^{T+2}, saving would become positive again, but remain low (point 2); the function would resume its movement to the right, say to $S^{T+3}S^{T+3}$, but the shift would be slight. In general, we see that, as long as income remains well below the previous peak, saving will be small (and may even be negative) and, therefore, the saving function will continue to coincide approximately with the function corresponding to the highest previous peak. As income rises back to the previous peak, say in the year $T + 3$, saving will also recover approximately to the earlier level (point 3 in our figure). The coincidence need not be perfect. Saving might be somewhat smaller if, as in our picture, a net accumulation of assets had occurred between the two years, or somewhat larger if, as is possible in a severe depression, there had been a reduction of assets.

With the recovery of saving, the saving function once more exhibits its characteristic shifts to the right as shown by $S^{T+4}S^{T+4}$. But if income also increases substantially, saving may well rise, temporarily, above the long run line $S(\rho)S(\rho)$ (point 4).

The scatter of points, 0, 1, 2, 3, and 4, exhibits the familiar steep "cyclical" saving-income relation. From this time on, however, the scatter will tend to flatten out. If income continues its rapid rise toward its trend value, saving will, for a time, remain abnormally high because, as a result of the low accumulation of the depression, the asset aggregate, $\mathcal{A}$, is below the dynamic equilibrium value represented by equation (2.15). However, as long as this is the case, $\mathcal{A}$ will rise at an abnormally fast pace, catching up with its equilibrium value and producing large shifts in the saving function (for example, $S^{T+5}S^{T+5}$). As the equilibrium value is neared, the observed points will again fall close to the flatter secular line, $S(\rho)S(\rho)$.

We should mention that occasionally the relationship between $\mathcal{A}$ and Y may be the reverse of the one just described. In the course of a war, patriotism, scarcity of goods, and the type of monetary-fiscal policy followed may result in an abnormally high accumulation of assets. In this case, $\mathcal{A}^T$ may exceed its trend value and become abnormally large relative to Y^T. With the return of peacetime conditions, saving will tend to be low until the growth in income, together with the retarded growth in assets, reestablishes dynamic equilibrium.

In conclusion, our model is capable of accounting for both the long-run stability of the saving ratio and for its pronounced cyclical variability. The reader may also have observed that the results of this section are very easy to reconcile with such empirical consumption functions as the so-called Duesenberry-Modigliani function and related types.

Before we proceed to a systematic comparison of our model with empirical findings, however, we will have to make sure that our conclusions are not substantially changed when we relax the simplifying assumptions to which we have adhered so far.

PART 3 Relaxation of the Assumptions

3.1 Variations in the Price Level and the Pigou Effect

In our analysis so far, we have assumed that prices were constant over the relevant past and were expected to be constant over the relevant future; it is for this reason that we did not find it necessary to distinguish between nominal and "real" values. In this section we will relax this assumption and examine the effect of changes in the price level of consumables on saving. The subject is one of special interest since it has been suggested that this effect, usually referred to as the "Pigou effect" because of the well-known contributions of that author, invalidates certain fundamental results of the Keynesian analysis.[57]

According to Keynes, if the schedule of the marginal efficiency of investment were sufficiently depressed, full employment equilibrium could not be brought about by the market mechanism, even if prices were perfectly flexible. Price flexibility might, indeed, lead to a continuous and indefinite deflation, but could not reestablish full employment equilibrium.[58] Professor Pigou has claimed that this conclusion must be rejected. He argued that the price deflation, by increasing the purchasing power of those assets with value fixed in money terms, would cause a reduction in saving at any given level of employment until a price level was reached in which full employment savings were no greater than could be absorbed in investment at the institutional minimum of the rate of interest. At this point, full employment equilibrium would be reestablished.

Even before this point had been forcefully brought forward by Pigou, it was treated with remarkable clarity by Tibor De Scitovszky,[59] who also realized the possible shortcomings of the argument and partly foresaw our own conclusions.

We shall start by summarizing the specific conclusions to which we are led by our model, illustrating our points with numerical examples. A rigorous proof of our statements will be postponed until after the analysis of the numerical example, at which point the reader who is not particularly interested in tedious proofs may proceed directly to the next section. Our conclusions are:[60]

(a) An unanticipated fall in prices that is expected to be permanent has exactly the same effect on the consumption of each age group as a nonpermanent addition to income by an amount equal to the percent change in prices multiplied by the net value of assets fixed in money terms. (''Net'' here means the difference between the gross value of assets and of liabilities fixed in money terms.) The effect of such an addition, it will be recalled, is to increase consumption, although the marginal propensity to consume with respect to such changes is very small.[61]

(b) Since the increase in consumption is not accompanied by an increase in income, the impact effect will be to decrease saving.

(c) The fall in saving will only be *temporary*. Just as we do not expect an increase in income lasting but one period to raise consumption permanently to a new level, so we cannot expect a once-and-for-all fall in prices to reduce saving permanently. In other words, the Pigou effect wears off.

(d) For saving to remain at the lower level to which it has been reduced by the impact effect, prices will have to continue to fall endlessly. In this sense the Keynesian conclusion is vindicated, although admittedly at a more complex level of analysis. Just how fast prices would have to fall depends on the entire history of the system previous to the point of time at which our endless deflation begins; but we can show that for any steady state (be it a stationary state or a state of steady growth) there exists—after a transitional period—a constant and calculable percentage rate of price decline that will keep the saving-income ratio at any desired level.

(e) The impact effect on the saving ratio of a once-and-for-all change in prices declines, and the rate at which this effect wears off rises with the proportion of income that would have been saved in the absence of the price decline. The first part of our statement essentially follows from the fact that, according to our model, saving results from the disequilibrium of income and assets (see equation (2.5a)); a high saving ratio implies a low level of assets relative to income and, therefore, less of an opportunity for the fall in prices to encourage consumption. Similarly, population and productivity growth quickly tend to regenerate those unbalances that are responsible for a high rate of saving in the absence of the price change.

Under these conditions, the tail of the effect of a given price change tends to be swamped. This justifies the second part of our statement.

(f) Since the net value of money-fixed claims is a relatively small proportion of total net worth, our model suggests that the effect of price changes on the saving ratio is of negligible magnitude. For instance, if we assume that money-fixed assets are as much as 20–25% of the total,[62] with an income growth of 3% per year, a price change as large as 10% (larger than actually occurred in the United States in any year between 1929 and 1952, except for 1947) would alter the saving ratio by an amount in the order of 1/2 of 1%.

Under these conditions it seems safe to conclude that, while in principle the short-run consumption function should include a price-change variable—see equation (2.3 π) below—for purposes of empirical testing, this variable can be neglected and our equations (2.3) and (2.5) can be utilized as they stand.[63]

Our conclusions (a) to (f) are illustrated in table 1. Column 1, as we have seen, shows the behavior of the various age groups and of the overall economy in a stationary state in which not only real income but also prices are at the level of previous periods. In column 2 we show what would happen in the decade T if prices had unexpectedly fallen. To bring our points home, we assume a price fall as large as 50%, and we also proceed as though all assets were in the form of money-fixed claims. Since real income is assumed unchanged and all variables are measured in terms of their purchasing power over consumables at prices of the decade $T - 1$, the effect of the price change is to double the initial assets of each age group. As a result, we see at the bottom of column 2 that consumption is higher than in the absence of the price change, and the saving ratio is reduced from 0 to 0.32. This fall illustrates our conclusion (b).

Column 3 shows that if in the next period prices fall no further, the saving ratio will climb back to -0.12, illustrating conclusion (c). If we were to follow our economy into later periods, we would find that with prices remaining constant, the ratio would continue to rise rapidly until, by period $T + 5$, it would be back at the initial level of zero. The economy recovers its old habits because the people who held assets and benefited from the price decline are replaced by those who must go through the process of collecting their own wealth. Moreover, although it takes a full lifetime for the effect to be completely dissipated, its "half-life" is rather short. In the example given, saving recovered more than half of the ground lost by the second period. The reason for the short half-life is that those who gained the greatest appreciation in real value were the oldest people in the society.

In columns 4, 5, and 6, the same analysis is repeated for the steady growth economy, whose behavior under stable prices was first illustrated in table 2. The data for column 4 are taken from the column labeled $T + 4$ in table 2, but, for convenience, the origin from which time is measured has been advanced by four decades. In column 5 we see what would happen in the same period T if prices had fallen by one-half. The saving ratio would drop from 0.197 to 0.073. The fall, although substantial, is smaller than for a stationary economy, 0.124 against 0.321. If prices declined no further—by the next period, $T + 1$, the saving ratio would be back to 0.173 (see column (6))—the recovery is much faster than in the stationary economy. This behavior substantiates both parts of our conclusion (e).

The reader can further verify that if prices had been cut again by 50% in period $T + 1$, the saving ratio, instead of recovering, as in column 6, would have moved closer to zero; if we continued to cut prices at this rate in every successive period, by period $T + 5$ the saving ratio would reach zero and remain at that level thereafter. Thus, to maintain the saving ratio at zero in an economy growing at 100% per decade, prices must eventually be cut at the rate of 50% per decade. This is a specific illustration of conclusion (d).[64]

Finally, the reader can verify that if we had assumed that only 20% of the asset holdings of each age group were in the form of money-fixed claims and had limited the price fall to only 20%, then the saving ratio would be 0.191 in period T, a fall of only 0.006. By period $T + 1$, the ratio would be back to 0.196. For a 10% fall in prices, the corresponding figures, to three decimal places, would be 0.194 and 0.197. This illustrates our conclusion (f).

We will now set out the mathematical foundations of our propositions. For this purpose, the following additional symbols are required:

P^T the price level of consumables in the year T;

$\pi^T = P^T / P^{T-1}$ (it is assumed that any change in prices between period $T - 1$ and T occurs at the very beginning of period T, and that prices remain constant for the rest of period T).

It will also be necessary to refine our notation with respect to assets. Although the assets held by any household at the beginning of period T are physically the same as those held at the end of period $T - 1$, their purchasing power will change if prices of consumables vary between the two periods. Our earlier notation, a_t^T and a_t will be reserved to denote the money values of the initial assets at the end of the year $T - 1$; that is, before a price change. Furthermore, it is now necessary to distinguish between assets whose values are fixed in money terms (money-fixed claims), a^{I}, and those assets whose market values change with the price level, a^{II}; clearly

$$a_t^T = a_t^{\text{I}T} + a_t^{\text{II}T}.$$

The money value of initial assets as of the beginning of period T will be denoted by the same symbols, but with an asterisk. Since the money value of money-fixed claims is unaffected by the price change, we have

$$a_t^{*\text{I}T} = a_t^{\text{I}T}.$$

For the remaining assets, we may assume that their market value changes in the same way as the price level of consumables.

Hence,

$$a_t^{*\text{II}T} = \pi^T a_t^{\text{II}T},$$

and,

$$a_t^{*T} = a_t^{*\text{I}T} + a_t^{*\text{II}T} = a_t^{\text{I}T} + \pi^T a_t^{\text{II}T}.$$

All other symbols are defined as before, except that they will represent real values in terms of prices of the year $T - 1$; that is, money values in the year T divided by π^T. The current money value itself will be denoted by an asterisk. Thus,

$$c^{*T} = \pi^T c^T, \qquad Y^{*T} = \pi^T Y^T, \qquad \text{etc.}$$ [65]

Finally, we will maintain throughout the assumption that the price level anticipated for any year beyond the current year is equal to the current price level,[66] so that

$$y_t^{e*T} = y^{e*T} = \pi^T y^{eT}.$$

Our individual consumption function, in current prices, becomes

$$c_t^* = \frac{y_t^* + (N - t)y^{e*} + a_t^*}{L_t}. \tag{1.8*}$$

Hence, making use of the above definitions and of Assumption V, the average consumption of age group t in the year T will be

$$\begin{aligned} c_t^{*T} &= \frac{y_t^{*T} + (N - t)y_t^{e*T} + a_t^{*T}}{L_t} \\ &= \frac{y_t^{*T} + (N - t)y_t^{e*T} + a_t^{\text{I}T} + \pi^T a_t^{\text{II}T}}{L_t}; \end{aligned}$$

whence

$$\begin{aligned} c_t^T = c_t^{*T}/\pi^T = c_t^T(\pi) &= \frac{y^T + (N - t)y^{eT} + a_t^{\text{II}T} + a_t^{\text{I}T}/\pi^T}{L_t} \\ &= \frac{\{y^T + a_t^{\text{I}T}[(1 - \pi^T)/\pi^T]\} + (N - t)y^{eT} + a_t^T}{L_t}. \end{aligned} \tag{2.2π}$$

Comparing equation (2.2π) with (2.2), we see that when prices change, the real consumption of every age group is the same as though prices were unchanged but current income, and only current income, were increased by an amount $a_t^{\text{I}T}[(1 - \pi^T)/\pi^T]$. This proves conclusion (a).

Summing up over all individuals, we get the aggregate consumption function:

$$\begin{aligned} c^T(\pi^T) &= \alpha Y^T + \beta Y^{eT} + \mathcal{A}^T + \frac{1 - \pi^T}{\pi^T}\sum_{t=1}^{L} \frac{n_t^T a_t^{\text{I}T}}{L_t} \\ &= \alpha Y^T + \beta Y^{eT} + (1 + \phi^T \Pi^T)\,\mathcal{A}^T; \end{aligned} \tag{2.3π}$$

where α, β, and $\mathcal{A}^T$ are defined by equations (2.4) and

$$(3.1)\quad \mathcal{A}^{\pi T} \equiv \sum_{t=1}^{L} \frac{n_t^T a_t^{\pi T}}{L_t}, \qquad \phi^T \equiv \frac{\mathcal{A}^{\pi T}}{\mathcal{A}^T}, \qquad \Pi^T \equiv \frac{1 - \pi^T}{\pi^T} = \frac{P^{T-1} - P^T}{P^T}.$$

The variable ϕ^T represents the proportion of the asset aggregate at the end of period $T - 1$, which is accounted for by the "net money-fixed-claims aggregate."[67]

Using (3.1), our aggregate saving function can now be written

$$(2.5\pi)\qquad S^T(\pi^T) = [(1 - \alpha)Y^T - \beta Y^{eT} - \mathcal{A}^T] - \phi^T \Pi^T \mathcal{A}^T.$$

The expression in brackets on the right-hand side of (2.5π) is equal to $S^T(1)$. It is also identical to our original saving function defined by the right-hand side of equation (2.5); this is expected, since the function was derived under the assumption of no change in prices. Furthermore, if prices fall ($\pi^T < 1$ and, therefore, $\Pi^T > 0$), the last term in (2.5π) is negative; thus the impact effect of a price fall is to reduce saving, proving conclusion (b).

From (2.5π) we can derive the following expression for the saving ratio:

$$(3.2)\qquad \frac{S^T(\pi^T)}{Y^T} = \frac{S^T(1)}{Y^T} - \phi^T \Pi^T \frac{\mathcal{A}^T}{Y^T}.$$

If $Y^{eT} = Y^T$ (an assumption that we will generally maintain in this section because we are dealing primarily with steady-state economies), then from (2.5π), by putting $\pi^T = 1$ (therefore, $\Pi^T = 0$) and solving for $\mathcal{A}^T$, we obtain

$$\mathcal{A}^T = (1 - \alpha - \beta)\, Y^T - S^T(1)$$

or

$$\frac{\mathcal{A}^T}{Y^T} = (1 - \alpha - \beta) - \frac{S^T(1)}{Y^T}.$$

Consequently, the impact effect of a given change in prices, which by (3.2) is proportional to $\mathcal{A}^T/Y^T$, will be smaller the larger $S^T(1)/Y^T$, as stated in the first part of conclusion (e).

We have seen that $1 - \alpha - \beta$ may be expected to lie between 0.3 and 0.4 (the specific value depends on population growth). In an economy growing at 3% per year $S^T(1)/Y^T \approx 0.11$. Hence, $1 + \alpha - \beta - (S^T(1)/Y^T)$ can be placed at around 0.25. As for ϕ, we have suggested that its value is unlikely to exceed 0.2. Accordingly, the impact effect of the price change on the saving ratio can be placed at around $0.05\Pi^T$. For instance, a 10% price fall ($\Pi^T = 0.9$) would reduce saving by some 0.5%, or from 11 to 10.5%. To look at the same question from a different angle, it would take a deflation of more than 30% within the year T to reduce the saving ratio by as much as one quarter. These magnitudes justify conclusion (f) and also entitle us, without resort to more "realistic" arguments, to join the ranks of economists who feel that price deflation is hardly an adequate tool for the control of saving.

We must now show what happens to the saving ratio in the years $T+1, \cdots, T+j$ if prices remain at the new level P^T established at the opening of the year T. We shall let $S^{T+j}(\pi^T)$ denote the value of saving in the year $T+j$ for the given value π^T, with $\pi^{T+1} = \pi^{T+2} = \cdots = \pi^{T+j} = 1$.

Let us first consider the stationary case and let $\overline{Y}$ again denote the stationary level of income. For $j = 0$, we see from equation (3.2) (since $S^T(1) = 0$) that

$$\frac{S^T(\pi^T)}{Y^T} = -\phi^T\Pi^T\frac{\mathcal{A}^T}{\overline{Y}} = -\phi^T\Pi^T(1 - \alpha - \beta). \tag{3.3}$$

In order to proceed to the year $T+1$, we first observe that the consumption of every age group present in both the year T and $T+1$ is the same in both years. In fact, according to our model, the consumption of the year T is set at a level that can be continued through life *if* expectations are fulfilled; since prices change no further, expectations *are* fulfilled. The only change in aggregate consumption is that (a) the age group first entering in the year $T+1$ will consume an amount $(N/L)y^{T+1} = \overline{Y}/L$ (again assuming one household per age group); and (b) the group having age L in the year T will stop consuming altogether in $T+1$. The consumption of this group is

$$a_L^T + \Pi^T a_L^{1T} = a_L^T + \phi^T\Pi^T a_L^T,$$

assuming for convenience that the ratio a_t^{1T}/a_t^T is the same for all age groups and therefore equal to ϕ^T. But in the stationary economy, equation (2.7c) holds so that

$$a_L^T = a(y^T, L) = \frac{N}{L}y^T = \frac{1}{L}\overline{Y}.$$

Consumption, therefore, changes by an amount

$$C^{T+1}(\pi^T) - C^T(\pi^T) = \frac{\overline{Y}}{L} - (1 + \phi^T\Pi^T)\frac{\overline{Y}}{L} = -\frac{\phi^T\Pi^T}{L}\overline{Y} = -\phi^T\Pi^T a_L^T;$$

and since income is unchanged, saving rises by a corresponding amount. Thus, making use of (3.3),

$$\begin{aligned}\frac{S^{T+1}(\pi^T)}{Y^{T+1}} &= \frac{S^T(\pi^T)}{Y^T} + \phi^T\Pi^T\frac{a_L^T}{Y^T} \\ &= -\phi^T\Pi^T\frac{\mathcal{A}^T}{\overline{Y}}\left(1 - \frac{a_L^T}{\mathcal{A}^T}\right) \\ &= \frac{S^T(\pi^T)}{Y^T}\left(1 - \frac{a_L^T}{\mathcal{A}^T}\right).\end{aligned} \tag{3.4a}$$

Applying the same reasoning to later years, we obtain

$$\frac{S^{T+j}(\pi^T)}{Y^{T+j}} = \frac{S^T(\pi^T)}{Y^T} + \frac{\phi^T\Pi^T}{Y^T}\sum_{t=L+1-j}^{L}\frac{a_t^T}{L_t} \tag{3.4b}$$

$$= \frac{S^T(\pi^T)}{Y^T}\left[1 - \frac{\sum_{t=L+1-j}^{L} \frac{a_t^T}{L_t}}{\mathscr{A}^T}\right]$$

From (3.4a) and (3.4b), we see that saving starts recovering in the year $T + 1$ and continues to rise thereafter. As j increases from 1 to L, the proportion of the impact effect surviving becomes smaller and smaller. When, finally, j reaches the value L, we have

$$\sum_{t=L+1-j}^{L} \frac{a_t^T}{L_t} = \sum_{t=1}^{L} \frac{a_t^T}{L_t} = \mathscr{A}^T,$$

and the right-hand side of (3.4b) becomes zero. At this point the effect of the price change in the year T dies out altogether and saving is back at the stationary value of zero. This proves conclusion (c).

While the time required for the effect to be completely dissipated appears to be quite long—L years—most of the dissipation can be shown to occur in the early years. As long as $j \leq M$, so that the running index t in (3.4b) remains larger than N, we know from (2.7b) that

$$a_t^T = \frac{L_t N}{L} y^T = \frac{L_t}{L} \bar{Y},$$

and we also know that $\mathscr{A}^T = (1 - \alpha - \beta)\bar{Y}$. Therefore,

$$\frac{\sum_{t=L+1-j}^{L} \frac{a_t^T}{L_t}}{\mathscr{A}^T} = \frac{j \frac{\bar{Y}}{L}}{\mathscr{A}^T} = \frac{j}{L(1 - \alpha - \beta)}, \qquad 1 \leq j \leq M. \tag{3.5}$$

For $L = 50$, $1 - \alpha - \beta \approx 0.4$; thus, when $j = 10$, half of the impact effect has already disappeared.

The task of deriving expressions for the path of saving in the dynamic case when income grows at the rate $\rho - 1$ per year is considerably more tedious, and it does not seem worthwhile to carry it out here in detail. It will suffice to say that by a combination of the reasoning used in the stationary case and the method followed in developing the basic formulas for the dynamic case (Appendix 1), one can derive the following formula analogous to (3.4b):

$$\begin{aligned} \frac{S^{T+j}(\pi^T)}{Y^{T+j}} &= \frac{S^T(1)}{Y^T} - \phi^T \Pi^T \frac{A^T}{Y^T} \rho^{-j}\left[1 - \sum_{t=L+1-j}^{L} \frac{a_t^T}{\mathscr{A}^T L_t}\right] \\ &= \frac{M}{L} k_1(\rho) - \phi^T \Pi^T \left[1 - \alpha - \beta - \frac{M}{L} k_1(\rho)\right] \\ &\quad \times \frac{1}{\rho^j}\left(1 - \left(\frac{\sum_{t=L+1-j}^{L} \frac{a_t^T}{L_t}}{\mathscr{A}^T}\right)\right), \qquad 1 \leq j \leq L. \end{aligned} \tag{3.6}$$

For $j = 0$, this formula coincides with (3.2), as we should expect.[68]

We see again from (3.6) how the effect of the price change wears off with the passage of time. As j increases, the numerical value of the second term approaches zero and finally takes on the value zero when $j = L$. At this point the saving ratio is back at the normal level, $(M/L)k_1(\rho)$. It can be further shown that the rate at which the effect wears off is greater than in the stationary case. In the stationary case, as we see from (3.4b), the proportion of the impact effect surviving after j years is given by the expression

$$1 - \frac{\sum_{t=L+1-j}^{L} \frac{a_t^T}{L_t}}{\mathcal{A}^T},$$

while in the dynamic case, as we see from (3.6), it is given by the same expression multiplied by ρ^{-j}. It must be recognized that the ratio that forms the second term of the above expression does not necessarily have the same value in both cases. In the dynamic case, both terms of the ratio are smaller than in the stationary case. It can be verified, however, that the values of the ratios themselves are very nearly equal, so that the "stationary-state" ratio, whose value is given in equation (3.5), can also be taken as a close approximation to the "dynamic-state" ratio. Hence, on account of the factor ρ^{-j}, which appears in the dynamic case, the effect wears off faster. For instance, for $\rho = 1.03$, the time required for half the effect to be dissipated is approximately 7 years, against 10 years for the stationary case. This proves the second part of conclusion (e).

The only conclusion that remains to be proved is (d). This conclusion rests on the fact that, in an economy in which real income grows at the rate $\rho - 1$ per year and prices fall steadily at the rate $\pi - 1$ per year (that is, $P^T = P^o(\pi)^T$), the relationship between a_t^T and y_t^T, or $\mathcal{A}^T$ and Y^T, is exactly the same as the relationship that would prevail in an economy in which prices were constant and real income grew at a certain rate $\rho' - 1$ per year, where ρ' is given by

$$\rho' = \frac{\rho\pi}{\phi + \pi(1 - \phi)}. \tag{3.7}$$

This statement can be verified by following the reasoning used in Appendix 1 to derive the relationship between assets and income. Hence, if we have an economy growing at the rate $\rho - 1$, there will correspond to each value of π a constant saving ratio $(M/L)k_1(\rho')$, with ρ' defined by (3.7).[69]

3.2 The Effect of Relaxing Other Simplifying Assumptions

In this section we shall examine the effect of eliminating or relaxing other major simplifying assumptions. There are primarily three questions in which we are interested:

1. Does the relaxation change our conclusion that the individual function is linear in income, expected income, and assets?
2. If the linearity of the individual function is invalidated, does the aggregate consumption function remain linear? This question is distinct from the first because the linearity of the individual function is a sufficient but not a necessary condition for linearity of the aggregate function.
3. Does the relaxation bring to light any other major factors besides those treated thus far? And if it does, do these factors affect the numerical estimates of various critical quantities we derived earlier?

As in the previous section, we shall first set out a literary summary of our conclusions and supporting reasoning for the benefit of those who are primarily interested in the content rather than in the method of proofs. This summary will then be followed by a more rigorous analytical presentation of the argument to substantiate our conclusions.

A. Elimination of Assumption III, that the interest rate is zero

1. The removal of this assumption cannot affect the linearity of the individual consumption function, as the linearity was established in equation (1.4) before the introduction of the assumption.

2. Consequently, the aggregate function remains linear.

3. (i) We stated in our discussion of (1.4) that the γ_τ, and therefore in particular γ_t^t, depended on the rate of interest as well as on the specific form of the individual utility function. The influence of interest on γ_t^t can be analyzed in terms of the "income" and "substitution" effect.[70]

Because the households of our model are typically creditors, and plan to be creditors throughout their lives, an increase in interest rates will have a positive income effect; that is, it will make them better off. It must therefore increase consumption as a whole (because of Assumption I) and hence also increase the sum of the γ_t^t for a given t. Whether and to what extent γ_t^t will increase depends on the substitution effect. If we, for the moment, neglect this effect, (whose role will be indicated under B.3 below), then all the γ_τ^t (for given t) will change in the same proportion (because of Assumption II), and therefore γ_t^t must also increase. If we further retain the assumption that the individual plans to consume his resources at an even rate (Assumption IV), γ_t^t can be shown to be equal to $r/[1 - (1 + r)^{-L_t}]$. This expression reduces, of course, to $1/L_t$ in the limiting case where $r = 0$ (compare equation (1.7)) and, as we anticipated, its value increases with r.

(ii) Because of the accumulation of assets with age, if assets have a yield, average total income will tend to rise with age up to retirement, even if average nonproperty income remains constant. Hence, with a constant consumption pattern over life, the ratio of average saving to average total income will tend to rise with age up to retirement, contrary to the conclusion we reached in section 2.1 for an income stationary economy without interest.[71]

(iii) Because the γ_t^t depends on the rate of interest, the estimates of the income coefficients of the aggregate function, α and β, which are weighted sums of the γ_t^t must be expected to change when interest is introduced and, like the γ_t^t, to be monotonically increasing functions of the interest rate. For an interest of 3%, for example, we find the normal marginal propensity, $\alpha + \beta$, to be in the order of 0.69, against 0.61 for $r = 0$. However, a further increase of r to 0.05 raises $\alpha + \beta$ to only 0.73, suggesting that the marginal propensity is not very sensitive to fluctuations in r within its usual range.

(iv) Although the normal marginal propensity to consume has risen with interest, it does not follow that there must be dissaving in a stationary economy with a positive interest rate. When we recall that no one is leaving any bequests and that the population is balanced in a stationary state, it immediately follows that aggregate saving is zero, regardless of the yield of assets.

It must be recognized, however, that even in a stationary economy, changes in the interest rate may have a significant transient effect. It is shown that to each rate of interest, r, there corresponds a stationary equilibrium level of assets, $A(r)$, and this level falls with r. We have already shown in section 2.1, (note 38) that $A(0.00) = 5\ \bar{Y}$. It is further found that $A(0.03) = 4.1\bar{Y}$, $A(0.05) = 3.5\bar{Y}$, etc.

Now, if interest fell from 5% to 3%, a discrepancy would arise between the existing level of assets adjusted to a 5% interest and the level of assets required at 3%, which would be about 15% larger. It would appear, therefore, that such a fall in interest would generate positive savings during a transitional period (of L years) while the additional assets were being accumulated. But this conclusion is warranted only if the change in interest rate does not noticeably affect the value of the initial stock of assets; that is, if all assets were in the form of very short-term loans or such that their yield would fall pari passu with the interest rate. If, at the other extreme, all assets were in the form of perpetuities, the fall in interest from 5% to 3% would increase the value of assets by 5/3, or to $5.8\ \bar{Y}$, a figure well above the equilibrium level for $r = 3\%$. In this case, the fall in interest would generate negative transitory saving. The younger generations would have to step up their rate of saving, but this would be more than offset by the increased dissaving, or lower saving, of older generations who had benefited mostly from the unexpected "capital gain." Thus, changes in interest rates may produce a transient effect on saving, but the magnitude and even the sign of this effect are unpredictable without knowledge of the composition of assets.

(v) While our conclusion of zero saving for a stationary economy is unchanged when we introduce interest, we find that interest does affect the proportion of income saved in a growing economy. In the latter, there is an excess of saving by the younger generations over the dissaving of the retired generations. Since we have seen that positive interest generates less saving out of total income for young households than for old (A.3.ii), we should expect to find in a growing economy that the saving-total income ratio falls at higher rates of interest. Our actual findings for a population growth of 4% are (where $\tilde{Y}$ denotes total income):

r	$S/\tilde{Y}$
0.00	0.13
0.03	0.08½
0.05	0.07½

(vi) Although aggregate consumption remains a linear function of Y^T, Y^{eT}, and $\mathcal{A}^T$ (A.2), we must recall that Y^T and Y^{eT} refer exclusively to nonproperty income, and the normal marginal propensity to consume considered in (A.3.iii) is defined with respect to this component of the total income, $Y^T + r\mathcal{A}^T$. Property income does not appear explicitly in our aggregate function. This fact, however, does not imply that this income has no influence on consumption.

In our model, consumption depends on assets precisely because the current value of assets reflects the anticipated stream of receipts obtainable from these assets. It follows, to the extent that variations in current property income are accompanied by corresponding variations in the expected stream of receipts from existing assets, that such variations will also generate changes in current consumption by affecting the valuation of assets (as long as interest rates are relatively stable). We can therefore include as a variable in the consumption function either the current value of assets or the current and anticipated receipts from such assets; the choice between the two alternatives is largely a matter of convenience. So far in our development we have found it preferable to follow the first course. In the next section, where we face the problem of testing our model empirically, some use will be made of the alternative formulation.

B. Elimination of Assumption IV, that the individual plans to consume at an even rate throughout his remaining life

1. The removal of this assumption, like Assumption III, cannot affect the linearity of the individual consumption function, since the linearity was established before the introduction of the assumption.

2. In consequence, the aggregate function must remain linear.

3. The γ_t^t is no longer equal to $r/[1-(1+r)^{-L_t}]$ as indicated in (A.3.i). Its value will depend more generally on the preferred life pattern of consumption as well as on the interest rate. This generalization will, of course, affect the parameters of the aggregate consumption function. For example, it can be shown that a monotonically rising (falling) pattern of (planned and actual) consumption over life leads to a fall (rise) in the marginal propensity to consume $\alpha + \beta$, the quantitative effect again being small for reasonable patterns of the γ_t^t. But the preferred pattern of consumption is not likely to exhibit anything like a monotonic path.

Rather, the evidence available suggests a humped path rising to a peak in the mature period of life and then falling, first slowly and then abruptly, with retirement.[72]

The preferred pattern of consumption may also be affected by the interest rate through the substitution effect. This effect, if it exists, must be in the direction of raising consumption for large t and depressing it for small t. Such changes, as we have just seen, would tend to reduce the marginal propensity to consume, but the quantitative effect is unlikely to be significant. As long as the substitution effect is present, it will tend to offset the depressing effect on saving of the income effect.

C. Relaxation of Assumption Va and Vb, that every age group within the earning span has the same average income and expects the same average income over the remainder of its earning span

1. Since these assumptions are only introduced for the purpose of constructing the aggregate functions from the individual ones, their relaxation can only influence the former.

Assumption Va and Vb are clearly unrealistic in that casual observation, as well as systematic evidence, indicates the presence of a clear positive correlation between income and age within the earning span.[73] At the cost of just a slight complication in our formulas, these assumptions can be replaced by two much more reasonable ones.

ASSUMPTION Va′ Average income varies with age, but the relation between average incomes of different age groups remains (approximately) constant over time.

ASSUMPTION Vb′ The average income expected at any given future age is the same for all groups younger than that age, and the pattern of income expected over the life cycle does not change over time. We may suggest that this assumption is reasonable in that the recognized existence of a typical and stable life cycle of income will be accepted by most households as the basis for their own expectations.[74]

2. The aggregate function, when constructed from the individual functions by means of these more realistic assumptions, is still linear.

3. Thus, the only effect of our relaxation upon the aggregate function is possibly to invalidate our earlier numerical estimates of the coefficients of the aggregate function. In just what way these estimates will be affected depends, of course, on the specific life pattern of income. If, for example, income rises with age, and the expected life pattern is the same as the currently prevailing age pattern, then $\alpha + \beta$ tends to rise. However, under "reasonable" assumptions about the pattern of variation of income with age, the effect is likely to be small, especially if r is at all large.

D. Relaxation of Assumption I, that no assets are inherited and that the optimum life plan excludes bequests

1. We can relax this assumption by making either of two more realistic alternative assumptions.

(i) If we consider the utility over life to depend also on planned bequests but assume that it is a homogeneous function of this variable as well as of planned consumption, then the proportion of total resources at age t, which the individual plans to leave behind, is independent of the size of total resources. The individual consumption function, therefore, remains a linear homogeneous function of total resources; that is, of current income, discounted expected income, and initial assets.

(ii) This homogeneity assumption with respect to bequests is, however, not completely satisfactory; the proportion of total resources planned for bequests may tend to be greater for individuals with "large" resources. If this is so, the individual consumption function will not be a linear function of total resources, at least for sufficiently high values of this variable.

2. Under assumption (D.1.i), our aggregate function must remain linear. Even under (D.1.ii), the aggregate consumption function may well remain linear. We believe that the notion of "large" or "small" resources is a relative one and that the proportion of total resources earmarked for bequests is likely to be an increasing function of the individual's resources relative to the average level of resources of his age group. Furthermore, if the degree of inequality in the size distribution of resources is stable over time, we deduce that the average consumption for a given age group remains a linear function of the average resources of the group. Summing up over all ages, the aggregate consumption function is again linear.

3. Assuming either variant (D.1.i) or (D.1.ii), we see that the normal marginal propensity to consume will be smaller the greater the desire to leave an estate. Moreover, with respect to (D.1.ii), it appears that a more equal size distribution of resources will moderate the fall in the propensity to consume. Approximate computations again indicate, however, that for "reasonable" assumptions about the relationship between planned bequests and resources, even the relaxation of Assumption I would not very significantly affect the values of α and β.

E. Relaxation of the assumptions and the long run behavior of the saving ratio

Even with the elimination of Assumptions III and IV and the relaxation of V, our model is still capable of accounting for the long-run stability of the saving-income and asset-income ratio. More specifically we can show that (1) given the rate of interest, the life pattern of income, and the preferred pattern of consumption, the asset aggregate $\mathcal{A}^T$, under steady growth, will tend to be proportional to aggregate assets A^T and can be replaced in the consumption function by δA^T, δ being a constant; and (2) because of (1), if *income grows at a constant rate, saving and assets will be proportional to income*. These conclusions do not seem to be significantly affected even by the relaxation of Assumption I along either of the lines proposed.

The significance of the proportionality of saving and assets to income has already been illustrated in figure 2 by the long-run saving function $S(\rho)S(\rho)$, toward which saving always tends to return in spite of cyclical deviations of income from its growth trend.

To be sure, the specific long-run level of the saving ratio will be somewhat affected by the many factors that have been discussed in this section, and these factors are subject to some variation over long periods of time. In general, the long-run saving ratio will tend to vary in the same direction as the marginal propensity to save. However, our model suggests that the marginal propensity to save should tend to remain reasonably stable in time (see section 4.1). Therefore, changes in the long-run trend of saving that might take place would tend to be both gradual and modest, as long as no significant change occurs in the growth trend of income.

The full implications of the results presented so far in this section for the empirical analysis of the consumption function will be developed in part 4; the remainder of this section will be devoted to support these results analytically.

F. Analytical development of the relaxation of Assumptions III, IV, and V

As stated, the elimination of Assumption III affects the individual consumption function through the γ_t^t. Utilizing equation (1.4) and taking into account Assumption I, the budget equation (1.2) implies

$$v_t = \sum_{\tau=t}^{L} \bar{c}_\tau (1 + r)^{-(\tau+1-t)} = v_t \sum_{\tau=t}^{L} \gamma_\tau^t (1 + r)^{-(\tau+1-t)}, \tag{3.8}$$

and therefore

$$\sum_{\tau=t}^{L} \gamma_\tau^t (1 + r)^{-(\tau+1-t)} = 1. \tag{1.6r}$$

Since (1.6r) (of which equation (1.6) is a special case) tells us that the sum of the discounted γ_τ^t must equal unity, it is clear that a rise in the rate of interest must increase the sum of the γ_τ^t for given t.

If we retain Assumption IV, which is permissible as long as the substitution effect is neglected,[75] and remember that under these conditions $\gamma_\tau^t = \gamma_t^t$, $\tau = t + 1, \cdots, L$, we can derive from (1.6r) the following expression for γ_t^t:

$$\gamma_t^t = \left[\sum_{\tau=t}^{L} (1 + r)^{-(\tau+1-t)}\right]^{-1} = \frac{r}{1 - (1 + r)^{-L_t}}. \tag{3.9}$$

The expression $r/[1 - (1 + r)^{-L_t}]$ is the reciprocal of the present value of a unit annuity running for L_t years. Since expressions of this type will occur repeatedly, we will use the notation $V\{x, r\}$ to denote the present value of an annuity of x years with interest rate r.

Substituting for γ_t^t from (3.9) into (1.4), our individual consumption function at age t, for $r = 0$, becomes

$$c_t = \frac{1}{V\{L_t, r\}} v_t = \frac{(1+r)^{-1}}{V\{L_t, r\}} y_t + \frac{\sum_{\tau=t+1}^{N} y_\tau (1+r)^{-(\tau+1-t)}}{V\{L_t, r\}} + \frac{a_t}{V\{L_t, r\}}. \tag{1.8r}$$

Thus, as stated in (A.1), c_t remains a linear and homogeneous function of income, expected incomes, and assets.

It follows that the average consumption of the age group t, c_t^T, is the same linear function of the average values of these variables for the age group t. Remembering Assumption V, we can write

$$c_t^T = \frac{(1+r)^{-1}}{V\{L_t, r\}} y^T + \frac{(1+r)^{-1} V\{N-t, r\}}{V\{L_t, r\}} y^{eT} + \frac{a_t^T}{V\{L_t, r\}}. \tag{2.2r}$$

The middle term of this expression is obtained from the corresponding term of (1.8r) by observing that the average value of income for the age group t and for any future age τ, namely $y_{t\tau}^T$, reduces to y^{eT} (by Assumption V).

From equation (2.2r) we can readily derive the aggregate consumption function by summing over all age groups. It is a linear relation of the same form as our original equation (2.3), except that the coefficients α and β of the Y^T and Y^{eT} now represent the sums from $t = 1, \cdots, N$ of the corresponding coefficients of equation (2.2r) weighted by the $n_t^T/\mathcal{N}_1^T$. Similarly, $\mathcal{A}^T$ represents the sum over all age groups of the last term weighted by n_t^T. In particular, if population is growing at the constant rate $(\mu - 1)\%$ per year, the "normal" marginal propensity to consume, $\alpha + \beta$, reduces to

$$\alpha(\mu, r) + \beta(\mu, r) = \frac{\mu - 1}{(1-\mu^{-N})(1+r)} \sum_{t=1}^{N} \frac{\mu^{-t} V\{N+1-t, r\}}{V\{L_t, r\}}. \tag{3.10}$$

The values of $\alpha + \beta$ reported under (A.3.iii) were computed from (3.10) by means of an approximation formula of the type discussed in Appendix 2.

We may now analyze the effects of interest on the saving ratio starting again with the case of a stationary economy. By means of equation (2.2r), and following the same line of reasoning used to derive the equations (2.7), we can generalize these equations so that they will apply to an income-stationary economy with nonzero interest.[76]

Let us define $\sigma \equiv 1 - V\{N, r\}/V\{L, r\}$; let us also define $\hat{Y}$ and $(\tilde{y})$, as aggregate and individual property income plus nonproperty income so that

$$\tilde{y}_t^T \equiv y_t^T + ra_t^T = \begin{cases} y^T + ra_t^T, & t = 1, \cdots, N, \\ ra_t^T, & t = N+1, \cdots, L; \end{cases}$$

and remember that y^T coincides with $\bar{y}$, the stationary level of nonproperty income. Then:

$$\text{(2.7r}'\text{)} \qquad c_t^T = (1 - \sigma)y^T, \qquad t = 1, \cdots, L,$$

$$\text{(2.7r}''\text{)} \quad s_t^T = \begin{cases} (1+r)^{t-1}\sigma\, y^T = \dfrac{\sigma}{(1-\sigma)(1+r)^{-(t-1)} + \sigma}\,\tilde{y}_t^T, & t = 1, \cdots, N, \\ -(1+r)^{t-1}[(1+r)^{-N} - \sigma]y^T \\ \quad = -\dfrac{(1+r)^{-N} - \sigma}{(1-\sigma)(1+r)^{-(t-1)} - [(1+r)^{-N} - \sigma]}\,\tilde{y}_t^T, & N+1, \cdots, L, \end{cases}$$

$$\text{(2.7r}'''\text{)} \quad a_t^T = \begin{cases} \sigma\,\dfrac{(1+r)^{t-1} - 1}{r}\,y^T, & t = 1, \cdots, N, \\ \dfrac{1 - \sigma - (1+r)^{t-1}[(1+r)^{-N} - \sigma]}{r}\,y^T, & t = N+1, \cdots, L. \end{cases}$$

We see from (2.7r″) that the proportion of total income saved increases with age during the earning span, as stated in (A.3.ii), and then decreases with age during the retirement span.

In order to evaluate aggregate saving, let us recall that in a stationary economy population is constant so that we may conveniently assume a single household in each age group, and $y^T = Y^T/N$. Making use of (2.7r′), we obtain

$$S^T = \hat{Y}^T - C^T = Y^T + rA^T - \sum_{t=1}^{L} c_t^T = Y^T + rA^T - L(1 - \sigma)Y^T/N.$$

But from (2.7r‴) we have

$$\text{(3.11)} \qquad A^T = \sum_{t=1}^{L} a_t^T = \frac{1}{r}\left(\frac{L}{N}\frac{V\{N, r\}}{V\{L, r\}} - 1\right)Y^T,$$

and substituting into the previous equation, we find that aggregate saving is zero, regardless of the level of the interest rate.

Equation (3.11) also gives the relationship between the stationary equilibrium level of aggregate assets and the rate of interest from which we computed the values of $A(r)$ quoted in (A.3.iv).

Proceeding to examine the effect of interest on saving in a growing economy, let us suppose that the increase in income is due entirely to a population growth of $(\mu - 1)\%$ per year with a stationary per capita income. Then from (2.7r′), (2.7r‴), and (2.9), we deduce

$$\frac{C^T}{\hat{Y}^T} = \frac{\sum_{t=1}^{L} n_t^T c_t^T}{\sum_{t=1}^{N} n_t^T y^T + \sum_{t=1}^{L} n_t^T a_t^T}$$

$$= \frac{(1 - \sigma)(1 - \mu^{-L})}{(1 - \mu^{-N}) + \sigma F(L) - \mu^{-N} F(M)},$$

where

$$F(X) = \left[\frac{\left(\frac{1 + r}{\mu}\right)^x - 1}{(1 + r) - \mu} (\mu - 1) - (1 - \mu^{-x}) \right]$$

The values of the saving ratio given in (A.3.v) were computed by means of this formula. Approximate computations carried out for the case of productivity growth yield results of the same order of magnitude.

We now examine the effects of replacing Assumptions Va and Vb with some more reasonable hypotheses about the relationship between income, income expectations, and age. For this purpose, we first observe that in any year T, the actual relationship between y_t^T and Y^T can be expressed in terms of the identity

$$y_t^T \equiv \frac{i_t^T}{\sum_{t=1}^{N} n_t^T i_t^T} Y^T,$$

where

$$i_t^T \equiv \frac{y_t^T}{\left(\sum_{t=1}^{N} y_t^T\right) /N}$$

denotes the ratio of the average income of the age group t to the mean of the average incomes of all age groups. The first of our revised assumptions is that the age pattern of income changes slowly, if at all, over time so that i_t^T for given t can be approximated by a constant, i_t (for values of T within a reasonable range).

Accordingly, Assumption Va, $y_t^T = y^T$, will be replaced by the following assumption:

ASSUMPTION Va′

$$y_t^T = (i_t N_t^T / \sum_{t=1}^{N} n_t^T i_t) y^T.$$

Because of the existence of a typical life cycle of income, we may suppose that households in every age group will expect, on the average, that a similar pattern will apply to them. This suggests replacing Assumption Vb with another assumption.

ASSUMPTION Vb′ In any given year T, the average income expected at age τ, $y_{t\tau}^T$, is the same for each age group $t < \tau$, and the pattern of income expected at various ages does not change over time; that is,

$$\frac{y_{t\tau}^T}{y_{t(\tau+j)}^T} = \frac{y_{t\tau}^{(T+m)}}{y_{t(\tau+j)}^{(T+m)}}, \qquad \text{for all } m, \text{ all } t < \tau, \text{ and all } \tau \text{ and } j, \text{ such that } \tau + j \leq N.$$

These assumptions imply

$$y_{t\tau}^T = i'_\tau y^{eT}, \qquad \tau = 2, \cdots, N, \quad t = 1, \cdots, \tau - 1,$$

where i'_τ is a constant for given τ and such that

$$\sum_{\tau=1}^{N} i'_\tau = N \qquad \text{and} \qquad y^{eT} = \frac{1}{N-1} \sum_{\tau=2}^{N} y_{1\tau}^T.$$

(This definition of y^{eT} coincides with our original definition if all the i'_τ are equal, as originally assumed in Vb.) If the pattern of income expected over life is the same as the actual cross-section age pattern of income at time T, then

$$i'_\tau = i_\tau, \qquad \tau = 2, \cdots, N.$$

If we also drop our Assumption IV, so that γ_t^t is not necessarily equal to $1/V\{L_t, r\}$, then, from (1.4) and Assumptions Va′ and Vb′, we find the average consumption of the age group t expressed in terms of y^T and y^{eT} to be

$$\text{(2.2}'\text{)} \quad \begin{aligned} c_t^T &= \gamma_t^t v_t^T \\ &= \gamma_t^t \frac{(1+r)^{-1} i_t \mathcal{N}_1^T}{\sum_{t=1}^{N} n_t^T i_t} y^T + \left[\gamma_t^t \sum_{\tau=t+1}^{N} i_\tau (1+r)^{-(\tau+1-t)} \right] y^{eT} + \gamma_t^t a_t^T. \end{aligned}$$

Equations (2.2) and (2.2r) are now seen as special cases of (2.2′).

The aggregate consumption function obtained by summing (2.2′) over all age groups clearly remains of the same linear form as (2.3); its coefficients, α and β, are found as usual by the summation over the first N age groups. As stated in (B.3) and (C.3), $\alpha + \beta$ does not appear to be very sensitive to variations in the γ_t^t and in the i_t within "realistic" limits.

We will now proceed to show that our generalized model resulting from the relaxation or elimination of Assumptions III, IV, and V still implies that, with a steady growth of income, saving and assets will tend to represent a constant proportion of income. In order to prove this statement we shall first establish a proposition that will prove useful in both the present argument and the next section: If consumption is a linear and homogeneous function of aggregate income and *aggregate* assets, say

$$\text{(2.12)} \qquad C^T = \theta Y^T + \delta A^T,$$

and if income grows at a constant rate ρ, then both the ratio of saving to income and the ratio of aggregate assets to income are constant over time (except possibly for a transitional period).

To prove this proposition, we note that

$$S^T \equiv \hat{Y}^T - C^T = Y^T - \theta Y^T - \delta A^T = (1 - \theta)Y^T - (\delta - r)A^T,$$

or

$$\Delta S^T = (1 - \theta)\Delta Y^T - (\delta - r)\, \Delta A^T, \tag{2.13}$$

where

$$\Delta X^T \equiv X^T - X^{T-1}.$$

But clearly,

$$A^T = A^{T-1} + S^{T-1} \qquad \text{or} \qquad \Delta A^T = S^{T-1}.$$

Substituting into (3.13) and dividing by Y^T, we have

$$\frac{\Delta S^T}{Y^T} = (1 - \theta)\frac{\Delta Y^T}{Y^T} - (\delta - r)\frac{S^{T-1}}{Y^T}.$$

If income grows at a rate $(\rho - 1) \geq 0$, then $Y^T = \rho Y^{T-1}$. Denoting the saving ratio by δ^T in the year T, S^T/Y^T, we obtain

$$\sigma^T = (1 - \theta)\frac{\rho - 1}{\rho} + \frac{(1 + r - \delta)}{\rho}\sigma^{T-1}. \tag{3.14}$$

Equation (3.14) is a first order difference equation in σ^T whose solution can be written as

$$\sigma^T = (\sigma^{T_0} - \bar{\sigma})\left(\frac{1 + r - \delta}{\rho}\right)^{(T-T_0)} + \bar{\sigma}, \tag{3.15a}$$

$$\bar{\sigma} = \frac{(1 - \theta)(\rho - 1)}{\delta - r + (\rho - 1)}, \tag{3.15b}$$

and T_0 denotes the year in which the steady growth began. Hence, $\sigma^T = \bar{\sigma}$ if the $\sigma^{T_0} = \bar{\sigma}$. Even if this equality does not hold, σ^T will approach $\bar{\sigma}$ asymptotically provided $(1 + r - \delta)/\rho < 1$, a condition we find satisfied (see section 4.3).

By a similar process, we can establish that A^T/Y^T must be equal to, or approach asymptotically, the value

$$\frac{1 - \theta}{(\delta - r) + \rho - 1}, \tag{3.15.c}$$

which also equals $\bar{\sigma}/(\rho - 1)$, provided $\rho = 1$.

Having proved our proposition, if we can show that our generalized model implies that aggregate consumption can be represented by an equation of the form (3.12), then clearly this model can account for both the long-run stability of the saving income ratio and the income asset ratio. We already know our generalized model to be of the form (2.3). Since, in the long run, we can expect Y^{eT} to be approximately equal to Y^T, our function can be written as

$$C^T = (\alpha + \beta)\, Y^T + \mathcal{A}^T = (\alpha + \beta)\, Y^T + \frac{\mathcal{A}^T}{A^T}A^T.$$

The remaining link in our argument is the demonstration that $\mathcal{A}^T/A^T$ is constant.

From the definition of $\mathcal{A}^T$, we see that

$$(3.16) \qquad \frac{\mathcal{A}^T}{A^T} = \frac{\sum_{t=1}^{L} \gamma_t^t n_t^T a_t^T}{A^T} = \sum_{t=1}^{L} \gamma_t^t \frac{n_t^T a_t^T}{\sum_{t=1}^{L} n_t^T a_t^T}$$

can be regarded as an average of the coefficients γ_t^t, weighted according to the age distribution of assets. We must show that this age distribution is constant over time in a steady state economy.

Consider first an economy whose growth is due exclusively to population changes while per capita income remains stationary. In order to take into account our revised Assumptions Va′ and Vb′ and the elimination of IV, we can redefine an income-stationary economy as one in which income may change with age but average income at age t and income expected at age τ remain constant over time; that is,

$$y_t^T = i_t \bar{y}, \qquad y_{t\tau}^T = i_\tau \bar{y}, \qquad t \leq \tau \leq N, \text{ for all } T.$$

If we are further given the preferred pattern of consumption over the life cycle expressed by the coefficients γ_t^t, and if we repeat the procedure followed in deriving the equations (2.7) and (2.7r), we can again express average assets at an age t, a_t^T, in terms of y^T, say $a_t^T = a_t y^T$. Whence,

$$\frac{n_t^T a_t^T}{A^T} = \frac{\frac{n_t^T}{N_1^T} a_t}{\sum_{t=1}^{L} \frac{n_t^T}{N_1^T} a_t}.$$

But with a constant population growth, the quantities n_t^T/N_1^T depend only on t and not on T; hence, the age distribution of assets is constant over time and so is the ratio $\mathcal{A}^T/A^T$. We have, therefore, supported our contention that if growth is due only to population growth, the consumption function is homogeneous in income and aggregate assets.

On the other hand, if income grows because of increasing productivity, with population constant, one can again express a_t^T as a linear homogeneous function of y^T by the general procedure followed in Appendix 1. With a repetition of the reasoning used above, this relation implies that the age distribution of assets is again constant. Consequently, for any given combination of (steady) productivity and population growth, consumption is a homogeneous function in aggregate assets, and our generalized model is seen to imply a constant saving-income and asset-income ratio.

G. The estate motive

No essential new problem is encountered if we eliminate this assumption and replace it with the assumption that the utility function is homogeneous in $c_t, \cdots, c_L$ and planned bequests, a_{L+1}. We only must add to our $L + t - 1$ equations in (1.4) an additional equation of the same general form, namely

$$\bar{a}_{L+1} = \gamma^t_{L+1} v_t, \tag{1.4a}$$

and replace equation (1.6r) by

$$\sum_{\tau=t}^{L} \gamma^t_\tau (1 + r)^{-(\tau+1-t)} = 1 - \gamma^t_{L+1} (1 + r)^{-(L_t)}, \tag{1.6a}$$

where the quantities $\gamma^t_\tau, \tau = t, t + 1, \cdots, L + 1$, are again constants independent of v_t.

Because of this independence, the individual and aggregate consumption functions remain linear, although the coefficients α and β will tend to be reduced, since, as we see from equation (3.11a), if $\gamma^t_{L+1} > 0$, the discounted consumption coefficients, γ^t_τ for $\tau = t, \cdots, L$, must add up to a number less than unity. Just how large the effect would be depends, of course, on the utility derived from bequests. It can be shown, for instance, by following the general line of approach used earlier, that in a stationary economy (with Assumption IV holding) the value of $\alpha + \beta$ is given by

$$\alpha + \beta = \frac{1}{N} \sum_{t=1}^{N} \frac{\psi V\{N + 1 - t, r\}}{V\{L_t, r\} + (1 - \psi)(1 + r)^{t-1} V\{t - 1, r\}},$$

where $\psi \equiv 1 - \gamma^1_{L+1} (1 + r)^{-L_t}$ and $\gamma^1_{L+1} = \bar{a}_{L+1}/v_1$ represent the ratio of planned bequests to the present value of total life resources. For a value of $r = 0.05$ and $\psi = 0.95, \alpha + \beta$ amounts to about 0.63, against a value of 0.73 for our original model with $\gamma^1_{L+1} = 0$. But note that for ψ to reach a value of $0.95, \bar{a}_{L+1}/v_1$ would have to be as high as 0.57.

We can also observe that the assumption of a stationary state, which we have used in deriving the above result, is not at all inconsistent with the presence of the estate motive as represented by equation (1.4a). The net saving of the generation of the year T over its entire life is given by

$$\begin{aligned} a^{T+L+1}_{L+1} - a^T_1 &= \gamma^1_{L+1} v^T_1 - a^T_1 = \gamma^1_{L+1} [V\{N, r\} y^T + a^T_1] - a^T_1 \\ &= \gamma^1_{L+1} V\{N, r\} y^T - (1 - \gamma^1_{L+1}) a^T_1, \end{aligned}$$

so that

$$a^{T+L+1}_{L+1} - a^T_1 \gtreqless 0, \quad \text{as} \quad a^T_1 \lesseqgtr \frac{\gamma^1_{L+1} V\{N, r\}}{1 - \gamma^1_{L+1}} y^T \qquad (\text{assuming } \gamma^1_{L+1} < 1).$$

In other words, the amount of net accumulation over life depends on the relationship between average inherited assets and average income; saving will occur only if income is large relative to assets, while a low value of income relative to assets would generate dissaving. Thus, given γ_{L+1}^{1}, to each level of income there corresponds a value of assets that is just large enough to induce neither net saving nor dissaving. Once this level of assets has been accumulated, the value of assets bequeathed equals the value of assets inherited and net saving comes to an end. On the whole, then, the recognition of the estate motive in the form of equation (1.4a) does not seem to have a very significant effect on any of our conclusions.

Unfortunately, equation (1.4a) may not hold; it seems quite possible that γ_{L+1}^{t} is not independent of v_t but, rather, tends to rise with it. We suggest, however, that γ_{L+1}^{t} is an increasing function not simply of v_t but, say, of $v_t/\bar{v}_t$, where $\bar{v}_t$ denotes average resources of the age group t. If so, the size of bequests planned on the average at age t by those having total resources, v_t can be expressed as

$$\bar{a}_{L+1} = \left[\gamma_{L+1}^{t}\left(\frac{v_t}{\bar{v}_t}\right) \right] v_t, \tag{3.17.a}$$

where the function $\gamma_{L+1}^{t}\ (v_t/\bar{v}_t)$ has the property

$$\frac{\partial \gamma_{L+1}^{t}}{\partial\left(\frac{v_t}{\bar{v}_t}\right)} \geq 0. \tag{3.17b}$$

These assumptions, together with Assumption II, which we have no reason to modify, imply

$$c_t = \gamma_t^t\left[v_t = \frac{\bar{a}_{L+1}}{(1 + r)^{L_t}} \right] = \gamma_t^t\left[1 - \gamma_{L+1}^{t}\left(\frac{v_t}{\bar{v}_t}\right)\ (1 + r)^{-L_t} \right] v_t, \tag{3.18}$$

in which γ_t^t is again a constant independent of v_t. In other words, consumption at age t is again a linear and homogeneous function of total consumption planned over the balance of life; but it need not be a linear and homogeneous function of total resources, v_t. Thus, the replacement of Assumption I by equations (3.17a) and (3.17b) may affect, in an essential way, the form of the individual consumption function.[77]

The important point, however, is that even this modification need not disturb the linearity of the aggregate consumption function. This statement can be justified by examining the relationship, in any given year T, between the average consumption of the age group t, c_t^T, and the average resources of this group, v_t^T. Let $f_t^T(v/v_t^T)\ d(v/v_t^T)$ denote the frequency distribution of the households of age t by *relative* size of resources. We then have from (3.18)

$$(3.19) \quad c_t^T = v_t^T \gamma_t^t \int_{-\infty}^{\infty} \left[1 - (1+r)^{-L_t} \gamma_{L+1}^t \left(\frac{v}{v_t^T} \right) \right] \frac{v}{v_t^T} f_t^T \left(\frac{v}{v_t^T} \right) d \left(\frac{v}{v_t^T} \right).$$

Clearly, if the frequency distribution of relative resources, f_t^T, remains stable over time (that is, approximately the same for all T), then the expression multiplying v_t^T in (3.19) is also approximately time invariant and the equation reduces to

$$(3.20) \qquad c_t^T = \Gamma_t v_t^T;$$

c_t^T is therefore a linear homogeneous function of v_t^T, in spite of the nonlinearity of the individual consumption function.[78] It is not implausible that the size distribution of total resources, f, should satisfy approximately the above condition, although there is no way to test this statement at present, since no information is available on the variable v.[79] Taking into account the definition of v_t^T, it is clear that if Γ_t is a constant independent of v_t^T, then the average consumption of the age group t remains a linear homogeneous function of income, income expectations, and initial assets; and the same proposition must hold for the aggregate consumption function. However, the coefficients of these variables depend now, among other things, on the strength of the estate motive as well as on the size distribution of resources. In particular, the values of α and β may be increased by a more equal distribution of resources.

What effect does the relaxation of Assumption I have on the saving-income ratio and the asset-income ratio under steady growth? A precise answer to this question is difficult because we can no longer make use of the general method used in connection with the relaxation of Assumptions III, IV, and V. The crucial step of the proof, that under steady growth the age distribution of resources would remain constant, consists of showing that it is possible to express a_t^T uniquely in terms of y^T, and this possibility depends in an essential way on the fact that $a_1^T = 0$ for all T. Once we recognize the existence of the estate motive and thereby admit that $a_{L+1}^T \neq 0$, we can obviously no longer assume a_1^T to be zero, especially since we should now think of a_1^T not only as the assets immediately available at age one but, more generally, as the present value of assets that the individual expects to acquire by gift or inheritance over his entire life cycle.

Now it is true that our earlier argument will continue to hold if a_1^T, while not being zero, were nevertheless a fixed multiple of y^T independent of T. It is also true that as long as the ratio of planned bequests to the present value of resources does not exceed unity (even the top "resource group" is not likely to desire to make larger bequests than these),[80] the quantity a_1^T/y^T should tend to reach a definite limit. But the approach to this limit may be an asymptotic one and, in the absence of systematic information on the strength of the estate motive and on the nature of the size distribution of total resources, one cannot be certain, in the half century or so in which we are primarily interested, that we would be anywhere close to this limit.

Despite this breakdown of our earlier line of attack, there are other good reasons to support the conclusion that the ratio of $\mathscr{A}^T/A^T$ is likely to be quite stable over time. We have shown in section 3.2E that this ratio can be regarded as an average of the Γ_t weighted by the age distribution of assets. There are two reasons why this average should not change appreciably, given the Γ_t. In the first place, the age distribution of assets, if it does vary over time, can only change slowly; and in the second place, it is a well-known empirical observation that weighted averages are relatively insensitive to small changes in the weighting system. On the last point, some direct evidence will be provided in the next part.

We seem, therefore, to be on fairly solid grounds in suggesting that as long as the Γ_t are stable, the ratio $\mathscr{A}^T/A^T$ will still be nearly constant; as a very good first approximation, consumption may be regarded as a linear and homogeneous function in income, income expectations, and aggregate assets.

PART 4 Empirical Verification

4.1 The Function to Be Tested

We emerge from the analysis of part 3 with the conclusion that, although we have dropped or considerably relaxed our major simplifying assumptions, aggregate (real) consumption remains a linear function of current and expected real income (other than from assets), Y^T and Y^{eT}, and the real value of the asset aggregate at the end of the period $T-1$, $\mathscr{A}^T$; that is,

$$C^T = \alpha Y^T + \beta Y^{eT} + (1 + \phi^T \Pi^T)\mathscr{A}^T.$$

The only significant effect of the easing of our assumptions is that the values of α, β, and $\mathscr{A}^T$, defined on the basis of the original simplifying assumptions by equations (2.4), are now given by the following more general expressions:

$$\alpha = \frac{(1+r)^{-1}}{\sum_{t=1}^{N} n_t^T i_t} \sum_{t=1}^{N} \Gamma_t n_t^T i_t,$$

$$\beta = \frac{(1+r)^{-1}}{\mathscr{N}_1^T} \sum_{t=1}^{N} \Gamma_t n_t^T \sum_{\tau=t+1}^{N} i'_t (1+r)^{-(\tau+1-t)}, \qquad (2.4a)$$

$$\mathscr{A}^T = \sum_{t=1}^{L} \Gamma_t n_t^T a_t^T.$$

By way of summarizing the results of our theoretical construction, we may recall that

(a) Γ_t represents the proportion of total resources devoted to consumption at age t by the age group t, and depends on

(i) the length of the earning and retirement spans, N and M,

(ii) the yield of assets, r,

(iii) the preferred pattern of consumption over the life cycle,

(iv) the strength of the estate motive, and, possibly,

(v) the size distribution of resources;

(b) $i_t\,(i'_t)$ stands for the ratio of actual (expected) average income at age t to the mean of the actual (expected) average incomes at all ages;

(c) $n_t^T/\mathcal{N}_1^T$ is the ratio of households of the age t to the total number of earning households;

(d) ϕ^T measures the ratio of the money-fixed claims to the total asset aggregate;

(e) Π^T is the percentage change in the price of consumables in the year T relative to the year $T - 1$;

(f) $\mathcal{A}^T$ represents the asset aggregate, which is the sum of the average assets of each age group weighted by the coefficients $n_t^T\,\Gamma_t$. It is influenced in two ways by all the factors we have listed so far:

(i) through the weights $n_t^T\,\Gamma_t$ and,

(ii) through the fact that the quantities a_t^T depend in the long run on the Γ_t. The very same factors that make for an increase in the Γ_t make for a decrease in the a_t^T; however, these changes do not necessarily cancel out in $\mathcal{A}^T$.

(g) While productivity growth, in contrast to population growth, does not affect the parameters α and β, it does influence the long-run relationship between $\mathcal{A}^T$ and Y^T, which in turn affects the long-run trend of the saving ratio.

This represents an exhaustive list of the major factors that we should expect will exert a significant and systematic influence on aggregate consumption and saving.[81] To be sure, every one of these factors has been mentioned before with varying emphasis by other authors. But our model goes beyond merely telling us what factors are relevant; it also tells us how these factors enter and provides some idea of their quantitative significance. It is precisely from the quantitative analysis carried out in part 3 that we are enabled to move to the next and most significant conclusion: The coefficients α and β (and, in particular, $\alpha + \beta$) and the ratio $\mathcal{A}^T/A^T$ may be expected to change slowly, if at all, over time.

This last conclusion is based on the consideration that most of the variables affecting α, β, and $\mathcal{A}^T/A^T$ may themselves be expected to change, but slowly. This stability holds, for instance, for the lengths of the earning and retirement span, and their relation; the age distribution of population and of assets, the typical life pattern of income and consumption, and, possibly, the relevant characteristics of the frequency distribution of resources. Furthermore, movements in these variables as well as in the remaining relevant variable, the yield of assets, appear to have a rather minor influence on the value of these coefficients.[82] Taking into account the extent to which these variables are capable of changing and the effect of such changes, and remembering that the quantity $\phi^T\, \Pi^T$ is small enough to be neglected for the range of values to which Π^T is typically confined, we are led to the following conclusion: For purposes of empirical testing over a not-too-long stretch of time, the consumption function can be approximated by an equation of the form

$$(4.1) \qquad C^T = \alpha Y^T + \beta Y^{eT} + \delta A^T,$$

and the coefficients α, β, and δ can be treated as constant.[83]

We are now ready to test the fruitfulness of our hypothesis in explaining a number of well-known empirical findings and in providing guidance for further studies. In parts 2 and 3 we gave ample evidence of the model's ability to account for the long-run relative stability of the saving ratio and the asset-income ratio; we shall now concentrate on the short-run findings that have been reported for the years following the First World War.

4.2 Reinterpretation of the Duesenberry-Modigliani Function

Among the many consumption functions that have been suggested and tested in recent years, the one that has probably received the most extensive confirmation is the so-called Duesenberry-Modigliani (D-M) function, which has been tested in its original or variant forms for a number of Western countries.[84] This hypothesis in the Modigliani version states that saving is a linear function of current income, Y^T, with intercept determined by the previous peak of income, $\mathring{Y}^T$; that is,

$$(4.2) \qquad S^T = aY^T - b\mathring{Y}^T, \qquad a, b > 0.$$

According to (4.2), as long as income fluctuates below the previous peak ($Y^T < \mathring{Y}^T$), the saving function is represented by a fixed (linear) relationship between saving and income. Now, as we have hinted in section 2.2, this implication of the D-M function is very easy to reconcile with our model. As long as income remains significantly below its previous peak, saving and, therefore, the additions to assets will tend to be small and may even be negative; the year to year as well as the cumulative shift of the saving function will be slight.[85] In terms of figure 2, the saving function for periods $T + 2$ through $T + 4$ very nearly coincides with that of period $T + 1$. Furthermore, since cyclical fluctuations of income typically have large amplitudes, the wide swings may obscure the minor shifts of the function and the observed points will appear to lie on a straight line.

When income rises above its previous peak, the rate of saving recovers and the shift in the function is significant (for example, $S^{T+5}\, S^{T+5}$ in figure 2), a result that is again entirely consistent with the D-M function. Also, by and large, the shift will be larger the larger Y^{T-1} relative to Y^{T-2}, as is implied by the D-M hypothesis. In the limiting case in which income rises at a constant rate ρ so that $\mathring{Y}^T = Y^{T-1}$

$= Y^T/p$, the D-M function implies a constant saving ratio, $a - (b/p)$, as does our present model.

This analysis indicates that the D-M function may well be regarded as a close empirical approximation to our saving function (4.1), with the quantity $\mathring{Y}^T$ acting essentially as a convenient proxy for aggregate assets, or for $\mathcal{A}^T$ of equation (2.3).[86] Thus, the fact that the D-M function fits the data for several countries and periods quite well is fully consistent with our theory.

It should further be clear by now why variants of the D-M function, obtained by replacing highest previous income by the highest previous consumption, would also fit the data well.[87] More generally, our analysis helps to explain why the addition of slowly changing variables such as population, or even a linear time trend, to the simple correlation of saving and income has tended to improve the "explanation" of aggregate savings, especially for periods of time covering more than one cycle.[88] The fact that population grew more slowly during the thirties when income was depressed suggests this series as a good proxy for A^T and may explain the favorable results obtained with this variable.[89]

4.3 The Hamburger Test

The significance of the results just discussed is limited by the fact that they were based on definitions of income, consumption, and saving somewhat different from those underlying our model, and that the influence of assets was not tested explicitly. We now proceed to the only direct test of the influence of assets with which we are familiar. In a pioneering contribution, William Hamburger fitted a regression using estimates of consumption, income, and assets that are conceptually almost identical with our own, and produced (sometime before the genesis of this paper) a consumption function that compares favorably with the D-M function for the period 1929–1950 over which it was tested.[90]

In order to establish the relationship between Hamburger's test and our hypothesis, we first express (4.1) on a per capita basis and rewrite it as follows:

$$\frac{C^T}{\mathcal{N}^T} = (\alpha + \beta)\frac{1}{\mathcal{N}^T}\left(\frac{\alpha Y^T + \beta Y^{eT}}{\alpha + \beta}\right) + \delta\frac{A^T}{N^T}$$
$$= (\alpha + \beta)\frac{\hat{Y}^{eT}}{\hat{\mathcal{N}}^T} + \delta\frac{A^T}{\hat{\mathcal{N}}^T},$$

where $\hat{\mathcal{N}}^T$ denotes total population, and $\hat{Y}^{eT} = (\alpha Y^T + \beta Y^{eT})/(\alpha + \beta)$ may be regarded as the income per year expected over the relevant future with the current year included in "future." We can further express expected income per capita, $Y_{eT}/\hat{\mathcal{N}}_T$, as expected income per member of the labor force F^T multiplied by the proportion of the population in the labor force:

$$\frac{\hat{Y}^{eT}}{\hat{\mathcal{N}}^T} = \frac{\hat{Y}^{eT}}{F^T}\frac{F^T}{\hat{\mathcal{N}}^T}.$$

Substituting, we finally obtain

$$\text{(4.3)} \qquad \frac{C^T}{\hat{\mathcal{N}}^T} = \left[(\alpha + \beta) \frac{F^T}{\hat{\mathcal{N}}^T} \right] \frac{\hat{Y}^{eT}}{F^T} + \delta \frac{A^T}{\hat{\mathcal{N}}^T}.$$

The hypothesis actually tested by Hamburger, when translated into our notation, essentially reduces to

$$\text{(4.4)} \qquad \frac{C^T}{\hat{\mathcal{N}}^T} = a_0 + a_1 \frac{\hat{Y}^{eT}}{F^T} + a_2 \frac{A^T}{\hat{\mathcal{N}}^T}.$$

It follows that, provided $\hat{Y}^{eT}$ and A^T are measured with a reasonable degree of accuracy, the numerical coefficients of the Hamburger function should agree with the corresponding coefficients of equation (4.3). Let us now look at the range of values within which our model tells us these coefficients should fall.

Since (4.3) has no constant term, a_0 should not be significantly different from zero.

The second coefficient, a_1, corresponds to $(\alpha + \beta) F^T/\hat{\mathcal{N}}^T$, whose second factor is the ratio of the labor force to the total population. Over the period studied, this factor has remained quite constant, in the order of 0.4. The first factor, $\alpha + \beta$, has, according to our simplified model, a value of about 0.6. We have seen in part 3 that when we take into account the many factors originally neglected, this estimate is likely to be somewhat on the low side. Judging from several special cases for which numerical values have been computed, the value of $(\alpha + \beta)$ can be placed at around 0.7 and should not fall outside a band of 15% on either side of this figure. Thus, we arrive at an a priori estimate for a_1 of 0.24 to 0.30.

Proceeding to the last coefficient, a_2, what can we learn from our model about its value? This coefficient represents δ, the ratio of $\mathscr{A}^T/A^T$, which we have shown to be an average of the coefficients γ_t^t (or Γ_t, as we have called them in our most general formulation) weighted according to the age distribution of assets (see equation (3.16)). We have also shown in 3.2F that in a steady state process this age distribution is constant and, therefore, the value of δ is uniquely determined. Referring back to equation (3.15b) and solving for δ we find

$$\text{(4.5a)} \qquad \begin{aligned} \delta &= \frac{1 - \theta - \overline{\sigma}}{\overline{\sigma}} (\rho - 1) + r \\ &= \frac{(1 - \alpha - \beta) - \overline{\sigma}}{\overline{\sigma}} (\rho - 1) + r, \qquad \rho \neq 1, \end{aligned}$$

since $\theta = \alpha + \beta$.[91] We have already given the values of $\alpha + \beta$ and the steady-state saving ratio, $\overline{\sigma}$, for a number of special cases. Using the above formula, we can easily compute δ for these cases. In the following table we give values of δ obtained from the original simplified model with $r = 0$.

Table 3. Values of δ for $r = 0$

Cause of Growth	Rate of Growth (ρ)	δ
None	0% (stationary economy)	0.079
Population	3% per year	0.068
Productivity	3% per year	0.074
Productivity	4% per year	0.072

The most striking thing about this table is the stability of δ. But this stability is precisely what we should expect when we realize that, in every one of the four cases, δ is a weighted average of the same γ_t^t, namely $1/L_t$; the only thing that has changed is the weighting system, given by the age distribution of assets. For example, if population grows, there will be a preponderance of younger households and, therefore, a relatively larger proportion of total assets in their hands. This change increases the relative weights of the γ_t^t for small t; and because γ_t^t is a monotonically increasing function of t, there is a decline in δ, but it is slight.

Considering next a positive rate of interest, and remembering that the γ_t^t are increasing functions of r, we should expect δ to rise with r, but again to be affected to only a minor extent by variations in the weighting system resulting from different rates and causes of growth. The following table shows our results.

Table 4. Estimates of δ for Selected Values of r[92]

Yield of Assets (r)	Cause of Growth	Rate of Growth	δ
0.03	None	0	0.11
0.05	None	0	0.13
0.05	Population	0.03	0.12
0.05	Productivity	0.03	0.12
0.05	Productivity	0.04	0.12

These results wholly confirm our earlier conclusion that, as long as the γ_t^t are stable (which we have argued to be the case), the coefficient δ will be quite stable in spite of possible short-run changes in the age distribution of assets brought about by cyclical variations in income. Furthermore, reflecting on the preceding two tables and recalling that the estate motive should tend to reduce the γ_t^t somewhat below the values underlying these tables, we conclude that, according to our theory, the value of δ, and therefore a_2 in equation (4.4), can be placed at around 0.10 ± 0.03; values outside these limits would be hard to reconcile with our model.

We now look at Hamburger's results. In order to fit his consumption function, he had to tackle the problem of measuring consumption according to our definition and tackle the much more vexing problem of estimating expected income, $\hat{Y}^{eT}$, and aggregate assets, A^T. We shall say no more of his methods of estimation than is required for comparison with our model. In brief, he estimated consumption from the Department of Commerce's series of personal consumption expenditures by subtracting expenditures on durable goods and adding back an estimate of their depreciation. He handles $\hat{Y}^{eT}$ essentially by assuming that expected nonproperty income per member of the labor force, Y^{eT}/F^T, is equal to wage and salary income per employed person net of (estimated) personal taxes. This is tantamount to assuming that everybody in the labor force, whether employed or not, expects to be employed in the immediate future at the going annual wage. Finally, the problem of estimating A^T is treated by Hamburger through a combination of direct and indirect procedures. He estimates directly the value of the stock of consumers' durable goods (adjusted for depreciation) and the value of certain money-fixed assets (primarily government debt and monetary items). The remaining items of wealth he estimates indirectly by assuming that (a) their market value is proportional to the expected income from them, the proportionality factor representing the capitalization rate (assumed constant), and (b) the expected income can be measured in terms of the sum of current income from unincorporated enterprises, private interest, and dividends.

This brief description should be sufficient to indicate the remarkable degree of ingenuity and originality as well as some of the possible shortcomings of Hamburger's procedures. For example, in our view, his approach is likely to overestimate the cyclical *rigidity* of nonproperty income expectations and the cyclical *variability* of property income expectations and, therefore, of the value of aggregate assets. On the whole, while Hamburger should be given credit for doing as well as one could hope to do on the basis of the available data, the margin of error in his estimates must be regarded as substantial.

Nevertheless, Hamburger's empirical findings appear to agree remarkably well with our a priori estimates. The constant term a_0 is not significantly different from zero, being only about one half of its standard error. The coefficient a_1 is $0.191(\pm 0.0009)$; this figure is on the low side, but still within striking distance of our estimate. Finally, the coefficient of assets, the most interesting one for present purposes, is 0.096. No standard error is reported for this coefficient, which results from the combination of two others estimated by least sequares, but from his data one can surmise that the standard error can be put at less than 0.005. This coefficient falls squarely at the middle of our range.

4.4 Suggestions for Further Tests

While the test we have just described is of considerable interest, there is some real question as to whether, at present, the quality of the available information on aggregate personal net worth warrants any attempt at using equation (4.1) directly. We should, therefore, advance some suggestions as to how our hypothesis can be further tested and, if supported by such tests, utilized, in the absence of direct information on the variable A^T.

If we are willing to assume that the only source of variation in assets is net saving or dissaving, then this variable can be eliminated from the consumption function along the lines already developed in section 3.2F. Specifically, from (4.1) we derive

$$\Delta C^T = \alpha \Delta Y^T + \beta \Delta Y^{eT} + \delta \Delta A^T.$$

But, by assumption,

$$\Delta A^T = A^T - A^{T-1} = S^{T-1}. \tag{4.7}$$

Hence,

$$\Delta C^T = \alpha \Delta Y^T + \beta \Delta Y^{eT} + \delta S^{T-1}. \tag{4.8a}$$

If we again denote total income by $\tilde{Y}^T$, so that $S^T \equiv \tilde{Y}^T - C^T$, equation (4.8a) can also be written as

$$C^T = \alpha(Y^T - Y^{T-1}) + \beta(Y^{eT} - Y^{eT-1}) + (1 - \delta)C^{T-1} + \delta \tilde{Y}^{T-1}. \tag{4.8b}$$

The consumption function (4.8) may be convenient for certain purposes, notably for long-run theoretical analysis. In this case, one may reasonably take $Y^{eT} = Y^T$ and assume that nonproperty income is a stable proportion of total income[93] so that (4.8a, b) can be reduced to the linear difference equation

$$C^T = (\alpha^* + \beta^*)\tilde{Y}^T - (\alpha^* + \beta^* - \delta)\tilde{Y}^{T-1} + (1 - \delta)C^{T-1} \tag{4.9a}$$

or

$$S^T = (1 - \alpha^* - \beta^*)(\tilde{Y}^T - \tilde{Y}^{T-1}) + (1 - \delta)S^{T-1}. \tag{4.9b}$$

An interesting implication of equation (4.9a, b) is that, although we may still evaluate the short-run investment multiplier,

$$\frac{d\tilde{Y}^T}{dI^T} = 1 \bigg/ \frac{dS^T}{d\tilde{Y}^T} = \frac{1}{1 - \alpha^* - \beta^*},$$

there does not exist a corresponding finite long-run multiplier. One can verify that, to any given, indefinitely maintained level of investment, $\bar{I}$, there does not correspond (even asymptotically) a finite level of income but instead a constant arithmetic growth at the rate $\delta \bar{I}/(1 - \alpha^* - \beta^*)$.[94]

The equations (4.9a, b), however, may not be very satisfactory for short-run analysis and forecasting. In the first place, the value of assets may change for reasons other than current saving or dissaving, namely, as a result of changes in the current and anticipated yield on assets whose returns are not contractually fixed. Equation (4.7) is, therefore, not tenable, even as an approximation, in the short run and should be replaced by

$$\Delta A^T = S^{T-1} + G^T. \tag{4.7G}$$

The variable G^T denotes the change from the year $T - 1$ to the year T in the average value of those assets that were already in existence in the year $T - 1$. We shall refer to G^T as "capital gains" (or losses).[95] The only effect of this modification of (4.7) is that an additional term, δG^T, must be added to the right-hand side of the consumption function (4.8a, b).[96]

In the short run, there is also little justification, in a fluctuating economy, for assuming $Y^{eT} = Y^T$. In section 2.2 we suggested an approximation of the relationship between these two variables that we believe is reasonable. Our suggestion can be formalized by the following "expectation" equation:

$$Y^{eT} = w_1 Y^T + w_2 \mathring{Y}^T, \tag{4.10}$$

where $w_1 \leq w_1 + w_2 = 1 \leq 1 + w_1$. The variable $\mathring{Y}^T$ is defined as the highest level of income reached in any previous year up to and including the year T, unless current income exceeds the highest previous peak by more than the secular growth rate, $\rho - 1$, say 4%. In this case, $\mathring{Y}^T$ is ρ times the highest previous peak.

Taking into account equations (4.7G) and (4.10), our consumption function (4.8b) would become

$$\begin{aligned} C^T = {} & (\alpha + w_1\beta)(Y^T - Y^{T-1}) + \beta\, w_2(\mathring{Y}^T - \mathring{Y}^{T-1}) \\ & + (1 - \delta)C^{T-1} + \delta \bar{Y}^{T-1} + \delta G^T. \end{aligned} \tag{4.11}$$

The major difficulty in testing (4.11) is that of securing information on G^T. Nevertheless, we propose this particular form of our function in the belief that estimating G^T (or an index of it) will be easier than estimating A^T.[97]

We next suggest one transformation of our consumption function that could be tested even in the absence of information on G^T. First note that the current value of assets in the year T may be taken as the capitalized value of their average expected yearly return,

$$A^T = \chi R^{eT}, \tag{4.12}$$

where, in the year T, R^{eT} denotes the expected return and χ denotes the capitalization factor.[98] Unfortunately, R^{eT} is not observable, and to assume that it coincides with current property income, R^T, hardly seems warranted (compare with comment on Hamburger's procedure). The general experience is that the value of property fluctuates less than the income therefrom. We suggest instead that the quantity R^{eT} can be approximated reasonably well by

$$R^{eT} = u_1 R^T + u_2 R^{eT-1}, \qquad u_1, u_2 \geq 0, \qquad u_1 + u_2 = 1. \tag{4.13}$$

This hypothesis states that the currently expected average return is a weighted average of the current return, R^T, and of the previously expected average return, R^{eT-1}.[99] In view of the short-term variability in profits, we should expect u_2 to exceed u_1 considerably.

If we denote by A'^T the value in the year T of those assets that were in existence in the year $T - 1$, we can deduce from (4.12) and (4.13) that

$$A'^T = \chi R^{eT} = \chi\, [u_1\, R^T + u_2\, R^{eT-1}] = \chi\, u_1\, R^T + u_2\, A^{T-1}. \tag{4.14}$$

Our equation (4.7) now becomes

$$A^T = \chi u_1\, R^T + u_2\, A^{T-1} + \omega S^{T-1}. \tag{4.7R}$$

(The variable S^{T-1} appears with a coefficient $\omega \leq 1$, rather than unity, to adjust for the impossibility of eliminating from R^T income originating from assets acquired through S^{T-1}.)[100] With assumption (4.7R) and (4.10), and remembering that our basic equation (4.1) implies

$$\delta A^{T-1} = C^{T-1} - \alpha Y^{T-1} - \beta Y^{eT-1},$$

we obtain the following approximation to the consumption function:

$$\begin{aligned} C^T = {} & (\alpha + \beta w_1)\, Y^T - u_2\, (\alpha + \beta w_1)\, Y^{T-1} + \beta\, w_2\, \mathring{Y}^T \\ & - u_2\, \beta w_2\, \mathring{Y}^{T-1} + (u_2 - \delta\omega) C^{T-1} + \delta\, \chi\, u_1\, R^T + \delta\omega\, \tilde{Y}^{T-1}. \end{aligned} \tag{4.15}$$

This equation contains only variables which information is presently available or which can be approximated without serious difficulties from existing data. The large number of variables might present a statistical problem, but by appropriate approximations this number can be easily reduced. For instance, if one were willing to (a) drop the last term on the reasonable assumption that the coefficient $\delta\omega$ is quite small (in the order of 0.05) and on the grounds that $\tilde{Y}^{T-1}$ is highly correlated with Y^{T-1}; and (b) drop the variables $\mathring{Y}^T$ and $\mathring{Y}^{T-1}$ on the (less reasonable) assumption that w_2 is small and/or these variables are highly correlated with the corresponding Ys, then

$$C^T = \alpha_1\, Y^T + \delta \chi u_1\, R^T + (u_2 - \delta\omega)\, C^{T-1} - u_2 \alpha_1\, Y^{T-1}. \tag{4.15a}$$

The coefficient of Y^T should be approximately equal to $\alpha + \beta$, the coefficient of Y^{T-1} somewhat smaller, and the coefficient of C^{T-1} larger than 0.5 but certainly less than unity. As for the coefficient of property income, our theory is of limited help because it only tells us that δ should be about 0.1. With a capitalization rate of between 10 and 20, this coefficient could be anywhere between u_1 and $2u_1$. Since we speculate that u_1 is considerably less than 0.5, $\delta\chi u_1$, the "marginal propensity to consume" with respect to current property income R^T, may well be less than with respect to current nonproperty income, Y^T. But this lower value would arise *not* because property owners are richer and, therefore, save more, but because of the low value of u_1. Since property income is more volatile than nonproperty income, its current level is a less reliable indicator of longer-run prospects upon which consumption mostly depends; it may thus receive a smaller weight than current nonproperty income in current consumption decisions.[101]

In a recent paper, T. M. Brown has reported considerable success for Canada with a function that differs from (4.15a) only because of the emission of the last variable and because C^T is the conventional "consumers' expenditure" rather than the "consumption" of our model.[102] When an adjustment is made for the omitted variable, his coefficients agree quite well with our a priori estimates.[103] We hope that in the course of further work in this area, there will be an opportunity to test the influence of the variables neglected by Brown.[104]

One more method of handling the thorny problem of income expectations, which would eliminate the present asymmetry between property and nonproperty income expectations, and one that may be worth testing is, following Hamburger, to define a variable,

$$\hat{Y}^T = \frac{\alpha Y^T + \beta Y^{eT}}{\alpha + \beta},$$

representing expectations for the entire future including the current year. We suggest that the variable $\hat{Y}^T$ may be approximated by an equation analogous to (4.12), namely,

$$\hat{Y}^T = w_1 Y^T + w_2 \hat{Y}^{T-1}. \qquad (4.16)$$

The important advantage of (4.16) is that the nonobservable variable $\hat{Y}$ can be inferred from the data by the general method used in this section to infer the value of A^T and A^{T-1}. By applying the differencing process twice in succession, one obtains an equation relating C^T to the variables Y, C, R, and $\tilde{Y}$, current and/or lagged and/or double lagged.

In conclusion, we have shown in this section that (a) even in the absence of reliable information on assets, there are a variety of approximations that can be obtained from our theory, all of which should fit the data tolerably well; and that (b) those approximations that have been tested do, in fact, give satisfactory results and yield coefficients within range of those inferred a priori from our model. Only further empirical investigations can determine which of the various approximations to our model is the most useful. It is our hope that the framework developed in this paper will provide a practical tool for such research and will contribute to the construction of a much needed bridge between economic theory and the empirical study of micro- and macroeconomic saving behavior.

APPENDIX 1 Proof of Formula (2.8)

This formula can be established by first exhibiting the saving of each age group in the year T, and then summing up over all age groups.

Let us recall that our "productivity" growing economy with stationary population is characterized by the following relations in addition to Assumption V:

$$Y^T = Ny^T = \rho^j Y^{T-j}; \tag{A.1}$$

$$y^{eT} = \frac{Y^{eT}}{N} = y^T. \tag{A.2}$$

In order to determine the saving of each age group in a given year, we will first compute the saving at various ages of one specific generation, say the generation of the year T', by following it through its life cycle. At age 1 we have, by Assumption I, $a_1^T = 0$, and from equation (2.2), making use of (A.2), we find

$$S_1^T = \frac{My^{T'} - a_1^{T'}}{L_1} = \frac{M}{L} y^{T'}.$$

Initial assets at age 2 will then be given by

$$a_2^{T'+1} = a_1^{T'} + S_1^{T'} = \frac{M}{L} y^{T'} = \frac{M}{L} \rho^{-1} y^{T'+1} = \frac{M}{L} [1 - (\rho - 1)\rho^{-1}] y^{T'+1}.$$

Hence, again using (2.2) and (A.2),

$$s_2^{T'+1} = \frac{My^{T+1} - a_2^{T'+1}}{L_2} = \frac{M}{L} \left(\frac{L - 1 + (\rho - 1)\rho^{-1}}{L_2} \right) y^{T'+1}$$

$$= \frac{M}{L} \left(1 + (\rho - 1) \frac{\rho^{-1}}{L_2} \right) y^{T'+1}.$$

Similarly

$$a_3^{T'+2} = a_2^{T'+1} + s_2^{T'+1} = \frac{M}{L} \left[2 - (\rho - 1)\rho^{-1} \frac{L_2 - 1}{L_2} \right] \rho^{-1} y^{T'+2}$$

$$= \frac{M}{L} \left[2 - (\rho - 1) L_3 \left(\frac{2}{L_3} \rho^{-1} + \frac{1}{L_2} \rho^{-2} \right) \right] y^{T'+2}$$

$$= \frac{M}{L} \left[2 - (\rho - 1) L_3 \sum_{j=2}^{3} \frac{j - 1}{L_j} \rho^{-(4-j)} \right] y^{T'+2},$$

and

$$s_3^{T'+2} = \frac{M}{L} \frac{L - 2 + (\rho - 1) L_3 \sum_{j=2}^{3} \frac{j - 1}{L_j} \rho^{-(4-j)}}{L_3} y^{T'+2}$$

$$= \frac{M}{L} \left[1 + (\rho - 1) \sum_{j=2}^{3} \frac{j - 1}{L_j} \rho^{-(4-j)} \right] y^{T'+2}.$$

Proceeding thus, one can establish the following formula:

$$(\text{A.3})\quad s_t^{T'+t-1} = k_t y^{T'+t-1} = \begin{cases} \dfrac{M}{L}\left[1 + (\rho - 1)\displaystyle\sum_{j=2}^{t} \dfrac{j-1}{L_j}\, \rho^{-(t+1-j)}\right] y^{T'+t-1}, & t = 1, 2, \cdots, N; \\[2ex] -\dfrac{M}{L}\rho^{-(t-N-1)}\left[\dfrac{N}{M} - (\rho - 1)\displaystyle\sum_{j=2}^{N+1} \dfrac{j-1}{L_j}\, \rho^{-(N+2-j)}\right] y^{T'+t-1}, & t = N+1, \cdots, L; \end{cases}$$

which gives the saving at age t of the generation of the year T' in terms of average income prevailing in the year in which it reaches age t, namely the year $T' + t - 1$. Since the choice of T' is arbitrary, we can find the saving of every age group in the same year T by setting $T' = T - (t - 1)$ in (A.3). We thus obtain

$$s_t^T = k_t\, y^T,$$

where k_t represents the coefficient of $y^{T'+t-1}$ in the right-hand side expression of (A.3).

Remembering that with a stationary population we can conveniently assume a single household in each age group, our expression for aggregate saving is

$$S^T = \sum_{t=1}^{L} k_t y^T = \frac{Y^T}{N}\sum_{t=1}^{L} k_t = \frac{Y^T M}{NL}\left\{\sum_{t=1}^{N} 1 + (\rho - 1)\sum_{t=1}^{N}\sum_{j=2}^{t} \frac{j-1}{L_j}\, \rho^{-(t+1-j)} - \frac{N}{M}\sum_{t=N+1}^{L} \rho^{-(t-N-1)} + (\rho - 1)\sum_{t=N+1}^{L}\sum_{j=2}^{N+1} \frac{j-1}{L_j}\, \rho^{-(t+1-j)}\right\}.$$

We next observe $\Sigma_{t=1}^{N}\, 1 = N$; also

$$\sum_{t=N+1}^{L} \rho^{-(t-N-1)} = \frac{\rho(1 - \rho^{-M})}{\rho - 1};$$

and the sum of the two double summations can be rearranged as follows:

$$(\rho - 1)\left[\sum_{t=1}^{N}\sum_{j=2}^{t} \frac{j-1}{L_j}\, \rho^{-(t+1-j)} + \sum_{t=N+1}^{L}\sum_{j=2}^{N+1} \frac{j-1}{L_j}\, \rho^{-(t+1-j)}\right]$$

$$= (\rho - 1)\sum_{j=2}^{N+1} \frac{j-1}{L_j}\sum_{t=j}^{L} \rho^{-(t+1-j)}$$

$$= \sum_{j=2}^{N+1} \frac{j-1}{L_j}\left[1 - \rho^{-(L+1-j)}\right].$$

Hence

$$S^T = \frac{M}{L}\left\{1 - \frac{\rho(1 - \rho^{-M})}{M(\rho - 1)} + \frac{1}{N}\sum_{j=2}^{N+1}\frac{j-1}{L_j}\left[1 - \rho^{-(L+1-j)}\right]\right\}Y^T.$$

The last term of the summation in the right-hand side is $(1 - \rho\overline{M})/M$, which can be combined with the second term within the braces. We therefore finally obtain

$$S^T = \frac{M}{L}\left\{1 - \frac{1 - \rho^{-M}}{M(\rho - 1)} + \frac{1}{N}\sum_{j=2}^{N}\frac{j-1}{L_j}\left[1 - \rho^{-(L+1-j)}\right]\right\}Y^T,$$

from which equation (2.8) follows directly with a transformation of the running index, and corresponding change of limits, in the summation.

APPENDIX 2 Evaluation of k_1 (M, N, ρ)

We are interested in estimating the value of the expression

$$Z = \sum_{t=1}^{N-1}\frac{t}{L-t}\left[1 - \rho^{-(L-t)}\right]$$

without actually carrying out the indicated summation, which would be a cumbersome task, especially for large values of N. We first note that Z can be rewritten as follows

$$\begin{aligned} Z &= \sum_{t=1}^{N-1}\frac{t}{L-t} - \sum_{t=1}^{N-1}\left(\frac{L}{L-t} - 1\right)\rho^{-(L-t)} \\ &= \sum_{t=1}^{N-1}\frac{t}{L-t} - L\rho^{-L}\sum_{t=1}^{N-1}\frac{\rho^t}{L-t} + \frac{\rho^{N-1} - 1}{\rho^{L-1}(\rho - 1)}. \end{aligned} \tag{A.4}$$

In order to evaluate the two summations that still appear in the right-hand side of (A.4) we have made use of the so-called Euler-Maclaurin sum formula which permits one to approximate a summation in terms of integrals. The formula is

$$\begin{aligned} \sum_{k=1}^{m-1} f(k) &= \int_0^m f(x)dx - \frac{1}{2}\left[f(0) + f(m)\right] \\ &\quad + \sum_{s=1}^{n-1}\frac{B_{2s}}{(2s)!}\left[f^{(2s-1)}(m) - f^{(2s-1)}(0)\right] + f^{(2n)}(\theta m)\frac{mB_{2n}}{(2n)!}, \end{aligned}$$

where $f^{s}(a)$ denotes the sth derivative of $f(x)$ evaluated at $x = a$, B_{2s} denotes the Bernouili numbers ($B_2 = 1/6$, $B_4 = -1/30$, $B_6 = 1/42$, $\cdots$), and the last term is the remainder after $n - 1$ terms.[105]

Applying this formula to our first summation, and taking $n = 2$ (since the remainder appears to be already sufficiently small for this value of n), we obtain

$$\sum_{t=1}^{N-1} \frac{t}{L-t} \approx \int_0^N \frac{x}{L-x} dx - \frac{N}{2M} + \frac{1}{12}\left(\frac{L}{M^2} - \frac{1}{L}\right)$$

$$= L \ln \frac{L}{M} - \frac{N(2M+1)}{2M} + \frac{N(L+M)}{12\, M^2 L}.$$

For our second summation, again taking $n = 2$, we find

$$\sum_{t=1}^{N-1} \frac{\rho^t}{L-t} \approx \int_0^N \frac{\rho^x}{L-x} - \frac{1}{2}\left(\frac{1}{L} + \frac{\rho^N}{M}\right) + \frac{1}{12}\left(\frac{\rho^N(M \ln \rho + 1)}{M^2} - \frac{L \ln \rho + 1}{L^2}\right).$$

Unfortunately, the function $\rho_x/L - x$ does not have a general integral. However, by means of the transformation of variable $y = (L - x) \ln \rho$, $dy = -\ln \rho\, dx$, the integral $\int_0^N (\rho^x/L - x)dx$ is transformed into

$$\rho^L \int_{M \ln \rho}^{L \ln \rho} (e^{-y}/y)dy = \rho^L\left[\int_{M \ln \rho}^{\infty} (e^{-y}/y)dy - \int_{L \ln \rho}^{\infty} (e^{-y}/y)dy\right].$$

Values of the definite integral $\int_x^\infty (e^{-y}/y)dy$ have been tabulated for $0 \leq x \leq 10$.[106] For any values of L and ρ that are reasonable for the problem on hand, $L \ln \rho$ falls within this range.

In conclusion, therefore, the original summation can be reduced to

$$Z \approx L \ln \frac{L}{M} - \frac{N(2M+1)}{2M} + \frac{N(L+M)}{12M^2L}$$

$$- L\left(\int_{M \ln \rho}^{\infty} (e^{-y}/y)dy - \int_{L \ln \rho}^{\infty} (e^{-y}/y)dy\right)$$

$$+ \frac{1}{2\rho^L} + \frac{L}{2M\rho^M} - \frac{L}{12\rho^L}\left(\frac{\rho^N(M \ln \rho + 1)}{M^2} - \frac{L \ln \rho + 1}{L^2}\right) \tag{A.5}$$

$$+ \frac{\rho^N - 1}{\rho^{L-1}(\rho - 1)},$$

and the value of the two definite integrals can be found from the above mentioned tables.

Notes

1. John Maynard Keynes, *The General Theory of Employment, Interest, and Money,* Book III (Harcourt, Brace, 1936).

2. For example, John R. Hicks, *Value and Capital* An Inquiry into some Fundamental Principles of Economic Theory (Clarendon Press, 1946).

3. G. H. Orcutt and A. D. Roy, ''A Bibliography of the Consumption Function,'' mimeographed release (University of Cambridge: Department of Applied Economics, 1949).

4. *Bibliography on Income and Wealth, 1937–1947,* Daniel Creamer, ed. (International Association for Research in Income and Wealth, 1952).

5. Keynes, *General Theory,* p. 97.

6. For example, see Mordecai Ezekiel, ''Statistical Investigations of Savings, Consumption, and Investment, I,'' *American Economic Review,* March 1942; R. B. Bans, ''The Changing Relation of Consumer Income and Expenditure,'' *Survey of Current Business,* April 1942.

7. For example, see the series by Arthur Smithies, Morris S. Livingston, and J. L. Mosak, ''Forecasting Postwar Demand,'' *Econometrica,* January 1945.

8. Probably the opening gun in this campaign was the paper by W. S. Woytinsky, ''Relationship Between Consumers' Expenditures, Savings, and Disposable Income,'' *Review of Economic Statistics,* February 1946, pp. 1–12.

9. Simon Kuznets, *Uses of National Income in Peace and War,* NBER Occasional Paper 6, March 1942.

10. See Arthur Smithies, ''Forecasting Postwar Demand''; and Paul A. Samuelson, ''Full Employment After the War,'' *Postwar Economic Problems,* Seymour Harris, ed., p. 33.

11. For example, see Lawrence R. Klein, ''Savings Concepts and Their Relation to Economic Policy: The Viewpoint of a User of Savings Statistics,'' paper delivered at the Conference on Savings, Inflation and Economic Progress, University of Minnesota, 1952; and George Katona, *Psychological Analysis of Economic Behavior,* Part II (McGraw-Hill, 1963).

12. James S. Duesenberry, *Income, Saving and the Theory of Consumer Behavior* (Oxford University Press, 1947).

13. James Tobin, ''A Theoretical and Statistical Analysis of Consumer Saving,'' unpublished Ph.D. dissertation (Harvard University, 1947).

14. William Hamburger, ''Consumption and Wealth,'' unpublished Ph.D. dissertation (The University of Chicago, 1951).

15. Margaret G. Reid, ''The Relation of the Within-Group Permanent Component of Income to the Income Elasticity of Expenditures,'' preliminary draft. Some of the basic ideas underlying this paper are already found in her ''Effect of Income Concept upon Expenditure Curves of Farm Families,'' *Conference on Research in Income and Wealth,* XV, 1950, pp. 131–174. (Joint sponsorship of National Bureau of Economic Research and U. of Illinois.)

16. Tibor de Scitovszky, ''Capital Accumulation, Employment and Price Rigidity,'' *Review of Economic Studies,* VIII (February 1941): 69–88.

17. Duesenberry, *Income, Saving and the Theory of Consumer Behavior.*

18. Franco Modigliani, ''Fluctuations in the Saving-Income Ratio: A Problem in Economic Forecasting,'' part V, *Studies in Income and Wealth,* XI, Conference on Research in Income and Wealth (National Bureau of Economic Research: New York, 1949): 369–441.

19. T. M. Brown, ''Habit Persistence and Lags in Consumer Behavior,'' *Econometrica,* July 1952; and Tom E. Davis, ''The Consumption Function as a Tool for Prediction,'' *Review of Economics and Statistics,* August 1952.

20. Lawrence R. Klein, ''The Use of Econometric Models as a Guide to Economic Policy,'' *Econometrica,* April 1947.

21. Brown, ''Habit Persistence.''

22. Hamburger, ''Consumption and Wealth.''

23. Lawrence R. Klein, *Economic Fluctuations in the United States, 1921–1941* (John Wiley & Sons, Inc., 1950).

24. V. L. Bassie, ''Consumers' Expenditures in War and Transition,'' *The Review of Economic Statistics,* February 1939, pp. 1–12.

25. Irwin Friend, "Five Views on the Consumption Function," *The Review of Economic Statistics*, November 1946, pp. 208–215.

26. J. J. Polak, "Fluctuations in United States Consumption, 1919–1932," *The Review of Economic Statistics*, February 1939, pp. 1–12.

27. For another recent attempt in this direction that bears some similarity to our own, see Simon Kuznets, "Proportion of Capital Formation to National Product," *American Economic Review*, May 1952, pp. 507–526. An earlier but still valuable contribution is that of Gustav Cassel, *The Theory of Social Economy* (Harcourt, 1932), especially pp. 232–246.

28. Franco Modigliani and Richard Brumberg, "Utility Analysis and the Consumption Function: An Interpretation of Cross-Section Findings," *The Post Keynesian System: Essays in Honor of John Maynard Keynes*, Kenneth Kurihara, ed. (Rutgers University Press, 1954), pp. 388–436.

29. An extensive application of marginal utility analysis to the theory of saving is found in a series of valuable contributions of Umberto Ricci, dating almost thirty years back. See his "L'Offerta del Risparmio," Part I, *Giornale Degli Economisti*, February 1926, pp. 73–101; Part II, *ibid*, March 1926, pp. 117–147; and "Ancora Sull'Offerta del Rispanmio," *ibid*, September 1927, pp. 481–504.

30. See, for instance, Jacob L. Mosak, *General-Equilibrium Theory in International Trade*, Chapter VI (The Principia Press, Inc., 1944), especially pp. 116–117.

31. Compare Keynes, *General Theory*, p. 107.

32. For a more extensive formulation of these assumptions and their common sense, see Modigliani and Brumberg, "Utility Analysis and the Consumption Function." The reader who is interested in seeing how far one can go without introducing any specific assumption will find some valuable material in the contributions of Umberto Ricci cited earlier in note 29.

33. The assumption, as stated, is somewhat more stringent than necessary. All we really need for our purpose is equation (1.4) below, and Assumption II is a sufficient but not necessary condition for equation (1.4) to hold. Even the homogeneity condition could be stated in the following less restrictive form: The utility index is some monotonic increasing function of a function U homogeneous in $c_t, \cdots, c_L$. Furthermore, as will become apparent, we do not require that equation (1.4) be satisfied for each individual of age t, but only for the aggregate of all such individuals. Finally, even this assumption will be relaxed somewhat at a later point (see section 3.2).

34. For $t > N$, y_t and y_t^e are zero and only the last term remains in the numerator.

35. It will be noted that in developing our model of individual behavior, we have completely neglected the phenomenon of uncertainty. The reasons that justify this omission have been set out in the companion paper (Modigliani and Brumberg, "Utility Analysis and the Consumption Function") to which the reader is referred for a full discussion. Briefly, our argument is that the presence of uncertainty adds two motives for saving, the precautionary motive and the desire to enjoy the services of certain durable goods that can be secured more cheaply by holding at least a partial equity in them. But even under the certainty model, the household will tend to accumulate assets rapidly from the very beginning (see equation (2.7c). Also, since many such assets can be used to satisfy all the four motives simultaneously, the presence of uncertainty is unlikely to generate a saving behavior significantly different from that arising in a world of certainty.

36. The most complete aggregate data, those recently published by R. W. Goldsmith, cover reproducible tangible wealth rather than private net worth. See "The Growth of Reproducible Wealth of the United States of America from 1805 to 1950," *Income and Wealth, Series II*, Simon Kuznets, ed. (Bowes and Bowes, 1952).

37. This constancy does not imply, however, that the saving-income ratio is the same for every household, unless the households fulfill similarly defined "stationary" conditions. If individual incomes are subject to short-term fluctuations, a possibility not at all excluded by our definition of an income-stationary economy, then the saving ratio for individual households will tend to rise with income. The slope of the cross-section saving-income relationship would then give an upward biased estimate of the variation of aggregate saving with aggregate income. It can be shown that this bias is greater the greater the short-term variability of individual income. See Modigliani and Brumberg, "Utility Analysis and the Consumption Function."

38. From formula (2.6), it is easily verified that $A^T = \sum_{t=1}^{L} a_t^T = \frac{M}{2} Y^T$ in the stationary state. Thus the relation found in our table would hold also if each period consisted of one year and M were in the order of 10 (and L in the order of 50), as we shall be assuming hereafter for purposes of illustration.

39. This statement does not hold, of course, for the group just entering.

40. See Appendix 2. We wish to acknowledge the valuable help we have received from Dr. Albert Heins of the Department of Mathematics, Carnegie Institute of Technology, in developing the method discussed in this appendix. Many of the numerical applications of those as well as other formulas quoted in the text were carried out by William Holter.

41. Suppose that both population and productivity are increasing at the rates $(\mu - 1)$ and $(\rho - 1)$ per year, respectively; then income will grow at the rate $(\mu\rho - 1)$ per year and the saving ratio will be given by an expression of the form $S^T/Y^T = (M/L)k(M, N, \mu, \rho)$. From the relationship between $k(M, N, x)$ and $k_2(M, N, x)$ reported earlier, one can derive the following more general one:

$$(2.10') \qquad k(M, N, \mu, \rho) \approx k(M, N, \mu\rho, 1) \approx k(M, N, 1, \mu\rho),$$

for μ and ρ in the relevant range (say $1 \leq \mu \leq \mu\rho \leq 1.05$), which justifies the "and/or" statement in the text. To prove the approximation (2.10′) we may proceed as follows. From a Taylor expansion of $k(M, N, \mu, \rho)$ around the point $\mu = 1, \rho = 1$, after dropping terms of degree higher than one (since we are interested in the value of μ, ρ very close to unity), we obtain

$$(2.10'') \qquad k(M, N, \mu, \rho) = (\mu - 1)k_\mu(M, N, 1, 1) + (\rho - 1)k_\rho(M, N, 1, 1).$$

Here $k_\mu = \dfrac{\partial k}{\partial \mu}$, $k_\rho = \dfrac{\partial k}{\partial \rho}$, and the term $k(M, N, 1, 1)$ drops out since its value is proportional to the saving ratio in a stationary economy, which is zero. We have already shown in the text, by actual computations, that $k(M, N, \chi, 1) \approx k(M, N, 1, \chi)$; because of (2.10″), this implies $(\chi - 1)\, k_\mu(M, N, 1, 1) = (\chi - 1)k_\rho(M, N, 1, 1)$, or, $k_\mu = k_\rho$. Substituting into (2.10″), and observing that $\mu\rho - 1 = (\mu - 1) + (\rho - 1) + (\mu - 1)(\rho - 1) \approx (\mu - 1) + (\rho - 1)$ for the relevant range of μ and ρ, we get $k(M, N, \mu, \rho) \approx [(\mu - 1) + (\rho - 1)]\, k_\mu(M, N, 1, 1) \approx (\mu\rho - 1)\, k(M, N, 1, 1) = k(M, N, \mu\rho, 1) = k(M, N, 1, \mu\rho)$.

42. See table 34, column 6, in Simon Kuznets, "Long Term Changes in the National Income of the United States of America Since 1870," *Income and Wealth, Series II*, Simon Kuznets, ed. (Bowes and Bowes, 1952): 155.

43. For instance, the estimates taken from Kuznets do not include in saving the national addition to equities in consumers' durable goods, but they do include some capital formation by government that need not represent an addition to the private sector's net worth. On the whole, Kuznets's method yields a higher estimate of the saving ratio than can be deduced from the Department of Commerce's data.

44. See R. W. Goldsmith, "Trends and Structural Changes in Saving in the 20th Century," *Conference on Saving, Inflation, and Economic Progress*, W. Heller, F. Boddy, and C. Nelson, eds. (University of Minnesota Press, 1953).

45. By comparing Goldsmith's estimates of reproducible tangible wealth (R.T.W.) in (*Income and Wealth, Series II*, table 1A, p. 306) for the years given from 1880 to 1948, with Kuznets' decadal averages (*ibid.*, table 1, p. 30) for the early years, and the Department of Commerce estimates for more recent years, it is found that the ratio of R.T.W. to net national product has fluctuated between 3 and 4 with no clear trend. Of course, R.T.W. differs from our private net worth by the exclusion of privately held natural resources and public debt, and by the inclusion of publicly owned R.T.W. With these adjustments, the ratio presumably would be somewhat higher, especially for 1948 when the ratio of R.T.W. to net national product appears abnormally low.

46. The task of computing $\alpha(L, N, 1)$ from its definition would be rather forbidding for large values of N and L. We have, therefore, made use of the following approximation, which appears to give very close results, especially for large values of N and L:

$$\alpha(L, N, 1) \approx \int_{-1/2}^{N-1/2} \frac{dZ}{L+1-Z} = \frac{1}{N} \ln \frac{2L + 1}{2M + 1},$$

where ln denotes the natural logarithm. From this approximation, we find $\alpha(50, 40, 1) \approx 0.39$.

Similarly, $\alpha(L, N, 1) + \beta(L, N, 1)$ can be approximated with the formula

$$\frac{M}{N} \ln \frac{M}{L} + \frac{N + 1}{N} - \frac{N + 1}{2N(L + 1)},$$

based on the Euler-MacLaurin sum formula (see Appendix 2).

Hence $\alpha(50, 40, 1) + \beta(50, 40, 1) \approx 0.607$ and therefore $\beta(50, 40, 1) \approx 0.568$. The value of $\alpha(50, 40, \mu)$ and $\beta(50, 40, \mu)$ was approximated by the method used to evaluate k_1 (L, N, ρ) (see Appendix 2). In particular, for $\mu = 1.03$ we find $\alpha(1.03) \approx 0.64$.

47. We speak advisedly of "short-run" and of "impact" effects (that is, the effect within the year itself), for as we shall see later a permanent change in the level of investment in the year T need not maintain income at the level reached in the year T itself.

48. The increase in saving would be larger the older the household. For further detail see Modigliani and Brumberg, "Utility Analysis and the Consumption Function."

49. The process of adjustment would occupy $L - 1$ years (the time it takes for every individual who ever earned income at the original rate Y to disappear), although it can be shown that most of the adjustment would occur in the early years.

50. The figure 9.1 is obtained by observing that for $Y = 103$, $S^{T+1}(Y) = S^{(T+1)}(103) = 10.3$. The slope of the S^{T+1} function is 0.4 so that $S(100) = 10.3 - (.4 \times 3) = 9.1$.

51. See Brown, "Habit Persistence," p. 370.

52. For further elaboration of the relationship between income change and lagged adjustments from the microeconomic point of view, see Modigliani and Brumberg, "Utility Analysis and the Consumption Function," section II.3, pp. 406–418.

53. Hans Neisser has written of some flaws in the stagnation theory's preoccupation with high savings. He reasoned that the change in the age composition resulting from the cessation of population growth would, of itself, diminish saving. This paper is in complete agreement with Neisser's conclusion and we generalize that saving will fall if the rate of increase in income declines because of either population or productivity "stagnation." See Hans Neisser, "The Economics of a Stationary Population," *Social Research,* 11 (November 1944) 470–90. Needless to say, an adequate treatment of the stagnation thesis requires an analysis not only of the supply of saving but also of investment demand, a subject beyond the scope of this paper.

54. This view has been forcefully expressed by Bertil Ohlin, "Some Notes on the Stockholm Theory of Savings and Investment," *Readings in Business Cycle Theory* (Richard D. Irwin, Inc., 1951) 87–100.

55. A tone of confidence and optimism would tend to flatten the upper right portion of the function and steepen the lower left portion.

56. It is only an approximation because zero saving implies $A^{T+2} = A^{T+1}$, and not necessarily $\mathcal{A}^{T+2} = \mathcal{A}^{T+1}$. Whether or not the latter equality holds exactly can be shown to depend on the coefficient of expectations. On this point, see the discussion of the relationship between A^T and $\mathcal{A}^T$ in section 3.2F.

57. A. C. Pigou, "The Classical Stationary State," *Economic Journal,* 53 (December 1943): 343–51; A. C. Pigou "Economic Progress in a Stable Environment," *Economica,* n.s., 14 August 1947): pp. 180–90, and reprinted in *Readings in Monetary Theory,* 1951, pp. 241–51; Don Patinkin, "Price Flexibility and Full Employment," *American Economic Review,* 38, September 1948: 543–64, and reprinted in *Readings in Monetary Theory,* 1951, pp. 252–83.

58. Keynes, *General Theory,* especially chapter 19. For a brief treatment of the logical structure of the argument, see also F. Modigliani, "Liquidity Preference and the Theory of Interest and Money," *Econometrica,* 12 (January 1944) 1: 45–88, reprinted in *Readings in Monetary Theory,* 1951, pp. 186–239, especially section 16.

59. Scitovszky, "Capital Accumulation, Employment and Price Rigidity."

60. These conclusions are based on a strictly "partial equilibrium" analysis, abstracted from the question of whether there would be enough offset to saving to maintain the income at the postulated level. This is, of course, perfectly legitimate as long as we are interested only in studying the characteristics of the consumption function, one of the many equations that simultaneously determine the level of income.

61. See our discussion of equation (2.5a) in section 2.2.

62. Hamburger, "Consumption and Wealth," has made some estimates of the net value of money-fixed assets and total assets. According to his estimates, whose margin of error is probably large, the ratio of the former the latter quantity has risen gradually from 8% in 1929 to about 25% in 1950.

63. A factor that may become significant on occasions is short-term price expectations. In our analysis we have been concerned only with the effect of price changes that are considered permanent. Clearly, a fall in prices, which is considered strictly transitory, will have a very negligible effect on the value of assets, but it may nonetheless produce some reshuffling of the consumption plan by encour-

aging some anticipatory purchases to be made up by a corresponding reduction once prices have gone back to "normal." Such anticipations and postponements should be important primarily for durable goods, the purchase of which we do not include in consumption; as far as they affect nondurables, they are likely to be largely offset by countermovements of stocks in the hands of consumers. However, to the extent that we must rely on consumers' purchases as a measure of consumption, short-term price expectations might, on occasion, disturb saving behavior; however, once more we should not expect these disturbances to reach major proportions for aggregate consumption, except possibly for intervals considerably shorter than one year.

64. Our results under conclusion (d) imply, of course, that an increase in prices at a constant rate would tend to raise the proportion of income saved. However, in applying this result to any real situation one should carefully note the assumption of unit elasticity of price expectations. It does not necessarily follow, for instance, that if the government guaranteed a steady rise in prices of $(\pi - 1)\%$ per year, saving would necessarily go up. A price increase of $(\pi - 1)\%$ per year fully and firmly anticipated by everybody is equivalent to a negative rate of interest on money of $(\pi - 1)\%$ per year, with the further proviso that this negative interest could be avoided, at least partly, by shifting money-fixed holdings from cash into bonds whose yield should tend to increase somewhat if not by the entire amount $(\pi - 1)$. In the next section we will show that the level of the interest rate is not likely to affect the rate of saving significantly if interest income is included in income. Unfortunately, interest income arising from a steady price decline is not included in income; the additional consumption generated by it would therefore reduce saving. By the same token, to the extent that a guaranteed steady rise of prices creates a negative interest (because the rate on bonds, not of price changes, was still negative, or because people chose partly not to assume the additional risk associated with shifting from cash into bonds, this rise in prices would tend to cause some increase in saving. It can be shown, however, that the resulting increase in saving should be smaller than the increase generated by the same rate of change of prices if the change were always unanticipated (this last case is discussed in connection with equation (3.7)).

65. The real value of a variable in terms of prices of any year, $T - j$, can be obtained by dividing the real value in terms of $T - 1$ by P^{T-1}/P^{T-j}.

66. The effect of removing this assumption has been partly indicated in previous notes.

67. More generally, if C^T and Y^T, denote real consumption and income in terms of prices of any given year, $T - j$, then equation (2.3π) can be written as

$$C^T = \alpha Y^T + \beta Y^{eT} + (1 + \phi^T \Pi^T) \mathcal{A}^T / P^{T-1} / P^{T-j},$$

where $\mathcal{A}^T$, it will be recalled, represents current values at the end of the year $T - 1$ of the initial assets of the year T.

68. Provided the summation $\sum_{t=L+1}^{L}$, which is a sum of no terms, is assigned the value zero.

69. The relation (3.7) is strictly true only if ϕ is unity—that is, all assets are in the form of money-fixed claims—or if, as the deflation proceeds, the proportion of such assets remains ϕ. Since the deflation increases the value of money-fixed assets, this assumes that the households succeed in rearranging their balance sheets so as to bring about the above result. For the economy as a whole, however, this may not be possible and ϕ may grow toward unity. In this case, with a constant rate of change of prices, $\pi - 1$, S/Y would asymptotically approach the value $\frac{M}{L} k_1 (\rho\pi)$. It is hardly worthwhile to follow such questions further since we have already traveled far enough into the world of pure fancy.

70. See Hicks, *Value and Capital,* especially Chapter XVIII.

71. This conclusion appears to be supported by data on the proportion of income saved by age groups presented in Janet A. Fisher, "Income, Spending and Saving Patterns of Consumer Units in Different Age Groups," *Conference on Research in Income and Wealth,* XV, 1950, pp. 75–102, especially table 10, p. 92; table 11, p. 93. (Joint sponsorship of National Bureau of Research and University of Illinois.) Unfortunately, these estimates can provide only an indirect test. In Fisher's definition, saving does not include additions to equity in consumers' durables while income does include such items as pensions, a large portion of which we do not consider income in our definition. The first mentioned difference in definition produces a downward bias in her estimate of saving, which is likely to be particularly large in the younger age groups. The second difference tends to overestimate saving, especially in the oldest age group, 65 and over. There seems little doubt that with these adjustments,

her data would agree even more closely with the implications of our model. The observed age pattern of the saving-income ratio may also reflect, in part, the variation of both income and planned consumption with age, which is discussed in section 3.2B and 3.2C, as well as the secular productivity growth of income (compare table 1).

72. See, for instance, Fisher, "Income, Spending and Saving Patterns," especially Table 10, p. 92, from which it is possible to estimate average consumption per spending unit for five age groups. These data are of course subject to the qualifications about the treatment of durable purchases mentioned in note 71.

73. See, for instance, Fisher, "Income, Spending and Saving Patterns," especially table 1, p. 81. According to her figures, the average income per household rises to a peak figure for the age groups 35–44, a figure approximately twice as large as the average for her youngest group, 18–24; it then levels off to fall again sharply in the age group 65 and over, which presumably includes the bulk of retired people.

74. The shape of the actual (and, therefore, presumably of the expected) life cycle of income varies with occupation. However, since the occupational structure of the population changes at most slowly, this fact is not inconsistent with Assumptions Va′ and Vb′ for a period of reasonable length.

75. If a certain pattern in the distribution of consumption over time is strongly preferred to all others, an assumption that may not be altogether unrealistic, variations in interest rates within the normal range will fail to produce a significant substitution effect. In terms of the usual two-commodity indifference map, this amounts to assuming that the indifference curves exhibit a pronounced curvature in the neighborhood of the point at which they cross a certain radius vector representing the earlier mentioned "preferred pattern." With this property of the indifference map, and the other properties implied by Assumption II, changes in the interest rate will not sensibly affect the ratio of consumption planned for any year to consumption planned for any other. It is, therefore, logically permissible to maintain our Assumption IV for the time being, even if $r > 0$, at least as an approximation, and even if we permit r to vary, provided these variations are within reasonable limits.

76. For an economy to be income-stationary with nonzero interest, we require that actual and expected interest coincide at any point of time and have remained at the current level for a sufficient length of time (L years).

77. However, the value of the derivative given in (3.17b) may well be negligibly small for a considerable range of values of $v_t/\bar{v}_t$. Under this condition, for a cross-section of individuals that does not include extreme incomes to any significant extent, consumption would remain approximately proportional to total resources. These considerations help to reconcile the possibility mentioned in the text and the cross-section analysis and empirical findings presented in Modigliani and Brumberg "Utility Analysis and the Consumption Function."

78. The last two sentences represent a slight modification of the argument presented in the original text. I have taken the liberty of making the change because it is both shorter and more general. The original formulation relied on a Taylor expansion of the function $\gamma_{L+1}^T(v/v_t^T)$ and on the constancy of the moments (normalized by the mean) of the density function $f_t^T(v)$. The substitute formulation was actually outlined in the last sentence of note 79, which I have preserved for historic reasons.

79. This variable, it will be recalled, represents the sum of initial assets plus current and expected (discounted) income. For Γ_t to be constant, it is sufficient that if v_t^T and $v_t^{T\prime}$ represent two alternative values of the mean value of resources at any two points of time, and f_t^T and $f_t^{T\prime}$ represent the corresponding frequency distributions, then

$$f_t^{T\prime}(v)dv = f_t^T\left(\frac{v_t^T}{v_t^{\prime T}} v\right) \alpha\left(\frac{v_t^T}{v_t^{\prime T}} v\right).$$

80. A ratio larger than unity would imply a planned consumption less than the interest on the present value of total resources.

81. In addition to the factors listed, our model suggess two additional ones that we have felt justified in passing over in this already lengthy paper. These are variations over time in life expectancy and in the average size of the household.

The first of these factors should be taken into account by relaxing Assumption Vc and is of some importance, since a good deal of population growth in Western countries over the last century is attributable to increased life expectancy. Note, however, that much of this increase is due to the spectacular decline in infant mortality, while the gains in life expectancy for the age groups that are relevant to our model have been far more modest. It can be shown within the framework of our model that population and income growth through this channel tend to affect the saving ratio in much the same general direction as productivity growth.

As for the second factor, it is already indirectly taken into account in the model through the relaxation of Assumption IV, although with a fuller treatment, the Γ_t would turn out to be related to population growth. (In this connection, we want to express our thanks to Mr. David Gordon Tyndall of Carnegie Institute of Technology for some exploratory work on this problem.)

In conclusion, we should like to stress that both factors readily find their place within our theoretical framework and that we have reason to believe that their explicit recognition does not affect our major conclusions, either qualitatively or quantitatively.

82. The assumption of constancy of the coefficients is, of course, more risky for longer periods; if we have reliable information on the behavior of the relevant, slowly-changing variables, this information should be taken into account along the lines indicated by equation (2.4a).

83. With regard to the ratio $\mathcal{A}^T/A^T$, our contention of stability will be further supported in section 4.3.

84. For the United States, see Duesenberry, *Income, Saving and the Theory of Consumer Behavior;* Modigliani, "Fluctuations;" Hamburger, "Consumption and Wealth;" Davis, "Consumption Function;" and Robert Ferber, *A Study of Aggregate Consumption Functions* (National Bureau of Economic Research, Technical Paper 8, 1953), For Canada, see Brown, "Habit Persistence;" and Modigliani, "Fluctuations." For Sweden, see Modigliani, "Fluctuations."

85. For example, according to the Department of Commerce's estimates and definitions, cumulated (real) saving out of personal income for 1930–1935, inclusive, was somewhat less than in the single year 1936. If we were to take into account saving in the form of consumer durables, the comparison would be presumably even more striking, since the stock of durable goods was significantly depleted between 1930 and 1935, but rose in 1936. See Goldsmith, "The Growth of Reproducible Wealth," table X, p. 327.

86. Since the D-M function has usually been stated and tested on a per capita basis, the last term of (4.2) should be more accurately written as $b(\mathcal{N}^T/\hat{\mathcal{N}}^{oT})\mathring{Y}$, where $\mathcal{N}$ denotes total population. This refinement does not significantly affect the argument in the text; in fact, it may make the D-M function an even better approximation to our model. See the comments on the Bassie function in the next paragraph of text.

87. See Brown, "Habit Persistence;" and Davis, "Consumption Function." The highest previous consumption might well represent a slightly more accurate proxy for assets than does highest previous income. See section 4.4.

88. See Ferber, "Aggregate Consumption Functions."

89. See Bassie, "Consumers' Expenditures;" and Ferber, "Aggregate Consumption Functions."

90. Hamburger, "Consumption and Wealth."

91. Unfortunately, (4.5a) breaks down for a stationary state. For $\rho = 1$, we know that $\bar{\sigma} = 0$; consequently, the first term on the right-hand side is an indeterminate form. In this case, however, δ may be estimated by another route. We have shown in Section 3.2F that in steady state,

$$\frac{A^T}{Y^T} = \frac{1 - \theta}{\delta - r + \rho - 1}.$$

Putting $\rho = 1$ and solving for δ we get

$$\delta = \frac{1 - \alpha - \beta}{A^T/Y^T} - r. \tag{4.5b}$$

92. These values were computed by retaining Assumptions I, IV, and the original formulation of V. Most of the values of $\alpha + \beta$, $\bar{\sigma}$, and A^T/Y^T, required to compute δ from equations (4.5a,b) were given in part 3. The remaining values were computed by the procedures indicated there. Because most of these procedures involve approximation formulae, the value of δ is not deemed to be significant to more than two decimal places, and, in some cases, even the second decimal may be off by one point.

93. This proportionality is justified by the stability of the asset-income ratio under steady growth (see section 3.2E).

94. From equation (4.9b), by setting $S^{T-1} = S^T = \bar{I}$, we find that the path of income is given by the equation

$$\tilde{Y}^T = k_0 + \frac{\delta \bar{I}}{1 - \alpha^* - \beta^*}(T - T_0),$$

where k_0 may be regarded as the level of income prevailing in the year T_0 in which the constant level of investment, I, began.

95. Compare Keynes, *General Theory*, p. 92f.

96. Note that G^T includes all noncontractual appreciations and depreciations of assets, whether realized or unrealized.

97. As a first approximation, the term δG^T could be dropped altogether. It is true that this term may make a substantial contribution to consumption; with A^T in the order of four times income and δ in the order of 0.1, a 10% appreciation of assets would reduce the saving-income ratio by as much as 0.04. But G^T is likely to be well correlated with $Y^T - Y^{T-1}$ and, hence, its role might be proxied by the first "independent" variable.

98. If the expected yearly return is not constant over time, then by the average expected return we mean the constant yearly stream whose present value is equal to the present value of the actually expected stream.

99. A hypothesis of this nature was first advanced and successfully tested by Jan Tinbergen, "The Notions of Horizon and Expectancy in Dynamic Economics," *Econometrica*, (July 1933): 247–264. Some further confirmation was found in some as yet unpublished results of the Merrill project on "Expectations and Business Fluctuations." See also the forthcoming publication of this project, *The Railroad Shipper's Forecasts*, by Robert Ferber, Bureau of Economic and Business Research, University of Illinois.

100. Possible refinements of this equation will be omitted, as anyone actually carrying our tests would want to make adjustments suitable to his data.

101. See Modigliani and Brumberg, "Utility Analysis and the Consumption Function," especially section 3.2.

102. Brown, "Habit Persistence."

103. The value reported for α_1 is 0.61. The coefficient of nonproperty income, $\delta\chi u_1$, is 0.28, which suggests a value of around 0.2 for u_1. This inference implies $u_2 \simeq 0.8$ and, therefore, a coefficient of G^{T-1} in the order of 0.75. Unfortunately, Brown's reported coefficient cannot be readily compared with this estimate because of his omission of Y^{T-1}. We may expect the variables Y^T and C^T to be rather highly correlated and their relationship to be expressed by a regression equation

$$Y^T = -a + bC^{T-1}, \qquad a > 0, \qquad b > 1.$$

Substituting in (4.15) for Y^{T-1}, the last two terms become

$$(u_2 - \delta\omega)C^{T-1} - u_2\alpha_2(bC^{T-1} - a) = (u_2 - \delta\omega - u_2\alpha_1 b)C^{T-1} + u_2\alpha_1 a.$$

With $\alpha_1 = 0.6$ and b somewhat above 1, we should, therefore, expect to find in Brown's equation a positive constant term and a coefficient for C^{T-1} somewhat below 0.25. His equation does indeed contain a positive constant, and his coefficient of C^{T-1} is 0.22. Thus, the agreement appears to be quite satisfactory. On the basis of our model, we further predict that, with the inclusion of lagged nonproperty income (or lagged total income), his lagged-consumption coefficient should rise considerably and his constant term fall close to zero. We may add that Brown's interpretation of his results is radically different from ours.

104. A number of suggestions advanced in this section are also being tested by the junior author.

105. For a derivation of this formula see, for instance, P. Franklin, *Treatise on Advanced Calculus* (John Wiley and Sons, 1940) pp. 552–556.

106. *Tables of Sine, Cosine and Exponential Integrals*, vol. II, Federal Works Agency, Work Projects Administration for the City of New York, U.S. National Bureau of Standards Computation Lab, 1940.

Consumption Decisions under Uncertainty*

JACQUES H. DRÈZE

Center for Operations Research and Econometrics, Université Catholique de Louvain, Louvain, Belgium

AND

FRANCO MODIGLIANI

Massachussets Institute of Technology, Cambridge, Massachusetts 02139

Received May 15, 1970

INTRODUCTION

This paper deals with three issues related to consumption decisions under uncertainty, namely, (i) the determinants of risk aversion for future consumption; (ii) the impact of uncertainty about future resources on current consumption and (iii) the separability of consumption decisions and portfolio choices. These issues are discussed in the context of a simple model introduced, together with our assumptions, in Section 1. The first issue is motivated and treated in Section 2, the conclusions of which are summarized in Proposition 2.5. The other two issues are treated in Section 3 under the assumption that there exist perfect markets for risks, and in Section 4 under the converse assumption.

Some technical results needed in the text are collected in Appendices A, B and C; a simple graphical illustration of our major result, Theorem 3.3, is given in Appendix D.[1]

* The research underlying this paper was initiated while the authors were both affiliated with the Graduate School of Industrial Administration, Carnegie-Mellon University; the support of that institution, and at a later stage of the Sloan School of Management, Massachussets Institute of Technology, is gratefully acknowledged. The authors also wish to thank Albert Ando and Ralph Beals for their helpful assistance at an early stage of this work, as well as Louis Gevers, Agnar Sandmo and Joseph Stiglitz for their critical reading of the final manuscript.

[1] An earlier summary version of this paper, written in French, has appeared in the *Cahiers du Séminaire d'Econométrie* [5].

308

1. The Model and the Assumptions

1.1. Following Fisher [6], we study the problem faced by a consumer who must allocate his total wealth y between a flow of current (or "initial") consumption c_1 and a residual stock $(y - c_1)$ out of which future consumption c_2 (including bequests) will be financed. We restrict our attention to the aggregate values of present and future consumption, or equivalently to a single-commodity, two-period world.

We conceive of the consumer's wealth y as being the sum of two terms:

1. The (net) market value of his assets, plus his labor income during the initial period, to be denoted altogether by y_1;

2. The present value of his future labor income, plus additional receipts from sources other than his current assets.

Denote by y_2 the value of the second term, discounted back to the *end* of the initial period; and by r the real rate of interest prevailing over that initial period[2]; y and c_2 are then defined by

$$y = y_1 + y_2(1 + r)^{-1}; \quad c_2 = (y - c_1)(1 + r) = (y_1 - c_1)(1 + r) + y_2 . \tag{1.1}$$

Usually, when a decision about current consumption is made, y_1 may be taken as known with certainty, but y_2 and r may not: future labor income and real rates of return on assets are, in most cases, imperfectly known *ex ante*. In our simple two-period model, we conceive of the uncertainty about y_2 and r as being removed only at the end of the initial period—hence, *after* c_1 has been chosen. Accordingly, we refer to uncertain prospects for y_2 and/or *are* as *temporal uncertain prospects* (time will elapse before the uncertainty is removed), and we refer to this type of uncertainty as being "temporal" or "delayed." By contrast, if the uncertainty is to be entirely removed before the choice of c_1, we speak of *timeless uncertain prospects.*

1.2. Relying upon the theory of decision under uncertainty, as developed by von Neumann and Morgenstern [16], Savage [15], etc..., we start from assumptions about probability and utility, instead of the more natural axioms about choice.

For analytical convenience, their results are strengthened into

Assumption I. Every uncertain prospect is described by a (subjective) mass or density function $\phi(y_2, r)$ with finite moments of at least first and

[2] In a single-commodity world, real rates are well defined; a multiplicity of assets, with different rates of return, is introduced in Section 3.

second order. The distribution function corresponding to $\phi(y_2, r)$ will be denoted by $\Phi(y_2, r)$.[3]

ASSUMPTION II. There exists a cardinal utility function $U(c_1, c_2)$, real valued, continuous and continuously differentiable at least three times.[4]

In addition, we introduce two assumptions that go beyond consistency requirements but reflect behavior patterns that we regard as generally encountered in reality.

In the first place, we assume that neither present nor future consumption is an inferior commodity, so that both c_1 and c_2 increase when y (or y_1 with y_2 and r constant) increases. An alternative statement is that the "marginal propensity to consume," as defined in appendix formula (A.4), is everywhere positive but less than one, i.e.,

ASSUMPTION III. $1 > dc_1/dy_1 > 0$.

In the second place, we assume that the consumer's preferences among consumption vectors are convex, and that his choices among uncertain prospects reflect risk aversion, or possibly risk neutrality; that is,[5]

ASSUMPTION IV. U is concave.

Various properties of U, derived from assumptions II, III and quasi-concavity of U, are collected in Appendix A.

1.3. The (cardinal) indirect utility function corresponding to $U(c_1, c_2)$ may be written $V(y, r)$, where

$$V(y, r) =_{\text{def}} \max_{c_1} U(c_1, (y - c_1)(1 + r)).$$

Let $r = r^0$ be the sure and only rate of interest at which a consumer may lend and borrow; then $V(y, r^0)$, a function of y alone, is the *cardinal utility function for wealth* relevant to the analysis of choices among *timeless* uncertain prospects. In other words, if a cardinal utility function for wealth were derived from observations about choices between *timeless* uncertain

[3] For notational convenience, we use the integral symbol without introducing parallel statements in the notation of discrete random variables; the standard symbol E is used for the expectation operator when there is no ambiguity about the underlying mass or density function.

[4] Thus, U is defined up to a linear increasing transformation; if the consumer were to choose between the certainty of consuming (c_1, c_2) and the prospect of consuming either (c_1', c_2') or (c_1'', c_2'') with respective probabilities π and $1 - \pi$, he would never prefer the former alternative if $U(c_1, c_2) \leqslant \pi U(c_1', c_2') + (1 - \pi)U(c_1'', c_2'')$.

[5] As argued elsewhere by one of us [4], risk preference may be excluded without loss of generality, if one assumes the availability on the market of fair gambling opportunities.

prospects, when the market rate of interest for safe loans is r^0 and y_2 is known, then such a function would coïncide with $V(y, r^0)$ up to an increasing linear transformation.

In the language of demand theory, $V(y, r^0)$ measures utility cardinally for movements along the Engel curve corresponding to r^0, by assigning utility levels to the successive indifference curves crossed by that Engel curve. Provided dc_1/dy is continuous (as implied by assumption II) and satisfies assumption III, the Engel curve will have a point in common with every indifference curve and the assignment of utility levels to these curves will be exhaustive. One may then *construct* the cardinal utility function $U(c_1, c_2)$ by relying simultaneously on two independent and familiar tools, namely,

1. Indifference curves, as revealed by choices among sure vectors of present and future consumption;

2. A cardinal utility function for wealth, as revealed by choices among timeless uncertain prospects.

2. Temporal Prospects, the Value of Information and Risk Preference

2.1. If a consumer owns a temporal uncertain prospect $\phi(y_2, r)$ that he cannot or does not wish to exchange for some other prospect, his expected utility is given by

$$\max_{c_1} \int U\{c_1, (y_1 - c_1)(1 + r) + y_2\} \, d\Phi(y_2, r). \tag{2.1}$$

The solution to this maximization problem determines the optimal current consumption $\hat{c}_1$. Future consumption is a random variable defined by (1.1), with $c_1 = \hat{c}_1$. We shall assume that c_2 so defined is nonnegative, identically in y_2 and r, so that the density of c_2 is defined by

$$\psi(c_2) = \int \phi\{c_2 - (y_1 - \hat{c}_1)(1 + r), r\} \, dr \tag{2.2}$$

with first and second moments

$$\bar{c}_2 = (y_1 - \hat{c}_1)(1 + \bar{r}) + \bar{y}_2,$$

$$\sigma_{c_2}^2 = (y_1 - \hat{c}_1)^2 \sigma_r{}^2 + \sigma_{y_2}^2 + 2(y_1 - \hat{c}_1) \, \sigma_{ry_2}. \tag{2.3}$$

Had the *same* uncertain prospect been timeless, so that the value of y_2 and r were known to our consumer before his choice of c_1, then his expected utility would have been

$$\int \max_{c_1} U\{c_1, (y_1 - c_1)(1 + r) + y_2\}\, d\Phi(y_2, r)$$
$$= \int V\{y_1 + y_2(1 + r)^{-1}, r\}\, d\Phi(y_2, r). \tag{2.4}$$

It is immediately verified, by application of a well-known theorem,[6] that

$$\max_{c_1} \int U\{c_1, (y_1 - c_1)(1 + r) + y_2\}\, d\Phi(y_2, r)$$
$$\leqslant \int \max_{c_1} U\{c_1, (y_1 - c_1)(1 + r) + y_2\}\, d\Phi(y_2, r). \tag{2.5}$$

The difference between the right and left hand sides of (2.5) is "the expected value of perfect information" (EVPI), well known to the statisticians.[7]

The meaning of (2.5) may be conveyed somewhat informally, as follows:

PROPOSITION 2.1. *A temporal uncertain prospect is never preferred to the timeless uncertain prospect described by the same mass or density function, no matter what the consumer's utility function may be.*[8]

2.2. The general inferiority of temporal over timeless uncertain prospects has implications for the willingness to bear risk in a temporal context. One convenient way of capturing these implications rests upon the "risk aversion function" introduced by Pratt [12] for timeless uncertainty about total resources (wealth).

Let $r = r^0$ be given; Pratt's (absolute) risk aversion function is then given by $(-V_{yy}/V_y)_{r^0}$. This quantity, which is equal to "twice the risk

[6] See, e.g., Marschak [9, p. 201]. The theorem may be stated as follows: "Let g be a function of the decision variable d and of the random variable x with density $f(x)$; then: $\int_x \max_d g(d, x)f(x)\, dx \geqslant \max_d \int_x g(d, x)f(x)\, dx$."

[7] In order to get a measure that does not depend upon the choice of units for the utility function, one should divide both sides of (2.5) by some appropriate index of marginal utility — like $U_1 = V_y$, or U_2 — so as to measure the EVPI in the same units as consumption, either current or future.

[8] The mass or density functions must, of course, be kept identical, not only "theoretically" but also "practically," if spurious contradictions are to be avoided; thus, a consumer with strong risk aversion may prefer a temporal prospect that is marketable to a similar timeless one that is not; the appropriate density for the temporal prospect is then given by the certainty of its market value and our proposition is not applicable.

premium per unit of variance for infinitesimal risks" when the consumer's wealth is y and $r = r^0$, is a local measure of risk preference. It is, however, related to risk aversion in the large: if one consumer has a greater local risk aversion than another at all wealth levels y, then (and only then) he has greater risk aversion in the large—in the sense that he would exchange *any* timeless uncertain prospect $\chi(y)$ against the certainty of an amount which would be unacceptable to the other consumer.[9]

We shall now derive a (local) measure of risk aversion for *delayed* risks which, like the Pratt measure in the timeless context, represents "twice the risk premium per unit of variance for infinitesimal risks."

We begin with a given r (say $r \equiv r^0$) and income prospects $\phi(y_2)$. If such prospects are *timeless*, the random outcome will be known at time 1 but *paid* at time 2: the choice of c_1 still occurs under certainty. It is readily verified that the risk aversion function relevant for such prospects is

$$\frac{-1}{1+r^0}\left(\frac{V_{yy}}{V_y}\right)_{r^0} = \left(\frac{-V_{y_2y_2}}{V_{y_2}}\right)_{r^0}.$$

When such prospects become temporal, on the other hand, the appropriate risk aversion function is $(-U_{22}/U_2)_{\hat{c}_1}$. This can be verified as follows. Let $\hat{c}_1$ be the first period consumption that is optimal for a given temporal uncertain prospect $\phi(y_2, r)$, and let $\psi(c_2)$ be defined as in (2.2). The expected utility of the prospect is then $\int U(\hat{c}_1, c_2)\, d\Psi(c_2)$.

Clearly, if U_{22} does not change sign over the range of $\psi(c_2)$, then

$$\int U(\hat{c}_1, c_2)\, d\Psi(c_2) \gtreqless U(\hat{c}_1, \bar{c}_2) \text{ according as } U_{22} \gtreqless 0. \tag{2.6}$$

Confining attention to infinitesimal risks, we have

$$\int U(\hat{c}_1, c_2)\, d\Psi(c_2) \simeq U(\hat{c}_1, \bar{c}_2) + (\sigma_{c_2}^2/2)\, U_{22}(\hat{c}_1, \bar{c}_2) =_{\text{def}} U(\hat{c}_1, c_2'), \tag{2.7}$$

thereby defining c_2' implicitly.

Furthermore, $U(\hat{c}_1, c_2') \simeq U(\hat{c}_1, \bar{c}_2) + (c_2' - \bar{c}_2)\, U_2(\hat{c}_1, \bar{c}_2)$, so that

$$c_2' \simeq \bar{c}_2 + \frac{\sigma_{c_2}^2}{2}\frac{U_{22}(\hat{c}_1, \bar{c}_2)}{U_2(\hat{c}_1, \bar{c}_2)}, \quad \text{implying} \left(-\frac{U_{22}}{U_2}\right)_{\hat{c}_1, \bar{c}_2} \simeq \frac{2(\bar{c}_2 - c_2')}{\sigma_{c_2}^2}. \tag{2.8}$$

Thus, $(-U_{22}/U_2)_{\hat{c}_1, \bar{c}_2}$ is equal to "twice the risk premium per unit of variance y_2 for infinitesimal *delayed* risks." For given $\hat{c}_1$, the function

[9] See Pratt [12, p. 122] and Sections 3–5; Arrow has independently introduced the same concept in [2].

$(-U_{22}/U_2)_{\hat{c}_1}$ is a local measure of risk aversion at all levels of c_2 in the same sense as $-V_{y_2y_2}/V_{y_2}$ provides such a measure at all levels of y_2 for timeless uncertain prospects. One must, however, be careful to realize that the value of $(-U_{22}/U_2)_{\hat{c}_1}$ is in general not independent of $\hat{c}_1$[10]: It measures risk aversion along a particular cut of the utility function orthogonal to the c_1 axis, but the measure may not be the same, at a given level of c_2, for different choices of c_1 (different cuts of the utility function by parallel planes).

2.3. It follows from Appendix formula (A.15) that, *at any point in* (c_1, c_2) *space,*

$$\frac{-U_{22}}{U_2} = \frac{-V_{y_2y_2}}{V_{y_2}} + \left(\frac{dc_1}{dy_2}\right)^2 \left(\frac{d^2c_2}{dc_1^2}\bigg|_U\right) \geqslant -\frac{V_{y_2y_2}}{V_{y_2}}, \tag{2.9}$$

where $V_{y_2y_2}/V_{y_2}$ and dc_1/dy_2 are computed along the Engel curve going through *that point*, and where the inequality follows from assumptions III and IV.

The risk premium for a delayed risk must be equal to the sum of (i) the expected value of perfect information, and (ii) the risk premium for the same risk when timeless.[11] Thus the second term on the right hand side of (2.9) measures "twice the expected value of perfect information per unit of variance y_2 for infinitesimal risks." That second term is invariant under monotonic transformations of the utility function;[12] it is the product of two factors, of which the second one is most easily interpreted. $d^2c_2/dc_1^2\,|_U$ is a (local) measure of curvature of the indifference loci. As shown in the appendix formulas (A.5, A.6), it also measures the reciprocal of the substitution effect on c_1, of a rise in r.[13] That curvature of the indifference loci should be relevant to assess the superiority of timeless

[10] A necessary and sufficient condition for $-U_{22}/U_2$ to be everywhere independent of c_1 is that $U = f(c_1) + g(c_1)\,h(c_2)$.

[11] Indeed, the total premium paid to dispose of a given delayed risk should be the same, whether the uncertain prospect be exchanged outright for a sure amount, or whether it be exchanged first (at some premium) for an identical but timeless prospect, to be converted next into a sure amount.

[12] It is thus observed that, for *infinitesimal* risks, the expected value of perfect information depends only upon ordinal properties of U; of course, this strong and somewhat surprising result does not hold more generally.

[13] This effect is usually referred to as the "substitution term of the Slutsky equation;" it measures the response of c_1 to a *compensated* change in the rate of interest; the Slutsky equation, however, is typically expressed in terms of the "price" $(1 + r)^{-1}$ rather than in terms of the interest rate r.

over temporal uncertain prospects is readily seen if one contrasts extreme situations. At one extreme, suppose that the indifference curves are nearly linear in the vicinity of the equilibrium point: the consumer is almost indifferent about the allocation of his total resources between c_1 and c_2, which are almost perfect substitutes, the curvature is close to nil, and the response of c_1 to a compensated change in the rate of interest would be very large. Obviously, for such a consumer, delayed uncertainty is not appreciably different from timeless uncertainty, since the opportunity to gear c_1 exactly to total resources matters little to him. At the other extreme, suppose that the indifference curves are very close to right angles in the vicinity of the equilibrium point: the consumer has very exacting preferences for the allocation of his total resources between c_1 and c_2, which are strongly complementary, the curvature is very pronounced, and the response of c_1 to a compensated change in the rate of interest would be negligible. For such a consumer, delayed uncertainty is very costly, due to the imperfect allocation which it entails: the utility of a consumption plan with given present value $c_1 + c_2(1 + r)^{-1}$ decreases rapidly when the allocation departs from the preferred proportions. Thus, as formula (2.9) shows, *the aversion for delayed risks grows as curvature of the indifference loci increases*, or, to use more operational terms, consumers who would respond strongly to a (compensated) change in the rate of interest are *relatively* better suited to carry delayed risks.

The role of the other factor, the marginal propensity to consume, is again most easily understood by looking at limiting situations. If $dc_1/dy = 0$, then the optimum c_1 can be chosen without exact knowledge of total resources, so that perfect information is worthless. At the other extreme, a person who wants to consume all his resources now because he derives no satisfaction from later consumption is ill-suited to bear delayed risks: since he can only afford to consume now the resources he is sure to own, the uncertain prospect carries no more utility for him than the certainty of its worst outcome. In general, *the inferiority of temporal over timeless uncertain prospects will be the more severe, the larger the marginal propensity to consume (other things being equal).*

2.4. We now turn briefly to the case where y_2 is given (say $y_2 = \bar{y}_2$) and r is a random variable with density $\phi(r)$. Our problem is to compare timeless with temporal uncertain prospects about r. One can readily verify that the Pratt "risk-aversion function" for timeless gambles about r is $-(y_1 - c_1)(V_{rr}/V_r)_{\bar{y}}$.[14] Similarly, when $\sigma^2_{c_2} = (y_1 - \hat{c}_1)^2 \sigma_r^2$, we see from (2.7) that $-(y_1 - \hat{c}_1)^2(U_{22}/U_2)_{\hat{c}_1}$ is the appropriate corresponding meas-

[14] Note from (A.11) that $V_r = V_{y_2}(y_1 - c_1)$ has the same sign as $(y_1 - c_1)$: an increase in r affects utility positively for a lender, negatively for a borrower.

ure for temporal gambles. Furthermore, it follows from formula (A.15) that, *at any point in* (c_1, c_2) *space*,

$$-(y_1 - c_1)^2(U_{22}/U_2) = -(y_1 - c_1)(V_{rr}/V_r) + (dc_1/dr)^2(d^2c_2/dc_1^2 \mid_U) \geqslant -(y_1 - c_1)(V_{rr}/V_r), \tag{2.10}$$

where V_{rr}/V_r and dc_1/dr are computed along the offer-curve going through that point. Formula (2.10) admits of the same interpretation as (2.9), so that the second term on the right hand side measures "twice the expected value of perfect information per unit variance r for infinitesimal risks"—a nonnegative quantity that is again invariant under *monotonic* transformations of the utility function. We notice that this quantity vanishes when $dc_1/dr = 0$: if current consumption is insensitive to r, it is also insensitive to σ_r^2 (at least locally), and uncertainty about r is of no concern in choosing c_1. For people with positive asset holdings $(y_1 - c_1 > 0)$, dc_1/dr is unrestricted as to sign on *a priori* grounds; the absence of empirical evidence pointing strongly to either a positive or a negative sign is perhaps an indication that dc_1/dr, whatever its sign, may not be appreciably different from zero, thus pointing towards a small value for the expected value of perfect information about r, and *a less pronounced inferiority of temporal over timeless uncertainty in the case of rates of return than in the case of income.*[15]

2.5. Summarizing our discussion of (2.9)–(2.10), we have:

PROPOSITION 2.5. *A consumer's willingness to bear delayed risks, as measured by his risk aversion function for temporal prospects* $(-U_{22}/U_2)_{\hat{c}_1}$, *will be the lower:*

(i) *the lower his willigness to bear immediate risks, as measured by his risk aversion function for timeless prospects* $(-V_{yy}/V_y)_r$;

(ii) *the larger his marginal propensity to consume* dc_1/dy, *and/or the responsiveness of his current consumption to the rate of interest* $\mid dc_1/dr \mid$;

(iii) *the lower, in absolute value, the substitution effect of a change in the rate of interest on his current consumption* $\mid S \mid$.

[15] The general case of joint uncertainty about y_2 and r is a straightforward extension of the foregoing analysis; (2.9) and (2.10) combine to

$$\begin{aligned}(-U_{22}/U_2)\,\sigma_{c_2}^2 &= (-U_{22}/U_2)(\sigma_{y_2}^2 + (y_1 - c_1)^2\sigma_r^2 + 2(y_1 - c_1)\sigma_{ry_2}) \\ &= -\left(\frac{V_{y_2y_2}}{V_{y_2}}\sigma_{y_2}^2 + \frac{V_{rr}}{V_r}(y_1 - c_1)\sigma_r^2 + 2\frac{V_{ry_2}}{V_r}(y_1 - c_1)\sigma_{ry_2}\right) \\ &\quad + \left(\left(\frac{dc_1}{dy_2}\right)^2\sigma_{y_2}^2 + \left(\frac{dc_1}{dr}\right)^2\sigma_r^2 + 2\frac{dc_1}{dr}\frac{dc_1}{dy_2}\sigma_{ry_2}\right)\left(\frac{d^2c_2}{dc_1^2}\,\Big|_U\right).\end{aligned}$$

3. Consumption and Portfolio Decisions with Perfect Markets

3.1. We now turn to the following questions: (i) How does uncertainty about future resources affect current consumption? (ii) What is the relationship between consumption decisions and portfolio choices? The first question may be raised irrespective of the nature and source of uncertainty, but cannot be answered until some reference criterion is chosen; the second question is appropriate only when savings may be invested in a variety of assets, and the consumer is free to *choose* his portfolio mix.

The portfolio problem traditionally considered in the literature involves a perfectly safe asset, yielding a rate of return r_0, and n risky assets yielding uncertain rates of return. The consumer is free to allocate his savings (wealth) among these $n + 1$ assets. If there is no uncertainty about future income, then any uncertainty affecting future resources is "chosen" or "endogenous," since it results entirely from portfolio choices (all the savings could have been invested in the safe asset). And a natural reference criterion, in assessing the impact of uncertainty on current consumption, is the value of c_1 that would be optimal if indeed all the savings were yielding the *sure* rate r_0. This is a more natural reference than the (more traditional) optimal c_1, given the *expected* rate of return on the chosen portfolio. Indeed, under assumption IV, a consumer would not choose a risky portfolio unless its expected return were higher than r_0; but no portfolio yielding the certainty of that expected return is available on the market; and knowing how $\hat{c}_1$ stands relative to the expected value criterion would not tell us how endogenous uncertainty actually affects c_1.

This argument can be extended to income uncertainty if one assumes the existence of insurance markets where an uncertain future income with density $\phi(y_2)$ can be exchanged against the certainty of some sure income y_2^0. In the presence of perfect markets for both income and assets, all uncertainty is "chosen" or "endogenous," and it is natural to compare $\hat{c}_1$ with the consumption that would be optimal if c_2 were equal to $y_2^0 + (y_1 - c_1)(1 + r_0)$ with certainty.

Such is the case treated in this section. It turns out that with perfect markets, a particular *ordinal* property of the utility function determines unambiguously how uncertainty affects consumption, *and* whether consumption and portfolio decisions are separable.

First-order conditions for optimal decisions are given in 3.2. We then prove a certainty equivalence theorem in 3.3 and interpret it in 3.4. The property of the utility function mentioned above is discussed in 3.5. In Section 4, we then turn to the case where the uncertain prospect faced by a consumer is not chosen, but given "exogenously" (at least on the income side). And we conclude that section with some remarks on the response of current consumption to availability of market opportunities for sharing risks.

3.2. We now introduce a general model designed to analyze simultaneous decisions about $\phi(y_2, r)$ and $\hat{c}_1$ under perfect insurance and asset markets.[16] These decisions are assumed to maximize expected utility over the class of all prospects, the market value of which does not exceed that of $\phi(y_2, r)$.

Let there be one perfectly safe asset, yielding a rate of return r_0, and n risky assets yielding the uncertain rates of return r_j, $j = 1 \cdots n$. The amounts invested in these $n + 1$ assets will be denoted by $(x_0, x_1 \cdots x_n)$. Let furthermore future earnings y_2 be the sum of m components y_{i2}, $i = 1 \cdots m$; and let z_{i1} be the *present* value of y_{i2} on the insurance market.[17] Denote by $(1 - \alpha_i)$, $i = 1 \cdots n$, the *fraction* of y_{i2} that a consumer chooses to *sell* on the insurance market; his current wealth and future (net) earnings then become $y_1 + \sum_{i=1}^{m} (1 - \alpha_i) z_{i1}$ and $\sum_{i=1}^{m} \alpha_i y_{i2}$, respectively. Given a current consumption c_1, his portfolio of assets must satisfy the constraint

$$y_1 + \sum_{i=1}^{m} (1 - \alpha_i) z_{i1} - c_1 = x_0 + \sum_{j=1}^{n} x_j,$$

or (3.1)

$$x_0 = y_1 - c_1 + \sum_{i=1}^{m} (1 - \alpha_i) z_{i1} - \sum_{j=1}^{n} x_j,$$

[16] In [5, Section 6], we have used a slightly different formulation, based upon the notion that labor income (current and future) results from activities among which the consumer divides his *time*, of which a fixed quantity is available; it was also assumed that earnings from a given activity were proportional to the amount of time devoted to it, and that one of the activities entailed a perfectly safe income; the activities themselves did not appear as arguments of the utility function. Under that formulation, earnings per unit of time from the safe activity provide an implicit "insurance value" for the earnings per unit of time from any of the risky activities.

[17] This "insurance value" may be defined in a number of ways: one of them is straightforward insurance of professional income (including unemployment and medical insurance); another is suggested in footnote 16; another still is provided by the purchase (or short sale) of a portfolio of assets perfectly negatively (or positively) correlated with y_{i2}. One might also consider a "states of the world" model [1, 3, 7] with m states and define:

$$y_{i2} = \begin{cases} \text{future earnings, if state } i \text{ obtains,} \\ 0, \text{ otherwise;} \end{cases}$$

$z_{i1} = y_{i2}$ times the current price of a unit claim contingent on state i.

Our formal analysis is consistent with any of these interpretations, or combinations thereof, so long as z_{i1} is well-defined, independently of the amount of "coverage" that our consumer buys on y_{i2}.

and his future consumption is defined by

$$
\begin{aligned}
c_2 &= \sum_{i=1}^{m} \alpha_i y_{i2} + x_0(1 + r_0) + \sum_{j=1}^{n} x_j(1 + r_j) \\
&= \sum_{i=1}^{m} \alpha_i y_{i2} + \left(y_1 - c_1 + \sum_{i=1}^{m} (1 - \alpha_i)\, z_{i1}\right)(1 + r_0) + \sum_{j=1}^{n} x_j(r_j - r_0) \\
&= z_2 + (y_1 - c_1)(1 + r_0) + \sum_{i=1}^{m} \alpha_i(y_{i2} - z_{i2}) + \sum_{j=1}^{n} x_j(r_j - r_0), \qquad (3.2)
\end{aligned}
$$

where

$$
z_{i2} =_{\text{def}} z_{i1}(1 + r_0) \qquad \text{and} \qquad z_2 =_{\text{def}} \sum_{i=1}^{m} z_{i2}\,.
$$

Given the joint density $\phi(y_{12} \cdots y_{m2}, r_1 \cdots r_n)$, the simultaneous choice of an asset portfolio $(x_1 \cdots x_n)$, an insurance portfolio $(1 - \alpha_1 \cdots 1 - \alpha_m)$ and a consumption level c_1, is then arrived at by solving the following problem:

$$
\max_{c_1, \alpha_1 \cdots \alpha_m, x_1 \cdots x_n} \int U \left\{ c_1, z_2 + (y_1 - c_1)(1 + r_0) + \sum_{i=1}^{m} \alpha_i(y_{i2} - z_{i2}) + \sum_{j=1}^{n} x_j(r_j - r_0) \right\} d\Phi(y_{12} \cdots y_{m2}, r_1 \cdots r_n), \qquad (3.3)
$$

subject to whatever constraints prevail on the maximizing variables. We shall assume that such constraints, if any, are never binding, and that the solutions to (3.3) are given by the first-order conditions (3.4)–(3.6):[18]

$$
\partial EU/\partial c_1 = E(U_1 - U_2(1 + r_0)) = 0, \quad \text{or} \quad EU_1/EU_2 = 1 + r_0\,; \qquad (3.4)
$$

$$
\partial EU/\partial x_j = E(U_2(r_j - r_0)) = 0 \quad \text{or} \quad EU_2 r_j/EU_2 = r_0\,; \qquad (3.5)
$$

$$
\partial EU/\partial \alpha_i = E(U_2(y_{i2} - z_{i2})) = 0, \quad \text{or} \quad EU_2 y_{i2}/EU_2 = z_{i2}\,. \qquad (3.6)
$$

These results admit of the following economic interpretation:

PROPOSITION 3.2. *Under perfect insurance and asset markets, any solution to problem* (3.3) *has the following properties*:

(3.4) *The ratio of the expected marginal utilities of present and future consumption is equal to one plus the rate of return on the* safe *asset*;

[18] Thus, we assume that all solutions to (3.4)–(3.6) satify $c_1 \geqslant 0$ and $c_2 \geqslant 0$ identically in $(y_{12} \cdots y_{m2}, r_1 \cdots r_n)$, plus whatever conditions might be imposed on the α_i's and x_j's; clearly, the model lends itself to a more courageous formulation with inequality constraints. The second-order conditions follow naturally from Assumption IV.

(3.5) *The expected marginal utility of a unit investment in every asset is the same*; *the expected value of the rate of return on every asset*, weighted by the marginal utility of future consumption, *is equal to the rate of return on the safe asset*;

(3.6) *The expected marginal utility of a unit worth of insurance on every source of earnings is the same*; *the expected value of the earnings from any source*, weighted by the marginal utility of future consumption, *is equal to the insurance value of these earnings.*

Clearly, if there exist perfect asset markets, but no insurance markets, the solution to (3.3) with all α_i's equated to one's is still given by (3.4)–(3.5), and if there exist neither asset nor insurance markets, the solution is given by (3.4).

Furthermore, if the rate of return on the entire portfolio, namely,

$$r_0 + \left(\sum_{j=1}^{n} (r_j - r_0)\, x_j \bigg/ \left(x_0 + \sum_{j=1}^{n} x_j \right) \right),$$

is still denoted by r, and since $y_2 =_{\text{def}} \sum_{i=1}^{m} y_{i2}$, (3.5)–(3.6) imply

$$EU_2 r/EU_2 = r_0\,, \quad EU_2 y_2/EU_2 = z_2 = EU_2 \sum_{i=1}^{m} (\alpha_i y_{i2} + (1 - \alpha_i)\, z_{i2}) \Big/ EU_2\,. \tag{3.7}$$

3.3 We now state and prove a theorem that has an immediate bearing on consumption and portfolio decisions with perfect markets. It does, however, admit of a somewhat broader interpretation, which justifies the notation "y_2^*, r^*, c_1^*" introduced in the statement of the theorem.

THEOREM 3.3. *Let* $y_2^* =_{\text{def}} Ey_2U_2(\hat{c}_1, c_2)/EU_2(\hat{c}_1, c_2)$, $r^* =_{\text{def}} ErU_2(\hat{c}_1, c_2)/EU_2(\hat{c}_1, c_2)$ *and define* $c_1^* = c_1^*(r^*, y_2^*)$ *by*

$$U_1(c_1^*, (y_1 - c_1^*)(1 + r^*) + y_2^*)$$
$$- (1 + r^*)\, U_2(c_1^*, (y_1 - c_1^*)(1 + r^*) + y_2) = 0.$$[19]

Then

$$\partial^2 \frac{U_1}{U_2} \Big/ \partial c_2{}^2 \gtreqless 0 \text{ (identically in } c_2\text{, given } \hat{c}_1\text{) implies } \hat{c}_1 \gtreqless c_1^*.$$

Proof. The proof is based upon appendix Lemma C.2. Let $U_1(\hat{c}_1, c_2)/U_2(\hat{c}_1, c_2) - (1 + r^*) =_{\text{def}} f(c_2)$; we may rewrite (3.4) as

$$0 = \int U_2 f(c_2)\, d\Psi(c_2) =_{\text{def}} \int h(c_2)\, d\Psi(c_2), \tag{3.8}$$

[19] That is, c_1^* is the level of current consumption that would be optimal given $y_2 \equiv y_2^*$, $r \equiv r^*$; $\hat{c}$, is still the optimal level given $\phi(y_2, r)$.

where $U_2 = U_2(\hat{c}_1, c_2)$ is a function of c_2. Let then

$$c_2^* =_{\text{def}} \frac{Ec_2U_2}{EU_2} = \frac{E((y_1 - \hat{c}_1)(1 + r) + y_2)\, U_2}{EU_2}$$
$$= (y_1 - \hat{c}_1)(1 + r^*) + y_2^* \text{ by (3.7).}$$

Lemma C.2 then implies

$$f(c_2) \begin{array}{c}\text{concave}\\ \text{linear}\\ \text{convex}\end{array} \Rightarrow \int h(c_2)\, d\Psi(c_2) \begin{array}{c}\leq\\ =\\ \geq\end{array} f(c_2^*) \int U_2\, d\Psi(c_2). \qquad (3.9)$$

Now, $\int U_2\, d\Psi(c_2) > 0$, and $f(c_2)$ is a linear function of U_1/U_2, whose concavity properties (in c_2) are determined by the sign (assumed constant) of $\partial^2(U_1/U_2)/\partial c_2^2$; consequently, (3.8) and (3.9) together imply

$$\frac{\partial^2(U_1/U_2)}{\partial c_2^2} \begin{array}{c}\leq\\ =\\ \geq\end{array} 0 \Rightarrow U_1(\hat{c}_1, c_2^*)/U_2(\hat{c}_1, c_2^*) - (1 + r^*) \begin{array}{c}\geq\\ =\\ \leq\end{array} 0$$
$$\Rightarrow U_1(\hat{c}_1, c_2^*) - (1 + r^*)\, U_2(\hat{c}_1, c_2^*) \begin{array}{c}\geq\\ =\\ \leq\end{array} 0. \qquad (3.10)$$

Assumption III and the definition of c^* imply that

$$U_{11}(c_1^*, c_2^*) - (1 + r^*)\, U_{21}(c_1^*, c_2^*) < 0,$$

so that

$$U_1(\hat{c}_1, c_2^*) - (1 + r^*)\, U_2(\hat{c}_1, c_2^*) \gtreqless 0 \Leftrightarrow \hat{c}_1 \lesseqgtr c_1^*.$$

The theorem then follows from (3.10). Q.E.D.

3.4. When there exist perfect markets for income insurance and for assets, then (3.4)–(3.7) imply that y_2^* is equal to the insurance value of future income (z_2) and r^* is equal to the market sure rate of return (r_0).[20] Suppose that $\partial^2(U_1/U_2)/\partial c_2^2 = 0$; Theorem 3.3 then implies that current consumption $\hat{c}_1$ is equal to the level (c_1^*) that would be optimal if all income were insured ($y_2 \equiv y_2^*$) and all savings were held in the safe asset ($r \equiv r^*$). *This result holds independently of the actual insurance policy and asset portfolio chosen by the consumer.* Hence, endogenous uncertainty has no impact on consumption. Furthermore, y_2^* ($= z_2$) and r^* ($= r_0$) being directly observable market values, $\hat{c}_1$ ($= c_1^*$) may be chosen first (as a function of z_2 and r_0), the optimal insurance policy and asset portfolio being determined thereafter (jointly, for this given $\hat{c}_1$).

[20] Some readers may find it more convenient to transpose this interpretation to the situation where there is no uncertainty about future income, so that $y_2 \equiv y_2^*$.

Consumption and portfolio decisions may be taken sequentially and are "separable", in that sense.[21]

When $\partial^2(U_1/U_2)/\partial c^2_2 \neq 0$, then the sign of that quantity is also the sign of the impact of endogenous uncertainty on current consumption. It is noteworthy that U_1/U_2, hence its second derivative, is invariant under monotonic transformations of the utility function, and thus independent of risk aversion. There thus exist ordinal preferences, consistent with our assumptions, such that endogenous uncertainty results in increased consumption, and alternative preferences such that the opposite result holds. In the latter case, the consumer chooses an uncertain prospect which yeilds a higher expected utility than the sure prospect of identical market value, but he simultaneously chooses to consume less in the first period-postponing the (uncertain) benefit to the second period. Such behavior is consistent with risk aversion, in spite of the saying that "a bird in hand is worth two in the bush."

3.5. It is appropriate at this point to inquire about the meaning of the rather unfamiliar quantity $\partial^2(U_1/U_2)/\partial c_2^2$ which controls the response of consumption to endogenous risk, and to inquire whether there is ground for supposing that some sign is more plausible than another.

First we recall that U_1/U_2 is a familiar quantity, the slope of the indifference curve; hence $\partial(U_1/U_2)/\partial c_2$ is the rate of change of the slope of the indifference curves as we increase c_2 for fixed c_1. That derivative must have a positive sign by Assumption III (c_1 is not an inferior good). The function $(\partial^2(U_1/U_2)/\partial c_2^2)_{\hat{c}_1}$ measures the curvature of U_1/U_2 as a function of c_2.

An intuitive explanation of the relevance of $\partial^2(U_1/U_2)/\partial c_2^2$ for consumption decisions under uncertainty is provided in Appendix D, by means of a simple graphical illustration.

More generally, the following can be said:

(i) $\partial^2(U_1/U_2)/\partial c_2^2 = 0$ identically in c_1 and c_2 if and only if $U(c_1, c_2) = F(g(c_1) + h(c_1) \cdot c_2)$, $F' > 0$, $h > 0$ (see Appendix B). That is, $\partial^2(U_1/U_2)/\partial c_2^2 \equiv 0$ is the *ordinal* property of $U(c_1, c_2)$ that is *necessary* for risk neutrality in terms of c_2, and sufficient for such neutrality to obtain under a monotonic transformation of U.

(ii) given any $r > -1$, $y > 0$ and u, there exist y_1 and $y_2 = (y - y_1)(1 + r)$ such that $dc_1/dr = 0$; when $dc_1/dr = 0$, then d^2c_1/dr^2 has the sign of $\partial^2(U_1/U_2)/\partial c_2^2$ (see formulas A.7–A.8). That is, $\partial^2(U_1/U_2)/\partial c_2^2 = 0$ is the *ordinal* property of $U(c_1, c_2)$ that is *necessary* for

[21] An extension of these propositions to an n-period model, $n > 2$, has been provided by Pestieau [11], under the additional assumption of homothetic indifference surfaces.

a zero interest-elasticity of consumption at all r and *sufficient* for this situation to obtain under an appropriate time-distribution of income.

Concluding heuristically about the case of perfect insurance and asset markets, we would like to suggest as *a rough first approximation* that uncertainty has little impact on current consumption, and that consumption decisions are for practical purposes separable from portfolio decisions. The lack of empirical evidence pointing towards a substantial interest–elasticity of consumption and the intuitive appeal of the separability proposition lend support to this conclusion.

4. Consumption and Portfolio Decisions without Perfect Markets

4.1. When there do not exist perfect markets, with prices at which an arbitrary uncertain prospect can be evaluated and exchanged, then uncertainty is no longer endogenous, and a new reference criterion must be introduced to replace market value. Expected value then seems to be a natural criterion; it calls for comparing $\hat{c}_1$, that maximizes EU given $\phi(y_2, r)$, with $\bar{c}_1$ that would maximize U given $y_2 \equiv \bar{y}_2$ and $r \equiv \bar{r}$.

Theorem 3.3 has some implications for the relation of $\hat{c}_1$ to $\bar{c}_1$, but these implications are limited in scope. Specifically, it follows from the definition in Theorem 3.3 that

$$y_2^* = EU_2 y_2 / EU_2 = \bar{y}_2 + [\operatorname{cov}(U_2, y_2)/EU_2]. \tag{4.1}$$

When r is nonstochastic ($r \equiv r^*$), then it follows from $U_{22} < 0$ and $c_2 = y_2 + (y_1 - \hat{c}_1)(1 + r)$ that $\operatorname{cov}(U_2, y_2) < 0$ and $y_2^* < \bar{y}_2$. In view of Assumption III, this entails $c_1^* < \bar{c}_1$. Consequently, $\partial^2(U_1/U_2)/\partial c_2^2 \leqslant 0$ implies $\hat{c}_1 \leqslant c_1^* < \bar{c}_1$; the relationship of $\hat{c}_1$ to $\bar{c}_1$ is indeterminate only when $\partial^2(U_1/U_2)/\partial c_2^2 > 0$.

Unfortunately, when r is stochastic, this line of reasoning is no longer valid. Indeed, $\operatorname{cov}(U_2, y_2) = \operatorname{cov}(U_2, c_2) - (y_1 - \hat{c}_1)\operatorname{cov}(U_2, r)$. Whereas $\operatorname{cov}(U_2, c_2) < 0$ still follows from $U_{22} < 0$, the sign of the second term is indeterminate: both $y_1 - \hat{c}_1$ and $\operatorname{cov}(U_2, r)$ are arbitrary as to sign (r could be negatively correlated with c_2, if the returns on the *chosen* portfolio were negatively correlated with labor income).

4.2. A different line of analysis has been pursued, still for the case where r is nonstochastic, by Leland [8] and Sandmo [14]. Broadly speaking, their results point to diminishing absolute risk aversion as a sufficient condition for $\hat{c}_1 < \bar{c}_1$, where r is nonstochastic. Remember that $-U_{22}(c_2, \hat{c}_1)/U_2(c_2, \hat{c}_1)$ has been defined in Section 2 as the "absolute risk aversion" function relevant for temporal risks. Starting from any point in (c_1, c_2)-space, one may wonder whether $-(U_{22}/U_2)$ increases, decreases or remains constant when the starting point is displaced in some particular direction. Leland [8] considers a move along the (tangent to the) indifference curve through (c_1, c_2): c_2 increases and c_1 is simultaneously decreased to keep utility constant. Leland assumes that such a move *decreases* absolute risk aversion, and derives as an implication that current consumption diminishes if the variance of y_2 increases, the expectation of y_2 being kept constant. In other words, such an "increase in risk" reduces current consumption.

Sandmo [14] assumes that $-U_{22}/U_2$ decreases with c_2 and increases with c_1; he then defines an "increase in risk" as a multiplicative shift in the distribution of y_2 combined with an additive shift that keeps the mean constant. His assumptions imply that such an increase in risk reduces current consumption.[22]

We will now state and prove (Section 4.3) a theorem and a corollary that generalize the analysis of Leland and Sandmo. An interpretation of our results is given in 4.4, where it is also explained how Theorem 4.3 generalizes these related results. Finally, we come back in Section 4.5 to the relevance of market opportunities for consumption decisions under uncertainty.

4.3. The condition appearing in Theorem 4.3 refers to the behavior of the absolute risk aversion function along budget lines with slope $dc_2/dc_1 = -(1 + r^*)$. Define indeed

$$R(c_1, c_2, r^*) = \frac{\partial - (U_{22}/U_2)}{\partial c_1} - (1 + r^*) \frac{\partial - (U_{22}/U_2)}{\partial c_2} .$$

The sign of R determines whether absolute risk aversion increases (> 0), decreases (< 0) or remains constant ($= 0$) when c_1 increases and c_2 decreases along the budget line $c_2 = (y_1 - c_1)(1 + r^*) + y_2$. In this definition r^* is still given by (3.7) and satisfies $EU_1/EU_2 = 1 + r^*$.

THEOREM 4.3. *Let $y_2^\dagger$ be such that*

$$\max_{c_1} U(c_1, (y_1 - c_1)(1 + r^*) + y_2^\dagger) = EU(\hat{c}_1, (y_1 - \hat{c}_1)(1 + r) + y_2) \tag{4.2}$$

and let $c_1^\dagger$ be the value of c_1 maximizing the left hand side of (4.2). *Then $R \gtreqless 0$ (identically in c_2 given $\hat{c}_1$) implies $\hat{c}_1 \lesseqgtr c_1^\dagger$.*

[22] Related results have been established under the additional assumption of additive (cardinal) utility, e.g., by Mirman [10] or by Rothschild and Stiglitz [13]. The latter paper clarifies in a basic way the concept of "increase in risk."

Proof. The proof is based upon appendix Lemma C.1. For convenience, it is broken into three easy steps.

(i) We first notice that

$$U_1(\hat{c}_1, c_2) - (1 + r^*)\, U_2(\hat{c}_1, c_2) =_{\text{def}} h(c_2) = f(U(\hat{c}_1, c_2)), \tag{4.3}$$

with

$$f'(U) = [U_{12} - (1 + r^*)\, U_{22}]/U_2\,. \tag{4.4}$$

Indeed, differentiating both sides of (4.3) with respect to c_2, we verify: $dh/dc_2 = U_{12} - (1 + r^*)\, U_{22} = f'(U) \cdot U_2$, which satisfies (4.4);

$$\begin{aligned} d^2h/dc_2^2 &= U_{122} - (1 + r^*)\, U_{222} = f''(U) \cdot U_2^2 + f'(U) \cdot U_2 \\ &= df'(U)/dc_2 \cdot (dc_2/dU) \cdot U_2^2 + f'(U) \cdot U_{22} \\ &= \frac{(U_{122} - (1 + r^*)\, U_{222})\, U_2 - U_{22}(U_{12} - (1 + r^*)\, U_{22})}{U_2^2} \\ &\quad \times \frac{U_2^2}{U_2} + U_{22} \cdot \frac{U_{12} - (1 + r^*)\, U_{22}}{U_2}, \end{aligned}$$

and so on for higher derivatives. We notice in the process that

$$\begin{aligned} U_2 f''(U) &= \frac{(U_{122} - (1 + r^*)\, U_{222})\, U_2 - U_{22}(U_{12} - (1 + r^*)\, U_{22})}{U_2^2} \\ &= \frac{\partial(U_{22}/U_2)}{\partial c_1} - (1 + r^*) \frac{\partial(U_{22}/U_2)}{\partial c_2} = -R. \end{aligned} \tag{4.5}$$

(ii) In view of (4.5) and $U_2 > 0$, $R \gtreqless 0$ implies that f is a concave / linear / convex function of U. Let c_2' be such that $U(\hat{c}_1, c_2') = \int U(\hat{c}_1, c_2)\, d\Psi(c_2)$; Lemma C.1 then implies

$$R \gtreqless 0 \Rightarrow \int h(c_2)\, d\Psi(c_2) \lesseqgtr h(c_2'). \tag{4.6}$$

By (3.4) and the definition of h, $\int h(c_2)\, d\Psi(c_2) = 0$; therefore,

$$R \gtreqless 0 \Rightarrow h(c_2') = U_1(\hat{c}_1, c_2') - (1 + r^*)\, U_2(\hat{c}_1, c_2') \gtreqless 0. \tag{4.7}$$

(iii) By definition,

$$\begin{aligned} U(\hat{c}_1, c_2') &= U(c_1^\dagger, (y_1 - c_1^\dagger)(1 + r^*) + y_2^\dagger) \\ &= \max_{c_1} U(c_1, (y_1 - c_1)(1 + r^*) + y_2^\dagger). \end{aligned}$$

Since $d^2U/dc_1^2 < 0$, this implies

$$U_1(\hat{c}_1, c_2') - (1 + r^*)\, U_2(\hat{c}_1, c_2') \gtreqless 0 \Leftrightarrow \hat{c}_1 \lesseqgtr c_1^{\dagger}.$$

Combining this with (4.7), we conclude

$$R \gtreqless 0 \Rightarrow \hat{c}_1 \lesseqgtr c_1^{\dagger}. \qquad \text{Q.E.D.}$$

COROLLARY. $r = r^*$ implies $c_1^{\dagger} \leqslant \bar{c}_1$.

Proof. $U_{22} \leqslant 0$ implies

$$\begin{aligned} U(c_1^{\dagger}, (y_1 - c_1^{\dagger})(1 + r^*) + y_2^{\dagger}) &= EU(\hat{c}_1, (y_1 - \hat{c}_1)(1 + r) + y_2) \\ &\leqslant U(\hat{c}_1, (y_1 - \hat{c}_1)(1 + \bar{r}) + \bar{y}_2) \\ &\leqslant U(\bar{c}_1, (y_1 - c_1)(1 + r^*) + \bar{y}_2). \end{aligned}$$

It then follows from Assumption III that $c_1^{\dagger} \leqslant \bar{c}_1$. Q.E.D.

4.4. When $r = r^*$, $R < 0$ means that absolute risk aversion $(-U_{22}/U_2)_{\hat{c}_1}$ diminishes when c_2 increases *thanks to* the additional savings implied in a decrease of c_1. We shall refer to this situation as "endogenously diminishing absolute risk aversion." Combining Theorem 4.3 and its corollary, we have the result that $R \leqslant 0$ implies $\hat{c}_1 \leqslant \bar{c}_1$.

This conclusion is consistent with those reached by Leland and Sandmo. In the case of infinitesimal risks, the three conclusions are identical, although the assumptions are not quite identical—indicating that the assumptions used are sufficient, but not necessary, for the conclusion. Theorem 4.3 clarifies that issue, by showing that $R \leqslant 0$ is *necessary and sufficient* for $\hat{c}_1 \leqslant c_1^{\dagger}$; when $U_{22} < 0$ and $\sigma_{y_2}^2 > 0$, then $c_1^{\dagger} < \bar{c}_1$. Thus, $R < 0$ is not necessary for $\hat{c}_1 < \bar{c}_1$, but it is necessary for $\hat{c}_1 < c_1^{\dagger}$. The three-way implication in Theorem 4.3 is thus a generalization of the other results.

Our sharper result may be interpreted as follows. The impact of the uncertainty about future income on current consumption may be decomposed into an income effect and a substitution effect. The income effect corresponds to the fact that the expected utility of $\phi(y_2)$ is less than the utility of $\bar{y}_2$—it is only equal to the utility of $y_2^{\dagger} \leqslant \bar{y}_2$. This income effect alone would call for setting $\hat{c}_1 = c_1^{\dagger} < \bar{c}_1$: the income effect is always negative under risk aversion. But in addition there is room for a substitution effect: keeping expected utility constant, uncertainty about y_2 may still affect current consumption. Theorem 4.3 states that the sign of the substitution effect is the sign of R: risk aversion alone does not imply that the substitution effect is negative, but endogenously diminishing absolute risk aversion does. The implications of risk aversion are thus unambiguously defined.

A strong case may be made for regarding endogenous risk aversion as a meaningful, operational concept. Arrow [2] argues as follows that absolute risk aversion for total wealth may reasonably be expected to decrease with wealth: "If absolute risk aversion increased with wealth, it would follow that as an individual became wealthier, he would actually decrease the amount of risky assets held" (p. 35). In that argument, wealth is used as a primitive concept, and the increase in wealth is treated as exogenous. The argument may, however, be reformulated for the case where assets are acquired with savings and used to finance future consumption. One would then say: "If absolute risk aversion for c_2 increased with c_2 along a budget line, it would follow that as an individual accumulated more wealth, he would actually decrease the amount of risky assets held." One may thus consider that standard arguments invoked to discuss increasing versus decreasing absolute risk aversion for "wealth" apply almost verbatim to "risk aversion for c_2 along a budget line," that is, to endogenous risk aversion.

The arguments for decreasing absolute risk aversion are perhaps not compelling (the argument quoted above lacks generality when there are more than two assets), but it is a general conclusion that $\hat{c}_1$ is less than, equal to or greater than its "expected utility" certainty equivalent according to whether absolute risk aversion for c_2 decreases, remains constant or increases with c_2 along budget lines defined by r^*—with some plausibility arguments in favor of the "decreasing" case.

4.5. There remains now to relate the results of Sections 3 and 4. This will be done in three steps.

(i) *When there exist perfect insurance and asset markets*, then $y_2{}^*$ (as defined in Theorem 3.3) $\leqslant y_2{}^\dagger$ (as defined in Theorem 4.3). Indeed, define y_2^{00} by

$$\max_{c_1} \underset{r}{E} \cup (c_1, (y_1 - c_1)(1 + r) + y_2^{00}) = U(c_1{}^\dagger, (y_1 - c_1{}^\dagger)(1 + r^*) + y_2{}^\dagger)$$
$$= \underset{r, y_2}{E} U(\hat{c}_1, (y_1 - \hat{c}_1)(1 + r) + y_2).$$

Because r is the rate of return on the *chosen* portfolio, whereas the sure rate r^* was available, we must have $y_2{}^\dagger \geqslant y_2^{00}$. Similarly, because the chosen future income could have been exchanged against the certainty of $y_2{}^*$, $y_2^{00} \geqslant y_2{}^*$. It follows that $c_1{}^* \leqslant c_1{}^\dagger$. Furthermore, if $\hat{c}_1 \leqslant c_1{}^*$, then $\hat{c}_1 \leqslant c_1{}^\dagger$, revealing that $\partial^2(U_1/U_2)/\partial c_2{}^2 \leqslant 0$ implies $R \leqslant 0$. This may be verified through formula (A.16) which may be rewritten as

$$\frac{\partial^2(U_1/U_2)}{\partial c_2{}^2} = R - \frac{U_{22}}{U_2} \frac{\partial(U_1/U_2)}{\partial c_2} + \left(\frac{U_1}{U^2} - (1 + r^*)\right) \frac{\partial - (U_{22}/U_2)}{\partial c_2}. \tag{4.8}$$

On the right hand side of (4.8), the second term is positive, and the third vanishes when $U_1/U_2 = 1 + r^*$. Hence, at the value of c_2 for which $U_1/U_2 = 1 + r^*$, $\partial^2(U_1/U_2)/\partial c_2^2 \leqslant 0$ implies $R < 0$; if R does not change sign over the range of $\psi(c_2)$, that sign must be negative. We may then conclude that $\partial^2(U_1/U_2)/\partial c_2^2 \leqslant 0$ is consistent with endogenously diminishing absolute risk aversion.

(ii) *When perfect insurance markets do not exist*, then: if $\hat{c}_1 = c_1^\dagger$, the availability of insurance would definitely increase $\hat{c}_1$; if $\hat{c}_1 = c_1^*$, the availability of insurance would increase (decrease) $\hat{c}_1$ if the insurance prices were such that the consumer would buy (sell) some insurance on his whole future income.

The first proposition is immediate: new insurance opportunities could only raise expected utility, irrespective of the insurance prices; this would also raise $y_2^\dagger$, hence $c_1^\dagger$, hence $\hat{c}_1 = c_1^\dagger$. The second proposition can be verified as follows: To say that insurance becomes available at a price such that the consumer would buy some on his whole future income means that $EU_2(y_2 - z_2) < 0$, or $EU_2 y_2/EU_2 < z_2$ (where z_2 is still the insurance value of future income). Hence, y_2^* would increase from its present level to the level z_2, through insurance purchase, and $\hat{c}_1 = c_1^*$ would similarly rise. A similar reasoning applies to the selling case.[23]

(iii) In the absence of perfect markets for assets *and* insurance, separability of consumption and portfolio decision is rather implausible; actually, we do not know of any reasonable conditions under which that situation obtains.

Appendix A

Under certainty, the maximum of $U(c_1, c_2)$, under the budget constraint

$$c_2 = (y_1 - c_1)(1 + r) + y_2 \tag{A.1}$$

[23] The existence of markets with prices at which the consumer would *sell* insurance might seem remote, under generalized risk aversion. This remark is well-taken when the risks of different consumers or groups of consumers are sufficiently independent, or even negatively correlated, so that insurance can reduce everybody's risks simultaneously. On the other hand, when the risks of most consumers are strongly positively correlated, equality of supply and demand in the insurance markets calls for prices at which there will be sellers as well as buyers; the less risk-averse consumers will then be sellers: they will find it profitable to accept a greater variability of c_2 but will offset partly this added variability by reducing c_1 (for reasons indicated in Appendix D). In such cases, the organization of the insurance market need not stimulate total consumption.

is defined by the first- and second-order conditions

$$U_1 - U_2(1+r) = 0, \qquad U_{11} - 2U_{12}(1+r) + U_{22}(1+r)^2 < 0. \tag{A.2}$$

Let

$$S =_{\text{def}} U_2(U_{11} - 2U_{12}(1+r) + U_{22}(1+r)^2)^{-1} < 0. \tag{A.3}$$

Through total differentiation of the first-order condition in (A.2), we find

$$\frac{dc_1}{dy} = \frac{dc_1}{dy_1} = -S(1+r)\,\frac{\partial(U_1/U_2)}{\partial c_2},$$

$$\frac{dc_1}{dy_2} = S\,\frac{\partial(U_1/U_2)}{\partial c_2}, \qquad \text{where} \quad \frac{\partial(U_1/U_2)}{\partial c_2} = \frac{U_{12} - (U_1/U_2)\,U_{22}}{U_2}; \tag{A.4}$$

$$\begin{aligned} dc_1/dr &= ((y_1 - c_1)/(1+r))(dc_1/dy_1) + S \\ &= -S\left((y_1 - c_1)\,\frac{\partial(U_1/U_2)}{\partial c_2} - 1\right). \end{aligned} \tag{A.5}$$

In (A.5), $((y_1 - c_1)/(1+r))(dc_1/dy_1)$ measures the income effect, and $S\,(<0)$ the substitution effect, of a change in r on c_1. The absolute value of S is also a measure of curvature of the indifference surfaces:

$$-1/S = (d^2c_2/dc_1^{\,2})_U = (-1/U_2)(d^2U/dc_1^{\,2})_{U_1=U_2(1+r)}\,. \tag{A.6}$$

For any given values of r and $y = y_1 + y_2(1+r)^{-1}$, dc_1/dr is equal to 0 provided $y_1 = \hat{y}_1$ and $y_2 = (y - \hat{y}_1)(1+r)$, where

$$\hat{y}_1 = c_1 + \left(\frac{\partial(U_1/U_2)}{\partial c_2}\right)^{-1} > c_1\,. \tag{A.7}$$

One then finds that $(dc_2/dr)_{y_1=\hat{y}_1} = \hat{y}_1 - c_1 = (\partial(U_1/U_2)/\partial c_2)^{-1}$ and

$$\begin{aligned} \left.\frac{d^2c_1}{dr^2}\right|_{y_1=\hat{y}_1} &= \frac{\partial(dc_1/dr)}{\partial c_2}\,\frac{dc_2}{dr} = -S(\hat{y}_1 - c_1)\,\frac{\partial^2(U_1/U_2)}{\partial c_2^{\,2}} \\ &= -S\left(\frac{\partial(U_1/U_2)}{\partial c_2}\right)^{-1}\frac{\partial^2(U_1/U_2)}{\partial c_2^{\,2}}\,. \end{aligned} \tag{A.8}$$

This expression has the sign of $\partial^2(U_1/U_2)/\partial c_2^{\,2}$, where

$$\frac{\partial^2(U_1/U_2)}{\partial c_2^{\,2}} = \frac{U_{122} - (U_1/U_2)\,U_{222}}{U_2} - 2\,\frac{U_{22}}{U_2}\,\frac{\partial(U_1/U_2)}{\partial c_2}\,. \tag{A.9}$$

The indirect utility function $V(y, r)$ is defined by

$$V(y, r) = U(c_1(y, r), c_2(y, r) \mid U_1 = U_2(1+r)), \tag{A.10}$$

and its partial derivatives are evaluated by

$$\begin{aligned} V_y &= U_1(dc_1/dy) + U_2(dc_2/dy) \\ &= U_1(dc_1/dy) + U_2(1+r)(1-(dc_1/dy)) = U_2(1+r) = U_1\,, \\ V_r &= U_1(dc_1/dr) + U_2(dc_2/dr) \\ &= U_1(dc_1/dr) + U_2(y_1 - c_1 - (1+r)(dc_1/dr)) = U_2(y_1 - c_1). \end{aligned} \tag{A.11}$$

Proceeding further in this manner, one finds:

$$V_{yy} = U_{22}(1+r)^2 - (U_2/S)(dc_1/dy)^2 \geqslant U_{22}(1+r)^2; \tag{A.12}$$

$$V_{rr} = U_{22}(y_1 - c_1)^2 - (U_2/S)(dc_1/dr)^2 \geqslant U_{22}(y_1 - c_1)^2; \tag{A.13}$$

$$V_{ry} = U_{22}(1+r)(y_1 - c_1) - (U_2/S)(dc_1/dy)(dc_1/dr). \tag{A.14}$$

Since $dy/dy_2 = (1+r)^{-1}$, one may define $V_{y_2} = (1+r)^{-1} V_y = U_2$, $V_{y_2 y_2} = (1+r)^{-2} V_{yy}$, and write in view of (A.12)–(A.14):

$$\begin{aligned} -\frac{U_{22}}{U_2} &= -\frac{V_{y_2y_2}}{V_{y_2}} + \left(\frac{dc_1}{dy_2}\right)^2 \left(\frac{-1}{S}\right) \\ &= -\frac{V_{y_2y_2}}{V_{y_2}} + \left(\frac{dc_1}{dy_2}\right)^2 \left(\frac{d^2c_2}{dc_1^2}\Big|_U\right) \geqslant -\frac{V_{y_2y_2}}{V_{y_2}}, \\ -\frac{U_{22}}{U_2} &= -\frac{V_{rr}}{V_r(y_1 - c_1)} + \frac{1}{(y_1 - c_1)^2}\left(\frac{dc_1}{dr}\right)^2 \left(\frac{-1}{S}\right) \\ &= -\frac{V_{ry_2}}{V_r} + \frac{1}{y_1 - c_1}\frac{dc_1}{dy_2}\frac{dc_1}{dr}\left(\frac{-1}{S}\right). \end{aligned} \tag{A.15}$$

$-(U_{22}/U_2)$ is defined in the text as the absolute risk aversion function for future consumption. Its partial derivatives satisfy:

$$\begin{aligned} &\frac{\partial - (U_{22}/U_2)}{\partial c_1} - (1+r)\frac{\partial - (U_{22}/U_2)}{\partial c_2} \\ &= -\frac{U_{122} - (1+r)\,U_{222}}{U_2} + \frac{U_{22}}{U_2}\frac{U_{12} - (1+r)\,U_{22}}{U_2} \\ &= -\frac{\partial^2(U_1/U_2)}{\partial c_2^2} - \frac{U_{22}}{U_2}\frac{\partial(U_1/U_2)}{\partial c_2} + \left(\frac{U_1}{U_2} - (1+r)\right)\frac{\partial - (U_{22}/U_2)}{\partial c_2}, \end{aligned} \tag{A.16}$$

$$\begin{aligned} &\frac{\partial - (U_{22}/U_2)}{\partial c_1} - \frac{U_1}{U_2}\frac{\partial - (U_{22}/U_2)}{\partial c_2} \\ &= -\frac{U_{122} - (U_1/U_2)\,U_{222}}{U_2} + \frac{U_{22}}{U_2}\frac{U_{12} - (U_1/U_2)\,U_{22}}{U_2} \\ &= -\frac{\partial^2(U_1/U_2)}{\partial c_2^2} - \frac{U_{22}}{U_2}\frac{\partial(U_1/U_2)}{\partial c_2} \geqslant -\frac{\partial^2(U_1/U_2)}{\partial c_2^2}, \end{aligned} \tag{A.17}$$

as can be readily verified, starting from (A.9).

Appendix B[24]

Let $f(x, y)$ have the property that $f_x/f_y = a(x) + b(x)y$, $f_y \neq 0$. We wish to show that $f(x, y) = F(g(x) + h(x) \cdot y)$.

For $f(x, y) = \text{constant}$, we have $f_x + f_y y' = 0$, with $y' = dy/dx \,|_{f\,\text{constant}}$, or $y' = -(f_x/f_y)$, so that:

$$y' = -a(x) - b(x)y. \tag{B.1}$$

The solution of this ordinary differential equation is readily verified to be

$$y = e^{-B(x)}(-\textstyle\int a(x)\, e^{B(x)} dx + C), \tag{B.2}$$

where $B(x) = \int b(x)\, dx$; we may write (B.2) as

$$g(x) + h(x) \cdot y = c, \tag{B.3}$$

with $h(x) = e^{B(x)}$, $g(x) = \int a(x)\, e^{B(x)}\, dx$; since (B.3) is equivalent to "$f(x, y) = \text{constant}$," our hypothesis is verified.

Appendix C

Lemma C.1. *Let $h(x) = f\{g(x)\}$, where f is differentiable in g and g is continuous in x; let furthermore $\phi(x)$ be any density such that $\int h(x)\, d\Phi(x)$ and $\int g(x)\, d\Phi(x)$ exist and are finite. Define x^0 (not necessarily unique) implicitly by $\int g(x)\, d\Phi(x) = g(x^0)$. Then*

$$f\{g(x)\} \begin{matrix}\text{concave}\\ \text{linear}\\ \text{convex}\end{matrix} \text{ in } g \text{ over the range of } \phi \text{ implies } \int h(x)\, d\Phi(x) \begin{matrix}\leq\\ =\\ \geq\end{matrix} h(x^0).$$

Proof.

$$f\{g(x)\} \begin{matrix}\text{concave}\\ \text{linear}\\ \text{convex}\end{matrix} \text{ in } g \Rightarrow h(x) = f\{g(x)\}$$
$$\begin{matrix}\leq\\ =\\ \geq\end{matrix} f\{g(x^0)\} + \{g(x) - g(x^0)\} \cdot f'(g)|_{g(x^0)}\,.$$

This in turn implies

$$\int h(x)\, d\Phi(x) \begin{matrix}\leq\\ =\\ \geq\end{matrix} f\{g(x^0)\} + f'(g)|_{g(x^0)} \int \{g(x) - g(x^0)\}\, d\Phi(x)$$
$$= f\{g(x^0)\} = h(x^0),$$

since $\int \{g(x) - g(x^0)\}\, d\Phi(x)$ vanishes by definition of x^0. Q.E.D.

[24] We are grateful to Wlodzimierc Szwarc for this result.

LEMMA C.2. *Let* $h(x) = g(x) f(x)$, *where* f *is differentiable and* g *is continuous in* x, *let furthermore* $\phi(x)$ *be any density such that* $\int h(x)\, d\Phi(x)$, $\int g(x)\, d\Phi(x)$ *and* $\int x g(x)\, d\Phi(x)$ *exist and are finite. Define*

$$x^0 = \int x g(x)\, d\Phi(x) \Big/ \int g(x)\, d\Phi(x).$$

Then $f(x)$ $\begin{matrix}\text{concave}\\ \text{linear}\\ \text{convex}\end{matrix}$ *in* x *over the range of* ϕ *implies*

$$\int h(x)\, d\Phi(x) \begin{matrix}\leqslant\\ =\\ \geqslant\end{matrix} f(x^0) \int g(x) d\Phi(x).$$

Proof. $f(x)$ $\begin{matrix}\text{concave}\\ \text{linear}\\ \text{convex}\end{matrix}$ in $x \Rightarrow f(x) \begin{matrix}\leqslant\\ =\\ \geqslant\end{matrix} f(x^0) + (x - x^0) f'(x)|_{x^0}$.

This in turn implies:

$$\int h(x)\, d\Phi(x) \begin{matrix}\leqslant\\ =\\ \geqslant\end{matrix} f(x^0) \int g(x)\, d\Phi(x) + f'(x)|_{x^0} \cdot \int (x - x^0)\, g(x)\, d\Phi(x)$$

$$= f(x^0) \int g(x)\, d\Phi(x)$$

since $\int (x - x^0)\, g(x)\, d\Phi(x)$ vanishes by definition of x^0. Q.E.D.

APPENDIX D

Figure 1 may be helpful to illustrate the role of $\partial^2(U_1/U_2)/\partial c_2^2$ in our problem, as well as the way in which a reduction of c_1 is equivalent to a reduction in the risk about c_2.

In the figure, line I is the sure budget equation $c_2 = (y_1 - c_1)(1 + \bar{r}) + \bar{y}_2$ with slope $-(1 + \bar{r})$. The point $\bar{c}$ with coordinates $(\bar{c}_1, \bar{c}_2)$ represents the chosen point on this budget equation, and the rising line EE depicts the Engel curve through $\bar{c}$, drawn linear for graphical convenience. Now suppose $\bar{y}_2$ is replaced by a very simple uncertain prospect $\phi(y_2)$ in terms of which y_2 will assume the value $(\bar{y}_2 + \delta)$ or the value $(\bar{y}_2 - \delta)$ with equal probability. In the figure the lines labelled IIA and IIB represent the (mutually exclusive) budget equations corresponding to each of these alternatives. Suppose further that, when confronted with $\phi(y_2)$, the consumer wonders whether he should consume $\bar{c}_1$ or alternatively reduce his first period consumption from $\bar{c}_1$ to $c_1' = \bar{c}_1 - \epsilon$.

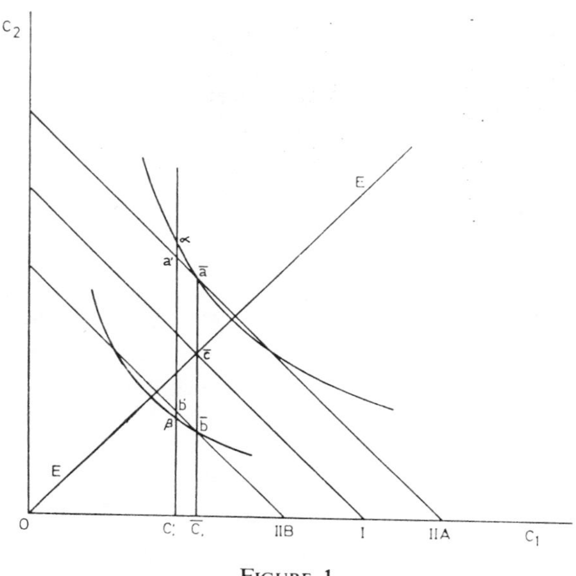

FIGURE 1

If the consumer stays at $\bar{c}_1$, we see from the figure that he will end up at the consumption points $\bar{a}$ or $\bar{b}$, with equal probability. Letting $\bar{a}$ and $\bar{b}$ denote also the c_2 coordinate of the corresponding points in the figure, the mutually exclusive and equally likely outcomes can be described by the two consumption vectors $(\bar{c}_1, \bar{a})$, $(\bar{c}_1, \bar{b})$ having expected utility: $\bar{U} = (1/2)(U(\bar{c}_1, \bar{a}) + U(\bar{c}_1, \bar{b}))$. Similarly, if he moves to c_1', we see that his expected utility can be expressed as $U' = (1/2)(U(c_1', a') + U(c_1', b'))$. To compare the two consumption decisions, first draw the indifference curve through $\bar{a}$ and let it intersect the line $c_1 = c_1'$ at the point α. Hence, by construction, $U(\bar{c}_1, \bar{a}) = U(c_1', \alpha)$. By drawing similarly the indifference curve through $\bar{b}$, we locate the point β such that $U(\bar{c}_1, \bar{b}) = U(c_1', \beta)$. Hence $\bar{U} = \frac{1}{2}(U(c_1', \alpha) + U(c_1', \beta))$. In other words, moving back from c_1' to $\bar{c}_1$ is entirely equivalent, in terms of $E(U)$, to remaining at c_1' but exchanging the random variable c_2' taking the values a' and b' with equal probability against a new random variable, call it γ_2, which takes the values α and β with equal probability. Thus our problem can be reduced to the question: Given c_1', is the prospect $\{c_2'\}$ better or worse than the prospect $\{\gamma^2\}$? One point is immediately apparent from Fig. 1: since $\beta < b' < a' < \alpha$, it follows that $\text{var}(\gamma_2) > \text{var}(c_2')$. In other words *increasing consumption* from c_1' to $\bar{c}_1$ has the effect of *increasing the variance* of the outcome. The reason is not far to seek. Increasing c_1 is equivalent to gearing current consumption more nearly to the higher income; this will produce an improvement *if* the larger y_2 obtains, but a deterioration if the smaller y_2 obtains. It will thus make things even brighter when they would be bright anyway and even more dismal if the worse turns out, hence it increases the variance of the outcome.[25] On this account then, if there is risk aversion, c_2' will be preferred to γ_2, and hence c_1' will be preferred to $\bar{c}_1$. Or, to put it differently, uncertainty tends to increase savings because the increase in savings has the effect of trimming the uncertainty of the outcome.

But this "variance effect" is not the end of the story: In choosing between the uncertain prospects $\{c_2'\}$ and $\{\gamma_2\}$, one must also compare their mean values.[26] If $\bar{\gamma}_2 = \frac{1}{2}(\alpha + \beta) < c_2' = \frac{1}{2}(a' + b')$, then c_2' dominates γ_2 in both respects and hence c_1' will be unequivocally preferred to $\bar{c}_1$ (even under risk indifference). But if the above inequality is reversed, then no definite conclusion can be reached. We will now show that the relation between $\bar{\gamma}_2$ and $\bar{c}_2'$ is precisely controlled by the sign of $\partial^2(U_1/U_2)/\partial c_2^2$.

To this end we first observe from Fig. 1 that the two mutually exclusive values of c_2', namely a' and b', can be expressed as follows:

$$a' = \bar{a} + \epsilon(1 + \bar{r}), \qquad b' = \bar{b} + \epsilon(1 + \bar{r}). \tag{D.1}$$

We further note that, for ϵ small, the slope of the chord joining the points $\bar{a}$ and α in the figure can be approximated by that of the indifference curve through $\bar{a}$, namely, $U_1(\bar{c}_1, \bar{a})/U_2(\bar{c}_1, \bar{a}) =_{\text{def}} (U_1/U_2)_{\bar{a}}$. Similarly, the slope of the chord joining $\bar{b}$ and β can be approximated by the slope of the indifference curve through $\bar{b}$, $(U_1/U_2)_{\bar{b}}$. We therefore have

$$\alpha \simeq \bar{a} + \epsilon(U_1/U_2)_{\bar{a}}, \qquad \beta \simeq \bar{b} + \epsilon(U_1/U_2)_{\bar{b}}. \tag{D.2}$$

Hence:

$$\begin{aligned} \bar{c}_2' - \bar{\gamma}_2 &\simeq \epsilon\left((1 + \bar{r}) - \frac{1}{2}\left(\frac{U_1}{U_2}\bigg|_{\bar{a}} + \frac{U_1}{U_2}\bigg|_{\bar{b}}\right)\right) \\ &= \epsilon\left(\frac{U_1}{U_2}\bigg|_{\bar{c}} - \frac{1}{2}\left(\frac{U_1}{U_2}\bigg|_{\bar{a}} + \frac{U_1}{U_2}\bigg|_{\bar{b}}\right)\right).^{27} \end{aligned} \tag{D.3}$$

Since $\bar{a}$ and $\bar{b}$ are symetrically located about $\bar{c}$, in the neighborhood of that point, it follows that

$$\frac{\partial^2(U_1/U_2)}{\partial c_2^2}\bigg|_{\bar{c}} \gtreqless 0 \Leftrightarrow \left\{\frac{1}{2}\left(\frac{U_1}{U_2}\bigg|_{\bar{a}} + \frac{U_1}{U_2}\bigg|_{\bar{b}}\right) \gtreqless \frac{U_1}{U_2}\bigg|_{\bar{c}=(a+b)/2}\right\} \Leftrightarrow \bar{c}_2' - \bar{\gamma}_2 \lesseqgtr 0. \tag{D.4}$$

[25] It can be verified from the figure that, for ϵ sufficiently small, the above conclusion must necessarily hold as long as the indifference curves are convex and the Engel curve has a finite positive slope. For an extension to more complicated densities, see Theorem 5.1 in [5].

[26] With infinitesimal risks, higher moments need not be considered.

[27] The last step follows from the fact that the point $\bar{c} = (c_1, c_2)$ is the point of tangency of the budget equation I with an indifference curve, hence at $\bar{c}$, the slope of the indifference curve $(U_1/U_2)_{\bar{c}}$ is precisely $(1 + \bar{r})$.

Accordingly, this "mean effect" will reinforce the "variance effect" whenever $\partial^2(U_1/U_2)/\partial c_2^2 \leqslant 0$, establishing unequivocally the superiority of c_1' over $\bar{c}_1$; but it will work in opposite direction when $\partial^2(U_1/U_2)/\partial c_2^2 > 0$. Theorem 3.3 may be interpreted as showing that the "variance effect" vanishes at c_1^*, through optimal choice of the prospect ϕ; the sign of $\hat{c}_1 - c_1^*$ is then determined by the "mean effect", i.e., by the sign of $\partial^2(U_1/U_2)/\partial c_2^2$.

REFERENCES

1. K. J. ARROW, Le rôle des valeurs boursières pour la répartition la meilleure des risques, *Econométrie* (1953), 41–48: English translation: The role of securities in the optimal allocation of risk bearing, *Rev. Econ. Studies* **31** (1964), 91–96.
2. K. J. ARROW, "Aspects of the Theory of Risk Bearing," Yrjö Jahnsson Foundation, Helsinki, 1965.
3. G. DEBREU, "Theory of Value," Wiley, New York, 1959.
4. J. DRÈZE, Market allocation under uncertainty, *European Econ. Rev.*, **2** (1971), 133–165.
5. J. DRÈZE AND F. MODIGLIANI, Epargne et consommation en avenir aléatoire, *Cah. Sém. Econ.* **9** (1966), 7–33.
6. I. FISHER, "Theory of Interest," Macmillan, New York, 1930.
7. J. HIRSHLEIFER, Investment decision under uncertainty: Choice theoretic approaches, *Quart. J. Econ.* **79** (1965), 509–536.
8. H. E. LELAND, Saving and uncertainty: The precautionary demand for saving, *Quart. J. Econ.* **82** (1968), 465–473.
9. J. MARSCHAK, Towards an economic theory of organization and information, in "Decision Processes" (Thrall, Coombs and Davis, Eds.), pp. 187–220, Wiley, New York, 1954.
10. L. J. MIRMAN, Uncertainty and optimal consumption decisions, *Econometrica* **39** (1971), 179–185.
11. P. PESTIEAU, Epargne et consommation dans l'incertitude: un modèle à trois périodes, *Recherches Economiques de Louvain* **2** (1969), 63–88.
12. J. W. PRATT, Risk aversion in the small and in the large, *Econometrica* **32** (1964), 122–136.
13. M. ROTHSCHILD AND J. E. STILGITZ, Increasing risk, I and II, *J. Econ. Theory* **2** (1970), 225–243; **3** (1971), 66–84.
14. A. SANDMO, The effect of uncertainty on saving decisions, *Rev. Econ. Studies* **37** (1970), 353–360.
15. L. J. SAVAGE, "The Foundations of Statistics," Wiley, New York, 1954.
16. J. VON NEUMANN AND O. MORGENSTERN, "Theory of Games and Economic Behavior," Princeton University Press, Princeton, 1944.

Printed by the St Catherine Press Ltd., Tempelhof 37, Bruges, Belgium.

Errata

Page 320, footnote 19, line 2: "$\hat{c}$, is still the optimal level" should read "$\hat{c}_1$ is still the optimal level."

Page 323, 2 lines from the bottom: equation should read "$-U_{22}(\hat{c}_1, c_2)/U_2(\hat{c}_1, c_2)$."

Page 325, line 9: after the second equality sign equation should read

$$\text{"}f''(U)\cdot U_2^2 + f'(U)\cdot U_{22}.\text{"}$$

Pages 326–328, sections 4.4 and 4.5: whenever "R" appears, including equation (4.8), it should be replaced by "$-R$."

Page 327, section 4.5, line 6: the left-hand side of the equation should read "$\max_{c_1} E_r\, U(c_1, (y_1 - c_1)(1 + r) + y_2^{00})$."

Page 329, line 7: "$\frac{dc_1}{dy_2} = S \frac{\partial(U_1/U_2)}{\partial c_2}$" should read "$\frac{dc_1}{dy_2} = -S \frac{\partial(U_1/U_2)}{\partial c_2}$."

Page 333, 6 lines from the bottom: "prospect $\{\gamma^2\}$ "should read "prospect $\{_2\}$."

Page 334, equation (D.4): the term "$\frac{U_1}{U_2}\Big|\bar{c} = (a + b)/2$" should read "$\frac{U_1}{U_2}\Big|\bar{c} = (\bar{a} + \bar{b})/2$."

PART III
Empirical Verifications

THE "PERMANENT INCOME" AND THE "LIFE CYCLE" HYPOTHESIS OF SAVING BEHAVIOR: COMPARISON AND TESTS*

Franco Modigliani
Carnegie Institute of Technology
and
Albert Ando
Massachusetts Institute of Technology

II — A RESTATEMENT OF FRIEDMAN'S "PERMANENT INCOME HYPOTHESIS" AND MODIGLIANI-BRUMBERG'S "LIFE CYCLE MODEL" AND THEIR CROSS-SECTIONAL IMPLICATIONS

II.1. Introduction: Purpose of This Section

Since publication of the article by Modigliani-Brumberg [19] and of the book by Friedman [9], more than a half decade has elapsed, and a number of empirical works have appeared which aim at testing the hypotheses formulated in these contributions. In our opinion, despite the ingenuity and the high degree of competence with which these tests have been carried out, they have been at best inconclusive. In retrospect, there are good reasons for this frustrating experience. The basic hypotheses of both Modigliani-Brumberg and of Friedman are stated in terms of unobservable magnitudes, such as permanent income and the total resources available to a household over its life span. Thus, in order to carry out satisfactory empirical tests it is necessary to derive from these hypotheses implications concerning the relations between variables which can be observed, and have actually been measured, in the empirical studies available to those attempting the tests of these hypotheses. This is a difficult task frequently requiring the introduction of further specification which cannot be directly derived from the basic model itself. The original authors in their papers did attempt to provide some testable propositions in terms of the available data but the subsequent empirical works proved their effort inadequate. This is especially true for the Modigliani-Brumberg hypothesis, since these authors did not devote as much attention as Friedman to the task of bridging the gap between the concepts of the pure theory and measurable magnitudes.

Finally, the fact that the two models have many common elements that distinguish them sharply from the previously accepted framework has tended to obscure the many important differences between the two theories. This in turn has made it difficult to sift out those tests which are relevant to both hypotheses from those which properly apply to only one.

The task we propose to carry out in this section is to provide a systematic comparison of the essential aspects of the Friedman [9] hypothesis and of the hypothesis first presented by Modigliani and Brumberg [19] and later elaborated by the present authors [17]. The latter model will be referred to hereafter for brevity as the M-B-A hypothesis. In carrying out this comparison we shall devote particular attention to bringing out explicitly implications of these hypotheses which are capable of being tested by means of data such as those provided by the BLS-Wharton Study. The results of several such tests will then be presented in Section III, while in the final section further promising tests will be outlined some of which we are already in the process of carrying out.

74

II.2. Fundamental Propositions

The point of departure of both models, as we see it, can be paraphrased—if only loosely—in terms of the following three basic propositions:

(i) The "scale of living" or in Friedman's terminology, the "permanent level of consumption," adopted by a household is determined by their perception of their current and prospective resources.

(ii) The actual consumption expenditure of the household over some arbitrary interval of time, such as a month or a year, will tend to fluctuate around the permanent level of consumption, or, equivalently, is determined by the permanent level of consumption up to a stochastic component. The statistical properties of this stochastic component will depend to an important extent on the length of the period over which we measure consumption as well as on our definition of consumption expenditure—e.g., whether we define it more nearly on a cash or on an accrual basis. Actual consumption may of course differ from reported or "measured" consumption because of errors of measurement *strictu sensu*.

(iii) The income received by the household over some arbitrary interval of time will obviously bear some relation to the overall level of resources to which the standard of living is anchored. Because both income and consumption are thus related to the underlying level of resources, we can expect these two variables to be systematically related. But to understand the nature of this relation, we must remember that current measured income is only an indirect measure of the true determinant of consumption, and unavoidably subject to considerable error.

These three propositions, we believe, are by now broadly acceptable to the majority of students of saving behavior even though their implications, some of which will be spelled out presently, are frequently not fully appreciated.

Before proceeding further, it will be useful to restate our three propositions in more formal language as follows:

Proposition (i)

$$\tilde{c} = F(x) \tag{2.1}$$

where $\tilde{c}$ denotes "permanent consumption" and x the level of current and prospective resources.

Proposition (ii)

$$c = \tilde{c} + \text{stochastic components} \tag{2.2}$$

where c denotes current measured consumption expenditure.

75

Proposition (iii)

$$y = G(x) + \text{stochastic component} \tag{2.3}$$

where y denotes current measured income.

(iv) In addition to the above propositions the Friedman and M-B-A model share in common a fourth hypothesis which we feel is the really controversial one. This is the hypothesis that the function F(x) defined in (2.1) takes (at least approximately) the specific form

$$F(x) = kx \tag{2.4}$$

where k is a proportionality factor which, as we shall see, may depend on various characteristics of the household but is independent of x (given these characteristics). In other words according to both models the ratio of permanent consumption to the level of resources should tend to be the same at all levels of resources. While this proposition is in a very real sense the essence of the Friedman model, it is less essential to the M-B-A construction. As will be indicated below, it could be relaxed, by making explicit allowance for the inheritance motive, with the effect of reducing but not destroying altogether the empirical content of the M-B-A model.

By substituting (2.4) into (2.2) we obtain

$$c = kx + \text{stochastic component} \tag{2.5}$$

which is the basic hypothesis of the Friedman model and one of the major implications of the M-B-A model in its simplest version.

II.3. The Relation between Measured and Permanent Consumption

In order to explore the empirical implications of (2.5), it is necessary to formulate some specifications about the nature of the stochastic component and to spell out more explicitly the interpretation of the non-observable variable x.

The error term in (2.5) is by assumption uncorrelated with x, but in addition, it seems reasonable to suppose that its absolute size is roughly proportional to the magnitude of x, suggesting a relation of the form

$$c = \tilde{c}\, u' = kxu' = kx(1 + u^*) \tag{2.6}$$

where

$$E(u') = 1;\ E(u^*) = 0;\ E(u^*x) = 0,\ \text{var}(u') = \text{var}(u^*) \tag{2.6a}$$

76

For some purposes we shall also find it convenient to assume—though this is not strictly essential—that the error component u' has a log-normal distribution.

Using capital letters to denote the logarithm of the quantity represented by the corresponding lower case letter, from (2.6) we derive

$$C = K + X + U'\text{[29]} \qquad (2.7)$$

By our previous assumption, the error component U' is normally distributed: its expected value, however, is not zero. It can be shown that the following relations obtain between the first two moments of the distribution of a log-normally distributed variable s and of its logarithm, S.[30]

$$E(S) = \ln[E(s)] - (1/2)\,\text{var}\,(S) \qquad (2.8a)$$

$$\text{var}\,(S) = \ln[1 + \frac{\text{var}(s)}{[E(s)]^2}] \qquad (2.8b)$$

where ln denotes the natural logarithm. Hence

$$E(U') = \ln E(u') - 1/2\,\text{var}(U') = -\,1/2\,\text{var}(U')$$

Defining for simplicity

$$\bar{\bar{U}}' \equiv E(U') \qquad (2.9a)$$

$$U \equiv U' - \bar{\bar{U}}', \qquad (2.9b)$$

we can finally write (2.7) as

$$C = (K + \bar{\bar{U}}') + X + U;\ E(U) = 0,\ E(UX) = 0 \qquad (2.10)$$

which states that, according to both models, the log of consumption is a linear function of the log of x, with unit slope (elasticity) and intercept depending both on the marginal (and average) propensity to consume, k, and the variability of the error term.

We must proceed next to the specification of the variable x, and it is at this point that significant differences emerge between the Friedman and the M-B-A formulations.

---

[29] The reader is reminded that in Parts II and III of this paper, the capital letters represent the logarithms of the variables denoted by the corresponding lower case letters, while in Part I, the capital letters represented the ratio to income of the variables denoted by the corresponding lower case letters.

[30] See Aitchison and Brown [1].

77

II.4. Friedman's "Permanent Income"

For Friedman, the variable x is the permanent component of income, a term that has a very specific meaning in his formulation. He observes that each household possesses an array of assets, human and non-human, from which it expects to receive streams of returns. For each stream, the household is assumed to have some appropriate rate of discount, not necessarily the same for different types of assets. For example, for those assets for which there exist active markets the subjective discount rates might be equal to the prevailing market rates of return on the respective assets. In the case of other assets for which there is no active market, particularly for human wealth, the discount rate is completely subjective and may be quite high. In fact, Friedman has suggested that this value might be as high as 33.3 per cent a year. The sum of the present values of these future streams of income is the total wealth of the household. By multiplying the present values of the future stream from each asset by its respective discount rates and summing up, we get the permanent income as Friedman defines it. Thus, according to Friedman [8]

$$x = \sum_j i_j \sum_{\tau=1}^{\infty} \frac{y_\tau^j}{(1+i_j)^{\tau-1}} \tag{2.11}$$

where y_τ^j is the expected return from the jth asset during the τth future period, and i_j is the subjective discount rate appropriate for the jth asset.

II.5. Total Resources and the Life Cycle in the M-B-A Model

According to the M-B-A hypothesis, on the other hand, consumption (or more precisely the systematic component thereof) over a given interval reflects the household's decision as to the most desirable allocation over time of the total value of resources available for consumption over life. Hence, in the most general formulation, the x of equations (2.1) - (2.4) can be defined as the amount available for consumption over life, which is the sum of the household's net worth at the beginning of the period, denoted by a, plus the present value of its non-property income, w, minus present value of planned bequests, q. If we further denote by y_τ^ℓ the expected non-property income at age τ, the present value of non-property income, for a household of age t, can be written as

$$w_t = \sum_{\tau=t}^{N} \frac{y_\tau^\ell}{(1+i)^{\tau+1-t}} \tag{2.12}$$

where N is the expected retirement age and i is again a measure of the yield of assets.

In line with this definition of x, the coefficient k of equation (2.4) represents the proportion of total resources x allocated to consumption within the span of time covered by the variable c. The value of k may be expected to differ as between different households because of differences in tastes and other circumstances (see below). But the model postulates that the value of k chosen by the household is uncorrelated with x, given the age of the household. Translated in more explicit behavioral terms, this assumption states that the proportion of total life consumption allotted by a household to a given interval of time is uncorrelated with the size of the household's life consumption.

In the simplest version of the model it is further assumed that the value of planned bequests, q, is of negligible magnitude as compared with (w + a) (or, alternatively, that the ratio of q to (w + a) is independent of (w + a)[31]. Under this further assumption equation (2.5) for the M-B-A model can be written in the specific form

$$c = k_t^* x_t + \text{stochastic component} \tag{2.13}$$

where

$$x_t = w_t + a_t, \tag{2.14}$$

and the stochastic component, reflecting interhousehold variations in k_t^*, as well as transitory consumption is uncorrelated with x_t. Two points should be noted in connection with these equations. In the first place, the proportionality factor in (2.13) differs in one important respect from the corresponding k of the Friedman model. In that model both c and x are flows and hence k is a pure number. In the M-B-A model, on the other hand, x is a stock and hence the proportionality factor has dimension (1/time); its value will depend on the length of time covered by the variable c. For this reason we have labelled it k* rather than k, and we shall continue to use the asterisk superscript whenever this difference in interpretation is of consequence. The second point to be noted is our explicit reference to the age of the household through the use of an age subscript in (2.13) and (2.14). The reason for doing so is that, in general, both k* and (w + a) may be expected to change systematically with age—the association being positive for k* and negative for (w + a).

That (w + a) will on the whole tend to fall with age should be self-evident, at least as long as bequests can be ignored. As for k* the association with age results from the fact that the household's choice of a consumption plan over the balance of life is limited by the budget constraint: the sum of the amounts allocated to every

[31] For an analysis of the effect of dropping this assumption see section II.11 below.

79

remaining "year" τ properly discounted must add up to the present value of resources available, x_t. If we denote by L the expected life span, and by $k_\tau^*(t)$ the proportion of x_t slated for consumption at age τ, $\tau = t + 1, t + 2, \ldots, L$, then the budget constraint implies

$$k_t^*(t) + \sum_{\tau=t+1}^{L} \frac{k_\tau^*(t)}{(1+i)^{\tau-t}} = 1 \qquad (2.15)$$[32]

The implication of this constraint can be most easily grasped by considering the special case where the household prefers an even rate of consumption over the balance of his life (i.e., $k_\tau^*(t) = k_t^*$ for all τ) and the rate of return i is taken as zero. Then k_τ^* becomes $1/(L+1-t)$, i.e., it is the reciprocal of the number of remaining years of life, and therefore must rise continuously with age t. But this conclusion will tend to hold as well if we take into account the yield of assets and if we replace the assumption of a constant planned rate of consumption with any other reasonable assumption; indeed it could fail to hold only if the consumption plan called for a rate of consumption falling rapidly over life.[33]

Besides age there are other characteristics that may be expected to affect k_t^* in a systematic fashion. One that is particularly worth mentioning is current and prospective family size. The effect of this variable can again be most easily grasped by considering the special case where the consumption plan calls for a constant rate of expenditure per equivalent adult. Let J(j) denote the adult equivalent consumption index; i.e., J(j)Z is the amount that a family of size j needs to spend in order to maintain the same standard of living as a one-person family spending Z. Let j_τ denote expected family size at age τ; then the coefficient k_t^* becomes $J(j_t)/\sum_{\tau=t}^{L} J(j_\tau)$.[34] In reality the index J(j) may depend also on the age composition of the household members, the number of full-time earners and on specific needs associated with specific stages of the family cycle, such as educational needs for children. These needs in turn may interact with other characteristics such as occupation and/or

---

[32] If we drop the assumption that planned bequests are negligible, we only need to extend the summation in (2.15) to L + 1 and interpret $k^*_{L+1}(t)$ as the ratio of planned bequests to x_t.

[33] To be precise, for any given household the proportion of resources devoted to current consumption, k_t^*, must rise monotonically with t, as long as its tastes as to the allocation of consumption over life are unchanged.

[34] This result holds under the assumption of zero return on capital. Otherwise the summation in the denominator becomes the present value of the number of equivalent adults.

80

education of the family head.[35] However, there is no need to develop further at this point a comprehensive analysis of the factors that may be expected to affect systematically the coefficient k^* within the M-B-A model. What has been said should be sufficient to indicate how inferences about the behavior of k^* can be derived from the basic proposition that consumption in any given interval is controlled by a broad life plan rather than by current income; and that saving (or dissaving)—i.e., $y - c$—over an interval, which is short in relation to the life span, is in the nature of a residual whose function it is to reconcile the life pattern of income with the preferred life pattern of consumption.

II.6. The Relation Between Measured Consumption and Income Implied by the Friedman Hypothesis

We have now completed our first task, restating and comparing the Friedman model and the M-B-A model in its simplest version. Though different definitions are attributed by the two models to the variable x, this variable, under either definition, has never been measured, and indeed may forever defy meaningful measurement. Hence, at least for the moment, the test of these hypotheses must rely on their implications as to the relation among observed variables, such as current income and current consumption.

We may begin by considering implications for the relation between current measured consumption c and current measured income y, which has attracted so much attention in recent years. In order to attack this question we need in turn to consider the relation between y and x—i.e., the nature of equation (2.3). Friedman explicitly specifies (a) that this relation takes the form

$$y = x + \text{stochastic component} \tag{2.16}$$

and (b) that the stochastic component, which he labels "the transitory component of income," is uncorrelated with x, the "permanent component of income.[36,37] These two specifications may appropriately be regarded as an integral part of Friedman's hypothesis,

---

[35] Because of this interaction and the further association between lifetime earnings and occupational-educational characteristics, it is conceivable that for certain classes there might arise a correlation between k^* and $(w + a)$; but the independence of k^* from $(w + a)$ is still postulated to hold within age-occupation-education cells. Note furthermore that if the above correlation is positive within some age groups, then it should be negative for other age groups, because of the overall constraint (2.15).

[36] Friedman, [9], pp. 25-30.

[37] The coefficient of x in (2.16) could be made different from unity without affecting the remainder of the argument in a significant

(Continued)

81

for in view of the non-measurability of x, it is these two further postulates that give empirical content to his model. Various writers have questioned the consistency of his second specification with his definition of permanent and transitory income. In his comment published in the present volume, Friedman has provided a rebuttal to this criticism.

It seems once more reasonable to suppose that the error component in (2.16) will tend to be proportional to x, and to rewrite therefore this equation in the more specific form

$$y = xv' = x(1 + v^*);\ E(v') = 1,\ E(v^*) = 0,\ E(v^*x) = 0 \qquad (2.17)$$

In addition, it will be convenient, though not essential, to assume that v' has a log normal distribution.[38] If this is done, making use of relations indicated in (2.8), we have

$$Y = X + V' = \bar{\bar{V}}' + X + V,\ E(V) = 0,\ E(VX) = 0 \qquad (2.18)$$

were $\bar{\bar{V}}'$ and V are defined by

$$\bar{\bar{V}}' \equiv E(V') = -\ 1/2 \text{ var } (V') \qquad (2.18a)$$

$$V = V' - \bar{\bar{V}}' \qquad (2.18b)$$

Friedman also assumes that the correlation between transitory income and transitory consumption is strictly zero, i.e.,

$$E(VU) = 0 \qquad (2.19)$$

Friedman seems to be very much attached to this further specification and argues most elequently for its defense in this volume. In our view, the status and role of the assumption (2.19) must be regarded as quite different from those of the assumptions we have reviewed so far. We shall show presently that (2.19) is not necessary to give empirical content to the model; indeed many important implications will hold whether or not (2.19) is satisfied.[39] This does not mean that this assumption is devoid of empirical

---

(Continued)

way. In fact, however, from Friedman's definition of x we should expect this coefficient to be close to unity, through it might be somewhat lower or somewhat larger than unity depending on whether the year under consideration was an unusually depressed or prosperous one.

[38] Since Y is known to be approximately normal, X must be normal if V is normal.

[39] See Section II.10 below.

82

content; it will be found that in principle this further hypothesis could be tested separately from the others, although in practice adequate tests are likely to be very hard to design.

For the moment, we shall accept this hypothesis for convenience of exposition, and only for convenience of exposition, until the argument has been sufficiently developed.

From equations (2.10), (2.18) and (2.19) we can readily derive the implication of the Friedman model as to the relation between C and Y. Let equation (2.18) be considered the regression equation of Y on X. Then we have, by the assumptions contained in (2.18), cov (X,Y)/var (X) = 1. If we run the regression of X on Y, on the other hand, we have

$$X = \beta_o + \beta_1 Y + V''; \; E(V'') = 0 \qquad (2.20)$$

where

$$\beta_1 = \frac{\text{cov}(X,Y)}{\text{var}(Y)} = \frac{[\text{cov}(X,Y)]^2}{\text{var}(Y)\,\text{var}(X)} \frac{\text{var}(X)}{\text{cov}(X,Y)} = r^2_{XY} \qquad (2.21)$$

$$\begin{aligned} \beta_o &= E(X) - \beta_1 E(Y) = (1 - \beta_1) E(Y) - \bar{\bar{V}}' \\ &= (1 - r^2_{XY}) E(Y) - \bar{\bar{V}}' \end{aligned} \qquad (2.21a)$$

We shall again assume, though this is not essential, that V'' is normally distributed.

Note also

$$\begin{aligned} r^2_{XY} &= \frac{[\text{cov}(X,Y)]^2}{\text{var}(X)\,\text{var}(Y)} = \frac{[\text{cov}(X,Y)]^2}{[\text{var}(X)]^2} \frac{\text{var}(X)}{\text{var}(Y)} \\ &= \frac{\text{var}(X)}{\text{var}(Y)} = \frac{\text{var}(X)}{\text{var}(X) + \text{var}(V)} \end{aligned} \qquad (2.21b)$$

Substituting (2.20) into (2.10), we get

$$\begin{aligned} C &= (K + \bar{\bar{U}} + \beta_o) + \beta_1 Y + V'' + U \\ &= b_o + b_Y Y + \omega; \; E(\omega) = 0 \end{aligned} \qquad (2.22)$$

In addition, if and only if (2.19) holds, then it follows that ω has the further characteristic

$$E(Y\omega) = 0 \qquad (2.22a)$$

and hence the regression coefficient of C on Y is in fact b_y.

83

Thus, the Friedman hypothesis, as embodied in equations (2.10), (2.18) and (2.19), implies that the regression of log consumption on log income should be linear, or, stated more loosely, that the relation between current consumption and current income should be linear in the logarithms. Also as long as there are any discrepancies between current measured income and permanent income—possibly arising in part from sheer error of measurement—the slope of this logarithmic regression equation, or elasticity of consumption with respect to income, will be less than unity. More generally, the elasticity will be smaller the larger the variability of the transitory relative to the variability of the permanent component of income, or equivalently, the smaller r^2_{XY}, the correlation between current measured income and the permanent component of income. Note that, since the log of the permanent component of consumption is $\tilde{C} = K + X$, and the correlation between Y and K + X is the same as that between Y and X, we have $r^2_{XY} = r^2_{\tilde{C}Y}$. Thus, we can also say that the elasticity is determined by the correlation between current measured income and the permanent component of consumption. The relevance of this alternative interpretation will soon become apparent.

The result expressed in (2.22) can be reached by an alternative approach that will prove useful in the analysis to follow. Supposing equations (2.10) and (2.18) hold, we wish to derive from them the population regression of C on Y, given by (2.22) expressing the parameters b_o and b_y in terms of the parameters of (2.10) and (2.18).

Now we know that

$$b_y = \frac{\text{cov}(C,Y)}{\text{var}(Y)}$$

and from (2.10) and (2.18)

$$C - E(C) = X - E(X) + U; \; Y - E(Y) = X - E(X) + V$$

Hence

$$b_y = \frac{\text{cov}[(X + U), (X + V)]}{\text{var}\,(X + V)} = \frac{\text{var}\,(X) + \text{cov}(U,V)}{\text{var}(X) + \text{var}(V)} \qquad (2.21')$$

If in addition, (2.19) holds, then this result simplifies to

$$b_y = \frac{\text{var}(X)}{\text{var}(X) + \text{var}(V)} = \frac{\text{var}(X)}{\text{var}(Y)} = r^2_{XY} = \beta_1 \qquad (2.23a)$$

Similarly we find

$$\begin{aligned} b_o &= E(C) - b_y\, E(Y) = (K + \overline{\overline{U}}') + \overline{X} - b_y\, \overline{Y} \\ &= K + \overline{\overline{U}}' + (1 - r^2_{XY})\, E(Y) - \overline{\overline{V}}' = K + \overline{\overline{U}}' + \beta_o \end{aligned} \qquad (2.23b)$$

84

Thus our alternative approach leads to results identical to the original approach without any special assumptions about the distribution of the error terms other than those embodied in (2.10) and (2.18).[40]

II.7. The Relation Between Measured Consumption and Income Implied by the M-B-A Hypothesis

We have now established the implications of the Friedman model as to the relation between current measured consumption and income. Before examining these results more closely, we will try to show that the M-B-A model, at least in its simplest version, has very similar implications: that is, the relation between the measured variables c and y is again of the form (2.22) and the regression coefficient b_y is again determined by the value of r^2_{CY}. Unfortunately this task will prove considerably more tedious than for the Friedman model. In part this results from the greater complexity of the M-B-A model. More importantly, however, Friedman's definition of the variable x, it would appear, was intentionally designed to bear a simple relation to the observables, whereas in the M-B-A model the definition of this variable is determined by the basic postulate of life time planning. The reader who is not interested in details of proofs may wish to accept our statement on faith and proceed directly to the next section.

In the M-B-A model the basic determinant of consumption is given by equation (2.13). Assuming again a multiplicative error component, this equation can be stated in the form (2.6) or (2.10). However, the constant k must now be regarded as varying systematically with age and certain other characteristics (though not directly with x); and the definition of x (in the simplest version) is given by (2.14).

Also, y, current measured income, can be written as

$$y = y^{\ell} + y^{n\ell} \tag{2.24}$$

where y^{ℓ} and $y^{n\ell}$ denote respectively measured non-property and property income. The latter quantity will clearly be related to a, and we may hypothesize a relation of the type

$$y^{n\ell} = i\, a\ (1 + \epsilon_1);\ E(\epsilon_1) = 0 \tag{2.25}$$

[40]It will be recognized that in this alternative approach we are in effect treating the error component V as an error of measurement in the "independent" variable X of equation (2.10).

85

To see what (2.13) - (2.14) and (2.24) - (2.25) imply as to the relation between y and x, let us limit ourselves first to the highly idealized case where all the households in our sample have the same age, and identical life pattern of income and consumption—both past and prospective—differing only in aggregate resources and, hence, in the level of consumption. In addition, let us for the next paragraphs assume that all error terms are identically zero.

Our assumption about the life pattern of income clearly implies

$$y^{\ell} = D_y w \tag{2.26a}$$

where D_y is a constant having the same value for all households. If we next use the assumption about the life pattern of consumption and supplement it with the assumption that the return on assets is the same (and has been the same) for all households, we can similarly deduce

$$a = D_a w \tag{2.26b}$$

Substituting these results into (2.24) and remembering (2.25), (2.14) and (2.13) we find

$$\begin{aligned} y &= D_y w + iD_a w = (D_y + iD_a) w = (D_y + iD_a) \frac{w}{w+a} x \\ &= \frac{D_y + iD_a}{1 + D_a} x = \frac{D_y + iD_a}{k^*(1 + D_a)} k^* x = \frac{D_y + iD_a}{k^*(1 + D_a)} c \end{aligned} \tag{2.27}$$

or

$$c = ky; \tag{2.27a}$$

$$k = \frac{k^* (1 + D_a)}{D_y + iD_a} \tag{2.27b}$$

That is, according to the M-B-A hypothesis, for such a "stationary" group of households c would be strictly proportional to current income y.[41]

Every one of the coefficients making up the proportionality factor k (except i) would of course depend on the age of the group under consideration, the association being generally positive, as can be readily verified.[42] They would further depend on the specific

[41] Note that since the coefficient of k* in the right hand side of (2.27b) has dimension time, the coefficient of proportionality k is a pure number, just as in the Friedman model.

[42] The only possible exception to this statement relates to the coefficient D_a, for in the early phases of life net worth might conceivably be negative and decrease with age.

86

cycle of consumption and income. If we suppose the prevailing tastes to call for a relatively stable rate of consumption per equivalent adult over life, the interplay of these coefficients will be such as to cause the overall proportionality factor k to be high in those phases of the life cycle where income is below average and family size above average, and conversely. It can be verified, however, that for life patterns of income and family size that are consistent with the empirical evidence the overall proportionality could be expected to fluctuate within relatively narrow limits over the life cycle, not departing radically from unity.[43]

It is of course impossible to locate groups of households having identical life cycles. It is, however, possible to classify all households of a given age into groups which may be expected to have similar life cycle, by relying on characteristics such as education, occupation, and family size which are known to be strongly associated with the life cycle of income and family needs. For each such group, equations (2.26) may be expected to hold but in stochastic form. Thus

$$y^{\ell} = D_y w(1 + \epsilon_2); \; a = D_a w(1 + \epsilon_3) \tag{2.28}$$

$$E(\epsilon_2) = E(\epsilon_3) = E(\epsilon_2 w) = E(\epsilon_3 w) = E(\epsilon_1 \epsilon_3) = 0 \tag{2.28a}$$

Substituting these equations and (2.25) into (2.24) we find:

$$\begin{aligned} y &= [D_y(1+\epsilon_2) + iD_a(1+\epsilon_1)(1+\epsilon_3)]\frac{w}{w+a}x \qquad (2.29)\\ &= \frac{(D_y+iD_a)\,(1+\eta_1)}{(1+D_a)\,(1+\eta_2)}\,x \end{aligned}$$

where

$$\eta_1 = \frac{D_y \epsilon_2 + iD_a(\epsilon_1 + \epsilon_3 + \epsilon_1\epsilon_3)}{D_y + iD_a}, \; E(\eta_1) = 0 \tag{2.29a}$$

$$\eta_2 = \frac{D_a \epsilon_3}{1+D_a}, \; E(\eta_2) = 0 \tag{2.29b}$$

Recalling further that, by hypothesis, the permanent component of consumption is $\tilde{c} = kx$, (2.29) can be rewritten as

$$y = \frac{D_y + iD_a}{k^* (1+D_a)}\tilde{c}\left[\frac{1+\eta_1}{1+\eta_2}\right] = \frac{1}{k}\,\tilde{c}\,v_1' \tag{2.30}$$

---

[43]Modigliani and Ando [17].

where

$$v_1' = \frac{1+\eta_1}{1+\eta_2} \tag{2.30a}$$

and k is defined by (2.27b).

If we let

$$V_1' = \ln v_1' = \ln(1+\eta_1) - \ln(1+\eta_2),$$

and

$$E(V_1') = \bar{\bar{V}}_1, \; V = V_1' - \bar{\bar{V}}_1,$$

then (2.30) can be expressed as

$$Y = -\ln k + \tilde{C} + V_1' = (-K + \bar{\bar{V}}_1) + \tilde{C} + V_1 \tag{2.31}$$

where

$$E(V_1\tilde{C}) \simeq 0.\text{[44]}$$

V_1 in (2.31) performs a function equivalent to that of V in (2.18) (Friedman's transitory component of income), and we shall generally omit the subscript of V_1 in what follows. However, it should be remembered that, conceptually, V and V_1 are quite different from each other, as is quite obvious from their derivations above.

With the help of (2.31) and (2.10) we can now exhibit the parameters of the regression equation of C on Y. For the regression coefficient, again denoted by b_y, we have

$$b_y = \frac{\text{cov}(C,Y)}{\text{var}(Y)} = \frac{\text{cov}(\tilde{C}+U,\ \tilde{C}+V)}{\text{var}(\tilde{C}+V)} = \frac{\text{var}(\tilde{C})+\text{cov}(U,V)}{\text{var}(\tilde{C})+\text{var}(V)} \tag{2.32}$$

$$= r^2_{\tilde{C}Y} + \frac{\text{cov}(U,V)}{\text{var}(Y)}$$

---

[44] We cannot assume $E(V_1C) = 0$, because $\tilde{C}$ is proportional to $(w + a)$ and a in turn is necessarily positively correlated with ϵ_3 --cf. equation (2.28)--which is a component of both η_1 and η_2. However (i) we can expect the correlation between a and η_1 and a and η_2 to be rather small, (ii) the correlation between V_1 and a can be expected to be even smaller since η_1 and η_2 affect V_1 in opposite direction, (iii) a is only a component of (w + a) and there is no reason to expect any correlation between w and η_1 or η_2. On the whole, therefore, the assumption $E(V\tilde{C}) \simeq 0$ does not seem unreasonable.

If we follow Friedman for the moment in assuming $E(UV)=O$, then we see that the M-B-A model, just like the Friedman one, implies

$$b_y = r^2_{\tilde{C}Y} \tag{2.32a}$$

i.e., the regression coefficient of C on Y is determined by the correlation between current measured income and the permanent component of consumption.

Proceeding to evaluate the constant term of the regression equation, b_o, we find

$$b_o = E(C) - b_y E(Y) = E(\tilde{C}) + \bar{\bar{U}}' - b_y E(Y)$$

Noting that (2.31) implies

$$E(\tilde{C}) = K - \bar{\bar{V}}_1 + E(Y)$$

we obtain

$$b_o = K + \bar{\bar{U}}' - \bar{\bar{V}}_1 + (1 - b_y) E(Y) \tag{2.33}$$

Thus, the M-B-A model implies that within a homogeneous cell the relation between C and Y is of the form (2.22); i.e.,

$$C = b_o + b_y Y + \omega^* \tag{2.22}$$

with b_o and b_y given respectively by (2.33) and (2.32). From these equations we see once more that, for a "stationary" group where all the error terms are zero, b_y is unity, b_o is K and the regression equation reduces to

$$C = K + Y, \text{ or } c = ky$$

which is precisely the result of equation (2.27). The presence of errors has the effect of reducing the slope (elasticity) and generally to increase the constant term.[45] It is also worth noting that, according to our model, an estimate of the parameter k can be secured from observables, independently of the estimate of the regression constant b_o. In fact from (2.6), (2.23) and (2.28) it follows

[45]Remembering that $\bar{V}_1$ and $\bar{U}'$ may be expected to be negative,--cf. equation (2.8)--we see that the terms following k in (2.33) are all positive, with the single exception of $\bar{U}'$. The sum of these terms will be positive unless var(V) is appreciably smaller than var (U), which we should generally not expect.

89

that

$$E(c) = k^*E(x) = k^*E(w + a) = k^*(1 + D_a)\ E(w)$$

while from (2.24), (2.25), and (2.28) we deduce

$$E(y) = E(y^{\ell}) + E(y^{n\ell}) = D_y E(w) + iD_a E(w) = (D_y + iD_a)\ E(w)$$

Hence,

$$\frac{E(c)}{E(y)} = \frac{k^*(1+D_a)}{(D_y + iD_a)} = k \tag{2.34}$$

i.e., a direct estimate of k for the group under consideration is provided by the ratio of mean consumption to mean income in the group.

We have so far been dealing with the relation between C and Y within any given cell of households with the same age and presumably similar life cycles of income and needs. The parameters b_o and b_y of the regression equation may, of course, be expected to take different values for different cells. For one thing the results embodied in (2.32) and (2.33) relate to "population" regression equations, and the values of the parameters estimated from a given sample could differ from the population value because of ordinary sampling fluctuations. But aside from this, we should also expect systematic differences among cells. This proposition is obvious for b_o since this parameter depends on k, which should vary systematically between cells in ways at least roughly predictable from the M-B-A model. The parameter b_y could also differ between cells because of variations in the correlation between $\tilde{C}$ and Y. Such variations might reflect differences in the dispersion of the error term, var(V), or merely differences in var(X) and hence, var($\tilde{C}$), since $r^2_{\tilde{C}Y}$ depends on the ratio of these variances. The M-B-A model in general does not provide direct inferences as to the behavior of these variances, and hence of b_y. Since $r^2_{\tilde{C}Y}$ in turn affects the constant term b_o, our inferences about b_o are accordingly weakened, although some "consistency" tests could be worked out from the joint estimate of b_o and b_y, making use of (2.34).

However, we do not propose at this point to pursue these issues. What we are mostly concerned with at the moment is to see the implications of our analysis for the relation between C and Y when we throw together the households from all, or at least a great many, cells. Roughly speaking—and what we seek at the moment is a rough answer—the result will depend on whether there are systematic associations between the parameters of the jth cell—$b_0^{(j)}$ and $b_y^{(j)}$—and the mean current income in the cell, $E(Y^{(j)})$. To illustrate, let us suppose all cells had roughly the same b_y but radically

90

different values for b_o. If $b_o^{(j)}$ were uncorrelated with $E(Y^{(j)})$, then the overall regression would have a slope—b_y—equal to the common value of b_y and a constant equal to the average of $b_o^{(j)}$ (weighted by the number of households in each cell). Otherwise, the overall slope would differ from the common slope, being larger if the above mentioned correlation is positive and smaller if it is negative.

Now there is one systematic factor tending to cause a positive correlation between $b_o^{(j)}$ and $E(Y^{(j)})$. As can be seen from (2.33), $(1-b_y)$ $E(Y)$ is one of the components of b_o. Since b_y is positive and less than unity the coefficient of $E(Y)$ is necessarily positive and is larger for smaller b_y. Thus, if $E(Y^{(j)})$ varies appreciably between cells, and $K^{(j)}$ were uncorrelated with $E(Y^{(j)})$, we should find that the slope of the overall regression of C on Y is somewhat larger than the common slope of the within cells regression. More generally, if the $b_y^{(j)}$ vary between cells, we should expect the overall slope to be somewhat larger than an "appropriately weighted" average of the $b_y^{(j)}$.[46] It should be noted, however, that while this conclusion can be regarded as a definite implication of the Friedman model, and has in fact been suggested by Friedman as one valid test of his hypothesis,[47] the same cannot be said for the M-B-A model. The reason is that Friedman's postulate that k is uncorrelated with x implies a lack of correlation between $K^{(j)}$ and $E(Y^{(j)})$.[48] The M-B-A model on the other hand only postulates lack of correlation between k and x within cells, which per se does not exclude the possibility of correlation between K and E(Y) over cells. Within the M-B-A model one can think of factors tending to make for some negative correlation between $K^{(j)}$ and $E(Y^{(j)})$—i.e., for a positive correlation between the average saving-income ratio and mean income over cells, the most obvious one being the prevailing shape of the life cycle of income and family size. In fact, if households endeavour to maintain over life a relatively stable rate of consumption per equivalent adult, then the saving ratio will be positively correlated with income per equivalent adult. But the latter quantity tends on the whole to be positively associated with income, over the life cycle.[49] The resulting negative correlation between $K^{(j)}$ and $E(Y^{(j)})$ is however, unlikely to offset fully the positive

---

[46] As has been shown by Eisner, the appropriate weight for each $b_y^{(j)}$ is $n^{(j)}$ var $[Y^{(j)}]$ where n^j is the number of observations in cells j. See Eisner [5], p. 979.

[47] Friedman [9], p. 216.

[48] Except possibly if cells are defined in some very "biased" way.

[49] Income per equivalent adult is lowest at the beginning and end of the life cycle when income is well below average, and tends to reach a peak toward the end of the earning span, when income is still close to its peak. See Modigliani and Ando [19].

relation between $b_o^{(j)}$ and $E(Y^{(j)})$ generated by the forces discussed above.

On the whole we can conclude that according to the M-B-A model the relation between C and Y within homogeneous cells should tend to be linear in the logs, with slope equal to $r^2_{\tilde{C}Y}$ and hence less than unity; and that this same result should hold for a very heterogeneous group of households, the slope of this overall regression being close to an average of the prevailing slopes within cells, though very likely somewhat higher.

This last conclusion concerning the slope of the overall regression line can also be reached by repeating for all cells combined the reasoning leading up to equation (2.32): An equation like (2.31) will hold for all households combined; but now K is an average of the K's for the individual cells, and accordingly the error terms will include an additional component resulting from the differences between the cell $K^{(j)}$ and the overall mean K. The additional error component will tend to increase the denominator of (2.32) but this effect can be totally or partially offset, or even more than offset by a simultaneous rise in var($\tilde{C}$). In particular if different cells had different $E(\tilde{C}^{(j)})$, but all the same (or roughly the same) K, as the Friedman model postulates, then the overall var(V) would be the same as within cells var(V) while var($\tilde{C}$) would be larger than within cells. Thus, $r^2_{\tilde{C}Y}$ for the heterogeneous group would be larger than within cells, causing the overall b_y to exceed the average of the $b_y^{(j)}$. Similarly if $K^{(j)}$ varied over cells but were uncorrelated with $E(Y^{(j)})$, then it would have to be positively correlated with $E(\tilde{C}^{(j)})$; under these conditions the error term V would also have to be negatively correlated with $\tilde{C}$. But then var ($\tilde{C}$) would rise more than var(Y) increasing the value of b_y above the within cells $b_y^{(j)}$.[50] Only a negative correlation between $K^{(j)}$ and $E(Y^{(j)})$ could offset this tendency in part, or even in toto, if it were sufficiently strong.

II.8. Tests Based on the Regression of Consumption on Income and Their Limitations

We have thus established that both the Friedman and the M-B-A models—plus the statistical assumption of multiplicative error terms—imply (i) that the relation between the logarithms of current measured consumption c and income y is approximately linear, and (ii) that the regression slope b_y is roughly equal to the square of the correlation between the logarithms of permanent consumption and current income, $r^2_{\tilde{C}Y}$. Since this correlation is

[50]Note that in this case b_y would not strictly coincide with $r^2_{\tilde{C}Y}$, since in (2.31) the regression coefficient of C would become less than unity, and b_y, which is equal to the reciprocal of this coefficient multiplied by $r^2_{\tilde{C}Y}$, would be larger than $r^2_{\tilde{C}Y}$.

92

necessarily less than one, (ii) implies that the elasticity of consumption with respect to income is less than one, or that the consumption income ratio should fall (the saving income ratio rise) with current income.

For the Friedman model $r^2_{\tilde{C}Y}$ can also be written as r^2_{XY} and interpreted as the correlation between permanent income and measured income; correspondingly the error term V can be interpreted as "transitory income."[51] This interpretation is not valid—at least strictu sensu—for the M-B-A model which does not make use of the notion of permanent income. Even for this model, within a cell of households homogeneous with respect to age and life cycle of income and family needs, $r^2_{\tilde{C}Y}$ can be written as r^2_{XY}, since $\tilde{C}$ is proportional to X within a cell. Furthermore X is not permanent income but the present value of total resources (in the simplest version—in the more general model it is the present value of total consumption). Hence, the error component, V, cannot be interpreted as transitory income but only as a measure of the dispersion of current measured income around the present value of total resources, within cells. This dispersion arises not only from purely transitory fluctuations in current income which will be reflected primarily in the error terms ϵ_1 of (2.25) and ϵ_2 of (2.28a), but also from much more permanent inter-household differences in the life cycle of income and needs as well as taste. These latter components of V cannot be altogether eliminated by our grouping of households into homogeneous cells, especially insofar as they reflect variations in the past history of the household. It is such differences that lie behind the error term ϵ_3 of (2.28b) and partly ϵ_2.

The implications of the two models concerning the relation between c and y which have just been spelled out—linearity in the logarithms, and a saving-income ratio rising with income—are readily testable, and as we shall see in the next section, are supported by the BLS-Wharton data. In fact, as is well known, at least the second of these conclusions is by and large consistent with all available data.

Unfortunately these favorable results do not provide much support for the Friedman and M-B-A models because these tests fail to discriminate between these hypotheses and most of the traditional and accepted models. In particular, the supporters of the view that the current income is the main determinant of current consumption[52] might take equation (2.22) as embodying their complete theory of the determinant of consumption behavior, while discarding the underlying structure represented by the reasoning leading to this equation.

---

[51] More precisely, (v' - 1) can be interpreted as the ratio of transitory to permanent income.

[52] We shall hereafter refer to this hypothesis as the strict current income hypothesis.

93

It does not follow, however, that all our effort in II.6 and II.7 has been wasted. In the first place it is important to establish that both models are at least consistent with well-known and established empirical regularities. But aside from this consideration, the analysis of these sections provides an interpretation of the parameter b_y and its determinants, which is radically different from that implied by the traditional models. For, those holding that (2.22) is a complete and adequate theory of consumption behavior would have to maintain that b_y is a meaningful measure of the response of individual households to a change in current income—regardless of the nature of this change. According to the Friedman and M-B-A models, on the other hand, this parameter has nothing to do with individual behavior, and is entirely determined by the relationship between the variability of the "error term" of income and the cross-sectional variability of resources, i.e., by the relationship between the variability of y around x and the variability of x.

Now it is true that the error term V is not directly observable, but it should frequently be possible to make sensible statements as to the behavior of var(V). Thus, we should expect var(V) to become smaller if we lengthen the period over which c and especially y are measured, if we increase the care with which both variables are measured, or when we measure them more nearly on an accrual rather than on a cash basis. Furthermore, var(V) should vary in a roughly predictable way depending on the type of households included in the sample. For instance, it should be larger for households whose head is engaged in an occupation with unstable income like self-employed entrepreneurs, than for those whose heads are in an occupation with considerable short-run stability of income, like civil service. Most of these implications are testable and a few of them have actually been tested with favorable results. In particular, the marginal propensity to consume with respect to income—when a linear rather than a logarithmic regression is used—has generally been found to be smaller for farmers and other self-employed groups than for other occupations.[53] When information on income is available for neighboring years, an indirect measure of the short-run stability of income for any given group can be obtained from the relation between the income of successive years, and we should expect the elasticity b_y to be closer to unity the greater the stability. Some such tests have been carried out mostly with favorable results.[54]

[53]See Fisher [6], Friedman [9] and Dorothy Brady in Goldsmith [12], Vol. III.

[54]One such test is reported by Margaret G. Reid in this volume [19b] pp. 16-17. Several other tests have been presented by the same author in an as yet unpublished manuscript. On the other hand the results of some tests reported by Friend and Kravis [10b] have not been too favorable.

94

Another type of test, suggested by the analysis in II.6 and II.7, consists in the comparison of the elasticity coefficient within cells, $b_y^{(j)}$, with the coefficient b_y obtained after combining the households from all the cells. As we have seen, it is a definite implication of the Friedman model that b_y will be larger than a weighted average of the $b_y^{(j)}$, except for sampling fluctuations. The M-B-A model yields a similar prediction but with certain qualifications relating to the nature of the individual cells. If these cells were the homogeneous cells of which we spoke in II.7, the result would be predicted as likely but not altogether sure because of a possible negative correlation between $E(Y^{(j)})$ and $K^{(j)}$. No such qualification would be needed, however, if each of the cells consisted of a group of households heterogeneous with respect to age and life cycle of income and needs, and the mixture were similar within each cell. This would be the case if, say, each cell consisted of a broad region of the U.S., or even of a city class as defined in the BLS-Wharton study; or if each cell were a different occupation provided in this case that all age groups were adequately represented, and the age distributions were reasonably similar within each cell.

A number of tests of this implication based on the BLS-Wharton data have actually been carried out by Eisner [5].[55] He has provided 23 different comparisons of the overall regression coefficient b_y with a weighted average of the corresponding cell coefficients $b_y^{(j)}$. In some of these tests the individual cells were city classes, in some occupation, in others age, and in others the cells were defined by age and city class and by occupation and city class. The prediction of the models was supported in every one of the 23 instances, though in some cases the differences were small.

These favorable results are encouraging and significant. It should be recognized, however, that all of the tests we have outlined so far—both those that have been carried out and those that have not—have in common one important shortcoming. They provide a test of the first three propositions underlying both the Friedman and M-B-A model (see Section II.2); but they do not throw much light on the fourth and by far the most controversial proposition, namely that (permanent) consumption is proportional to permanent income or total resources. To see this point let us suppose that equation (2.6) were replaced by

$$c = k\, x^m\, u'; \quad m < 1 \qquad (2.6^*)$$

[55] Similar tests were attempted earlier by Houthakker [13] and Watts [23] but were not altogether adequate because the authors compared the overall coefficient b_y with the individual coefficients $b_y^{(j)}$, rather than with an appropriately weighted average of such coefficients.

and correspondingly (2.10) were replaced by

$$C = K + mX + \bar{\bar{U}}' + U \qquad (2.10^*)$$

This equation differs from the currently prevailing view by stating that current consumption is determined (up to the stochastic component) by x, rather than by current measured income, but it accepts the prevailing view that the elasticity of (permanent) consumption with respect to x is less than unity, and the ratio of c to x falls with x. One can then readily verify, by repeating the reasoning leading to (2.21) or (2.34), that (2.10*) implies a linear regression of C on Y, but that the coefficient b_y now becomes

$$b_y = m\, r^2_{\tilde{C}Y} \qquad (2.22b)$$

so that b_y would still reflect partly the stochastic properties of the error term V. It immediately follows that all of the inferences or predictions established earlier in this section as to the behavior of b_y would be equally valid if (2.6*) instead of (2.6) were true. In short, these tests cannot help to discriminate between (2.6) and (2.6*).

In the next section we will outline a class of tests which at least in principle should enable us to select between (2.6) and (2.6*) and thus test the validity of the controversial fourth proposition common to the two models.

II.9. A Critical Test Based on the Relation Between Cell Means

Suppose that instead of classifying families into current income classes we group them into say H classes according to some characteristics other than income. The specific criterion of classification is for the moment immaterial; it might be, for instance, the geographical location of the family, or its age, or the level of expenditure on some class of commodities or services, like housing or insurance.

Let us denote by $\bar{z}_h$ the mean value of a variable z for all households in our sample belonging to class h, h=1, . . ., H; similarly, let $\bar{Z}_h$ denote the sample mean value of ln z in class h. The corresponding population means will be denoted by the conditional expectations E(z|h) and E(Z|h).

Suppose now that for each of the H classes we compute $\bar{C}_h$ and $\bar{Y}_h$, and that we then compute the regression equation of $\bar{C}_h$ on $\bar{Y}_h$. Let B_y and B_o denote respectively the slope and the constant term of this regression equation fitted to the cells means. We will show that, provided the criterion of classification satisfies a certain set of conditions spelled out below, the values of B_y and B_o will provide a powerful test as to whether the observed regression equation (2.22) between C and Y is after all an adequate direct explanation of the consumption-saving behavior of households, or, on the contrary, this behavior is more adequately accounted for by equations (2.1) to (2.6) of the Friedman and M-B-A model, and equation (2.22) is merely a statistical figment bearing very little relation to the true casual structure of individual behavior. We will further show that this test should in principle enable us also to discriminate between equations (2.6) and (2.6*) and thus provide a direct test of the fourth proposition of the two models.

In order to establish this result, let us suppose that (2.22) did in fact provide a complete explanation of the determinants of consumption, and let us see what this would imply as to the relation between $\overline{C}_h$ and $\overline{Y}_h$. From the linear form of (2.22) we deduce immediately

$$\overline{C}_h = b_o + b_y \overline{Y}_h + \overline{U}_h \tag{2.35}$$

where $\overline{U}_h$ is the mean value of the error term in class h. Now suppose that the criterion of classification is some characteristic like geographical location, which presumably should not affect consumption, given income. Then the mean value of the error term, $\overline{U}_h$, should be zero in each class, except for sampling fluctuation, i.e., $E(\overline{U}_h) = 0$ for all h, and hence, $E(\overline{U}_h \overline{Y}_h) = 0$. It then follows from (2.35) that the parameters B_o and B_y of the regression equation fitted to the cell means should coincide with these of (2.22), or

$$B_o = b_o, \; B_y = b_y,$$

except for sampling fluctuations.

This result can be restated less technically as follows. Suppose that we compute and graph the overall regression equation (2.22). If this equation is a complete explanation of the final systematic determinants of consumption, then, except for sampling fluctuations, the cell means $(\overline{c}_h, \overline{y}_h)$ should fall right on the regression equation (2.22) and the regression equation fitted to these cell means should coincide with the overall regression equation.

Suppose, on the other hand, that equation (2.6*) and hence (2.10*) express the true determinant of consumption behavior (leaving open for the moment the question of whether in fact m is unity, reducing (2.6*) and (2.10*) respectively to (2.6) and (2.10)). What can we infer about the value of B_y?

97

Let us begin by answering this question under the Friedman interpretation of x. First from equation (2.10*) we derive

$$\bar{C}_h = (K + \bar{\bar{U}}') + m\bar{X}_h + \bar{U}_h \tag{2.36}$$

If we let n_h stand for the number of observations in class h, and N for the overall sample size, then

$$\frac{\sum_{h=1}^{H} n_h \bar{C}_h}{N} = \bar{C}; \quad \frac{\sum_{h=1}^{H} n_h \bar{X}_h}{N} = \bar{X}; \quad \frac{\sum_{h=1}^{H} \bar{U}_h}{N} = \bar{U}$$

i.e., the weighted average of the cell means is the overall sample mean. In order to conserve space we will assume that $\bar{U}$ can be taken as zero. Next, from (2.18) we similarly deduce

$$\bar{Y}_h = \bar{\bar{V}}' + \bar{X}_h + \bar{V}_h \tag{2.37}$$

and the mean of $\bar{Y}_h$ is again $\bar{Y}$. Now the regression coefficient of $\bar{C}_h$ on $\bar{Y}_h$ is given by

$$B_y = \frac{\sum_{h=1}^{H} n_h(\bar{C}_h - \bar{C})(\bar{Y}_h - \bar{Y})}{\sum_{h=1}^{H} n_h(\bar{Y}_h - \bar{Y})^2} \tag{2.38}$$

Substituting into this equation (2.36) and (2.37), we find

$$B_y = \frac{\sum_{h=1}^{H} n_h[m(\bar{X}_h - \bar{X}) + \bar{U}_h][(\bar{X}_h - \bar{X}) + \bar{V}_h]}{\sum_{h=1}^{H} n_h(\bar{X}_h - \bar{X} + \bar{V}_h)^2} \tag{2.39}$$

$$= m\,\frac{\sum_{h=1}^{H} n_h(\bar{X}_h - \bar{X})^2 + \sum_{h=1}^{H} n_h(\bar{X}_h - \bar{X})\bar{V}_h + \frac{1}{m}\sum_{h=1}^{H} n_h(\bar{X}_h - \bar{X})\bar{U}_h + \frac{1}{m}\sum_{h=1}^{H} n_h(\bar{U}_h\bar{V}_h)}{\sum_{h=1}^{H} n_h(\bar{X}_h - \bar{X})^2 + \sum_{h=1}^{H} n_h\bar{V}_h^2 + 2\sum_{h=1}^{H} n_h(\bar{X}_h - \bar{X})\bar{V}_h}$$

B_y is of course a random variable whose value may change from sample to sample. We are interested in its central tendency, $E(B_y)$. This is the expected value of the ratios on the right hand

98

side of (2.39) which, to a first approximation, can be replaced by the ratio of the expected values.[56]

Now suppose we can find a criterion of classification that satisfies, at least approximately, the following conditions

$$E(\overline{V}_h) = 0, \tag{2.40a}$$

$$E(\overline{X}_h - \overline{X})\overline{U}_h = 0; \; h=1, \ldots, H. \tag{2.40b}$$

Then, on taking the expected value of the numerator all the product moments will vanish, and we are left only with the first term which represents the variance of the sample cell means around the overall sample mean (multiplied by N). We shall denote the expected value of this sample variance by $\text{var}(\overline{X}_h)$.[57] Taking similarly the expected value of the denominator, from (2.39) we derive

$$E(B_y) \approx m \frac{\text{var}(\overline{X}_h)}{\text{var}(\overline{X}_h) + \frac{\sum_h n_h E(\overline{V}_h^2)}{N}} \text{ [58]} \tag{2.41}$$

Let us take a closer look at the second term in the demoninator. Since $\overline{V}_h$ is the mean error in class h, and by (2.40) the expected value of this mean error is zero, $E(\overline{V}_h{}^2)$ is the variance of the

[56] This approximation should not be too bad as long as the number of observations in each cell is reasonably large, for then the sampling variance of the denominator will be small.

[57] This should not be confused with the variance of the sample mean in cell h around the population mean in class h, to be denoted by $\text{var}(\overline{X}_h | h)$.

[58] It may be noted that, for many purposes, the conditions (2.40) are unnecessarily strong. For much of what follows all that is required is, in essence, that $\overline{V}_h$ and $\overline{U}_h$ should be uncorrelated with $\overline{X}_h$ and with each other. In particular this condition is all that is required for (2.41) to hold. On the other hand (2.42) below is valid only if (2.40a) holds.

We should also like to point out that $E(\overline{V}_h)$ depends in general not only on the mean value but also on the variance, within each cell, of the error term v* defined in (2.17). In fact, by applying (2.8), we find that

$$E(V' | h) = E(\overline{V}_h') = \ln [1 + E(v^* | h)] - (1/2)\ln \left[1 + \frac{\text{var}(v^* | h)}{[1 + E(v^* | h)]^2}\right]$$

Hence, $E(\overline{V}_h) = E(\overline{V}_h') - \overline{V}'$ may vary between cells as a result of inter-cell variations in either or both $E(v^*)$ or $\text{var}(v^*)$. It is only if $\text{var}(v^*)$ is approximately the same in all cells that $E(\overline{V}_h)$ depends only on $E(v^* | h)$. Similar considerations apply to $E(\overline{U}_h)$.

99

sample mean around the population mean for a sample of size n_h. Hence, making use of the standard formula for the variance of a sample mean, we can write

$$E(\overline{V}_h^2) = \frac{var(V|\ h)}{n_h}$$

If the variance of the error term were the same in all cells, we would have var $(V|\ h) = var(V)$ and hence,

$$\sum_{h=1}^{H} n_h\ E(\overline{V}_h^2) = \sum_{h=1}^{H} n_h \frac{var(V)}{n_h} = H\ var(V) \qquad (2.42)$$

Even if the cell variances are not all the same, the above equation will hold as an approximation, since var(V) is the weighted average of the cell variances, $var(V|\ h)$. Substituting in (2.41), we then finally have [59]

$$E(B_y) \simeq m \frac{var(\overline{X}_h)}{var(\overline{X}_h) + \frac{H}{N} var(V)} = m \frac{1}{1 + \frac{H}{N}\frac{var(V)}{var(\overline{X}_h)}} = mr^2_{\overline{X}_h \overline{Y}_h} \qquad (2.43)$$

The reasoning leading up to (2.43) can be repeated step by step for the M-B-A model using equation (2.31) in place of (2.18). It can be verified that the only effect of this substitution is to replace everywhere $\overline{X}_h$ and $\overline{X}$ by $\overline{\overline{C}}_h/m$ and $\overline{\overline{C}}/m$ respectively. In particular, (2.43) becomes

$$E(B_y) \simeq m \frac{1}{1 + \frac{H}{N} \frac{var(V)}{var\left(\frac{\overline{\overline{C}}_h}{m}\right)}} = mr^2_{\tilde{\overline{C}}_h \overline{Y}_h} \qquad (2.43a)$$

In what follows we shall make explicit reference only to equations (2.39) to (2.43); but it should be understood that any result

[59] Our formula is not exact for two reasons. First, we have not made the proper allowance for the loss of degrees of freedom in deriving equation (2.43). Second, we have ignored the variances of variables within cells. The exact formulae are given in Madansky [16] pp. 189-194 in a slightly different context. The comparison of our formulae and those of Madansky indicate that biases due to these two sources will not be very severe provided (1) that the number of observations in each cell is fairly large; (2) that the observations are fairly evenly distributed over the cells.

100

obtained can be extended to the M-B-A model by making the above mentioned replacement if necessary.

It should be noted that we have not restricted the criterion h to quantitatively measurable variables. More specifically, h may be a variable such as occupation of the head of household, or the locality in which household resides, which cannot be expressed in numerical terms. It can also be some such variable as the value of the house owned, which can be measured numerically, at least in principal. If we choose a numerically measurable variable as the criterion of classification, however, we can also use it as the instrumental variable to obtain an estimate B_y.[60] In Part III, we shall present estimates of m using the criterion of classification as an instrumental variable whenever this is possible and appears desirable.

The result expressed by (2.43) has very useful implications. Provided that the cell means are appreciably different from each other so that var$(\overline{X}_h)$ is not too close to zero, the second term in the denominator will approach zero as the overall sample size N increases, and will in fact be negligibly small if N is large. Under these conditions $E(B_y)$ will be approximately m; or, to put it in more operational terms, the regression coefficient of the cell means of C on the cell means of Y will provide an estimate of the true elasticity m of equation (2.10*), differing from m only because of sampling fluctuations, (and because of a systematic downward bias which will be small if N is large). In particular, if the Friedman and M-B-A proposition (iv) is valid and m is in fact unity, then this regression coefficient B_y should be close to one.

Summing up, if the traditional view is correct and (2.22) is a complete explanation of saving behavior, then the slope B_y of the regression fitted to the cell means should be approximately the same as b_y, the slope of the overall regression. If, on the other hand, the Friedman and M-B-A propositions (i) to (iii) are correct and consumption is determined by X rather than by current income

[60] When h is a numerical variable, let $\bar{h}$ represent the mean value of h in the class h. Then, we compute the estimate B_y by the formula

$$B_y = \frac{\sum_{h=1}^{H} n_h (\overline{C}_h - \overline{C})\bar{h}}{\sum_{h=1}^{H} n_h (\overline{Y}_h - \overline{Y})\bar{h}}$$

Here again, this formula is not exact for the same reasons given in footnote 59, p. 100. For extensive discussion of this method and for the exact formula, see Madansky [16], pp. 185-194.

Y, and provided the criterion of classification satisfies conditions (2.40), we will have

$$b_y = m \frac{1}{1 + \frac{\text{var}(V)}{\text{var}(X)}} = mr^2_{XY}$$

$$B_y = m \frac{1}{1 + \frac{H \text{ var}(\bar{V}_h)}{N \text{ var}(\bar{X}_h)}} = mr^2_{\bar{X}_h \bar{Y}_h}$$

Hence, the two regression coefficients should have distinctly different values—i.e., the cells means should <u>not</u> lie on the overall regression equation. In particular B_y but not b_y, should increase with sample size; and as long as var $(\bar{X}_h) >> 0$, and N is large, B_y will be larger than b_y. Finally, if proposition (iv) of the Friedman and M-B-A model is also correct, then, at least for sufficiently large samples, B_y should turn out to be close to unity.

In part III we will report the results of a number of empirical tests based on the method we have just outlined. As should be clear, the main problem with such tests consists in finding suitable criteria of classification. It is, therefore, worthwhile to take a somewhat closer look at the properties that a satisfactory criterion of classification should satisfy.

Consider first condition (2.40a). Since for the Friedman model, the error term V can be interpreted as the transitory component of income, this condition states that there should be no association between the transitory component of income and the classification criterion. Unfortunately it is not possible to test explicitly whether this condition is satisfied by a given criterion, because permanent income, and hence V, is not an observable. However, in many instances it should be possible to arrive at a fairly reliable assessment as to whether the condition is likely to be satisfied on the basis of indirect evidence, judgment and experience. It is clear, e.g., that the number of days the head of the household was sick in the course of the period would be a very poor criterion to use, while at the other extreme any very permanent characteristics like height of the head, years of schooling or even geographical location could normally be expected to fulfill condition (2.40a) within the scope of Friedman's model.[61] For the M-B-A model the

[61] It should be remembered in this connection that for (2.40a) to hold the classification criterion must also be such that the variance of the transitory component v* should not vary appreciably between cells. However for B_y to be a nearly unbiased estimate of m it is sufficient that var (v*) should not be correlated with $\bar{X}_h$ and $\bar{U}_h$, and similarly that var (u*) should not be correlated with $\bar{X}_h$ or $\bar{V}_h$. Cf. footnote 58, p. 99.

102

situation is somewhat more complicated, since V must be interpreted as the dispersion of current income around the present value of resources w + a within each homogeneous cell. As we have noted earlier, this dispersion can be caused by many factors besides purely transitory disturbances, like temporary sickness. The task of assessing whether (2.40) is fulfilled is accordingly harder, although by and large any very permanent characteristic is likely to prove adequate, at least within fairly homogeneous groups of households.

Condition (2.40b), in the Friedman formulation, requires that there should be no correlation between the mean value of permanent income and the mean transitory component of consumption $\bar{U}_h$ over the cells.[62] This condition is again not explicitly testable, since neither **X** nor U is observable, and we must rely on indirect evidence and judgment. As an example of classification criteria which are likely to be poor in this respect one might quote the number of children attending college, the amount spent on the purchase of a car, at least when consumption is defined to include expenditure on durables—or even liquid asset holdings at the beginning of the year, since this variable is likely to be correlated with permanent income as well as with intentions to undertake extraordinary expenditure in the near future. On the other hand, very permanent characteristics are gain likely to fulfill the condition. Similar considerations apply to the M-B-A formulation, except that this model explicitly recognizes that the error term U reflects not only the variability of current measured consumption around permanent consumption, but also possible variability in the ratio of permanent consumption to x—that is in the k of equation (2.6) or the k_t^* of equation (2.15)—due to differences in tastes and other circumstances. Presumably this source of variation in U should be recognized also in the Friedman formulation.

Last, but not least, the classification criterion should be such as to generate large differences between the mean permanent consumption in the various cells, so that var $(\tilde{\bar{C}}_h)$ will be large—the larger the better. Unfortunately many of the classificatory criteria that could be counted on to satisfy (2.40a) and (2.40b) will prove unacceptable on this score: e.g., the height of the household head, or the second digit of age. However, as far as this third desideratum is concerned we can at least establish how well it is being fulfilled by relying on the observed variance of $\bar{Y}_h$, the mean measured income in the cells. The reason is that var$(\bar{Y}_h) = (1/m)^2$ var $(\tilde{\bar{C}}_h)$ +(H/N) var(V), so that the sample variance of $\bar{Y}_h$ is an estimate of var $(\tilde{C}_h)$ except for a constant depending on sample size, and the constant of proportionality. Thus, among alternative criteria of classification satisfying (2.40), the most useful one is that for which

[61] But $\bar{U}_h$ depends partly also on cov (u*h). See footnote.

103

the observed variance of $\overline{Y}_h$ is the largest. It is the most useful in the sense that the value of B_y estimated for this criterion will provide an estimate of the true parameter m with the smallest downward bias and least subject to sampling fluctuations.

Since the conditions (2.40) are not directly testable, it is never possible to be sure that any given criterion will in fact satisfy them. For this reason the best that we can do is to repeat the test for a variety of criteria and rely on the consensus of the result. Even if some of the criteria used in these tests are unlikely to fulfill those conditions, we may get some useful information from the test if we can make some sensible conjectures about the behavior of the product moment terms in (2.39), and thus assess whether B_y is likely to be an upward or downward biased estimate of m.

II.10 The Effects of Correlation Between the Transitory Components of Income and Consumption

Before we proceed to the task of presenting some empirical tests, we should like to examine the effect of relaxing two assumptions introduced earlier. The first of these assumptions is that embodied in equation (2.19), that the transitory component of consumption is uncorrelated with the transitory component of income; or, stated differently, that the propensity to consume out of transitory income is zero. We shall investigate this problem with special reference to the Friedman model, but the results are equally valid for the M-B-A model. We shall take as our point of departure equation (2.10*) instead of (2.10) in order to separate issues pertaining to the first three propositions from those pertaining to the last.

Suppose then that term U' of (2.10*) is in fact correlated with the error V' of (2.18) and for the sake of concreteness let us suppose the relation between the two errors can be expressed as

$$U' = \xi_0 + \xi V' + e', \tag{2.44}$$

where ξ_0 and ξ are some constants with $\xi > 0$ and

$$\text{cov}(e'V') = \text{cov}(e'X) = 0$$

The regression coefficient ξ is a measure of the elasticity of consumption with respect to transitory income. Substituting (2.44) into (2.10*), we obtain

$$C = K + mX + U' = K + MX + \xi_0 + \xi V' + e' \tag{2.45}$$

Notice that according to (2.45) the elasticity of consumption with respect to transitory income is constant, which implies, since ξ is presumably less than unity, that the marginal propensity to consume out of transitory income decreases with the size of the transitory component. This would seem a more reasonable hypothesis than to assume a constant marginal propensity, and meets some of the objections raised by Friedman [7] in his comment on Bodkin's paper. Remembering that $V = Y - X$, we can rewrite (2.45) as

$$\begin{aligned} C &= (K + \xi_0) + mX + \xi(Y - X) + e' \\ &= (K + \xi_0) + (m - \xi)X + \xi Y + e' \end{aligned} \tag{2.46}$$

or also as

$$c = k' x^{m-\xi} y^{\xi} e^* \tag{2.46'}$$

We can see from this equation that, if (2.44) holds, then in effect consumption is a function of both current and permanent income—unless of course $\xi = m$ in which case the coefficient of X (or the exponent of x) vanishes. It follows that even if we discard (2.19) and replace it with the much weaker proposition $\xi < m$, the Friedman and M-B-A model still imply a consumption function quite different from the accepted form (2.22).

Let us next examine the implications of replacing (2.19) with (2.44) on b_y, the regression coefficient of C on Y. This question is most easily answered by referring back to equation (2.21'), and using (2.44) to evaluate cov(U,V). We have

$$U = U' - E(U') = \xi V + e; \; e = e' - E(e') \tag{2.44a}$$

and hence

$$E(UV) = E\left[(\xi V + e)V\right] = \xi \, \text{var}(V) \tag{2.47a}$$

Substituting this result in (2.21')—and remembering that in the numerator of this equation var(X) must be replaced with m var(X) because we have replaced (2.10) with (2.10*)—we obtain

$$b_y = \frac{m \, \text{var}(X) + \xi \, \text{var}(V)}{\text{var}(X) + \text{var}(V)} = m r_{XY}^2 + \xi(1 - r_{XY}^2) < m, \text{ if } \xi < m. \tag{2.47}$$

This result has a number of interesting implications: (1) Even if (2.19) is discarded, the Friedman and M-B-A models still imply that b_y is not a meaningful estimate of individual behavior, but is at best a mongrel measuring neither the marginal propensity to consume with respect to transitory nor that with respect to permanent income; (2) As long as $\xi < m$, b_y will necessarily underestimate the effect on consumption of a permanent change in income, the extent of the underestimate depending again on r_{XY}^2; (3) In particular, if m

105

were unity and ξ, though positive, were less than unity, the two models would predict that b_y would be less than unity, so that the proposition (iv) of the two models is still perfectly consistent with the well-known fact that b_y is in fact less than unity.

We can finally ask how the discarding of (2.19) affects the test based on the coefficient B_y of the regression equation fitted to the cell means, discussed in Section II.9. The answer to this question is exceedingly simple. Equation (2.39) shows that $E(B_y)$ does not involve $E(UV)$ but only $E(\bar{U}_h \bar{V}_h)$. It follows that, as long as the criterion of classification satisfies condition (2.40a), $E(B_y)$ is completely unaffected by whether or not (2.19) holds. The common sense of this result is not far to seek. If (2.40a) holds, $\bar{Y}_h$ coincides with $\bar{X}_h$; hence, the difference in $\bar{C}_h$ between cells can reflect only the effect of the differences in $\bar{X}_h$ and cannot reflect the effects of "transitory" income, since average transitory income is the same in all cells, namely zero. It also follows that our discussion of the relation between b_y and B_y implied by the two models remains valid. In particular, if we can find suitable criteria of classification, B_y will be a nearly unbiased estimate of m, the elasticity of consumption with respect to "permanent" changes in income, and therefore should be larger than b_y.

The conclusion that $E(B_y)$ is unaffected by whether or not (2.19) holds has one further implication that is worth noting: namely, that tests based on regression on cell means can provide very little information concerning ξ. If B_y is significantly larger than b_y, we can conclude that ξ is at most smaller than m. But we cannot estimate the value of ξ, or test whether it is zero and the Friedman hypothesis (2.19) is valid. This raises the question as to whether there is any other device to estimate the correlation between u and v, or otherwise test the hypothesis (2.19). As indicated in the concluding section, we believe that such tests exist, although the task of designing adequate ones is by no means trivial.

II.11 The Role of The Estate Motive in The M-B-A Model

The other assumption that we wish to scrutinize further is the proposition that the estate motive can be neglected. This assumption (or at least the weaker one that planned bequests are proportional to $x + a$) underlies the "simplest version" of the M-B-A model with which we have been concerned so far. We feel that this assumption has a good deal of a priori plausibility within the range of incomes that are adequately covered by most family budget studies,[63]

[63]This conjecture receives some support from answers to questions on reasons for saving raised in several consumers surveys. Thus according to Katona, [13c] Table 1, the proportion of (Continued)

106

but we are ready to concede that it is less plausible as a general feature of saving behavior. It is therefore important to stress that what gives theoretical as well as empirical content to the M-B-A model is not the absence of the estate motive, but the notion of life planning plus the postulate that k^*_t is uncorrelated with lifetime consumption. To make this point clear, let us suppose we drop this simplifying assumption and go back to the most general formulation of the model:

$$\tilde{c}_t = k^*_t (w_t + a_t - q_t);\ k^*_t \text{ independent of } (w_t + a_t - q_t). \quad (2.48)$$

If q is not zero, presumably it can be expressed as a function of (w + a), say

$$q = f(w + a), \text{ with } 1 > f' > 0,\ f'' \geq 0$$

Hence

$$\begin{aligned} w+a-q &= w+a-f(w+a) = g(w+a) = g(x), \\ g' &= 1-f' > 0,\ g'' = -f'' \leq 0 \end{aligned} \quad (2.49a)$$

Here g(x) expresses the relation between (the present value of) lifetime consumption and lifetime resources. Accordingly g' (x) might be labeled the "over life marginal propensity to consume" and we might expect that

$$g'(x) \leq \frac{g(x)}{x}, \quad (2.49b)$$

i.e., the over life <u>marginal</u> propensity to consume will be no larger than the <u>average</u>, or equivalently the elasticity of over life consumption with respect to total resources will not exceed unity.

(Continued)
families reporting that their purpose for saving was "to bequeath money" amounted to only 2%; and while the proportion rises with income, even in the income class over $10,000, it was but 5%. Similar results have been reported by Katona and Mueller [13b], Table 34. On the other hand in an interim report recently issued by the Inter-University Committee for Research on Consumer Behavior (Interim Report No. 1, January 1959), the proportion of families giving as one of the reasons for saving "to leave an inheritance to children" was reported to be 29%. This much higher percentage might reflect the "disproportionately high representation from the upper income groups" in the sample, although the data provided are insufficient to test this conjecture.

Equations (2.49) and (2.48) imply (2.50) $c_t = k_t^* g(x)$ and the right hand side is precisely the function F(x) of equation (2.1). Substituting (2.51) into (2.2) and assuming again a multiplicative error term, we can further write

$$C_t = \tilde{C} + U' = K_t^* + \ln g(x) + U' \tag{2.50'}$$

It is apparent from (2.50) that even if we recognize the estate motive, the consumption function implied by the M-A-A model does not reduce to the conventional form (2.22), for it asserts that consumption is determined by total resources x and not by current income y. Furthermore, the various propositions about the behavior of k_t^* over the life cycle discussed in II.7 should still apply. On the other hand, the independence of k_t^* from w + a - q no longer enables us to conclude that the ratio of (permanent) consumption $\tilde{c}$ to total resources x is independent of x or, equivalently, that the elasticity of permanent consumption with respect to total resources is unity within a homogeneous cell. In fact, from (2.50) we find

$$\frac{d \log \tilde{c}_t}{d \log x} = \frac{d\tilde{C}_t}{dX} = \frac{g'(x)}{g(x)/x}$$

which, according to (2.49b), is smaller than unity—unless the equality holds in (2.49b). But the equality cannot hold for all x, except under the assumption of the simplest model that g(w + a) is proportional to (w + a).

Suppose, for the sake of illustration, that g(w + a) can be approximated by

$$g(w + a) = (w + a)^m = x^m, \tag{2.51}$$

Then, (2.50') becomes

$$C = K_t^* + mX + U' \tag{2.50''}$$

which is precisely of the form (2.10*), instead of (2.10). Now, we have shown that, through the test based on regression on cell means, we should in principle be able to discriminate between (2.10) and (2.10*), at least for large samples, because B_y is a nearly unbiased estimate of the coefficient m. Even if (2.51) is not strictly valid, the regression of $\overline{C}_h$ on $\overline{Y}_h$ should provide some information on the nature of the function g(x); in particular, if the inequality in (2.49b) holds within the range of incomes covered by the sample, we should expect to find that B_y is decidedly less than unity. It appears therefore that the regression over the cell means can provide not only a test of the M-B-A model as against the traditional

108

III.4 Tests Based On Classification by Housing Expenditure

The question raised in the last section can be answered if we can find other classification criteria, in addition to education and occupation, that satisfy the condition (2.40). We can use such criteria in two ways. First, we can apply them to the sample as a whole to compute new values of B_y. These new values of B_y may be: (a) close to unity; (b) close to the values obtained using occupation or education; or (c) neither. If the possibility (a) materializes, we would have some fresh support for the proposition (iv), and for the conjecture that there is some bias inherent in education and occupation as classification criteria.

Furthermore, we can put the new classification criteria to a second use, and test explicitly the last mentioned conjecture. For this purpose, we first group households into education (occupation) classes and then use the new criteria to estimate B_y within each educational (occupational) class. If B_y's within each educational (occupational) class so obtained are all close to unity, we have a strong support for the contention that, within each educational (occupational) class the parameter k is independent of the level of x. This in turn would imply that the low value of B_y obtained with education (occupation) as the criterion of classification is due to a correlation between k and the criterion—or, between errors of measurement and the criterion—rather than to the correlation between k and x.

The first and main classification criterion we propose to use in our further tests is the size of resources devoted to housing, which can be measured by expenditure on rent for renters and by the estimated value of the house for home owners.[78] The criterion looks very promising from several points of view. We know that generally families plan to change their living quarters very intermittently at best, especially when this requires buying and selling a house. In particular, we have no reason to suppose that housing expenditure will change in response to purely transitory changes in income. We can therefore be confident that if we group families into housing expenditure classes, the mean transitory income in each class will be zero (or will at least be uncorrelated with the mean income in the class) except possibly for sampling fluctuations. We also have good grounds to expect a substantial correlation between housing expenditure and x, and hence a relatively large var($\overline{X}_h$) when h is the variable representing housing expenditure.

Against these advantages of housing expenditure as the classification criterion, there is one possible shortcoming. It is conceivable that the error term $\overline{U}_h$ may be positively correlated with the level of housing expenditure. This danger is especially serious in the case of renters for here the classification criterion is a component of total consumption expenditure and reasonably important one, at that.[79] It is therefore conceivable that the higher rent classes might include households who tend to have a high consumption relative to their resources, while the opposite might be true in the lower expenditure classes. Since housing expenditure is correlated with $\overline{X}_h$, there may arise some correlation between $\overline{U}_h$ and $\overline{X}_h$, so that the condition (2.40b), cov($\overline{U}_h \overline{X}_h$) = 0, may not be exactly satisfied. To the extent that this possibility materializes the coefficient B_y may provide a somewhat upward biased estimate of the true elasticity, m. In the case of homeowners the danger of bias from this source would seem much smaller, because here the criterion is the value of the house which is not directly an item of expenditure. While it is true that this variable will be correlated with certain items included in consumption such as taxes, insurance and repairs, it must also be remembered that, for owners who are in the process of repaying their mortgage debt, the value of the house may well be positively associated with saving.[80]

---

[78] The idea of using this criterion of classification was first suggested to us by Margaret Reid several years ago.

[79] The rent item accounts for about 13 per cent of total consumption expenditure of renters. Cf. Vol. 18, Table 6-4.

[80] The use of the value of the house, as the criterion of classification, does however pose some further problems in relation to the M-B-A model. Especially when the house is fully paid for, it is likely to represent an important component of net worth. Accordingly, there may well be a systematic association between the value of the house and the ratio of net worth to income. Unfortunately the effects of such an association are extremely hard to trace through (Continued)

139

In any event we shall have to keep this possibility of bias in mind as we analyze the results.

The relevant information for renters is presented in Table III.5.A.[81] It will be noted that this criterion is indeed effective in producing a relatively large spread in mean income over classes. The value of var$[\log(\bar{y}_h)]$ for this classification is .0178, while it is .0088 for classification by occupation, and even smaller for all other classifications. These values can be compared to .0464 for classification by current income. In spite of the wide variation in income, there is no systematic tendency for the consumption-income ratio to fall as income rises, and this is confirmed by the value of B_y which is extremely close to unity.

Parts B and C of the table provide similar information for the two main home owners groups classified by value of house. Once more our criterion generates a sizable spread in mean income, especially for the third group. However, an examination of the figures of the third column now reveals a mild downward drift of the consumption-income ratio as income rises. In fact, the value of B_y turns out to be .93 for the first group and .94 for the second, which is much larger than the corresponding value of b_y given in Table III.1—.83 and .82 respectively—but still appreciably short of unity. We must recall at this point, however, that measured consumption for home owners is systematically downward biased because of the omission of any allowance for the depreciation of the house. While this omission is always troublesome, it becomes critical when the classification criterion is the value of the house, for then the magnitude of the bias is correlated with the criterion, which in turn is correlated with X. Thus, in this case, the omission of the depreciation from consumption leads to a violation of the condition (2.40), i.e., we would expect $E(\overline{X}_h \overline{U}_h)$ to be negative, causing a downward bias in the value of B_y. Since we know neither the

(Continued)

because they depend partly on age. The complications are further increased since in our data income does not include an allowance for the return on the capital invested in the house. We suspect that this possible source of bias is not too serious but we have not been able to establish this proposition beyond doubt. In the last analysis the only really satisfactory test of the M-B-A model would require explicit information on net worth.

[81] Both renters and home owners are divided into nine housing expenditure classes, as shown in the table. While these particular divisions are not the most convenient for our purposes, producing very uneven distributions of households among the cells, these are the only divisions provided by the BLS-Wharton data. For renters only eight classes are shown in Table III.5A, because the last class, $3,000 and over contained but one observation, and was therefore lumped with the preceding class, $2,000 to $3,000.

140

TABLE III.5

Tests of the Friedman and M-B-A Models Based on Classification by Housing[1]

A — Renters

Yearly Rental (h)	(1) Number of Families	(2) $\bar{y}_h$	(3) $\bar{c}_h/\bar{y}_h$	(5) Average Family Size
Under 250	733	1,832	.99	1.8
250- 499	2,335	2,725	1.02	2.7
500- 749	2,154	3,706	1.01	3.0
750- 999	804	4,659	1.01	3.1
1,000-1,249	216	5,203	1.08	3.2
1,250-1,499	75	6,861	1.05	2.8
1,500-1,999	40	7,004	1.13	2.8
over 2,000	12	13,788	.94	3.0

Variance of cell means: .0178
Elasticity (B_y): 1.033
r^2: .9977

B — Home Owners (bought after 1946)

Value of House	(1) Number of Families	(2) $\bar{y}_h$	(3) $\bar{c}_h/\bar{y}_h$ unadjusted	(4) $\bar{c}_h/\bar{y}_h$ adjusted for dep.	(5) Average Family Size
Under 5,000	297	3,033	.95	.97	3.6
5,000- 7,499	403	3,728	.97	1.00	3.5
7,500- 9,999	442	4,216	.95	.99	3.4
10,000-12,499	406	4,685	.99	1.04	3.4
12,500-14,999	191	5,555	.92	.97	3.4
15,000-17,499	153	5,990	.90	.96	3.7
17,500-19,999	61	7,424	.84	.89	3.3
20,000-24,999	82	6,591	.89	.98	3.3
over 25,000	68	9,519	.93	1.00	3.5

Variance of cell means: .0134
Elasticity without adjustment for depreciation: .927
Elasticity - adjusted for depreciation: .975
r^2 - adjusted for depreciation: .989
Elasticity - adjusted for depreciation and return on equity: .981

[1] For the description of the data used in this table, see footnote to Table III.8.

141

TABLE III.5—Continued

Tests of the Friedman and M-B-A Models Based on Classification by Housing

C — Home Owners (bought before 1946)

Value of House	(1) Number of Families	(2) $\bar{y}_h$	(3) $\bar{c}_h/\bar{y}_h$ unadjusted	(4) $\bar{c}_h/\bar{y}_h$ adjusted for dep.	(5) Average Family Size
Under 5,000	510	2,658	1.00	1.02	3.2
5,000- 7,499	688	3,436	.98	1.02	3.2
7,500- 9,999	635	4,023	.99	1.03	3.2
10,000-12,499	718	4,567	.97	1.02	3.0
12,500-14,999	214	5,189	.99	1.04	3.1
15,000-17,499	288	5,333	.98	1.04	3.0
17,500-19,999	109	6,333	.93	.99	3.0
20,000-24,999	126	6,416	.88	.95	3.0
over 25,000	110	10,601	.91	.97	3.0

Variance of cell means:	.0168
Elasticity - without adjustment for depreciation:	.938
Elasticity - adjusted for depreciation:	.972
r^2 - adjusted for depreciation:	.9962
Elasticity - adjusted for depreciation and return on equity:	.975

D — All Families

(Adjusted for depreciation and return on equity)

Variance of cell means:	.0235
Elasticity:	1.000
r^2:	.9960

exact value of the house nor the appropriate rate of depreciation for each household, it is difficult to make a reliable adjustment. However, some adjustment in the right direction would seem better than no adjustment at all. Accordingly, we have computed an alternative estimate of mean consumption in each class by adding to the original figure an imputed depreciation equal to 2 per cent of the mean value of the house in each cell, assumed to be equal to the mid value of the cell.[82] The adjustment appears to eliminate to a

[82]For the lowest class the mean value of the house was taken as $3,000 and for the open-ended class as $32,500.

142

large extent the downward drift of the consumption-income ratio, as well as the very marked discrepancy between the consumption-income ratio of renters and that of home owners which exists when this adjustment is not made. Accordingly, the value of B_y rises appreciably for both owner groups, becoming remarkably close to unity.

Even the adjustment just described is not adequate from a conceptual point of view, for the revised estimate still fails to include the full rental value of the house. To do so, we should add to both consumption and income the return on the owners' equity. There is unfortunately no adequate way of making such an adjustment. We have nonetheless attempted a very crude adjustment, primarily to check whether it would significantly affect the results. The adjustment was made by assuming, conservatively, that on the average the owners' equity is equal to half the value of the house and that the return on this equity averages 6 per cent per year. We can then adjust the reported mean consumption and income in each class by adding to each respectively 5 per cent and 3 per cent of the mean value of the house, estimated as above. Since the adjustment is so crude, the resulting values of income and the consumption-income ratio are hardly worth reporting. We report, however, the values of B_y based on these figures. It is seen that for both groups this final adjustment brings the value of B_y still closer to unity, though the magnitude of change is quite negligible. In the light of this result, we shall not attempt to make this last adjustment hereafter. We will, however, continue to adjust consumption of home owners by the estimated depreciation of the house, whenever the value of the house is the criterion of classification. Also, since the results obtained for the two owner groups are so nearly the same, we shall hereafter lump these two groups together and refer to them as home owners. While we may lose some information in the process, we gain in terms of increased frequencies in the cells, which will prove important in dealing with individual education and occupation groups where the total number of observations is very small.

There is, however, one further test based on the adjustment for return on equity which is worth reporting. With this adjustment the definitions of consumption and income are conceptually the same for renters and home owners. We can therefore combine all three tenure classes and compute the regression coefficient B_y based on all observations. The results of this correlation are reported in Part D of the table; the value of B_y now turns out to be unity to three decimal places.

This result is illustrated in graphical form in the scatter diagram of Figure III.2. The purpose of this figure is to contrast the behavior of the saving-income ratio in relation to income when families are classified by the conventional current income criterion, with the behavior found when the classification criterion

143

is housing expenditure. The points marked by asterisks show the relation between $\bar{s}_h/\bar{y}_h$ and log $\bar{y}_h$ using the current income classification. The underlying data are those reported in Table III.4 part A; $\bar{s}_h/\bar{y}_h$ is obtained by subtracting column (3) of that table from unity. As usual the lowest income class is omitted. It can be readily shown that if the relation between mean consumption and mean income is linear in the logarithms and the saving-income ratio is fairly small—both of which are approximately true for our data, once the lowest income class is dropped—then the relation between the saving-income ratio and log($\bar{y}_h$) will be approximately linear. The scatter of asterisks indicate that the relation is indeed very close to linear. It can be shown further that the slope of this linear relation can be approximated by subtracting the slope of the regression of log ($\bar{c}_h$) on log($\bar{y}_h$) from unity and multiplying the result by ln 10 or approximately 2.3.[83] Using this relation, remembering that $b_y = .85$ (cf. Table III.1, last column), the slope of the line through the asterisks was computed as $(1 - .85) \times 2.3 = .35$. Thus, when the criterion of classification is current income, an increase in income by a factor of 10 (an increase in log y of 1) should be accompanied by a rise in the saving-income ratio of about .35. It can, in fact, be verified from the figures in Table III.1 that as income rises from about $1,600 to $16,000, the saving-income ratio rises from - 15 percent to + 25 per cent, a rise only slightly larger than .35.

The points showing the relation between the saving-income ratio and log $\bar{y}_h$, when the criteria of classification is housing, are marked by crosses: x is used to denote renters classes, while $\underline{x}$ and $\bar{x}$ denote home owners having bought before and after 1946 respectively. For the two owners groups both income and consumption are adjusted for imputed depreciation and return on equity, as explained earlier. Finally, the crosses with circles around them indicate the cells with less than 100 observations.

---

[83] We have, omitting the stochastic terms,

$$\ln c = b_o + b_y \ln y$$

$$\ln \left(\frac{c}{y}\right) = \ln c - \ln y = b_o + (b_y - 1) \ln y$$

But, for $\frac{s}{y}$ close to zero, we also have

$$\ln \left(\frac{c}{y}\right) = \ln \left(1 - \frac{s}{y}\right) \simeq -\frac{s}{y}$$

Hence,

$$-\frac{s}{y} = b_o + (b_y - 1) \ln y$$

$$\frac{s}{y} = -b_o + (1 - b_y) \ln 10 \log y$$

144

Figure III.2

Relation between the Saving Income Ratio and Income for Two Alternative Classification Criteria

*Classification by current income
x, $\bar{x}$, $\underline{x}$ Classification by housing (x: renters; $\bar{x}$: owners, post '46; $\underline{x}$: owners, pre '46)[1]

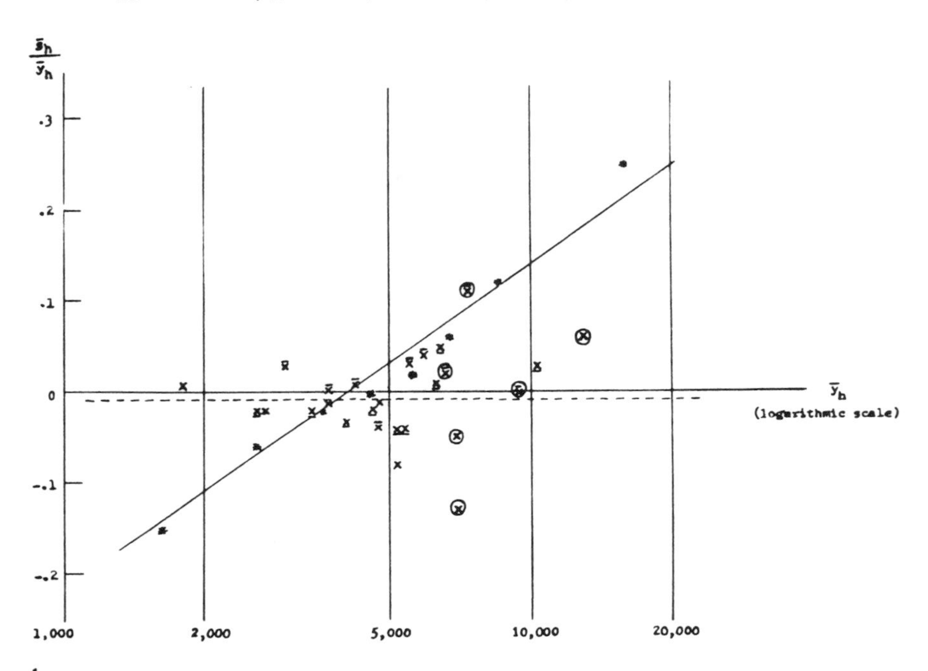

[1]Circled points relate to cells with less than 100 observations.
Source: See Text.

The broken line through the scatter of the crosses was derived again from the regression of C_h on Y_h; since as shown in Part D the coefficient of this regression is precisely unity, the slope of the broken line is zero. It is seen that there is a fair amount of scatter in the crosses. This is to be expected due to sampling fluctuations. This is especially true for cells where the number of observations is relatively small. It will be seen that most of the scatter is, in fact, generated by cells with relatively few observations. For the 20 cells containing more than 100 observations the scatter is distinctly smaller, as 18 fall within the ±4 per cent limit and only one fall outside the 5 per cent limit. Furthermore, for these more reliable observations there is absolutely no evidence

145

of an upward or downward drift in the saving-income ratio as income rises, even though the range of income spanned is quite large, from $1,800 to nearly $12,000.

Before we try to assess the implications of these seemingly favorable results, we must pay some attention to the possibility envisaged earlier of a positive correlation between the error term $\overline{U}_h$ and the variable $\overline{X}_h$. Such a correlation would cause an upward bias in B_y as an estimate of the true elasticity m, possibly more than offsetting the downward bias coming from the sampling variance of $\overline{V}_h$. Since the error terms $\overline{U}_h$ and $\overline{V}_h$ are not observable, it is not possible to make a reliable estimate of this bias in a straight-forward manner.[84]

There are nonetheless a number of considerations suggesting that if the bias exists, it is very unlikely to be strong enough to affect materially our estimate of m. From the analysis presented in Section II.9, we can express m as a function of B_y, the unobservable correlation coefficient between $\overline{U}_h$ and $\overline{X}_h$—denoted by $r_{\overline{UX}}$ —and other observable quantities:

$$m = g[B_y - \frac{r_{\overline{UX}}}{(1-r^2_{\overline{UX}})^{1/2}} \quad (1 - r^2_{\overline{CY}}\, g)^{1/2} \quad (\frac{var(\overline{C}_h)}{var(\overline{Y}_h)})^{1/2} g^{1/2}]$$

where

$$g = 1 + \frac{var(\overline{V}_h)}{var(\overline{X}_h)};$$

$r_{\overline{CY}}$ = correlation coefficient between $\overline{C}_h$ and $\overline{Y}_h$.

The second term in the brackets is a measure of the bias in B_y coming from a possible positive value for $r_{\overline{UX}}$.[85] Now the terms multiplying the fraction $r_{\overline{UX}}/(1-r^2_{\overline{UX}})^{1/2}$ are uniformly quite small in our tests, because the variances of $\overline{C}_h$ and $\overline{Y}_h$ are roughly equal and $r^2_{\overline{CY}}$ ranges from .989 to .9977 as shown in Table III.5. Under these circumstances, $r_{\overline{UX}}$ would have to be quite large before it could produce an appreciable upward bias in B_y. In the case of

[84]We have given some thought to the possibility of making some inferences on the size of the variances of $\overline{V}_h$ and $\overline{U}_h$, and of the covariance between them, from the available data. We believe that this is not an impossible task, though the procedure involved will by no means be a simple one. We hope to be able to report some progress on this score, including some estimates, in a later paper.

[85]g, of course, represents the bias due to the non-zero value of var. $(\overline{V}_h)$.

renters, for example, if we assume the value of g to be 1.001, and the value of $r_{\bar{X}\bar{U}}$ to be as high as .7, the second term in the brackets will be somewhat less than .04, changing the elasticity from 1.033 to .995.

For the two owner groups, the effect of the bias would be a little more serious since $r_{\bar{C}\bar{Y}}$ is slightly lower and the value of B_y is slightly below unity to begin with, if we assume the same value of $r_{\bar{U}\bar{X}}$ for them as for the renters. However, as pointed out at the beginning of this section, for home owners there is much less ground to fear a significant positive correlation between $\bar{X}_h$ and $\bar{U}_h$.

On the whole, then, the battery of tests reported in this section provides some fresh support for the first three propositions of the Friedman and M-B-A model. They also reinforce the evidence already provided by the classification by city class in support of the fourth proposition, namely, that the true elasticity m is very nearly unity. We cannot, however, accept this latter conclusion with full confidence. In the first place, it is subject to doubt because of the possible bias inherent in the classification by housing discussed above. In the second place, we have not yet dealt with the major problem that has resulted from our findings in the previous section, namely, to see if we can find a convincing explanation for the much lower values of B_y obtained with education and occupation as the criteria of classification. It is to these remaining questions that we must now turn our attention.

Errata

Page 80, 5 lines from the bottom: "$J(j\tau)$" should read "$J(j_\tau)$."

Page 82, line after (2.18): "were $\bar{V}'$ and V" should read "where $\bar{\bar{V}}'$ and V."

Page 89, footnote 45, line 2: "following k" should read "following K."

Page 89, footnote 45, line 3: "single exception of $\bar{U}'$" should read "single exception of $\bar{\bar{U}}'$."

Page 92, footnote 50, line 2: "coefficient of C" should read "coefficient of $\bar{C}$."

Page 103, paragraph 2, line 14: "are gain likely" should read "are again likely."

Page 103: footnote should be numbered 62, not 61. The second sentence of the footnote should read "See footnote 61."

Page 104, equation (2.45): the "M" on the right-hand side of the equation should read "m."

Page 108, line 1, equation (2.50): "c_t" should read "$\bar{c}_t$."

Page 108, line 3: "(2.51) into (2.2)" should read "(2.50) into (2.2)."

Page 108, line 7: "M-A-A model" should read "M-B-A model."

THE "LIFE CYCLE" HYPOTHESIS OF SAVING: AGGREGATE IMPLICATIONS AND TESTS

By ALBERT ANDO AND FRANCO MODIGLIANI*

The recent literature on the theory of the consumption function abounds with discussions of the permanent income hypothesis of Friedman and other related theories and attempts at their empirical verification. Friedman's formulation of the hypothesis is fairly well suited for testing against cross-section data, though numerous difficulties are associated with this task, and there is now a rapidly growing body of literature on this subject [5] [8] [11] [12] [14] [16] [17] [21] [25]. Friedman's model, on the other hand, does not generate the type of hypotheses that can be easily tested against time series data.

More or less contemporaneously with Friedman's work on the permanent income hypothesis, Modigliani and Brumberg developed a theory of consumer expenditure based on considerations relating to the life cycle of income and of consumption "needs" of households [34] [35]. Several tests of the Modigliani-Brumberg theory using cross-section data have been reported in the past including a comparative analysis of the cross-section implications of this hypothesis as against the Friedman model [8] [12] [32] [33].

Modigliani and Brumberg have also attempted to derive time series implications of their hypothesis in an as yet unpublished paper [34], and their theory appears to generate a more promising aggregative consumption function than does Friedman's. However, at the time of their writing the unavailability of data on net worth of consumers made empirical verification exceedingly difficult and indirect [6] [7] [20]. Since then, this difficulty has been partially eliminated as a result of the work of Goldsmith [18] [19].

In Part I of this paper, we give a brief summary of the major aggregative implications of the Modigliani-Brumberg life cycle hypothesis of saving. In Part II, we present the results of a number of empirical tests

* The authors are, respectively, assistant professor of economics and professor of industrial management, Massachusetts Institute of Technology. They are indebted to a number of their colleagues and students for comments and suggestions, particularly to Robert Ferber of the University of Illinois, Fred Westfield of Northwestern University, Franklin M. Fisher, Ralph Beals, and Stephen Goldfeld of the Massachusetts Institute of Technology, who read an earlier draft of this paper and suggested a number of improvements. The final phase of the research for this paper was partially supported by a grant from the National Science Foundation.

for the United States which appear to support the hypothesis.[1] The reader who is not interested in the derivation and statistical testing of the aggregate Modigliani-Brumberg consumption function may proceed directly to Part III, where we develop some features of the model which, in our view, make it particularly suitable for the analysis of economic growth and fluctuations, as indicated in our past and forthcoming contributions [1] [2] [3] [4] [29] [31].

I. *Theory*

A. *Derivation of the Aggregate Consumption Function*[2]

The Modigliani and Brumberg model starts from the utility function of the individual consumer: his utility is assumed to be a function of his own aggregate consumption in current and future periods. The individual is then assumed to maximize his utility subject to the resources available to him, his resources being the sum of current and discounted future earnings over his lifetime and his current net worth. As a result of this maximization the current consumption of the individual can be expressed as a function of his resources and the rate of return on capital with parameters depending on age. The individual consumption functions thus obtained are then aggregated to arrive at the aggregate consumption function for the community.

From the above brief description, it is quite apparent that the most crucial assumptions in deriving the aggregate consumption function must be those relating to the characteristics of the individual's utility function, and the age structure of the population. The basic assumptions underlying the shape of the utility function are:

Assumption I: The utility function is homogeneous with respect to consumption at different points in time; or, equivalently, if the individual receives an additional dollar's worth of resources, he will allocate it to consumption at different times in the same proportion in which he had allocated his total resources prior to the addition.[3]

Assumption II: The individual neither expects to receive nor desires to leave any inheritance. (This assumption can be relaxed in either of

[1] Since this paper was submitted and accepted for publication, a model that bears some similarity to the one proposed here has been presented by Alan Spiro in "Wealth and Consumption Function," *Jour. Pol. Econ.*, Aug. 1962, *70*, 339–54.

[2] The theory summarized here is essentially the same as that developed by Modigliani and Brumberg in [7] and [34]. Because of the untimely death of Richard Brumberg in August 1954, the original paper by Modigliani and Brumberg [34] has never been published, and it is not likely to be published in the near future. Because of this, we present here a summary. However, the aggregation procedure developed here is different from that followed by Modigliani and Brumberg. This is because they are largely concerned with numerical prediction of parameters while we are interested only in exhibiting the conditions for existence of a particular form of the aggregate consumption function.

[3] This equivalence holds on the assumption that consumers deal in perfect markets.

two ways. First, we may assume that the utility over life depends on planned bequests but assume that it is a homogeneous function of this variable as well as of planned consumption. Alternatively, we may assume that the resources an individual earmarks for bequests are an increasing function of the individual's resources relative to the average level of resources of his age group, and that the relative size distribution of resources within each age group is stable over time. It can be shown that either of these generalized assumptions implies an aggregate consumption function similar in all essential characteristics to the one obtained from the stricter assumption stated here.)

These two assumptions can be shown to imply (cf. [35, pp. 390 ff.]) that, in any given year t, total consumption of a person of age T (or, more generally, of a household headed by such a person) will be proportional to the present value of total resources accruing to him over the rest of his life, or:

$$c_t^T = \Omega_t^T v_t^T . \tag{1.1}$$

In this equation[4] Ω_t^T is a proportionality factor which will depend on the specific form of the utility function, the rate of return on assets, and the present age of the person, but not on total resources, v_t^T. The symbol c_t^T stands for total consumption (rather than for consumer's expenditure) in the year t. It consists of current outlays for nondurable goods and services (net of changes if any in the stock of nondurables) plus the rental value of the stock of service-yielding consumer durable goods. This rental value in turn can be equated with the loss in value of the stock in the course of the period plus the lost return on the capital tied up. Finally the present value of resources at age T, v_t^T, can be expressed as the sum of net worth carried over from the previous period, a_{t-1}^T, and the present value of nonproperty income the person expects to earn over the remainder of his earning life; i.e.,

$$v_t^T = a_{t-1}^T + y_t^T + \sum_{\tau=T+1}^{N} \frac{y_t^{eT\tau}}{(1 + r_t)^{\tau-T}} \tag{1.2}$$

where y_t^T denotes current nonproperty income; $y_t^{eT\tau}$ is the nonproperty income an individual of age T expects to earn in the τth year of his life; N stands for the earning span and r_t for the rate of return on assets.[5]

In order to proceed further, it is convenient to introduce the notion of "average annual expected income," y_t^{eT}, defined as follows:

[4] For the sake of simplicity, we shall not display the stochastic component of these relations explicitly in this section.

[5] To be precise $y_t^{eT\tau}$ is the income the person expects to earn at age τ, measured in prices prevailing in the year t, and r is the "real" rate of return on assets. In (1.2) the expected real rate is assumed to remain constant over time, but the formula can be generalized to allow for changing rate expectations.

$$(1.3)\qquad y_t^{eT} = \frac{1}{N-T}\sum_{\tau=T+1}^{N}\frac{y_t^{eT\tau}}{(1+r_t)^{\tau-T}}.$$

Making use of this definition and of (1.2) we can rewrite equation (1.1) as:

$$(1.4)\qquad c_t^T = \Omega_t^T y_t^T + \Omega_t^T (N-T) y_t^{eT} + \Omega_t^T a_{t-1}^T.$$

To obtain an expression for aggregate consumption we proceed to aggregate equation (1.4) in two steps, first within each age group and then over the age groups.

If the value of Ω_t^T is identical for all individuals in a given age group T, then it is a simple matter to aggregate equation (1.4) over an age group, obtaining:

$$(1.5)\qquad C_t^T = \Omega_t^T Y_t^T + (N-T)\Omega_t^T Y_t^{eT} + \Omega_t^T A_{t-1}^T$$

where C_t^T, Y_t^T, Y^{eT}, and A_{t-1}^T are corresponding aggregates for the age group T of c_t^T, y_t^T, y_t^{eT}, and a_{t-1}^T. If Ω_t^T is not identical for all individuals in the age group, however, the meaning of the coefficients in equation (1.5) must be reinterpreted. It has been shown by Theil [41] that under a certain set of conditions the coefficients of (1.5) can be considered as weighted averages of the corresponding coefficients of (1.4).[6]

Next, taking equation (1.5) as a true representation of the relationship between consumption and total resources for various age groups, we wish to aggregate them over all age groups to get the consumption function for the whole community. Consider the equation:

$$(1.6)\qquad C_t = \alpha_1' Y_t + \alpha_2' Y_t^e + \alpha_3' A_{t-1}$$

where C_t, Y_t, Y_t^e and A_{t-1} are obtained by summing respectively C_t^T, Y_t^T, Y_t^{eT} and A_{t-1}^T over all age groups T, and represent therefore aggregate consumption, current nonproperty income, "expected annual nonproperty income," and net worth.

The theorems given by Theil again specify the conditions under which the coefficients in equation (1.6) are weighted averages of the corresponding coefficients of equation (1.5). In this case, it is likely that the conditions specified by Theil are not satisfied, because both net worth and its coefficient in equation (1.5) are positively correlated with age up to the time of retirement. However, a much weaker set of conditions can be specified which are sufficient to insure stability over time

[6] See Theil [41, pp. 10–26]. More precisely, the least squares estimates of the parameters of equation (1.5) will be weighted averages of the least squares estimates of the corresponding parameters of equations (1.4) only if the set of conditions specified by Theil in the reference cited above is satisfied. Roughly speaking, these conditions require that there be no systematic relations between parameters and variables of equation (1.4) over individuals.

of parameters in equation (1.6). In particular one such set of conditions is the constancy in time of (i) the parameters of equation (1.5) for every age group, (ii) the age structure of population, and (iii) the relative distribution of income, of expected income, and of net worth over the age groups.

B. *A Priori Estimates of the Coefficients of the Aggregate Consumption Function*

Modigliani and Brumberg [34], in order to obtain a priori estimates of the order of the magnitude of the coefficients of equation (1.6) implied by their model, introduced a number of rather drastic simplifying assumptions about the form of the utility function and life pattern of earnings, to wit:

Assumption III: The consumer at any age plans to consume his total resources evenly over the remainder of his life span.

Assumption IV: (a) Every age group within the earning span has the same average income in any given year t. (b) In a given year t, the average income expected by any age group T for any later period τ, within their earning span, is the same. (c) Every household has the same (expected and actual) total life and earning spans, assumed to be 50 and 40 respectively for the purpose of numerical computation.

Assumption V: The rate of return on assets is constant and is expected to remain constant.

Under these assumptions, if aggregate real income follows an exponential growth trend—whether due to population or to productivity growth—the sufficient conditions for the constancy in time of the parameters of (1.6) are satisfied. The value of these parameters depends then only on the rate of return on assets and on the over-all rate of growth of income, which in turn is the sum of population growth and the rate of increase of productivity.[7]

Table 1 gives some examples of the numerical value of the coefficients under the assumptions described above.

It should be emphasized that assumptions III to V have been introduced only for the sake of numerical estimation of the coefficients and are by no means necessary to insure the approximate constancy in time of the parameters in (1.6). A change in the assumptions would lead to somewhat different values of the parameters. But both a priori considerations and rough numerical calculations suggest that these values would not be drastically affected, and that it is generally possible to

[7] Strictly speaking the values of the parameters would vary somewhat depending on whether the growth of income results from population or from productivity growth. However, for rates of growth within the relevant range, say 0 to 4 per cent per year, the variation turns out so small that it can be ignored for present purposes.

TABLE 1—COEFFICIENTS OF THE CONSUMPTION FUNCTION (1.6) UNDER STATED ASSUMPTIONS[a]

Yield on assets (per cent)	0	0	0	3	5	5	5
Annual rate of growth of aggregate income (per cent)	0	3	4	0	0	3	4
$\alpha_1+\alpha_2$	.61	.64	—	.69	.73	—	—
α_3	.08	.07	.07	.11	.13	.12	.12

[a] Missing values have not been computed because of the complexity of calculation.

infer the direction in which these values would move when a specific assumption is changed. The recognition of the estate motive would tend to yield lower values for both coefficients, especially that of assets.[8]

On the whole, then, the values shown in Table 1 should be regarded as a rough guide to the order of magnitude of the coefficients consistent with the basic model; i.e., radically different values would cast serious doubts on the adequacy of the life cycle hypothesis.

C. *The Measurement of Expected Income*

The last point that must be clarified before we proceed to the discussion of the empirical tests is the measurement of expected nonproperty income, Y^e, which, at least at present, is not directly observable. A "naive" hypothesis is to assume that expected nonproperty income is the same as actual current income, except for a possible scale factor. Thus, we have:

$$Y_t^e = \beta' Y_t; \qquad \beta' \simeq 1.$$

Substituting the above expression into (1.6), we obtain the aggregate consumption function

$$C_t = (\alpha_1' + \beta'\alpha_2') Y_t + \alpha_3' A_{t-1} = \alpha_1 Y_t + \alpha_3 A_{t-1}$$
$$\alpha_1 = \alpha_1' + \beta'\alpha_2' \simeq \alpha_1' + \alpha_2'.$$

We designate this formulation as hypothesis I.

A similar but somewhat more sophisticated formulation is to assume that expected income is an exponentially weighted average of past income, weights adding up to one, or slightly more than one in order to reflect the expected growth [15] [16]. But it is quite difficult to deter-

[8] On the other hand, if we assume (i) that the preferred pattern of allocation of consumption and the pattern of income over life are the type suggested by the available cross-section data, (ii) that income expectation is consistent with the prevailing pattern of income, again suggested by the cross-section data over age groups, then the resulting coefficients of income and assets in equation (1.6) would be somewhat higher than those reported in Table 1.

mine the weights from the data we have at our disposal, and Friedman, who favors this formulation, has acknowledged its shortcomings [15].

The third possible formulation is a slight modification of the first. Under our definitions, Y, and expected income, Y^e, are nonproperty or labor income, excluding, for instance, profits. We may hypothesize that for those currently employed, average expected income, y_t^e, is current income adjusted for a possible scale factor, i.e.,

$$y_t^e = \beta_1 \frac{Y_t}{E_t} \tag{1.7}$$

where E_t is the number of persons engaged in production. We should expect β_1 to be quite close to unity.

For those individuals who are currently unemployed, we hypothesize that expected income is proportional to the average current income of those who are employed. The proportionality constant in this case represents three factors. First, as before, there may be some influence from expected growth. Second, and probably most important, the incidence of unemployment is likely to be smaller for higher-paid occupations than for lower-paid, less-skilled workers; hence, the average earnings the unemployed can look forward to, if reemployed, are likely to be lower than the average earnings of those currently employed. Third, it seems reasonable to suppose that some of the currently unemployed persons would expect their current unemployment status to continue for some time and, possibly, to recur. We shall therefore assume:

$$y_t^{eu} = \beta_2 \frac{Y_t}{E_t} \tag{1.8}$$

where y_t^{eu} is the average expected income of unemployed persons; and, for the reasons given above, we expect the constant β_2 to be substantially smaller than β_1. The aggregate expected income is then given by:

$$\begin{aligned} Y_t^e &= E_t y_t^e + (L_t - E_t) y_t^{eu} = E_t \beta_1 \frac{Y_t}{E_t} + (L_t - E_t) \beta_2 \frac{Y_t}{E_t} \\ &= (\beta_1 - \beta_2) Y_t + \beta_2 \frac{L_t}{E_t} Y_t \end{aligned} \tag{1.9}$$

where L_t denotes the total labor force.[9]

Substituting (1.9) into (1.6), we obtain the following variant of hypothesis I,

$$C_t = \alpha_1 Y_t + \alpha_2 \frac{L_t}{E_t} Y_t + \alpha_3 A_{t-1} \tag{1.10}$$

[9] See Ando [1]. Mincer in [28] relied on a similar device, except that he used population in place of labor force.

where

$$\alpha_1 = \alpha_1' + \alpha_2'(\beta_1 - \beta_2)$$
$$\alpha_2 = \alpha_2'\beta_2; \qquad \alpha_3 = \alpha_3'.$$

We designate the formulation embodied in equation (1.10) above as hypothesis II.

Since β_1 is thought to be close to unity, we have

$$\alpha_1 + \alpha_2 = \alpha_1' + \beta_1\alpha_2' \simeq \alpha_1' + \alpha_2'. \tag{1.11}$$

The individual values of the observable coefficients α_1 and α_2 are, however, dependent on the nonobservable value of β_2, about which there is little we can say a priori.

II. *Empirical Verification and Estimation*

In this section we report results of a number of tests of our model for the United States.[10] Unless otherwise stated, the period of observation is 1929 through 1959 excluding the Second World War years 1941–46.[11] Consumption, C, labor income net of taxes, Y, and net worth, A, are all measured in billions of current dollars as called for by our hypothesis.[12]

In recent years, economists have become increasingly aware of the many sources of bias, inconsistency, and inefficiency that beset prevailing estimation procedures, e.g., the existence of simultaneous relations, errors of observations in the "independent" variables, spurious correlation, multicollinearity, and heteroscedascity.[13] As a result, the simple-minded and straightforward least-squares approach is being replaced by a host of alternative procedures. Unfortunately most of these alternative procedures are designed to cope with one specific source of difficulty, and they often do so at the cost of increasing the difficulties arising from other sources. Under these conditions, we feel that the best course is to utilize a variety of procedures, exploiting our knowledge of the structure of the model and the nature of data to devise methods whose biases are likely to go in opposite directions. By following such a procedure, we can at least have some confidence that the

[10] The data and the procedure by which they have been obtained will be found in Ando, Brown, Kareken, and Solow [3, Data App.]. The derivation of labor income after taxes is particularly troublesome and is based in part on methods suggested by [13] and [38].

[11] A few experiments were made using data including the Second World War years, and equation (1.6) appears to explain consumption behavior during these years better than any other consumption function to our knowledge. However, the fit is still not very good, and, at any rate, we do not feel that these years are relevant because of their obviously special characteristics.

[12] In this section, the time subscript will be omitted whenever there is no danger of confusion.

[13] See, for instance, Theil [40].

estimates obtained by different methods will bracket the value of the unknown parameters being estimated.

The main alternative procedures used and the estimates obtained are summarized in Table 2. Row (1) shows the results of a straightforward least-squares fit of hypothesis I.[14] The coefficients of both independent variables are highly significant and R^2 extremely high. But in other respects, the results are not altogether satisfactory. The coefficient of Y, which is an estimate of $\alpha_1+\alpha_2$, is somewhat higher and that of A appreciably lower than our model would lead us to expect. Furthermore, the Durbin-Watson statistic [10] falls considerably short of 2, suggesting the presence of pronounced serial correlation in the residuals.

As can be seen from row (2), the results do not change appreciably if we replace hypothesis I with II by introducing an additional variable Y_E^L. Although the coefficient of Y_E^L has the right sign it does not appear to contribute significantly to the explanation of C. Meanwhile, it reduces still further the estimate of the coefficient of net worth, and increases the estimate of $\alpha_1+\alpha_2$ which, it will be recalled, is approximately given by the sum of the coefficients of Y and Y_E^L. Also, the serial correlation of the residuals does not change at all. As will soon become apparent, much of the difficulty with hypothesis II can be traced back to multicollinearity, which makes it rather hard to obtain reliable estimates of the individual coefficients.

Note also that in both (1) and (2) the constant term is very significantly different from zero by customary standards, a result which would seem inconsistent with the hypothesis tested. In our view, however, this result is not as serious as might appear at first glance. The constant term is numerically rather small, amounting to only about 5 per cent of the mean value of the dependent variable. Furthermore, we know that the least-squares estimate of the constant term is upward-biased in the present instance because of the simultaneous-equations bias as well as because of errors of measurement in the independent variables.[15] While the size of these biases cannot be directly estimated, we suspect it to be appreciable. Accordingly, on the basis of presently available evidence, we see no compelling reason to reject the hypothesis that consumption is in fact roughly homogeneous in income and assets. Under these circumstances, a more reliable estimate of the coefficients of these variables might be obtained by suppressing the constant term in accordance with the specification of our model.

The constrained estimation results in the equations reported in rows (3) and (5) of Table 2. A comparison of row (1) and row (3) shows that this procedure leads to estimates which are more nearly of the order

[14] In this section, we shall refer to equations by the rows in Table 2.

[15] See footnote 17.

TABLE 2

ESTIMATES OF THE COEFFICIENTS OF THE CONSUMPTION FUNCTION

Rows	Hypothesis Tested	Mode of Regression[a]	Coefficients and Their Standard Errors of Estimates[b]						$\alpha_1+\alpha_2$	Standard Error of Dependent Variable	Standard Error of Estimate	R^2[c]	Durbin-Watson Statistic
			Constant	Y (α_1)	XY (α_{1x})	$Y(L/E)$ (α_2)	A (α_3)	XA (α_{3x})					
(1)	I	A	8.1 (1.0)	.75 (.05)	—	—	.042 (.009)	—	.75	88.289	2.233	.998	1.26
(2)	II	A	7.3	.65 (.11)	—	.13 (.13)	.037 (.011)	—	.78	88.289	2.188	.998	1.26
(3)	I	A	—	.56 (.09)	—	—	.081 (.015)	—	.56	88.289	4.414	.997	.33
(4)	I	A	—	.87 (.08)	—	—	.046 (.012)	−.018 (.003)	.87	88.289	2.826	.998	1.13
(5)	II	A	—	.59 (.16)	—	.19 (.12)	.036 (.017)	—	.78	88.289	3.443	.998	.74
(6)	I	B	—	.52 (.11)	—	—	.072 (.018)	—	.52	8.292	2.208	.929	1.85
(7)	I	B	—	.60 (.16)	−.11 (.13)	—	.074 (.018)	—	.60[d]	8.292	2.177	.931	1.92
(8)	I	B	—	.51 (.12)	—	—	.089 (.031)	−.017 (.024)	.51	8.292	2.184	.930	1.91
(9)	II	B	—	.44 (.12)	—	.24 (.15)	.049 (.022)	—	.68	8.292	2.090	.936	1.74
(10)	II	B	—	.39 (.13)	—	.31 (.16)	.076 (.029)	−.033 (.024)	.70	8.292	1.994	.942	1.91
(11)	I	C	—	.44 (.05)	—	—	.105 (.008)	—	.44	.092	.030	.899	.34
(12)	I	C	—	.69 (.07)	−.07 (.02)	—	.071 (.009)	—	.69[d]	.092	.021	.948	.93
(13)	I	C	—	.69 (.06)	—	—	.071 (.009)	−.012 (.003)	.69	.092	.020	.953	.95
(14)	II	C	—	.62 (.09)	−.06 (.02)	.10 (.08)	.065 (.011)	—	.71[d]	.092	.021	.948	.93
(15)	II	C	—	.63 (.09)	—	.09 (.08)	.066 (.010)	−.011 (.003)	.71	.092	.020	.953	1.03

[a] A: Regressions in which variables are used in the original form.
B: Regressions in which variables are used in the first-difference form.
C: Regressions in which variables are used in the form of ratios to labor income.

[b] Figures in parentheses underneath the estimates are estimated standard errors of respective estimates. Number of observations = 25. Where no estimate is shown, the variable is excluded from the equation.

[c] The ratio of the variance of the residual to the variance of the dependent variable.

[d] Figures given do not include the coefficient of XY. In other words, the estimate of the coefficient pertains to the period 1929–40.

of magnitude suggested by our model. Unfortunately the serial correlation is now so high that the reliability of the estimate is open to serious question. From row (5) it also appears that the addition of the variable Y_E^L is again not very helpful. Though its contribution is still hardly significant, it again lowers the coefficient of A, and the serial correlation remains high.

A common procedure in time-series analysis when serial correlation of errors is high is to work with first differences. In the present instance this procedure also serves to reduce drastically the degree of multicollinearity and provides a more meaningful test for the adequacy of the hypothesis as a causal explanation of consumption. The results, reported in rows (6) and (9) and in Figure 1, appear quite favorable to the hypothesis. The multiple correlation remains quite high and the coefficient of net worth is highly significant. Also the Durbin-Watson statistic improves considerably and there is no longer any reason to suspect that the reliability of the estimate is seriously affected by serial correlation of residuals. Furthermore, a comparison of row (6) with row (3) reveals a relatively minor change in the estimates of the coefficients of both Y and A, tending to increase our confidence in these estimates. Also from row (9), we see that the introduction of the variable Y_E^L produces now a much less drastic change in the estimates of the coefficients: the estimate of α_3 in particular is reduced only from .07 to .05, while that of $\alpha_1+\alpha_2$ is raised from .52 to .68. On the other hand, a comparison of row (5) and row (9) reveals that the relatively small change in the estimate of $\alpha_1+\alpha_2$ from .78. to .68 is accompanied by a marked shift in the relative size of the coefficients of Y and Y_E^L, the first falling and the second rising appreciably.

An interpretation and explanation of these various results is readily found. When we deal with actual values the movements of all the variables are dominated by their common trend. On the other hand, when dealing with first differences we are primarily focusing on short-run or cyclical variations. Now with respect to such variations, consumption is much more stable than income, even labor income. This stability is accounted for in our model by the fact that both net worth and expected labor income are more stable than current income in the short run, even though all the variables move together in the longer run. These considerations help to explain why in row (9) the coefficient of current income is appreciably lower than in row (5), while the coefficients of the two remaining, cyclically more stable, variables are correspondingly increased. Equation (9) suggests that consumption may be less sensitive to purely cyclical and temporary swings in current labor income than the estimates reported in row (5) indicate. At the same time the fact that both Y_E^L and A perform a similar function in stabilizing consump-

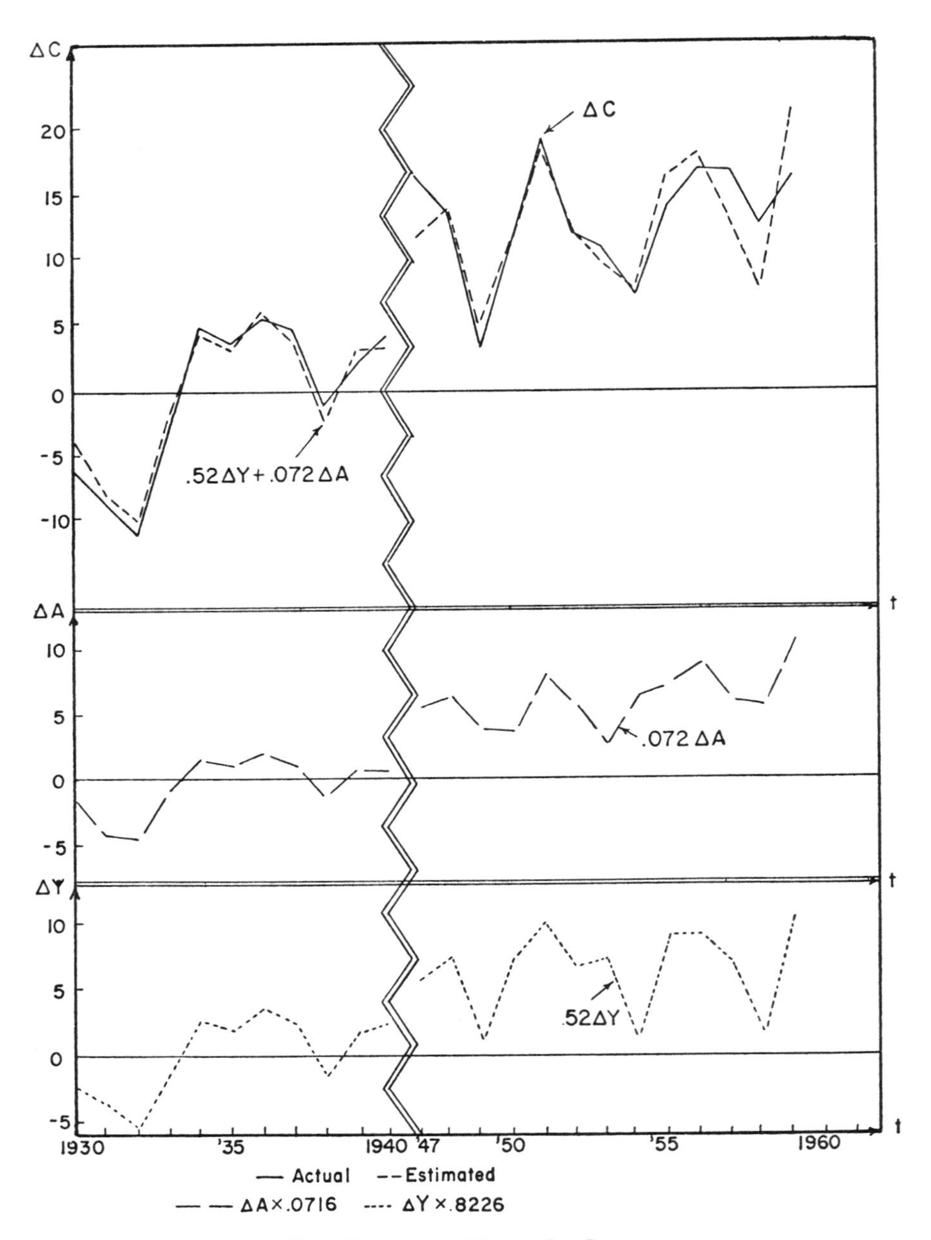

FIGURE 1. TIME PROFILE OF (6) AND ITS COMPONENTS

tion with respect to short-run variations in Y helps to explain why the addition of the latter variable generally tends to reduce not only the coefficient of Y but also that of A, even though its own contribution is statistically not very significant. It would thus seem that from the available data we cannot obtain a very reliable estimate of the role of each variable separately.[16]

All the estimates reported so far are based on the least-squares method applied to a single equation. As is well known this method leads to estimates which are biased, even in the limit, when one or more of the "independent" variables are related to the dependent variable by other simultaneous relations. In the present instance the variable A can be taken as predetermined, but the same is not true of labor income which is related to consumption via total income. That is, the true error component of the consumption function cannot be assumed to be uncorrelated with Y, and hence the least-squares estimates of its parameters are not consistent. Specifically, it can be shown that, asymptotically, the estimator of the coefficient of Y is upward-biased and that of the coefficient of A downward-biased.[17]

The only really adequate way of resolving this difficulty would be to construct a complete model of the U. S. economy and then apply an appropriate simultaneous-equations estimation procedure. This approach would lead at least to consistent estimates, except to the extent that the model was incomplete or misspecified and the exogenous variables were subject to errors of measurement. Furthermore, the effi-

[16] The simple correlation between ΔA and $\Delta(Y_E^L)$ is .93, higher than that between ΔY and $\Delta(Y_E^L)$, .89.

[17] Let us denote the *true* error term in equation (1.6) by ϵ. Then, under the assumption that the correlation between Y and A and that between Y and ϵ are positive, while A and ϵ are uncorrelated with each other, it can be readily shown that

$$\text{plim}\ \hat{\alpha}_1 = \alpha_1 + \text{plim} \frac{\sum A^2 \sum Y\epsilon}{\sum A^2 \sum Y^2 - (\sum AY)^2} \geq \alpha_1$$

$$\text{plim}\ \hat{\alpha}_3 = \alpha_3 - \text{plim} \frac{\sum Y\epsilon \sum AY}{\sum A^2 \sum Y^2 - (\sum AY)^2} \leq \alpha_3$$

where $\hat{\alpha}_1$ and $\hat{\alpha}_3$ are the least squares estimates of α_1 and α_3, respectively.

The above formulae are stated for the case in which the constant is suppressed, but for the case where the constant is not suppressed, it is only necessary to reinterpret the symbols as deviations from respective means. The asymptotic bias for the constant term can then be expressed in terms of the above limits and the means of the variables involved. Denoting the constant term and its least squares estimate by γ and $\hat{\gamma}$ respectively, it can be shown that

$$\text{plim}\ (\hat{\gamma} - \gamma) = \text{plim} \frac{\sum Y'\epsilon}{\sum A'^2 \sum Y'^2 - (\sum A'Y')^2} (\bar{A} \sum A'Y' - \bar{Y} \sum A'^2)$$

where the primed symbols denote the deviations from the mean. The estimate from our data of the probability limit of the expression inside the parenthesis is positive and fairly large, so that the asymptotic bias of the least squares estimate of the constant term is most likely to be positive.

ciency of the estimates might be reduced, particularly if the theory and data relating to other sectors of the economy were less reliable than those relating to the consumption sector. Whatever the merits of this approach, however, we regard the specification of a complete model beyond the scope of this paper.

A compromise followed by some authors is to introduce an accounting identity relating consumption, saving, and income, note that saving is equal to investment, assume that investment is autonomous, and estimate the parameters of the consumption function from the regression of consumption on saving [39] [43]. Now in our view this procedure is likely to lead to bias in the estimates of the parameters which is more serious than that resulting from the conventional regression on income. The arguments supporting this conclusion are developed formally in Appendix, section B and can be summarized here as follows:

1. When the "independent" variable is subject to errors of measurement, the resulting estimate of the regression coefficient is biased toward zero, the more so the greater the variance of the error of measurement of the independent variable relative to its true variance. Now since personal saving is in the order of one-tenth of disposable income, it is reasonable to suppose that the variance of true (as distinguished from measured) personal saving is a good deal smaller than the variance of disposable income. At the same time, personal saving, as actually measured in the national income accounts, represents the difference between largely independent estimates of disposable income and of personal consumption. Hence the error of measurement of personal saving is likely to be even larger than that of disposable income. We can therefore be rather confident that the bias toward zero due to errors of measurement will be a good deal more serious when consumption is regressed on personal saving than when it is regressed on disposable income. Furthermore, given the estimating procedure, the error of measurement of consumption is likely to be negatively correlated with the error of measurement of saving, and this negative correlation will produce a further downward bias in the estimate of the true regression coefficient.

2. Personal saving is *not* identically equal to investment either conceptually or in terms of actual measurement, and investment is *not* exogenous, or independent of consumption, even in the short run, especially when account is taken of investment in inventories. At least over a very short period of time, such as a quarter or less, it is quite likely that random variations in consumption behavior will be accompanied by random variations in personal saving in the opposite direction, and, to the extent that this is true, an estimate of the propensity to consume based on the regression of consumption on saving will be seriously downward-biased, even in the absence of errors of measurement.

For the problem at hand, there exists an alternative and relatively simple way of securing consistent estimates of the parameters in hypothesis I. Relying on the specification that the constant term is zero and that the true error is uncorrelated with A, this procedure consists in (i) regressing income on assets, and obtaining computed values of Y from this regression, say Y_c; (ii) then regressing C on Y_c and on A. The coefficients of Y_c and A so obtained can be shown to be consistent estimators of the coefficients of Y and A respectively.[18]

Unfortunately the application of this procedure to our problem yields rather meaningless results (the point estimate of the coefficient of Y turns out to be negative!). This outcome is not entirely surprising in view of the high degree of multicollinearity present and the fact that this procedure is probably not a very efficient one. Since multicollinearity is reduced by first-differencing data, we have applied this procedure to the first differences, though the assumptions which assure the consistency of the estimates are no longer strictly tenable in this case.[19] The resulting estimates of α_1 and α_3 turned out to be .67 and .05.

Another possible way of coping with the problem of bias in the estimates resulting from a known cause but of unknown magnitude is to construct an alternative estimation procedure in which the same cause may be expected to produce a bias in the opposite direction. If this can be done, then the unknown parameters may be bracketed by the estimates generated by the two alternative procedures, and if they are close together, then we may conclude with some confidence that the bias in either procedure is not too serious. For this purpose, suppose that

[18] Suppose that we estimate the parameters of the following equation by the method of least squares:

(a) $$Y = b_y A + a_y + \eta_y$$

where η_y is the error term.

The substitution of the value of Y estimated by (a) into equation (1.6) yields

(b) $$C = \alpha_1(b_y A + a_y) + \alpha_3 A + \epsilon = (\alpha_1 b_y + \alpha_3)A + \alpha_1 a_y + \epsilon.$$

Comparison of equation (b) with the regression of C on A

(c) $$C = b_c A + a_c + \eta_c$$

results in

(d) $$\alpha_1 b_y + \alpha_3 = b_c$$

(e) $$\alpha_1 a_y = a_c$$

(d) and (e) can then be solved to give the estimated values of α_1 and α_3. These estimates are identical with those resulting from the two-stage least-squares procedure described in the text.

[19] Since $A_{t-1} = A_{t-2} + S_{t-1}$ and S_{t-1} depends on Y_{t-1} and C_{t-1}, it must be admitted that the possibility of a positive correlation between A_{t-1} and ϵ_{t-1}, and hence between ΔA_{t-1} and $\Delta\epsilon_t$, cannot be ruled out. However, it seems safe to assume that this correlation, if it exists, is reasonably small.

we divide both sides of equation (1.6) by Y, obtaining

$$\frac{C}{Y} = \alpha_1 + \alpha_3 \frac{A}{Y}$$

and then proceed to estimate the parameters of this equation by the conventional least squares method. It can be shown that, in so far as the bias due to the positive correlation between Y and the true error of the consumption function is concerned, the least-squares estimate of α_3 will be upward-biased, and hence, that of α_1 will be downward-biased. Thus, for both coefficients, the bias is in the direction opposite to that resulting from other procedures reported so far. This approach has also other desirable properties: it eliminates the difficulties arising from the presence of strong multicollinearity, and the homoscedasticity condition is more likely to be satisfied. Furthermore, it eliminates altogether the common trend in the variables, thus providing a rather stringent test of the relevance of net worth as a determinant of consumption. Its main drawback is that the above-mentioned bias in the estimates may be appreciably reinforced by error of measurement in the variable Y, although error of measurement in A will tend to work in the opposite direction.[20]

The results of this test reported in row (12) are rather mixed. The still remarkably high value of R^2 provides strong support for the hypothesis. Also, as expected, the procedure yields a higher estimate of α_1 and lower estimate for α_3. But the gap between the estimates obtained in this manner and those reported earlier is so wide as to provide little useful information as to the true value of these coefficients. Furthermore, the very high serial correlation of errors casts serious doubt on the reliability of the estimates.

The high serial correlation in the estimated errors, in this and to a lesser extent in other procedures, suggests the desirability of testing for evidence of a significant change in the parameters of our consumption function as between the prewar and the postwar period. Individual tastes as well as the demographic structure and the rate of return on assets, on which the theoretical values of the coefficients depend, may have changed sufficiently over the two periods to cause a measurable change in the parameters. In addition, there exists a statistical problem arising from the fact that the data, particularly the net worth estimates, are based on somewhat different estimating procedures for the two periods. To test the hypothesis of a shift in parameters we have computed a number of regressions involving a "dummy" variable X, with value zero for the years 1929–40 and value one for the years 1947–59.

The results given in rows (4), (7), (8), (10), and (12) to (14), which

[20] For possible problems arising from the use of ratios, see [26] and [37].

constitute a representative sample of the tests we have carried out, show that the coefficient of the dummy variable is consistently negative, suggesting a moderate downward shift in the "measured" consumption function in the postwar period.[21] In the first-difference test the shift is not statistically significant and the coefficients of the other variables are altered only slightly. In the constrained and the ratio estimates, the downward shift is generally significant, and the serial correlation of the observed errors is reduced appreciably though it still remains high;[22] there also occur some sizable changes in the coefficients of the other variables. At least in the case of the ratio estimates, these changes tend on the whole to increase the agreement between the various results, which we may now endeavor to summarize.

In the first place, all of the tests seem, by and large, to support the basic hypothesis advanced in this paper, and in particular, the importance of net worth as a determinant of consumption. Unfortunately, serious difficulties arise in the attempt to secure reliable estimates of the coefficients of the "independent" variables, although some tentative conclusions seem to stand out. First, the different estimation procedures when applied to hypothesis I generally yield a similar estimate of the coefficient of net worth for the period as a whole, somewhere between .07 and .08. [Cf. rows (3), (6), (7), and (12), but note (11).]

At the same time, the estimate of the coefficient of income is definitely

[21] Our model provides one possible clue to this apparent downward shift. An examination of the figures reported in [3] reveals a distinct decline in the ratio of nonlabor income to net worth, which can be taken as a measure of the rate of return on capital. This is presumably attributable in large measure to increases in corporate taxes and in the extent and progressiveness of personal income taxation. An examination of the values of the coefficients of income and net worth implied by our model, reported in Table 1, suggests that both coefficients should tend to decline as the rate of return on assets declines. However, we do not wish to press this point, especially since we cannot even be sure whether the apparent decline in the coefficients reflects anything more than error of measurement.

[22] Another possible explanation for the high serial correlation in some of the tests is that consumption does not adjust fully to changes in income and assets within the arbitrary time unit of one year. To allow for this possibility hypothesis I might be written as

$$C_t - C_{t-1} = \delta(\alpha_1 Y_t + \alpha_3 A_{t-1} - C_{t-1}), \text{ or } C_t = (1-\delta)C_{t-1} + \delta\alpha_1 Y_t + \delta\alpha_3 A_{t-1},$$

where the constant δ, with the dimension 1/time, measures the speed of adjustment of consumption and may be expected to approach unity as the time unit increases. This hypothesis was tested in ratio form (to avoid increasing further the already extremely high multicollinearity prevailing in the direct form) with the following results:

$$\frac{C_t}{Y_t} = .46 + \underset{(.077)}{.177}\frac{C_{t-1}}{Y_t} + \underset{(.016)}{.072}\frac{A_{t-1}}{Y_t}$$

implying $\delta = .82$, $\alpha_1 = .56$, $\alpha_3 = .087$.

The relatively low coefficient of C_{t-1} (which is only moderately significant) suggests that a span of one year is long enough for most of the adjustment to take place. Also the estimates of the remaining coefficients are not greatly affected and move closer to the first difference estimates. However, somewhat surprisingly, the serial correlation is increased still further.

unstable [see rows (3), (4), (6), (8), (10), and (12)]. This instability is appreciably reduced under hypothesis II, where the third variable, Y_E^L, apparently helps to disentangle the effect of purely cyclical and transitory changes in nonproperty income from that of long-run or permanent changes. The various estimates for the long-run marginal propensity, $\alpha_1+\alpha_2$, are fairly consistent—between .68 and .71 for the first-difference and the ratio estimates [rows (9), (11), and (15)], and only moderately higher for the straight estimate with constant suppressed [row (5)]. There is however much less consistency in the values of α_1 and α_2 separately and hence in the estimates of the short-run marginal propensity to consume with respect to labor income, α_1. The first-difference approach yields figures of .39 and .44 [rows (9) and (11)], while the estimates from straight regression with the constant suppressed and from regression on ratios [rows (5) and (15)] are about .6. On the whole we are inclined to regard the first estimates as somewhat more reliable, in part because of the high serial correlation present in rows (5) and (15), but no firm conclusion seems warranted with the available data and methods. At the same time we observe that the introduction of the third variable, Y_E^L, tends to reduce somewhat the estimate of the coefficient of net worth. It would appear that the value .07 to .08 obtained for hypothesis I, where Y_E^L is not present, may be somewhat too high—since the cyclically sluggish variable A acts partly as a proxy for expected nonlabor income—and the true value may be closer to .06 or even somewhat lower.

Our tests also agree in suggesting a moderate downward shift in both parameters, $\alpha_1+\alpha_2$, and α_3 of the measured consumption function from the prewar to the postwar period, although it does not seem possible at present to estimate reliably the distribution of this downward shift between $\alpha_1+\alpha_2$ and α_3.

As indicated earlier, a few tests of hypothesis I have also been carried out for the period 1900–28. Because the data for this period are mostly obtained from different sources and are subject to very wide margin of error, we have seen little point in combining them with the series relating to the period since 1929. In fact, we are inclined to attach rather little significance to the results of these tests, which are accordingly confined to Appendix section A. For whatever they are worth, these results do not appear grossly inconsistent with those for the period after 1929, especially when account is taken of error of measurement and its likely effects on different estimation procedures. In particular, the contribution of net worth appears again to be significant, its coefficient being of the same order of magnitude as in the later period except in the first-difference test which is obviously most seriously affected by the error of measurement.

Finally, our empirical results are also roughly consistent with the a priori numerical predictions reported in Table 1. The fact that the coefficients of both variables, especially that of net worth, are on the low side may be accounted for by reference to the estate motive which was ignored in the numerical calculations for Table 1, while it probably plays a nonnegligible role at least for the high-income and/or self-employed groups.[23]

III. *Some Implications*

A. *Relation to the Standard Keynesian Consumption Functions*

The standard Keynesian consumption function [23] is usually written in the form:

$$C = \gamma Y^* + \gamma_0 \tag{3.1}$$

where Y^* denotes personal income net of taxes or disposable income and the γ's are constants.[24] A more sophisticated variant of this hypothesis, which has become quite popular of late, consists in separating income into two parts, disposable labor income Y, and disposable nonlabor or property income, which we shall denote by P. Thus,

$$C = \gamma_1 Y + \gamma_2 P + \gamma_0. \tag{3.2}$$

This variant, which reduces to (3.1) when $\gamma_1 = \gamma_2$, is usually advocated on the ground that property income accrues mostly to higher-income and/or entrepreneurial groups who may be expected to have a lower marginal propensity to consume. Accordingly, γ_2 is supposed to be smaller than γ_1 and this supposition appears to be supported by empirical findings.

It is immediately apparent that (3.2) bears considerable similarity to hypothesis I discussed in this paper, i.e.,

$$C = (\alpha_1 + \alpha_2) Y + \alpha_3 A. \tag{3.3}$$

The main difference lies in the constant term which appears in (3.2) but not in (3.3), and in the fact that the wealth variable A in (3.3) is replaced in (3.2) by a closely related variable, income from wealth, P. We can avoid dealing with the first source of discrepancy by working with both hypotheses in first-difference form,

$$\Delta C = \gamma_1 \Delta Y + \gamma_2 \Delta P \tag{3.2a}$$

$$\Delta C = (\alpha_1 + \alpha_2) \Delta Y + \alpha_3 \Delta A. \tag{3.3a}$$

Equations (3.2a) and (3.3a) are quite useful since they allow a straightforward test of the usefulness of the Modigliani-Brumberg hypothesis

[23] See for instance the results of cross-section studies reported in [24] and [32].

[24] Keynes' own formulation (See [23, Book 3]) was considerably more general than that contained in equation (3.1).

as compared with the standard Keynesian one. We have already exhibited in Table 2, row (6), the results obtained by fitting (3.3a) to the data. In order to complete the test we need to estimate the parameters of (3.2a). If the standard Keynesian version is correct, the net worth variable in (3.3) and (3.3a) is merely a proxy variable for the return from wealth, P, and hence substitution of ΔP for ΔA should improve the fit. On the other hand, if (3.3) and (3.3a) are closer to the truth than (3.2), then the substitution of ΔA by a proxy variable ΔP should reduce the correlation.

The estimate of P needed for this test is given in [3].[25] The definition of consumption on which we rely, however, is somewhat different from that customarily used in the standard Keynesian formulation in that it includes the current consumption—depreciation—of the stock of consumer durables, while excluding expenditure for the purchase of such goods.[26] The results obtained for hypothesis (3.2a) are as follows:

$$\Delta C = \underset{(.07)}{.93\Delta Y} + \underset{(.29)}{.07\Delta P} \qquad R^2 = .86. \tag{3.4}$$

Comparison of this result with those reported in Table 2, row (6), strongly suggests that net worth is definitely not a mere proxy for current property income. While the coefficient of P is positive and smaller than that of Y as expected, this variable is much less useful than A in explaining the behavior of consumption. In fact, its contribution is not significantly different from zero.[27]

[25] Our estimates of Y and P do not add up exactly to disposable personal income as usually defined because we include in disposable personal income contributions to, instead of benefits from, the social security system. However, this discrepancy is quite minor.

[26] Also, our data are in current dollars, while the standard Keynesian version of the consumption function is usually stated in terms of constant dollars.

[27] For the sake of completeness several other variants of (3.2a) were tested by adding variables that were included in the test of our hypothesis and which are consistent with the spirit of the Keynesian model. The addition of the variable ΔY_E^L, which might help to sort out the effect of long run from that of purely cyclical variations in income, yields

$$\Delta C = \underset{(.18)}{.47\Delta Y} + \underset{(.13)}{.49\Delta (Y_E^L)} + \underset{(.23)}{.17\Delta P} \qquad R^2 = .921. \tag{3.4a}$$

If we also include the dummy variable X to allow for possible shifts from the prewar to the postwar period, its coefficient is uniformly less than its standard error, and in general hypothesis (3.2) does not fare any better. This conclusion can be illustrated by the following result which is the most favorable to that hypothesis among the battery we have run:

$$\Delta C = \underset{(.14)}{.46\Delta Y} + \underset{(.14)}{.51\Delta (Y_E^L)} + \underset{(.28)}{.26\Delta P} - \underset{(.39)}{.21X\Delta P} \qquad R^2 = .921. \tag{3.4b}$$

The fact that in (3.4a) and (3.4b) the coefficient of the variable ΔY_E^L is a good deal higher and statistically more significant than in the corresponding tests reported in Table 2 is readily accounted for by the high correlation between this variable and A which, in the absence of A, makes this variable act partly as a proxy for A. (The correlation in question is .93. See also footnote 16.)

These results, besides supporting our hypothesis, serve also to cast serious doubts on the conventional interpretation of the empirical coefficients of ΔY and ΔP in (3.2); namely, that incremental labor income is largely consumed while incremental property income is largely saved. For our tests of the Modigliani-Brumberg model indicate that consumption is quite responsive to variations in the market value of wealth, which, in turn, must largely reflect the capitalization of property income. Note, however, that the market valuation of assets will be controlled by expected long-run returns, say $\overline{P}$, which will tend to be a good deal more stable than *current* property income, P. We suggest therefore that the coefficient of P in (3.2) is small not because property income is largely saved but because short-run changes in P are dominated by transitory phenomena and hence are a poor measure of changes in the relevant long-run, or permanent, property income, which will be reflected far more reliably in the market valuation of assets. Put somewhat differently, the low coefficient of P does not imply a low marginal propensity to consume out of property income but merely a low propensity to consume out of transitory income. Correspondingly the extremely high coefficient of labor income in (3.3) is equally misleading, reflecting the fact that Y acts partly as a proxy for the permanent component of property income, $\overline{P}$.

One might be tempted to estimate the marginal propensity to consume with respect to permanent property income $\overline{P}$ by relying on the estimates of the coefficient of net worth in (3.3a) provided in Table 2, and on the relation

$$\overline{P} \simeq rA \quad \text{or} \quad A \simeq \frac{\overline{P}}{r}.$$

Following this reasoning, the coefficient of $\overline{P}$ in the consumption function would be given by $\frac{\alpha_3}{r}$, where r is the rate at which the market capitalizes the return from assets. If we are willing to approximate r with the average realized rate of return on assets, then, from the figures given in [3], we find that r was about .04 in the prewar period and somewhat lower (around .03) in more recent years.[28] Combining this estimate with our estimate of α_3, which is in the order of .06, we seem to be led to the conclusion that the marginal propensity to consume with respect to permanent property income $\frac{\alpha_3}{r}$, far from being low, is actually well above unity.

This result may appear preposterous if judged in terms of the standard Keynesian framework underlying (3.2), with its emphasis on the relation

[28] See, however, our comment below on the shortcomings of our estimate of P given in [3] as a measure of return on assets.

between flows. It is however possible to interpret this result in terms of the Modigliani-Brumberg framework. For, in this model, wealth affects consumption not only through the stream of income it generates but also directly through its market value which provides a source of purchasing power to iron out variations in income arising from transitory developments as well as from the normal life cycle. It is therefore not surprising that this model implies a marginal propensity to consume with respect to assets, α_3, larger than the rate of return r (cf. Table 1), an inference which, as we have just seen, is supported by empirical tests. It should be noted however that $\frac{\alpha_3}{r}$ should not be interpreted as the marginal propensity to consume with respect to permanent property income in the same sense in which $(\alpha_1+\alpha_2)$ can be said to measure the propensity with respect to permanent nonproperty income, for it measures the *joint* effect on consumption of a change in property income, r constant, and of the accompanying change in assets. It is not possible to infer the two effects separately from knowledge of α_3 and of the average value of r. Although we cannot pursue this subject here, we wish to point out that the effect on C of a change in $\overline{P}$ will be quite different depending on the behavior of A and hence r, as $\overline{P}$ changes.

B. *Cyclical versus Long-Run Behavior of the Consumption-Income Ratio —Relation to the Duesenberry-Modigliani Consumption Function*

As is well known, one of the major difficulties encountered with the standard Keynesian consumption functions (3.1) or (3.2) lies in the constant term γ_0. This constant term is needed to account for the observed cyclical variability in the saving-income ratio, but it also implies a long-run tendency for the saving ratio to rise with income, which is contradicted by empirical findings. The lack of any positive association between income and the saving-income ratio in the long run, at least for the U. S. economy, was first uncovered by Kuznets, and has more recently been confirmed by the extensive investigation of Goldsmith [19], focusing on the years 1896–1949. In his summary recapitulation, he lists as the first item: "Long-term stability of aggregate personal saving at approximately one-eighth of income, and of national saving at approximately one-seventh."[29]

The consumption function proposed here is capable of accounting both for the long-run stability and the cyclical variability of the saving-income ratio. In order to exhibit its long-run properties, let us suppose that Y were to grow at a constant rate n, in which case Y^e can be taken as equal or proportional to Y. Suppose further that the rate of return on assets r is reasonably stable in time. Then the consumption function

[29] Goldsmith [19, Vol. 1, p. 22].

(1.6) implies that the income-net worth ratio, Y_t^*/A_{t-1} will tend to a constant h, related to the parameters of the consumption function by the equation:[30]

$$h = \frac{n + \alpha_3 - \alpha r}{1 - \alpha}; \qquad \alpha = \alpha_1 + \alpha_2 \cdot \tag{3.5}$$

When the ratio $\frac{Y_t^*}{A_{t-1}}$ is in fact equal to h, then income and net worth grow at the same rate, n, and the saving-income ratio will be a constant given by:

$$\frac{S_t}{Y_t^*} = \frac{A_t - A_{t-1}}{A_{t-1}} \frac{A_{t-1}}{Y_t^*} = n \frac{1}{h} \cdot \tag{3.6}$$

Similarly, we find:

$$\frac{Y_t}{A_{t-1}} = \frac{Y_t^* - rA_{t-1}}{A_{t-1}} = h - r \tag{3.7}$$

$$\frac{C_t}{Y_t} = \frac{Y_t^* - S_t}{A_{t-1}} \frac{A_{t-1}}{Y_t} = \frac{h - n}{h - r} \cdot \tag{3.8}$$

Thus the model implies that if income fluctuates around an exponential trend the income-net worth ratio will tend to fluctuate around a constant level h, and the saving-income ratio around a constant $\frac{n}{h}$.

The empirical estimates reported in Section II suggest that α is around .7, and α_3 close to .06. The average rate of return, r, is much more difficult to guess. If we are willing to rely on the ratio $\frac{P}{A_{t-1}}$ for this purpose, then r would be around or somewhat lower than .04. But this

[30] Under the stated assumptions we have $Y_t^* = Y_t + P_t$, and $P_t = rA_{t-1}$. Hence, saving can be expressed as

$$S_t = Y_t^* - C_t = Y_t + P_t - C_t = (1 - \alpha)Y_t^* - (\alpha_3 - \alpha r)A_{t-1}. \tag{a}$$

We also have $S_t = A_t - A_{t-1}$. Substituting this definition for S_t in (a), dividing through by A_{t-1}, adding and subtracting n, and then rearranging terms, we obtain

$$\frac{A_t - A_{t-1}}{A_{t-1}} = n + (1 - \alpha)\left[\frac{Y_t^*}{A_{t-1}} - \frac{n + \alpha_3 - \alpha r}{1 - \alpha}\right]. \tag{b}$$

Comparison of (b) above with equation (3.5) shows that if Y_t^*/A_{t-1} were larger than h, the second term in the right-hand side would be positive, and hence net worth would grow at a rate larger than that of income, n, causing Y_t^*/A_{t-1} to fall toward h: and conversely if Y_t^*/A_{t-1} were smaller than h.

This argument is oversimplified and incomplete, particularly since it ignores the interaction between the behavior of consumers and the production process in the economy. A more complete analysis of this growth process is given in Ando [2].

ratio is very likely to understate the true value for r, since the estimate of P given in [3] corresponds to the conventional definition of personal income and omits a number of items whose exclusion is appropriate for the standard Keynesian model but not for the Modigliani-Brumberg model. Among those items, the more important are imputed net rent on consumer durables and undistributed corporate profits.[31] These adjustments suggest an average value for r slightly over .04. If we further take for n, the rate of growth of income, a value in the order of .03, then from (3.6), (3.7), and (3.8) we obtain the following estimates for the various ratios under discussion: (i) total income to net worth, $h \simeq .2$; (ii) nonproperty income to net worth, $h-r \simeq .16$; (iii) saving to income, $\frac{n}{h} \simeq .15$. It can be seen that the first two of the above figures are in fact close to the values around which the ratios

$$\frac{Y_t^*}{A_{t-1}} \quad \text{and} \quad \frac{Y_t}{A_{t-1}}$$

fluctuate according to the data given in [3] while the third, the saving-income ratio, is consistent with the findings of Goldsmith reported earlier.

Needless to say, these calculations are very crude and are given here primarily to bring out certain interesting testable implications of the consumption function discussed in this paper. Among these implications the long-run stability of the ratio of net worth to income is particularly significant, for it paves the way for an explanation of the historical stability of the capital-output ratio in terms of the supply of capital, thereby challenging the prevailing notion that the behavior of this ratio is explained by technological requirements [1] [2] [5] [29].

As for the cyclical implications of our model, we need only observe that at any given point in time net worth A_{t-1} is a given initial condition. Hence, retaining for the moment the assumption that $Y^e \simeq Y$, (1.6) implies that the aggregate consumption function for any given year is a straight line in the C-Y plane with slope α and intercept $\alpha_3 A_{t-1}$. It is shown in Figure 2 for the year 0 as the line labeled $\overline{C}_0$, and looks like the orthodox Keynesian version. Yet, it differs from the latter in one essential respect, namely, that its intercept will change in time as a result of the accumulation (or decumulation) of wealth through saving. As we have shown in preceding paragraphs, so long as income keeps rising on its exponential trend, the growth in net worth will shift the function in such a way that the observed consumption-income points will trace out the long-run consumption function (3.8) represented in

[31] The rationale for including corporate saving in property income and personal saving is given in Modigliani and Miller [36].

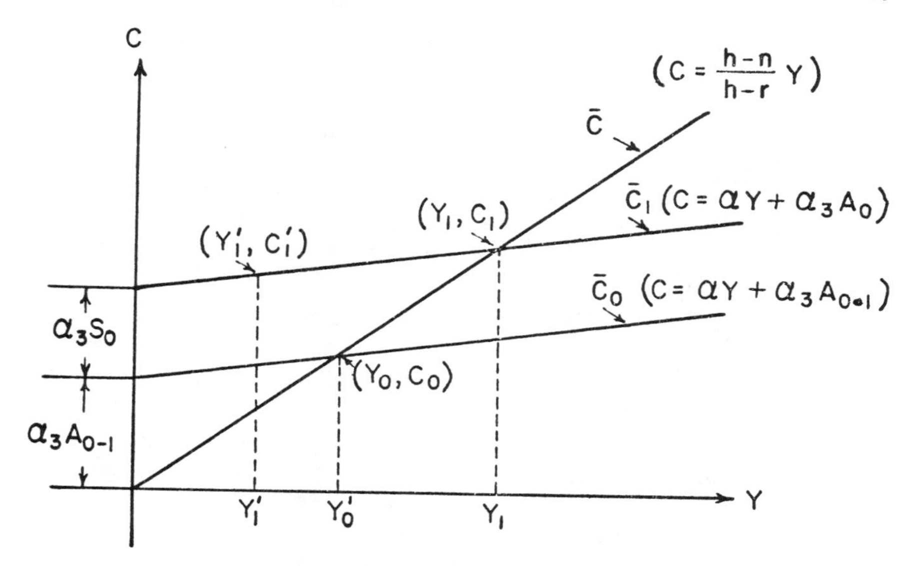

FIGURE 2. CONSUMPTION INCOME RELATIONS: LONG-RUN AND SHORT-RUN

our graph by the line $\overline{C}$ through the origin. This point is illustrated in Figure 2 for two years, 0 and 1. However, suppose that a cyclical disturbance caused income to fall short of Y_1, say to the level Y'_1. Then the consumption C'_1 given by the short-run consumption function $\overline{C}_1$ implies a higher consumption-income ratio and a lower saving-income ratio.

Thus, cyclical swings in income from its long-run trend will cause swings in the saving-income ratio in the same direction,[32] especially since the position of the function will not change appreciably when income is cyclically depressed below its previous peak due to the small or negative saving that would prevail.[33] After income has recovered beyond the previous peak, it may for a while rise rapidly as it catches up with

[32] This phenomenon will be further accentuated when we recognize the possibility that a cyclical fall in Y is likely to bring about a smaller change in Y^e. Also, because property income may be expected to fluctuate cyclically even more than labor income, the ratio of saving to total income will fluctuate even more than the ratio of saving to labor income. See footnote 30, equation (a).

[33] Some downward shift of the consumption function might occur even in the absence of dissaving, if there is some downward revaluation of the market value of assets, as the depressed level of property income tends to bring about less favorable evaluation of the long-run prospects for return from assets.

Because of this dependence of the value of assets on property income, the statement made earlier to the effect that A_{t-1} can be taken as a given initial condition in the year t is only approximately true. Also the relation $\Delta A_t = S_t$ does not hold in the presence of capital gains and losses. Note however that what is relevant in the present connection is the change in the value of assets in terms of purchasing power over consumption goods and not the change in terms of money value, which may be considerably more severe.

its trend, running ahead of the slowly adjusting wealth. In this phase we may observe points to the right of $\overline{C}$, and the corresponding high saving will tend to make A catch up with Y.

Thus the model advanced here may be expected to generate a behavior of consumption and saving which is very similar to that implied by the earlier Duesenberry-Modigliani type of hypothesis, in which consumption was expressed as a function of current income and the highest previous peak income (or consumption) [9] [30]. If we interpret the role of the highest previous income as that of a proxy for net worth, then the Duesenberry-Modigliani consumption function can be considered as providing a good empirical approximation to the consumption function discussed in this paper, and to this extent the empirical support provided for the Duesenberry-Modigliani type of hypothesis can also be considered as empirical support for the consumption function advanced here, and vice versa. At the same time the present model has the advantage that the hypotheses on which it rests are explicitly stated as specifications of the consumer's utility function. It is also analytically more convenient as a building block in models of economic growth and fluctuations, as we have endeavored to demonstrate in various contributions [1] [2] [3] [29] [31].[34]

Appendix

A. *Some Statistical Results for Earlier Years*

The following are the estimates obtained using data for 1900–28, excluding years 1917, 1918, and 1919. As stated in the text, the data used are very rough, and may not be compatible with the data for the period since 1929. The data and their derivation are described in Ando [2, App.], except for the adjustments needed for different treatments of the government sector. This adjustment is self-explanatory from the description given in [2]. The data presented in [2] are in turn based largely on [18] [19] [22] [27] and [42].

(a)
$$C = \underset{(.134)}{.755Y} + \underset{(.020)}{.073A} \qquad R^2 = .995 \qquad DW = 1.63$$

(b)
$$\Delta C = \underset{(.180)}{.731\Delta Y} + \underset{(.037)}{.047\Delta A} \qquad R^2 = .44 \qquad DW = 2.48$$

(c)
$$\frac{C}{Y} = \underset{(.144)}{.505} + \underset{(.021)}{.112}\frac{A}{Y} \qquad R^2 = .51 \qquad DW = 1.05$$

[34] On the other hand, because up-to-date estimates of wealth are not readily available, at least for the present, some variant of the Duesenberry-Modigliani model may well be more useful for short-run forecasting.

B. *Biases in Estimating the Consumption Function by Regressions on Saving*

Suppose that true consumption c^* and true income y^* are related by a linear function (all variables being measured from their means),

$$c^* = \alpha y^* + \epsilon \tag{a}$$

and measured income and measured consumption are related to their respective true values by

$$c = c^* + \eta \tag{b}$$

$$y = y^* + \xi \tag{c}$$

where ϵ, η, and ξ are random variables. For simplicity, let us assume that ϵ is uncorrelated with y^*, η, and ξ; η and ξ are uncorrelated with c^* and y^*. We also have the definitions

$$s^* = y^* - c^* \tag{d}$$

$$s = y - c = y^* - c^* + \xi - \eta \tag{d'}$$

Using (a) and (d), we have

$$c^* = \frac{\alpha}{1-\alpha} s^* + \frac{\epsilon}{1-\alpha} \equiv \beta s^* + \epsilon'. \tag{e}$$

In order to concentrate first on the effect of errors of measurements, let us momentarily accept the unwarranted assumption that saving is equal to investment which in turn is truly exogenous. Under this assumption s^* can be taken as independent of ϵ' and therefore, if we could actually observe s^* and c^*, by regressing c^* on s^* we could secure an unbiased estimate of β from which we could in turn derive a consistent estimate of α. If however we estimate β by regressing c on s, then remembering that s is obtained as a residual from y and c, we obtain the estimate

$$\hat{\beta} = \frac{\sum cs}{\sum s^2} = \frac{\sum (\beta s^* + \epsilon' + \eta)(s^* + \xi - \eta)}{\sum (s^* + \xi - \eta)^2} \tag{f}$$

$$= \frac{\beta \sum s^{*2} + \sum \eta(\xi - \eta)}{\sum s^{*2} + \sum (\xi - \eta)^2}.$$

The term $\sum\eta(\xi-\eta)$ arises from the fact that when there is a statistical error η in measuring consumption, there will be an error $-\eta$ in measuring saving, except in so far as this is offset by an error ξ in measuring income. This term will tend to be negative and introduces a downward bias into β. The term $\sum(\xi-\eta)^2$ in the denominator is the well-known result of an error of measurement of the independent variable, and it introduces an unambiguous bias towards zero into β.

However, as pointed out in the text, the assumption that personal saving is exogenous is completely unwarranted. In order to bring out the nature of the bias resulting from this misspecification, let us make the other extreme and equally unwarranted assumption that disposable income is truly exogenous. We can then regard y^* as independent of ϵ and by substituting (a) and (d) into (d′) we find

(g) $$s = s^* + \xi - \eta = (1 - \alpha)y^* - \epsilon + \xi - \eta.$$

Equation (f) is then replaced by

(h) $$\beta = \frac{\alpha(1 - \alpha)\sum y^{*2} - \sum \epsilon^2 + \sum \eta(\xi - \eta)}{(1 - \alpha)^2 \sum y^{*2} + \sum \epsilon^2 + \sum (\xi - \eta)^2}.$$

The presence of the term $\sum \epsilon^2$ in both numerator and denominator is the result of the fact, discussed in the text, that when there is residual error ϵ in the consumption-income relationship, there will be residual error $-\epsilon$ in the saving-income relationship. Because of the signs, this effect, too, will bias β downward.

Since all these biases are downward and there is no offsetting upward bias of any significance, it is not surprising that recent applications of this approach [39] [43] lead in a number of cases to a negative estimate of the marginal propensity to consume.

References

1. A. Ando, *A Contribution to the Theory of Economic Fluctuations and Growth.* Unpublished doctoral dissertation, Carnegie Institute of Technology, 1959.
2. ———, "An Empirical Model of the U.S. Economic Growth: Exploratory Study in Applied Capital Theory," Conference on Income and Wealth, National Bureau of Economic Research (forthcoming).
3. ———, E. C. Brown, J. Kareken and R. M. Solow, *Lags in Fiscal and Monetary Policy.* Monograph prepared for the Commission on Money and Credit (forthcoming).
4. A. Ando and F. Modigliani, "Growth, Fluctuations, and Stability," *Am. Econ. Rev., Proc.,* May 1959, *49,* 501-24.
5. R. Bodkin, "Windfall Income and Consumption," *Am. Econ. Rev.,* Sept. 1959, *49,* 602-14.
6. R. E. Brumberg, "An Approximation to the Aggregate Saving Function," *Econ. Jour.,* Mar. 1956, *46,* 66-72.
7. ———, *Utility Analysis and Aggregate Consumption Function: An Empirical Test and Its Meaning.* Unpublished doctoral dissertation, The Johns Hopkins University, 1953.
8. *Bulletin of the Oxford University Institute of Statistics,* Savings Behavior; A Symposium, May 1957, *19,* (2), 99-199.
9. J. S. Duesenberry, *Income, Savings, and the Theory of Consumer Behavior.* Cambridge 1959.
10. J. Durbin and G. S. Watson, "Testing for Serial Correlation in Least Squares Regression, I and II," *Biometrika,* Dec. 1950, *37,* 409-28; and *ibid.,* June 1951, *38,* 159-78.
11. R. Eisner, "The Permanent Income Hypothesis: Comment," *Am. Econ. Rev.,* Dec. 1958, *48,* 972-89.
12. M. R. Fisher, "Exploration in Savings Behavior," *Bull. Oxford Univ. Inst. Stat.,* Aug. 1956, *18,* 201-77.

13. L. FRANE AND L. R. KLEIN, "The Estimation of Disposable Income by Distributive Shares," *Rev. Econ. Stat.*, Nov. 1943, *35*, 333-37.
14. M. FRIEDMAN, "Comment on R. Bodkin's Windfall Income and Consumption," in *Proceedings of the Conference on Consumption and Saving*, Vol. 2. Philadelphia 1960.
15. ———, "The Concept of 'Horizon' in the Permanent Income Hypothesis," in *Proceedings of the Conference on Consumption and Saving*, Vol. 2. Philadelphia 1960.
16. ———, *A Theory of the Consumption Function*. Princeton 1957.
17. I. FRIEND AND I. KRAVIS, "Consumption Patterns and Permanent Income," *Am. Econ. Rev. Proc.*, May 1957, *47*, 536-54.
18. R. W. GOLDSMITH, *The National Wealth of the United States in the Postwar Period*, National Bureau of Economic Research (forthcoming).
19. ———, *A Study of Saving in the United States*. Princeton 1951.
20. W. HAMBURGER, "The Relation of Consumption to Wealth and the Wage Rate," *Econometrica*, Jan. 1955, *23*, 1-17.
21. H. S. HOUTHAKKER, "The Permanent Income Hypothesis," *Am. Econ. Rev.*, June 1958, *48*, 396-404.
22. M. S. KENDRICK, *Productivity Trends in the United States*. London 1960.
23. J. M. KEYNES, *General Theory of Employment, Interest, and Money*. London 1937.
24. L. R. KLEIN, "Entrepreneurial Savings," in I. Friend and R. J. Jones, ed., *Proceedings of the Conference on Consumption and Saving*. Philadelphia 1960.
25. M. E. KREININ, "Windfall Income and Consumption," *Am. Econ. Rev.*, June 1961, *51*, 310-24.
26. EDWIN KUH AND J. R. MEYER, "Correlation and Regression Estimates When the Data Are Ratios," *Econometrica*, Oct. 1955, *23*, 400-16.
27. S. LEBERGOTT, "Earnings of Non-Farm Employees in the United States, 1890-1946," *Jour. Am. Stat. Assoc.*, Mar. 1948, *43*, 74-93.
28. J. MINCER, "Employment and Consumption," *Rev. Econ. Stat.*, Feb. 1960, *42*, 20-26.
29. F. MODIGLIANI, "Comment on 'A Survey of Some Theories of Income Distribution' by T. Scitovsky," in *Conference on Income and Wealth*, National Bureau of Economic Research (forthcoming).
30. ———, "Fluctuations in the Saving-Income Ratio: A Problem in Economic Forecasting," *Studies in Income and Wealth*, Vol. 11. National Bureau of Economic Research, New York 1949.
31. ———, "Long-run Implications of Alternative Fiscal Policies and the Burden of the National Debt," *Econ. Jour.*, Dec. 1961, *71*, 730-55.
32. ———, AND A. ANDO, "The 'Permanent Income' and the 'Life Cycle' Hypothesis of Saving Behavior: Comparison and Tests," in *Proceedings of the Conference on Consumption and Saving*, Vol. 2. Philadelphia 1960.
33. ——— AND ———, "Test of the Life Cycle Hypothesis of Saving," *Bull. Oxford Univ. Inst. Stat.*, May 1957, *19*, 99-124.

34. ——— AND R. BRUMBERG, *Utility Analysis and Aggregate Consumption Functions: An Attempt at Integration,* unpublished.
35. ——— AND ———, "Utility Analysis and the Consumption Function: An Interpretation of Cross-section Data," in K. K. Kurihara, ed., *Post-Keynesian Economics.* New Brunswick 1954.
36. ——— AND M. MILLER, "Dividend Policy, Growth and the Valuation of Shares," *Jour. Bus.,* Oct. 1961, *34,* 411-33.
37. K. PEARSON, "On a Form of Spurious Correlation Which May Arise When Indices Are Used in the Measurement of Organs," *Proc. Royal Soc. London,* 1897, *60,* 484-98.
38. L. H. SELTZER, *Interest as a Source of Personal Income and Tax Revenue,* National Bureau of Economic Research, New York 1955.
39. D. SUITS, *The Determinants of Consumer Expenditure: A Review of Present Knowledge,* prepared for the Commission on Money and Credit, (forthcoming).
40. H. THEIL, *Economic Forecasts and Policy.* Amsterdam 1958.
41. ———, *Linear Aggregation of Economic Relations.* Amsterdam 1954.
42. UNITED STATES BUREAU OF THE CENSUS, *Historical Statistics of the United States: Colonial Times to 1957.* Washington 1960.
43. A. ZELLNER, "The Short-Run Consumption Function," *Econometrica,* Oct. 1957, *25,* 552-67.

The Consumption Function in a Developing Economy and The Italian Experience

By F. MODIGLIANI AND E. TARANTELLI*

The many models that have been proposed since J. M. Keynes' *General Theory* to explain aggregate consumption and saving have been largely developed with reference to mature, western-type, capitalistic economies. This paper examines, in the first place, how well the various models can account for the behavior of saving in a country undergoing rapid development such as Italy in the postwar period. It next reviews a number of "stylized facts" characterizing the process of development, which, in turn, lead to some needed extensions of existing models.

Our main conclusions can be summarized as follows: 1) All major models, starting from the standard textbook consumption function, provide a reasonably good approximation to the behavior of aggregate consumption in the two decades terminating in the early 1970's. At the same time, the successive vintages of the consumption function do yield some improvements. 2) On the whole, the model that appears to provide the most fruitful framework for a consistent understanding of saving behavior, both at the aggregate and the cross-sectional level, is the life cycle hypothesis of consumption (*LCH*) in its more general form, according to which consumption depends on expected income from labor, wealth, and "permanent" income from wealth. 3) However, even this model needs to be modified along Ricardian-Marxian lines to take account of the consumption behavior of the reserve army of the structurally unemployed, which gradually dwindles in the process of development. 4) Our other major result is to provide overwhelming evidence against the standard Kaldorian two-casts parable of hard-pressed workers consuming all and plush capitalists saving almost all, which so far had been held to provide the most satisfactory explanation of the behavior of aggregate saving in Italy. 5) The crucial piece of evidence supporting the proposition stated in (4) is that the consumption coefficient of "expected" profits is not only larger than that of expected labor income, but is in fact larger than one. This result is not merely inconsistent with the Kaldorian hypothesis but altogether uninterpretable in that framework, whereas it is shown to be fully consistent with the implications of the life cycle model. In this model every household is typically both a worker and a recipient of property income during at least some phase of the life cycle and may be expected to respond differently to these two differing sources of income. 6) It is shown that the coefficient measuring the response of consumption to property in-

* Massachusetts Institute of Technology. Some of the equations proposed here are part of the Econometric Model of the Bank of Italy, which partly supported the present work, and whose aid is gratefully acknowledged. We also wish to thank the National Bureau of Economic Research for use of the TROLL System for Applied Econometric Research, and, finally, to express our appreciation to many colleagues of the Research Division of the Bank of Italy for useful discussion and advice. In particular Bruno Sitzia contributed importantly to the development of the tests discussed in Section IV. The main issues examined in this paper are dealt with in greater detail in our forthcoming book.

come cannot be interpreted as a marginal propensity in the customary sense of the word and reflects, at least in part, the degree of substitution between current and future consumption in the utility theoretic sense.

I. The "Old Theories," the "Permanent Income" Hypothesis, and the Kaldorian Model

The first conclusion listed in the introduction can be readily established by an inspection of Table 1 which shows the result obtained by fitting to Italian aggregate data the standard Keynesian model (equation 1), the Duesenberry-Modigliani (D-M) 1949 model in its original form (equation 2), and the Tillman Brown-Tom Davis (B-D) version (equation 3). Strictly speaking, the explanatory variable called for by the D-M model is, besides current income, the highest previous income. But, in the case of Italy, as for any continuously growing economy, the highest previous income reduces to lagged income. Similarly, for the B-D model the highest previous consumption coincides with lagged consumption.

For every model, two alternative estimates of the parameters are provided, first using the linear form (equations labeled L),

Table 1—Estimates of Parameters of Consumption Function: Italy, 1952–70

Consumption Function		Coefficients of						
		Constant	Y	Y_{-1}	C_{-1}	$P(Y/YN)$	$S.E.$	$D.W.$
Elementary Keynes	1L	1355.4	.78				322.3	1.41
		(246.8)	(.011)					
	1R	1687.7	.76				.0154	.98
		(224.9)	(.012)					
Duesenberry Modigliani (D-M)	2L	1254.3	.23	.58			250.3	1.23
		(193.8)	(.16)	(.17)				
	2R	1571.5	.33	.46			.0134	.95
		(200.5)	(.17)	(.18)				
Brown-Davis Friedman (B-D)	3L	499.1	.40		.52		260.9	1.66
		(337.1)	(.12)		(.17)			
	3R	648.5	.37		.55		.0122	1.32
		(356.9)	(.12)		(.16)			
Kaldor (KH)	4L	2927.2	1.02			−.70	245.1	1.17
		(468.5)	(.068)			(.19)		
	4R	3448.9	1.06			−.83	.0106	1.07
		(421.5)	(.067)			(.19)		

Note: The figure in parentheses underneath each coefficient is the standard error of the coefficient. $S.E.$ and $D.W.$ denote, respectively, the standard error of the regression and the Durbin-Watson coefficient. C, Y, and $P(Y/YN)$ denote, respectively, total private domestic consumption, total disposable income, and "independent labor income" (national income less wages and salaries) multiplied by the ratio of disposable to net national income. All variables were measured in billions of lire at 1963 prices. (Over the period of analysis, 1 billion lire was roughly equivalent to 1.6 million dollars at the official exchange rate.) The average value for C in the period under consideration was 18,340 billions of lire. Dividing $S.E.$ by this value one can calculate the percentage standard error of the linear equations. For the equations expressed in ratio form (R), the dependent variable is C/Y, and $S.E.$ gives the root mean square error as a percentage of income. Disposable income was defined as national income plus government transfers minus personal and corporate income taxes. Note that this definition differs from the standard one because it includes undistributed corporate profits.

and second dividing both sides of the equation by income (equations labeled R). This alternative estimate is provided because, over the period of observation, both consumption and income have grown very substantially (roughly by a factor of three) and, therefore, the error term may be more nearly homoscedastic in the ratio than in the linear form. Note also that the models tested would generally call for the use of per capita rather than aggregate real data. However, since population has changed very little over the period of observation, we find it convenient to use aggregate data, expressed in real terms using as a deflator the implicit price index of private domestic consumption. It is apparent that even the standard Keynesian function fits well, as its standard error is well below 2 percent of consumption (see the footnote to Table 1). The next two models yield appreciably smaller standard errors. Note also that in terms of fit, the B-D model is an improvement over the D-M model only in its ratio version. However, it does yield a much smaller and barely significant constant term which accords better with the specification of the hypothesis and the nowadays widely held view that the saving ratio should, in the long run, be independent of the level of income (though not of its rate of growth). Note that in both the D-M and B-D equations the coefficient of the lagged variable is distinctly larger than that of the current variable, implying a long lag in the response of consumption which will play an important role in what follows.

The three models discussed so far belong to the empirically oriented tradition of the early post-Keynesian period, that is, they belong to what has since come to be known, in Michael Farrell's words, as the "old theories of the consumption function." However, equation 3 can also be interpreted as providing a test of one version of the "new theories," namely, Milton Friedman's Permanent Income Hypothesis. As is well known, Friedman suggested that permanent income could be approximated by an exponentially weighted average of past incomes, a formulation which, making use of the L. M. Koyck transformation, leads to an autoregressive equation of the form of equation 3.

Equation 4 provides a test of Nicholas Kaldor's hypothesis (hereafter KH) that the propensity to consume of the recipients of property income, the "capitalists," is significantly lower than that of the recipients of labor income, the "workers." Denoting by a_p the propensity to consume out of net of tax property income P^*, and by a_w the corresponding propensity for wage income W^*, KH can be stated as

$$(4) \qquad C = a_w W^* + a_p P^*, \quad a_p < a_w$$

Recalling that $W^* + P^* = Y$, (4) can be rewritten in ratio form as

$$(4') \qquad C/Y = a_w + (a_p - a_w)P^*/Y$$

which shows that the saving ratio $S/Y = 1 - C/Y$ does not depend on income as such, but instead on income distribution, P^*/Y.

The national income accounts do not provide explicit measures of W^* and P^*, i.e., labor and property income net of taxes, but provide only estimates of *dependent* labor income (wages and salaries) and of other incomes (with various breakdowns) gross of personal taxes. These variables have, therefore, been approximated by relying on the assumption that the ratio between P^* and W^* and the corresponding measures gross of taxes, P and W, are approximately equal, i.e., that the incidence of taxes is roughly the same on the two sources of income. This assumption, though risky, finds some justification in the tax structure of the country taking into account the phenomenon of widespread tax evasion, especially on property income. Thus,

$$\frac{P^*}{P} \simeq \frac{W^*}{W} \simeq \frac{Y}{YN} \tag{5}$$

where YN is "real" (net) national income. From (4) and (5) and since $W+P=YN$, one derives

$$C = (a_p - a_w)P\frac{Y}{YN} + a_w Y \tag{6}$$

Following studies made by A. Niccoli and S. Vinci, for the Bank of Italy in 1970, testing KH for the Italian economy, a constant was added to (6) even though it presumably should be close to zero. It is apparent from equation 4 that both the scaled and unscaled equations fit the data somewhat better than the previous models, though in both equations the Durbin-Watson statistic still indicates the existence of substantial positive serial correlation.

These results, and similar ones obtained by others, have often been interpreted as providing strong support for the Kaldorian model. They imply, in fact, a marginal propensity to consume out of labor income of 1.02 to 1.06, and corresponding propensities to consume out of property income of only .32 to .23. Yet these estimates show a number of grave inconsistencies and dubious implications. First, the estimated marginal propensity to consume out of wage income appears unreasonably high. Second, the estimated marginal propensity to consume for nonlabor income as low as .23—i.e., four to five times lower than that out of wages--is rather dubious. It is, in fact, glaringly inconsistent with the results of budget studies.

One of the most complete and comprehensive series of these studies for the Italian economy, conducted by A. Ulizzi for the Bank of Italy, classifies families into two groups, dependent workers and the self-employed, which correspond to those underlying the National Income classification of dependent and independent workers. The behavior of savings within each class is very much in line with what one would expect on the basis of the permanent income or life cycle hypothesis of savings. Specifically, for the dependent families whose income may be presumed to be relatively stable over time, the proportion of income saved is roughly independent of income and around 7 to 8 percent (see Ulizzi, p. 424, Table 3.4 and Graph 2), at least for incomes above 1 million lire. (Even for income recipients below 1 million, which undoubtedly contain a sizable proportion of the transiently poor, saving is positive and around 3 percent.) For the group as a whole, average saving amounts to 5.8 percent, which is clearly inconsistent with the results given above implying a *negative* average propensity to save of 2 to 6 percent. On the other hand, for the self-employed, including farmers and other entrepreneurs whose income is notoriously subject to wide short-run fluctuations, the saving ratio tends to rise markedly with income, being negative for incomes up to 2 million lire and increasingly positive for the remaining two groups. This is precisely what one would expect for a group whose income is uncertain and fluctuating, if consumption depends on "permanent income" (Friedman), or "life resources" (Modigliani-Ando, 1960). For such groups, a better estimate of the average and marginal propensity to save is provided by the sample average which turns out to be 8.4 percent.[1] These results indicate a roughly similar average propensity to consume for the two groups, and contradict those suggested by the Kaldorian equation (4).

[1] These figures were kindly provided by Ulizzi and are consistent with the results shown in Table 3.4 of his work. In his definition, the self-employed include workers in agriculture and other sectors, entrepreneurs, and professionals. Dependent labor includes wage earners and employees. Pensioners are excluded from both definitions of income. This, together with other characteristics of the sampling procedure adopted, leads to an underestimate of the average propensity to save which should not, however, appreciably affect the magnitude of the propensities to save relative to each other.

Finally, in equation (4), the constant term is by far the highest of all the estimates presented so far and is statistically highly significant. This result plays havoc with the well-known Kaldorian theory of income distribution. Indeed, adding a constant a to (4), the Kaldorian saving function can be written as: $S=(1-a_w)W^*+(1-a_p)P^*-a=I$, where I denotes investment. Substituting for W^* from the identity $Y=W^*+P^*$ and solving for P^*, the share of profits implied by the Kaldorian theory of income distribution can be written as:

$$\frac{P^*}{Y}=\frac{1}{(a_w-a_p)}\left[\frac{I}{Y}-(1-a_w)+\frac{a}{Y}\right]$$

which, in turn, implies that given a_p and a_w, and for a given investment ratio, the long-run share of profits is a decreasing function of income and not a constant as implied by the theory. (See Kaldor, p. 229.)

It is the contention of this paper that the improbable estimates of the parameters of (6) result from the failure to take into account a number of fundamental characteristics of a developing economy, like Italy's, in the period under consideration and their implications for an understanding of consumption behavior. These characteristics are reviewed below.

II. Some "Stylized Facts"

A

First, it is wrong to identify dependent labor income with Kaldorian labor income and the remaining income with profits, because of the well-known fact that in an undeveloped economy such as Italy's in the early postwar years, the *independent* labor pool contained a substantial portion of self-employed, of marginally employed, and/or of "disguised" unemployed. Indeed, in 1951, the number of supposedly "capitalist" independent workers amounted to 7,700,000 on a total labor force of some

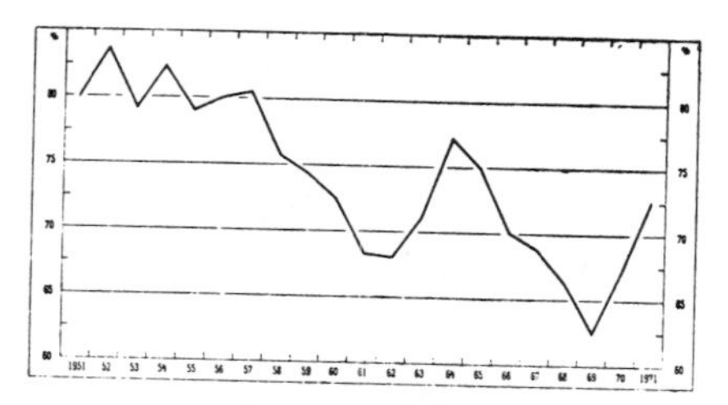

FIGURE 1. RATIO BETWEEN PER CAPITA DEPENDENT LABOR INCOME AND OTHER INCOMES

17 million.[2] Furthermore, in the early 1950's, the per capita income of the independent workers was quite close to that of the dependent workers as shown by Figure 1, which traces the behavior of the ratio of per capita income of dependent workers to that of the independent workers. Thus, in 1951, per capita dependent labor income equalled \$720 as against only \$890 for per capita "profits." (In other words, according to the conventional definition, the capitalists would have shared the misery of the workers!)

As also indicated by the budget studies mentioned previously, these small differences in the average per capita earnings of the two groups cannot account for the extreme gap in the two propensities to consume suggested by the "naive" Kaldorian equation. The narrow differences in earnings[3] suggest, in fact, that there has been and still is a whole group, conventionally included in the independent labor category, for which average per capita income and saving behavior are likely to be

[2] We have been told that in some parts of the south, this group of people is jokingly referred to as "gli industriali, perchè si industriano" which can be roughly paraphrased as "the managers, because they manage." For a stimulating and enlightening discussion of the "class composition" of the Italian labor force and its development in time, see P. Sylos-Labini (1972).

[3] In 1971, per capita dependent "labor income" averaged \$4000, as against only \$5400 for per capita "profits." See Tarantelli (1973a, b).

roughly similar to those of the dependent labor group.[4]

B

The measured share of wages and salaries as a proportion of net national income has increased remarkably in the period under consideration. As the Annual Report of the Bank of Italy for 1971 has shown,[5] this change does not arise from an increase in the average per capita earnings of this group relative to the income of independent labor: the ratio between the two has, in fact, fallen, as shown by Figure 1. It arises instead from the increase in the share of dependent labor in the total labor force, as one might expect for a developing economy,[6] as a consequence of two major features of development: a) the continuous flow of marginal and low-income independent workers into the dependent labor pool; b) the substantial fall, up to the beginning of the 1960's, in the number of structurally unemployed who were also largely absorbed into the dependent labor pool. The report of the Bank of Italy also suggests that once the data are "purged" of the bias due to the change in the composition of employment, the long-run trend in favor of wages shown by Figure 2 disappears. The "corrected" distribution of income shows modest cyclical fluctuations around a constant, as shown by Figure 3.

C

It seems plausible to assume, à la Karl Marx, that the marginal and average propensity to consume of the structurally un-

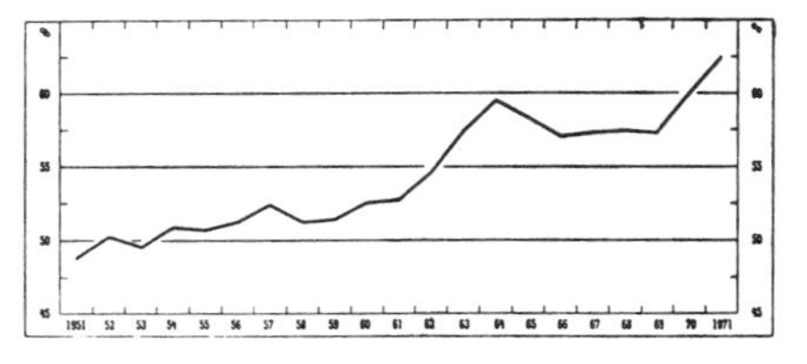

FIGURE 2. SHARE OF WAGES AS A PROPORTION OF NET NATIONAL INCOME

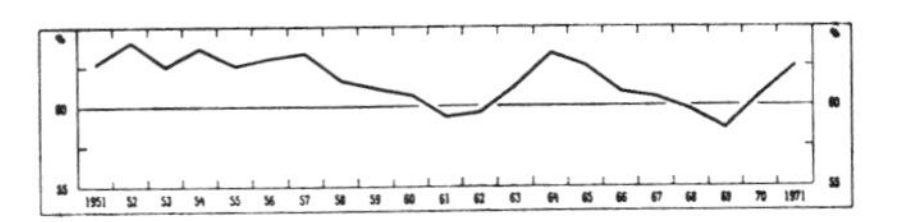

FIGURE 3. WAGE SHARE "CORRECTED" FOR THE VARIATIONS IN THE COMPOSITION OF EMPLOYMENT

employed in a developing economy equals one. This group is a receiver of dependent and independent labor income from occasional gainful employment and from low earnings in unrecorded activities and of transfer income from the gainfully employed.

Because of the higher propensity to consume of the structurally unemployed, one would expect that in a developing economy, the gradual absorption of this group into the labor pool would involve a corresponding fall in the average propensity to consume of the system as a whole.[7] This presumption is fully verified by the Italian postwar experience. As Figure 4 shows, the average propensity to consume has substantially fallen from 1951 to the beginning of the 1960's, while following a cyclical pattern thereafter. Figure 4 also shows the remarkable fall in the number of the structurally unemployed in the 1950's. The parallelism of the two series in the graph would seem to support the

[4] Along similar lines, Sylos-Labini (1967) suggested that "dependent workers have a propensity to consume near to unity, that the independent workers receive an income that moves together with that of the dependent ones and have a propensity similarly high" (p. 360).

[5] See Banca d'Italia (1971, p. 147).

[6] By 1971, the number of independent workers had shrunk from 7.7 to 5.7 million, representing 30 percent of the labor force, as against 46 percent in 1915.

[7] For earlier interest in this evidence, see F. Di Fenizio and A. Graziani.

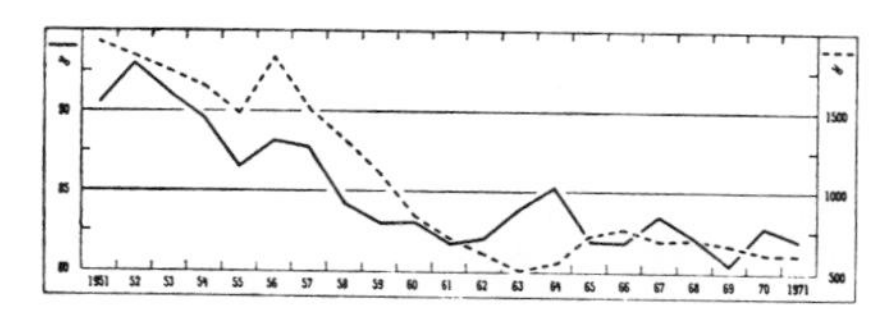

– – – – – – Number of Unemployed (in thousands)
———— Average Propensity to Consume

FIGURE 4

Ricardian-Marxism hypothesis proposed above.[8]

These "stylized facts" suggest two major modifications of (6). First, following the procedure of the Bank of Italy, total labor income is estimated as the sum of dependent labor income and an *imputed* labor income of the *independent* workers measuring, in essence, their "opportunity cost" of self-employment. This opportunity cost is assumed to equal, on the average, the average wage income of dependent workers W/LD, where LD stands for the number of dependent workers. Thus, letting LL denote total employment, our measure of the "corrected net of tax labor income" becomes $(W/LD)LL(Y/YN)$.[9]

Second, one needs to account for subsistence consumption of the dwindling army of the unemployed, U.[10] Thus, equation (6) must be modified to:

$$C = a_w \hat{W} + a_p \hat{P} + a_u U \tag{7}$$

where U denotes the number of unemployed and

$$\hat{W} = \frac{W}{LD} LL \frac{Y}{YN}; \quad \hat{P} = Y - \hat{W} \tag{7'}$$

Equation (7) can be used directly for linear estimation, and the coefficients a_p and a_w of $\hat{P}$ and $\hat{W}$ provide direct estimates of the Kaldorian marginal propensity to consume (MPC) of the capitalists and the rest of the population, respectively. For ratio estimation, in order to preserve the same dependent variable used in the test of the other models, namely C/Y, it is necessary to perform a transformation by adding and subtracting $a_p\hat{W}$, which yields

$$\frac{C}{Y} = a_p + (a_w - a_p)\frac{\hat{W}}{Y} + a_u \frac{U}{Y} \tag{7''}$$

III. Empirical Test of the Modified Kaldorian Model

Empirical tests of equations (7) and

[8] It seems worth noting that the recognition of the above *stylized facts* can readily account for the relatively good mechanical fit of the naive Kaldorian equation 4 and some of its properties. The large constant term in equations $4L$ and $4R$ of Table 1 mechanically accounts for the higher than average and falling average propensity to consume up to the beginning of the 1960's. To be sure, this constant would imply, on the other hand, a fall in the average propensity to consume also for the rest of the period under consideration, contrary to what has in fact happened. Equations $4L$ and $4R$ account for this pattern by assigning an unreasonably high weight to the share of wages, which as can be seen from Figure 2, increased but little up to 1960 (from .49 to .52), but substantially in the second half of the period (from .52 to .61), thus offsetting the depressing effect of the constant term.

[9] This approach assumes that there is no appreciable number of "pure capitalists." This conjecture is supported by the estimates produced by Sylos-Labini (1972). In any event, we have also computed an alternative estimate of labor income assuming that pure capitalists represented 30 percent of employment, the proportion of self-employed at the close of the sample period. To this end, the average income of dependent labor was imputed to only 70 percent of the labor force. This alternative was used in all the tests reported below, but since in no case did it lead to qualitatively different conclusions, the results (and their implications for shares of the dependent labor force included between these two alternatives) are omitted here, though they can be found in the authors' forthcoming book. The measure used here also coincides with that discussed in Tarantelli (1970). See also Tarantelli (1973a,b).

[10] As shown in the more extensive version of our model cited earlier, the unemployment component should in principle distinguish between structural and cyclical unemployment and account for the variations of the average income per capita of dependent labor. See also the same reference for a discussion of the issues involved and for a detailed derivation of equation (7) from the aggregation of the relevant income subgroups. The distinction between structural and cyclical unemployment is also elaborated by the authors (1973).

(7″) are reported in the equations labeled 1 and 2, Table 2. In equation 1, we omit the unemployment variable, mainly for purposes of comparison with the standard Kaldorian equation reported in Table 1, 4*L* and 4*R*. While the estimated coefficients have the expected sign, all equations give a somewhat poorer fit than the equations of Table 1. The estimated *MPC* out of wages falls to a more reasonable .85, while that out of profits is unaffected. But the constant terms remain highly significant in all cases.[11]

The addition of the variable relating to structural unemployment in equation 2 improves substantially the general characteristics of the equations. The constant becomes of negligible magnitude and statistically insignificant, implying a long-run consumption-income ratio independent of income for given distributive shares. As a result, if the constant term is suppressed as is shown in equations 3*L* and 3*R*, the coefficients of the variables are essentially unaffected and the standard error adjusted for degrees of freedom is actually reduced. Similar results were found to hold also for the other versions of the model reported in Table 2. In view of this, and since a priori considerations suggested that the constant term should in fact be zero, further results are reported only for equations estimated constraining the constant term to be zero.

The order of magnitude of the point estimates of the coefficient of U implies an average "subsistence minimum" slightly above half a million lire ($800) which is somewhat high, but not altogether beyond reason. However, the estimated marginal propensity of "capitalists" remains rather small, .42, still only half as large as a_w. Thus the results of row 3 would seem to provide strong support for Kaldor's model.

But these equations still suffer from one serious shortcoming, namely that they make no allowance for the possibility of a gradual response of consumption to income, especially property income, as suggested by a number of earlier studies on this topic and by previous considerations. This could, in part at least, explain the relatively low *t*-ratio of property income, and the autocorrelations of residuals in equation 3 of Table 2.

An operationally simple approach to allow for this possibility is to amend (7) as follows

$$(8)\ C = a_w\hat{W} + a_p\hat{P} + a_p'\hat{P}_{-1} + a_uU + dC_{-1}$$

This formulation allows for consumption to respond with an exponentially distributed lag to past labor income, while the response to profits can be expressed as the sum of *two* distributed lags, which allows for the possibility of a longer average lag for this variable. In (8), a_w and a_p measure the short-run *MPC* out of wages and profits, respectively, while the corresponding long-run propensities are given by

$$\hat{a}_w = \frac{a_w}{1-d}; \qquad \hat{a}_\pi = \frac{a_p + a_p'}{1-d}$$

The tests for equation (8) in both linear and ratio form are shown in Table 2 as equations 4*L* and 4*R*.

The results of the linear form confirm that the short-run *MPC* for labor income (around .60) is much larger than that for current profit, around .22. However, the long-run *MPC* out of labor income (.8) is now *lower* than that out of property income which comes to .90. If the coefficients are estimated in ratio form, the results are even more striking: $\hat{a}_w = .8$, $\hat{a}_\pi = 1$. Clearly, these results are entirely inconsistent with the Kaldorian hypothesis—indeed they

[11] The estimates of *LD* and *LL* were calculated in full-time equivalent employees. The number of full-time equivalent employees is estimated by adding to the number of full-time employees one-third of so-called "marginal employees," essentially defined as those with less than 32 hours worked per week (even though they would be willing to work longer hours). Source: *Relazione Generale sulla Situazione Economica del Paese.*

TABLE 2—KALDORIAN TESTS: ITALY, 1952–70

	Coefficients of									
	Constant	$\hat{W}$	$\hat{P}$	U	$\hat{P}_{-1}$	C_{-1}	λ	$L(\hat{P}_{-1})$	$S.E.$	$D.W.$
$1L$	1043.4	.85	.40						290.5	1.07
	(4.)	(23.5)	(2.4)							
$1R$	1350.7	.85	.35						.0142	.80
	(5.1)		(1.7)							
$2L$	−87.4	.88	.41	.49					263.2	1.45
	(−.2)	(24.6)	(2.7)	(2.1)						
$2R$	−70	.88	.43	.55					.0127	1.05
	(− .1)		(2.3)	(2.3)						
$3L$		.88	.42	.45					255.	1.44
		(33.)	(2.9)	(5.)						
$3R$		.88	.43	.52					.0123	1.04
			(2.4)	(6.3)						
$4L$		.59	.22	.40	.43	.28			202.9	1.70
		(3.3)	(1.7)	(3.2)	(3.1)	(1.4)				
$4R$		.55	.23	.44	.45	.31			.0103	1.58
			(1.4)	(3.1)	(2.5)	(1.3)				
$5L$		.73	.37	.61			.7	1.11	210.8	1.68
		(13.1)	(3.1)	(6.6)				(2.9)		
$5R$		.68	.41	.68			.7	1.48	.0086	1.77
			(3.2)	(9.8)				(4.2)		

Note: In the ratio form, the coefficient a_w is obtained by fitting (8) to the data and then adding the coefficient of W/Y to the constant term. For this reason, the regression program does not provide an explicit value of the standard error of a_w, although such a standard error could be computed from the variance-covariance matrix of the errors of the coefficients. We have felt it unnecessary to perform this computation since the t-ratio of a_w is uniformly very large, and of the same order of magnitude as that reported for the linear form. The values in parentheses below the coefficients indicate t-ratios for the corresponding estimates.

are impossible to interpret in that framework.[12]

To be sure, hypothesis (8) is rather restrictive as to possible shapes of the distributed lag for the two components, though the result, implying a very rapid decay for the weights of past labor income, and hump-shaped weights, rising at first then decaying more slowly for $\hat{P}_{-1}$, are certainly consistent with what one might expect a priori. In addition, the previous estimates have one further econometric shortcoming in that the equation is estimated in autoregressive form, which could in principle bias the point estimates of the lagged dependent variables. As an alternative, we assumed that expected labor income could be identified with the current value $\hat{W}$, especially since the possible effects of cyclical variations in employment are taken into account through the unemployment variable. We relied on the specification,

$$C = a_w \hat{W} + a_p \hat{P} + \gamma L(\hat{P}_{-1}) + a_u U \tag{9}$$

in which L is an exponentially distributed lag beginning with $\hat{P}_{-1}$.[13] The rate of decay λ was estimated by scanning over the range $0<\lambda<1$ for the value minimizing the residual variance.[14]

[12] The approach of equation (8) was first pursued in a yet unpublished study of Bruno Sitzia. He also pursued some alternative methods of estimating $\hat{a}_r$ all of which confirmed that this coefficient is as large or larger than $\hat{a}_w$. His valuable contribution as well as his advice in designing the tests reported here are gratefully acknowledged.

[13] The Koyck variable for the first year in the sample was obtained by extrapolating backward the positive trend of the profit variable estimated for the first five years (1951–55), until it tended to vanish, and by applying the Koyck transformation to the sample.

[14] As a check, we estimated separate exponentially distributed lags for W; whenever this procedure was tried, the estimate of λ for this component turned out to be around 1 while the estimate of λ for the $\hat{P}$ component was basically unchanged.

From the tests of (9) and of its ratio form reported in equation 5,[15] Table 2, it appears that the distributed lag makes a substantial contribution to the explanation of C; the value of λ in both linear and ratio form indicates a rather slow rate of decay, much as one would expect in view of the short-run variability of profits. The coefficient of current profit is again only half as large as that of labor income. But when we add to it the very high coefficient of lagged profits, we arrive at an estimate of a_p not merely higher than a_w, but actually between 1.5 and 2. This is likely to be a shocking and inadmissible result for those who try to interpret $\hat{a}_\pi$ in the Kaldorian framework as the *MPC* out of property income. As we shall see presently, it is perfectly consistent with the *LCH* framework, which implies an altogether different interpretation.[16] The coefficient of unemployment is again highly significant,[17] though somewhat high, probably reflecting some upward bias.[18]

To summarize, the Kaldorian-type equation of equations 4 and 5 appear to fit quite well the data of the postwar Italian experience. They also yield a sensible estimate of the *MPC* out of labor income and of the effect of structural unemployment. At the same time, the estimated coefficient of profits is of an order of magnitude which is altogether inconsistent with the Kaldorian hypothesis. Hence, if we are to accept this equation as a valid description of saving behavior, it must be on the basis of a framework other than the Kaldorian one. In the following sections, we shall show that such a framework can be provided by the life cycle hypothesis of saving, once the hypothesis is generalized to take into account the stylized facts of development discussed earlier.

IV. The Life Cycle Hypothesis

The life cycle hypothesis (*LCH*), (see Modigliani and Richard Brumberg, 1954), rests on the proposition that the consumption of the representative household reflects the endeavor to achieve the preferred allocation of its life resources to consumption over the life cycle. Together with some further simplifying assumptions, this hypothesis leads to an aggregate consumption function linear in current and expected labor income, YL and YL^e, and in net worth A:

$$C = a'YL + a''YL^e + \delta A \simeq \alpha YL + \delta A \tag{10}$$

where α and δ in principle depend on the rate of growth of income and the rate of return on assets.

There are serious problems in attempting to test an equation of the form (10) for Italy since at present there is no available estimate of total consumers' net worth at market prices. The closest proxy available for the period of observation is an estimate of the aggregate value of financial wealth held by households. This estimate,[19] de-

[15] For the ratio estimate, (9) was transformed to $C/Y = a_p + (a_w - a_p)\hat{W}/Y + \gamma L(P_{-1})/Y + a_u U/Y$.

[16] Similar results were found to hold in the course of the first stage of this research by Tarantelli (1973), even though it was then chosen to give only regression estimates in the neighborhood of the value minimizing the standard error sufficient to reject the Kaldorian hypothesis. An analysis of the results reported here would have implied a framework totally different from the Kaldorian model (see Tarantelli, 1973, note 44, p. 133), and which will be developed in the following pages.

[17] Following similar lines, T. Ter-Minassian, in a yet unpublished study, tested the hypothesis according to which the average propensity to consume for durables should tend to increase as the structural unemployment army decreases. Some preliminary results would also seem to support the symmetrical hypothesis of a fall in the average propensity to consume foodstuffs.

[18] The upward bias may result from our failure to separate the effect of structural and cyclical unemployment, as would be called for by our model. This separation, however, must await the availability of quarterly data, which would provide additional degrees of freedom and thereby also enable us to allow for a subsistence minimum varying as an increasing function of per capita earnings.

[19] Data were based on F. Cotula and M. Caron.

noted by A^*, falls considerably short of total consumers' net worth A, omitting such items as equity in noncorporate business, and in tangibles directly held by households—residential real estate, land, and the stock of durable goods. Judging from American experience and other very indirect evidence, one might guess that on the average, over the relevant postwar period, A^* has been in the order of one-half to two-thirds of A; but this is no more than an educated guess and, furthermore, this figure might well have fluctuated and also has probably tended to increase in the process of development with the spread of financial intermediation.

As for the variable YL, since what is conceptually needed is a measure of income from "human capital" which clearly includes not only wages and salaries but also the imputed labor income of farmers and other self-employed (independent) workers, we used the same measure $\hat{W}$, used for the Kaldorian test. Further, in testing the *LCH* equation (10) for a developing country like Italy, we must again allow for the effect of structural and cyclical unemployment. Considerations entirely analogous to those set out in connection with the test of the Kaldorian hypothesis led us to approximate this effect by adding the number of unemployed U to the right-hand side of (10). Thus, the equation finally tested was:

$$(10') \qquad C = \alpha\hat{W} + \delta A^* + \beta U$$

where $\hat{W}$ is defined by equation (7′) and A^* denotes financial wealth deflated, like C and W, by the implicit price deflator for private domestic consumption.

A test of this equation in both linear and ratio form is reported in equations $1L$ and $1R$ of Table 3. The results are rather interesting considering the shortcomings of the data. In the first place, in both cases the equation fits the data appreciably better than any of the "old theories" or, for that matter, the permanent income model tested in Table 1.[20] Second, the coefficient of wealth is highly significant and its value is of the right order of magnitude. The fact that it is somewhat larger than that observed for the United States (.06 ± .02, see Albert Ando and Modigliani, 1963) is to be expected since A^* underestimates private net worth A. In fact, it is probably somewhat on the low side, though this too could be accounted for by the attenuation effect resulting from the "noise" in A^* as a measure of A. Similarly, the coefficient of α is somewhat on the high side but again not by a large factor. One may suspect that the underestimate in the coefficient of A^*, because of attenuation, is absorbed in part by the coefficient of YL and in part by that of U, which is again highly significant but clearly on the high side.[21]

V. The *LCH* versus the Kaldorian Hypothesis

In the test of (10′), as in similar tests for the United States and other countries, it was assumed that the coefficients α and δ could be taken as constant in time. Actually, as mentioned earlier, both coefficients should in principle depend also on r, the rate of return on assets, as was confirmed

[20] The reader might wonder to what extent the superiority of the *LCH* results of equation 1, Table 3, over those of the old theories of Table 1 is due to the inclusion of the unemployment variable rather than to the replacement of income with labor income and wealth. To answer this question, the variable U has been added to the equations of Table 1, rows 2 and 3. In both cases, the addition of the unemployment variable improved the fit, but the *S.E.* remained substantially higher than in the life cycle test of row 1, Table 3.

[21] In equation 1 as in all the remaining equations (except 3) in Table 3, we report estimates with the constant term constrained to zero. This specification is consistent with the hypothesis, at least if wealth could be measured directly. Some question about the appropriateness of this specification may, however, arise because of the use of A^* as a proxy for A. In any event, when equation (10′) was estimated with a constant term, this term was uniformly insignificant while the other coefficient estimates hardly changed. For a further discussion of possible bias arising from the use of A^*, see the authors (forthcoming).

TABLE 3—ESTIMATES OF PARAMETERS OF CONSUMPTION FUNCTION: ITALY, 1952–70

	Dependent Variable	Coefficients of									
		YL	P	λ	$L(\hat{P}_{-1})$	P^p	A^*	U	Constant	$S.E.$	$D.W.$
1L	C	.74					.092	1.04		210.	1.19
		(16.)					(4.4)	(6.)			
1R	C/Y	.77					.078	.99		.0113	1.00
							(3.1)	(5.)			
2L	C	.75	.07				.083	1.		216.	1.19
		(14.)	(.4)				(2.7)	(4.6)			
2R	C/Y	.78	.14				.063	.92		.012	.94
			(.6)				(1.8)	(3.9)			
3L	A^*		4.75	.7	11.9	16.6			− 9.374	2648.	.77
			(3.2)		(5.9)				(− 5.1)		
3R	A^*/Y		6.2	.6	10.3	16.5			−11.208	.118	.86
			(4.)		(5.1)				(− 7.4)		
4L	C	.64	.13	.8	1.21	1.34	.060	.97		191.	1.60
		(9.2)	(.8)		(2.3)		(2.1)	(5.1)			
4R	C/Y	.59	.28	.8	1.9	2.18	.03	.85		.0085	1.86
			(1.6)		(3.7)		(1.1)	(4.9)			

Note: The values in parentheses below the coefficients are t-ratios.

by some numerical calculations in the unpublished paper by Modigliani and Brumberg, reported in Ando and Modigliani (1963). However, the nature of this dependence is rather complex. The difficulty here is the familiar one that a rise in r (which should be interpreted here as the long-term *real* rate of return, since variations in the short-term rate around a stable long-run level would have negligible effects), labor income constant, affects the life profile of consumption both through an income effect, tending to raise consumption at all ages, and a substitution effect tending to shift consumption away from the present and toward a later age. In the case of current consumption these two effects go against each other and the net effect cannot be ascertained unless one is prepared to make specific assumptions about the nature of the utility function. The numerical results cited above were obtained for the limiting case in which the substitution effect was assumed zero (corner indifference curves or strict complementarity). As expected, they showed that an increase in r would in steady state lead to a fall in the wealth-income ratio A/Y, and thus to a fall in the saving ratio $S/Y=\rho A/Y$, for any given rate of growth ρ. In terms of the consumption function (10), it was found that a rise in r tended to raise both α and δ. The effect on α was relatively minor but on δ it was proportionately quite large. Specifically, δ appeared to increase linearly with r, or $\delta(r)=\delta^*+\mu r$, with μ roughly unity (and δ^* around .08).

These results of the unpublished paper have since led Modigliani (1973) to conjecture that the effect of r on the *LCH* consumption function might be approximated by rewriting (10) in the form,

$$(11)\qquad C_t = \alpha YL_t + (\delta^* + \mu r_t)A_t = \alpha YL_t + \delta^* A_t + \mu(r_t A_t)$$

with the value of μ depending on the substitution effect between current and future consumption.[22] The value of μ in turn is

[22] An expression analogous to (11) has also been derived as a linear approximation by W. H. Somermeyer and R. Bannink, starting from an additive logarithmic utility function except that α is also replaced by α_0+

critical in determining the steady-state response of the saving ratio to changes in r. Indeed, as shown in Modigliani (1973), equation (11) implies the following steady-state relation between the saving ratio, μ, r, and ρ.

$$\frac{S}{Y} = \frac{\rho(1-\alpha)}{\delta^* + \rho + (\mu - \alpha)r} \tag{11'}$$

The calculations of Modigliani-Brumberg reported above suggest that μ might have an upper bound of one in the limiting case of no substitution. Since $\alpha < 1$, it is seen from (11′) that such a value of μ implies that a rise in r reduces S/Y, as expected. But μ would be lower in the presence of substitution. Some simulations reported by James Tobin and Walter Dolde, assuming an iso-elastic additive utility function with an elasticity of 1.5, suggest a value of μ close to zero (see Table 3, simulation 13), which implies that S/Y is an increasing function of r. Another set of calculations reported by Tobin (1967), assuming a logarithmic utility function, implying an elasticity of one and hence greater substitution, shows a stronger positive responsiveness of S/Y to r, suggesting a negative value of μ. Unfortunately, there is no way to establish a priori just how strong the substitution effect might be in reality, and hence what value μ should take—except that it should not exceed unity. Because of a hunch that the substitution effect is unlikely to be strong relative to the income effect, we would rather expect μ positive and not very different from α (which, as can be seen from (11′) would imply that S/Y is roughly independent of r). However, in principle, it could be a good deal lower and even negative.

The generalization of the *LCH* embodied in equation (11) is likely to be especially useful for a developing economy, since the process of development might tend to be accompanied by systematic changes in the rate of return on assets. In addition, it provides a useful link to the Kaldorian form of the consumption function. This can best be seen by noting that $r_t A_t$ may be thought of as the long-run expectation of the flow of profits out of current assets, call it P^p, the capitalization of which at the long-term rate r determines the market value of wealth, i.e., $A_t = P_t^p / r_t$. Hence, (11) can be rewritten in the form

$$C_t = \alpha Y L_t + \delta^* A_t + \mu P_t^p \tag{12}$$

Comparing (12) with (4), it is apparent that there are some important similarities between *LCH* and *KH* in that both models assert that C is a linear homogeneous function of labor income and profits, and with different coefficients. The main differences are:

(i) In terms of the arguments in the consumption function: For *LCH*, they are the expected rate of earnings from human effort, closely related to Friedman's return from human capital, and the expected long-run return from current private wealth, in addition to the value of wealth itself. In *KH*, the last variable does not appear and the first two variables supposedly denote current "wages" and "profits"—or, at any rate, no distinction is made between current measured values and long-run expectations.

(ii) In terms of interpretation: For *KH*, the coefficients of YL and P are different because YL and P are received by the members of different castes. The coefficients of these variables can rightly be interpreted as marginal propensities to consume of the members of each caste. In the *LCH*, on the other hand, every household typically earns both kinds of income during at least part of its life cycle, and the coefficient of P^p *cannot* be interpreted

---

$\alpha_1 r_t$. They also show that μ should be negative, but this result reflects the special assumption of a logarithmic utility function. See text below.

as a marginal propensity. It measures, instead, the strength of the substitution effect between current and future consumption. The *LCH* per se has little to say about the value of this coefficient or even about its sign.

Yet the *LCH* permits some inferences about the results that one might expect to find if one were to estimate the coefficient of P^* in the Kaldorian equation (4). Consider first the quantity dC/dP^p which measures the response of C to a change in expected property income. Differentiating (12) totally with respect to P^p, and remembering the relation $P^p - rA = 0$, one obtains

$$\frac{dC}{dP^p} = \mu + \frac{\delta^*}{r} E_{AP} \equiv c_p \tag{13}$$

where E_{AP} is the elasticity of A with respect to P^p. Thus, according to the *LCH* the response of consumption depends on the nature of the change in P^p. If it changes because of a change in A, r constant—which is presumably the most common source of change—then E_{AP} will be one and $dC/dP^p = \mu + \delta^*/r$. But if it changes only because of a change in r, then E_{AP} is zero and $dC/dP^p = \mu$. Thus an increase in profit due to a change in A is sure to increase C and the derivative is likely to exceed α; but, if due to a change in r, it might well be less than α and it could be even negative.

If, as in the present case, the observations are time-series of aggregates for a given country, presumably most of the observed variation in profits must come from variations in A (through saving and dissaving) rather than from variations in r. Hence c_p of (13) must be close to $\mu + \delta^*/r$. Now, as we have seen, the value of δ^* seems to be in the order of .07 and hence δ^*/r is certainly positive and of the order of unity—and could easily be above one. On the other hand, the value of μ is quite uncertain: it is unlikely to exceed unity, but it could be smaller and even negative. Thus c_p could be larger than α and, in fact, it *might well exceed unity*. However, c_p is the coefficient of P^p. On the other hand, in testing the Kaldorian model, it has been customary to use *current* labor income and *current* profit. The difference is not too important in the case of YL because labor income is quite stable; hence, expected income will tend to be roughly proportional to current YL. But the situation is entirely different in the case of P. As was pointed out by Ando and Modigliani (1963), since P tends to fluctuate substantially in response to fluctuations in aggregate demand, P^p must be based on an average experience from the past (as well as other information). Hence, $dC/dP = c_p dP^p/dP$ will be distinctly smaller than c_p, since dP^p/dP is certainly smaller than one and may be close to zero if P exhibits much short-run variation. Thus, independently of the relation of c_p to α, a regression of C on YL and P is most likely to yield a P coefficient much smaller than that of YL, especially since YL will tend to proxy in part for P^p. In the case of the United States, for example, Ando and Modigliani (1963) obtained a coefficient of YL of .93 and a coefficient of P of .07 (totally insignificant). This was true even though A, in contrast to P, contributed very significantly to the explanation of C.

The results of a similar test for Italy have already been reported in connection with our test of the Kaldorian hypothesis and appear in Table 2, equations 2L and 2R. From those results, one can infer that the coefficient of current profit is only .43, and hence much lower than the coefficient of wages. But according to *LCH*, this low coefficient does not reflect a purportedly low *MPC* out of property income, but rather the fact that current profit P is a poor proxy for wealth and/or expected long-run profit P^p, the truly relevant variables. The supposition receives some indirect support from the fact that the coefficient of P is not only low but also has a

t-ratio which is relatively low, especially when compared with that of $\hat{W}$ (see equation 2) or with that of A in equation 1, Table 3. These results are thus in line with those of Ando-Modigliani (1963) for the United States. But a more telling test, reported in equations $2L$ and $2R$ of Table 3, consists in adding the variable A to the Kaldorian model (or equivalently P to the LCH model); in the linear estimate, the coefficient of P then falls from .42 to .07 and is insignificantly different from zero whereas the A coefficient falls only from .092 to .083 and is still quite significant. Similar results hold for the ratio estimate. These results are consistent with the LCH interpretation that P, in the Kaldorian equations 2 of Table 2, is but a poor proxy for the relevant variables A and P^p.

The validity of this inference is supported by the other results which are reported in Table 2. Indeed, we can now interpret these tests as an endeavor to estimate the coefficient c_p of equation (13), by replacing both A^* and P by an approximation to P^p. As we have already seen in commenting on the results of Table 2, we find that the coefficient of P^p is uniformly larger than that of wages, and that in fact most of the time our estimate is above unity. In particular, when using the more refined approach of equation 5, relying on a Koyck distributed lag on $\hat{P}_{-1}$, our estimate of c_p is as high as 1.5 to 1.9, a value which is perfectly consistent with the LCH framework, as is apparent from (13). This consistency can also be verified by relating the estimate of c_p to the estimate of the coefficient of A^*, δ, in equation 1, Table 3. From equations (10), (11), and (13) it is seen that δ, and the coefficient of P^p, c_p, should be related by

$$(14)\qquad c_p \simeq \frac{\delta^*}{\bar{r}} + \mu \equiv \frac{1}{\bar{r}}(\delta^* + \mu\bar{r}) = \frac{1}{\bar{r}}\delta$$

where $\bar{r}$ is the average value of the return on wealth, $r = P^p/A$ or equivalently the capitalization rate relating the market value of wealth to expected profits, $A = P^p/r$.

Relying on the assumption that r was reasonably stable in the relevant period and that, as in Table 2, P^p can be approximated by a linear combination of $\hat{P}$ and a Koyck lag beginning with $\hat{P}_{-1}$,[23] we can obtain an estimate r, $\hat{r}$, from the regression

$$(15)\qquad A^* = \mu'\hat{P} + \mu'' L(\hat{P}_{-1}) + a$$

where $\mu' + \mu'' \simeq 1/\hat{r}$. The results obtained in estimating (15) are shown in equations $3L$ and $3R$, Table 3. The fit is reasonably good considering the rough approximation to A. The estimate of $1/\hat{r}$ implied by $\mu' + \mu''$, 16.5, is not unreasonable (though somewhat on the high side).[24] It is seen from (15) that this estimate of $1/r$ together with the estimate of δ of Table 3 would lead us to expect a value of c_p of around 1.5 (.092x16.6 relying on the linear estimates, .078x16.5 for the ratio estimates), which is quite consistent with the actual estimate.[25]

An attempt was also made to estimate the coefficients of the LCH function in its more general form (12), which includes both A and P^p, in the hope of gaining some

[23] We allow for a constant term on the ground that what we measure is not A, but financial wealth A^*, and we hypothesize that the relation of A^* to A can be approximated by

$$A^* = a_0 A - a_k = \frac{a_0}{r} P^p - a_1; \quad 0 < a_0 < 1, a_1 > 0$$

since, in the process of development, financial wealth is likely to rise proportionately faster than A (see fn. 21).

[24] Especially since from fn. 23, it is seen that $\mu_1 + \mu_2$ is an estimate of a_0/r and $a_0 < 1$.

[25] Since in the test equations 1 and 2, A^* denotes the value of assets at the end of the *preceding* year, the same is true in (15), and equation 3 of Table 3. Nonetheless, the explanatory variables include *current* profits $\hat{P}$. This was done on the ground that the variable $\hat{P}$ appears in equation 5 of Table 2 and the estimate of c_p is the sum of the coefficient of profits including the current value $\hat{P}$. The very significant contribution of current $\hat{P}$ to the explanation of earlier A^* can be readily accounted for on the hypothesis that $\hat{P}$ is a good proxy for profit expectations for the coming year held at the end of the previous year, which are reflected in A^*.,

information on the sign and size of the coefficient of P^p, an estimate of μ in (12) which reflects the strength of the substitution effect.

This attempt runs into serious difficulties because of the unavoidable collinearity of A and P^p, a problem made more serious in the present instance by our use of A^* as a proxy for A. The results are reported in equation 4, Table 3, although we regard them as rather unreliable. They do suggest that the value of μ is positive; however, the point estimate, greater than unity, is above the a priori upper limit, probably as a result of upward biases arising from the fact that our approximation to A is very rough, and hence P^p may partly act as a proxy for A.

On the whole, and subject to the caveat at the beginning of the previous paragraph, the results of equation 4, Table 3 seem to warrant the conclusion that a generalized version of the life cycle model can provide an explanation of consumption in postwar Italy which is substantially superior to that offered by any of the competing hypotheses. They also confirm and throw light on the inference that c_p is well above one. They further suggest that μ of equation (12) is positive at least in the case of Italy, though its numerical value (and therefore, in particular, its relation to α) cannot be reliably estimated with the presently available data.

While these striking results for Italy have not yet been replicated, they receive some support from scattered evidence for other countries. First, Richard Stone, in his 1966 paper, provides us with an explicit estimate of δ^* and μ of equation (12) for the United Kingdom, though his results are based on some rather stringent assumptions which may limit their reliability for our purpose.[26] His estimate of α is .79 and that of μ is positive and in fact only moderately lower, .67; at the same time, the separation of income into labor and property income does not affect the estimate of δ^* which remains .06. It is readily apparent from these estimates that for any reasonable value of the rate of return r, the quantity $.67+.06/r$ will exceed the estimated MPC out of labor income of .79, and in fact will exceed unity. These results have been confirmed by his later paper extending the analysis to 1970. In particular, when relying on the alternative measure of consumption excluding durables, the estimates of both α and μ are reduced as expected, but, in addition, the difference between them shrinks further to only about .10 (and with a very small t-ratio).

Finally, for the United States, Warren Weber, following a rather different method of estimation, but allowing explicitly for the effect of the interest rate, has concluded that the partial derivative of C with respect to r is positive, implying again a positive value of μ and, hence again, a value of c_p most probably above unity or at least above α.

One suggestive implication of these conclusions should be to relieve the schizophrenia of many economists and other social scientists who have been torn in the past between advocating a redistribution of income in favor of labor on grounds of equity, and reluctantly accepting a redistribution in favor of profits on the ground that this would increase savings and capital formation and, hence, the potential rate of economic development. Our evidence suggests that a sheer redistribution of a given income from wages to profits would increase savings only in the short-run, but would decrease it in the longer run (since c_p is larger than α). Furthermore, a reduction in the rate of return or

[26] The most sensitive assumptions for our purpose are that: (i) permanent labor income can be approximated by a Koyck lag of the wage and salary component of National Income; (ii) permanent property income P^p is a Koyck distributed lag of the remaining components of income; and (iii) the weights of the distributed lag are the same for the two components.

rate of profit resulting from a lower productivity of capital or from taxation of property income might also increase saving, although this inference is uncertain since the available evidence does not enable us to conclude with confidence that μ exceeds α in (12), (see equation (11')).

REFERENCES

C. Ackley, "The Wealth-Saving Relationship," *J. Polit. Econ.*, Feb./Dec. 1951, *59,* 155–61.

A. Ando and F. Modigliani, "The 'Life Cycle' Hypothesis of Saving: Aggregate Implications and Tests," and "Correction," *Amer. Econ. Rev.*, Mar. 1963, *53,* 55–84 and Mar. 1964, *54,* 111–13.

D. S. Brady and R. D. Friedman, "Savings and the Income Distribution," Nat. Bur. Econ. Res. *Stud. in Income and Wealth,* Vol. 10, New York 1947, 247–65.

T. M. Brown, "Habit Persistence and Lags in Consumer Behavior," *Econometrica,* July 1952, *20,* 355–71.

R. E. Brumberg, "An Approximation to the Aggregate Saving Function," *Econ. J.*, May 1956, *66,* 66–72.

G. Carlucci and G. M. Rey, "La funzione aggregata del consumo in Italia," *Riv. Polit. Econ.*, Nov. 1963, *53,* 3–23.

F. Cotula and M. Caron, "I conti finanziari dell'Italia. Dimensioni e struttura della riccheza e del risparmio finanziari dell'-economia," Banca d'Italia *Bollettino,* Nov.-Dec. 1971, *6,* 839–919.

T. E. Davis, "The Consumption Function as a Tool for Prediction," *Rev. Econ. Statist.*, Aug. 1952, *34,* 270–77.

F. Di Fenizio, "La funzione del consumo in Italia come legge di lungo periodo," *L'Industria,* Jan.-Feb. 1958, *1,* 37–59.

J. S. Duesenberry, *Income, Saving and the Theory of Consumer Behavior,* Cambridge, Mass. 1949.

M. J. Farrell, "The New Theories of the Consumption Function," *Econ. J.*, Dec. 1959, *69,* 678–96.

I. Fisher, *The Theory of Interest,* New York 1930.

M. Friedman, *A Theory of the Consumption Function,* Princeton 1957.

R. W. Goldsmith, *A Study of Saving in the United States,* Princeton 1956.

A. Graziani, *Reddito Nazionale, Moneta e Consumi Nell'economia Italiana: Saggi,* Naples 1961.

N. Kaldor, "Alternative Theories of Distribution," in his *Essays in Value and Distribution,* London 1960.

J. M. Keynes, *The General Theory of Employment, Interest and Money,* New York and London 1936.

L. M. Koyck, *Distributed Lags and Investment Analysis,* Amsterdam 1954.

S. Kuznets, *Uses of National Income in Peace and War,* Occas. Paper 6, Nat. Bur. Econ. Res., New York 1942.

F. Modigliani, "Fluctuations in the Saving-Income Ratio: A Problem in Economic Forecasting," Nat. Bur. Econ. Res. *Stud. in Income and Wealth,* Vol. 11, New York 1949.

———, "The Life Cycle Hypothesis of Saving, the Demand for Wealth and the Supply of Capital," *Soc. Res.*, Summer 1966, *33,* 160–217.

———, "The Life Cycle Hypothesis of Saving and Inter-Country Differences in the Saving Ratio," in W. A. Eltis et al., eds., *Induction, Growth and Trade: Essays in Honour of Sir Roy Harrod,* Oxford 1970, 197–225.

———, "The Life Cycle Hypothesis of Saving Twenty Years Later," *Proc. AUTE Conference,* Univ. Warwick, England, Mar. 1973.

——— **and A. Ando,** "The Permanent Income and the Life Cycle Hypothesis of Saving Behavior: Comparisons and Tests," *Consumption and Savings,* Vol. 2, Philadelphia 1960, pp. 156–59.

——— **and** ———, "Tests of the Life Cycle Hypothesis of Saving," *Bull. Oxford Univ. Inst. Econ. Statist.*, May 1957, *19,* 99–124.

——— **and R. Brumberg,** "Utility Analysis and the Consumption Function: An Interpretation of Cross-Section Data," in K. Kurihara, ed., *Post Keynesian Economics,* New Brunswick 1954.

——— **and** ———, "Utility Analysis and Aggregate Consumption Function: An Attempt at Integration," unpublished paper, 1954.

——— and E. Tarantelli, "A Generalization of the Phillips Curve for a Developing Country," *Rev. Econ. Stud.*, Apr. 1973, *40*, 203–23.

——— and ———, *Mercato del Lavoro, Distribuzione del Reddito e Consumi Privati*, il Mulino, Bologna (forthcoming).

A. Niccoli, "Consumi privati," in *Analisi quantitativa per la programmazione di breve periodo*, Istituto Nazionale per lo Studio della Congiuntura (ISCO), Rome 1971.

D. Ricardo, "On the Principles of Political Economy and Taxation," in P. Sraffa, ed., *Works and Correspondence of David Ricardo, 1*, Cambridge 1953, 96–97.

B. Sitzia, "A Note on Consumption Functions in Econometric Models," unpublished study, Rome 1974.

W. H. Somermeyer and R. Bannink, *A Consumption-Savings Model and Its Applications*, Amsterdam and London 1973.

R. Stone, "Spending and Saving in Relation to Income and Wealth," *L'Industria*, Oct.-Dec. 1966, *4*, 471–99.

———, "Personal Spending and Saving in Postwar Britain," in W. Sellekaerts, ed., *Economic Development and Planning: Essays in Honour of J. Tinbergen*, White Plains 1974.

P. Sylos-Labini, "Prices, Distribution and Investment in Italy, 1951–1966: An Interpretation," *Banca Naz. Lavoro Quart. Rev.*, Dec. 1967, *23*, 316–70.

———, "Sviluppo economico e classi sociali in Italia," *Quaderni di Sociologia*, Oct.-Dec. 1972, *4*, 371–443.

E. Tarantelli, "Produttività del lavoro, salari e inflazione," Ente per gli Studi Monetaria, Bancari e Finanziari L. Einàudi, *Quaderni di Richerche*, Jan. 1970, *5*, 1–128.

———, (1973a) "Note sul consumo nella teoria economica e nuove linee di ricerca per l'esperienza italiana," *Riv. Int. Sci. Soc.*, Jan.-Apr. 1973, *81*, 115–33.

———, (1973b) "Distribuzione del reddito e rinnovi contrattuali nell'esperienza italiana," *Riv. Int. Sci. Soc.*, July-Oct. 1973, *81*, 345–72.

T. Ter-Minassian, "Effects of Tax Changes on the Real Variables of the Economic System in Italy," unpublished study, Rome 1973.

J. Tobin, "Life Cycle Saving and Balanced Growth," in *Ten Economic Studies in the Tradition of Irving Fisher*, New York 1967.

———, "Asset Holdings and Spending Decisions," *Amer. Econ. Rev. Proc.*, May 1952, *42*, 109–37.

——— and **W. C. Dolde**, "Wealth, Liquidity and Consumption," in *Consumer Spending and Monetary Policy: The Linkages*, Fed. Reserve Bank Boston, Monetary Conference Series, No. 5, Boston 1971.

A. Ulizzi, "Income, Saving and Expenditure of Italian Households in 1968: Review of the Economic Conditions in Italy," *Banco di Roma*, Nov. 1970, *24*, 410–38.

S. Vinci, "Consumi e distribuzione del reddito," *L'Industria*, Jan.-Mar. 1971, *1*, 21–39.

W. R. Weber, "The Effect of Interest Rates on Aggregate Consumption," *Amer. Econ. Rev.*, Sept. 1970, *60*, 591–600.

Banca d'Italia, *Relazione Annuale*, Rome 1971.

———, Gruppo per lo Studio della Politica Monetaria e Fiscale, "Un modello econometrico dell'economia italiana M.2B.1," mimeo., Rome 1974.

Ministero del Bilancio, *Relazione Generale sulla Situazione Economica del Paese*, annual issues, 1950–70.

Errata

Page 839, column 2, paragraph 2, line 6: "an estimate r, $\hat{r}$" should read "an estimate of r, r̂."

[Reprinted from SOCIAL RESEARCH, Vol. 33, No. 2, Summer, 1966]

THE LIFE CYCLE HYPOTHESIS OF SAVING, THE DEMAND FOR WEALTH AND THE SUPPLY OF CAPITAL*

BY FRANCO MODIGLIANI

INTRODUCTION AND SUMMARY

A NUMBER of recent papers have been devoted to developing the life cycle hypothesis of saving, deriving some of its testable implications, both at the household and at the aggregate level, and to testing some of these implications (See especially [3], [4], [7], [8], [2], [22], [17], [19], [20]). The purpose of this present contribution is to exhibit some further aggregative implications of the model concerning both the long run and the short run, or cyclical,

* AUTHOR'S NOTE—Part of the material of the present paper was first presented in my presidential address to the Econometric Society in December, 1963. An extended and revised version is contained in a document prepared for presentation at the First International Congress of the Econometric Society, held in Rome, Italy in September, 1965. This version contained a third part devoted to tests based on a cross-section of countries. That portion will appear shortly elsewhere and is referred to hereafter as the "sequel paper."

I wish to thank Mr. Richard Sutch for reading an early draft of the manuscript and making many useful suggestions concerning both form and content, and my research assistants, Farid Saad and Lawrence Kilham, for helping with the collection of the data and taking responsibility for the computations.

Part of the research was undertaken while I held a Ford Foundation Faculty Fellowship. I also wish gratefully to acknowledge research support from a Ford Foundation grant to the Sloan School of Management for research in Finance, and from the National Science Foundation.

Last but not least, I wish to record here my gratitude to Hans Neisser and Adolph Lowe, who witnessed my first interest in problems of consumption and saving behavior, and who through the past twenty years have provided constant encouragement, intellectual stimulation and valuable criticism.

behavior of the saving-income and the wealth-income ratio, and to provide empirical tests of some of these implications.

In Part I.1 it is shown that the life cycle model, assuming that prevailing tastes as to the pattern of allocation of life resources to consumption over life remain stable in time, has the following implications: if income grows at a constant rate, then both aggregate private saving and aggregate private wealth will tend to grow at the same rate and therefore the saving and the wealth-income ratio will tend to remain constant. Furthermore, both ratios will depend on the rate of growth of income, though in the case of saving the association will tend to be positive, while in the case of wealth it will be negative. In Part I.2, it is then shown that if income fluctuates cyclically around its growth trend, the saving-income and the wealth-income ratio will also fluctuate around the constant long run value derived in I.1, but the saving ratio will fluctuate procyclically, while the wealth ratio will move countercyclically.

Part II is devoted to some empirical tests of behavior of the wealth-income ratio established in Part I. It relies on historical data for the United States, an economy for which some estimates are available over a span of some sixty years and which over this span has exhibited cyclical fluctuations around a reasonably stable long run trend. It is found that the life cycle model accounts remarkably well for the observed behavior of aggregate wealth. It is further shown that this behavior of aggregate wealth may account, to a substantial extent, for the purported long run stability of the so-called capital-output ratio. It is argued that these results cast doubt on the generally accepted notion that the stability of the capital-output ratio reflects rigid technologically imposed capital requirements. It is suggested, instead, that the limited stability observed may, at least in good part, reflect the adjustment of the amount of capital in use to the supply of wealth resulting from consumption and saving behavior of the type formalized by the life cycle model.

The final section of Part II applies the results of the analysis to the classical issue of the burden of the national debt. It provides some impressive, if preliminary, empirical evidence that the national debt does indeed tend to displace other components of wealth, and through this route may reduce the income capability of later generations.

No attempt is made in this paper to test the implications of the model concerning the long run relation between the saving ratio and the rate of growth of income. This task is, however, carried out in a sequel paper relying on a cross section of some thirty-six countries, where it is shown that the inter-country differences in reported saving ratios bear little relation to the level of per capita income but are, instead, largely accounted for by differences in the rate of growth of income, and that both the sign and the order of magnitude of the empirical coefficients agree rather well with the implications of the life cycle model derived in Part I of this paper.[1]

PART I. IMPLICATIONS OF THE LIFE CYCLE HYPOTHESIS FOR THE BEHAVIOR OF THE SAVING RATIO AND THE WEALTH-INCOME RATIO

I.1. The "Life Cycle" Model and the Long Run Determinants of Saving and Private Wealth

The point of departure of the life cycle model is the hypothesis that consumption and saving decisions of households at each point of time reflect a more or less conscious attempt at achieving the preferred distribution of consumption over the life cycle, subject to the constraint imposed by the resources accruing to the household over its lifetime. In the strictest version of the model it is also hypothesized that the amount allocated to consumption exhausts resources, there being no planned bequests. While this assumption will be relaxed below, we first wish to establish that, even in the absence of bequests, the model can account for the existence of a very substantial aggregate stock of wealth. To this

[1] These results are reported in the paper read at the First International Congress of the Econometric Society, referred to in the Author's Note.

end it is sufficient to add the reasonable assumption that, on the average, earning power tends to dry up well before the termination of life and that the preferred allocation of resources over life will typically call for a rate of consumption, after this drying up, on a scale commensurate with earlier consumption. Under these conditions households must, on the average, save in the earlier part of their life in order to accumulate a stock of wealth (possibly in some form of retirement insurance) which will eventually be used to support consumption through dissaving in the later part of their life.

In order to establish the implications of the life cycle model and the above assumptions, both as to the stability of the wealth-income and saving-income ratios and as to the order of magnitude of these ratios, it is convenient to start out by considering a "stationary" economy, in which both population and productivity are constant through time, and then to relax these assumptions one by one. The argument set out below in literary form is developed in more rigorous analytical form in Appendix A.

a) Saving and Wealth with Stationary Income and Population

In an unpublished paper written with R. Brumberg [22] it was shown that if one makes some reasonable guesses about the typical length of earning life and retired life (say forty years and ten years, respectively), and combines this guess with the simplest possible life pattern of earning and consumption—a constant rate of earning up to retirement, a constant rate of consumption through life, and a zero rate of return on net worth—one finds that in a stationary economy of constant population and productivity the aggregate stock of wealth would be quite significant, some five times yearly national income (see below). At the same time, under these conditions the aggregate rate of saving would be zero as the positive saving of the younger households, in their accumulation phase, would be precisely offset by the dissaving of the retired households drawing down their earlier accumulation. Thus, wealth will remain constant in the aggregate, though it is continuously being transferred from dissavers to savers in exchange for current resources.

This conclusion of zero net aggregate saving in an economy of stationary per capita income and population will hold even if we drop the assumptions of a constant rate of earning and consumption over life and zero rate of return and replace them with the following much weaker assumptions: (1) the proportion of total life income earned and consumed at each age remains stable for successive cohorts of households, and (2) the rate of return is also constant through time. Under these conditions, a stationary per capita income implies that the per capita rate of saving of each age class T present at any date t, coincides with the per capita rate of saving of any one cohort as it reaches that same age T. If, in addition, population is stationary, in the sense that each successive cohort has the same size at birth and the same mortality experience, then the aggregate rate of saving at any date t, say S_t, will coincide with the aggregate net saving of any one cohort over its entire life cycle. But since under our assumption of no bequests the net over-life saving of each cohort must be zero, S_t itself must be zero.[2] Note also that the stock of wealth will again be proportional to aggregate income (since both variables remain constant in time) although the proportionality factor will depend on the specific path of average earning and consumption over the life cycle.

These results are illustrated graphically in Figure 1 under the simplest set of assumptions. The mortality rate is assumed to be zero up to age L and one at age L. The solid curve labeled Y(T) shows per capita income from labor as a function of age, which is assumed constant at the rate $\overline{Y}$ up to age N and zero over the rest of the life. On the further assumption of a zero rate of return on assets, this locus represents also total per capita income. The dashed line shows the rate of per capita consumption which is assumed to be constant through life; since life consumption must exhaust income, the constant rate must be $(N/L)\overline{Y}$. The distance between Y(T) and C(T), shaded in the figure, is per

[2] *Cf.* Appendix A, a).

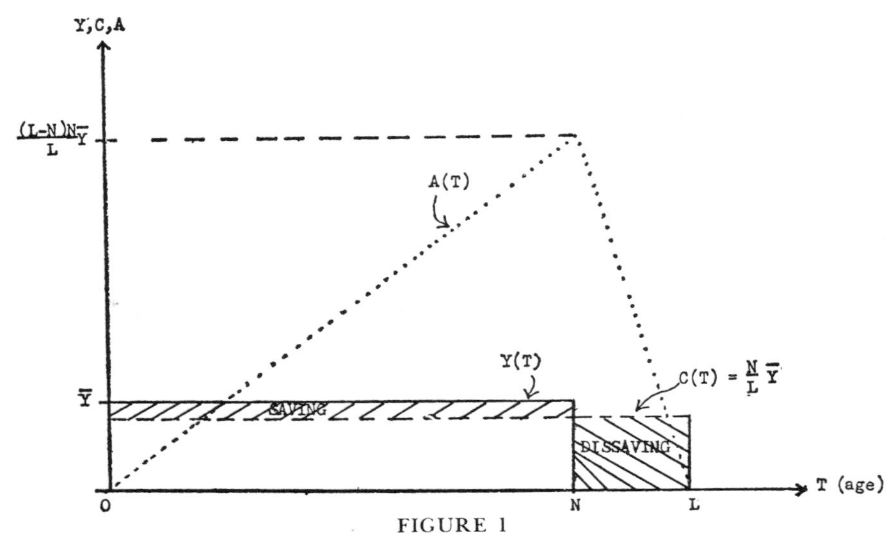

FIGURE 1

INCOME, CONSUMPTION, SAVING AND WEALTH AS A FUNCTION OF AGE

capita saving (or dissaving). Finally, the dotted locus shows per capita net worth, the cumulant of saving, as a function of age; it starts at zero, rises linearly to a peak at the age of retirement, N, and then falls linearly back to zero at age L. In addition to showing the life history of any one cohort the graph can also be interpreted as representing average income, consumption and net worth of the various age cohorts present at any given date t. Hence, under the mortality assumptions stated above, and the stationarity assumption that each age cohort has the same size at age zero, say P_0, the area under the Y(T) curve, $N\bar{Y}$, also represents aggregate income in the year t, Y(t), up to a proportionality factor P_0. Similarly, the algebraic sum of the two shaded areas is total saving up to the factor P_0, and this sum is of course zero. Finally, the area under A(T) is the aggregate net worth A(t) up to the factor P_0. It can readily be seen from the figure that this area is $\frac{(L-N)N}{2}\bar{Y}$, so that the wealth income ratio at any date t, is

$$A(t)/Y(t)=[\frac{(L-N)N}{2}\bar{Y}]/[N\bar{Y}]=(L-N)/2$$

Thus, for an earning span of, say, forty years, and a life span of fifty years (from the date of entering the labor force), aggregate wealth in our stationary society would come to five times annual income.

b) The Effect of Population Growth

Suppose that we retain assumptions (1) and (2), but let income grow as a result of population growth or of growth in income per employed resulting from increasing productivity. We can then show that saving will become positive, even in the absence of bequests. Consider first the effect of pure population growth, while retaining the assumption of a life cycle of earning and consumption constant through time. Suppose that the size of the cohorts born in successive years grows at the rate p. As a result, both population and aggregate income will also grow at the rate p. The effect of this growth will be to increase the ratio of younger households in their accumulation phase to older households in their dissaving phase, giving rise to a positive net flow of saving. It should also be apparent that if the rate of growth of population is constant in time then aggregate saving, $S(t)$, and wealth, $A(t)$, will also grow at the rate p and hence will be proportional to aggregate income.[3] We can thus write: $S(t)=sY(t)$ and $A(t)=aY(t)$. In the case of saving, the proportionality factor s, or saving-income ratio, may be expected to increase with p, as the relative frequency of households in their accumulation phase will tend to increase monotonically with p—a conclusion which was anticipated by Hans Neisser in a 1944 contribution [23]. On the other hand, since on the whole wealth may be expected to be markedly concentrated in the hands of older households (as suggested by Figure I.1), the increase in the relative frequency of younger households may be expected to reduce the ratio of wealth to income. In other words, a will tend to be negatively associated with the rate of growth, p. Note also that since saving is the rate of change of wealth, if wealth is rising at the rate p, we must have $S(t)/A(t)=p$, implying $S/Y=pA/Y$, or $s=pa$. From this equation we deduce

$$\frac{ds}{dp}=a+p\frac{da}{dp}=\frac{s}{p}(1+\frac{p}{a}\frac{da}{dp}).$$

Since, as was just indicated, we may expect $\frac{da}{dp}<0$, it follows that

[3] *Cf.* Appendix A, b).

while s may be expected to rise with p (as long as $\frac{p}{a}\frac{da}{dp} > -1$), it will tend to rise less than in proportion, i.e., its elasticity with respect to p, $\frac{p}{s}\frac{ds}{dp}$ must be less than one.

c) The Effect of Productivity Growth

Let us consider now the case where population is stationary but average income earned at each age, and hence also aggregate income, rises gradually in time, as a result of increasing productivity. This cause of growth will also tend to result in a positive rate of saving and a growing stock of wealth. This is because each successive cohort will enjoy life earnings larger than the preceding ones, and therefore a larger level of consumption at each age, since by assumption the distribution of consumption over life remains constant in time. It follows in particular that the currently active households will be aiming at a level of consumption in their retirement period larger than the consumption enjoyed by the currently retired households belonging to a less affluent generation. To support this future level of retired consumption the active households will have to save currently on a scale exceeding the dissaving of retired households. Thus, even if population were stationary, net aggregate saving will tend to be positive. In fact, if income tends to grow at a constant rate, say y, then both saving and wealth will tend to grow at the same rate, implying a constant saving-income and wealth-income ratio.[4] Furthermore, the saving ratio will again tend to rise with y as a faster rate of growth will tend to increase the excess of positive saving over dissaving. This tendency will be particularly pronounced if in estimating life resources each cohort does not take into account, to a significant extent, the future productivity growth of income. Anticipation of future growth by extrapolation of past trends will tend to reduce the saving ratio associated with each rate of growth by delaying and reducing the accumulation of each cohort; how-

[4] *Cf.* Appendix A, c). A very lucid discussion of this mechanism is given by Bentzel [6], pp. 39–40.

ever, this effect is most unlikely to destroy the positive association between the two variables.[5]

d) *Some* A Priori *Estimates of the Relation of s and a to Growth Rates*

In the unpublished paper written with R. Brumberg [22] cited earlier, we were able to derive quantitative estimates of the relations of the saving ratio s and the wealth ratio a to the rates of growth p and y, under a number of convenient simplifying assumptions and "reasonable" guesses about the values of relevant parameters. A sample of results of these calculations is reported in columns 2 and 3 of Table 1. These results are rather striking on two accounts. First, they suggest that, at least for rates of growth in the empirically relevant range, the relation between the saving ratio and the rate of growth is quite similar whether the growth is due to population only, productivity only, or, consequently, some mixture of the two.[6] In the second place, it is

[5] *Cf.*, the last paragraph of Appendix A, c).

[6] The analytical results of Appendix A b) and c) help to throw some light on this finding. In the first place, the expressions for total income (10b) and (10c) are actually identical for population and for productivity growth, except for the trivial difference that the rate of growth is denoted in one case by p, in the other by y; in other words, for any given rate of growth, ρ, the time path of total income is the same whether that growth results from pure population or pure productivity growth (and therefore also from any mixture of the two). In the case of S(t) and A(t), by comparing (8b) and (9b) with (8c) and (9c), respectively, we note that the only source of difference is the substitution of the function s(T) by $s^*(T,y)$. Since, in general, these two functions cannot be supposed identical in T, we cannot generally conclude that the saving-income ratio, s, and the wealth-income ratio, a, depend only on growth, independently of its source. In particular, $s^*(T,y)$ depends also on the rate of growth y, and, as noted in the text, the nature of this dependence will reflect in part (through the function σ (T)) the extent to which income expectations, that in turn control current consumption decisions, take into account the future productivity growth of income. At the same time there are good reasons to suppose that the saving ratio implied by (8b) and (8c) would be rather close for realistic values of the rate of growth, say between zero and 5 per cent. This is because (i) the bracketed expressions on the right hand side of (8b) and (8c), respectively, can be looked at, essentially, as weighted sums of the variable $h(T)e^{-\rho T}$; (ii) the weighting functions, s(T) and $s^*(T,y)$, respectively, are identical in T for y=0; and (iii) for any value of y the weighting functions are related to each other by the condition of no bequests, or zero over life saving, implying

$$\int_0^L s(T)\ h(T)\ dT = \int_0^L s^*(T,y)\ h(T)\ dT = 0$$

TABLE 1

RELATION OF THE SAVING-INCOME RATIO, s, AND THE WEALTH-INCOME RATIO, a, TO THE RATE OF GROWTH OF INCOME, DERIVED FROM THE LIFE CYCLE MODEL

Rate of Growth of Income (ρ)	*By Direct Aggregation*[a]				*Based on parameters of U. S. Aggregate Consumption Function*[b]			
	Source of Growth				*Estimate A* $\sigma=.35$, $\delta=.05$		*Estimate B* $\sigma=.28$, $\delta=.029$	
	Population (p)		*Productivity (y)*					
	s(%)	a	s(%)	a	s(%)	a	s(%)	a
(1)	(2a)	(2b)	(3a)	(3b)	(4a)	(4b)	(5a)	(5b)
0	0	5	0	5	0	7	0	10
1	4.5	4.5			6	6	7	7
2	8	4.0	8	4	10	5.1	11	5.7
3	11	3.6			13	4.5	14	5.1
4	13	3.3	14	3.5	16	4.0	16	4.2
5	15	3.0			18	3.7	18	3.7
10	19	1.9			23	2.6	22	2.5

[a] The main assumptions underlying the figures reported in columns 2 and 3 are as follows:

(i) For both columns: Earning life (N) 40 years, life span (L), 50 years; mortality rate, zero up to age 50 and unity at age 50. Zero rate of return on net worth; constant planned rate of consumption over the remaining life.

(ii) For column 2: Constant income over the earning life. It is shown in [28] and in the sequel paper that under these assumptions the relation between s and p is given by

$$s=\frac{L-N}{L}-\frac{N}{L}\frac{1-(1+p)^{-(L-N)}}{(1+p)^{N}-1}$$

(iii) For column 3: Stationary population; in any given year the same rate of earning for every age up to 40; expected annual income over the balance of the working life equal to current income (i.e., no extrapolation of past growth trends). It is shown in [2] that under these assumptions the relation between s and y is given by

$$s=\frac{M}{L}\left\{1-\frac{1-e^{-yM}}{My}+\frac{1}{N}\sum_{t=1}^{N-1}\frac{t}{L-t}\left[1-e^{-y(L-t)}\right]\right\}$$

The summation term was approximated by means of integrals and evaluated from values of the definite integral

$$\int_{x}^{\infty}\frac{e^{-y}}{y}dy$$

tabulated in *Table of Sines, Cosines, and Exponential Integrals*, Vol. II, Work Projects Administration of the City of New York.

(iv) The value of a is given by s/ρ. For $\rho=0$, this expression is indeterminate and a was computed from the formula $a=(L-N)/2$ derived in the text in relation to Figure 1.

[b] s and a are computed from formulas (I.4) and (I.3) of section I.2.

apparent that for growth rates of the order of that observed for the United States in recent decades, somewhere between 3 and 3.5 per cent, the saving ratio derived from the model is strikingly similar to those which have been reported for the United States.

In summary, then, the life cycle hypothesis, plus the assumption of stability in time in the distribution of income by age, in the preferred allocation of consumption over life and in the rate of return, implies that the saving-income and the wealth-income ratios are independent of the level of income and related instead to the growth trend of income. Furthermore, the saving ratio will be zero for stationary income and will tend to rise with the growth trend.[7] By contrast, the wealth-income ratio will tend to be nega-

[7] It is of some interest to compare the above implications of the life cycle model with the following conclusions that Friedman has derived from his "permanent income hypothesis" in [10]. "According to it [the permanent income hypothesis] the saving ratio is independent of the level of income" (p. 234); and "Although, on the permanent income hypothesis, a low level of real income does not make for a low savings ratio, a rapid rate of rise in income, whatever the level, may do so. The reason is that a rise expected to continue tends to raise permanent income relative to measured income and so to raise consumption relative to measured income." (*Ibid.*) Thus the two models agree about the relation of saving to the level of income. But they seem to lead to sharply divergent implications about the effect of income growth, which is somewhat surprising considering that they have a great deal in common and are frequently lumped together as if they were minor variants on the same theme. To account for the differences in conclusions let us note first that the Friedman argument clearly applies only to growth of income resulting from productivity; his formulation does not have any immediate implications about the effects of population growth which, in our model, generate a positive association between income growth and the saving ratio. As for the radically different conclusions about the effects of per capita income growth, they can be traced to the fact that according to the life cycle model the "permanent income" which is supposed to control the rate of consumption of a household at any given point can be basically identified with its life earnings, which include current, future and *past* earnings. In this sense the effect of (permanent) growth of income on the relation of current to "permanent income" depends very much on the age of the household. For younger households for which most of the income is still to accrue, it will indeed be the case that income growth will tend to raise permanent income relative to current per capita income and the Friedman effect will tend to hold (subject to limitations on the ability to build up a negative net worth). But for older households, and especially for retired households, for which most or all of the earnings have already accrued at a time when productivity and income were lower than currently, the very opposite will be true; income growth will tend to *reduce* permanent income and consumption relative to current per capita income.
Under these conditions, the considerations developed in the text and in the above

tively associated with the rate of growth, being highest for a zero growth rate. Finally, some rough estimates of the saving and wealth-income ratios that one would expect to prevail if the life cycle model were a reasonable approximation to actual behavior yield values of s and a of the order of magnitude of those observed for the United States.

I.2. Alternative Derivation Via the Aggregate Consumption Function—Cyclical Implications of the Model

The conclusions reached above can also be established through an alternative route, namely, by deriving from the life cycle model an aggregate consumption function and then exhibiting its long run implications. This approach, which was followed in [4], does not bring out as clearly the role of the life cycle, but it has certain advantages. In particular, it permits relaxing the assumption of no bequests, and also makes it possible to derive implications about the short run or cyclical behavior of the saving and wealth-income ratios.

a) The Aggregate Consumption and Saving Function Implied by the Life Cycle Model

It was shown in [4] that the aggregate consumption function implied by the life cycle model can be written in the form

$$C_t = \alpha_1 L_t + \alpha_2 L^e_t + \alpha_3 A_{t-1} \tag{I.1}$$

where L and L^e denote respectively the aggregate current and anticipated rate of nonproperty income.[8] It was also indicated that

footnote and in Appendix A, c), suggest that s can be counted upon to be an increasing function of y, at least in the neighborhood of $y=0$, and in the relevant range of y.

[8] In equation (I.1) all variables may be thought of as measured in current money prices. However, under the assumption that the expected real rate of return on assets, measured in terms of consumables, is independent of the current price level of consumables, the life cycle hypothesis implies that consumption is homogeneous of first degree in L_t, L^e_t, A_t and the price level of consumables. Under these conditions we can divide through both sides of (I.1) by an index of the money price of consumables, thus expressing all variables in "real terms." In what follows it will actually be convenient to think of all variables as measured in real terms, i.e., as measured in terms of baskets of consumables.

Note also that in this section we find it convenient to treat time as discrete, in-this equation remains valid if the assumption of no bequests is replaced with the assumption that "the resources an individual earmarks for bequests are an increasing function of the individual's resources relative to the level of resources of his age group, and the relative size distribution of resources within each age group is stable over time." This assumption will be recognized as a variant of the so-called "relative income" hypothesis, but applied to aggregate life consumption rather than to short run consumption decisions.

The coefficients α_1, α_2, α_3 of (I.1) depend, in general, on preferences as to the distribution of consumption over life (and to bequests), on the rate of return on assets, on the age structure of population and on the previous history of income. If the rate of return and tastes are constant, and population grows at a constant rate p and income per worker at a rate y, then the coefficients will be constant in time (once steady state has been reached), though their value will depend in principle on r, p and y. Furthermore, with steady growth of income, L^e_t can be taken as equal, or at least proportional, to L_t and therefore the first two terms of (I.1) can be replaced by a single term, αL_t. Then from (I.1), letting Y_t denote aggregate current income, the sum of labor income L_t and of property income, and noting that property income can be expressed as rA_{t-1}, we derive the aggregate saving function

$$S_t = Y_t - C_t = Y_t - \alpha L_t - \alpha_3 A_{t-1} = Y_t - \alpha(L_t + rA_{t-1}) - (\alpha_3 - \alpha r)A_{t-1}.$$

Letting $\sigma \equiv (1-\alpha)$, $\delta = \alpha_3 - \alpha r$

the saving function can be simplified to

$$\text{(I.2)} \qquad S_t = \sigma Y_t - \delta A_{t-1}$$ [9]

It was also shown in [3] and [4] that the saving function (I.2) im-

stead of continuous, as in section I.1, and to replace the notation X(t) with X_t. When X denotes a stock, X_t is the value at the *end* of period t.

[9] A consumption function of the general form (I.2) has been hypothesized by a number of authors on a variety of grounds. A very useful and compact account of its history will be found in Lydall [14]. However, stress on its derivation from, and relation to, the life cycle hypothesis seems to be largely confined to the literature cited in the introduction, except for passing references (e.g., [14], p. 231).

plies that if income is growing at a constant rate $\rho = p + y$, then wealth will also tend to grow at the same rate and hence the asset income ratio and the saving ratio will each tend to a constant value, which depends on the parameters of the consumption function and on ρ. Specifically,

$$A_t/Y_t \to a \equiv \frac{\sigma(1+\rho)}{\delta+\rho} \tag{I.3}$$

$$S_t/Y_t \to s \equiv \frac{\rho\sigma}{\delta+\rho} \tag{I.4}$$ [10]

b) Implications for the Short Run Behavior of the Saving and Wealth-Income Ratios

For purposes of empirical testing, however, these results are of limited value, for one is unlikely to find situations in which income grows at a constant rate for any extended period of time. We propose, therefore, to exhibit the implications of the model for the empirically relevant case in which income fluctuates moderately around a stable growth trend. In this process, we shall also be able to derive equations (I.3) and (I.4) as limiting cases where the fluctuations of income approach zero. In our derivation, the parameters of (I.2) will be treated as constants on the

[10] The derivation of (I.3) and (I.4) from (I.2) relies on the proposition that saving in any given period is equal to the change in the values of assets (measured in terms of consumables). This proposition is strictly valid only insofar as there are no real capital gains or losses, i.e., no net changes in the market value of initial assets relative to the price index of consumables. Insofar as there are capital gains of a systematic and predictable character, it would seem best to think of them as being included in the return on assets (and hence in property income). As for capital gains which are in the nature of unpredictable and unsystematic windfalls, their effect will be that the equation $S = \frac{dA}{dt}$ (or $A_t - A_{t-1}$) will hold up to a random component which may be expected to be small and close to zero on the average, if expectations are not too far off, and which can be disregarded for purposes of long run analysis. It should be noted that since we define hereafter property income to include corporate profit net of taxes, whether paid out in dividends or not, (real) changes in the market value of corporate equity are to be regarded as capital gains (or losses) only insofar as they differ from corporate saving.

It may also be noted that (I.3) and (I.4) imply $a = \frac{s}{\rho}(1+\rho)$ instead of s/ρ as in section I.1. This follows from the fact that time is now treated as discrete and a is defined as the ratio of income to *terminal* assets.

ground that, for moderate fluctuations of income, changes in these parameters may be expected to remain of an order of magnitude sufficiently small to be neglected.

Focusing first on the behavior of the wealth-income ratio we observe that equation (I.2) implies [11]

(I.5) $$A_t = A_{t-1} + S_t = \sigma Y_t + (1-\delta)\, A_{t-1}$$

Applying (I.5) recursively, we can express A_t as an exponentially weighted average of past incomes,

$$A_t = \sigma Y_t + \sigma(1-\delta)\, Y_{t-1} + (1-\delta)^2 A_{t-2} = \sigma \sum_{\tau=0}^{T} (1-\delta)^\tau Y_{t-\tau} + (1-\delta)^T A_{t-T}$$

Since $(1-\delta)$ is between zero and unity, the last term must approach zero as T tends to infinity, so that we can write

(I.5a) $$A_t = \sigma \sum_{\tau=0}^{\infty} (1-\delta)^\tau\, Y_{t-\tau}.$$

Now let $Y^*_t \equiv Y_0\,(1+\rho)^t$ denote the exponential trend around which current income fluctuates. Let us further define

(1.6a) $$q'_t = (Y_t - Y^*_t)/Y^*_t$$

as the relative deviation of income from trend in period t. Obviously q'_t is a measure of cyclical position of the economy. Now substituting $q'_{t-\tau}\, Y^*_{t-\tau} + Y^*_{t-\tau}$ for $Y_{t-\tau}$ in (I.5a), and recalling that

$$Y^*_{t-\tau}/Y^*_t = (1+\rho)^{-\tau}$$

we find

$$A_t = \sigma \sum_{\tau=0}^{\infty} (1-\delta)^\tau\, Y^*_{t-\tau} + \sigma \sum_{\tau=0}^{\infty} (1-\delta)^\tau\, q'_{t-\tau}\, Y^*_{t-\tau} =$$

$$= Y^*_t \left[\sigma \sum_{\tau=0}^{\infty} \left(\frac{1-\delta}{1+\rho}\right)^\tau + \sigma \sum_{\tau=0}^{\infty} \left(\frac{1-\delta}{1+\rho}\right)^\tau q'_{t-\tau}\right]$$

[11] Neglecting capital gains and losses, as noted in footnote 10.

Carrying out the summation and using definition (I.3), we find

$$\sigma \sum_{t=0}^{\infty} \left(\frac{1-\delta}{1+\rho}\right)^{\tau} = \sigma \frac{1+\rho}{\delta+\rho} \equiv a.$$

Substituting in the previous equation and factoring a leads to

$$A_t = aY^*_t \ (1+u'_t) \tag{I.7}$$

where

$$u'_t = \frac{\delta+\rho}{1+\rho} \sum_{\tau=0}^{\infty} \left(\frac{1-\delta}{1+\rho}\right)^{\tau} p'_{t-\tau} \tag{I.8}$$

can be thought of as the error involved in approximating A_t by aY^*_t.

The behavior of the wealth-income ratio can now be finally expressed as

$$\frac{A_t}{Y_t} = a\frac{Y^*_t}{Y_t}(1+u'_t) = a - a\left(\frac{Y_t - Y^*_t}{Y_t}\right) + a\frac{Y^*_t}{Y_t}u'_t = a - a\ q_t + au_t \tag{I.9}$$

where

$$q_t = \frac{Y_t - Y^*_t}{Y_t} \tag{I.6b}$$

can be thought of as a variant of the cyclical income index q' and $u_t = u'_t \frac{Y^*_t}{Y_t}$.

Equation (I.7) also enables us to derive an approximation to the saving function (I.2) in which wealth does not appear explicitly and is replaced instead by the cyclical index q. This is clearly a very useful approximation in view of the extreme scarcity of information presently available on aggregate wealth. By substituting (I.7) into (I.2) one obtains

$$S_t = \sigma Y_t - \delta a Y^*_{t-1}\ (1-u'_{t-1}) = \sigma\ Y_t \frac{\delta a}{1+\rho}\ Y^*_t - [\delta a\ Y^*_{t-1}\ u'_{t-1}]$$

Noting that (I.3) and (I.4) imply $\frac{\delta a}{1+\rho} = \frac{\delta}{\rho}$, from this equation, after adding and subtracting $\frac{\delta}{\rho} Y_t$, one finally derives

$$\frac{S_t}{Y_t} = s + \frac{\delta}{\rho} s\, q_t - \frac{\delta}{\rho} s\, \nu_t \tag{I.10}$$

where $\nu_t = \frac{(1+\rho)Y_{t-1}}{Y_t} u_{t-1}$.

c) Steady Growth Implications

In order to bring out the implications of (I.9) and (I.10) consider first the special case where income follows exactly its growth trend. Then q_t will be zero and so will be the current and lagged values of q'_t and hence u_t and u'_t. (I.9) and (I.10) then imply that the wealth-income ratio will assume and retain the value a, and the saving ratio the value s, given by equations (I.3) and (I.4). (More generally, if income has followed its trend for the last n periods, then these values will be approached asymptotically as n grows.)

These implications are seen to agree with, and confirm, the results obtained in section 1 by the alternative approach. In particular, it is apparent from (I.4) that (1) the saving ratio will be zero for zero growth; and (2) that it will tend to rise with $\rho = p + y$, but at a decreasing rate. On the other hand, the wealth-income ratio will tend to fall with ρ, assuming a maximum value σ/δ, at zero growth.[12]

It is also instructive to compare the *a priori* estimates of the saving and wealth-income ratios which were presented in columns 2 and 3 of Table 1 with the values implied by equations (I.3) and (I.4) and the empirical estimates of the parameters of the consumption function (I.1) which were reported in [4] and [5] on the basis of U. S. data, mostly for the period 1929–59. While different methods of estimation lead to somewhat different results, most procedures yield a value of α in the immediate neighborhood of .65 and of α_3 between .077 and .08 (*cf.* [5, Table A]). Some alternative procedures, however, lead to a somewhat higher value of α, around .72 and to a lower value for α_3, just below .06. Assum-

[12] These implications of (I.3) and (I.4), however, need to be qualified insofar as the parameters σ and δ may themselves vary with ρ, or more precisely with p and y.

ing for r a value of .04, which is roughly the value of the ratio of net-of-tax property income to wealth, implied by the U.S. data, the first set of estimates imply a value of σ of .35 and a value of δ of approximately .05. Columns (4a) and (4b) of Table 1 show the value of the saving and the wealth ratio obtained by substituting these estimates in equations (I.3) and (I.4). The corresponding values obtained from the alternative estimates, which imply a value of σ of .28 and value of δ just below .03, are shown in columns (5a) and (5b). The broad similarity in the behavior of the figures of columns 2 to 5 is readily apparent. These results, among other things, confirm our earlier conjecture that although the value of the coefficients σ and δ depend in principle on ρ and its components, p and y, in practice these coefficients, or at least their ratio, may be fairly insensitive to variations in p and y, at least within the empirically relevant range.[13]

d) Cyclical Implications

Proceeding next to consider the implications of (I.9) and (I.10) when income fluctuates cyclically around its trend, let us first dis-

[13] Some estimates of the parameters σ and δ for the United States as well as for two other countries, the United Kingdom and Australia, and their implications for the relation between the saving ratio and the rate of growth have been recently presented by Lydall [14]. Because of significant differences in the concepts used as well as in the method used to estimate income and wealth (e.g., his interpolation between bench mark years by cumulating saving in current prices, neglects capital gains which at least for the U.S. leads to appreciable year to year errors in the estimates of wealth in *current* prices) we must conclude that his estimates are not comparable with ours, or directly relevant for our present purposes. Even his alternative estimates derived in footnote 3, p. 241, which do not rely on a direct estimate of wealth are not comparable with ours because of his use of total (rather than labor) income and the neglect of capital gains. Both differences are likely to be quite important for year to year movements, though they should tend to wash out in the longer run. Note in particular that the neglect of capital gains should tend to bias up his estimate of b (roughly the equivalent of our δ) which might account for his higher estimate of this parameter (though it obviously does not help to account for the U. K. results). It is relevant however that he finds the wealth variable to be highly significant in every instance (for this only requires that his measure of wealth be well correlated with the "true measure"). Also his table V (p. 244), confirms once more the relative insensitivity of the saving ratio even with respect to the values of σ and ρ, for moderate values of the rate of growth.

regard the error term u′. Equation (I.9) is then seen to imply that the wealth-income ratio will tend to fluctuate *countercyclically* around its long run "equilibrium" value a, the relative deviations from a being equal to q. Similarly, from (I.10), we see that the saving ratio will tend to fluctuate *cyclically* around s, with a relative amplitude somewhat greater than that of q, since as a rule ρ is likely to be smaller than δ. The common sense of these results is not far to seek. The purpose and effect of accumulated wealth are to stabilize consumption, insulating it from short run fluctuations of income which are therefore reflected in corresponding pro-cyclical fluctuations in saving. On the other hand, wealth can change only very slowly in time since (annual) saving can only amount to a small fraction of total existing wealth A; along the trend, when S is sY, this fraction is precisely ρ; and even allowing for the cyclical swings in S, the rate of change of A cannot deviate appreciably from ρ. Hence in the course of cyclical fluctuations, income will tend to fall and rise faster than A, causing A/Y to move *countercyclically*.

Taking into account the error terms $-u_t$ of equation (I.9) and ν_t of (I.10) does not require changing these conclusions qualitatively—as long as the fluctuations of income around trend are of moderate magnitude and duration and reasonably stable in character—except that the relations (I.9) and (I.10) must now be recognized as stochastic in nature. In particular, by relying on standard statistical formulae, on certain approximations and on the empirical estimate of δ, one can establish that both in (I.9) and in (I.10) the variance of the error term should be much smaller than that of the explanatory variable q_t, or, equivalently, that the cyclical index q should account for a large fraction of the variance of A/Y and S/Y.[14]

[14] In the first place, by the very definition of a stable trend, the fluctuations around it must tend to cancel out. Letting E denote "mathematical expectation," this can be formalized as

$$E(q'_t) \simeq 0 \; E(q_t) \simeq 0$$

implying also

$$E(u'_t),\; E(u_t) \simeq 0.$$

While the above considerations suggest that (I.9) should already provide a very good approximation to the short run behavior of the wealth-income ratio, there is reason to believe that a yet better approximation can be secured by replacing the trend of income Y^*_t by a "rachet" trend of the kind embodied in the so-called Duesenberry-Modigliani consumption function, [9] [16] namely, $(1+\rho)\mathring{Y}_t$ where $\mathring{Y}_t$ denotes the highest value reached by Y in any year preceding t. With this substitution the cyclical indices q and q′ are replaced by

$$\text{(I.6')} \qquad Q_t = \frac{Y_t - (1+\rho)\mathring{Y}_t}{Y_t} \qquad\qquad Q'_t = \frac{Y_t - (1+\rho)\mathring{Y}_t}{(1+\rho)\mathring{Y}_t}$$

Equations (I.7) and (I.9) now become

$$\text{(I.7')} \qquad A_t = a(1+\rho)\mathring{Y}_t(1+\epsilon'_t)$$

$$\text{(I.9')} \qquad \frac{A_t}{Y_t} = a\,\frac{(1+\rho)\mathring{Y}_t}{Y_t}(1+\epsilon'_t) = a - aQ_t + a\epsilon_t$$

Similarly, the condition that the amplitude of the cyclical fluctuations is stable in time can be formalized as

$$E[q'^2_t] \cong \text{var}(q') \text{ for all t}$$

where var is short for variance. If we also assume for the moment that the q'_t's are not serially correlated, from (I.8) we can deduce

$$\text{var}(u'_t) = \text{var}(q')\left(\frac{\delta+\rho}{1+\rho}\right)^2 \sum_{\tau=0}^{\infty}\left(\frac{1-\delta}{1+\rho}\right)^{2t} = \frac{\delta+\rho}{2+\rho-\delta}\,\text{var}(q').$$

As we have seen, empirical estimates for the United States (as well as *a priori* estimates, cf. [4, Table 1]), suggest that δ is below .1. With ρ in the order of .03, we can conclude that $\text{var}(u'_t)$ should be at most around 5 per cent of var(q′). Since, in addition, at least for the United States, the variance of the cyclical income index q′, will be shown in Part II to be quite small (on the order of .01)—cf., footnote 22, we can also conclude that var(q) and var(u) will be of the same order as var(q′) and var(u′).

Indeed, from the definition of q′ and q it follows that $q = q'/(1+q')$. If var(q′) is quite small compared with unity, we may infer that var(q) is of the same order of magnitude as var(q′). Similarly, from (I.9), $\text{var}(u) = \text{var}(\frac{Y^*}{Y}u') = \text{var}[(1+q)u'] = \text{var}(u')\,[1+\text{var}(q)]$, if u'_t and q_t are uncorrelated, so that var(u) will be of the same order as var(u′).

The specification that u'_t and q_t are uncorrelated may not hold exactly since u'_t includes q'_t, which is obviously highly correlated with q_t. However, since u'_t is an exponentially weighted moving average of all past values of q′ and with weights declining fairly slowly, the above specifications might be expected to hold, at least approximately.

where

$$\epsilon_t = \frac{(1+\rho)\overset{\circ}{Y}_t}{Y_t}\,\epsilon'_t$$ [15]

and we suggest that var(ϵ_t) will tend to be somewhat smaller than var (u_t), i.e., that $a - aQ_t$ will yield a somewhat better approximation to A_t/Y_t than is provided by $a - aq_t$. To support this proposition, we first note that if income follows its rising trend exactly, then $(1+\rho)\overset{\circ}{Y}_t = (1+\rho)Y_{t-1} = Y_t = Y^*_t$ and $Q_t = 0$. In this case, clearly, (I.9) and (I.9′) are equivalent and they both hold exactly, i.e., the error terms u and ϵ are zero. Suppose next that income rises year after year, though at a rate fluctuating around ρ. Then, again $(1+\rho)\overset{\circ}{Y}_t = (1+\rho)Y_{t-1}$ cannot depart much from Y^*_t, and since the rate of saving cannot depart widely from s, A_t will also tend to grow at approximately the same rate ρ. We may therefore expect to find $A_t \simeq aY^*_t \simeq a(1+\rho)\overset{\circ}{Y}_t$, and hence approximations (I.9) and (I.9′) will be roughly as good. Consider, however, what happens if, following some year t′, income should undergo a significant cyclical contraction falling below Y_t, and remain there for some time, say n periods. Then since $\overset{\circ}{Y}_{t'+\tau} = Y_{t'}$, $\tau = 1 \ldots n$, approximation (I.9′) implies that wealth will remain constant at the level $a(1+\rho)Y_{t'}$ whereas (I.9) implies that it will continue to grow at the rate ρ. Now we know from the saving equations that in fact, when income is depressed the saving ratio will tend to be below the equilibrium value and in fact may even be negative.

[15] By a repetition of the reasoning leading from (I.5a) to (I.7) and (I.8) but replacing q'_t with Q'_t one finds that ϵ'_t can be expressed as

$$\text{(I.8')} \qquad \epsilon'_t = \frac{\delta+\rho}{1+\rho}\sum_{\tau=0}^{\infty}\left(\frac{1-\delta}{1+\rho}\right)^{\tau}\left[\frac{\overset{\circ}{Y}_{t-\tau}(1+\rho)^{\tau} - \overset{\circ}{Y}_t}{\overset{\circ}{Y}_t}(1+Q'_{t-\tau}) + Q'_{t-\tau}\right] \simeq$$

$$\frac{\delta+\rho}{1+\rho}\sum_{\tau=0}^{\infty}\left(\frac{1-\delta}{1+\rho}\right)^{\tau} Q'_{t-\tau}$$

since with a stable growth trend and moderate fluctuations, we can expect

$$\overset{\circ}{Y}_t/\overset{\circ}{Y}_{t-\tau} \cong (1+\rho)^{\tau}.$$

Thus ϵ'_t bears much the same relation to Q'_t as u'_t bears to q'_t (cf. equation (I.8)).

Thus assets may be expected to rise moderately at best, and therefore more in accordance with (I.9′) than with (I.9). Similarly, once income recovers passing the previous peak it is likely for a while to grow faster than ρ as it catches up with its trend. In this period the wealth-income ratio will tend to be above average, causing A to rise faster than Y^*_t (though possibly not quite as fast as $\mathring{Y}_t$). On the whole, then, at least in the presence of cyclical movements of some magnitude and duration, approximation (I.9′) may be expected to prove somewhat superior to (I.9) and it is therefore the hypothesis that we propose to test from United States data in Part II.

The substitution of Y^*_t with $(1+\rho)\mathring{Y}_t$ leading to approximation (I.7′) also implies that the short run behavior of saving and the saving ratio can be approximated closely by a Duesenberry-Modigliani (D-M) type of consumption function in which, again, aggregate wealth does not appear explicitly. In fact, from (I.7′) and (I.2) we can obtain

$$S_t = \sigma Y_t - \delta a \mathring{Y}_t + \eta'_t,$$ [16]

from which, using the definitions of s and a given by (I.3) and (I.4) and the definition of Q in (I.6′), we also derive

$$\frac{S_t}{Y_t} = \frac{\sigma\rho}{\delta+\rho} + \frac{\delta\sigma}{\delta+\rho} Q_t + \eta_t \tag{I.10′}$$

These equations are precisely of the D-M form except that the parameters are related explicitly to those of the "true" long run saving function (I.2) and to the rate of growth. It should be noted, however, that the definitions of S and Y in (I.10′) differ somewhat from that commonly used in connection with the D-M function, notably by the inclusion in S of corporate saving, as well as net investment in consumers' durables.

[16] Substitution of (I.7′) into (I.2) yields $S_t = \sigma Y_t - \delta\, a(1+\rho)\, \mathring{Y}_{t-1}(1+\epsilon'_{t-1})$ which can be reduced to the form shown in the text by letting

$$\eta'_t = \delta a \left[\mathring{Y}_t - (1+\rho)\, \mathring{Y}_{t-1}(1+\epsilon'_{t-1})\right]$$

e) Some Qualifications

Before proceeding to the empirical test, we must call attention to certain limitations in the argument leading up to (I.9′) which are relevant in assessing the domain of applicability of this approximation.

(1) It should be apparent from the formal and the heuristic argument supporting (I.9) and (I.9′) that the approximation might not perform too well in the case of extreme fluctuations such as characterized the period 1929–1941. If income remains below previous peak for a lengthy period, then wealth can gradually drift away to an appreciable extent, in either direction, from the level reached at previous peak. Similarly, when income recovers, piercing the previous peak, it may grow for a while at such a fast rate that (I.7′) may tend to overstate wealth.

(2) The derivation of (I.7′), (I.9′) and (I.10′) relies on (I.2) and (I.5) which in turn were obtained under the "long run" assumption that expected labor income L^e_t is proportional to current income L_t, that property income can be measured by rA_{t-1} and that changes in the (real) value of assets other than from saving, i.e., capital gains or losses, can be disregarded. These assumptions lose some of their justification once we allow for cyclical fluctuations in income. In [4] it was hypothesized that expected labor income would tend to fluctuate cyclically less than current income and this hypothesis was found to receive some—though not overwhelming—empirical support. If so, saving will be more responsive to cyclical fluctuations in income than implied by (I.2) and (I.10′). The fact that current property income will tend to fluctuate cyclically more than expected property income, rA_{t-1}, will also tend to affect saving in a similar fashion. Finally, since cyclical variations in property income may give rise to some corresponding variations in the value of assets, A_t/Y_t may tend to fluctuate somewhat less than in proportion to $\mathring{Y}_t/Y_t$ as implied by (I.9′). This phenomenon, in turn, would tend to reduce the

cyclical variability of the saving ratio, counteracting the two tendencies noted earlier.

On the whole, these various qualifications do not seem to call for any qualitative modification of hypotheses (I.7′) and (I.9′), with which we are primarily concerned in Part II. They do indicate, however, that our derivation may tend to overstate the closeness of the approximation [17] and the error may be especially large for exceptionally severe cyclical disturbances.

PART II—TESTS OF THE BEHAVIOR OF PRIVATE WEALTH: THE UNITED STATES, 1900–1958

II.1. Data and Basic Tests

The United States presents an opportunity—rather unique at the present time—to test the implications of the life cycle model for the behavior of private wealth, which were derived in Part I and are embodied in hypotheses (I.7′) and (I.9′). For this country, it is possible to piece together annual estimates of the market value of private wealth and of income for some six decades, namely, from 1900 to 1958—though admittedly the estimates are of limited reliability, especially for the earlier years. Furthermore, hypotheses (I.7′) and (I.9′) should hold for this period, since the available evidence indicates that income has tended to fluctuate around a fairly stable growth trend.

Before proceeding to a review of the evidence, it will be useful to set out certain notational conventions:

1. Aggregates measured in *constant prices* are denoted by letters with an asterisk;

[17] Note in this connection that the estimate of var(u′) relative to var(q′) derived in footnote 14 relies on the assumption that the q'_t's are serially independent. Since cyclical fluctuations tend to have some continuity, some positive correlation between the q_t is, in fact, likely, and therefore $\frac{\text{var}(u')}{\text{var}(q')}$ is likely to be somewhat higher than indicated there.

2. The same letter without asterisk denotes the corresponding aggregates measured in *current* prices. It should be noted that, unless the contrary is stated, these symbols may equally be interpreted as denoting aggregates measured in terms of consumables as *numéraire*—i.e., current values deflated by a price index of consumables. This is because our equations are equally valid whether variables are measured consistently in current dollars or in terms of consumables.[18]

3. Whenever it is necessary to make the distinction, a caret will be used to denote variables measured in terms of consumables.[19]

The stability of the growth trend of income can be inferred from the estimates of Private Gross National Product in constant prices—denoted hereafter by X^*—reproduced in the Appendix. According to these estimates, X^* grew over the entire period at a rate of just about 3 per cent per year, and very nearly at the same rate during each half of the period 1900–29, 3.1 per cent, and 1929–58, 3 per cent.

To be sure, the measure of income called for by our model is not private GNP but more nearly private domestic income net of direct taxes. The closest approximation to this concept that one can readily derive from available series is so-called "personal income" less dividends plus corporate income minus direct personal and corporate taxes or, equivalently, disposable income plus corporate savings. It is this measure which we shall use in this section as an empirical approximation to the variable Y of the model of Section I. The inclusion of corporate saving in income (and hence in saving) is dictated by the consideration that corporate saving, just like personal saving, will tend to result, at least in the long run, in an increase in private net worth by way

[18] See, however, footnote 19.

[19] If in (I.7′) and (I.9′), A_t (and Y_t) are measured in current prices, $\dot{Y}_t$ must be interpreted as the highest previous peak of income measured in terms of consumables, adjusted for any change in the price level of consumables intervening since the previous peak.

of its effect on the market value of corporate equity (*cf.* Modigliani and Miller [15]).

In order to estimate the long run growth trend, Y should be first expressed in terms of consumables, through deflation by an appropriate price index of consumables p^c. Unfortunately, there is no readily available continuous measure of p^c for the entire period. Using as our approximation to p^c the BLS cost of living index as far as available (1913) and the Rees index[20] for earlier years, one finds that the trend of $\hat{Y}=Y/p^c$ is fairly similar to that of X^*. In particular, the rate of growth for the entire period turns out to be 2.9 per cent, and for the first and second half of the period 2.9 and 3 per cent, respectively.

a) *The Long Run Behavior of the Wealth-Income Ratio*

The ratio of wealth to income, A/Y, implied by our estimates, is shown as a time series by the solid curve of Figure 2. The years of the First and Second World Wars, 1917–18 and 1942–45, are

[20] See *Historical Statistics of the United States,* p. 127.

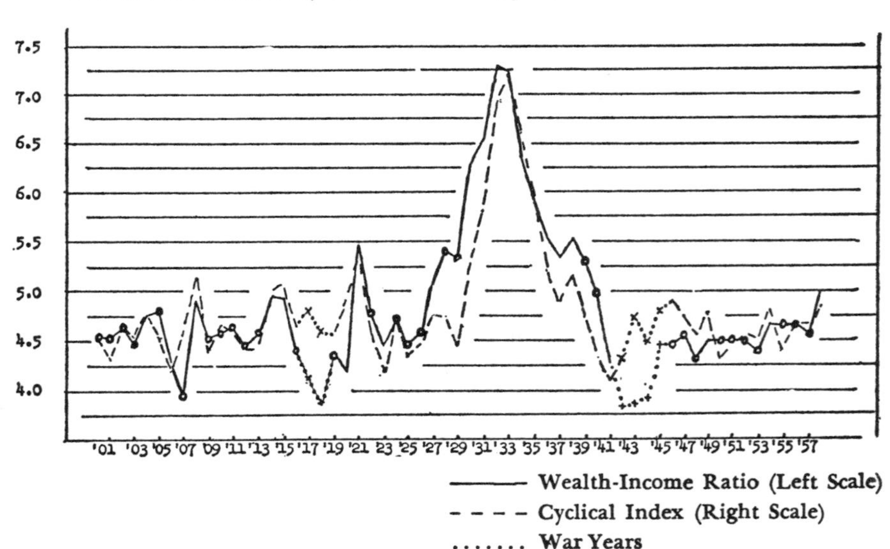

FIGURE 2

THE WEALTH-INCOME RATIO AND THE CYCLICAL INCOME INDEX, U. S., 1900–1958

denoted by crosses and omitted from all subsequent analysis. It is apparent that over the sixty years covered by the data, A/Y has tended to fluctuate around an essentially constant level, as implied by the model. It starts out at around 4.5 in 1900–01 and winds up at around 4.6 in 1956–57 (the somewhat higher value in 1958 can be accounted for by the cyclical contraction of that year). Between these terminal points there have been rather wide swings, from a low of 3.9 in 1907 to a high of 7.3 in 1932. But, as implied by (I.9′), these fluctuations appear to be largely accountable for by cyclical fluctuations in income, as can be inferred by comparing the graph of A_t/Y_t with the behavior of the dashed curve in Figure 1, which is a graph of the cyclical income index Q_t, plotted with sign inverted. For a number of reasons related to the reliability of the data and to convenience in connection with some later tests, our empirical measure of the cyclical index Q has been based on X^* rather than on Y. In other words, Q_t is defined as $(X^*_t-(1+\rho)\mathring{X}^*_t)/X^*_t$ rather than as $(\hat{Y}_t-(1+\rho)\mathring{\hat{Y}}_t)/\hat{Y}_t$. This choice makes little practical difference as the two indices parallel each other very closely. In computing Q, ρ was assigned a value of .03.

As a check on the long run stability of A/Y, we may at first confine our attention to "normal years," i.e., years in which Q_t was close to zero; according to (I.9′) A/Y should then be close to a. Such years, operationally defined by the condition that current income should be at least as high as the previous peak but not more than 10 per cent above it—which implies a value of Q between —3 and 7—are circled in Figure 1. It is apparent that A/Y is remarkably stable in these years, and this is confirmed by the following statistics:

(II.1) $\overline{(A/Y)}=4.62$ $\sigma(A/Y)=0.29$ coefficient of variation (cv)$=$

$$\frac{.29}{4.62}=.063$$

The mean value is seen to agree quite well with the *a priori* estimate of a derived in Table 1 from the parameters of the consumption function and a 3 per cent rate of growth, and the dispersion around the mean is quite moderate, as indicated by a coefficient of variation of about 6 per cent.[21]

[21] The data plotted in the figure and reproduced in Appendix B extend only to 1958 because at the time the empirical tests were carried out, estimates of net worth were not available beyond that date. Since then, some preliminary quarterly estimates of the net worth of the household sector have been prepared by Albert Ando, of the Wharton School, University of Pennsylanvia, which extend to the end of 1963. These estimates, which are at present unpublished, kindly have been made available to me. The method by which they are obtained is similar to that used in deriving the annual series, *cf.* Appendix B. Conceptually, the figure for a given quarter is an estimate of the net worth at the beginning of the quarter at average market prices of that quarter. Unfortunately, one cannot readily derive from this series an estimate conceptually comparable to the one we have used in the text which, for a given year, represents an estimate of net worth at the end of that year at average prices of the year. Nonetheless, in order to provide some rough idea of the behavior of the wealth-income ratio since 1958, we give below figures for the years 1959 to 1963, computed as follows:
Wealth, A_t: Ando's estimate for last quarter of the year t; Private income, Y_t: Disposable Personal Income plus Corporate Saving from *Survey of Current Business*, July 1964. It will be noted that the above wealth estimate may have a downward bias in that Ando's last quarter figure relates to the stock at the end of the third quarter rather than at the end of the year; on the other hand, it may be upward biased in that wealth is valued at average prices of the *last* quarter instead of average prices of the year and, on the whole, prices of assets have been rising significantly over the relevant period. In order to provide some idea of the amount of distortion that may arise from these conceptual discrepancies, the wealth-income ratio computed from Ando's quarterly series is shown also for the "overlapping" years 1957 and 1958.

Year	A_t/Y_t	
(1)	(2) Based on Ando's Quarterly Estimates	(3) Estimates Used in Statistical Tests
1957	4.53	4.58
1958	4.87	4.97
1959	4.78	
1960	4.76	
1961	4.92	
1962	4.62	
1963	4.75	

These very rough and preliminary estimates suggest that the stability of the wealth-income ratio has continued also after 1958. In fact, the ratio has tended to remain within five per cent of the mean value. The only exception is 1961, when it was 6 per cent above. But then this high value might be in part accounted for by cyclical developments; in fact, according to the National Bureau chronology, the contraction that began in the second quarter of 1960 reached its trough in early 1961.

Close examination of the circled points also reveals that a good deal of the dispersion is attributable to five extreme observations: a very low value in 1907 and very high ones in 1928–29 and 1939–40. The large deviations for the last mentioned two years can be readily accounted for by the severity of the depression, as noted in section I.2 e. The high values of 1928 and 1929 seem to be largely accounted for by the stock market boom, leading to a sudden temporary increase in assets via capital gains. Such developments must be regarded as exogenous to our model. There is, on the other hand, no ready explanation for the low value of 1907, unparalleled in any other peacetime year, unless it reflects errors of measurement. In the remaining "normal" years the range of variation of A/Y is only about 10 per cent, and some of this variation can be accounted for by movements in Q_t, which, by our definition of normal years, is allowed a play of 10 per cent.

b) The Cyclical Behavior of the Wealth-Income Ratio

There remains to test how well the variations of A/Y in other years can be accounted for by Q as implied by (I.9′). This test utilizes all the observations (except war years) and has been carried out both in arithmetic and logarithmic form. In the arithmetic test we fit to the data by least squares an equation of the form

(II.2) $$A_t/Y_t = B_o + B_1 Q_t$$

According to (I.9′) we should find $B_o \simeq -B_1 \simeq a \simeq 4.6$. The empirical results are as follows:

(II.2a) $$A_t/Y_t = \underset{(0.5)}{4.7} - \underset{(0.4)}{4.9}\, Q_t \quad r = .80; \; S_e = .34; \; \frac{S_e}{\overline{(A/Y)}} = .069$$

where r is the correlation coefficient and S_e the standard deviation of the residual error.[22]

[22] The correlation is, in fact, not radically different from what might be inferred from the argument developed in footnote 14 suggesting that the qualifications mentioned in footnote 17 are quantitatively of moderate significance. We may also note in this connection that the standard deviation of the cyclical index Q for the entire period is .125, implying a variance of .016. These figures, however, are heav-

These results are seen to be quite favorable to the hypothesis. First, the correlation is quite high, considering that the dependent variable is a trendless ratio. Second, the coefficients are also quite close to *a priori* expectations. Note also that the relative dispersion of the error term is about the same as for normal years, some 7 per cent of the mean value.

These favorable results are confirmed by the logarithmic test. Using lower case letters to denote the logarithm of the variable represented by the corresponding capital letters, from (I.7′) we infer

$$(II.3)\quad (a_t - y_t) = \ln\,[a(1+\rho)] - (y_t - \overset{o}{y}_t) + \epsilon^*_t = \ln\, a(1+\rho) - q^*_t + \epsilon^*_t$$

where $q^*_t = (y_t - \overset{o}{y}_t)$ will be recognized as a cyclical index analogous to Q. Hence if we calculate the regression coefficients of the equation

$$(a_t - y_t) = b_o + b_1\, q^*_t$$

we should find $b_o \simeq \ln\, a(1+\rho) \simeq 1.56$, $b_1 \simeq -1$. In carrying out this test, q^*_t was again approximated by $(x^*_t - \overset{o}{x}{}^*_t)$. The results

$$(II.3a)\quad (a_t - y_t) = \underset{(.01)}{1.57} - \underset{(.08)}{1.03}\, q^*_t \quad r = .86 \quad S_e = .068$$

conform closely to expectation. In particular, the estimated elasticity of the wealth-income ratio with respect to the cyclical index is very close to unity [23] and the dispersion of the error term is again less than 7 per cent.

In summary, the evidence available for the first six decades of this century accords well with the implications of the life cycle model. With income fluctuating around a stable growth trend of some 3 per cent, the wealth-income ratio has fluctuated around a stable level of about 4.7, consistent with (I.3) and the fluctua-

ily affected by the great depression; dropping the worst years of the depression, say 1931 to 1935, would reduce the variance below .01.

[23] Though the considerations developed in section I.2 e) suggested that the elasticity of A/Y with respect to $\overset{\bullet}{Y}/Y$ might tend to fall somewhat short of unity, our data provide no evidence for such a tendency.

tions have been largely countercyclical and roughly proportional to those of the cyclical index Q, as implied by (I.7′) and (I.9′).

II.2. The Behavior of the Wealth-Income Ratio and the Constancy of the Capital-Output Ratio: Cause or Effect?

a) The Issue

Though the evidence we have reviewed is in close agreement with our model, its relevance may be questioned because of a serious "identification" problem. It may be argued that the wealth-income ratio we have been dealing with is in reality but a different name for the capital-output ratio and the stability of this ratio has long been recognized and accounted for on quite different grounds, namely, as reflecting the prevalence of a fixed technological relation between the flow of output and the stock of capital necessary to produce that output. In its simplest form, this technological hypothesis can be stated as

$$K^*_t = gO^*_t \qquad \text{(II.4)}$$

where K^* is the real stock of capital, O^* some measure of aggregate real output, and g is the so-called "capital coefficient."

It is readily apparent that if we were dealing with a simple kind of society in which the only form of private wealth were reproducible tangible capital and in which output coincided with net of tax income, then the long run implications of the life cycle model would be essentially indistinguishable from those of the technological hypothesis. That is, if one observed a constant capital-output ratio it would be impossible to tell whether this stability reflected the accumulation and wealth holding pattern resulting from the life cycle mechanism leading in turn to the choice of technologies having the appropriate capital intensity; or whether, instead, it reflected rigid technological requirements leading, through some other mechanism, to the accumulation and holding of the appropriate amount of wealth.

b) Conceptual Differences Between the Ratios

Fortunately, there are, in fact, a number of significant differences between the variables A and Y appearing in (I.9′) and the variables K^* and O^* of (II.4). Although the definition of K^* and O^* are seldom made very precise, we believe that a reasonable operational approximation to K^*_t is the reproduction cost, at prices of some base year, of the net stock of private plant (including residential housing), equipment and inventories existing in the year t. Denoting further by K_t the current reproduction cost of the same stock and by p^k_t the index of reproduction cost in the year t relative to the chosen base year, we have the definitional relation

(II.5) $$K_t \equiv p^k_t K^*_t$$

The relation between K and private net worth at market value, A, can be expressed as

(II.6) $A \equiv K +$ value of private land $+$ consumers' durables $+$ privately held government debt $+$ net claims on foreigners $+$ valuation discrepancy

The last item reflects mainly the discrepancy, if any, between the current market value of firms as going concerns—notably the current market value of the stock of corporate enterprises—and the value of their assets (net of debts) at current reproduction cost. We shall refer to the difference between A and K as "other wealth" denoted by Ao and summarize (II.6) as

(II.6′) $$A \equiv K + Ao.$$

Ao may be expected to be positive and in fact of non-negligible magnitude. For instance, according to the Goldsmith estimates on which we rely, for the period 1900–58 it was on the average more than two-thirds as large as K, accounting for some 40 per cent of net worth, with a minimum of 35 per cent in 1919 and a (peacetime) maximum of 47 per cent in 1946.

For output, O^*, a reasonable definition consistent with that of

K would seem to be private gross national product at constant prices, X^*. The relation between X^* and Y can be expressed by the two definitional relations:

$$(II.7) \qquad X_t \equiv p^x_t X^*_t$$

where p^x is the implicit price deflator, and

$$(II.8) \quad Y \equiv X + \text{Compensation of government employees} + \text{interest on the national debt} - \text{net taxes} - \text{capital consumption allowances} \equiv X + Yo$$

The quantity Yo, summarizing the discrepancy between Y and X, has been consistently negative, though of moderate size, between 10 and 20 per cent of Y.

Combining the definitions (II.5) to (II.8), the relation between the wealth-income ratio A/Y, and the capital-output ratio K^*/X^* can be expressed as

$$(II.9) \quad A/Y = \frac{K+Ao}{X+Yo} = \frac{K^*p^k(1+\frac{Ao}{K})}{X^*p^x(1+\frac{Yo}{X})} = \frac{K^*}{X^*} \cdot W; \; W \equiv \frac{1+Ao/K}{1+Yo/X}\frac{p^k}{p^x}$$

or, in logarithmic form, as

$$(II.9') \qquad a - y \equiv (k^* - x^*) + w$$

The quantity W measuring the discrepancy between A/Y and K^*/X^* will be referred to as the "wedge." Over the period covered by our data, W has been quite substantial; its average value is 2.15, reflecting the fact that the A/Y is a good deal larger than K^*/X^*, the mean values of the two ratios being, respectively, 4.9 and 2.3.

The existence of such a wide gap is ample cause for doubting that the long run stability of A/Y could be a mere reflection of the purported, technologically determined, long run stability of the capital-output ratio. These doubts are considerably reinforced by the test reported below, which leads to the conclusion that, over the period covered, K^*/X^* has, in fact, been decidedly *less* stable than A/Y.

c) The Relative Stability of the Two Ratios

In carrying out such a test, we must again face the problem that the hypothesized long run stability of K^*/X^* is not inconsistent with substantial cyclical variability. That is, (II.4) must be understood as a long run relation which need not hold closely in the short run. In particular, in the course of a cyclical contraction of income, the stock of capital might be expected to contract proportionally much less, if at all, if only for the reason that K^* can only fall through the time consuming process of gradual wear and tear. Similarly, in a cyclical upswing K^*/X^* might, for a while, fall below g, reflecting a temporary strain on capacity. It appears, therefore, that even under the technological hypothesis, the short run relation between K^* and X^* might be best approximated by a modification of (II.4) analogous to (I.7′), or

$$K^*=g(1+\rho)\,\mathring{X}^*_t\,(1+V'_t)$$

where V'_t is a residual error. This equation, in turn, implies

$$K^*_t/X^*_t=g-gQ_t+V_t \tag{II.10}$$

or also

$$k^*_t-x^*_t=\ln[g(1+\rho)]-(x^*_t-\mathring{x}^*_t)+v_t=\ln[g(1+\rho)]-q^*_t+v_t \tag{II.11}$$

Thus, in order to assess the relative stability of the capital-output and the wealth-income ratio, we must either confine ourselves to "normal" years when Q_t is small, or else fit (II.10) or (II.11) to the data and rely on a comparison of the residual variance with that of (II.2a) or (II.3a).

Confining first attention to the "normal" years, one finds

$$(\overline{K^*/X^*})=2.18,\ \sigma=.36,\ \frac{\sigma}{(\overline{K^*/X^*})}=.165$$

Comparison with (II.1) reveals that the absolute variability of the capital coefficient is 20 per cent larger than that of A/Y. When proper allowance is made for the much lower mean values of

K^*/X^*, the coefficient of variation is nearly 2½ times larger. These results are confirmed by the tests using all years and the cyclical income index:

$$\text{(II.10a)} \quad K^*_t/X^*_t = \underset{(0.5)}{2.2} - \underset{(0.4)}{2.2}Q_t \quad r=.65,\ S_e=.35,\ \frac{S_e}{\overline{(K^*/X^*)}}=.149$$

$$\text{(II.11a)} \quad (k^*_t - x^*_t) = \underset{(.02)}{.82} - \underset{(.021)}{1.01}\, q^*_t \quad r=.57 \quad S_e=.165$$

Comparison with the results of (II.2a) and (II.3a) shows that the relative dispersion of the residual is again more than twice as large.

These results seem to have a fairly clear implication: if the capital-output ratio has been distinctly less stable than the wealth-income ratio, the stability of the latter cannot be accounted for as a mere reflection of the stability of the former. On the contrary, this evidence suggests that the causation might well be running the other way! That is, the long noted stability of the capital-output ratio might well be the result of the stability of the wealth-income ratio generated by the life cycle mechanism in the presence of a reasonably stable long run growth trend. This hypothesis does, in fact, receive strong support from one further and rather telling test.

d) A Test of the Direction of Causation

Before we set out our test formally, it is useful to lay bare its common sense. Suppose that over some interval of time the wedge W should increase, say because of an increase in the national debt, or in the value of land, or in the price ratio p^k/p^x. Then, as is clear from (II.9) or (II.9′), A/Y and K^*/X^*, or their logarithms (a—y) and (k^*—x^*) cannot both remain constant; at least one of these quantities must change to make room for the larger W. Now, according to the technological (or T) hypothesis, the change in w should not affect (k^*—x^*), which is controlled by technological requirements. Hence the "accommodating" must occur in (a—y): the amount of wealth that the private sector is willing to hold must *rise* relative to income. Thus, *under the T hypothesis, w should tend to be uncorrelated with (k*—x*) and positively correlated with (a—y).* On the other hand, according to the life cycle (or L) hypothesis (a—y), the amount of wealth the private sector wishes to hold, relative to income, is determined by life cycle requirements. Hence the accommodating must occur in (k*—x*); i.e., an increase in the wedge for whatever reason must tend to result in a *reduction* in the capital coefficient. This means that *under the L hypothesis, w should be uncorrelated with (a—y) and negatively correlated with (k*—x*).* The test about to be presented consists essentially in correlating w with (a—y) and (k*—x*), respectively, and comparing the outcome with the above predictions of each model.

The heuristic reasoning above can be formalized as follows. According to the T model, the behavior of (k*—x*) can be accounted for by (II.4), or, allowing for cyclical effects, by (II.11). Furthermore, the error term v_t should bear no systematic relation to w_t which reflects forces having little relation to the technological requirements of production. This implication can be formalized by adding to (II.11) the specification

$$\text{(II.11}') \qquad \text{cov}(v_t w_t)=0$$

(where cov is short for covariance)

Substituting (II.11) into identity (II.9′) we derive

$$\text{(II.13)} \qquad (a_t-y_t)=\ln[g(1+\rho)]-q^*{}_t+w_t+v_t$$

Suppose we fit this equation to the data, obtaining the regression equation

$$\text{(II.14)} \qquad (a_t-y_t)=c_o+c_1 q^*{}_t+c_2 w_t$$

In view of specification (II.11′) the regression coefficients of (II.14) should be unbiased estimates of the coefficients of (II.13) or $E(c_1)=-1$ $E(c_2)=1$, $E(c_o=\ln g(1+\rho)\simeq .8$ (from equation (II.11a)). Consider, on the other hand, the implications of the L hypothesis for these same coefficients. According to L, (a—y) is explained by

(II.3). Furthermore, the error term ϵ^*_t is supposed to reflect the past history of the cyclical income index and therefore should bear no systematic relation to w_t. Hence we can add to (II.3) the specifiction

(II.3′) $$\text{cov}(\epsilon^*_t, w_t) = 0$$

But (II.3) and (II.3′) imply that w_t should contribute nothing to the explanation of $(a - y)$ or that the coefficient c_2 of w_t in (II.14) should not differ significantly from zero. As for the remaining coefficients, from (II.3) we can infer $E(c_1) = -1$, $E(c_o) = \ln a(1+\rho) \approx 1.5$. Thus, as suggested by the heuristic argument, the T and L hypotheses have quite different implications for the effect of w_t on $(a_t - y_t)$: for L the effect should be none, while for T the effect should be positive and the elasticity c_2 should be around unity.

A parallel test can be applied by estimating the coefficients of the regression equation

(II.15) $$(k^*_t - x^*_t) = d_o + d_1 q^*_t + d_2 w_t$$

From the T model hypothesis (II.11) and the specification (II.11′) it follows that w_t should be uncorrelated with $(k^*_t - x^*_t)$ or that $E(d_2) = 0$. For the L model instead, from (II.3) the specification (II.3′) and the identity (II.9′) one can deduce that this correlation should be negative and that $E(d_2) = -1$. Again the critical difference between the two models lies in the implications about the coefficient of w_t, d_2. According to T, K^*/X^* should be independent of W, whereas according to L it should be negatively related to W with an elasticity of minus one.

Table 2 summarizes the implications of the alternative hypotheses and compares them with the empirical results obtained. Each of the test equations (II.14) and (II.15) has been estimated for all years and also for "normal years" only, in which case the cyclical index q^* can be dropped.

Before turning to the results, it should be observed that the test might show that neither of the hypotheses is an adequate approximation by itself. That is, it could turn out that an increase

TABLE 2

IMPLICATIONS AND TESTS OF THE LIFE CYCLE HYPOTHESIS (L) VERSUS THE TECHNOLOGICAL HYPOTHESIS (T)

Equation Number (1)	Dependent Variable (2)	Years Included (3)	Coefficient (elasticity) of: Wedge (W) Implied by T	Wedge (W) Implied by L	Wedge (W) L.S. Estimate	Cyclical Index T L	Cyclical Index L.S. Estimate	Constant Term Implied by T	Constant Term Implied by L	Constant Term L.S. Estimate	$\overline{R}$	S_e
(II.14a)	$(a_t - y_t)$	Normal	1.0	0.0	.05 (.07)	...	....	.80	1.5	1.49 (0.05)	.05	.063
(II.14b)	$(a_t - y_t)$	All	1.0	0.0	.08 (.06)	−1.0	−1.03 (0.08)	.80	1.5	1.51 (0.04)	.87	.068
(II.15a)	$(k^*_t - x^*_t)$	Normal	0.0	−1.0	−.95 (.07)	...	....	.80	1.5	1.49 (0.05)	.94	.063
(II.15b)	$(k^* - x^*_t)$	All	0.0	−1.0	−.92 (.06)	−1.0	−1.03 (.08)	.80	1.5	1.51 (0.04)	.94	.067

in the wedge instead of leading just to a contraction in K^*/X^* as implied by L, or just to an increase in A/Y, as implied by T, might be accompanied by both effects. In this case neither the L specification (II.3′) nor the T specification (II.11′) is valid, and both c_2 and d_2 would turn out somewhere between the limits of zero and unity corresponding to each model. This same outcome might result even if one of the two models was, in fact, valid purely as a consequence of errors of measurement in the components of the wedge. Fortunately, it is not necessary to pursue these troublesome possibilities, for the results shown in Table 2 are clearcut. Every one of the tests confirms quite clearly the implications of the L model and rejects squarely the implications of the T model. Particularly striking are the results of tests (II.15a) and (II.15b); not only is the coefficient of the wedge very close to unity, but in addition the very high correlation coefficients indicate that the variations of the capital-output ratio over the last sixty years can be largely accounted for along the lines implied by the L model, namely, as a response to variations in the wedge in the face of a stable wealth-income ratio.

In summary, then, all of the tests of this section indicate that the long run stability of the wealth-income ratio cannot be accounted for by a purported technologically determined, long run constancy of the capital-output ratio. It can, instead, be accounted for by the life cycle hypothesis and is, therefore, valid evidence in support of that model. The tests further suggest that the long noted rough stability of the capital-output ratio in the United States may have stemmed not from rigid technological requirements but, at least in part, from the stability of the wealth-income ratio, predicted by the life cycle model in the presence of a stable long run growth trend, and actually verified for the United States.

It should be emphasized, however, that this is at best a partial explanation. For the limited stability of K^*/X^* reflects as well the fact that the share of wealth absorbed by the wedge, in the form of competing types of assets and through relative price movements has also fluctuated within moderate limits. The life cycle model does not throw any direct light on the behavior of the wedge. While some of its components are largely exogenous, such as the national debt, others are not. To this extent the wedge and the stock of capital are best regarded as simultaneously determined under the over-all constraint imposed by the life cycle determined aggregate stock of private wealth. This leaves open the possibility that the observed relative stability of the wedge may reflect in part limitations imposed by technology on the feasible variations of the capital-output ratio.[24]

II.3. *Some Implications for the Burden of the National Debt, and Tests*

In a recent contribution [18] it was suggested that the economic effects of deficit financing can be better understood by tying together the conventional short term analysis in terms of flows with a long term analysis in terms of stock. Pursuing this approach it was argued that the national debt tends to generate a (gross) burden by causing a reduction in the stock of private tangible capital, which in turn reduces the flow of output, if capital is productive. For present purposes, the underlying argument can be boiled down to the consideration that private tangible wealth K^p is the

[24] It should also be acknowledged that technology, and more generally the demand conditions for physical capital, may also contribute to determination of the capital-output ratio by contributing to the determination of the rate of return to capital which in turn, at least in principle, could affect the supply side through the wealth-income ratio. Unfortunately, the likely quanitative impact of the rate of return on capital on the wealth-income ratio is hard to gauge, not only as to magnitude, but even as to sign. The basic model cannot by itself throw much light on this question; as in the case of the rate of saving, we can only say that a rise of the rate of interest will tend to increase the wealth-income ratio through its substitution effect, but to decrease it through its income effect. It is tempting to argue that these two effects will largely tend to offset each other, making the wealth-income ratio roughly invariant with respect to the level of the interest rate—at least within the empirically prevailing range—and this view does not seem to be grossly inconsistent with the empirical evidence. However, at present this issue must be regarded as far from settled.

difference between aggregate net worth A and privately held national debt G, or

$$K^p \equiv A - G \qquad \text{(II.16)}$$

(K^p also includes net claims on foreigners which, however, for the United States are of negligible entity.) By differentiating the above equation, we find that the effect of G on K^p is

$$\frac{dK^p}{dG} = \frac{dA}{dG} - 1$$

Since there is no convincing *a priori* reason to suppose that the amount of wealth the private sector is prepared to hold should, in the long run, depend on the supply of national debt, it was suggested that, as a rule and on the average, dA/dG can be supposed equal to zero. This in turn implies that $dK^p/dG = -1$, or that the national debt will tend to displace private tangible capital on a dollar per dollar basis.

a) Tests of the Effect of the National Debt on Private Tangible Wealth

The conceptual framework and empirical data of the last two sections provide an opportunity to carry out some empirical tests of these conclusions. Clearly, under the life cycle hypothesis, the proposition $dA/dG = 0$ and the implication $dK^p/dG = -1$ should hold, since according to the life cycle model the forces controlling aggregate wealth are quite unrelated to the size of the national debt. This hypothesis is amenable to a simple test if, as in the case of the United States, income has been fluctuating around a stable growth trend, for then the forces controlling A can be approximated by (I.7′). Furthermore, the error term of this equation should be uncorrelated with G. Hence, if we estimate the parameters of the equation

$$A_t = b_1 (1 + \rho)\mathring{Y}_t + b_2 G_t \qquad \text{(II.17)}$$

we should find $b_1 \simeq a$, $b_2 \simeq 0$.

Substituting the right hand side of (II.17) for A in (II.16), it then follows that

$$\text{(II.18)} \qquad K^{p}_{t}=b_1(1+\rho)\mathring{Y}_t-(1-b_2)\,G_t$$

If $b_2 \simeq 0$, as suggested by the life cycle model, then the coefficient of G_t should be close to minus one, i.e., an increase in G should tend to be accompanied by a roughly equal fall in private tangible wealth, as indicated earlier. Because the dispersion of the error term in (II.17) and (II.18) may be supposed proportional to $(1+\rho)\mathring{Y}_t \simeq Y_t$, and Y_t exhibits wide variations over the period of observation, we can increase the efficiency of the test if we divide both sides of (II.18) by Y_t. We then obtain

$$\text{(II.17')} \qquad \frac{K^{p}_{t}}{Y_t}=b_1(1+\rho)\mathring{Y}_t/Y_t-(1-b_2)\,G_t/Y_t=$$

$$b_1-b_1\,\frac{Y_t-(1+\rho)\mathring{Y}_t}{Y_t}-(1-b_2)\,\frac{G_t}{Y_t}$$

and the first variable on the right hand side can be approximated as usual by the cyclical index Q. Thus, if we estimate the coefficient of the regression equation

$$\frac{K^{p}_{t}}{Y_t}=c_o+c_1\,Q_t+c_3\,G_t,$$

the life cycle model would lead us to expect

$$c_o \simeq -c_1 \simeq a,\; c_3=-(1-b_2)=-1.$$

The empirical result is

$$\text{(II.18a)} \qquad \frac{K^{p}_{t}}{Y_t}=\underset{(0.4)}{4.7}-\underset{(0.4)}{4.9}Q_t-\underset{(0.22)}{1.08}\,(G_t/Y_t).\quad R=.91,\ S_e=.34$$

which is remarkably close to the predictions of the L model; in particular, the critical coefficient c_3 is very close to minus one numerically and relative to its standard error. Thus the evidence for the United States over the last sixty years appears to support the inference that the national debt has tended to displace private tangible wealth roughly on a dollar per dollar basis.

b) The Effect of the National Debt on the Real Stock of Private Capital

This significant conclusion, however, is only partially relevant for assessing the economic burden of the debt. For that purpose, what would seem relevant is not the effect of G on the *market value* of the stock of *private* tangibles, K^p, but rather its effect on K^*, the *physical stock* of *reproducible producers'* capital and, through this avenue, on real output, X^*. An attempt at deriving from our results a reliable estimate of this "real output" effect would take us far afield, since clearly this effect depends on many forces besides those controlling the aggregate supply of wealth. We shall, however, suggest a possible line of attack which, though very crude, may at least help to clarify the nature of the relation between $\frac{dK^p}{dG}$ and $\frac{dX^*}{dG}$.

First, from the definitional equation (II.6) we note that K^p can be expressed as

$$K^p = K + (Ko)$$

when (Ko) denotes the sum of the value of land, consumers' durables, net foreign claims and the valuation discrepancy. The above equation and (II.5) in turn imply

$$\text{(II.19)} \qquad K^* = \frac{K^p - (Ko)}{p^k} = \frac{\hat{K}^p - (\hat{K}o)}{\hat{p}^k}$$

where the caret, it will be recalled, indicates that variables are measured in terms of consumables. For our purpose, this equation can be further restated in the form

$$\text{(II.20)} \qquad K^*_t = \frac{\hat{K}^p_t}{\bar{p}^k} - W^k_t, \quad W^k_t \equiv \frac{(\hat{K}o)_t}{\bar{p}^k} + \frac{\hat{p}^k - \bar{p}^k}{\bar{p}^k} K^*_t$$

Here $(\bar{p}^k)$ stands for the mean value of $\hat{p}^k_t$, and W^k can be regarded as a "wedge" analogous to that used in the last section, but falling now between K^* and $\hat{K}^p$. It reflects the behavior of tangibles other than K and of the relative price of capital goods.

Now $\hat{K}^p_t$ can be expressed in terms of $\hat{G}_t$ by means of (II.18), leading to

$$K^*_t = \frac{b_1}{(\bar{p}^k)}(1+\rho)\,\mathring{Y}_t - \frac{(1-b_2)}{(\bar{p}^k)}\,\hat{G}_t - W^k_t \tag{II.21}$$

From equation (II.18a) we know that the value of $(1-b_2)$ can be estimated at around -1; it would appear, therefore, that the effect of $\hat{G}$ on K^* could be estimated at $-1/(\bar{p}^k)$, or approximately $-.9$, since for our sample $(\bar{p}^k) \simeq 1.1$.[25] But this conclusion would be valid only if one could suppose the wedge W^k to be uncorrelated with $\hat{G}$ (given $\mathring{Y}_t$). Such an independence cannot be taken for granted. On the contrary one might readily conceive of a variety of mechanisms through which $\hat{G}$ might tend to affect systematically one or more components of $(\hat{K}o)$ as well as $\hat{p}^k$, and hence W^k_t, causing the average effect of G on K^* to be either larger or smaller than $-1/(\bar{p}^k)$. We do not propose here to spell out and test these conceivable mechanisms which are likely to be rather complex. We may, however, endeavour to gain some rough notion of their combined quantitative impact by estimating directly the average effect of $\hat{G}$ on K^* as measured by the coefficient of $\hat{G}$ in a regression equation analogous to (II.18) but in which K^p is replaced by K^*, i.e.,

$$K^*_t = d_1\,(1+\rho)\,\mathring{Y}_t + d_2\hat{G}_t \tag{II.22}$$

By comparing with (II.21) it is apparent that if W^k were uncorrelated with $\hat{G}$ we should find that $d_2 \simeq -(1/\mathring{\hat{p}}^k) \simeq -.9$. If, however, W^k is correlated with $\hat{G}$, then d_2 could be larger or smaller, depending on the sign and size of that association.

[25] The value of $(\bar{p}^k)$ depends, of course, on the basis chosen for the price indices p^k and p^e. In the present instance the base year is 1929, so that $(\bar{p}^k)$ is the mean value of the terms of trade between GNP and its capital goods component, taking the 1929 terms of trade as unity.

Because of the usual problem of heteroscedasticity for purposes of estimation, both sides of (II.23) have been divided by $\hat{Y}_t$ and the term $d_1(1+\rho)\ \mathring{\hat{Y}}_t/\hat{Y}_t$ has been approximated again by $d'_o - d'_1 Q_t$. The empirical result is

$$\text{(II.22a)} \quad \frac{K^*_t}{\hat{Y}_t} = \underset{(0.4)}{2.9} - \underset{(0.2)}{3.3}\ Qt - \underset{(.06)}{.65}\frac{G_t}{Y_t} \quad R = .93,\ S_e = .20$$ [26]

The coefficient d_2 is thus again very significantly negative. None-theless, it is appreciably smaller than —.9, by some 30 per cent. In other words, over the period of observation there has, in fact, been a substantial negative correlation between G and the wedge W^k. Or, to summarize our findings in different words, while (II.18a) appears to confirm that an increase in G has tended to depress K^p by a roughly equal amount, (II.22a) suggests that the depressing effect on K* has been attenuated to the extent of about 30 per cent by a tendency for changes in G to be absorbed by offsetting movements in the wedge.

It should be emphasized that the above estimate of the effect of $\hat{G}$ on K* is a very crude one; it rests, in effect, on the empirically observed covariation between $\hat{G}_t$ and W^k_t over the period of observation, which could be a poor estimate of the strength and character of true causal mechanisms.[27] One particular cause for concern is that over the period of observation the relevant variables exhibit marked time trends, positive for G/Y and negative for $K^*/\hat{Y}$, related in part to a pronounced shift of level between the periods preceding and following the Second World War. While the behavior of G/Y can presumably be taken as largely exogenous, the trend of the other variable might reflect a causal association with G/Y but might also reflect quite different causes,

[26] $\hat{Y}_t$ for this regression was actually estimated by deflating Y by the private GNP deflator p^x.

[27] For one thing, our estimate is an average for the period and different mechanisms may have been operating at different times. For instance, as pointed out in [18] the effect of G on K_o may be affected by the kind of taxes levied to pay the interest on the debt.

in which case the negative correlation of K^*/Y and G/Y might be spurious.[28]

c) *Implications for the "Burden" of the National Debt*

Although the above considerations indicate that the empirical estimate provided by (II.22a) is subject to a wide margin of error, it is worth pointing out what these results, taken at face value, would imply for the (gross) burden of the national debt measured in terms of its effect on real income ($\hat{Y}$) and output (X^*). Since we are concerned with long run effects, we can put $Q_t=0$ and thus rewrite (II.22a) as

$$K^*=3\hat{Y}-.65\hat{G} \tag{II.23}$$

As observed earlier, G may be expected to affect output by way of affecting the stock of capital which, in turn, affects output, or

$$\frac{dX^*}{d\hat{G}}=\frac{dX^*}{dK^*}\frac{dK^*}{d\hat{G}}=i\frac{dK^*}{d\hat{G}},\ \frac{d\hat{Y}}{d\hat{G}}=\frac{dX^*}{d\hat{G}}\frac{d\hat{Y}}{dX^*} \tag{II.24}$$

Here i is a measure of the marginal productivity of capital, which together with $\frac{d\hat{Y}}{dX^*}$, we may take as given parameters. The long run effect of $\hat{G}$ on K^* can be inferred from (II.23), though it cannot be simply identified with the coefficient of $\hat{G}$ in that equation. For that coefficient measures only what might be called the "displacement effect" of $\hat{G}$, i.e., its effect on K^* *given* aggregate wealth, $\hat{A}$ or its determinant, $\hat{Y}$. To get the "total" effect we must take into account the feedback of $\hat{G}$ on $\hat{A}$ by way of its effect on $\hat{Y}$, that is, we need to differentiate (II.23) totally with respect to $\hat{G}$, obtaining

[28] As a crude check against this type of spuriousness, we have added a time trend to equation (II.22a) to see whether this would lead to very different values of the coefficients. The outcome of this test

$$\frac{K^*_t}{Y^*_t}=\underset{(0.4)}{2.9}+\underset{(.2)}{3.3}\,Q_t-\underset{(.16)}{.70}\frac{G}{Y}+\underset{(.0040)}{.0015}t$$

is clearly reassuring, insofar as it goes—which is probably not very far.

$$(II.25) \qquad \frac{dK^*}{d\hat{G}} = \frac{3d\hat{Y}}{dX^*} \frac{dX^*}{d\hat{G}} - .65$$

Equations (II.25) and (II.24) can be solved simultaneously to yield

$$(II.26) \qquad \frac{dX^*}{d\hat{G}} = \frac{-.65i}{1-3\frac{d\hat{Y}}{dX^*}i}, \quad \frac{d\hat{Y}}{d\hat{G}} = \frac{-.65\frac{d\hat{Y}}{dX^*}i}{1-3\frac{d\hat{Y}}{dX^*}i}, \quad \frac{dK^*}{d\hat{G}} = \frac{-.65}{1-3\frac{d\hat{Y}}{dX^*}i}$$

Although our analysis does not directly provide information on the marginal productivity of capital i, other studies have suggested that it may be a good deal higher than average net of tax returns on aggregate wealth r, which we have estimated earlier as being in the order of 4 to 5 per cent. The value of $d\hat{Y}/dX^*$ depends on fiscal arrangements and has no doubt been different at different times. On the whole, however, the equations (II.26) suggest that, once we take into account both direct and feedback effects, our estimates of the parameters of (II.23) imply that $\frac{dK^*}{d\hat{G}}$ might not be too different from -1, i.e., that a dollar of national debt may tend to displace roughly a dollar's worth of private reproducible capital. By the same token, $\frac{dX^*}{d\hat{G}}$ might not be very different from $-i$, i.e., a dollar of debt would tend to reduce annual output by the marginal productivity of capital. If, in fact, because of taxes and other reasons, i exceeds significantly the interest rate the government has to offer the holders of the debt, then the (gross) real burden of the national debt could well be substantially higher than might be inferred from the annual interest charges.[29]

[29] Note that in deriving formula (II.26), on which these conclusions are based, we have again not taken into account explicitly the possible effect of interest rates on the wealth-income ratios—*cf.* footnote 24. It is, however, conceivable that this effect, if any, may be implicitly reflected, at least in part, in the empirically estimated parameters of (II.23) and therefore also in (II.26).

BIBLIOGRAPHY

1. Ando, A. *A Contribution to the Theory of Economic Fluctuations and Growth.* Doctoral Dissertation, Carnegie Institute of Technology, 1959.
2. ———. "An Empirical Model of the U. S. Economic Growth: Exploratory Study in Applied Capital Theory," in *Models of Income Determination, Studies in Income and Wealth,* Vol. 28, National Bureau of Economic Research, 1964.
3. ——— and F. Modigliani. "Growth Fluctuations and Stability," *American Economic Review, Proceedings,* Vol. 49, May 1959, pp. 501–524.
4. ——— and F. Modigliani. "The Life Cycle Hypothesis of Saving: Aggregate Implications and Tests," *American Economic Review,* Vol. 53, May 1963, pp. 53–84.
5. ——— and F. Modigliani. "The Life Cycle Hypothesis of Saving: A Correction," *American Economic Review,* Vol. 54, No. 2, Part I, March 1964, pp. 111–113.
6. Bentzel, R. "Några Synpunkter på Sparandets Dynamik," in *Festskrift Tillagnad Halvar Sundberg* (Uppsala Universitetes Arsskrift 1959:9) Uppsala, 1959.
7. Brumberg, R. E. *Utility Analysis and Aggregate Consumption Function: An Empirical Test and Its Meaning.* Doctoral Dissertation, The Johns Hopkins University, 1953.
8. ———. "An Approximation to the Aggregate Saving Function," *Economic Journal,* Vol. 46, May 1956, pp. 66–72.
9. Duesenberry, J. S. *Income, Saving and the Theory of Consumer Behavior.* Harvard University Press, 1949.
10. Friedman, M. *A Theory of the Consumption Function.* Princeton University Press, 1949.
11. Goldsmith, R. W. *A Study of Saving In the United States.* Princeton, 1956.
12. ———. *The Wealth of the United States in the Postwar Period.* National Bureau of Economic Research, Princeton, 1962.
13. *Historical Statistics of the United States, Colonial Times to 1957.* U. S. Government Printing Office, Washington, D.C., 1960.
14. Lydall, H. F. "Saving and Wealth," *Australian Economic Papers,* December 1963, pp. 228–250.
15. Miller, M. H. and F. Modigliani. "Dividend Policy, Growth and the Valuation of Shares," *Journal of Business,* Vol. 34, No. 4, October 1961, pp. 411–433.
16. Modigliani, F. "Fluctuations in the Saving-Income Ratio: A Problem in Economic Forecasting," in *Studies in Income and Wealth,* Vol. XI, National Bureau of Economic Research, 1949.
17. Modigliani, F. "Comment on 'A Survey of Some Theories of Income Distribution' by T. Scitovsky," *Studies in Income and Wealth,* Vol. 27, National Bureau of Economic Research, 1964.
18. ———. "Long Run Implications of Alternative Fiscal Policies and the Burden of the National Debt," *The Economic Journal,* Vol. 71, December 1961, pp. 730–765.
19. ——— and A. Ando. "Tests of the Life Cycle Hypothesis of Saving," *Bulletin of the Oxford University Institute of Statistics,* Vol. 19, May 1957, pp. 99–124.
20. ——— and A. Ando. "The Permanent Income and the Life Cycle Hypothesis of Saving Behavior: Comparisons and Tests," in *Proceedings of the Conference on Consumption and Saving,* Vol. 2, Philadelphia, 1960.

21. ——— and R. Brumberg. "Utility Analysis and the Consumption Function: An Interpretation of Cross-Section Data," in K. Kurihara (Ed.), *Post-Keynesian Economics*, New Brunswick, 1954.

22. ——— and R. Brumberg. "Utility Analysis and Aggregate Consumption Functions: An Attempt at Integration," unpublished.

23. Neisser, H. P. "The Economics of a Stationary Population," *Social Research*, November 1944, pp. 470–490.

APPENDIX A

Analytical Derivation of the Relation of Saving and Wealth to Income for Exponential Growth of Income

Assumptions

As in the text, we make the following four assumptions:

1. The rate of return on assets remains constant through time.

2. No bequests, which implies in particular that every cohort consumes all of its income over life.

3. "Tastes" remain constant through time in the sense that every cohort chooses the same age pattern of allocation of life resources to consumption over its life. More precisely stated, for any given rate of return, the ratio of per capita consumption at age T to per capita "life resources" is the same for all cohorts. Life resources is defined as the present value of life earnings from labor, computed as of the date when the cohort enters the labor force. The chosen allocation will in general be a function of the rate of return and must of course satisfy the over-life budget constraint that the present value of consumption must equal the present value of resources (in view of 2 above).

4. Every cohort has the same mortality experience, i.e., the proportion surviving at age T is the same for all cohorts.

Definitions and Notation

$P(\theta)$	The number of people reaching working age in the year θ. The members of this group are referred to as the "cohort θ."
$h(T)$	Proportion of every cohort surviving at age T, where T is measured from entering the labor force. T is assumed to have an upper bound L, in the sense that $h(T)=0$ for $T \geqq L$.
$y(T, \theta)$	*Per capita* rate of income of the cohort θ at age T
$c(T, \theta)$	*Per capita* rate of consumption of the cohort θ at age T
$s(T, \theta)$	*Per capita* rate of saving of the cohort θ at age T
$Y(t), C(t), S(t)$	*Aggregate* Income, Consumption and Saving in the year t
$A(T, \theta)$	*Aggregate* net worth at age T of the cohort θ
$A(t)$	*Aggregate* net worth in the year t (the sum over all cohorts present)

p	Rate of growth of population
y	Rate of growth of labor productivity

All variables (other than those relating to population) should be thought of as measured in "real" terms or more precisely in terms of purchasing power over consumables (which thus act as *numéraire*). Since we are dealing with steady state implications, we also rule out (real) capital gains and losses so that $S(t) \equiv \frac{dA}{dt}$.

From the above definitions, noting that the population having age T in the year t belongs to the cohort t—T, we derive the following useful relations

$$S(t) = \int_0^L s(T,t-T)P(T-t)h(T)dT \tag{1}$$

$$A(t) = \int_0^L A(T,t-T)dT \tag{2}$$

Also, since assumption 2 implies that no bequests are received, we have that $(A(\tau,\theta)$, the aggregate assets at some given age τ of the cohort θ, can be expressed as

$$A(\tau,\theta) = \int_0^\tau s(T,\theta)P(\theta)h(T)dT \tag{3}$$

which implies, in particular,

$$A(L,\theta) = \int_0^L s(T,\theta)P(\theta)h(T)dT = 0 \tag{4}$$

The last equality follows from the fact that $A(L,\theta)$ represents the terminal wealth, or over-life saving, of the cohort θ, and the assumption of no bequests clearly implies that this terminal wealth must be zero.

(a) The Case of Stationary Income and Population

The assumption of stationary population can be expressed as

$$P(\theta) = P_o \tag{5a}$$

Similarly, the absence of change in productivity over time can be formalized in the assumption that $y(T,\theta)$ depends only on age T but not on θ. This assumption in turn can be conveniently expressed as follows:

$$y(T,\theta) = y(T) \tag{6a}$$

But assumption 3, when combined with (6a), clearly implies that $s(T,\theta)$ also depends only on T and not on θ, which we can again express as

$$s(T,\theta)=s(T) \tag{7a}$$

If we now substitute (5a) and (7a) into (1) and (4), we obtain

$$S(t)=P_0\int_0^L s(T)h(T)dT=A(L,\theta) \tag{8a}$$

But since $A(L,\theta)$ is zero for all θ, we conclude that $S(t)$ is also zero. Q.E.D.

With zero aggregate saving, wealth must of course be constant in time, and since income is also constant so must be the wealth-income ratio. This conclusion can also be derived by substituting (5a) and (7a) into (3) and (2), which yields

$$A(t)=P_0\int_0^L\int_0^T s(\tau)h(T)d\tau dT \tag{9a}$$

Since the right hand side expression does not depend on time, we can infer that $A(t)$ is constant in time. The implication of zero saving under stationary income and population could be deduced from this result.

(b) Population Growth (at a Constant Rate p)

If population grows at the rate p, while productivity is stationary, then (5a) can be replaced by

$$P(\theta)=P_0e^{p\theta} \tag{5b}$$

while (6a) and therefore (7a) still hold. Substituting (5b) and (7a) into (1), we find

$$S(t)=P_0\int_0^L s(T)h(T)e^{p(t-T)}dT=P_0e^{pt}\left[\int_0^L s(T)h(T)e^{-pT}dT\right] \tag{8b}$$

and substituting into (3) and (2)

$$A(t)=\int_0^L\int_0^T s(\tau)h(\tau)P_0e^{p(t-T)}d\tau dT=P_0e^{pt}\left[\int_0^L\int_0^T s(\tau)h(\tau)e^{-pT}d\tau dT\right] \tag{9b}$$

Since the expressions in brackets in the right hand side of (8b) and (9b) are independent of t, we can conclude that both S and A grow at the exponential rate p. But this is also the growth rate of aggregate income since

$$(10b)\quad Y(t)=\int_0^L y(T)h(T)p_0 e^{p(t-T)}dT=P_0 e^{pt}\int_0^L y(T)h(T)e^{-pT}dT$$

Thus both the saving and the wealth-income ratios will remain constant in time. Once more, the fact that S(t) will be positive when population grows could be deduced directly from the behavior of A(t).

Note finally that the proposition advanced in the text that the saving ratio s should tend to rise with p, can be supported by reference to (8b). In fact, in view of the typical life profile of earnings, we should expect s(T) to be prevailingly positive before retirement, i.e., for $T<N$, and prevailingly negative for $N<T<L$. But, the larger p, the smaller the relative weight assigned to s(T) for large T.

(c) Productivity Growth of Income (at a Constant Rate y)

An explicit proof of the stability of the saving and wealth-income ratios will be provided for the simpler case where the rate of return on assets is zero, so that income coincides with income from labor. An analogous reasoning can, however, be applied even if the rate of return is non-zero, though the proof becomes somewhat more cumbersome.

The assumption that per capita income from labor at each age grows in time at the exponential rate y (and property income is zero) can be formalized as follows:

$$y(T,t-T)=y(T)e^{yt} \text{ or } y(T,\theta)=y(T)e^{y\cdot(\theta+T)}$$

(Note that the function $y(T,t-T)$, regarded as a function of T for fixed t, is simply the age profile of average income in the year t.)

Since the assumption of stationary population implies that (5a) holds, we deduce

$$(10c)\quad Y(t)=\int_0^L y(T,t-T)P_0 h(T)dT=P_0\int_0^L h(T)y(T)e^{yt}dT= P_0 e^{yt}\int_0^L y(T)h(T)dT$$

which shows that aggregate income grows at the rate y. Similarly, letting $Y(\theta)$ denote the *aggregate* income earned by the cohort θ over its lifetime, we find

$$Y(\theta)=P_0\int_0^L y(T,\theta)h(T)dT=P_0\int_0^L h(T)y(T)e^{y(\theta+T)}dT= P_0 e^{y\theta}\left[\int_0^L y(T)h(T)e^{yT}dT\right]$$

so that total life resources of successive cohorts also rise at the rate y. Next, from the assumption that the distribution of consumption over life remains constant in time, we can deduce that *aggregate* consumption of any one cohort at age T can be expressed as some fraction, say $\gamma(T)$, of its aggregate life resources, or that

$$c(T,\theta)P_o h(T)=\gamma(T)Y(\theta)$$

It follows that

$$s(T,\theta)=y(T,\theta)-c(T,\theta)=y(T)e^{y(\theta+T)}-\frac{\gamma(T)Y(\theta)}{P_o h(T)}=$$

$$=e^{y\theta}[y(T)e^{yT}-\frac{\gamma(T)}{h(T)}\int_o^L y(\tau)h(\tau)e^{y\tau}d\tau]$$

Once again the coefficient of the exponential is not a function of time; it is instead a function of age T, depending also on the rate of growth y. To stress this dependence we will denote the expression in brackets by $s^*(T,y)$, and thus rewrite the above expression for $s(T,\theta)$ in the form

$$s(T,\theta)=s^*(T,y)e^{y\theta} \tag{7c}$$

an equation which replaces (7a) of the previous two cases.

Substituting (7c) and (5a) in (1), we finally obtain

$$S(t)=P_o\int_o^L s^*(T,y)e^{y(t-T)}h(T)dT=P_o e^{yt}[\int_o^L s^*(T,y)h(T)e^{-yT}dT] \tag{8c}$$

Similarly, from (3) and (2), we deduce

$$A(t)=P_o e^{yt}[\int_o^L \int_o^T s^*(\tau,y)h(\tau)e^{-yT}d\tau dT] \tag{9c}$$

Thus both aggregate saving and net worth rise at the same rate y as aggregate income, implying again that the saving-income and the wealth-income ratio remain at a constant level through time.

The proposition that the level of the saving ratio is likely to increase with the rate of growth of income y, can again be supported by inspection of (8c), since it is seen that the larger y, the smaller is the relative weight of $s^*(T,y)$ for large T. However, the validity of this reasoning is now less certain than in the case of productivity growth, if in estimating life resources each cohort takes partially or fully into account the future productivity growth of its income. While it remains true, regardless of y, that $s^*(T,y)$ will be negative for $T>N$, extrapolation of past productivity growth may result in a large rate of consumption in the earliest part of life. Hence for small values of $T, s^*(T,y)$ will tend to fall with y and may even become negative. Under these conditions, the relation between s and y may not be monotonic. For small values of y, the association must be positive, since for $y=0$, $A(t)$ is a positive constant, and $S(t)=0$, while, at least for y sufficiently small, $A(t)$ must still be positive, but since it grows at the rate y, $S(t)$ and s must be positive. However, beyond some point, the growth in y could reduce the rate of saving of the younger age group to the point of causing a fall in the saving-income ratio. But this result seems unlikely within the relevant range of y, say between zero and 5 per cent, especially if institutional arrangements severely limit the ability of the younger age group to pile up a significant negative net worth.

APPENDIX B

Basic Data on Wealth and Income Underlying the Tests of Part II

Year (1)	A[1] (2)	Y[2] (3)	K[3] (4)	X[4] (5)	p^K[5] 1929=100 (6)	p^X[6] 1929=100 (7)	G[7] (8)	$\mathring{X}^*_t / X^*_t$[8] (9)	Year[9] type (10)
1900	78.2	17.2	49.4	19.3	49.5	50.5	2.8	.956	1
1901	86.0	19.0	50.6	21.1	49.9	50.6	2.7	.914	0
1902	92.6	19.9	54.1	22.0	50.7	51.5	2.8	.974	0
1903	95.6	21.3	56.4	23.8	51.0	53.2	2.9	.957	0
1904	97.8	20.5	58.5	22.8	51.8	51.9	2.9	1.009	1
1905	107.2	22.4	62.8	24.9	53.5	53.1	3.0	.953	0
1906	114.9	26.9	68.4	29.7	55.7	56.6	3.2	.893	1
1907	115.9	29.6	72.0	32.5	56.2	60.1	3.3	.970	0
1908	122.4	25.0	73.4	28.2	56.0	56.3	3.6	1.080	1
1909	135.4	29.9	77.3	32.9	57.4	56.9	3.7	.934	0
1910	142.3	30.8	80.9	34.6	57.7	58.4	4.0	.978	0
1911	145.7	31.2	83.1	35.1	58.1	57.8	4.2	.975	0
1912	155.4	34.9	87.1	38.6	58.9	59.9	4.4	.942	0
1913	159.6	34.6	90.6	38.7	59.0	59.7	4.5	.941	0
1914	163.2	33.3	93.1	37.6	59.0	60.8	4.9	1.048	1
1915	172.9	35.2	100.9	39.1	62.6	63.9	5.4	1.058	1
1916	195.8	44.7	121.2	47.4	73.6	71.6	5.6	.980	0
1917	223.5	54.2	152.8	58.9	89.5	90.1	12.1	1.012	2
1918	255.1	66.4	178.3	72.0	102.4	106.4	26.1	.966	2
1919	323.3	74.6	209.4	81.3	117.6	115.3	31.0	.960	0
1920	324.0	77.1	208.9	89.0	113.0	130.5	29.9	1.034	1
1921	244.6	54.6	177.1	67.1	95.5	108.2	29.9	1.137	1
1922	303.8	63.6	182.4	71.9	96.0	98.8	30.7	.968	0
1923	324.3	73.0	197.9	83.0	99.3	101.1	30.1	.887	1
1924	338.1	72.0	203.7	82.5	99.0	100.9	30.0	1.004	0
1925	356.1	79.6	213.2	91.0	99.1	102.2	30.2	.922	0
1926	374.4	81.3	220.9	94.9	98.1	100.7	29.8	.945	0
1927	400.5	79.1	228.0	92.6	97.8	98.8	29.5	1.008	1
1928	436.1	81.0	237.5	94.7	99.1	100.3	29.6	.998	0
1929	455.3	85.5	242.8	100.1	98.4	100.0	29.5	.943	0
1930	449.1	71.4	226.5	86.6	91.1	96.5	30.1	1.116	1
1931	383.1	58.4	198.6	71.6	80.9	86.5	33.3	1.208	1
1932	310.7	42.7	178.8	54.0	75.3	77.6	37.4	1.938	1
1933	313.0	43.3	184.4	51.3	80.5	76.5	40.5	1.491	1
1934	321.3	50.4	188.8	59.4	84.6	81.4	44.4	1.371	1
1935	338.0	57.5	190.4	66.6	85.8	82.3	46.6	1.237	1
1936	366.9	66.0	203.9	75.5	91.5	82.7	50.6	1.096	1
1937	383.7	71.5	214.6	83.9	94.5	85.7	53.4	1.023	1
1938	360.1	64.8	213.5	77.6	94.6	84.2	55.4	1.086	1
1939	379.7	71.6	219.4	83.5	96.5	83.2	58.2	.997	0
1940	388.1	78.5	234.0	92.8	100.7	84.6	61.5	.915	0
1941	418.7	97.9	262.1	116.4	108.7	92.4	74.2	.871	1
1942	469.1	122.7	280.0	144.0	114.9	105.1	128.8	.920	2
1943	538.1	139.5	288.6	167.0	120.5	116.1	185.0	.953	2
1944	593.1	152.5	298.1	179.2	125.7	118.2	246.2	.948	2
1945	689.1	154.0	375.6	178.4	134.7	118.9	292.4	1.011	2
1946	752.3	168.2	399.6	189.1	159.1	128.3	273.1	1.028	0
1947	831.7	181.8	483.1	217.6	186.5	143.6	271.4	1.001	0
1948	876.6	202.6	530.7	242.0	196.0	153.5	269.1	.962	0

1949	888.9	198.2	530.2	238.7	191.6	152.2	275.3	1.006	1
1950	992.9	221.3	612.5	263.8	211.9	154.1	277.4	.916	0
1951	1072.9	238.2	670.9	301.7	221.2	166.2	282.8	.943	0
1952	1107.1	247.0	699.8	316.0	223.1	169.1	293.2	.971	0
1953	1143.6	261.4	728.5	333.6	225.2	170.1	303.8	.952	0
1954	1236.8	263.9	754.2	330.8	227.2	171.4	312.2	1.017	1
1955	1341.9	286.3	808.9	363.5	234.5	172.9	319.2	.933	0
1956	1423.8	304.2	878.6	382.8	245.6	178.1	319.2	.979	0
1957	1459.7	318.5	941.6	403.8	254.8	184.4	321.7	.981	0
1958	1612.4	324.3	981.3	402.6	260.7	187.7	333.9	1.021	1

[1] Private Net Worth in Current Prices:

1945–58: R. W. Goldsmith, R. E. Lipsey and M. Mendelson, *Studies in the National Balance Sheet of the United States*, Vol. II, Princeton University Press, 1963, sum of the estimate of "Equities" of Non-Farm Households, Table III-1, p. 118–9 and of Agriculture, Table III-3, pp. 130–131.

1929–44: Ando, Brown, Solow & Kareken, "Lags in Fiscal and Monetary Policy" in *Stabilization Policies*, prepared for the Commission on Money and Credit, Prentice Hall, 1963, Appendix, Table I-A1, p. 150.

1900–28: Unpublished estimates kindly made available by A. K. Ando. The derivation of these estimates is described in Ando and Modigliani [4], Appendix A, p. 80; and in Ando [2], Appendix. The above two series (covering the years 1900 to 1944) are intended to provide an estimate of net worth at the *beginning* of the year, at *average prices* of that year. For the purpose of our tests, however, what is needed is an estimate of net worth, in current prices, at the *end* of the year. We have therefore added to the above estimates an estimate of net private saving during the year, defined as the sum of personal and corporate saving. Since the original series are based on benchmark year estimates by Goldsmith [11], the estimate of saving was also taken from Goldsmith [11], Vol. I, Table T 1, Col. (2) plus Col. (6). It will be noted that the resulting series represents, conceptually, an estimate of net worth at the end of the year at average prices of that year rather than at year end prices. No attempt was made to correct for this conceptual discrepancy; the resulting error is deemed to be negligible as compared with the error of estimate, which is undoubtedly considerable.

[2] Private Income Minus Net Taxes, in Current Prices:

1929–58: Sum of Disposable Personal Income and Undistributed Profits. Through 1955 the two estimates are taken from *U. S. Income and Output*, U. S. Department of Commerce, 1958, Table II-1, line 24, and Table I-17, line 9. For 1956–58 they are taken from *Economic Report of the President* January 1964, Tables C–15 and C–63.

1900–28: Gross National Product minus an estimate of the discrepancy between Gross National Product and Disposable Income plus Undistributed Corporate profits: For 1909–28 the estimate of GNP in current prices is from *U. S. Income and Output*, Table I-16, line 1. For 1900–08 the estimate of GNP of R. W. Goldsmith [11], Table N.1, Col. (1), was spliced to the Department of Commerce series by multiplying Goldsmith series by the blowup factor 1.084. This factor is the ratio of Goldsmith's to the Department of Commerce estimate of GNP in current prices for the overlapping years 1909–14. The estimate of the discrepancy is obtained from R. W. Goldsmith [11] by subtracting from his estimate of GNP the sum of his estimate of Disposable Personal Income, Table N.1, Col. (5), and Undistributed Corporate Profits, Table N.5, Col. (8).

[3] Stock of Private Productive Reproducible Tangible Capital at Current Reproduction Cost:

1945–58: Derived from the estimates in R. W. Goldsmith [12] as follows: Private Structures, Table A 5, Col. (3) plus (4); *plus* Producers Durables, Table A 5, Col. (6); *plus* Live Stock and Inventories, Table A 5, Col. (8) plus (9); *minus* Government Inventories, Table A 39, Col. (5) plus (6).

1900–44: Derived from the estimates in R. W. Goldsmith [11] Table W 1 as follows: Reproducible Tangible Assets, Col. (2); *minus* Government Structures, Col. (9); *minus* Consumers Durables, Col. (12); *minus* Monetary Gold and Silver, Col. (18). It may be noted that the estimates for this earlier period implicitly include Producers Durables held by the Government, which conceptually should be excluded (as we have done for the later period), but for which no separate estimate is available.

[4] Private Gross National Product (or GNP minus GNP originating in General Government), in Current Prices:

1956–58: *Survey of Current Business,* July 1962, Table 1–2, line 49 *minus* line 61.

1929–55: *U. S. Income and Output,* op. cit., Same tables and lines

1909–28: *U. S. Income and Output,* Table I-16, line 1, *minus* line 2.

1900–08: GNP estimated by splicing Goldsmith estimate in [11] to the Department of Commerce estimate, as explained in 2, above, minus a crude estimate of GNP orginating in General Government taken from worksheets kindly made available by A. K. Ando, (at the users' risk!)

[5] Price Index of Private Productive Reproducible Tangible Wealth:

1900–44: Ratio of the estimate of K as derived in 3, above, to the estimated stock in 1929 prices, from Goldsmith [11] Table W 3, Col. (2) *minus* Col. (9) *minus* Col. (12) *minus* Col. (18).

1945–58: Ratio of the estimated stock at current reproduction cost as derived in 3, above, to the estimate of the stock in 1947 prices provided in Goldsmith [12], Table A 6, same columns as indicated under 3, and Table A 39, "constant prices" section, col. (5) *plus* (6). This ratio yields a price index relative to 1947 prices and with a 1947 base. To convert this index to an index of prices relative to 1929 prices we have multiplied it by an estimate of reproduction cost in 1947 relative to 1929, obtained by dividing the estimate of the 1947 stock in current prices by an estimate of the 1947 stock in 1929 prices derived from Goldsmith [12], Table A 6 and A 39.

[6] Index of Prices of Private GNP:

1909–58: Ratio of Private GNP in current dollars as described in 4, to Private GNP in 1954 dollars, obtained as follows: 1956–58, *Survey of Current Business,* July 1962, Table I.13, line 1 *minus* line 3; 1929–55, *U. S. Input and Output,* Table I-13, line 1 *minus* line 3; 1909–28, *op. cit.,* Table I-16, line 5 *minus* line 6. The series was then converted to a 1929 base by dividing through by the price index for 1929 as computed above.

1900–08: Implicit GNP deflator in 1929 prices estimated from Goldsmith in [11], as the ratio of GNP in current prices to GNP in 1929 prices, spliced to the Department of Commerce estimate by multiplying the Goldsmith estimate by 1.1075, the ratio of the two indices for 1909.

[7] Net Public Debt:

1942–58: U. S. Government Gross Public Debt, *Economic Report of the President,* January 1963, Table C-53, *plus* State & Local Government Debt, *ibid.,* Table C-52.

1916–41: U. S. Government Gross Debt, *Banking and Monetary Statistics,* Board of Governors of the Federal Reserve System, 1943, Table 146, December figure, *plus* State & Local Debt, *Historical Statistics of the United States, Colonial Times to 1957,* series X 426, p. 664.

1900–15: Federal Government Total Gross Debt, *Historical Statistics, op. cit.,* series Y 257, p. 711 *plus* Net State & Local Debt estimated from Goldsmith [11], Vol. I, as follows: Gross Debt Outstanding, Table G-21, Col. (1) plus (2), *minus* Local Government holdings of Federal, State & Local Debt, Table G-8, Col. (3) *plus* (4) *plus* (5) *minus* State Government Holdings of Federal, State & Local Debt, Table G-17, Col. (3) plus (4) plus (5).

It will be noted that throughout we have included in G the Gross Federal Debt, on the ground that, conceptually, the amounts owed to Trust Funds are, for our purpose, a relevant component of the National Debt. It should be acknowledged, however, that in other respects the estimate of G we have used is rough and not entirely consistent; thus State and Local ownership of Federal debt was excluded (as appropriate) up to 1915, but not thereafter, and similarly, guaranteed issues are included (as, by and large, they should be) only after 1942. While it would be desirable eventually to run tests with a more refined and consistent measure of G, it is believed that inconsistencies in our series are minor enough not to affect the results materially.

[8] X^*_t=col. (5)÷col. (7); $\mathring{X}^*_t$ highest value of X^*_t preceding the year t.

[9] 0=normal year
1=cyclically High or Low (see text)
2=war year (excluded from correlations).

Errata

Page 169, note (ii), line 1: "[28]" should read "[21]."

Page 169, note (iii), line 4: "[2]" should read "[21]."

Page 174, line 10: the upper limit of the summation should be "$T - 1$" rather than "T."

Page 175, equation (I.8) should read "$\mu'_t = \frac{\delta + \rho}{1 + \rho} \sum_{\tau=0}^{\infty} \left(\frac{1 - \delta}{1 + \rho}\right)^{\tau} q'_{t-\tau}$."

Page 175, 3 lines from the bottom: equation should read

$$\text{"}S_t = \sigma Y_t - \delta a Y^{\circ}_{t-1}(1 + u'_{t-1}) = \sigma Y_t - \frac{\delta a}{1 + \rho} Y^{\circ}_t - \delta a Y^{\circ}_{t-1} u_{t-1}.\text{"}$$

Page 175, 2 lines from the bottom: equation should read "$\frac{\delta a}{1 + \rho} = \frac{\delta}{\rho} s$."

Page 175, last line: "$\frac{\delta}{\rho} Y_t$" should read "$\frac{\delta}{\rho} s Y_t$."

Page 176: second line should read "where $\nu_t = \frac{(1 + \rho) Y^{\circ}_{t-1}}{Y_t} u_{t-1}$."

Page 179, 8 lines from bottom of footnote: "var[$(1 + q)u'$]" should read "var[$(1 - q)u'$]."

Page 195, 3 lines from the bottom: "$E(c_0 = \ln g(1 + \rho)$" should read "$E(c_0) = \ln g(1 + \rho)$."

Page 198, line 14: "very close to unity" should read "very close to minus one."

Page 204, line 2: "both sides of (II.23)" should read "both sides of (II.22)."

Page 205, footnote 28, line 4: the "+" after 2.9 should be a minus.

Page 210, second line after equation (2): "that $(A(\tau, \theta)$" should read "that $A(\tau, \theta)$."

Page 211: equation (9a) should read "$A(t) = P_0 \int_0^L \int_0^T s(\tau) h(\tau)\, d\tau dT$."

Page 212: equation (10b) should read "$Y(t) = \int_0^L y(T) h(T) P_0 e^{p(t-T)} dT = \ldots .$"

14

THE LIFE CYCLE HYPOTHESIS OF SAVING AND INTERCOUNTRY DIFFERENCES IN THE SAVING RATIO*

FRANCO MODIGLIANI

1. *Introduction*

In Chapter 2 of *Towards a Dynamic Economics*, Sir Roy Harrod made a pioneering contribution to the study of aggregate saving by analysing the implications of the basic assumption that current saving decisions of households reflect an endeavour to achieve the preferred allocation of lifetime resources to consumption (and bequests) over the life cycle. Since that time, this approach has been pursued by a number of authors, both at the theoretical level and for the analysis of empirical data.[1] In particular, in Goldsmith (1956) and Modigliani (1966) it was found that this hypothesis is quite effective in accounting for the behaviour of aggregate saving and wealth in the United States both in the short and in the long run. The purpose of the present paper is to show that this approach appears equally fruitful for an understanding of observed inter-country differences in the average saving ratio.

A number of implications of the hypothesis of life cycle planning have been derived in Modigliani (1966) by combining that hypothesis with the assumption that the preferred pattern of allocation of consumption over life and the rate of return on assets remain reasonably stable in time. The following are directly relevant to the tests presented here:

(1) If productivity (output per employed person) tends to grow at a

* The tests reported in this paper were first presented in a paper entitled 'The Life Cycle Hypothesis of Saving, The Demand for Wealth and the Supply of Capital' prepared for the First International Meeting of the Econometric Society, Rome, Italy, September 1965. Other parts of that paper have since been published in Modigliani (1966). I am greatly indebted to Dr. Antonio Fazio of the Bank of Italy for advice and help in the design and execution of the statistical tests. Research support from a Ford Foundation grant to the Sloan School of Management for research in Finance is gratefully acknowledged.

[1] A partial list of references is given in Modigliani (1966). Among the contributions that have appeared since publication of that paper Meade (1966) and Tobin (1967) are particularly noteworthy.

constant rate, say y, and population at the rate p, and if aggregate output fluctuates cyclically around the growth trend $\varrho = y + p$, then the saving income ratio will tend to fluctuate *cyclically* around a constant level, say s.

(2) The value of s is independent of real income (aggregate or per capita) and depends instead on y and p or, more precisely, on y and the age structure of population, which, however, is uniquely related to p if population is in balanced growth. Furthermore the 'long run' saving ratio will be zero if y and p are zero (stationary economy) and will tend to grow with both y and p, though less than in proportion.

Implication (1) has long been known to be at least broadly consistent with the American experience over the last century or so; the available estimates of income and saving suggest in fact (i) a reasonably stable overall growth trend of real income; (ii) a saving income ratio characterized by marked cyclical movements but no significant overall upward or downward trend, despite the enormous rise in both aggregate and per capita real income. Implication (2), on the other hand, cannot be readily tested from U.S. data for the very same reason that makes the U.S. experience relevant for a test of implication (1), namely the overall stability of the growth trend of income over the period covered by the available data. More generally, there seems to be little chance that a satisfactory test of this set of implications can be carried out at present from time series data for individual countries because income is unlikely to exhibit very different growth trends within the span of time for which the required information is typically available. In what follows we propose instead to test these propositions by an analysis of intercountry differences in the saving ratio, and to show that they seem to account for a substantial proportion of the observed variations.

The raw material for our test is provided by the extensive compilation of data assembled in the United Nations *Yearbook of National Accounts Statistics*. With the help of this source and a few auxiliary ones, it has been possible to assemble usable data for a sample of some 36 countries. These are listed in the Data Appendix together with the values of the variables which will be used in our tests. It is readily apparent from this table and from the last column of Table 3, which provides a number of summary statistics, that the variables relevant to our tests exhibit a very wide variation, even though each of these variables represents an average over a span of several years, mostly seven to nine years (see below). In particular, the saving ratio, which averages 11·2 per cent for the sample as a whole, ranges all the way from −2·1 to 21·0 per cent, while the rate of growth of real income, averaging 4·7 per cent per year, varies between 1·5 and 9·9 per cent. Equally striking is the variation in estimated real per capita income in U.S. dollars, which ranges from \$65 to \$1,700, compared with a mean value of \$790.

In assembling, as well as in analysing, the data, we have relied heavily on the methodology proposed and followed by Houthakker in two recent papers (see list of References) dealing with the determinants of inter-country differences in saving behaviour. The second of these papers contains the first attempt of which we are aware at testing the specific implications of the life cycle hypothesis with which we are presently concerned. In the following section we briefly review Houthakker's methodology and some of his results, and in the remaining ones we rely on the same methodology to extend the tests in a variety of directions.

2. *Review of Houthakker Methodology and Results*

The method used by Houthakker in deriving the observations for each country is explained in the above references. The sample consists of all countries for which the required information is reported in the U.N. *Yearbook of National Accounts Statistics.* The saving and income variable for each country is an average of annual data for as many years as were available between 1952 and 1959, converted into real per capita U.S. dollars by means of population data, appropriate price indices and official exchange rates. The use of official exchange rates is, of course, a crude approximation, and probably subject to considerable error; fortunately, in most of our own tests we are able to rely on ratios which are unaffected by the choice of exchange rates. The most serious error is likely to occur in the estimates of per capita real income, though even here the spread between countries is so wide that we doubt that this source of error can affect the results to a significant extent.

Of the numerous results reported by Houthakker, the relevant ones for our purpose are those in which he has tested the effect of per capita income and of the rate of growth of income. These tests consist in fitting to the sample equations of the form

$$(S_{\text{pers}})_i = b_0 + b_1(Y_{\text{pd}})_i + b_2(\Delta Y_{\text{pd}})_i \tag{1}$$

and

$$\frac{(S_{\text{pers}})_i}{(Y_{\text{pd}})_i} = c_1 + c_2(\Delta^* Y_{\text{pd}})_i, \tag{2}$$

where $(S_{\text{pers}})_i$ and $(Y_{\text{pd}})_i$ denote, respectively, average annual *per capita* personal saving and disposable personal income for country i (measured in \$/year), ΔY_{pd} is the average annual increment in Y_{pd} (with dimension \$/(year)^2), and $\Delta^* Y_{\text{pd}}$ is the average annual rate of growth of *aggregate* personal income (with dimension 1/year).

Before we examine his empirical results we may stop to inquire whether the life cycle hypothesis can provide us with some notion as to the plausible range of values for the parameters of equations (1) and (2). To answer this question we must turn to a number of results established in Modigliani (1966).

14—I.G.T.

It was shown there that, if income fluctuates cyclically around the growth trend $\varrho = y + p$, the behaviour of the saving income ratio implied by the life cycle model can be approximated by

$$S_t/Y_t = \frac{\sigma\varrho}{\delta + \varrho} + \frac{\delta\varrho}{\sigma + \varrho} Q_t, \tag{3}$$

where S denotes private saving, Y private income net of taxes, σ and δ are constants and Q_t stands for the 'cyclical income index'

$$Q_t = \frac{Y_t - (1 + \varrho)^n \mathring{Y}_t}{Y_t},$$

$\mathring{Y}_t$ being the highest value reached by real income Y in any year preceding t and n the number of years from then to t. Since Q measures deviations from the growth trend, it must average out to zero over a sufficiently long span of years. Therefore, from equation (3), we can infer that, provided the number of years utilized in computing the average saving ratio for each country in our sample is sufficiently large to wash out roughly the cyclical effects, the life cycle hypothesis would imply

$$S_i/Y_i = \frac{\sigma_i\varrho_i}{\delta_i + \varrho_i}. \tag{4}$$

The parameters σ and δ might differ from country to country, as implied by the subscript i, since, in principle, they depend on such forces as the overall rate of growth and its distribution between y and p, the rate of return on assets, and, of course, tastes. However, a number of results reported in Modigliani and Brumberg (unpublished) and Modigliani (1966, Table 1) suggest that these parameters may not be, in fact, very responsive to the above forces, within the relevant range of variation. Indeed, it is found that there are broad similarities in the relation between s and ϱ implied by alternative assumptions about the source of growth (i.e., y versus p) and the representative life profile of income and consumption.[2] Furthermore, this relation is also similar to that implied by equation (4) by assigning to σ and δ the values estimated for the U.S. in the post-war period, namely, around 0·35 for σ and 0·05 for δ.[3] Such results suggest that intercountry differences in

[2] See also footnote 15.

[3] These values are derived in Modigliani (1966) from estimates obtained in Ando and Modigliani (1963 and 1964), by fitting to the U.S. data the consumption function

$$C_t = \alpha L^e_t + \beta A_{t-1}$$

where L^e is expected labour income and A is private wealth. The parameters σ and δ are related to α and β by

$$\sigma = 1 - \alpha \qquad \delta = \beta - \alpha r$$

where r is the rate of return on assets. The relation between s and ϱ implied by (4) for

the parameters σ and δ may be sufficiently small and unsystematic to be impounded in the error term without destroying the explanatory and predictive value of the model[4]. Under these assumptions, (4) can be rewritten as

$$S_i/Y_i = \frac{\sigma \varrho_i}{\delta + \varrho_i} + e_i. \tag{5}$$

By further noting that the ratio of per capita saving to per capita income is the same as the ratio of aggregate saving to aggregate income, we can conclude that Houthakker's equation (2) is simply a linear approximation to (5) with ϱ_i approximated empirically by the rate of growth of personal income, $\Delta^* Y_{\mathrm{pd}}$. A rough idea of the magnitude of the coefficient c_1 and c_2 implied by the model can then be obtained by expanding the right-hand side of (5) linearly around $\bar{\varrho}$, the mean value of ϱ in the sample, and relying on the estimates of σ and δ obtained for the United States, which is one of the countries included in the sample. Let

$$s(\varrho) \equiv \frac{\sigma \varrho}{\delta + \varrho}, \quad \text{and} \quad s'(\varrho) = \frac{\mathrm{d}s}{\mathrm{d}\varrho}.$$

Then

$$s(\varrho) \simeq s(\bar{\varrho}) + s'(\bar{\varrho})(\varrho - \bar{\varrho}) = [s(\bar{\varrho}) - \bar{\varrho}s'(\bar{\varrho})] + s'(\bar{\varrho})\varrho;$$

$$s(\bar{\varrho}) = \frac{\sigma \bar{\varrho}}{\delta + \bar{\varrho}} \qquad s'(\bar{\varrho}) = \frac{\sigma \delta}{(\delta + \bar{\varrho})^2}. \tag{6}$$

Substituting the U.S. estimates, $\sigma \simeq 0{\cdot}35$, $\delta \simeq 0{\cdot}05$, and the value of $\bar{\varrho}$ for

$\sigma = 0{\cdot}35$, $\delta = 0{\cdot}05$, is shown below for selected values of ϱ

ϱ (%)	0	1	2	3	4	5	10
s (%)	0	6	10	13	16	18	23

It should be noted that the life profile of consumption assumed in deriving the relation between s and ϱ referred to in the text imply no bequests and hence the only source of saving is Harrod's 'hump-saving' [Harrod (1948), p. 49]. However, as shown in Modigliani and Brumberg (unpublished) and Modigliani (1966) the above consumption function, and hence equation (4), also hold if we allow for bequests, under appropriate assumptions.

[4] Tobin (1967) also exhibits the relation between p and y and the saving ratio (derivable from his wealth income ratio) under rather different assumptions about income expectations and life consumption than those used in Modigliani (1966) and referred to above. His findings confirm that, generally, s tends to rise with both p and y and less than in proportion. However, they imply a far greater positive responsiveness of s to r than suggested by calculations carried out in Modigliani and Brumberg (unpublished). The difference seems to arise from the fact that contrary to what was assumed in the latter, he assumes (at least in part for computational convenience) that consumption is rather responsive to changes in r. As a result even for moderate values of r his values of s tend to be substantially above those shown in Table 1 of Modigliani (1966) and in footnote 3 above.

Houthakker's sample, 0·04, we find[5]

$$(7)\quad \begin{aligned} c_2 &\simeq s'(\bar{\varrho}) = \frac{(0{\cdot}35)(0{\cdot}05)}{(0{\cdot}05 + 0{\cdot}04)^2} = 2{\cdot}2, \\ c_1 &\simeq s(\bar{\varrho}) - \bar{\varrho}s'(\bar{\varrho}) = \frac{(0{\cdot}35)(0{\cdot}04)}{0{\cdot}05 + 0{\cdot}04} - (0{\cdot}04)(2{\cdot}2) = 0{\cdot}067. \end{aligned}$$

These *a priori* estimates of c_1 and c_2 would be directly applicable if S and Y were measured in accordance with the definitions underlying our model and the parameter estimates for the United States. There are, in fact, a number of significant differences. The income measure in Houthakker's tests is 'disposable personal income', which differs from our 'private income net of taxes' primarily by the exclusion of corporate saving. Similarly, his 'personal saving' differs from our concept by the exclusion of corporate saving as well as of the net addition to the stock of consumers' durables. Some idea of the extent to which these differences may affect the values of c_1 and c_2 can be gathered from an examination of Table 1. The statistics in column (1) are

TABLE 1

Saving Ratios and Growth Rates for Different Concepts of Saving and Income—22 Countries

(*a*) *Mean Values*	*Our Sample* (1)	*Houthakker Sample* (2)
Ratio of corporate saving to private income (%)	4·2	
Ratio of private saving to private income (%)	11·7	
Ratio of personal saving to personal income (%)	7·8	7·3
Rate of growth of private income (% per year)	4·6	
Rate of growth of personal income (% per year)	4·5	4·0
(*b*) *Correlations*		
Rate of growth of private income with rate of growth of personal income	0·995	
Private saving ratio with personal saving ratio	0·92	

based on a 22-country subsample of the sample used in our own analysis for which it is possible to estimate both private and corporate saving, and hence also personal saving. This sample overlaps to a considerable extent with the 28-country sample used by Houthakker, for which the available information is reported in column (2). It is apparent that the substitution of personal income for private income is unlikely to affect the results materially, but the difference in the definition of saving is important; the personal saving ratio is on the average only about two-thirds as large as the private saving ratio, although the correlation between the two measures is fairly high.

[5] Note that the result for c_1 implies that the constant term of the linear approximation to (5) should be positive even though (5) implies zero saving for a zero rate of growth. It reflects the fact that, according to (5), s rises proportionally less than ϱ.

The omission of saving in the form of additions to the stock of durable goods is common both to Houthakker's personal saving and to the measure of private saving used in Table 1 and in the rest of our analysis. Estimates for the United States based on Goldsmith (1956 and 1962) as well as on the Flow of Funds series (1961, Table 2), suggest that this form of saving is far from negligible and has tended to account for some 15 to 20 per cent of private saving, although this figure may not be very typical for other countries. On the whole, however, we should not be very far off in concluding that Houthakker's saving ratio is likely to be, on the average, 40 to 50 per cent lower than if he had used the measure called for by the model.

In the light of the above considerations it is significant that the mean saving ratio of Houthakker's sample, 7·3 per cent, is just below one-half the value of $s(\bar{\varrho})$ implied by equation (6) with U.S. parameters, namely, $[(0{\cdot}35)(0{\cdot}04)]/[(0{\cdot}05) + (0{\cdot}04)] = 15{\cdot}5$ per cent, considering also that $s(\bar{\varrho})$ will tend to overestimate the mean value of s implied by the model because of the negative curvature of $s(\varrho)$. These results also suggest that the coefficients of equation (2) should be on the order of 40 to 50 per cent lower than implied by (7), or around 1·1 to 1·3 for c_2, the coefficient of ϱ, and around 0·03 to 0·04 for the constant term c_1.[6] The result reported by Houthakker (1965, p. 218, equation (7)) is

$$\text{(2a)} \qquad \frac{S_{\text{pers}}}{Y_{\text{pd}}} = \underset{(0{\cdot}012)}{0{\cdot}020} + \underset{(0{\cdot}28)}{1{\cdot}36}\Delta^* Y_{\text{pd}}.$$

(The figure in parentheses underneath each coefficient is the standard error of the coefficient.) The coefficient of the rate of growth term is highly significant as indicated by a t-ratio of nearly 5, and what matters most, both this coefficient and the constant term agree rather well with the values implied by the hypothesis. The results reported by Houthakker for equation (1) are equally suggestive even though the variables used here are further removed from those called for by the model. A rough idea of the value of the coefficients of this equation implied by the model can be obtained by observing that the rate of growth of total income $\Delta^* Y_{\text{pd}}$, can be approximated as the sum of per capita income and population growth. Substituting this approximation in (2) and multiplying through by Y_{pd} we find

$$(S_{\text{pers}})_i = c_1(Y_{\text{pd}})_i + c_2\left[\frac{(\Delta Y_{\text{pd}})_i}{(Y_{\text{pd}})_i} + \left(\frac{\Delta P}{P}\right)_i\right](Y_{\text{pd}})_i$$

$$= c_1(Y_{\text{pd}})_i + c_2(\Delta Y_{\text{pd}})_i + c_2\left(\frac{\Delta P}{P}\right)_i(Y_{\text{pd}})_i.$$

This equation differs from equation (1) on account of the last term, which

[6] In the case of c_1 the estimate should presumably be reduced somewhat further because, as noted, $s(\bar{\varrho})$ is likely to overstate $\bar{s}$.

is omitted in Houthakker's test, and because of the absence of the constant term. We can conclude, therefore, that provided the omitted variable is not markedly correlated with the remaining two, our model would lead us to expect the following approximate relation between the parameters of (1) and (2)

$$b_1 \simeq c_1, \qquad b_2 \simeq c_2, \qquad b_0 \simeq 0.$$

The relation $b_0 \simeq 0$ deserves particular note for it expresses in operational form the independence of the saving *ratio* from the *level* of per capita income, implied by the model. According to the traditional view, instead the saving function should have a substantial negative intercept, i.e., $b_0 < 0$, implying that the saving ratio is an increasing function of per capita income.

A simple correlation of per capita income and per capita saving yields (Houthakker, 1965, p. 215, equation (1))

$$S_{\text{pers}} = \underset{(2\cdot3)}{-1\cdot1} + \underset{(0\cdot011)}{0\cdot081}\, Y_{\text{pd}}. \tag{1a}$$

It is apparent that the constant term is negligibly small and insignificant, as predicted by the hypothesis and contrary to prevailing views.[7]

Addition of the variable ΔY_{pd} leads to (Houthakker, 1965, p. 218, equation (5))

$$S'_{\text{pers}} = \underset{(1\cdot6)}{-1\cdot0} + \underset{(0\cdot010)}{0\cdot040}\, Y_{\text{pd}} + \underset{(0\cdot28)}{1\cdot59}\, \Delta Y_{\text{pd}}. \tag{1b}$$

Once more, the contribution of the rate of growth variable is highly significant and the values of the coefficients are rather close to those implied by the model.[8]

3. *Replication of the Basic Test for Private Saving*

The major shortcoming of Houthakker's tests for our purposes is that they are based on a definition of income and especially saving, which differs appreciably from that called for by our model. While it does not seem feasible at present to estimate saving in the form of net additions to durables for any significant number of countries, there is no serious difficulty in obtaining

[7] The independence of the saving ratio from per capita income is also confirmed by the logarithmic regression (*ibid.*, page 216, equation (3)),

$$\log C_{\text{pers}} = \underset{(0\cdot021)}{-0\cdot035} + \underset{(0\cdot0076)}{1\cdot004} \log Y_{\text{pd}},$$

where C_{pers} is per capita consumption, which shows that the elasticity of consumption with respect to income is remarkably close to unity.

[8] Houthakker's comment [1965, p. 218] that the 'large coefficient' of the growth term in (lb) and (2a) is 'disturbing' is very hard to understand and seems to be based on heuristic considerations which fail to take into account the dimension of the variable ΔY_{pd} namely, $\$/(\text{year})^2$ rather than \$/year, as his comment seems to imply.

estimates of private income and of private saving excluding durables. Indeed, relying on the U.N. *Yearbook* and on auxiliary data generously provided by Houthakker, we have found it possible to estimate these variables for 36 countries including all but three of the 28 countries in Houthakker's sample.[9] We have also included in our averages the year 1960, whenever available. In estimating the regression equations reported below, the observations for each country were weighted following the procedure recommended by Houthakker. Since in our tests the dependent variable is always the saving ratio, application of Houthakker's procedure leads to a weight equal to the product of average population times the number of years included in the country's average. This weight is shown in the Data Appendix (Column 4).

We may begin by testing whether the enlarged sample provides any support for the conventional view, rejected by our model, that the proportion of income saved tends to be an increasing function of, and can be largely explained by, per capita income. To this end we could replicate test (1a), and check whether the constant term is significantly negative. Since hereafter we intend to focus on the behaviour of the saving ratio, S/Y, or, more precisely, of the percentage of income saved, $s = 100(S/Y)$, it is convenient to rely on a simple variant of the above test obtained by dividing both sides of the equation by per capita income. We thus obtain the test equation

$$s = 100(S/Y) = 100(S'/Y') = 100(b_0/Y' + b_1) = b_0(100/Y') + (100b_1), \tag{8}$$

where primed symbols denote per capita values. The empirical result is

$$s = \underset{(2\cdot4)}{-2\cdot6}\,\frac{100}{Y'} + 12\cdot1 \qquad (r = -0\cdot18). \tag{8a}$$

It confirms that b_0, though negative, is negligible and that variations in per capita income account, at best, for a negligible proportion of the variation in the saving ratio.

Our next step is to add to the test equation (8a) the variable ϱ, i.e., to estimate the parameters of

$$s = c_0\left(\frac{100}{Y'}\right) + c_1 + c_2\varrho, \tag{9}$$

[9] The three countries we lose are Ghana, Mauritius, and Sweden. The loss of Sweden is especially regrettable and results from the fact that the available data yield an estimate of gross but not net private saving.

For those countries for which both estimates of personal saving and of corporate saving are available, private saving was defined as the sum of these two flows, while private income was defined as Houthakker's personal income plus corporate saving. For the remaining countries private income was derived from national income by subtracting all personal and corporate income taxes and adding transfers. Private saving was then obtained by subtracting consumption expenditure from private income.

where ϱ is an estimate of the rate of growth of income (expressed as per cent per year). This estimate was computed from the formula

$$\varrho_i = \{[(Y_t)_i/(Y_0)_i]^{1/(n_i - 1)} - 1\}\,100,$$

where $(Y_0)_i$ and $(Y_t)_i$ denote, respectively, real private income in the initial and terminal year, and n_i is the number of years available for country i.

According to our model in (9), c_0 should still be zero while rough *a priori* estimates of c_1 and c_2 can again be obtained from formula (6), but using for ϱ the value of 0·047, which is the mean for our sample. This yields for c_2 a value of 1·8 and for c_1 a value of 100 × (0·085) or 8·5. Both values, however, should again be reduced by some 10 to 20 per cent to allow for the fact that saving does not include the addition to the stock of durables.

A least squares estimate of the parameters of (9) yields

$$\text{(9a)} \qquad s = \underset{(1\cdot7)}{-2\cdot6}\,\frac{100}{Y'} + \underset{(1\cdot4)}{5\cdot4} + \underset{(0\cdot25)}{1\cdot42}\varrho \qquad (R = 0\cdot69;\ S_e = 3\cdot53).$$

Thus, (i) the coefficient c_0 remains very close to 0 (though it is statistically somewhat more significant than in (8a)), confirming the approximate independence of the saving ratio from per capita income; (ii) the variable ϱ is highly significant; (iii) the point estimate of c_2 and c_1 are quite close to the values suggested by the model. For later reference, dropping the barely significant income variable yields

$$\text{(9b)} \qquad s = \underset{(1\cdot3)}{4\cdot5} + \underset{(0\cdot25)}{1\cdot42}\varrho \qquad (r = 0\cdot67;\ S_e = 3\cdot59).$$

4. *The Identification Problem: The Interaction between Saving, Investment, and the Growth Rate*

While the above results seem to provide strong support for the life cycle model it must be acknowledged that they are open to an entirely different interpretation. Specifically, the rate of saving could be determined by some mechanism entirely different from the one we postulate and the strong association between the rate of saving and the rate of growth could result from the dependence of the rate of growth on the rate of investment $i = I/Y$ and the identity of saving and investment. Indeed, assuming a reasonably stable 'capital requirement', C_r (cf. Harrod, 1948, p. 82), ϱ is related to i by the well-known formula

$$\text{(10)} \qquad \varrho = \frac{i}{C_r}$$

which is commonly stated in the form $\varrho = s/C_r$ by relying on the identity of saving and investment. (A third possible interpretation for the association between s and ϱ provided by the Kaldorian model, according to which growth determines investment which determines saving through the share of profit, will be considered briefly in 6 (iii) below.)

It must be immediately acknowledged that the empirical evidence appears to provide rather good support for hypothesis (10). Estimates of the rate of investment I, which we may identify with domestic capital formation, are available for all 36 countries in our sample and from these we can readily compute the investment ratio i. Correlation of ϱ with i yields the regression equation

$$\varrho = \underset{(0\cdot 72)}{0\cdot 52} + \underset{(0\cdot 042)}{0\cdot 265i} \qquad (r = 0\cdot 73). \tag{10a}$$

The implied capital requirement, just below 4, may be somewhat on the high side, but not unrealistically so. But the interpretation of this empirical result is open to the very same question that applies to (9b): it could be the indirect outcome of the relation between s and ϱ hypothesized by the life cycle model.

It is readily apparent that *if* s were the same as i, it would be impossible to answer the question: does ϱ cause s or does i cause ϱ, or, quite conceivably, are both mechanisms simultaneously at work? At least from the kind of data under consideration, the parameters of equations (9b) and (10) could not be 'identified'. Fortunately, the rate of domestic capital formation I is not identical with S. It differs by two major components, to wit, the net foreign deficit on current account, or net capital imports, and government surplus on current account, or excess of government capital formation over government borrowing. Denote the difference between I and S by N, and let $n = N/Y$, implying

$$i = s + n. \tag{11}$$

It will be seen from the Data Appendix that the 'wedge' n between s and i is by no means negligible for our sample; its mean value, 4·5 per cent, is about 40 per cent as large as mean s, and, what is even more important, its variability is considerable, the standard deviation being about 70 per cent as large as that of s. This substantial discrepancy between s and i can be exploited to untangle the causal mechanism underlying the observed association between ϱ on the one hand and s and i on the other.

To this end, let us use (11) to eliminate i from (10) and rewrite that equation in the general form

$$\varrho = g_1 + g_2(s + n) + v. \tag{12}$$

Taking also into account the relation postulated by the life cycle model

$$s = c_1 + c_2\varrho + u \tag{13}$$

we have a system of two simultaneous equations in the two endogenous variables s and ϱ and the exogenous variable n.[10] Solving this system for s and ϱ in terms of n yields the 'reduced form' equations[11]

$$s = \frac{c_1 + c_2 g_1}{\Delta} + \frac{c_2 g_2}{\Delta} n + \frac{u + c_2 v}{\Delta} \tag{14}$$

$$\varrho = \frac{g_1 + g_2 c_1}{\Delta} + \frac{g_2}{\Delta} n + \frac{v + g_2 u}{\Delta} \tag{15}$$

$$\Delta = 1 - c_2 g_2.$$

From these reduced forms one can obtain unbiased estimates of the 'structural' coefficients of equations (12) and (13), provided one is willing to assume that the variable n can be regarded as exogenous to the system in the sense of being uncorrelated with the error terms u and v. This is because the coefficients of the system (12), (13) turn out to be just identified, though these equations contain but one exogenous variable, n. Identification is ensured by the fact that n does not appear in (13) and that the coefficients of n and s must be the same in (12). Accordingly, a least squares estimate of (14) and (15) yields four coefficients from which we can estimate uniquely the four structural coefficients g_1, g_2, c_1, c_2.

The coefficients of the reduced forms are

$$s = 9{\cdot}2 + 0{\cdot}44n$$

$$\varrho = 3{\cdot}2 + 0{\cdot}33n,$$

which imply the following structural estimates of (12) and (13)

$$s = 4{\cdot}9 + 1{\cdot}35\varrho \tag{13a}$$

$$\varrho = 1{\cdot}1 + 0{\cdot}23i. \tag{12a}$$

Comparison with (9b) and (10a) shows that in the present instance the structural estimates do not differ appreciably from those obtained by direct least square. In particular, the estimate of c_2, 1·35, remains broadly consistent with the *a priori* estimate given in the last section.

It may be argued that because of the conceptual and statistical problems involved in obtaining a meaningful estimate of depreciation (D), equation (10) should be stated in terms of gross capital formation $I_g = I + D$. Under this formulation, i should be replaced everywhere by $i_g = (I + D)/Y = i + d$,

[10] We rely here on this system as a device to check for possible gross biases in least square estimates of coefficients such as those of equations (2a) and (9b). This does not mean, however, that we regard the assumption underlying (12) that the (marginal) capital coefficient is a given constant and roughly the same for all countries, as a valid one.

[11] In what follows, it will be taken for granted that Δ is positive (which is also supported by the empirical estimates). A negative value of Δ would imply that the solution to the system (12) to (13) for given n corresponds to a dynamically unstable equilibrium.

and n by $n_g = n + d$. It is apparent that with this substitution, the equations (12), (13) still form a system whose four parameters are just identified, if n_g is taken as exogenous, and can be estimated from reduced forms obtained by regressing s and ϱ respectively on n_g. The alternative structural estimates obtained in this way are[12]

$$(13b) \qquad s = 2{\cdot}5 + 1{\cdot}83\varrho$$

$$(12b) \qquad \varrho = 0{\cdot}33 + 0{\cdot}163 i_g.$$

These results, on the whole, confirm and support our earlier ones. In particular, the two alternative structural estimates of c_2 (1·35 and 1·83) are seen to bracket narrowly the range of *a priori* estimates.

5. *Refinements of the Basic Hypothesis: Productivity Growth, Population Growth and Age Structure*

In our tests so far we have been focusing on the effects of the overall rate of growth of income, on the presumption that the two sources of income growth, productivity growth and growth in labour force, were likely to have a similar quantitative effect on the saving ratio. This conjecture, however, deserves explicit testing, especially since the mechanism through which the two sources of growth affect saving is really quite different.

A straightforward test consists of breaking up ϱ into its two components, growth in productivity or output per person employed, y, and growth in employment, p, and regressing s on p and y separately. If our conjecture is valid, the partial regression coefficient of the two variables should be roughly equal.

Unfortunately, there are serious difficulties in carrying out the test, since periodic estimates of employment are not available for a substantial proportion of the countries in our sample. The closest alternative might be to approximate p by the growth of population of working age and y by $\varrho - p$. Even this approximation presents problems, as it requires information on the age distribution of population for at least two years reasonably close to the beginning and end of the period covered by the national income estimates. This information could be secured only for 24 of the 36 countries, as shown in the Data Appendix. For these countries, p was measured as the growth of population aged 20 to 65, which we shall label hereafter as 'working age population', and y was computed as $\varrho - p$. The only information that could be secured for the entire sample was an estimate of growth in total population

[12] The direct least square estimate of equation (12b) is:

$$\varrho = \underset{(1{\cdot}1)}{-1{\cdot}0} + \underset{(0{\cdot}038)}{0{\cdot}210} i_g \qquad (r = 0{\cdot}68)$$

(United Nations *Demographic Yearbook*), denoted by p', and hence of growth in income per capita $y' = \varrho - p'$.

It might appear that p and p' ought to be close to each other and excellent proxies for the growth in the labour force. This would actually be the case if population were in 'balanced growth', by which we mean that the number of persons born in each successive age cohort grows at a constant rate and that age specific mortality is constant; indeed, in this situation p and p' would be identical and could not differ significantly from growth in the labour force, since labour force participation is unlikely to change appreciably in the span of a few years. In fact, this close association between alternative measures of growth cannot be counted upon for our sample in view of the sudden post war spurt in the birth rate in many countries and the simultaneous decline in other countries which were previously growing rapidly. As a matter of fact, for the 24 countries for which we were able to compute both p and p', the correlation between the two measures turns out to be only 0·47. Under these circumstances, the best that can be done is to regress s on y' and p' for the entire sample and check the results by using instead y and p for the subsample of 24 countries for which the information is available—denoted hereafter as 'sample p'.

The results obtained are set forth in Table 2, rows (a) to (e). It is apparent that they fail to provide any support for the hypothesis. Although the effect of per capita income growth on saving is confirmed, there is no evidence that population, whether measured by p or p', plays a similar role; indeed, its coefficient is consistently negative, though hardly significant.

There are, however, ample grounds for holding that this test does not do justice to the model. For, according to the model, the saving ratio does not depend on population growth *per se*, but rather on the relative frequency of active and retired households. The association between s and p was deduced from the fact that, under balanced growth, that relative frequency will be a well-defined function of p. But, as we have seen, for many countries in our sample population growth departed widely from a balanced pattern, and under these conditions p can no longer be supposed a good proxy for the relevant age composition. This point can be clarified with the help of a very simple model (cf. Modigliani and Audo, 1957), which will also prove useful in suggesting an alternative, more relevant test.

Denote by w and r, respectively, the expected number of working and retired years for a person at the beginning of his active span, and let ω denote the ratio r/w. Clearly, ω can be taken as a parameter reflecting prevailing practices affecting the customary working span and mortality experience. Similarly, denote c_w and c_r the planned (and realized) rate of average annual consumption during the working and retirement span, and let $\chi = c_r/c_w$. Finally, let e denote the average rate of earnings from labour during the working span. Since for present purposes, we can abstract from productivity

TABLE 2

Tests of the Effect of Different Sources of Income Growth on the Rate of Saving (s)[a]

Equation Number	Sample	Coefficient of y'	y	p'	p	R/W	M/W	$\frac{100}{Y'}$	Constant Term	$\bar{R}$	S_e
(1)	(2)	(3)	(4)	(5)	(6)	(7)	(8)	(9)	(10)	(11)	(12)
(a)	A	1·34							7·0	0·73	3·31
		(0·20)							(0·8)		
(b)	A	1·24		−0·67					8·4	0·73	3·32
		(0·25)		(0·87)					(2·0)		
(c)	p		1·90						4·3	0·83	2·68
			(0·26)						(1·2)		
(d)	p	1·33		−0·98					8·4	0·83	2·65
		(0·23)		(0·85)					(1·8)		
(e)	p		1·98		−0·60				4·6	0·82	2·71
			(0·29)		(0·81)				(1·3)		
(f)	A	1·15				−45	−12·7		23·1	0·81	2·88
		(0·19)				(16)	(3·6)		(4·9)		
(g)	p	1·03				−78	−18·9		32·9	0·88	2·24
		(0·23)				(30)	(5·8)		(9·0)		
(h)	p		1·31			−88	−20·0		33·7	0·89	2·16
			(0·28)			(28)	(5·4)		(8·5)		
(i)	A	1·10				−101	−15·4	−8·0	35·4	0·84	2·68
		(0·17)				(25)	(3·4)	(2·8)	(6·2)		
(j)	p		1·51			−96	−16·3	−6·0	32·9	0·90	2·09
			(0·29)			(27)	(5·7)	(3·9)	(8·2)		
(k)	A	(1·06)				−102	−15·7	−8·1	35·9		2·70
	TLS	(0·22)				(25)	(3·5)	(2·9)	(6·4)		
(l)	p		1·86			−78	−11·7	−8·2	26·0		2·22
	TLS		(0·80)			(45)	(11·3)	(5·8)	(16·0)		

[a] The dependent variable is s. For sample A, including 36 countries, s has a mean of 11·2 and standard deviation 4·87. For sample p, which includes 24 countries, the mean is 12·0 and the standard deviation 4·69.

growth, we can take c_w, c_r, and e as constant over time. We will also assume a zero rate of return, as this greatly simplifies the exposition while the implications would not be significantly affected if we allowed for a positive rate (as long as it were also constant in time).[13] Then, we is aggregate lifetime earning and, in the absence of bequests, the value of c_w can be inferred from the lifetime budget equation

$$we = wc_w + rc_r = c_w[w + r\chi],$$

which implies

$$c_w = \frac{we}{w + r\chi} = \frac{e}{1 + \omega\chi}. \tag{16}$$

Now, let W and R denote, respectively, the number of persons of working and retired age present in a given year. Then (assuming that income and

[13] See footnote 14, below.

consumption are not significantly correlated linearly with age within the active and the retired span), aggregate consumption and income can be approximated by

$$C = Wc_w + Rc_r = c_w(W + \chi R)$$
$$Y = We.$$

These relations, together with (16) imply

$$\frac{C}{Y} = \frac{c_w}{e}\left(1 + \chi\frac{R}{W}\right) = \frac{1 + \chi\,(R/W)}{1 + \omega\chi},$$

or

$$\frac{S}{Y} = 1 - \frac{C}{Y} = \frac{\omega\chi}{1 + \omega\chi} - \frac{\chi}{1 + \omega\chi}\left(\frac{R}{W}\right) \tag{17}$$

i.e., the saving ratio is a *linear* function of the ratio of retired to working age population with parameters depending on tastes (χ) and mortality experience and working span (ω).[14]

If population is in balanced growth, then there will be a one–one relation between R/W and the rate of population growth p, say $R/W = \Omega(p)$. Hence, the saving ratio s is itself a well-defined function of p,

$$s = 100\left[\frac{\chi\omega}{1 + \chi\omega} - \frac{\chi}{1 + \chi\omega}\,\Omega(p)\right] = s(p), \tag{18}$$

with the properties: (i) $s(0) = 0$ (since Ω (0) is precisely ω, reflecting the fact that, with a stationary population, the ratio R/W is the same as the ratio of retired to active men years for any given age cohort); (ii) $s'(p) > 0$ (since clearly $\Omega'(p) < 0$).[15]

[14] As indicated earlier, a similar conclusion holds if we allow for a non-zero rate of return on assets, as long as this rate, say i, is itself constant in time. The constant term and the coefficient of R/W in (17) will be functions of i in addition to χ, r, and w.

[15] Equation (18) was used to compute the relation between s and p reported in Modigliani (1966, Table 1, column (2)). For that computation, χ was taken as unity and it was assumed that every person had a life span of exactly 50 years, 40 in the labour force and 10 after retirement. To check whether the resulting relation between s and p would be significantly changed by more realistic assumptions about mortality, we computed the value of R/W for different values of p (the annual rate of growth in the number born) by relying on the Italian mortality experience of the early fifties (*Annuario Statistico Italiano*, 1961) with W defined as population aged 20 to 65 and R as population over 65. Substituting these values of R/W in (17) (and still assuming $\chi = 1$) one obtains the values of s reported below. For later references we also show the value of M/W where M is defined as population below age 20.

Rate of growth, p	R/W	s	M/W
%	%	%	%
0·0	23·7	0·0	48·0
1·0	17·2	5·7	66·0
2·0	12·2	9·7	89·0
3·0	8·6	12·6	118·0
4·0	6·0	14·7	155·0

[*continued opposite.*

But if, as in the case of our sample, population growth is prevailingly far from balanced, equation (18) or a linear approximation thereof cannot be expected to hold, since when such is the case p need not bear any stable relation to the relevant variable R/W. Equation (17) suggests that under these conditions p should be replaced by R/W and that according to the life cycle model, s should be a decreasing linear function of this variable.

As already noted, explicit estimates of active and retired population are not available for most countries. Accordingly, we shall approximate the variable R with population aged over 65 and W with population aged 20 to 65. Ideally, for each country we would want the mean value of R/W for the years used in computing the other averages. Since information is generally not available on a yearly basis, we have used for the 24 countries in sample p the mean value of R/W in the two years used to compute p. For the remaining countries we have to rely on a single year, choosing the one closest to the middle of the period. Since the age structure can be expected to change but slowly, this approximation should be adequate.

Some rough notion of the order of magnitude of the coefficient of R/W implied by the model can be inferred from (17). For ω a reasonable guess might be between 1/4 and 1/5 (cf. footnote 15 above). The value of χ is much harder to guess, but a casual perusal of survey data would suggest that 0·5 and 1·0 constitute safe outside limits, at least for the United States. Substituting these values in the coefficients of (17) yields an estimate of the slope between 45 and 80, the corresponding values of the constant term being 10 and 20 (in the absence of *productivity* growth).

Before we proceed to an empirical test, we need to pay some attention to the possible role of the third component of the population, namely, the portion which has not yet reached working age (operationally defined as age 20). Since this group, denoted hereafter by M (for minors!), contributes to consumption without contributing to income, one would conjecture that the saving ratio might be negatively associated with the size of M in relation to W. This conjecture can be checked by a straightforward generalization of the approach used in establishing the effect of retired population. That is, denote by m the average number of 'minor' years attached to a household over its life cycle, and let $\mu = m/w$; similarly, let χ_m denote the average yearly rate of consumption expenditure per minor relative to the rate of expenditure per active adult. Then by a repetition of the reasoning leading

The value of ω in (17) was taken as 0·24, which is the value of R/W corresponding to a stationary population.

The relation between s and p exhibited above is again quite close to that obtained neglecting the force of mortality, though it moves closer to that reported in footnote 3, based on equation (5) and the U.S. estimates of σ and δ. One can also readily verify that varying the assumed value of χ within reasonable limits, say between one-half and unity, would still lead to results broadly similar to those reported above and in Table 1 of Modigliani (1966).

up to (17) we arrive at the following generalization of that equation

$$(19) \quad \frac{S}{Y} = \frac{\omega\chi + \mu\chi_m}{1 + \omega\chi + \mu\chi_m} - \frac{\chi_m}{1 + \omega\chi + \mu\chi_m}\frac{M}{W} - \frac{\chi}{1 + \omega\chi + \mu\chi_m}\frac{R}{W}.$$

Under balanced growth M/W will again be uniquely related to p, and therefore s remains a well-defined function of p. Of course, M/W in contrast to R/W should tend to rise with p (as is confirmed by figures reported in footnote 15 above) and this will tend to affect adversely the saving ratio. Still, (19) suggests that, for reasonable guesses about χ_m and χ, s will rise with p and at a decreasing rate.

In the absence of balanced growth (19) suggests that (i) p should be replaced by two measures of age structure, R/W and M/W; (ii) s should be a decreasing function of both variables; (iii) the coefficient of R/W should be somewhat smaller than what was inferred earlier from (17) because of the additional term χ_m in the denominator; and (iv) since χ_m is likely to be less than χ, one might expect the coefficient of M/W to be smaller (in absolute value) than that of R/W.[16]

The empirical results are summarized in rows (f), (g), and (h) of Table 2. It is seen that the variables R/W and M/W contribute substantially to the explanation of s; for the entire sample the correlation rises to 0·81 as compared with a value of 0·67 when using as a single explanatory variable the overall rate of growth, ϱ. Also, the estimated coefficients agree rather well with the implications of the model derived above.[17] Finally comparison of row g and h suggests that the theoretically more relevant measure of income growth, y, performs somewhat better than y' as its coefficient is more in line with *a priori* estimates and the correlation is a little higher, though not significantly. The only mildly surprising results in this battery are those reported in rows (i) and (j), in which we test once more the effect of per capita income. The reliability of this result will be taken up in the next section.

The estimates presented in rows (a) to (j), are based on direct least squares, a procedure that might yield biased estimates in view of the simultaneous presence of a second relation between the growth rate and saving by way of investment, noted in section 4. These estimates were therefore recomputed by an alternative two-stage procedure which takes account of this second relation. These results were found to agree sufficiently closely with those shown in the table, so that they are not worth reporting separately. Just for the sake of

[16] This conclusion is reinforced by the consideration that μ in contrast to ω cannot be taken as a constant but must instead be positively associated with M/W. Under these conditions, the coefficient of M/W obtained by least square will be smaller (and that of R/W larger) than might be inferred from (18) by assigning to μ the mean value for the sample.

[17] Note that the constant term cannot be directly identified with that of (19), since it includes effects of productivity growth assumed absent in deriving that equation.

illustration we exhibit in rows (k) and (l) the alternative estimates obtained for the most inclusive equations, (i) and (j).[18]

6. *Some Further Tests*

(i) *The Role of Differences in Socio-Economic Structure and Possible Biases Resulting Therefrom*

In the test described so far, we have used every country for which the required information could be obtained from the above-mentioned sources. While this procedure has the advantage of being objective and maximizing sample size, it has the drawback of lumping together countries differing radically in terms of socio-economic structure and stage of economic development. Now the life cycle model does not purport to represent a universal theory of individual and aggregate saving formation and wealth holding, but is instead basically designed to apply to private capitalistic economies in which at least the bulk of income, consumption, and accumulation transactions occur through markets. Furthermore, even for economies satisfying this requirement, significant differences in economic structure might be associated with differences in such factors as tastes, life cycle profiles of earnings, and family structure, which, in turn, affect the parameters of the long run saving function.

Even at a very superficial level of analysis the countries in our sample can be classified into at least four major groups, namely, (1) Western and/or industrialized (W), (2) Latin American (L), (3) Far Eastern (E) and (4) Colonial African (C). The group to which a given country has been classified is shown by the letter entered in column (3) of the Data Appendix. In the first group we have included the 19 countries of Western culture outside Central and South America, plus Japan and, with some questions, South Africa; this is the largest group numerically and accounts for almost four-fifths of the total weight under the weighting scheme discussed in section 3. The second group consists of ten Central and South American countries and accounts for some 11 per cent of the weight. The third includes China (Taiwan), Korea, and the Philippines, with 7½ per cent of the weight. The remaining two countries, Congo and Rhodesia, with some 3 per cent of the weight, are combined in the last group.

It is apparent from the information summarized in Table 3 that the differences in cultural and socio-economic characteristics are accompanied by

[18] To derive the alternative estimates we started from the two simultaneous relations:

$$s = c_1 + c_2 y + c_3(100/Y') + c_4(R/W) + c_5(M/W) + u$$

$$y = g_1 + g_2(n_g + s) + g_3 p + v$$

in the jointly dependent variables s and y (for sample A, y and p were replaced by y' and p'). Accordingly, the instrumental variables used in the first stage were: R/W, M/W, $100/Y'$, $n_g = i_g - s$, p.

15—I.G.T.

TABLE 3

Means and Standard Deviations of Selected Variables for Four Groups of Countries

Variable	Statistic	Group W	L	E	C	All
Saving Ratio (s)	Mean (%)	12·5	7·1	3·3	13·2	11·2
	std. dev.	4·1	4·3	*	*	4·9
Growth Rate (ϱ)	Mean (%)	5·1	3·2	4·8	2·5	4·7
	std. dev.	2·5	1·1	*	*	2·4
Productivity Growth Rate (y)	Mean (%)	3·8	0·8	1·7	0·1	3·2
	std. dev.	2·7	1·0	*	*	2·7
Population Growth Rate (p)	Mean (%)	1·2	2·4	2·9	2·4	1·5
	std. dev.	0·56	0·55	*	*	0·6
Ratio of Retired to Working Population (R/W)	Mean (%)	15·6	6·1	4·7	4·0	13·4
	std. dev.	3·3	1·3	*	*	5·2
Ratio of Minors to Working Population (M/W)	Mean (%)	64	116	126	57	75
	std. dev.	10·7	7·8	*	*	24·2
Per Capita Income (Y)	Mean (U.S. $)	970	156	108	83	790
	std. dev.	200	42	*	*	360
Number of Countries		21	10	3	2	36
Relative Weight		78·5	11·4	7·3	2·8	100·0

* Standard deviation was not computed when there were three or less observations.

equally wide differences in the mean values of most of the variables which are called for by our analysis.

These marked differences, together with the fact that, for most variables the within-group dispersion is distinctly smaller than the overall dispersion, imply that our observations tend to fall into more or less tight clusters, a situation which may give rise to spurious correlations and seriously biased parameter estimates. It is conceivable, for instance, that the low rate of saving and per capita income growth prevailing for L and E countries as compared with the W group might be the result of certain cultural and socio-economic characteristics and not be casually related to each other through the mechanisms envisaged by our model. In this case the regression coefficient of equation (a) in Table 2 would be measuring the slope of the line joining the two clusters of points in the (s, y) plane rather than measuring the true effect of income growth on the saving ratio, an effect which might be totally non-existent. Similar doubt must be entertained about the other parameter estimates presented in Table 2.

A simple and yet fairly effective way of testing for the possible effect of this type of spuriousness consists of introducing into the various regression equations we have estimated in the last section dummy variables, taking the value 1 if the country belongs to a given group and 0 otherwise. In view of the fact that the E group contains but three countries and the C group but two, we have felt it advisable to apply this method to the 31-country subsample consisting of 21 W countries and 10 L countries. In this case, one needs a single dummy variable, say D, taking the value 0 if the country belongs to the W group and the value 1 if it belongs to the L group. To illustrate the method, suppose we retest equation (a) of Table 2 by fitting

$$s = b_0 + b_1 y + b_2 D.$$

Then the regression coefficient b_1 will provide an estimate of the relation between s and y uncontaminated by possible clusters effect. It measures, in effect, the average relation existing *within* the two clusters, while the dummy variable takes care of any differences between the mean values of s in the two clusters, say $\bar{s}_1 - \bar{s}_2$, which cannot be explained by the within-clusters slope, i.e., by $b_1 (\bar{y}_1 - \bar{y}_2)$.

The salient results of this test are summarized in Table 4. From rows (a) and (b) we can infer that the relation between the rate of saving and the rate of growth is not significantly contaminated by cluster effects. However, a re-estimation of the most inclusive hypothesis represented by equations (i) and (j) of Table 2, produces some rather striking results. Row (c) shows that merely dropping the five countries of the E and C groups results in a coefficient of M/W which is a good deal smaller and hardly significant. When the dummy variable is added in row (d) its coefficient is fairly large and significant, and while the coefficients of y' and R/W are only affected to a minor extent and remain within, or close to, the range of *a priori* estimates, the coefficient of the income variable becomes small and insignificant and that of M/W even has the wrong sign. Furthermore, the effect of income remains rather insignificant, even if we drop the variable M/W (row (e)). These results suggest that the effects of M/W and per capita income are unimportant (or else appreciably different) within each cluster of countries.

In an attempt to shed further light on this result we report in the remaining rows of Table 4 some estimates obtained when the test is repeated separately for each of the two groups of countries. Of particular interest are the results for the 21 W countries where the sample is more sizeable, the data probably more reliable, and the life cycle hypothesis is more clearly relevant.[19] The simple correlation between s and per capita income is substantial but in the

[19] For this sample the measure of income growth used is y rather than y'. An estimate of y is directly available for all but three of the 21 W countries. For the three remaining ones y was estimated by interpolation from a regression of y on y' computed for the remaining 18 countries. As a check the tests reported in row (f) to (i) were repeated using y' but in no case were the results appreciably different from those reported.

wrong direction! (row (f)). By contrast, the two principal variables suggested by the life cycle model have coefficients broadly consistent with the model and explain 80 per cent of the variance (cf. row (g)). (The remaining population variable M/W is consistently quite insignificant and with the wrong sign,

TABLE 4

Tests of the Effect of Country Type[a]

Equation Number	Sample	Coefficient of y'[b]	R/W	M/W	$100/Y'$	Dummy (D)	Constant Term	$\bar{R}$	S_e
(a)	31 W and L Countries	1·32					7·4	0·79	2·75
		(0·18)					(0·8)		
(b)	,,	1·25				−1·7	7·8	0·79	2·74
		(0·19)				(1·6)	(0·9)		
(c)	,,	1·29	−66·7	−5·4	−8·3		23·0	0·82	2·57
		(0·24)	(31·7)	(7·4)	(4·2)		(9·8)		
(d)	,,	1·11	−52·1	1·0	−3·8	−5·7	16·5	0·84	2·46
		(0·25)	(31·7)	(8·0)	(4·9)	(3·3)	(10·1)		
(e)	,,	1·10	−55·1		−3·8	−5·5	17·7	0·84	2·43
		(0·23)	(19·1)		(4·8)	(2·8)	(3·6)		
(f)	21 W Countries[b]				18·3		9·2	0·61	3·24
					(4·7)		(1·1)		
(g)	,,	1·39	−44·6				13·9	0·88	1·93
		(0·22)	(13·9)				(2·7)		
(h)	,,	1·44	−49·0		−1·8		14·7	0·88	1·98
		(0·27)	(18·3)		(4·8)		(3·5)		
(i)	,, TLS	1·78	−50·0		−5·3		13·9		2·12
		(0·65)	(19·0)		(7·6)		(3·7)		
(j)	10 L Countries				0·37		4·6	0	4·27
					(0·98)		(6·8)		
(k)	,,	1·45	−329				26·0	0·71	3·01
		(0·22)	(98)				(5·4)		
(l)	,,	1·29	−354		−6·2		31·8	0·69	3·07
		(1·26)	(104)		(7·1)		(8·7)		

[a] The dependent variable is s. For the 31 countries' sample its mean is 11·9 and its standard deviation 4·5. For 21 W countries the mean is 12·5 and the standard deviation is 4·1. For the 10 L countries the mean is 7·1 with a standard deviation of 4·3.

[b] For the tests reported in rows (f) to (i) the rate of growth of income was measured by y rather than y'. See footnote 19.

and has therefore been omitted.) Row (h) suggests that, given these variables, the net contribution of per capita income is nil. These inferences are broadly supported if the coefficients are re-estimated by a two stage procedure (row (i)) except for a somewhat higher estimate of the effect of per capita income.[20]

[20] Concern with the possibility that the results for the W countries might be swayed by one extreme observation, that of Japan—which has by far the largest saving ratio (21%) and per capita rate of growth (7·8%), the lowest R/W ratio (0·10) and the second lowest per capita income (after Portugal) led us to repeat the tests of rows (g) and (h) omitting Japan. The results seem to us on the whole to be reassuring, though not unmistakably so,

[*continued opposite*.

Finally, rows (j) to (l) indicate that similar results are obtained also for the sample of 10 L countries, except that the simple correlation between s and per capita income is essentially zero. This supporting evidence, however, is of limited value in view of the small size of the sample and the very limited variation of the key variables (cf. Table 3).

In summary, all the evidence supports both qualitatively and quantitatively the role of the two principal variables suggested by the life cycle model, productivity growth of income, and the age structure of the adult population. Furthermore, these variables appear to account for two-thirds to four-fifths of the inter-country variance in the saving ratio. There remains, instead, considerable doubt about the role of the proportion of 'youngs', suggested by the model, and of per capita income, which cannot be accounted for by the model. There is some prima facie evidence from Table 2 that these variables have some effect on the observed differences in s, but the more probing tests of Table 4 suggest that this effect may be spurious or at any rate considerably over-estimated.

(ii) *Test of Saving Concepts: Private, Personal and Corporate Saving*

In our tests the measure of saving utilized has been private saving—the sum of personal saving (S_p) and corporate saving (S_c). The reasons for focusing on this total have been clearly stated by Harrod (1948, Chapter 2). In short, the life cycle model endeavours to account for aggregate saving by focusing on the forces that lead individual households to accumulate and decumulate wealth over the life cycle. Now '. . . while the motive for this kind [i.e., corporate and business] saving is different, the result is that individuals . . . are provided with additional capital resources which may serve to meet their private needs as already classified. For this reason corporate saving may not be additional to personal saving, but part of it' (Harrod, 1948, p. 47). This implication of the life cycle model is in contrast with a widely held view that personal saving is unrelated to corporate

as is well illustrated by the following replication of the test of row (h)

$$s = \underset{(0{\cdot}33)}{1{\cdot}07y} - \underset{(21)}{30\,(R/W)} - \underset{(4{\cdot}5)}{2{\cdot}9\,(100/Y')} \qquad (\bar{R} = 0{\cdot}56;\ S_e = 1{\cdot}93).$$

The multiple correlation is a good deal lower and so are the t ratios for individual coefficients—but this result was to be expected in view of the appreciable reduction in the variance of both the dependent and the independent variables (*e.g.*, the variance of s is reduced from 16·8 to 5·4). On the other hand the point estimates of the coefficients are not drastically changed, the standard error of the residuals is very nearly the same, and, what is probably most significant, the above equation does help to explain the extremely high saving ratio of Japan. Indeed if we substitute the values of the independent variables for Japan in that equation we obtain a computed value of s of 17, which, though some two standard deviations below the actual value of 21, is still distinctly higher than for any other country in the sample. Furthermore the Life Cycle model may help to provide an explanation for the underestimate, as related to an abnormally depressed wealth-income ratio, as a consequence of the war experience (Cf. [Modigliani, 1961, p. 753]).

retention policies and therefore total private saving is the sum of two largely independent components. It seems, therefore, desirable, before concluding this investigation, to test which of these two rival views seems more nearly consistent with the empirical evidence, thereby also verifying the appropriateness of using the private saving ratio as the dependent variable throughout our analysis.

The most direct way of carrying out such a test is to examine whether, and to what extent, the private saving ratio $s = S_p/Y + S_c/Y$ is affected by variations in the corporate component, $S_c/Y = s_c$. If personal saving is unaffected by corporate retention, total private saving should tend to increase with corporate saving, and roughly by a dollar per dollar on the average. Thus the addition of s_c to the variables we have used so far should contribute significantly to the explanation of s and its regression coefficient should be close to unity.[21] On the other hand, if corporate saving is a close substitute for personal saving as implied by our model, the contribution of s_c should be insignificant and its coefficient should be close to zero.

Unfortunately, the above test cannot be carried out for our entire sample since estimates of corporate saving are available only for a sub-sample of 24 countries, basically Houthakker's original sample. This sub-sample consists of 14 of the 21 W countries (the seven countries lost including Germany and Italy and accounting for some one-fourth of the weight), eight of the ten L countries and the two C countries. In the interest of homogeneity, it seems advisable to discard the two C countries, which leaves a sample of 22 countries.

The results of our tests for this sub-sample are recorded in Table 5. A comparison of rows (a) and (b) shows that when s_c is added to the variables called for by the model, its coefficient is close to zero and totally insignificant. Equivalently the partial regression coefficient of corporate saving, s_c on the personal saving ratio is $-0{\cdot}8$, almost three times its standard error of $0{\cdot}3$, and not significantly different from the value of -1 implied by the model. This is a rather striking result considering also that, for most countries, private saving is estimated as the sum of personal and corporate saving and hence errors of measurement in corporate saving will tend to bias the result against our model. However, a comparison of rows (c) and (d) reveals that the addition of per capita income to the list of explanatory variables, though adding little to the explanation, has the effect of increasing a good deal the point estimate of the coefficient of s_c. Accordingly, the test of row (d) turns out to be somewhat of a draw. The contribution of s_c is quite small as implied by the model, and its coefficient is clearly much smaller than implied by the rival hypothesis. At the same time, it is distinctly larger than zero, and

[21] Because increased corporate saving will reduce personal income, the level of private saving will be increased not by one but by one minus the marginal propensity to save out of personal income (about 0·1).

in view of some reasonable doubts about the role of per capita income (and M/W) and of the large standard error, no clear-cut conclusion can be reached from our data. However, some further evidence in support of our hypothesis is provided by the last four rows of Table 5, which replicate the test for the more nearly homogeneous, though very thin, sample represented by the 14 W countries. It might be added that this hypothesis also receives some confirmation from other empirical studies. Particularly noteworthy in this connection are the results reported by Denison (1958) working with time series data for the United States, which suggest that total (gross) private saving is 'not affected by changes in the proportion of corporate profits paid out as dividends' (p. 264).

TABLE 5

Tests of Alternative Saving Concepts[a]

Equation Number	Coefficient of: y	R/W	M/W	$100/Y'$	s_c	Constant Term	$\bar{R}$	S_e
(1)	(2)	(3)	(4)	(5)	(6)	(7)	(8)	(9)
			A—22 Countries					
(a)	1·05	−85	−18·1			34	0·87	2·09
	(0·22)	(33)	(7·5)			(11)		
(b)	1·02	−77	−16·7		0·20	31	0·86	2·13
	(0·23)	(36)	(7·9)		(0·32)	(12)		
(c)	1·17	−88	−14·0	−4·6		32	0·87	2·09
	(0·25)	(34)	(8·5)	(4·5)		(11)		
(d)	1·19	−71	−7·8	−8·0	0·48	24	0·87	2·04
	(0·25)	(35)	(9·5)	(5·1)	(0·35)	(12)		
			B—14 W Countries					
(e)	1·42					7·4	0·90	1·68
	(0·18)					(0·8)		
(f)	1·33				0·23	6·8	0·88	1·80
	(0·23)				(0·34)	(1·2)		
(g)	1·05	−37			0·25	13·5	0·92	1·50
	(0·24)	(18)			(0·30)	(3·4)		
(h)	1·60	−47		−13	0·30	15·0	0·92	1·47
	(0·52)	(19)		(11)	(0·29)	(3·6)		

[a] The dependent variable is s. In part A of the table its mean is 7·8 and the standard deviation is 4·20. In part B the mean is 8·6 and the standard deviation is 3·82.

(iii) *Tests of the Effect of the Functional Distribution of Income*

We will conclude by reporting briefly on a battery of tests, admittedly rather crude, of one alternative hypothesis which has recently received a good deal of attention, according to which the proportion of income saved is related to, and explained by, the distribution of income as between profits (P) and labour income (L). This model, which provides the foundations for the well-known Kaldorian theory of income distribution (see e.g., Kaldor, 1960 (i), esp. essay 10, and 1960 (ii), esp. essay 13), rests on the proposition that the long-run, average propensity s_P to save out of profits P is substantially higher than the propensity s_L to save out of labour income, L. Thus

$$S = s_L L + s_P P, \qquad L + P = Y, \tag{20}$$

or, denoting by $\pi = P/Y$ the share of income going to profits,

$$S/Y = s_L + (s_P - s_L)\pi \qquad (s_P - s_L \gg 0), \tag{21}$$

i.e., the saving ratio is an increasing function of the share of profits.

This hypothesis is not necessarily unreconcilable with the life cycle model, unless it purports to be the sole or major explanation of saving behaviour. It is quite conceivable that, given income growth and age structure, the saving ratio might be somewhat affected by the distribution of income. This might occur in particular because persons engaged in entrepreneurial capacity might tend to have a more delayed pattern of life consumption (implying a life pattern of wealth holding relative to income higher than for other income receivers through all or most of the life cycle) and/or a higher propensity to leave bequests at any given level of income.[22] In other words, inter-country differences in the saving ratio could reflect in part differences in both s_L *and* s_P accounted for by the life cycle hypothesis, and, in part, differences in the distribution of income affecting savings, through differences *between* s_L and s_P.

There are, unfortunately, a number of serious problems in testing (21), among which is the fact that profits plus labour income do not exhaust income, unless profits is understood to embrace all property income, including interest and rents. Even if P be so interpreted, the only approximation to π that we can readily derive from our source of data is the ratio $Y_{nw}/(Y_w + Y_{nw})$ where Y_w denotes compensation of employees and Y_{nw} all other private income. This ratio differs from P/Y in two major respects: (1) Y_w and Y_{nw} are before taxes and transfers, as there is no way of allocating these between the two components; (2) Y_{nw} includes, in addition to all types of property income, the total earnings of the self-employed, a good portion of which cannot be considered as property income in the usual economic sense.

The discrepancy under (1) is hopefully not too serious since $Y_{nw}/(Y_w + Y_{nw})$ is likely to be, on the whole, a reasonably good proxy for the corresponding net of tax ratio. The difference under (2), however, could be a serious shortcoming *if* the hypothesis is interpreted literally to mean that income recipients save a larger fraction of income arising from property

[22] Evidence that persons engaged in entrepreneurial activity tend to save more at given levels of income has been reported in many studies, though much of the evidence is open to question since it may simply reflect the greater short run variability of measured income typically associated with entrepreneurship. However, these results have recently received some support from analysis relying on instrumental variable techniques such as Modigliani and Ando (1960).

than of income arising from labour services. For, if the proportion of labour income included in Y_{nw} varies appreciably between countries, then $Y_{nw}/(Y_w + Y_{nw})$ could be a poor proxy for P/Y. One might suppose, however, that differences in the propensity to save would be associated with whether the income recipient was engaged in an entrepreneurial activity (including risk bearing) rather than with whether the income received could be traced to the ownership of property or to the performance of labour services.[23] Under this interpretation the variable $Y_{nw}/(Y_w + Y_{nw})$ might well be a somewhat more relevant measure of the distribution of income than P/Y.

A breakdown of national income (less government income from property and entrepreneurship) between Y_w and Y_{nw} could be estimated for all but two countries of the W group (Portugal and South Africa) and one of the L group (Chile), leaving us with a sizeable sample of 33 countries. The results obtained for this sample are summarized in part A of Table 6. The constant term in column (2) can be interpreted as an estimate of $100s_L$, the propensity to save—expressed as a percentage—out of Y_w, the earnings of employees, while the coefficient of $Y_{nw}/(Y_w + Y_{nw})$, in column (3) is an estimate of $100(s_P - s_L)$, the differential propensity to save out of other income. According to the Kaldorian hypothesis this coefficient should be significantly positive. It is apparent that our data provide absolutely no support for the hypothesis

TABLE 6

Test of the Effect of the Functional Distribution of Income[a]

Equation Number	Constant Term	Coefficient of $\frac{Y_{nw}}{Y_w + Y_{nw}}$	y	ϱ	R/W	M/W	$100/Y'$	$\bar{R}$	S_e
(1)	(2)	(3)	(4)		(5)	(6)	(7)	(8)	(9)
				A—33 Countries					
(a)	12·1	−1·8						0·0	4·70
	(3·3)	(7·8)							
(b)	9·8	−7·0	1·37					0·77	3·00
	(2·1)	(5·0)	(0·20)						
(c)	28·5	−10·7	1·25		−60	−11·7		0·84	2·54
	(5·3)	(7·5)	(0·19)		(17)	(3·4)			
(d)	35·7	1·1	1·06		−101	−16·1	−7·8	0·87	2·35
	(5·8)	(8·5)	(0·23)		(23)	(3·7)	(3·2)		
				B—19 W Countries					
(e)	−0·4	35·2						0·67	3·00
	(3·2)	(8·4)							
(f)	4·2	4·2		1·35				0·88	1·91
	(2·2)	(8·1)		(0·26)					
(g)	14·7	−1·0	1·10		−38			0·91	1·77
	(4·0)	(8·0)	(0·25)		(15)				
(h)	15·0	1·3	1·21		−43		−4·3	0·91	1·76
	(4·1)	(9·3)	(0·32)		(18)		(8·0)		

[a] The dependent variable is s. In Part A, its mean value is 11·1 and the standard deviation 4·72. In Part B, the mean is 12·6, the standard deviation 4·05.

[23] Cf. footnote 22.

of systematic differences between the average propensity to save out of wage income and out of property and self-employment income. The simple correlation between s and our measure of π reported in row (a) is actually negative, though entirely negligible and rows (b) to (d) show that this coefficient remains equally negative and/or insignificant when we take into account the variables called for by our model.

We must, however, again face the possibility that this unfavourable outcome might be the spurious result of clusters, especially since the less developed countries of the L, E, and C groups which, as we know from Table 3, tend to have a lower saving ratio, also tend to have a large share of self-employed—partly reflecting the importance of the agricultural sector. Accordingly, in Part B of Table 6 we report results for the more nearly homogeneous sub-sample of the 19 W countries. It appears from row (e) that for this sub-sample the simple correlation of s with the non-wage share is positive, and in fact quite substantial (though the estimated coefficients do not make much sense!). However, as can be verified from rows (f) and (g), once we take into account the main variables suggested by our model—income growth, or per capita income growth and population age structure—the coefficient of π drops close to zero and becomes totally insignificant. This result holds whether or not we include per capita income, the other main variable suggested by the traditional view (cf. row (h)). There is, in short, no evidence that inter-country differences in the distribution of income between wage and non-wage income contribute to the explanation of differences in the saving ratio or, equivalently, no evidence of systematic differences in the average propensity to save out of these two sources of income.

Summing up, the outcome of this last battery of tests confirms our earlier results, whereas it provides no support for the hypothesis that the saving ratio is controlled or even significantly affected by the functional distribution of income. This negative verdict must, no doubt, be qualified first in recognition of the considerable margin or error to which our data are subject and because the measure of income distribution we have been forced to use may not be the most suitable one.[24]

[24] With all due regard to the above qualifications, the tests presented in Table 6 do serve as useful complements to the other tests reported in this paper because they help to come to grips with an identification problem analogous to that discussed in Section 4. It could be argued in fact that the strong association between the rate of saving and the rate of growth of income revealed by our tests is equally consistent with the Kaldorian model and hence is not an effective way of discriminating between that model and the life cycle model. However, the tests of Table 6 do help to make this discrimination. For the full sample of Part A the Kaldorian model is inconsistent with the simple correlation of row (a). But even in Part B, where the simple correlation is substantial, that model is not consistent with the results of rows (f) to (h). For in the Kaldorian model the rate of growth is supposed to affect the rate of saving *through the link of the profit share*. Thus, while s should be correlated both with π and ϱ, in a multiple regression of s on π *and* ϱ, as in row (f), the partial regression coefficient of π should be the same as the simple

[*continued opposite*.

DATA APPENDIX

Basic Data on Saving, Income Growth, and Demographic Characteristics

(1) Country	(2) Years	(3) Country Type	(4) Weight	(5) Y (\$)[1]	(6) s (%)[2]	(7) ϱ (%)[3]	(8) y' (%)[4]	(9) y (%)[5]	(10) p' (%)[6]	(11) p (%)[7]	(12) R/W[8]	(13) M/W[9]	(14) i_n (%)[10]	(15) i_g (%)[11]
1 Australia	54–60	W	67·5	977	13·20	2·68	0·42	1·14	2·25	1·52	0·15	0·66	26·42	37·61
2 Austria	52–60	W	63·0	432	12·11	5·85	5·55	6·11	0·29	−0·26	0·22	0·48	19·81	29·53
3 Belgium	54–59	W	53·8	909	13·60	2·22	1·58	2·14	0·63	0·08	0·20	0·48	17·38	27·94
4 Brazil	53–58	L	355·2	136	10·20	2·56	0·19	n.a.	2·37	n.a.	0·05	1·16	11·93	18·57
5 Canada	52–60	W	145·3	1,273	10·67	4·46	1·78	2·45	2·64	1·96	0·14	0·76	17·60	34·52
6 Chile	54–60	L	49·5	204	−1·64	1·93	0·14	n.a.	1·79	n.a.	0·08	0·96	4·16	14·61
7 China (Taiwan)	54–60	E	67·0	99	6·19	6·38	2·75	3·05	3·53	3·23	0·05	1·16	11·93	18·57
8 Colombia	54–60	L	92·7	208	6·09	3·66	1·72	n.a.	1·91	n.a.	0·07	1·20	11·87	23·30
9 Congo	52–59	C	102·0	65	13·47	1·49	−0·81	n.a.	2·32	n.a.	0·02	0·57	25·60	38·53
10 Costa Rica	53–60	L	8·1	262	7·10	4·42	−0·20	1·13	4·63	3·25	0·07	1·28	17·75	24·44
11 Denmark	54–59	W	31·4	719	8·28	5·92	5·26	5·58	0·63	0·32	0·18	0·59	12·99	23·29
12 Ecuador	52–60	L	34·4	138	6·28	5·69	2·39	n.a.	3·22	n.a.	0·08	1·19	13·41	19·41
13 France	54–60	W	309·2	893	9·10	4·53	3·53	3·97	0·97	0·54	0·21	0·54	14·45	26·67
14 Germany (West)	54–60	W	360·4	642	14·93	8·13	6·86	6·90	1·19	1·15	0·17	0·50	22·24	34·68
15 Greece	54–60	W	56·7	266	9·40	5·23	4·30	3·71	0·89	1·47	0·13	0·61	19·19	24·42
16 Honduras	51–58	L	13·1	166	7·76	4·69	1·48	n.a.	3·16	n.a.	0·09	1·12	11·65	17·84
17 Ireland	54–60	W	20·2	428	9·25	2·25	1·63	n.a.	0·61	n.a.	0·21	0·75	11·86	18·15
18 Italy	55–60	W	292·0	385	14·01	5·34	4·79	4·08	0·53	1·21	0·15	0·58	16·56	29·25
19 Jamaica	54–60	L	10·6	259	5·59	6·45	5·38	5·03	1·02	1·35	0·08	0·98	18·28	26·97
20 Japan	54–60	W	634·9	224	21·05	9·93	8·88	7·84	0·96	1·94	0·10	0·79	28·81	40·95
21 Korea (South)	54–60	E	159·5	83	3·59	2·99	0·90	n.a.	2·07	n.a.	0·02	1·18	8·32	13·69
22 Luxemburg	54–59	W	1·9	882	13·94	4·62	3·81	3·35	0·78	1·23	0·16	0·41	15·77	38·20
23 Malta	54–60	W	2·2	317	20·87	3·39	2·92	2·62	0·46	0·75	0·15	0·95	19·67	24·09
24 Netherlands	52–60	W	98·2	513	15·38	6·56	5·39	5·62	1·11	0·89	0·16	0·70	20·06	33·68
25 New Zealand	54–60	W	15·6	958	11·17	2·92	0·80	1·53	2·10	1·37	0·17	0·75	22·45	31·83
26 Norway	54–60	W	24·4	707	14·02	2·52	1·60	2·29	0·91	0·22	0·18	0·56	27·74	41·90
27 Panama	52–60	L	6·8	301	−2·08	5·41	2·45	3·20	2·89	2·14	0·07	1·19	8·97	16·19
28 Peru	54–59	L	59·0	103	−0·72	4·49	1·11	n.a.	3·34	n.a.	0·07	1·30	4·10	30·37
29 Philippines	54–60	E	177·4	135	1·52	4·86	1·63	2·04	3·18	2·59	0·07	1·37	5·12	10·89
30 Portugal	54–60	W	62·2	172	4·16	2·37	1·93	1·44	0·43	0·92	0·13	0·68	12·72	19·42
31 Rhodesia and Ny'd	54–60	C	54·1	116	12·47	4·58	2·00	n.a.	2·53	n.a.	0·08	0·67	28·62	37·64
32 South Africa	54–60	W	102·9	295	14·05	3·45	1·01	n.a.	2·43	n.a.	0·10	0·92	20·17	32·21
33 Spain	54–57	W	116·3	245	8·70	5·10	4·29	n.a.	0·78	n.a.	0·13	0·63	13·00	21·80
34 Trinidad	54–60	L	4·5	308	9·19	8·37	5·01	5·91	3·20	2·32	0·08	1·10	26·24	39·19
35 United Kingdom	54–60	W	360·5	820	11·03	3·32	2·80	3·18	0·51	0·14	0·20	0·49	11·78	22·35
36 United States	52–60	W	1,520·9	1,718	9·90	3·21	1·52	2·61	1·67	0·58	0·16	0·67	11·80	24·51

[1] Y: real per capita income. [2] s: private saving ratio.
[3] ϱ: rate of growth of income. [4] y': per capita income growth.
[5] y: 'productivity' growth. [6] p': population growth.
[7] p: rate of growth of 'working age' population (age 20 to 65).
[8] R/W: ratio of 'retired' to working age population.
[9] M/W: ratio of population below age 20 to working age population.
[10] i_n: ratio of domestic net capital formation to private income.
[11] i_g: ratio of domestic gross capital formation to private income.

It is conceivable that better data and/or a different measure of income shares would have led to different results. However, the presently available evidence does suggest that such variables are unlikely to supplant or even add significantly to the mechanism suggested by the life cycle model.

REFERENCES

ANDO, A. and MODIGLIANI, F., 'The Life Cycle Hypothesis of Saving: Aggregate Implications and Tests', *American Economic Review*, Vol. 53, May 1963, pp. 55–84, and Vol. 54, Part I, March 1964, pp. 111–13.

DENISON, E. F., 'A Note on Private Saving', *The Review of Economics and Statistics*, Vol. 50, No. 3, August 1958, pp. 261–7.

Flow of Funds/Savings Accounts, 1946–1960, Supplement 5, Board of Governors of the Federal Reserve System (Washington, 1961).

GOLDSMITH, R. W., *A Study of Saving in the United States* (Princeton University Press, Princeton, 1956).

——, *The National Wealth of the United States in the Postwar Period*, National Bureau of Economic Research (Princeton University Press, Princeton, 1962).

HARROD, R. F., *Towards a Dynamic Economics* (London, Macmillan, 1948).

HOUTHAKKER, H. S., 'An International Comparison of Personal Saving', *Bulletin of the International Statistical Institute*, Vol. 38, pp. 56–9.

——, 'On Some Determinants of Saving in Developed and Underdeveloped Countries', in *Problems in Economic Development*, edited by E. A. G. Robinson (London, Macmillan, 1965), Chapter 10, pp. 212–24.

INSTITUTO CENTRALE DI STATISTICA, *Annuario Statistico Italiano*, 1961.

KALDOR, N., *Essays in Value and Distribution* (London, 1960) (i).

——, *Essays on Economic Stability and Growth* (London, 1960) (ii).

MEADE, J. E., 'Life Cycle Saving, Inheritance and Economic Growth', *Review of Economic Studies*, Vol. 33 (1966), pp. 61–78.

MODIGLIANI, F. and ANDO, A., 'Tests of the Life Cycle Hypothesis of Saving', *Bulletin of the Oxford University Institute of Statistics*, Vol. 19, May 1957, pp. 99–124.

——, 'The Permanent Income and the Life Cycle Hypothesis of Saving Behavior: Comparisons and Tests', in *Proceedings of the Conference on Consumption and Saving*, Vol. 2, Philadelphia, 1960.

MODIGLIANI, F. and BRUMBERG, R., 'Utility Analysis and Aggregate Consumption Functions: An Attempt at Integration', unpublished.

MODIGLIANI, F., 'Long Run Implications of Alternative Fiscal Policies and the Burden of the National Debt', *The Economic Journal*, Vol. 71, December 1961, pp. 730–65.

——, 'The Life Cycle Hypothesis of Saving, the Demand for Wealth and the Supply of Capital', *Social Research*, Vol. 33, No. 2, Summer 1966, pp. 160–217.

TOBIN, J., 'Life Cycle Saving and Balanced Growth', in *Ten Economic Essays in the Tradition of Irving Fisher* (Wiley, New York, 1967), Chapter 9.

United Nations Department of Economic and Social Affairs, Statistical Office, *United Nations' Yearbook of National Accounts Statistics*, United Nations, New York.

——, *United Nations' Demographic Yearbook*, United Nations, New York.

regression coefficient of row (e), while the partial regression coefficient of ϱ should vanish. The result found in row (f) is just about the reverse. (This test could break down if ϱ and π were colinear, which however is not the case for our sample, as indicated by the result of row (f).) The tests of rows (g) and (h) are even more telling in this respect, for here ϱ is replaced by per capita growth and population structure, variables whose effect on s, as far as we can see, cannot be accounted for by the Kaldorian model.

Errata

Page 210, 10 lines from the bottom: ''Audo'' should read ''Ando.''
Page 216, 8 lines from the bottom: ''casually'' should read ''causally.''

PART IV
Policy Applications

LONG-RUN IMPLICATIONS OF ALTERNATIVE FISCAL POLICIES AND THE BURDEN OF THE NATIONAL DEBT[1]

I. Introduction

The time-honoured controversy over the burden of the National Debt has flared up once more. The view, almost unchallenged a few years back, that the National Debt is no burden on the economy and that the real cost of government expenditure, no matter how financed, cannot be shifted to " future generations " has been on the retreat under a powerful counter-attack spearheaded by the contributions of J. M. Buchanan,[2] J. E. Meade [3] and R. A. Musgrave.[4] These authors, while relying to a considerable extent on older arguments, have significantly enriched the analysis by blending the traditional approach with the new insights provided by the Keynesian revolution. But even these most recent contributions have failed, in our view, to provide an altogether adequate framework—a failure resulting at least in part from the Keynesian tendency to emphasise flows while paying inadequate attention to stocks. It is the purpose of this paper to propose a fresh approach to this problem, and to show that, unlike its predecessors, it leads to a consistent and yet straightforward answer to all relevant questions.

Unless otherwise noted, the National Debt will be defined here as consisting of: (1) all claims against the Government held by the private sector of the economy, or by foreigners, whether interest bearing or not (and including therefore bank-held debt and (government currency, if any);

[1] A number of colleagues at Massachusetts Institute of Technology and other institutions have greatly helped me with their comments on a preliminary draft of this paper. I wish particularly to acknowledge the many useful suggestions of Ralph Beals, James Buchanan, Sukhamoy Chakravarty, Margaret Hall and Merton Miller.

[2] J. M. Buchanan, *Public Principles of the Public Debt* (Homewood, Illinois: Richard D. Irwin, 1958).

[3] J. E. Meade, " Is the National Debt a Burden? " *Oxford Economic Papers*, Vol. 10. No. 2, June 1958, pp. 163–83, and " Is the National Debt A Burden: A Correction," *ibid.*, Vol. 11, No. 1, February 1959, pp. 109–10.

[4] R. A. Musgrave, *The Theory of Public Finance* (McGraw-Hill, 1959), especially Chapter 23. Other recent contributions include: the reviews of Buchanan's book by A. P. Lerner, *Journal of Political Economy*, Vol. 47, April 1959, pp. 203–6; E. R. Rolph, *American Economic Review*, Vol. 49, March 1959, pp. 183–5, and A. H. Hansen, *Review of Economics and Statistics*, Vol. 41, June 1959, pp. 377–8; also " The Public Debt: A Burden on Future Generations? " by W. G. Bowen, R. G. Davis and D. H. Kopf, *American Economic Review*, Vol. 50, September 1960, pp. 701–6; and the forthcoming note by A. P. Lerner, " The Burden of Debt," *Review of Economics and Statistics*, Vol. 54, No. 2, May 1961.

Since the completion of this paper, three comments on the Bowen, Davis and Kopf communication by W. Vickrey, T. Scitovsky and J. R. Elliott and a reply by the authors have also appeared in the March 1961 issue of the *American Economic Review*, pp. 132–43.

less (2) any claims held by the Government against the private sector and foreigners.[1]

From a methodological point of view, the central contention of our analysis is that to grasp fully the economic effects of alternative fiscal policies and of the National Debt, we must pay proper attention to stocks as well as to the usual flow variables and to the long-run as well as to the impact effects. Among the substantive implications of this line of approach, the following may be mentioned here by way of a rough summary: (1) Given the government purchase of goods and services, an increase of the (real) National Debt, whether internal or external, is generally advantageous to those present at the time of the increase (or to some subset thereof). (2) Such an increase will generally place a " gross burden " on those living beyond that time through a reduction in the aggregate stock of private capital, which, as long as the (net) marginal productivity of capital is positive, will in turn cause a reduction in the flow of goods and services. Furthermore, this loss (as well as the gain under (1) above) will tend to occur even when lack of effective private demand would prevent the maintenance of full employment in the absence of the deficit, though the relative size of gain and losses may be quite different in these circumstances. (3) These conclusions hold in reverse in the case of a reduction in the real National Debt. That is, such a decline is burdensome on those present at the time of the reduction and tends to generate a gross gain for those living beyond. (4) *If* the rate of interest at which the Government borrows can be taken as a good approximation to the marginal productivity of private capital, then the gross burden (or gain) to " future generations " referred to under (2) and (3) can be *measured* by the interest charges on the National Debt. (5) The gross burden may be offset in part or *in toto*, or may be even more than offset, in so far as the increase in the debt is accompanied by government expenditure which contributes to the real income of future generations, *e.g.*, through productive public capital formation.[2]

This summary is very rough indeed and is subject to numerous qualifications and amendments, many of which will be noted below. In any event, I should like to emphasise that the stress of this paper is on developing a method of analysis rather than on presenting a body of doctrines. For this reason I will try to relate my analysis to earlier points of view whenever this seems helpful in clarifying the issues involved. At the same time I will endeavour to stay clear of many traditional but somewhat sterile controversies, such as whether the analogy between private and public debt is true or false.

[1] This definition implies that the National Debt could in principle be negative. Even in this case we shall refer to it by the same name, although its magnitude will be expressed by a negative number. Similarly, we refer to an operation that reduces the algebraic value of the National Debt as a " reduction," even if the debt was initially zero or negative.

[2] The difference between the increase in the National Debt in a given interval and the Government expenditure contributing to future income corresponds roughly to the net increase in what Professor Meade has called the " deadweight " debt. Cf. *op. cit.*

II. A Bird's Eye View of the Classical and Post-Keynesian No-transfer and No-burden Argument

We begin by reviewing the very persuasive arguments supporting the doctrine that the cost of the current government use of resources cannot be transferred to future generations and that the National Debt is no burden on them. Since these arguments have been presented many times in the last couple of centuries and have been extensively restated in recent years, we can afford to recapitulate them very briefly in terms of the three propositions presented below—at the cost of glossing over some of the fine points and of foregoing the pleasure of citing " chapter and verse." [1]

(1) Individuals or sub-groups within an economic system can, by means of borrowing, increase the current flow of goods available to them and pay for this increase out of future output. But they can do so only because their borrowing is " external," *i.e.*, matched by a lender who yields current goods in exchange for later output. But a closed community cannot dispose of more goods and services than it is currently producing. It certainly cannot increase this flow by paying with future output, for there is no way " we can dispose to-day of to-morrow's output." Hence the goods and services acquired by the Government must always be " paid for " by those present at the time in the form of a reduction in the flow of goods available to them for private use, and cannot possibly be paid for by later generations, whether the acquisition is financed by taxes or by internal borrowing. Only through external borrowing is it possible to benefit the current generation and to impose a burden on the future.

(2) Although internal borrowing will leave in its wake an obligation for future tax-payers to pay the interest on the National Debt and, possibly, to repay the principal, this obligation is not a net burden on the community as a whole, because these payments are but transfers of income between future members of the community. The loss of the tax-payers is offset in the aggregate by the gain of the beneficiary of the payment. These transfers may, of course, occur between people of different ages and hence of different " generations," and in this sense internal borrowing may cause " inter-generations transfers," but it will not cause a net loss to society.

The above two arguments, or some reasonable variant thereof, have provided the cornerstone of the no-transfer, no-burden argument over the last two centuries or so. It was left for Keynesian analysis to provide a third argument, removing thereby a potentially troublesome objection to the first two. If the cost of government expenditure always falls on the current generation, no matter how financed, why not forego altogether the painful activity of levying taxes? Yet our common sense rebels at this

[1] The reader interested in establishing just who said what will find much useful material in Buchanan, *op. cit.*, especially Chapters 2 and 8, and in B. Griziotti, " La diversa pressione tributaria del prestito e dell'imposta " in *Studi di scienza delle finanze e diritto finanziario* (Milano: Giuffre, 1956), Vol. II, pp. 193–273.

conclusion. A partial answer to this puzzle was provided by recognising that taxes, even when paid back in the form of transfers, generate some "frictional loss," because most if not all feasible methods of raising tax revenue tend to interfere with the optimum allocation of resources.[1] Presumably the ever-increasing level of the National Debt resulting from full deficit financing of current expenditure would require raising through taxes an ever-growing revenue to pay the interest on the debt. Eventually the ratio of such taxes to national income plus transfers would exceed the ratio of government expenditure to national product, giving rise to frictional tax losses which could have been avoided through a balanced budget. While these considerations do provide a *prima facie* case for a balanced-budget policy, the case is not tight, for could not the interest itself be met by further borrowing?

However, we need not follow these fancy possibilities, for the Keynesian analysis has provided a much more cogent argument to support the need for an "appropriate" amount of taxation, although not necessarily for a balanced budget. This argument, which reaches its most elegant formulation in the so-called principle of "functional finance" enunciated by Lerner,[2] can be roughly summarised as follows.

(3) Given the full employment output, say $\bar{X}$, and given the share of this output which it is appropriate to allocate for government use, say $\bar{G}$, there is a maximum amount of output that is left available for the private sector, say $\bar{P} = \bar{X} - \bar{G}$. Now the private sector demand for output, say P, is a function of income and taxes, say $P = \mathscr{P}(X, T)$, with $\frac{\delta P}{\delta T} < 0$. Taxes are then to be set at that level, say $\bar{T}$, which satisfies the equation $\mathscr{P}(X, T) = P$. A higher level of taxes would generate unemployment and a lower level would generate inflation, both evils which it is the task of the Government to avoid. $\bar{T}$ may turn out to be larger than $\bar{G}$, calling for a surplus, or smaller than $\bar{G}$, or even perchance just equal to $\bar{G}$, implying a balanced budget. But in any event, the purpose of taxes is not to make the current members of the community pay for the government use of goods, which they will do in any event, the real reason we need to put up with the unpleasantness of taxes is to prevent the greater social evil of inflation.

III. A Bird's Eye View of the Classical and Post-Keynesian Transfer and Burden Argument

The basic contention of this school of thought, which itself has a long tradition, is that in general—though possibly with some exceptions—a

[1] See, *e.g.*, J. E. Meade, "Mr. Lerner on 'The Economics of Control,'" Economic Journal, Vol. LV, April 1945, pp. 47–70.

[2] See, *e.g.*, "Functional Finance and the Public Debt," *Social Research*, Vol. 10, No. 1, and "The Burden of the National Debt" in *Income Employment and Public Policy* (New York: Norton & Company, 1948).

debt-financed public expenditure will place no burden at all on those present at the very moment in which the expenditure takes place, and will instead place a burden on all tax-payers living thereafter. This burden may fall in part on those present at the time of the expenditure, but only in so far as they are present thereafter. The arguments which support this position have also been repeatedly stated and have been thoroughly reviewed quite recently by Buchanan. It will therefore again be sufficient to summarise them very briefly in the following two propositions:

(1) The cost of a tax-financed expenditure is borne currently, for the resources obtained by the Government come from a forcible reduction in the resources of current tax-payers. But an expenditure financed by debt, whether internal or external, as a rule places no burden on those present at the time of the expenditure in that, and in so far as, the resources acquired by the Government are surrendered in a voluntary exchange by the savers, who thereby acquire government bonds (in lieu of some other asset).

(2) The burden is imposed instead on all future tax-payers, who will have to pay taxes to service the debt. These taxes are *not* a mere transfer of income, but a net burden on society, for, in the absence of the debt-financed expenditure, the taxes would not have been levied, while the investors in bonds would have received the income just the same, directly or indirectly, from the return on the physical assets in which their savings would have been invested. This argument *does not* imply that a debt-financed expenditure will necessarily affect future generations unfavourably. In order to assess the " net outcome," we must subtract from the gross burden represented by the extra taxes benefits, if any, resulting from the expenditure. Thus the net outcome might even be positive if the expenditure undertaken produced greater benefits than the private capital formation which it replaces. But the argument does imply that, through deficit financing, the expenditure of the Government is being " paid for " by future generations.

A careful application of the *reasoning* underlying (1) and (2) will reveal circumstances in which the above conclusions do not hold and the allocation of the burden may be independent of the form of financing used. There are in particular two important cases which are treated at some length by Buchanan and which bring to light the contribution of Keynesian analysis also to this side of the argument. The first is the case of debt-financed expenditure in deep depressions, when private capital formation could not, in any event, provide an adequate offset to full-employment saving. Here, according to Buchanan, not even a gross burden need result to future tax-payers, for the expenditure could in principle be financed by interest-free issuance of currency. The second exception discussed by Buchanan is that of a major war. Unfortunately, the chapter on war financing is one of the least convincing in his book, and what follows may represent more nearly my application of his framework than a faithful summary of his argument. Suppose the war effort is sufficiently severe so that the allocation of resources to various uses, and to capital formation in particular, is completely determined by war necessities. In such a situation the way in which the Government finances its expenditure cannot affect private consumption or capital formation. It would seem therefore that the burden of reduced consumption must be borne by the current generation, even if the reduction is achieved not through taxes but through a combination of rationing and voluntary increases in saving and the unspent disposable income is invested in claims against the Government. Similarly, the burden of the reduction in useful capital formation is borne by those living after the war, again independently of financing. In this case, as well as in the case of depression financing, the taxes levied to pay the interest on the increased debt would indeed seem to result in a pure transfer, for the income associated with the bonds would *not* have come to exist had the Government decided respectively to tax, or to print money, instead of borrowing.

J. E. Meade has also lately associated himself with those maintaining that the National Debt is a burden,[1] but his argument is quite different from the classical one, and bears instead all the marks of post-Keynesian analysis. He is not concerned with the differential effect of deficit versus tax financing, but asserts none the less that government debt in excess of government-owned physical capital—the so-called deadweight debt—is a burden on the economy. Unfortunately his contribution, which is so stimulating in analysing the effects of a major capital levy, is less than convincing in its attempt to establish that the deadweight debt is a burden. For his demonstration seems to rely entirely on the proposition that elimination of the debt would be a blessing for the economy in that it would encourage saving through a " Pigou type " effect, besides reducing the frictional costs of transfers. Now the tax-friction proposition, though valid, is not new,[2] and had already been generally accepted as a second-order amendment to the no-burden argument. On the other hand, the first and central argument is rather unconvincing. For, as Meade himself recognises, a reduction in National Debt, be it through a capital levy, budget surplus or inflation, would spur saving whether or not the debt reduced thereby was " deadweight " debt. In fact, at least the first two means would tend to increase saving, even if they were applied in a situation where the National Debt was zero to begin with, and the outcome would be that of driving the economy into a position of net indebtedness *vis-à-vis* the Government. Finally, Meade's analysis throws no light on whether the increase in saving following the capital levy is a permanent or a purely transitory phenomenon, nor on who, if anyone, bears the burden of a debt reduction. In spite of these apparent shortcomings, I am encouraged to think that Professor Meade's views are fundamentally quite close to those advanced here. I hope this will become gradually apparent, even without much further explicit reference to his argument.

[1] Meade, *op. cit.*

[2] See, *e.g.*, the references in footnote 1, p. 733, above, and in Buchanan, *op. cit.*, p. 14, footnote 8.

IV. Fallacies in the No-transfer No-burden Argument

The classical argument summarised in the last section appears so far rather convincing, and if so we should be able to pinpoint the fallacies in one or more of the three propositions of Section II.

The fallacy in proposition (1) is not difficult to uncover. It is quite true that a closed community cannot increase its current resources by relying on to-morrow's unproduced output. None the less, the way in which we use to-day's resources can affect in three major ways the output that will result to-morrow from to-morrow's labour input: (i) by affecting the natural resources available to the future; (ii) by improving technological knowledge; and (iii) by affecting the stock of man-made means of production, or capital, available to future generations. Hence government expenditure, and the way it is financed, *can* affect the economy in the future if it affects any of the above three items.

The argument in (3) is also seriously inadequate, and the post-war experience has brought this home sharply. For the demand of the private sector consists of consumption C and capital formation I, and at least the latter component depends not only on income and taxes but also on monetary policy. Once we acknowledge this point, the principle of Functional Finance no longer implies a unique level of taxes. To demonstrate this point and its implications, it will be convenient—though it is not essential—to suppose that monetary policy affects P exclusively through the intermediary of the rate of interest r, *i.e.*, that $P = \mathscr{P}(X, T, r)$ with $\frac{\delta P}{\delta r} < 0$; and that r in turn depends on X and the quantity of money M. But once we admit that r enters not vacuously in $\mathscr{P}$ we must also recognise that the equation

$$(1) \qquad \mathscr{P}(\bar{X}, T, r) = P$$

will be satisfied not by one but by many possible values of T, each value being accompanied by the appropriate value of r, say $r(T)$. Now in most circumstances—that is, except possibly in very deep depression—there will be a range of values of T such that the corresponding $r(T)$ is achievable by an appropriate monetary policy. There is therefore not one but a whole schedule of values of T which are consistent with the maintenance of full employment and price stability, each value of T being accompanied by an appropriate monetary policy. Furthermore, within this range there will tend to be a direct connection between T and the capital formation component of $\bar{P}$. If, starting from a correct combination of T, r and M, we lower taxes we will increase consumption, and to offset this we must reduce capital formation by appropriately tightening monetary policy. Conversely, by increasing taxes we can afford to have a larger capital formation. Thus, given the level of government expenditure, the level of taxes, and

TABLE I

A. *Effects of Government Expenditure and Financing on Private Saving and Capital Formation*

(Full Employment—All variables measured in real terms)

Method of Financing.	Income, X. (1)	Government Expenditure, G. (2)	Taxes, T. (3)	Disposable. Income, Y. $(X - T)$ (4)	Consumption, C. $(c_0 + cY)$ $(c = 0{\cdot}6)$ (5)	Saving $S = \Delta W$ $(Y - C)$ (6)	Deficit, D. $(G - T)$ (7)	Private capital formation $I = \Delta K$ $(S - D)$ (8)
(a) Initial situation	2,000	300 (G_0)	300	1,700	1,500 (C_0)	200 (S_0)	0	200 (S_0)
(b) Increased expenditure-deficit financed	2,000	400 $(G_0 + dG)$	300	1,700	1,500 (C_0)	200 (S_0)	100 (dG)	100 $(S_0 - dG)$
(c) Increased expenditure—tax financed	2,000	400 $(G_0 + dG)$	400	1,600	1,440 $(C_0 - cdG)$	160 $(S_0 - sdG)$	0	160 $(S_0 - sdG)$

B. *Comparative "Burden" Effects of Alternative Budgetary Policies*

Budgetary policy.	Effect on Private capital formation.	Effect on "Burden."
1. Joint effect of increased expenditure *and* deficit financing	$I(b) - I(a)$ [1] $= (S_0 - dG) - S_0 = -dG$	$r^*(dG)$
2. Joint effect of increased expenditure and taxes	$I(c) - I(a) = (S_0 - sdG) - S_0 = -sdG$	$r^*s(dG)$
3. Differential effect of deficit financing	$I(b) - I(c) = (S_0 - dG) - (S_0 - sdG) = -(1 - s)dG = -cdG$	$r^*c(dG)$

[1] $I(a)$ means investment in situation (a), and similarly for $I(b)$ and $I(c)$.

hence of budget deficit, does affect " future generations " through the stock of capital inherited by them.

Having thus brought to light the weaknesses in arguments (1) and (3), it is an easy matter to establish that, at least under certain conditions, the Keynesian framework is perfectly consistent with the classical conclusion stated in Section III. Suppose we take as a starting-point a given G, and some given combination of T and r consistent with full employment. Suppose further, as is generally assumed in Keynesian analysis, that to a first approximation consumption responds to taxes but not to interest rates. Now let the Government increase its expenditure by dG while keeping taxes constant. Then the deficit will increase precisely by $dD = dG$. What will happen to capital formation? If we are to maintain full employment without inflation we must have

$$dG + dC + dI = 0$$

and since, by assumption, taxes are constant and hence $dC = 0$, we must have

$$dG = dD = -dI$$

i.e., the debt-financed expenditure must be accompanied by an equal reduction in capital formation (with the help of the appropriate monetary policy).

This outcome is illustrated by a numerical example in Table I. Row (*a*) shows the behaviour of the relevant flows in the initial situation, taken as a standard of comparison: here the budget is assumed to be balanced, although this is of no particular relevance. In row (*b*) we examine the consequence of an increase of expenditure by 100, with unchanged taxes, and hence consumption. The amount of resources available for, and hence the level of private capital formation, is cut down precisely by the amount of the deficit-financed expenditure. It is also apparent that this expenditure puts no burden on the " current " members of the community. Their (real) disposable income is unchanged by the expenditure, and consequently so is their consumption, as well as the net current addition to their personal wealth or private net worth. But because capital formation has been cut by the amount of the deficit, the community will thereafter dispose of a stock of private capital curtailed to a corresponding extent.

Thus the deficit-financed expenditure will leave in its wake an overall burden on the economy in the form of a reduced flow of income from the reduced stock of private capital.

V. Interest Charges and the " True " Burden of Debt Financing

The analysis of the last section is seen to agree with the classical conclusion that debt financing transfers the burden of the government expenditure to those living beyond the time of the expenditure. At the same time it indicates that this burden consists in *the loss of income from capital* and not in *the taxes levied on later members to pay the interest charges*, as the classical argument contends.

In some respects this amendment to the classical burden position may be regarded as rather minor, for it can be argued that, under reasonable assumptions, the interest charges will provide a good *measure* of the true burden. Indeed, as long as the amount dD is not large in relation to the stock of capital (and the flow of saving), the loss in the future stream of output will be adequately approximated by $r^*(dD)$, where r^* denotes the marginal productivity of capital. Now if the Government borrows in a competitive market, bidding against other seekers of capital, then the (long-term) interest rate r at which it borrows will also be a reasonable approximation to r^*. Hence the annual interest charges $r(dD)$ will also be a good approximation to the true social yearly loss, or opportunity cost, $r\ (dD)$ [1]—provided we can also establish that the initial reduction in the stock of capital will not be recouped as long as the debt is not repaid.

One can, however, think of many reasons why the interest bill might not even provide a good *measure* of the true loss. To begin with, if the government operation is of sizeable proportions it may significantly drive up interest rates, say from r_0 to r_1, since the reduction in private capital will tend to increase its marginal product. In this case the interest on the debt will overstate the true burden, which will lie somewhere between $r_0(dD)$ and $r_1(dD)$. More serious are the problems arising from various kinds of imperfections in the commodities as well as in the capital markets. In particular, the Government may succeed in borrowing at rates well below r^* by forcing banks and other intermediaries to acquire and hold bonds with yields below the market, or, as in war-time, by effectively eliminating the competition of private borrowers. In the first-mentioned case, *e.g.*, we should add to the interest bill the lost income accruing to the bank depositors (or at least to the bank's stockholders). There is also the rather nasty problem that, because of uncertainty, the rate of interest may not be a good measure of the productivity of physical capital. To put it very roughly, r is at best a measure of return net of a risk premium, and the actual return on capital is better thought of as a random variable whose average value is, in general, rather higher than r.[2]

Besides the relation of r to r^* there is another problem that needs to be recognised. In our discussion so far, and in our table, we have assumed that consumption, and hence private saving, were unaffected because taxes were unchanged. But once we recognise that the borrowing may increase the interest rate, we must also recognise that it may, through this route, affect consumption even with unchanged taxes. This problem might well be quickly dismissed under the principle of "*de minimis.*" For, though economists may still argue as to whether an increase in interest rates will

[1] This is precisely the position taken by Musgrave, *op. cit.*, p. 577.

[2] Cf. F. Modigliani and M. H. Miller, "The Cost of Capital, Corporation Finance and the Theory of Investment," *American Economic Review*, Vol. 58, No. 3, June 1958, pp. 261–97. However, Miller has suggested to me that r may be the more relevant measure of return on capital as it deducts an appropriate allowance for the "cost" of risk bearing.

increase or decrease saving, they generally agree that the effect, if any, will be negligible.[1] But even if the rate of saving were to rise from, say, S_0 to $S_0 + e$ and the level of capital formation were accordingly reduced only by $dD - e$, one could still argue that r^*dD and not $r^*(dD - e)$ is the relevant measure of the true loss to society. This is because, as suggested by Bowen *et al.*,[2] the income generated by the extra capital formation e may be quite appropriately regarded as just necessary to offset the extra sacrifice of current consumption undertaken by those who responded to the change in r.

Thus it would appear that the classical-burden position needs to be modified to the extent of recognising that the burden of deficit financing consists not in the increased taxes as such, but rather in the fall in income generated by the reduction in the stock of capital. But this modification would seem rather innocuous, since, admittedly, rdD will generally provide a reasonable approximate *measure* of the true burden. In fact, however, the amendment we have suggested turns out to have rather far-reaching implications as we will show presently.

VI. Shortcomings of the Classical Transfer and Burden Argument: The Differential Effect of Deficit Versus Tax Financing

The classical conclusion that deficit financing of an expenditure places the burden on the future seems to imply that, if the expenditure were financed by taxes, there would be no burden in the future. Interestingly enough, Buchanan's book provides nowhere a systematic treatment of the temporal distribution of the burden from a tax-financed expenditure. Nor is this really surprising, for if the burden were in fact the interest of the debt, then tax financing could generate no burden on the future.[3] But if the relevant criterion is instead the loss of capital formation, then in order to find the true differential effect of debt financing versus tax financing, we must inquire about the effects of tax financing on private saving and capital formation. Only if this effect were nil or negligible would the classical conclusion be strictly valid.

Now, to an economist steeped in the Keynesian tradition, it is at once obvious that raising taxes to finance the government expenditure cannot fail to affect significantly private saving and capital formation. While tax financing will reduce disposable income by the amount of the expenditure, it will reduce consumption only by an amount $cdT = cdG$, where c is the marginal propensity to consume. The rest of the tax will be borne by a reduction in saving by sdT, where $s = 1 - c$ is the marginal propensity to save. Accordingly, if the initial position was one of full employment, as we are assuming, and inflation is to be avoided, private capital formation

[1] This is especially true if current consumption is appropriately defined to include the rental value and not the gross purchase of consumers' durables.

[2] Bowen, Davis and Kopf, *op. cit.*, p. 704.

[3] See, however footnote 1, p. 746, for a different explanation of Buchanan's omission.

must itself be reduced by the amount sdG (through the appropriate monetary policy).[1] This outcome is illustrated numerically in row (c) of Table I. By comparing the outcomes (a), (b) and (c) as is done in part B of the table, we find that the differential effect of the deficit versus tax financing is to decrease capital formation by $dG - sdG = cdG$. The balance of the reduction, namely sdG, must be attributed to the expenditure as such, independently of how financed.[2] Hence, even if we are willing to regard the interest rate paid by the Government as a good approximation to r^*, the differential burden of debt financing on the future generations is not rdG but only $rcdG$.

It can readily be seen that the above result is not limited to the case we have explicitly discussed so far, in which the deficit arises from an increase in expenditure. If, for whatever reason, a portion dD of the government expenditure is not financed by taxes but by deficit, capital formation tends to be reduced by approximately $c(dD)$. This conclusion is, however, subject to one important qualification, namely that for $T = \bar{G}$, *i.e.*, with a level of taxation balancing the budget, there exists a monetary policy capable of achieving full employment—or, in terms of our previous notation, of enforcing the required rate of interest $r(\bar{T})$. When this condition is satisfied we shall say that there is a " potentially adequate private demand," or more briefly, an " adequate demand." We shall for the moment concentrate attention on this case, reserving the task of examining the implications of a lack of adequate demand to a later point.

Our result so far, then, is that even with an adequate demand, the net or differential burden placed on the future by debt financing is not nearly as large as suggested by the classical conclusion. But note that the implied error is poor consolation for the no-transfer proponents, for they maintained that the burden is always " paid as you go." The error we have uncovered would seem to lie instead in not recognising that a part of the burden of the expenditure is always shifted to the future. This last conclusion, however, is somewhat puzzling and disquieting. And this uneasiness can be easily increased by asking ourselves the following embarrassing question: roughly how large is the coefficient s which determines the unavoidable burden on the future? This question is embarrassing because recent empirical as well as theoretical research on the consumption function suggests that the answer depends very much on the length of time which is allowed for the adjustment. In the long run, the average propensity to save has remained

[1] The need to curtail investment when government expenditure is increased at full employment, even though it is fully tax covered, is the counterpart of the so-called multiplier effect of a balanced budget when starting from less than full utilisation of resources. The tax-financed expenditure *per se* increases the aggregate real demand for goods and services by a dollar per dollar of expenditure. But if we start from full employment, this extra demand could only result in inflation. Hence it must be offset by a fall in investment of s dollars per dollar of expenditure, which, taking into account the multiplier effect, will reduce total demand by $s/s = 1$ dollar per dollar, as required.

[2] This conclusion has also been reached by W. Vickrey, *op. cit.*

pretty constant in the general order of 0·1, meaning that the marginal propensity is of the same order. But the quarterly increase in saving associated with a quarterly increase in income seems to be of a much larger order of magnitude, with estimates ranging as high as 0·5 and even higher.[1] Which is the relevant figure and why? Or does the answer depend on whether we look only at the impact effect of taxation or also at its delayed and ultimate effects? We will argue that this is indeed the case, and that in so far as we are interested in the distribution of the burden over time and between generations, the total effects are paramount.

VII. Impact Versus Total Effects of Deficit and Tax Financing

Let us come back to a comparison of rows (*b*) and (*c*) in Table I, but this time let us concentrate on the effect of taxation on the terminal net worth position of the households. We can see that if the expenditure is debt-financed this terminal position is (at least to a first approximation) the same as if the expenditure had not been undertaken. On the other hand, in the case of tax financing, in addition to the concomitant fall in consumption, we find that saving, and hence the increase in net worth, was also cut down from 200 to 160. What effect will this have on later consumption and saving behaviour?

In order to answer this question we need to go beyond the standard Keynesian emphasis on current flows and try to understand why consumers wanted to add 200 to their net worth in the first place and how they will react when this goal has to be scaled down in response to higher taxes. I have elsewhere proposed some answer to these questions by advancing the hypothesis that saving (and dissaving) is not a passive reaction to income but represents instead a purposive endeavour by the households to achieve a desirable allocation of resources to consumption over their lifetime.[2] However, in what follows we do not need to rely, to any significant extent, on that model or any other specific theory of saving behaviour. All that we need to keep before our eyes is the logical proposition that there are, in the final analysis, only two ways in which households can dispose of any addition to their net worth achieved through current saving: namely, either through later consumption or through a bequest to their heirs.

Now let us suppose at first that the bequest motive is small enough to be neglected and that, as a rule and on the average, each household tends to

[1] See, *e.g.*, the following two recent and as yet unpublished studies prepared for the Commission on Money and Credit: D. B. Suits, " The Determinants of Consumer Expenditure: a Review of Present Knowledge "; and E. C. Brown, R. M. Solow, A. K. Ando and J. Kareken, " Lags in Fiscal and Monetary Policy," Part II.

[2] F. Modigliani and R. Brumberg, " Utility Analysis and the Consumption Function: An Interpretation of Cross-section Data," in *Post-Keynesian Economics*, K. Kurihara, ed. (Rutgers University Press, 1954).

consume all of its income over its lifetime. This assumption can be conveniently restated in terms of the notion of the " over-life average propensity to consume " (*oac*), defined as the ratio of (the present value of) life consumption to (the present value of) life resources, and of the " over-life marginal propensity to consume " (*omc*), defined as the ratio of marginal increments in the same two variables. With this terminology, our current assumption is that both *omc* and *oac* are unity. It should be noted that, under reasonable hypotheses about the typical individual life cycle of earnings and consumption, an *oac* of unity for each household is consistent with a sizeable stock of aggregate assets, in the order of several times national income. With a stationary population and unchanged technology—stationary economy—this aggregate stock would tend to be constant in size, implying zero net saving in the aggregate, but it would be undergoing a continuous reshuffling of ownership from dissavers, such as retired persons, to those in the process of accumulating assets for retirement and short-run contingencies. On the other hand, with a rising population and/or technological progress, there would tend to be positive saving and a rising stock; in fact, the ratio of saving to income and of assets to income would tend to be constant in the long run if the above two forces resulted in an approximately exponential growth trend for aggregate income.[1]

Let us now consider the consequences of a non-repetitive increment in government expenditure dG, financed by a deficit, limiting ourselves at first to a stationary economy. Fig. 1 (*a*) illustrates graphically the effects of this operation on aggregate private net worth W, and on the net stock of privately owned capital K. The horizontal dashed line AA represents the behaviour of net worth in the absence of dG. It is constant by our assumption of a stationary economy, implying zero net saving, or gross saving and gross investment just sufficient to offset the wear and tear of the capital stock. If we make the further convenient assumption that there is initially no government debt (and ignore non-reproducible tangible wealth), then W coincides also with K. The incremental expenditure dG is supposed to occur in the interval t_0 to t_1 at the constant rate $dG/(t_1 - t_0)$, and is financed by tapping a portion of the gross saving otherwise devoted to capital maintenance. As a result, between t_0 and t_1 K falls, as shown by the solid curve. But the net worth W remains at the same initial level as the fall in K is offset in the consumers' balance sheet by the government debt of dG. By t_1 the gap between W and K amounts to precisely dG, and thereafter the curves remain unchanged until and unless some further disturbance occurs. The final outcome is that the debt-financed expenditure, by generating a permanent wedge $dG = dD$ between W and K,[2] causes the entire cost of the expenditure to be borne by those living beyond t_1 in the form of a reduction

[1] Cf. A. K. Ando and F. Modigliani, " Growth, Fluctuations and Stability," *American Economic Review*, May 1959, pp. 501–24.

[2] Permanent in the sense that it persists as long as the debt remains outstanding.

in the stock of private capital by dG and in disposable income by $r^*(dG)$.[1] If, in addition, $r^* = r$, then before-tax income will be unaffected and the fall in disposable income will equal the tax collected to pay the interest, as claimed by the classical-burden doctrine.[2]

Consider now the effect of full tax financing of dG, illustrated in Fig. 1 (*b*). The line AA has the same meaning as before. The impact effect of the tax-financed expenditure—*i.e.*, the effect within the interval t_0t_1—is to reduce consumption by cdG and saving and private capital formation by sdG. Hence, as shown by the solid line, by t_1 both W and K have fallen by sdG. As we had already concluded, this fall in K partly shifts the effect of the expenditure to those living beyond t_1. However, by following up the delayed effect of the tax, we can now show that in this case: (*a*) the shift of the burden is only temporary, as W, and hence K, will tend to return gradually to the original pre-expenditure level, and (*b*) the burden transferred to the period following t_1 is borne, at least to a first approximation, entirely by those who were taxed between t_0 and t_1.

To establish this result we need only observe that since those taxed have suffered a loss of over-life (disposable) income amounting to dG as a result of the tax, they must make a commensurate reduction in over-life consumption. If the consumption is cut initially only by $c(dG)$ the balance of the tax, or $s(dG)$, is financed out of a reduction in accumulation—including possibly borrowing from other households—which at first reduces the net worth at time t_1 by $s(dG)$, but eventually must be matched by a corresponding reduction of consumption over the balance of the life span. Let L denote the length of time until the taxed generations die out. In the interval t_1 to $t_1 + L$, then, the consumption of this group will be smaller relative to its income, and hence its rate of saving will be larger, or its rate of dissaving smaller, than it would have been in the absence of the tax. On the other hand, over the same interval, the income consumption and saving of households who have entered the scene after t_1 will be basically unaffected by the operation. Hence, in the L years following t_1 there will arise some positive saving which will gradually die down as the taxed generation disappears. The precise path of aggregate saving will depend on the way the taxed generation chooses to distribute the reduction of consumption over its life. But, in any event, the cumulated net saving over the entire interval

[1] Actually the fall in disposable income consequent upon the fall in K is likely to give rise to a further fall in W and hence in K, but this indirect effect will tend to be of secondary magnitude. See on this point footnote 1, p. 750.

[2] If the reduction in K results in a significant rise in r^* and hence r, then, as pointed out by Vickrey (*op. cit.*, p. 135), there will tend to occur a shift in the distribution of *pre-tax* income. Labour income will tend to shrink and property income to increase—and, incidentally, this increase will tend to more than offset the fall in labour's earnings. It does not follow, however, as Vickrey has concluded, that the " primary burden of diminished future income will be felt by future wage earners." For the burden consists in the reduction of *disposable* income, and this reduction will depend on the distribution of the taxes levied to pay the interest as between property and non-property income.

FIG. 1
Effect of Deficit and Taxes on Net Worth, W, and Capital, K,
(unity over-life propensity to consume)

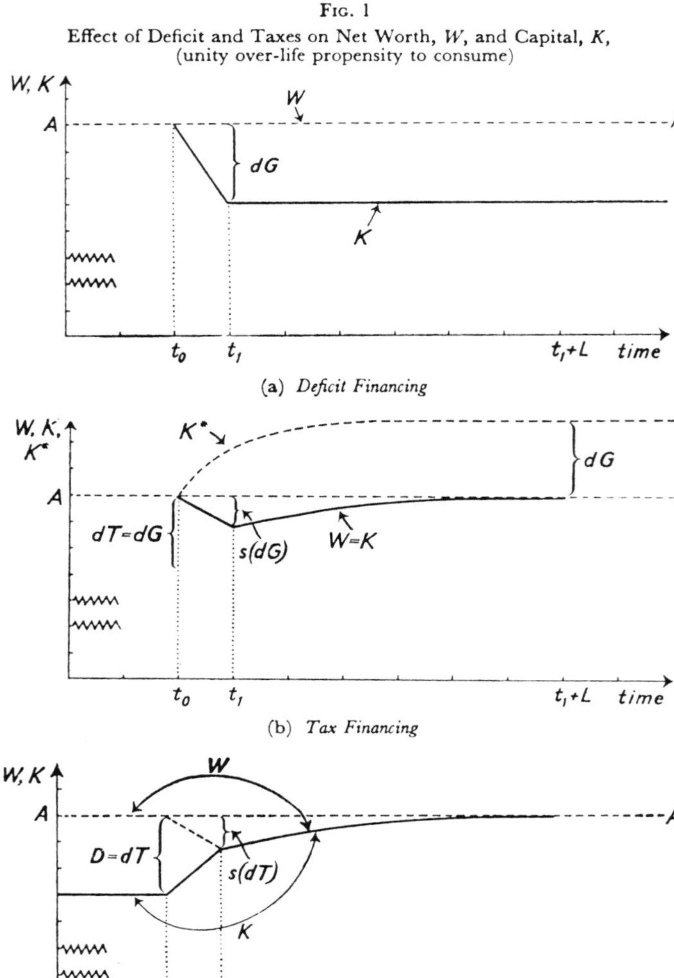

(a) *Deficit Financing*

(b) *Tax Financing*

(c) *Debt Retirement*

t_1 to $t_1 + L$ must come to precisely $s(dG)$, representing the required reduction of consumption relative to income of the taxed generation.[1] This

[1] It may be noted that the cumulated reduction in consumption will tend to be somewhat larger than $s(dG)$ because the taxed generation will also lose some income as a result of the reduction in their wealth, amounting initially to $s(dG)$. However, the cumulated increase in saving over the interval is still $s(dG)$ because the additional loss in consumption just matches the reduction in income from this source. Actually $s(dG)$ measures essentially the ***present value*** as of t_1 of the required reduction in consumption.

cumulated saving is just sufficient to make up for the initial fall in the stock of $s(dG)$, so that by $t_1 + L$ the stock of capital (as well as W) has returned to the original level, as shown in Fig. 2 (*b*), and we are back in the original stationary state.

The above framework can be readily applied to analyse the effects of deficit or surplus generated under different conditions, *e.g.*, by varying taxes, expenditure constant. Fig. 1 (*c*), for instance, depicts the outcome of an increase in taxes in the interval t_0 to t_1, utilised to retire the debt D outstanding at t_0. Here again the entire burden of the retirement falls on the taxed generation—although it is spread between t_0 and $t_1 + L$—and the gain accrues to those living after t_1 in the form of an increase in the stock of capital by an amount which eventually approaches the amount of debt retired and reflects the elimination of the wedge between W and K.

It is also easy to verify that our results remain valid for a growing economy, the only difference being that the dashed line AA would turn into an upward-sloping curve. With debt financing the graph of K would, from t_1 on, run at a distance dG below this line, while with tax financing the graph of $K = W$ would initially fall below it by $s(dG)$, but would tend to return to it at $t_1 + L$.

In summary, then, under unit *oac* the cost of an expenditure financed by debt, whether internal or external, tends to fall entirely on those living beyond the time of expenditure, as asserted by the classical-burden position, though it is best measured by r^*dD rather than by the incremental tax bill rdD. This burden may be eliminated at a later date by retiring the debt through a budget surplus, but thereby the full cost of the original expenditure is shifted to the later tax-payer, who financed the surplus. On the other hand, the cost of a tax-financed expenditure will tend to be borne by society as a whole, partly at the time and partly for some finite period thereafter. But the burden beyond t_1 still falls primarily on those who initially paid the tax and reflects the spreading of the burden over their lifetime.[1]

In the analysis so far we have concentrated on examining who bears the cost of the expenditure. To complete the picture we must, of course, also reckon the yield, if any, produced by dG beyond t_1. In particular, if dG results in a (permanent) addition to the stock of capital we must distinguish

[1] In a stimulating comment to a preliminary draft of this paper, Mr. Buchanan has provided an explanation for his failure to analyse the temporal distribution of the burden of a tax-financed expenditure. He points out that in line with the classic tradition, he defines the burden as the subjective loss of utility suffered by the tax-payer because of the initial loss of resources. The burden in this sense occurs entirely when the tax is levied and the later reduction of consumption cannot be separately counted as burden, as it is merely the embodiment of the original burden. I have serious reservations about the usefulness of this definition. It has, for instance, the peculiar implication that, when as a result of tax financing an heir receives a smaller inheritance or as a result of debt financing he is saddled with a larger tax bill, this cannot be counted as burden on him, as the entire burden is already accounted for in the guise of his father's grief that his heirs will enjoy a smaller net income. It is this peculiar reasoning that underlies Ricardo's famous conclusion that the cost of the government expenditure is always fully borne by those present at the time.

between W, K and K^*, the latter denoting the total stock of private- plus government-owned capital. K^* will exceed K by dG. Thus in the case of a debt-financed capital expenditure, K^* will everywhere tend to coincide with W, the government capital formation simply replacing the private one. For the case of tax financing, the behaviour of K^* is shown by the broken line in Fig. 1 (*b*). Here the burden on the taxed generation results in a permanent gain for those living beyond t_1, which will gradually approach the yield on dG. In this sense one might well say that the cost of current government services can be paid for not only by the current and future generations but even by past generations.

There remains to consider how far our conclusions need to be modified if the *omc* is less than unity. Since a debt-financed expenditure does not affect the behaviour of net worth, our analysis of this case basically stands, although one can conceive of some rather fancy circumstances in which modifications would be necessary.[1] In the case of tax financing, however, an *omc* of less than one implies that part of the burden of the expenditure will fall on later generations, who will receive a smaller bequest. It can be readily seen that the reduction in $K = W$ available to them will be of the order of $(oms)(dG)$, where *oms* denotes now the over-life marginal propensity to save. The differential burden of debt versus tax financing on society will correspondingly be of the order of $r(omc)(dG)$ instead of rdG.[2] In other words, the propensities to consume and save relevant to the long-run effect are precisely the over-life ones.[3] Unfortunately, these are propensities about which information is currently close to zero, both in terms of order of magnitude and stability, although some attention has begun to be devoted to this question.[4]

Our analysis of the differential burden of tax versus debt financing could stand a great deal of refinement and qualifications to take proper account of the specific nature of the taxes levied to pay for dG or for the interest on the

[1] It is conceivable that, *e.g.*, the tax newly imposed to defray the interest cost might reduce the bequests. To this extent an even greater burden is placed on later generations, which will inherit a smaller K for two reasons: because of the smaller W and because of the wedge dG between W and K. An even fancier possibility is that the new tax might spur the initial generation to increase its bequests to help their heirs pay for the new tax. This would, of course, increase the burden on the current generation and decrease that on posterity.

[2] Note that, regardless of the value of *omc*, the current generation must always fare at least as well, and generally better, under debt than under tax financing, even if it capitalised fully the new taxes that must be raised to pay the interest bill on the new debt. For, even in the highly unlikely event that the amount $r(dD)$ per year necessary to pay the interest bill were levied entirely on the initial generations, as long as they lived, this liability is limited by life, and hence represents a finite stream whose present value must be less than the amount dD which would have been taken away in the case of tax financing. See on this point also footnote 1, p. 746.

[3] Even with an *omc* of less than unity it is likely that the impact of the tax on bequests handed down from one generation to the next would gradually disappear so that W and K would eventually be unaffected by the tax-financed expenditure. But this is in the *very* long run indeed.

[4] See, *e.g.*, J. Tobin and H. W. Guthrie, " Intergenerations Transfers of Wealth and The Theory of Saving," Cowles Foundation Discussion Paper No. 98, November 1960.

debt. But it is clear that these refinements can in principle be handled by proper application of the framework set out in this section. We shall therefore make no attempt at working out a long list of specific cases,[1] and will proceed instead to point out the implications of our framework for a somewhat different class of problems, namely where the change in debt occurs without any accompanying change either in government purchases or taxation.

VIII. "Gratuitous" Increases in Debt, Repudiation and Inflation

For analytical convenience we may start out by considering a case which has admittedly rather limited empirical relevance: namely, where the government debt is increased at some date t_0 by an amount dD by a "gratuitous" distribution of a corresponding amount of bonds.[2] Presumably, at least in this case, the proponents of the classical burden argument, if they apply their reasoning consistently, would have to agree with the proponents of the classical non-burden argument that the increment in the National Debt puts *no burden on the economy as a whole*, either at the time of issuance or thereafter, except for frictional transfer costs. For while it is true that from t_0 on, tax-payers are saddled with extra taxes to defray the interest bill, it is also true that the receipt of interest would not have arisen without the creation of extra debt. Note that this conclusion does not rule out the possibility that the operation may result in some transfer between generations, if by a generation we mean the set of members of the economy born at a particular date: thus the interest accruing to those receiving the gift will very likely be paid, at least partly, by a younger generation. But these are still mere income transfers involving no overall burden.

But once we recognise that the overall burden of the National Debt derives from its effects on the private stock of capital, then it becomes clear that, by and large, both classical doctrines agree with the wrong conclusion. This is indeed quite obvious in the case of a unity *oac*, a case illustrated graphically in Fig. 2 (*a*). The solid line AA shows as usual the behaviour of $W = K$ in the absence of the gift. For the sake of variety, we deal here with a growing economy with positive saving and rising wealth.[3] If the gift is distributed all in one shot at point t_0, then at that point W will rise by dD, with no change in K. But now between t_0 and $t_0 + L$ the members of the generation that received the gift will gradually dispose of the bonds (or of other assets that they may have exchanged against the bonds) by selling them to current savers and using the proceeds to increase consumption over what it would have been otherwise. As this takes place, the aggregate

[1] By so doing we are also deliberately by-passing the other major issue of fiscal policy, that of the distribution of the burden between income classes.

[2] In order to avoid side issues, we will assume that the coupon rate on these bonds is such as to make their market value also equal to dD, and that no change occurs in the government purchase of goods and services, G.

[3] Just for reference, we may note that according to the Modigliani–Brumberg model, if income were growing at approximately exponential rate, W would be growing at the same rate.

rate of saving, and hence the accumulation of net worth and capital, is reduced. The result is that W gradually approaches the base path AA, while K, which is always lower by the wedge dD, falls below it. By $t_0 + L$

Fig. 2

Effect of "Gratuitous" Changes in Debt on Net Worth, W, and Capital, K, (unity over-life propensity to consume)

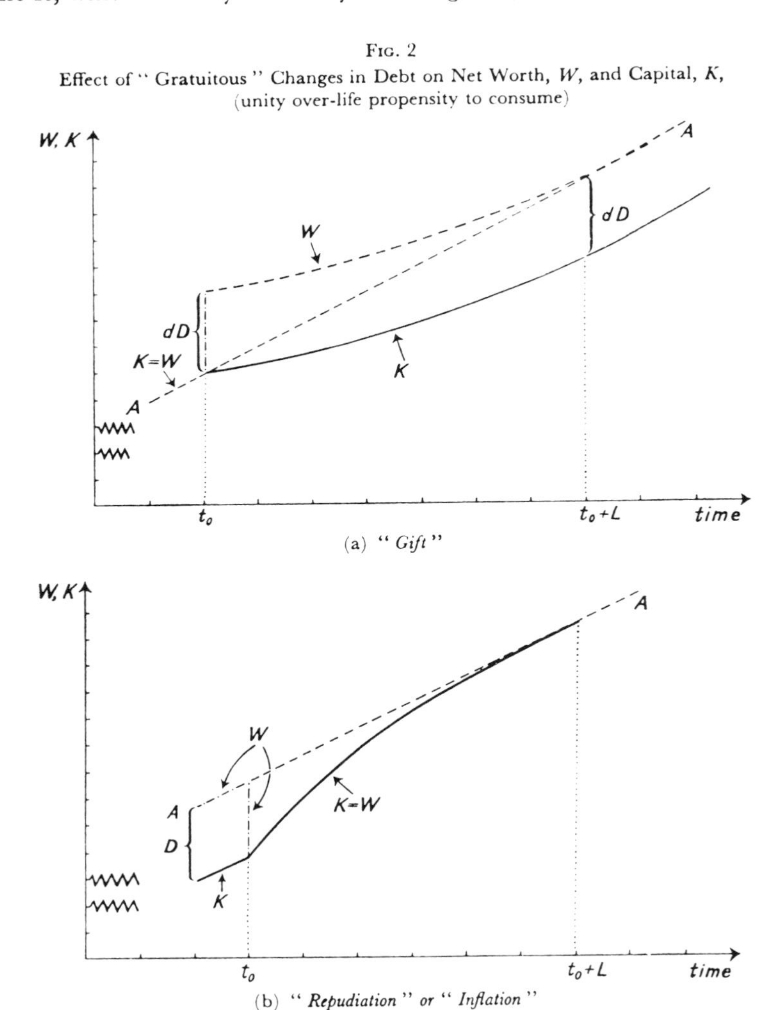

(a) "*Gift*"

(b) "*Repudiation*" or "*Inflation*"

the cumulated rate of saving and physical capital formation will have been reduced by (approximately) dD, so that W will tend to coincide with AA and K to be dD lower, a position that will tend to be maintained thereafter. Thus an increase dD in the National Debt, even if it arises from a free gift, will put a burden on the economy as a whole. Under unity *oac*—after a transient period in which W is increased as a result of the gift—this burden will approach the level $r^*(dD)$, and hence approximately equal the interest on the debt.[1]

If the *omc* is less than unity, then the burden will be smaller, tending to $(omc)(r^*dD)$, because the gift will tend to increase W " permanently " by $(oms)(dD)$ and hence K will tend to fall only by $(omc)(dD)$. As usual, this burden can be removed at any later point by taxation and retirement of the debt, but only at the cost of putting the burden on the taxed generation, which in effect will be paying for the benefits enjoyed by the beneficiaries of the gift.

Our conclusion applies directly, but for an appropriate change of " sign," to the case of a " gratuitous " one-shot reduction in the National Debt, as indicated in Fig. 2 (b). Such a reduction might be accomplished by repudiation, total or partial, or by a capital levy, or, much more importantly and frequently, by the simple device of (unanticipated) inflation.

[1] This conclusion is strictly valid only in so far as the fall in disposable income brought about by the fall in K is matched by an equal fall in consumption. To the extent, however, that consumption falls somewhat less, cumulated saving may fall somewhat more, pushing W and K to a lower position than in our figure: but this extra adjustment will in any event tend to be of a second order of magnitude. The nature and size of this adjustment can be exhibited explicitly with reference to the Modigliani–Brumberg model of consumption behaviour. As indicated earlier, this model implies that, in the long run, the aggregate net worth of consumers tends to be proportional to their (disposable) income, or (1) $W = gY$, where the proportionality constant is a decreasing function of the rate of growth of income. Suppose initially income is stationary as population and technology are both stationary. We also have the identity (2) $W = K + D$, where D denotes the National Debt. With population and technology given, the effect of capital on income can be stated by a " production function " (3) $Y = f(K)$. We have stated in the text that a gratuitous increase in D, or more generally an increase in D which does not result in government capital formation or otherwise change the production function, will tend to reduce K by dD and Y by r^*dD: *i.e.*, we have asserted $\frac{dK}{dD} \simeq -1$ and $\frac{dY}{dD} \approx -r^*$, where $r^* = \frac{df}{dK} = f' \simeq r$. By means of equations (1)–(3) we can now evaluate these derivatives exactly. Solving (2) for K and using (1) and (3) we have $K = gf(K) - D$. Hence $\frac{dK}{dD} = gf'\frac{dK}{dD} - 1$ or $\frac{dK}{dD} = \frac{-1}{1-gf'} = \frac{-1}{1-gr^*}$. Similarly, $\frac{dY}{dD} = \frac{-r^*}{1-gr^*}$ and $\frac{dW}{dD} = \frac{-gr^*}{1-gr^*}$. Thus, if $r^* \simeq r = 0{\cdot}05$ and g is in the order of 4, then $\frac{dK}{dD}$ is $-1{\cdot}25$ instead of -1 and $\frac{dY}{dD}$ is $-0{\cdot}625$ instead of $-0{\cdot}05$.

I am indebted to Ralph Beals, presently a graduate student at Massachusetts Institute of Technology, for pointing out that these formulæ are not entirely general, for, within the Modigliani–Brumberg model, the second-order effect is not independent of the nature of taxes employed to defray the interest bill. In fact, the formulæ derived above are strictly valid only if the revenue is raised entirely through an income tax on non-property income. With other kinds of taxes, one obtains somewhat more complicated formulæ. For instance, if the taxes are levied on property income this will depress the net yield of wealth below r, which in turn will, in principle, affect the proportionality constant g of equation (1). However, exploration of several alternative assumptions suggests to me that the outcome is unlikely to be appreciably different from that derived above, at least in the case of direct taxes.

It can also be shown that the above formulæ will tend to hold, at least asymptotically, for an expanding economy in which population grows at an approximately constant rate and/or so does productivity as a result of technological change which is neutral in Harrod's sense (cf. *Toward a Dynamic Economics* (Macmillan, 1949), p. 23). The main features of such a growth model are discussed in Ando and Modigliani, *op. cit.*

Thus a (once and for all) doubling of the price level is entirely equivalent to a repudiation of one-half of the National Debt at the original price level—although it has, of course, all kinds of other widespread economic effects. As far as the National Debt is concerned, this operation puts a burden on the owners of the bonds by reducing the real value of their interest income as well as the real value of the principal. In so far as the first effect is concerned, we have a mere transfer from the bond-holders to the tax-payers, with no overall effect. But the reduction in the principal generates an unmatched reduction in consumption, and hence a *transient* higher rate of saving. The resulting increase in the capital stock will benefit all those living after the inflation—provided, of course, private capital has a positive marginal product and the potentially higher rate of saving is utilised for capital formation rather than being wasted in depressed income and unemployment.

From the content of this section and the previous one it should also be apparent that our analysis basically supports Meade's conclusion concerning the burden of the deadweight debt, although this conclusion is derived by a very different line of reasoning. The deadweight debt is a burden because: (*a*) it generates a corresponding gap between aggregate net worth W and the aggregate stock of capital K^*, and (*b*) we can expect that this gap will result primarily in a fall in K^* rather than in an offsetting rise in W. Thus, if we conceive two communities A and B identical with respect to natural endowments, technical know-how and habits of private thrift, and which differ only in that A has a deadweight debt D' and B has none, community A will be poorer, roughly, by D' times the marginal productivity of capital plus frictional transfer costs.

IX. Deficit Financing in War and in Depression

In this concluding section we propose to apply our tools to see what light they shed on the two classical and empirically relevant issues: the pre-Keynesian problem of war financing and the post-Keynesian problem of deficit created as part of a counter-cyclical stabilisation policy.

In order to face squarely the core issue of war financing, let us be concerned with the case of a major war effort of the type outlined earlier in Section III, in which the stock of capital in existence at the termination of the war is independent of the methods used to finance it. It follows immediately that, independently of financing, the war will impose a burden on post-war society as a whole to the extent that the stock of capital in existence at its termination—counting only whatever portion is useful to satisfy the post-war requirements—is less than what would have been there in the absence of war. In order to examine the residual effects, if any, of methods of financing, we must suppose that, in spite of the war's severity, we have some choice as to the extent of taxation. Also, to keep separate for the moment the possible role of inflation, we must suppose that untaxed income in excess of the predetermined consumption level is prevented from bidding up the price of goods—whether through voluntary abstention or through a fully successful system of rationing. In these conditions the unspent income must result in an increase in government debt held by the private sector, either directly or through financial intermediaries. Thus the level of taxation versus deficit financing determines essentially the size of the increment in government debt, dD. Now suppose, for the sake of the argument, that the war had been entirely financed by taxes, dD being accordingly zero. It then follows from our earlier analysis that the burden of the war will be borne almost entirely by members of the war generation. For, in addition to the sacrifice of consumption and other amenities *during* the war, they will also bear the brunt of the reduced capital stock, their accumulation of net worth being limited to the permitted privately financed capital formation. Thus the burden falling on society as a whole after the war will fall primarily directly on the members of the war generation (affecting others only to the extent that the reduction in the stock of capital reduces total income by more than the return on capital). They will be forced after the war to maintain a reduced level of consumption over the rest of their life, tending to save heavily in their remaining earning span and to dissave at a greatly reduced rate thereafter. This behaviour in turn will produce, after the war, an abnormally large rate of aggregate saving, gradually declining with the disappearance of the war generation. As a result, by the time the war generation has disappeared, the war-time reduction in capital formation may have been substantially made up—this being more nearly true the closer the *oac* is to unity and the smaller the initial loss of capital.

If, on the other hand, through lower taxes the war generation is permitted to increase its terminal net worth by an additional amount dD, the effect, with respect to the present issue, is essentially the same as though at war's end it had been handed down gratuitously a corresponding amount of government bonds.[1] As usual, this will enable them to maintain a higher post-war consumption, reducing capital formation, by an extent that can range as high as dD, if the *oac* is unity. Thus the debt financing will generate both: (i) a transfer from the post-war to the war generation to the extent of taxes levied on the former to pay interest to the latter, and (ii) a permanent burden on society as a whole to the extent that the stock of capital is permanently reduced by dD—less any increase in W resulting directly from dD.[2] In so far as in the immediate post-war period the

[1] If the bonds issued during the war carried an exceptionally low rate of interest because of the monopoly position of the Government in the market the gift in question should be regarded, for present purposes, as represented by the market value of the bonds.

[2] Note that the incremental debt dD could be regarded as a burden on society even if the economy tended to suffer from long-run stagnation, *i.e.*, a chronic tendency for a very low or zero marginal productivity of capital. For while it is true that the larger consumption bestowed on the war generation would help to sustain consumption, and thus full employment, the same result could be achieved by reducing the taxes and expanding the consumption and saving of whoever was present at the appropriate later time.

Government, to speed up the reconstruction, pushes capital formation by raising taxes and creating a surplus, the long-run effect is eliminated. But the burden of debt financing is placed to that extent on those living in the relevant post-war period, which may again consist in part of the very same war generation.

If inflation is permitted to develop in the course of the war or immediately following it our analysis remains valid, provided the increment in the debt is measured in real, rather than money, terms. This net real increment can be expressed as $\frac{D_0 + dD}{1 + dP} - D_0$, where D_0 is the pre-war debt and dP is the relative increase in the price level in the course of the war inflation. The above quantity, it will be noted, may even be negative if $dP > \frac{dD}{D_0}$, *i.e.*, if the increase in prices exceeds the relative increase in the debt. In this case the war generation will be made to carry even more than the cost of the war (unless its plight is improved by post-war transfers of income); and later generations may conceivably end up by benefiting from the war, at least following the transient period of high saving rates and rapid capital accumulation. Perhaps the picture we have been drawing has some relevance for an understanding of the post-war experience of such countries as Germany, Italy and Japan.

It seems hardly necessary to point out that our analysis in no way implies that in financing a war the use of debt should necessarily be minimised. Quite aside from obvious incentive considerations, there may be perfectly good equity reasons for lightening the burden of the generation that suffered through the war by granting them a more comfortable life after the war, at the expense of later generations.

We come finally to the effects of debt generated as a counter-cyclical measure. In view of the complexity of the problem, we shall have to limit ourselves to a sketchy treatment of a limited class of situations. Our main concern is to show that, even in this case, debt financing, though quite advantageous to the current generation, will generally not be costless to future generations, at least in terms of gross burden.

Consider a situation where, in spite of the easiest possible monetary policy and with the whole structure of interest rates reduced to its lowest feasible level, the demand for private capital formation is inadequate to absorb full-employment saving with a balanced budget. But let us suppose that the situation can be counted upon to be temporary and not to recur for a long time to come. If the Government does not step in there will be a temporary contraction of employment accompanied by a contraction of consumption and of addition to net worth, which is limited to the amount of private capital formation. Suppose, on the other hand, the Government expands its expenditure to the extent needed to fill the deflationary gap, and thereby runs into a deficit dD. Let us also imagine that it succeeds in choosing its action perfectly so as to maintain full employment without inflation. Hence consumption will be kept at the full-employment level and so will the accumulation of net worth; except that this accumulation will now take the form of an addition to the National Debt to the extent dD. Thus the government action involves a current gain to society which can be measured by the income which would have been lost otherwise. What we wish to know is whether this gain places any cost on later generations (and if so, how it can be valued).

Under the assumed conditions the answer would have to be affirmative at least under unity *oac*. In this case, in fact, we can see that the cost which was spared to society would have fallen entirely on the members of the depression generation. They would have been forced over their lifetime to cut their consumption by an amount (whose present value is) equal to the lost income. This reduction would be distributed partly within the depression but partly *after* the recovery, to an extent equal to the loss in accumulation of net worth in the depression. This reduction of consumption would in turn give rise to a somewhat higher rate of capital formation after the recovery, so that by the time the depression generation disappears the stock of capital would tend to be back to where it would have been without depression. In other words, under the assumed conditions failure of the Government to act, though costly to the depression generation, tends to be costless to later generations. On the other hand, if the Government acts, the depression generation does not have to maintain a lower consumption after the recovery, and accordingly, the lost private capital formation during the depression is never made up. The creation of dD introduces again a corresponding wedge between W and K which will tend permanently to reduce the amount of physical capital available to future generations. Hence there is a loss to them to the extent that at later points of time an increment to the stock of capital would make any net positive addition to output. If the debt is never meant to be retired, then at least with well-functioning capital markets, the consol rate, being an average of anticipated future short rates, may provide at least a rough measure of the (appropriate time average) annual loss. And in this sense if the Government borrows long, the interest bill on the incremental debt may provide a rough measure of the average future (gross) burden placed on society as a whole.[1]

Once more, recognising that the government action may involve a gross cost to future society does not imply that the action should not be taken. In the first place, because of multiplier effects the gain in income to those present is likely to be appreciably larger than the lost stock of capital

[1] Of course, under our present assumptions the burden as measured by the opportunity cost will be essentially zero during the period in which the debt is created, regardless of whether it takes the form of long-term debt, short-term debt or currency creation. But in the last two cases the current interest cost will not appropriately reflect the average future burden, unless we also take into account the rate the Government will have to pay on bonds sold at later points of time to re-finance the short-term debt or to reduce the money supply in order to prevent inflation.

which approximates the present value of the sacrificed income stream. In the second place, if the Government spends on projects which produce a yield in the future, then the gross burden will be offset by the gross yield and the net outcome may even be positive. In the third place, the gross burden can be eliminated if at some future point of time the Government runs a surplus and retires the debt. It is true that this will tend to place the burden of the original deficit on those who pay the taxes financing the surplus. But if the surplus follows the deficit in short order these people will be, to a large extent, the very same ones that benefited from the original deficit; thereby the questions of inter-generation equity are minimised. The case for eradicating the deficit with a nearby surplus is, of course, strongest if the government expenditure provides nothing useful for the future, or if the deficit reflects a reduction in the tax bill, expenditure constant, resulting either from built-in flexibility arrangements or from *ad hoc* tax rebates. Thus, our analysis turns out to provide a strong case in favour of what used to be called the cyclically balanced budget.

Although we cannot pursue further here the complex issues raised by the burden aspects of counter-cyclical fiscal operations, we hope to have succeeded in showing how the tools we have developed may provide some insight into the problem. One point should be apparent even from our sketchy treatment: namely, that in so far as counter-cyclical fiscal policy is concerned, our analysis does not require any significant re-evaluation of currently accepted views. Yet, by reminding us that fiscal operations involve considerations of inter-generation equity even when used for stabilisation purposes, it may help to clarify some issues. It does, for example, establish a *prima facie* case, at least with respect to *ad hoc* measures as distinguished from built-in stabilisers, for a course of action that will minimise the " deadweight " deficit and stimulate investment rather than consumption.[1] More generally, considerations of inter-generation equity suggest the desirability of a compromise between the orthodox balanced-budget principle and the principle of functional finance, which might be couched roughly as follows: as a rule, the Government should run a " deadweight " deficit only when full-employment saving exceeds the amount of capital formation consistent with the most favourable feasible monetary policy; and it should run a surplus, in so far as this is consistent with full employment, until it has wiped out previous deficits accumulated in the pursuance of this policy.

FRANCO MODIGLIANI

Northwestern University,
Evanston, Illinois.

[1] These considerations, *e.g.*, cast some doubt on the desirability of relying on personal tax cuts explicitly announced to be but temporary. For there is at least some ground for supposing that the temporary nature of the cut will tend to reduce the desirable impact effect on consumption and increase instead short-run saving and the (possibly) undesirable delayed consumption.

Errata

Page 730, last line of text: delete the left parenthesis preceding "government."

Page 739, line 12: "$r(dD)$" should read "$r^*(dD)$."

Page 750, footnote 1, paragraph 1, last line: the number "-0.625" should read "-0.0625."

Monetary Policy and Consumption:

Linkages via Interest Rate and Wealth Effects in the FMP Model

FRANCO MODIGLIANI

I. Introduction and Outline

The purpose of the present paper is to examine the implications of the Federal Reserve-MIT-Penn Model (hereafter referred to as the FMP model) with respect to the central question with which this conference is concerned, namely whether and, if so, to what extent, monetary policy affects economic activity through its direct impact on consumers' expenditure. For the purpose of this paper we have chosen to concentrate on three major monetary policy variables: bank reserves, money supply and short-term interest rates. The model, however, incorporates several other variables within the control of the Federal Reserve such as reserve requirements, the discount rate and ceiling rates under regulation Q.

It will be shown that according to the FMP model the answer to the above question is decidedly affirmative and that indeed consumption is one of the most important, if not *the* most important, single channel through which the above tools affect

*While I bear the full responsibility for the main text, I wish to stress that the model construction and estimation, the method of analysis, and the specific results of simulations are the outcome of a close collaboration with many other persons who have contributed to making the FMP model possible. The present version of the model is primarily due to the efforts of Albert Ando, Robert Rasche, Edward Gramley, Jared Enzler and Charles Bischoff, besides myself. The consumption sector is primarily the result of collaboration with Albert Ando. However, we owe a substantial debt to earlier collaborators, and notably Frank deLeeuw and Harold Shapiro, who were responsible for part of the earlier work on this sector, Morris Norman had a leading role in developing the simulation program that made possible the simulation results reported here.

Mr. Modigliani is a Professor of Economics at the Massachusetts Institute of Technology.

directly and indirectly the level of aggregate real and money demand and thus, the level of output, employment, and prices.

The rest of this paper is divided into three parts plus a long epilogue. In Part I, we provide a summary description of the consumption sector of the model which differs in several important

TABLES and FIGURES

Figure 1a Time Path of Multipliers for Alternative Specifications of the Consumption and Tax Functions 28

Figure 1b Time Path of Multipliers for Alternative Specifications of the Consumption and Tax Functions 31

Figure 2a Response of Demand to an Exogenous Change in Net Worth .35

Figure 2b Response of Demand to a Change in Interest Cost of Durable Services 35

Figure III.1 Expenditure Multipliers 42

Figure III.2A Response of GNP to an Exogenous Change in the Stock of Demand Deposits (Decrease) 47

Figure III.2B Response of GNP to an Exogenous Change in the Stock of Demand Deposits (Increase) 51

Figure III.3 Response of GNP to a 0.5 Billion Change in Unborrowed Reserves 55

Figure III.4 Response of GNP to a Change of 0.5 Billion in the Treasury Bills Rate 57

E.1 Reduced Form Tests of the FMP Model Specification of the Monetary Mechanism 64

E.2 Simulation Test of Reduced Form Estimates of True Structure 67

E.3 Simulation Test of Reduced Form Including Government Expenditure (G$) – Dependent Variable: Change in GNP$ 73

Appendix A Equations of the Consumption Sector of the FMP Model 75

Figure A.1 Dynamic Simulation of Real Consumption (1958 Dollars) ...78

Appendix B.1 Dividend-Price Ratio and Value of Corporate Shares 80

Dividend Price Ratio (RPD, 126) 80

Appendix B.2 Term Structure Equation for Corporate Bond Rate (RCB,91) .81

respects from the corresponding sector of other existing models. We review both the major equations of this sector and the basic hypothesis that underlie these empirical equations. We do not, however, go into the details of the procedures used in the testing and estimation of parameters and in constructing some of the variables; these topics are dealt with in a chapter ot a forthcoming monograph describing the FMP model which is being prepared jointly with Albert Ando. A preliminary draft of that chapter is available on request.

The major novelty of the FMP consumption sector consists in introducing explicitly aggregate private net worth as a major determinant of consumption. As will become apparent, it is primarily (though not exclusively) through this channel – the so-called wealth-effect – that monetary policy has a direct impact on consumption. In order to grasp fully the nature of this channel, it is necessary to review also the channels through which monetary policy variables affect consumer's net worth. This review completes Part I.

In Part II, we examine certain "partial equilibrium" implications of our consumption sector, and especially the implications of the wealth variable. In particular, we are concerned with the magnitude and pattern of response of consumption and income to a change in "autonomous" expenditure or, in other words, with the so-called Keynesian consumption multiplier. The need for this analysis stems from the fact that the introduction of wealth in consumption, coupled with the recognition of the feedback of consumption on wealth via saving, has some rather unusual implications which must be grasped to understand and evaluate the dynamic response of the entire system examined in Part III. For instance, it will be shown that if tax revenue is independent of income, then under an accommodating monetary policy (i.e. one that adjusts the money supply so as to keep interest rates constant) the long-run conventional Keynesian multiplier is *infinite;* while, with taxes, the size of the long-run multiplier is basically controlled entirely by the marginal tax rate. Also provided in Part II is an analysis of two further partial mechanisms which are important in understanding the links between monetary policy and consumption. One is the response of consumption and income to a change in net worth; the other is the effect of a change in interest rates via expenditure on durable goods, on the assumption that all other components of demand, as well as wealth, are unaffected by the change in interest rates.

With the background provided by Parts I and II, we proceed in the last part to examine the full response of the system to a change in the various policy variables. Our focus here is both on the magnitude and path of response and on the contribution of the consumption sector, especially via wealth effect, to this total response. This last question is analyzed by comparing the path of response of the full system with the response of a fictitious system in which we sever the link between interest rates and wealth via the effect of interest rates on the market value of corporate equity. The upshot of this section is a clear indication that in the FMP model the wealth effect is a crucial link in the response of aggregate output and employment to the policy variables, both in terms of magnitude and in terms of speed of response.

The epilogue endeavors to shed further light on the reliability of the results reported in the main text, through a number of tests dealing with certain critical issues raised by the so-called "reduced form" approach.

I. The Structure of the Consumption Sector – A Summary View

I.1 – Consumption

The structure of the consumption sector of the FMP model basically rests on the life-cycle hypothsis of consumption and saving which has been set forth in a number of previous papers.[1] This hypothesis states that the consumption of a representative household over some arbitrary short period of time, such as a year or a quarter, "reflects a more or less conscious attempt at achieving the preferred distribution of consumption over the life cycle, subject to the constraint imposed by the size of resources accruing to the household over its lifetime" (Modigliani, 1966). This hypothesis implies that consumption – defined as the sum of expenditure on non-durable goods and services plus the rental value of the stock of durable goods owned by the household – can be expressed as a linear function of labor income (net of taxes) expected over the balance of the earning span, and of the net worth (including the value of claims to pensions, etc.), with coefficient which depend on age, allocation preferences and, in principle, the rate of return on net worth (Modigliani and Brumberg).

For our present purpose we are interested in the aggregate consumption function which is obtained by aggregating over

[1] For a fairly up-to-date bibliography on the life cycle hypothesis, see the references cited in Modigliani (1970).

households in all age groups. It has been shown in Ando and Modigliani, that aggregate consumption can be expressed as a linear function of aggregate expected income and of aggregate net worth. Furthermore, the coefficients of the two mentioned variables can be expected to be reasonably stable in time under the further assumption (which is sufficient though not necessary) that tastes, the age distribution and the real rate of interest are reasonably stable over the relevant time horizon. We regard the first two assumptions as reasonable; the third assumption is much more open to question and will be touched upon again below.

The above considerations lead to the hypothesis that aggregate consumption can be approximated by a linear function of aggregate net worth and expected income.

Aggregate consumers' net worth is in principle directly observable, and we have endeavored to develop an explicit measure, with the cooperation of the Flow of Funds Section of the Board of Governors of the Federal Reserve System. Our measure is obtained, basically, by adding to the flow of funds estimate of money fixed assets, less debt, of the household sector, an estimate of the market value of corporate equity, of the market value of consumers' tangibles (consumers' durables plus residentail structures and land), and of net equity in farm and non-farm non-corporate business. The estimate of corporate equity is obtained by capitalizing the national income account estimate of net dividends by the Standard and Poor index of dividend yields, and coincides fairly closely with the estimate provided in the Flow of Funds series. In dynamic simulations of the model, net worth is endogenized by a perpetual inventory method; i.e., by adding to the beginning of period wealth, current household personal saving, an estimate of capital gains on tangibles, (computed from the endogenous change in the stocks and the endogenous change in price) and of the change in the market value of corporate equity. (See I.3 below). These changes do not unfortunately totally exhaust the sources of changes in wealth (they leave out, for example, capital gains on non-corporate business and on land and also on long-term bonds which, incidentally, are omitted also in the flow of funds estimates); there is, therefore, a small and rather erratic residual difference between actual changes in wealth and those obtained by the above method which, in historical simulations, we take as exogenous, and in projections we estimate as best we can.

In previous empirical estimates, dealing with annual data (Ando and Modigliani), the measure of wealth used in the consumption function was net worth at the beginning of the year, valued at average prices of the current year. Since in the FMP model the dependent variable is quarterly consumption, we use average wealth in the year preceding the current quarter, obtained as a weighted average of net worth at the end of each of the previous four quarters. The weights, which were estimated empirically, assign about half the weight to the current quarter with the rest distributed over the remaining three quarters with a rapidly declining pattern.

Expected labor income on the other hand is not directly observable; in previous work (Ando and Modigliani) we have approximated this variable by a measure of current net-of-tax labor income, adjusted for the effect of unemployment. In the FMP model, for a number of reasons explained in the forthcoming monograph, we have been led to replace labor income with personal income net of taxes and contributions, which essentially coincides with the standard measure of disposable income (except for the fact that we treat personal taxes on an accrual rather than on a cash basis). Because this measure includes a substantial portion of property income, which is subject to large transient fluctuations, we have approximated "expected" income with a distributed lag of actual income over the previous three years. Our final estimate of the consumption function can then be summarized as follows:

(1) CON = 0.67 x a weighted average of disposable income over the previous three years + 0.053 x a weighted average of net worth over the previous year.

The actual pattern of the weights is given in Appendix A, equation I.1. Figure A.1 compares the actual behavior of consumption with that computed from equation I.1.

Since the results of Section III concerning the role of consumption in the response to monetary policy depend critically on the presence of wealth in the consumption function and on the size of its coefficient, it is proper at this point to inquire about the reliability of equation (1) above. We summarize here a few major considerations which, in our view, provide solid ground for confidence in our estimates, both qualitatively and quantitatively.

(i) From a narrow statistical point of view we can report that the coefficients of wealth in the above equation are highly significant by customary statistical standards; (the t-ratios of the individual coefficients reach a value of around 8 for the two middle coefficients).

(ii) Not only does the addition of wealth improve the explanation of consumption but in addition it produces a fairly dramatic reduction in the serial correlation of the errors, from over .8 to .6.

(iii) Furthermore, both the size of the coefficient and their significance is quite sturdy under variations in the detailed specification of the equation or variations in the period of time chosen for the estimation, provided the period is sufficiently long and includes some cyclical fluctuations.

(iv) The coefficients reported above, which were estimated over the period 1954-1 to 1967-4, are quite consistent with the results for annual data for the period 1929-59 reported in Ando and Modigliani, and with evidence on the stability of the wealth-income ratio in the United States at least since the beginning of the century, analyzed in Modigliani (1966). To be sure, the coefficient of the wealth variable is somewhat lower than reported in the papers cited; but this decline is readily accounted for both in principle and in order of magnitude, by the change in the definition of income which now includes the return on property, (cf. Modigliani, 1966, pp. 176-177).

(v) The basic form of our equation is a fairly straightforward implication of the life-cycle model which has by now passed a number of favorable tests. See, for example, in addition to the references already cited, Houthakker; Modigliani (1970); Leff; Weber; Landsberg; Singh et al.

(vi) Finally, aggregate consumption functions of the general form (1) above have by now been estimated for a number of countries, despite the serious difficulties encountered in securing estimates of private wealth, and have confirmed fairly uniformly the importance of wealth in explaining the behavior of consumption. In particular, to the author's knowledge such estimates have been carried out for the United Kingdom, Australia, (Lydall), India, the Netherlands, Canada, and Germany, (Singh et al) and the wealth variable has been found to be highly significant with the possible single exception of India. The coefficients of the wealth variable have an appreciable scatter (though they are generally higher than our coefficient) but this is not too surprising in view of differences in the comprehensiveness of the concept used and in the quality of the basic statistics.

Quite recently the role of wealth in consumption for the United States has been challenged at least implicitly by some authors, and in particular by Fair (cf. Fair (1971b) and the references therein) on the ground that the wealth variable may really be proxying for some measure of "consumer sentiment." First, Fair (1971a) has shown that an index of consumer sentiment based on the series compiled by the Michigan Survey Research Center, and which he refers to as MOOD, makes a significant contribution to his equations explaining, respectively, expenditure on consumer durables, non-durables, and services (though in his service equation the highly significant contribution of the MOOD variable is somewhat marred by the fact that its coefficient is *negative*). Next, Fair (1971b) reports the finding that both durable and non-durable expenditure (in current dollars) are more or less significantly correlated with the Standard and Poor index of stock prices, but that when the variable MOOD is added to the equations, with appropriately chosen lags (one and two quarters for durables, and two quarters for non-durables but, surprisingly enough, never contemporaneous) then the S&P index becomes altogether insignificant. He concludes from this evidence that "the level of stock prices does not have much of an independent effect" (p. 22). These results and conclusion can give rise to some justified concern, for while our measure of wealth is total consumer net worth, it is nonetheless true that movements in the stock market contribute non-negligibly to the short-run movements of this total.

In assessing the relevance of Fair's conclusions for our present purpose, it should be noted that, as Fair and others have found, the consumer sentiment index is significantly correlated with an index of stock market prices (cf. Friend & Adams, Hyman). The direction of causality in this observed association could of course run either way. Fair has actually faced this issue and provides some interesting evidence that the causation runs, at least in part, from the stock market to MOOD (1971(b), pp. 11-13, and Table 1). Under these conditions, if monetary policy can affect the level of stock prices, it would still have a direct impact on consumption by way of its effect on consumers' sentiment – and whether this effect on sentiment, and thus finally on expenditure, is a nondescript psychological response or instead the consequence of an improved financial position is a rather idle question of little operational significance. In any event, we are able to report here a more direct response to Fair's challenge. We have actually taken Fair's MOOD index and added it to our consumption function. For the sake of completeness, tests were run both with the current value of MOOD and with the value lagged one and two periods. In either case, the addition of MOOD has a hardly noticeable effect on our estimates of the wealth coefficients or their significance. Specifically, when the current value of MOOD is added, the sum of the wealth coefficient drops but by .004, and the individual coefficients as well as the sum remain highly significant. The coefficient of MOOD has a t-ratio of somewhat over two, but the point estimate implies that an increase of 1 percent in the MOOD index would increase real per capita consumption at annual rates, now running at around $2,300, by only about one dollar (or aggregate consumption by $.2 billion.) Since in 50 of the 60 quarters for which MOOD is available, it has remained in the range 90-100, and its extreme values are 78 and 103, it is seen that the contribution of MOOD is at best rather negligible. (By contrast a 1 percent change in wealth, now running at around $3 trillion, changes per capita consumption by some four dollars in the first quarter and some eight dollar within a year). When we add instead the value of MOOD lagged one and two quarters – which is more consistent with Fair's specifications – the t-ratios of these coefficients are respectively 2.2 and 2.7 but both signs are *negative*! The point estimates are in both cases – 1 dollar per point of the index. In view of this result it is not surprising that the sum of the wealth coefficients actually rises somewhat, by .012, while the sum of the income coefficients drops by .1.

We thus seem to be fairly safe in concluding that the wealth effect does not exhaust itself on changing consumers' sentiment. We have, at the moment, no plausible explanation for the negative sign of lagged MOOD and merely note that it is consistent with the negative sign for MOOD lagged two quarters reported by Fair in his service equation. Finally, in view of its modest and marginally significant contribution, we do not plan at the moment to add MOOD to our consumption function, especially since this would require adding an equation to explain MOOD itself. However, for purposes of short-run forecasting one might gain a little by making use of the actual value of the index, if one is not bothered by the negative sign.[2]

One final point deserves brief mention in relation to our present consumption function. We have noted earlier that, in principle, the coefficients of this function and, in particular, the coefficient of wealth could be a function of the rate of return on wealth. We have made some sporadic attempts at testing this possibility but since they met with little success, mostly because of multicollinearity problems, they have been abandoned for the moment. In part, this decision was motivated by the consideration that it is not possible to establish a priori whether a higher rate of return should increase or decrease consumption. However, a recent contribution (Weber) reports some evidence that the rate of return may matter at least marginally and

[2]It is interesting that the addition of lagged MOOD has the effect of reducing the autoregression coefficient of the error term from 0.5 to 0.3; in part for this reason the standard error S_u drops from 9 to 7 dollars per capita.

that it may actually have a *positive* effect on consumption (i.e. a negative effect on saving). It is our intention to look further into this matter, but at the present this possible effect has been ignored.

I.2 Consumer Expenditure

Consumption, the dependent variable of equation (1), is not directly a component of aggregate demand. The relevant component is instead personal consumption expenditure (EPCE) which is obtained by subtracting from CON the rental value of the stock of durables and adding consumers' expenditure on durable goods (ECD) or gross consumers' investment is durables. This expenditure is accounted for by a model analogous to that used for several other investment sectors – vis., a stock adjustment or flexible accelerator model. That is, expenditure is proportional to the gap between the "optimum stock" and the initial stock of durables, after allowing for depreciation, which in the case of consumers' durables is estimated to be quite high, 22.5 percent per year. The optimum real stock in turn is a linear function of consumption in which the coefficients of consumption is itself a linear function of the real rental rate. Finally the real rental rate per year is measured by the ratio of the price index of durable goods to the consumption deflator multiplied by the sum of three terms: the depreciation rate, plus a measure of the opportunity cost of capital minus a measure of the expected rate of change of consumers' durable prices. As a measure of the (risk-adjusted) opportunity cost of capital we have used the corporate bond rate (RCB).

Our model also allows for a short-run dynamic effect, by adding to the argument of the durable equations the current level of saving. The rationale for this term is that some portion of transient variations in income, and hence saving, will be reflected in corresponding variations in ECD. The resulting equation for consumers' durable expenditure is reported in Appendix A.1, equation I.2, while further details about the model and its estimation are provided in the forthcoming monograph. We may finally note that from the expenditure on durables and the depreciation rate we can compute endogenously the current stock of consumers' durables which is then used to estimate the rental component of consumption – see Appendix A.1, equations I.3 to I.6.

It is apparent from the above description that our durable equation is not directly affected by wealth (or the stock market) except through its effect on consumption. In the light of the results of Fair and Hyman, we have been led to test the possible effect of MOOD, which might indirectly bring the behavior of stock prices to bear also on this component of expenditure. Preliminary results indicate that this variable has a positive coefficient with a t-ratio of around 2. The point estimate implies that a 1 percent change in the index would increase expenditure by some 3/100 of 1 percent of consumption or roughly $100 million at current rates. This is again rather small compared with the current rate of over $80 billion, but may bear further analysis. Since the MOOD variable is not at present in the model, for the present analysis we ignore the possible role of MOOD on durable expenditure. As a result we may perhaps tend to underestimate the wealth effect via the stock market, but the bias would seem to be of a second order of magnitude at best.

I.3 Monetary Policy, Interest Rates and the Market Valuation of Corporate Equity

As we have indicated, the main channel through which monetary policy affects consumption via wealth is through its effect on the market valuation of corporate equity which is an important component of net worth – roughly one-third at the present time. We need therefore to provide an outline of the nature of this mechanism in the FMP model.

a) Corporate Equities

Conceptually, the market value of equity is obtained by capitalizing the expected flow of profits generated by the existing corporate assets at a capitalization rate which depends on the real rate of interest, a risk premium and expected growth opportunities. Expected profits is a function of dividends (on the ground that under prevailing payout policies dividends tend to be roughly proportional to expected long-run profits) and of current corporate profits. The real rate of interest is approximated by the corporate bond rate and adjusted for the expected rate of change of prices.

We have had, perhaps not surprisingly, a great many problems in translating this conceptual framework into an operational one and the actual structure of the model and estimated coefficients leave us far from satisfied. On the whole we must consider this sector of the model as unfinished business, and we are continuing work on it even if with some qualms as to whether it will ever be finished to our satisfaction.

For the moment the market value of corporate equity is obtained by capitalizing net dividends by an index of dividend price ratio. This dividend yield in turn is estimated as a linear function of the bond rate with a short distributed lag (5 quarters) and of a measure of the expected rate of change of prices. This measure is simply a weighted average of past rates of change of prices with weights derived from coefficients estimated in the term structure equation (see below). In our empirical estimates, however, we have been unable to uncover any significant effect of price expectations until 1966; for earlier years therefore the real rate coincides with the money rate up to a constant. This procedure is clearly a rather arbitrary one though it finds some faint support in survey data on price expectations of business economists collected by Livingston and analyzed both in a forthcoming paper on the investment function and by Turnovsky. Finally the list of interdependent variables includes the ratio of current profits to dividends; as expected this variable has a negative sign on the ground that when current profits are high relative to current dividends, then expected profits are also high relative to dividends, which raises the price of stocks relative to dividends thus reducing the dividend yield. We have had no success in measuring variations in growth expectations except insofar as these may be captured by the last mentioned variable. Finally we have not made much headway in measuring changes in the risk premium except through a decreasing time trend terminating in 1960, which accounts mechanically for the sustained decline in dividend yields during the Eisenhower era.

The specific form of the equation and its estimated coefficients are reproduced in Appendix B.1. The one slightly cheering aspect of the equation for present purposes is that the estimate of the effect of change in interest rates is both quantitatively sensible and statistically fairly significant (a t ratio of about 4). Finally the equation fits the data better than one might have expected; however, we take limited satisfaction in a good fit when the equation rests on somewhat shaky theoretical underpinnings.

As a final remark we should point out that there exists an alternative version of the stock market equation which we have occasionally used in simulation and extrapolations. This equation differs from the one in Appendix B by one main feature, namely that it contains a short distributed lag on the rate of change of the money supply. The addition of this variable makes a non-negligible contribution to the fit (though it also tends to increase the serial correlation of the errors). This is not surprising in view of the findings reported by several investigators and in particular, Sprinkle.

However, we can find little justification for the role of this variable – unless it is proxying for some other variable or variables, e.g. for the level of the stock market credit or for short-term interest rates. Unfortunately every attempt at testing such variables directly leads to most disappointing results as these variables were consistently insignificant while the money supply remained significant. We still cannot see any direct mechanism through which the rate of change of money could affect market values – except possibly because operators take that variable as an indicator of things to come. But even this explanation is hardly credible except, perhaps, in the last couple of years, when watching every wiggle of the money supply has suddenly become so fashionable. For this reason we do not use this alternate equation in the analysis reported here. We can report however that comparison of simulation of changes in money supply using the alternative equation indicates that this equation implies a somewhat stronger but mostly a somewhat faster response (especially to monetary expansion. See below).

b) The Money Market and Short-term Interest Rates

To complete our picture we need still to review the channels through which monetary policy affects the long-term rate which enters the stock market equation. In the FMP model the point of impact of monetary policy on the system centers on the money market in which the short-term rates (represented in the model by the three-month Treasury bill rate and by the commercial paper rate) are determined by the interaction of the money demand equation and the money supply. The modeling of these markets needs only brief mention since it has been discussed in detail in a recent paper (Modigliani, Rasche, Cooper). In the current version of the model this section differs only in minor details from the structure presented there.

In short, the money demand depends basically on the short-term rate (r) and the level of income. Hence, if we take the money supply as the policy variable, then the short-term rate is determined by the given money supply relative to the level of money GNP; furthermore, since there is but a small simultaneous (i.e. within the same quarter) feedback from short-term rates to GNP, one may say that, in the shortest run, r can be made to take any desired value by an appropriate level of M. In the construction of the model, however, we have actually assumed that, normally, the policy variable controlled by the Federal Reserve is unborrowed bank reserves; in this situation the money supply is itself endogenous and is determined together with r by the simultaneous solution of the money demand and supply equations. The money supply depends – given enough time for adjustment – on unborrowed reserves (adjusted for reserve requirements) and on r relative to the discount rate (which controls target free reserves). Thus, in the last analysis, r and the stock of money are determined by unborrowed reserves relative to GNP and, to a minor extent, by the discount rate. However, because the money supply as well as the demand have rather complex patterns of gradual adjustment, at any point of time these variables depend also on the recent rates of change of unborrowed reserves, of GNP and of commercial loans (which in turn are closely related to changes in GNP).

The gradual adjustment of money demand to interest rates has the well known implication that a given change in the stock of money causes the short-term rate to overshoot considerably the new equilibrium level which is reached with a one quarter lag by the bill rate and somewhat more gradually by the commercial paper rate. (For the bill rate the overshooting in the first quarter is by a factor of roughly 6, while for RCP it is somewhat below 4). The situation is strikingly different in terms of the response to a change in unborrowed reserves; the gradual response of banks to a change in reserves implies that the money stock responds gradually and smoothly. For instance, in a dynamic simulation of the money sector alone (i.e. with GNP and commercial loans exogenous) the increase in the stock of demand deposits per billion dollar increase in unborrowed reserves is but $1.3 billion in the same quarter and rises gradually to $4.5 billion at the end of one year and to somewhat over $7 billion by the end of the second year. As a result the response of interest rates is also gradual and smooth. For instance, in the above mentioned simulation it is found that both short rates decline fairly sharply in the first quarter but then continue their decline till the third or fourth quarter; furthermore while the level reached then is lower than the equilibrium level the overshooting is by a factor of less than two. These rather different patterns of response must be kept in mind when we proceed to examine in Section III the response of the system to alternative policy variables, especially since the differences are amplified by the mechanism determining the long-term rate to which we now finally turn.

The long-term rate in the model is at present measured by Moody's yield on AAA rated corporate bonds. (We are no longer entirely satisfied by this measure which is distorted by tax effects and hope at some point to replace or augment it by an index of new issue rates). This rate is essentially generated through a term structure equation accounting for the spread between the short-and the long-term rate. We think of this spread as equalizing the short-term rates with the expected holding yield of long term securities plus a risk premium to induce investors with pervailingly short interest to participate in holding the existing stock of long-term securities. The spread thus reflects primarily the expectation of capital gains or losses arising from expected changes in long-term rates. It is well known that this formulation implies that the long-term rate can be expressed as an average of the current short-term rate and of expected future short-term rates (or equivalently of the expected future long-term rate) plus risk premium. Following, and somewhat generalizing, the approach set forth in Modigliani and Sutch, and in Sutch, we hypothesize that expected future rates are the sum of the expected *real* rates plus the expected rate of change of prices ($\dot{p}$), and that both the expected real rate and the expected rate of change of prices are largely determined by the past history of the real rate, and of the rate of change of prices, respectively. This leads to an equation in which the long rate is finally accounted for by a long moving average of short-term past money rates measured by the commercial paper rate, RCP, and of past $\dot{p}$. The underlying theory would lead us to expect that the sum of the coefficients of the distributed lag on RCP should be close to unity, while the sum of the $\dot{p}$ coefficients should be around zero. This conclusion follows from the consideration that if both RCP and $\dot{p}$ remain constant for a sufficiently long time (and hence the real rate is itself constant) then future short-term money rates should also be expected to remain constant at the current level. Finally, the risk premium is approximated by a constant, plus a measure of instability of the short-term rate over the recent past.

The resulting equation, reproduced in Appendix B.2, is found to fit the data remarkably well (the standard error is but 8 basis points) and the coefficients satisfy rather closely the above specifications. (The sum of the r coefficients is .94 and that of the $\dot{p}$ coefficients .07).[3]

Two points are worth stressing in connection with our term structure equation. First, the presence of the $\dot{p}$ term implies that, even though the short-term rate in our model is basically a monetary phenomenon, which can be manipulated through monetary policy, the long-term rate cannot be so readily manipulated. For, if the Central Bank, by holding down short-term rates, endeavors to make the long-term rate artificially low, the resulting excess demand will cause accelerating inflation which, in turn, will cause the long-term rate to rise even if the short-term rate is prevented from rising by a sufficiently fast (and accelerating) growth of the money supply.

The second point concerns the role of the variable representing the recent instability of the short-term rate (which we measure operationally by an eight quarter moving standard deviation of RCP). The coefficient of this variable is quite significant (t ratio of roughly four); it is also again quite sturdy under alternative specifications and periods of fit as long as they are long and with varied experience. We stress this point because it turns out, somewhat to our own surprise, that this term has an important effect on the response of the system to monetary policy because it creates a significant *asymmetry* between *expansionary* and *contractionary* policies. The reason is simply that, through that term, any substantial *change* in short-term rates tends to produce an increase in the long-term rate; thus a restrictive policy tends to raise long-term rates in two ways, namely by increasing expectations of future rates and by initially increasing the risk premium; on the other hand the effect of reduction in short-term rates is partly offset in the short run by the increased risk premium. We are inclined to the view that, qualitatively, this mechanism is a real one and limits the feasibility of a fast reduction in the long rate, even if short rates are made to fall fast; this certainly seems to square well with certain recent experiences. We have of course much less confidence in our numerical estimate of the size of this effect; some of the results reported below suggest that we may be overestimating it and that further effort at refining the estimates may be very much worthwhile.

[3]The sum of the p weights reported in the Appendix is 28.9, but this figure must be divided by 400 to convert the index of prices used to a percentage at annual rate, so as to have the same dimensions as the interest rate.

Having thus reviewed the sectors of the model that are essential for an understanding and evaluation of the results reported in III, we proceed in Part II to the analysis of certain crucial component mechanisms of the total effect.

II. Analysis of Some Partial Mechanisms

II.1 The Consumption Multiplier: Implications of Wealth in the Consumption Function

The multiplier is generally defined as the increment in output brought about by a change in "exogenous" expenditure -- i.e. in any component of demand that is not itself directly related to income -- usually expressed per dollar of increment in the exogenous expenditure. The excess of the multiplier over unity is thus a measure of the amplification of the exogenous change, whether brough about by a policy variable or otherwise. In the most elementary text book version of the Keynesian system only consumption is directly dependent on current disposable income and taxes are independent of income: thus

$$(1) \qquad Y = C + E$$

$$(2) \qquad C = c_0 + c(Y - T)$$

where E is exogenous expenditure and tax revenue, T, is also exogenous. Then

$$(s.1)\ C = [c_0 + c(E - T)]/(1 - c),$$

$$(s.2)\ Y = [c_0 + E - cT]/(1 - c)$$

so that the income multiplier is $\frac{dY}{dE} = \frac{1}{1 - c}$ and the consumption multiplier is $dC/dE = c/(1 - c)$.

However, as soon as we generalize the consumption function (C.F.) to allow for some lag of consumption behind income, income will respond but gradually in time to a one time change in E. Hence the multiplier must be described by the difference between two paths; namely the path of income with and without the exogenous change. This difference expressed as ratio to dE can be thought of as the multiplier path and generally changes in value with t, the length of time elapsed since the change in E; *the* multiplier is then frequently defined as the limit reached by this ratio as t grows, if such a limit exists.

Let us denote by $[Y^*(t), C^*(t)]$ the path followed by [Y,C] after the change in E at t = 0. Then the income multiplier at date t can be expressed as $\frac{Y^*(t) - Y(t)}{dE} \equiv M_y(t)$, where Y(t) is the path in the absence of the exogenous change (i.e. for dE = 0); and the consumption multiplier at date t is $M_c(t) \equiv [C^*(t) - C(t)]/dE$. *The* multiplier could then be defined as $M_y = \lim_{t \to \infty} M_y(t)$; and similarly for M_c. For the above elementary model we find

$$\text{(s.3)} \qquad M_y(t) = \frac{1}{1 - c} \text{ for all } t = M_y$$

and

$$\text{(s.4)} \qquad M_c(t) = \frac{c}{1 - c} \text{ for all } t = M_c$$

Suppose now we replace the elementary consumption function (2) with a simplified version of our C.F. in which we neglect the lags: thus

$$\text{(2')} \qquad C(t) = c[\,Y(t) - T(t)] + w\,W(t)$$

where W(t) is net worth at the beginning of period t, and w a constant. Assuming no capital gains or losses, we also have the identity

$$\text{(3)} \qquad W(t) - W(t-1) = S(t-1) = Y(t-1) - T(t-1) - C(t-1),$$

where S denotes personal saving. In turn (3) implies

$$W(t) = W(0) + \sum_{\tau=0}^{t-1} S(\tau) \qquad t = 1,2, \ldots$$

Substituting from (1) we then find

$$S(t) = E(t) - T(t)$$

and

$$C(t) = c[C(t) + E(t) - T(t)] + w\left\{W(0) + \sum_{\tau=0}^{t-1} [E(\tau) - T(\tau)]\right\} + c_o$$

Solving the last equation for C(t):

$$\text{(s.1')} \quad C(t) = \frac{1}{1-c} \left\{c[E(t) - T(t)] + w\,W(0) + w \sum_{\tau=0}^{t-1} [E(\tau) - T(\tau)]\right\} + \frac{c_o}{1-c}$$

Similarly $C^*(t)$ is given by the right hand side of (s.1′) but with E(t), T(t) replaced by $E^*(t)$, $T^*(t)$. Suppose that at t = 0 a once and for all increment dE is added to E so that $E^*(t) = E(t) + dE$. Then, from (s.1′) we find

$$C^*(t) - C(t) = \frac{1}{1-c} \left[c(dE) + w \sum_{\tau=0}^{t-1} dE\right]$$

and therefore

$$\text{(s.4')} \qquad M_c(t) = \frac{C^*(t) - C(t)}{dE} = \frac{1}{1-c}[c + wt] = \frac{c}{1-c} + \frac{w}{1-c}\, t$$

$$\text{(s.3')} \qquad M_y(t) = \frac{Y^*(t) - Y(t)}{dE} = \frac{1}{1-c}(c + wt) + 1 = \frac{1}{1-c} + \frac{w}{1-c}\, t\,.$$

Thus if the C.F. includes wealth linearly the *multiplier increases with time, linearly at the rate w/(1 - c);* and as t grows the *multiplier also grows without bound.* This apparently paradoxical result can actually be readily understood. The increase in the exogenous expendtiure dE can be looked at as an increase in "offset to saving" which causes saving in every period to increase by the same amount dE. But the increase in saving in turn increases wealth which again increases consumption and income, forever. The relation between the multiplier implied by standard C.F. and that implied by (2′) is shown graphically in figure 1a below by the two solid lines.

If we allow for consumption to depend on an average of past income and wealth and let c and w denote respectively the sum of the income and wealth coefficients, then, in general, the multipliers

Figure 1a
TIME PATH OF MULTIPLIERS
FOR ALTERNATIVE SPECIFICATIONS OF THE CONSUMPTION AND TAX FUNCTIONS

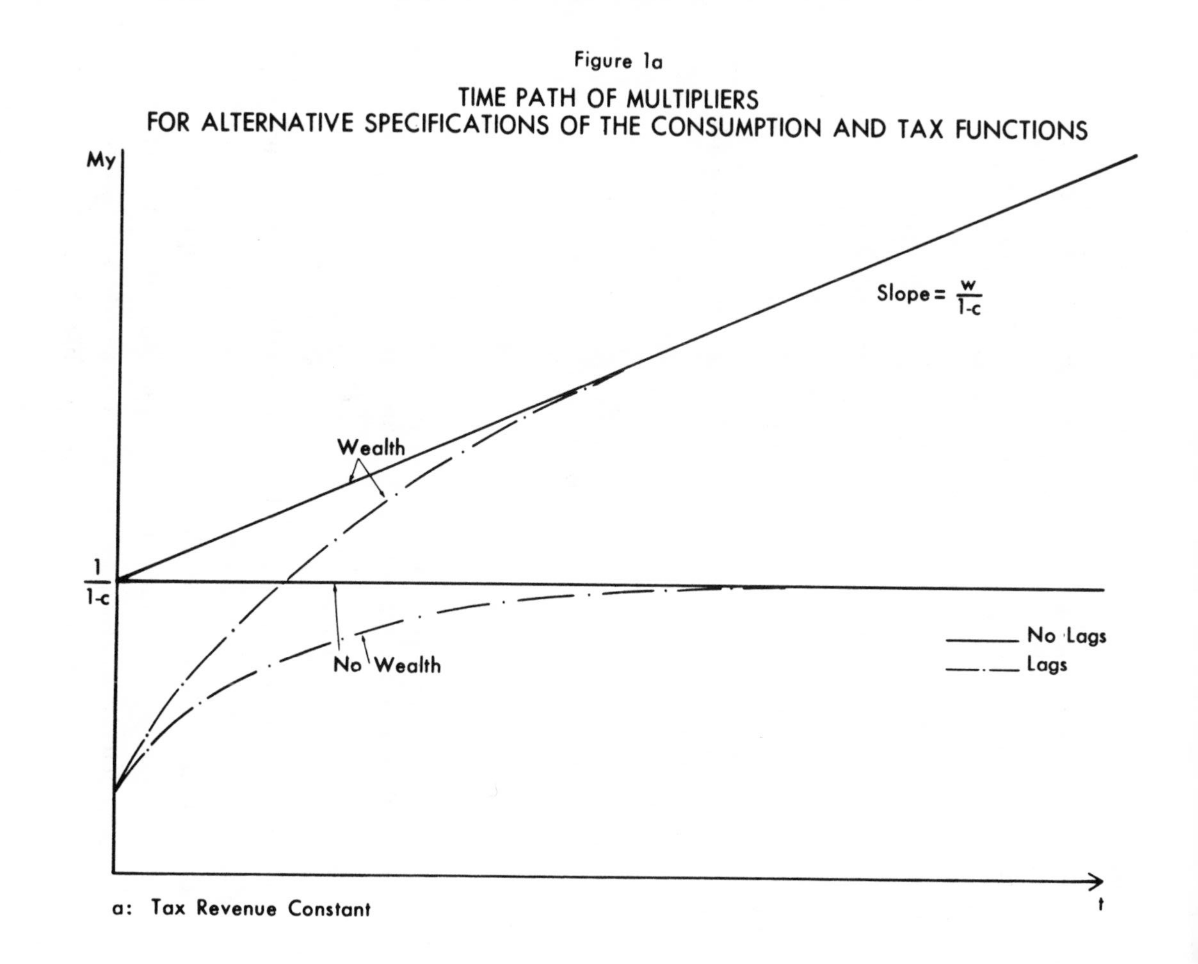

will approach asymptotically the graph obtained in the no lag case, as shown by the dotted lines in figure 1a.[4]

If, instead of taking tax revenue as a constant, we assume, more realistically, that it is proportional to income, say

$$(4) \quad T = \theta Y$$

then, with the standard consumption function (2) one gets the well-known result

$$(s.3.\theta) \qquad M_y(t) = 1/[1 - c(1 - \theta)] \qquad \text{for all } t \geq 0 .$$

On the other hand with our function (2′) one can readily establish that the result is

$$(s.3'.\theta) \qquad M_y(t) = \frac{1}{1 - c(1 - \theta)} + \frac{\frac{1 - \theta}{\theta}(1 - c)(1 - \lambda^t)}{1 - c(1 - \theta)} ,$$

$$\lambda = 1 - \frac{\theta w}{1 - c(1 - \theta)} < 1 .$$

Thus again the multiplier keeps growing in time (since $\lambda < 1$); however, in this case it approaches an asymptote:

$$M_y = \lim_{t \to \infty} M_y(t) = \frac{1 + \frac{1 - \theta}{\theta}(1 - c)}{1 - c(1 - \theta)} = \frac{1}{\theta} .$$

It is seen that, in this case, the addition of wealth makes the limiting value of the multiplier, M_y, *totally independent* of the parameters of the consumption function and simply equal to the reciprocal of the (marginal) tax rate θ (though the time path $M_y(t)$ does depend on these parameters). What happens in this case is that, as consumption and income rise under the impact of the original change dE and the

[4] Our result about the long-run multiplier follows directly from the fact that wealth appears in the C.F. with constant coefficients. It is not obvious, however, that this result is consistent with the life cycle model. Indeed, to derive from that model a C.F. of the form (2′), one needs a number of additional assumptions of "constancy" which might fail to hold when E is changed by a fixed amount once and for all. It can, in fact, be shown that our result is fully consistent with the life cycle model.

induced increase in saving and wealth, tax revenue also rises and this reduces disposable income and saving, and hence accumulation. The process comes to an end when the increase in income has become large enough so that the increase in tax take, $\theta M_y dE$, is just enough to offset the increase in dE. This obviously occurs when M_y is $1/\theta$. At this point dE is exactly offset by an increase in government receipts at the rate dE, the incremental saving is reduced to zero, and wealth stops growing. In figure 1b the solid rising curve c shows the approximate multiplier path implied by our C.F. (1) of part I, assuming an instantaneous response to income and wealth: it is computed by taking $c = .7$, $w = .05$ and $\theta = .5$. The assumed value θ is a rough approximation to the marginal tax rate for the U. S. economy for the mid-sixties, when account is taken of both the personal tax rate, (Federal plus state and local) social security contributions, and the tax rate on corporate profits. Then from equation (s.3′ .θ), $M_y(0) \simeq 1.5$, $M_y \simeq 2.0$. Also $\lambda \simeq .96$ so that the approach to equilibrium is rather slow, around 4 percent per quarter. The solid horizontal line a shows by contrast the multiplier implied by the standard C.F. assuming the same values of c and θ.

The lower dotted curve d in figure 1b shows the actual multiplier path computed from a dynamic simulation of the FMP model in which an exogenous component of expenditure – specifically exports – was increased by $10 billion above its actual value, beginning with 1962.1, while all other components of demand, except consumers' expenditure, were taken at their historical level. This path differs from the theoretical path c for two main reasons: i) the gradual response of consumption to income, and, to a minor extent, to wealth; ii) the fact that consumers' expenditure includes durable goods and the response of this conponent includes "accelerator effects." For an interim period ECD has to rise enough to generate the desired addition to the stock of durables, though eventually the increment settles down to what is necessary to offset the depreciation of the increased stock. It is this accelerator effect that is responsible for the overshooting of the accelerator path, though this overshooting is quite modest because of the very gradual response of consumption.

Figure 1b

TIME PATH OF MULTIPLIERS FOR ALTERNATIVE SPECIFICATIONS OF THE CONSUMPTION AND TAX FUNCTIONS

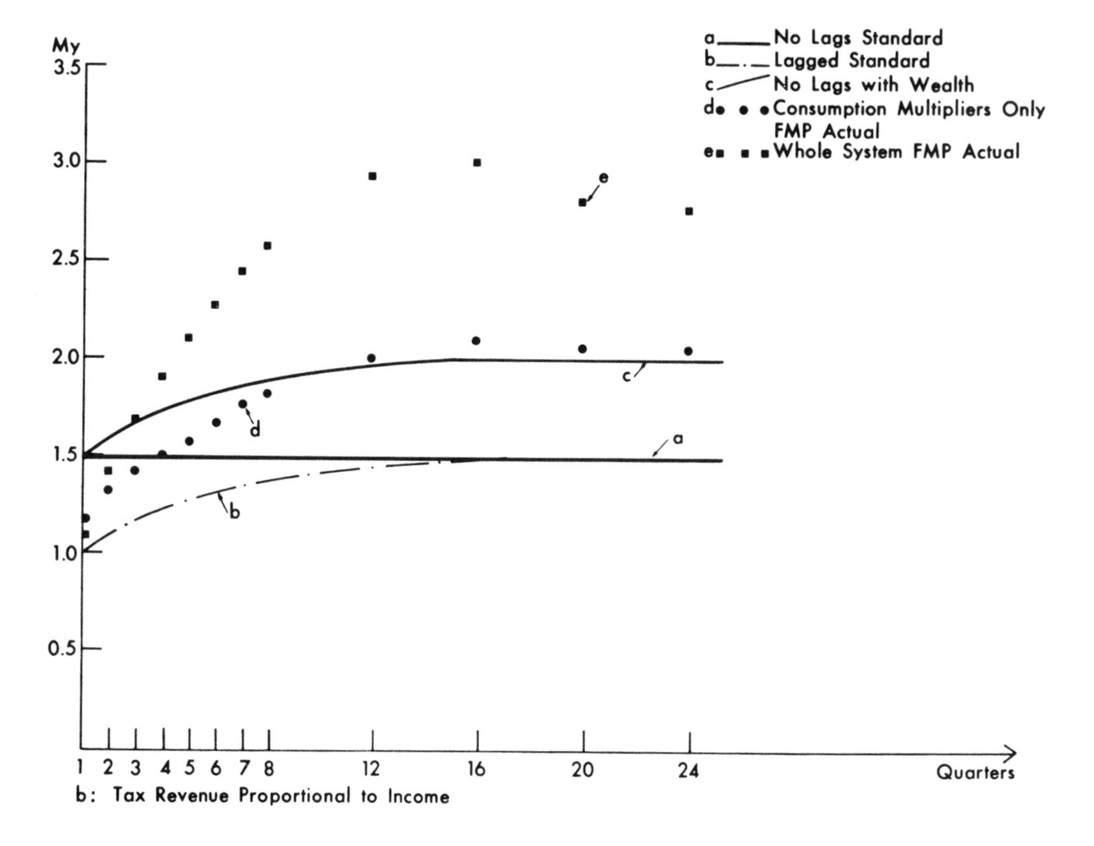

As expected, the multiplier M_y is around 2. This rather modest multiplier reflects the powerful stabilizing effect of our very high marginal tax rate (combined with the assumption that neither the Federal nor state and local governments respond to the increased tax take by changing either tax rates or expenditure). It is also seen that the response is fairly fast, with some 75 percent of the total effect occuring within one year.

To complete the picture we also show by the upper dashed line c in figure 1b the multiplier response when we allow all other components of demand (except real Federal Government expenditure) to respond to the increase in output. We thus allow for i) "accelerator effects" on plant and equipment expenditure and inventories, ii) effects on residential construction, iii) for response of state and local government expenditure to the increase in the tax base, [5] and also iv) for larger imports (which reduces the multiplier). However since we keep the financial sectors and, in particular, *interest rates unchanged,* we are implicitly assuming a "permissive" monetary policy which accomodates the higher money income resulting from the increase in real output (and from the increase in prices which would accompany the expansion of employment) by an appropriate expansion of the money supply. Or, to put it in familiar text book language, we are measuring the effect of a change in exogenous expenditure on shifting the Hicksian IS curve, rather than the shift in equilibrium resulting from the intersection of the shifted IS curve with an unchanged LM curve.

It is not surprising that the resulting multiplier is distinctly larger, somewhat slower, and exhibits more pronounced overshooting than when only consumers' expenditure is endogenous. The peak value of the multiplier rises roughly from two to three. About 2/3 of the peal effect is reached within the first year, and by the second year the proportion rises to over 90 percent. In section III we shall have occasion to compare this response with the path resulting from a different monetary policy; viz. a constant money supply, and thus

[5] In the FMP model, both expenditure and receipts of state and local Government are explained endogenously.

assess the restraining effect of a non-accommodating monetary policy.[6]

II.2 Real System Response to Change in Wealth

Another useful way of assessing the role of wealth in the consumption function is to examine the effect on GNP of an exogenous shift in that variable. The direct effect on consumption can of course be estimated directly from the coefficients of the consumption function reproduced in Appendix A. From these we can infer e.g. that a $10 billion change in W would change CON by some $.3 billion in the same quarter and by $.53 by the end of one year. At current level of net worth this means that a 1 percent increase in W, roughly $30 billion, changes consumption by about $.8 billion in the same quarter and by $1.5 billion within a year. However, this measures only the direct effect on CON. To get the direct effect on consumers' expenditure one needs to add the effect on consumers' durables which is more spread in time. Finally, to get the full effect on GNP, one should take further into account the multiplier effect which we have seen to reach a value of roughly 3, but over an even longer span.

In order to see how these various lags interact we have carried out a simulation in which W was increased by $50 billion in 62.1 and all real sectors were taken as endogenous while the financial sectors are again exogenous. Since in 62.1 wealth was nearly $2 trillion, the assumed increase amounts to 2.5 percent. Figure 2a reports the results of this simulation for GNP, expenditure on durable goods (ECD) and total consumers' expenditure (EPCE) all in constant prices.

In assessing the results it is helpful to remember that the direct effect on CON should be around $1.5 billion in the first quarter, grow to some $2.5 billion by the end of one year, and then remain there. (These figures are only approximate because the change in W is

[6]It should be noted that since the multiplier reported in Figure 1b represents the response of the system to an exogenous change in any component of aggregate demand for real private GNP, it measures, in particular, the response to a change in government purchase of goods – provided, however, that the change in expenditure did not result from defense procurement. This is because in the FMP model defense procurement begins to affect GNP, through inventories, beginning with the time at which the order is placed, and hence well in advance of actual expenditure. The expenditure occurs only when the goods are delivered, at which time inventories are reduced, largely offsetting the expenditure. Similarly, expenditure on compensation of employees, which is not a component of private GNP, also generates a somewhat different multiplier path.

in money terms and hence the real effect is somewhat reduced in time by the increase in CON deflator; however in the chosen period this increase was small -- of the order of 1 percent per year). It is seen that, through the various amplifying mechanisms, GNP actually rises by 4.3 within two quarters (an elasticity η of .3) to 7 in one year ($\eta = .5$) and reaches a peak effect of just over 8 by the seventh quarter ($\eta \simeq .6$), staying around that level till the end of the third year. It then declines slowly -- through this decline is, no doubt, due in part to increasing prices. Thus the direct effect on consumption, which is already sizable, gets amplified to a very substantial total. To illustrate, at current levels of W and GNP a 1 percent change in W would generate a change in GNP of nearly $3 billion within two quarters, over $4 billion within a year and nearly $5 billion before the end of two years. As for the composition of the total effect, it appears that, typically, around 2/3 is accounted for by consumers' expenditure and 1/3 by all other demand sectors (investment, plus state and local government, minus imports), though the share varies somewhat over time. It reaches its lowest point around the fourth quarter when the acceleration effects are most important. Some acceleration effects occur within the consumer expenditure sector itself through durables, though this is seen to be modest: the peak rate of durable expenditure is only some 30 percent higher than the steady state effect of about $1 billion.

In the light of these results it should not be surprising if a substantial portion of the impact of monetary policy were to occur through the role of wealth in the consumption function.

II.3 Real Systems Response to a Change in Interest Rates Via the Relative Cost of Durable Goods Services

The last partial effect to be examined here is the effect a change in interest rates on the rental rate of durables and thus on durable expenditure. We wish to stress from the outset that we have much less confidence in the numerical results about to be presented than in those given in the last subsections, because we do not regard our estimate of the coefficients of the rental rate in the durable equation as very reliable, especially with respect to the lag structure. We hope nonetheless that these results provide at least a bearable approximation to the order of magnitudes.

A first answer to the question posed could again be gleaned directly from the coefficients of the ECD equation given in

Figure 2a

RESPONSE OF DEMAND TO AN EXOGENOUS CHANGE IN NET WORTH

NET WORTH INCREASED BY 50 BILLION IN 1962.1

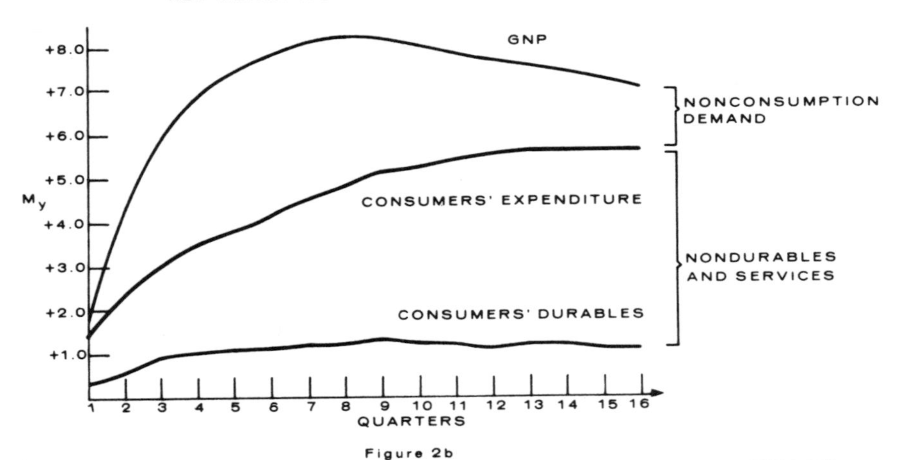

Figure 2b

RESPONSE OF DEMAND TO A CHANGE IN INTEREST COST OF DURABLE SERVICES

INTEREST RATE COMPONENT OF RENTAL RATE INCREASED BY 100 BASIS POINTS IN 1962.1; [SIGN REVERSED]

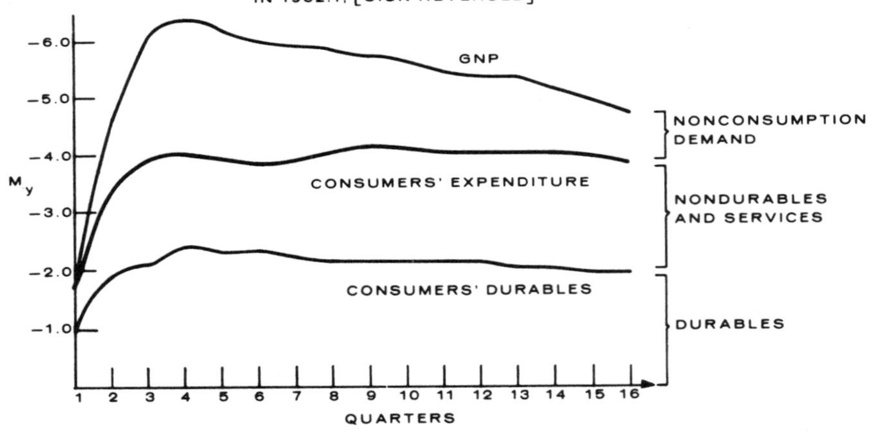

Appendix A: these tell us that a change of 100 basis points in the long-term rate (price expectation constant) would decrease durable expenditure by .002 of CON in the same quarter, and by more in the following quarter until the full impact effect of .0066 CON is reached in the fifth quarter. At current rates of CON, just below $500 billion, this would be a reduction of roughly $1 billion in the same quarter and over $3 billion by the fifth. These are again non-negligible magnitudes, though of course a change of 100 basis points in the long rate is a rather large one. But again these are only the direct effects, which do not even allow for the feedback effects through a change in the stock of durables. To estimate the total impact we must also allow for multiplier effects, and their distribution in time. Again we have endeavoured to throw light on these total effects through a simulation in which we have increased the long-term rate (RCB) by 100 basis points from 1962.1 on, while at the same time keeping it at the historical level for every other component of demand in which this rate appears, directly or indirectly, including the stock market. Our simulation therefore depicts the total effect of a change in RCB *only through its effect on the rental rate of durables.*

The results of the simulation are given in Figure 2b (with sign reversed). As background we may note that, since in the period '62–'65 CON was running around $330-380 billion, the direct effect should come to $.7 billion in the first quarter and rise to around $2 by the fifth quarter.

It can be seen from the table that initially, ECD rises a little more than these figures, reflecting the feedback of the multiplier effect on the desired stock of durables via CON; the peak effect is about $2.3 billion reached in the third quarter and maintained for the next year or so. But, because of the multiplier, the total effect on GNP soon becomes two to nearly three times larger, reaching nearly $5 billion by the second quarter and around $6 1/2 billion by the end of the year. Thereafter it declines very slowly returning to $5 billion at the end of four years.

Note that, given enough time, ECD declines again toward a long run level which is probably in the order of $1 billion. The overshooting in the first few quarters reflects a type of accelerator or rate of change effect of RCB. This can be seen as follows. The rise in RCB reduces the desired stock of durable goods. It can be shown that equation I.2 implies a long-run elasticity of the stock of durables with respect to RCB somewhat below .1. Since a change of RCB of 100 points is roughly a 20 percent change, the desired stock should change by some 2 percent or around $4 billion. Thus, in the long run, ECD should decline by the depreciation on 4 billion of stock, or around 1 billion. Initially, however, the decline must be larger so as to generate a decline of $4 billion in the stock itself. This is the acceleration effect referred to above.

In summary, the impact of interest rates via consumers' durable alone in the FMP model is again surprisingly strong, especially once we allow for direct and indirect effects. As an order of magnitude it appears that a 10 percent change in the real long rate would tend, within three quarters, to change real GNP by around six-tenths of 1 percent or around $4 1/2 billion at current rates, and this effect would be roughly maintained for a couple of years.

III. System Response to a Change in Policy Variables and the Role of Linkages Through Consumption

III.1 The Basic Approach

Our major interest here is in examining the implications of the FMP model concerning the role of the wealth effect in the response of the system to a change in policy variables, especially those traditionally associated with monetary policy. The basic technique by which we propose to analyze this problem consists in comparing the response of the entire system with the response to a "fictitious system" in which monetary effects through wealth are suppressed. This suppression is accomplished by the simple device of severing the connection between interest rates and the rate (RDP) at which dividends are capitalized. That rate is instead taken as exogenous (i.e. at its historical value, see below). Note that this is *not* equivalent to taking wealth as exogenous, since wealth contains many assets beyond equity in corporate enterprises; indeed as noted earlier, in recent years that component has amounted to roughly 1/3 of the total. Nor is it strictly equivalent to taking the market value of equity as exogenous. For, that value is obtained by capitalizing dividends and we continue to treat dividends as endogenous; thus any policy change which affects GNP will affect wealth by changing the flow of dividends both via real and via price effects. We proceed to list below a number of further operational aspects of our method of analysis which are essential for an understanding of the results, their scope, and limitations.

(i) For present purposes, we choose to measure "response" by the broadest conventional measure namely GNP, as defined in the

National Income Accounts. However, we exhibit the response of both real GNP (XOBE) and GNP in current dollars (XOBE$) from which one can also infer the price response. In principle, of course, we could also exhibit the response of any other endogenous variable of the system – say consumption or investment, or imports, or tax revenue, or other financial variables. However, because of limitation of space the results reported in figures and tables and the discussion in the text will focus exclusively on the two above mentioned measures of GNP.

(ii) The response is computed by the method of comparative dynamic simulations inside the historical period. That is, we first simulate the model with the policy variable on their historical path. We refer to this simulation as an "historical" one and denote the GNP so computed by GNP^c. Next, we run a second simulation with one or more policy variables changed in some specified way. We refer to this second simulation as a "policy" run and denote the resulting GNP by GNP^*. Finally, to complete the multiplier we subtract GNP^c from GNP^*, and, possibly, divide the difference by some measure of the change in the policy variable, in order to normalize the result. It will be recognized that, in the special case where the policy variable is an exogenous component of expenditure such as government expenditure on goods and services, the result of this operation is precisely the multiplier M_y, as defined in II.1. However, when the policy variable is a different one, then the notion of a multiplier will generally be ill-defined since the unit of measurement for the change in the policy variable is arbitrary, especially if that variable has a different dimension than the numerator, (as for instance if it were the stock of money, or the short-term rate). We still find it convenient to refer to the change in GNP as a policy multiplier but we shall have to make explicit the unit in which we measure the change in the policy variable.

(iii) Since our system contains a number of essential non-linearities, the multiplier response is in general not independent of "initial conditions," that is, of the state of the system at the beginning of the policy simulations or of the actual path of the exogenous variables over the period of the policy experiment. Because of limitations of space, we focus our attention on a single policy experiment generally starting in the near past, around the beginning of '67. The reason for choosing this particular period as the basic period of analysis is explained in (iv) below. We recall here that 1967 is a year in which unemployment was already quite low, and which was followed, historically, by a prevailing expansionary fiscal and monetary policy which further increased the inflationary pressures in the economy. To assess the sensitivity of our results to the specific initial and historical conditions we shall report, for comparison, selected results of a policy simulation beginning around 1962, a period of considerable slack of the economy followed by a very gradual expansion of aggregate demand, reduction of unemployment, and reasonably stable prices until 1965. The comparison also helps to assess whether the above described difference in initial conditions produces differential effects that are a priori credible and "sensible."

(iv) As we have indicated, several of our sectors allow for price expectational effects. In particular, such effects play a significant role more or less explicitly on (1) the stock market through RDP; and hence on any other variable that is directly related to RDP such as consumption, and plant and equipment expenditure; (2) equipment expenditure; (3) on expenditure on durable goods, (4) to some extent on housing starts; and finally (5) on long-term interest rates, both corporate, municipal and mortgage rates. We have also mentioned that, empirically, we have not been able to detect a significant direct effect of price expectations on either RDP or equipment and durable expenditures, until around 1966. On the other hand, the evidence suggests that price expectations were important throughout in affecting the relation between short-and long-term interest rates. As will soon become apparent, and is hardly surprising, the presence of a price expectational terms in sectors (1), (2) and (3) above is apt to be highly unstabilizing, especially for certain types of policies. We, therefore, felt it desirable to present multipliers both for the full system and for an artificial system in which the price expectational effects in (1), (2) and (3) are suppressed. These effects are automatically absent for any policy simulation which terminates before 1966. For simulations beginning on or after 1966, we can suppress the "price expectational mechanism" by the device of taking the rate of change of price term which appears in (1) (2) and (3) as a measure of expected p, as exogenously given at its historical value, instead of calculating it endogenously from the history of prices generated by the simulation. These simulations ex-price expectational mechanism enable us to assess the role of this mechanism. In addition, they also provide information on multipliers under initial conditions of price stability, since, in general, the price expectational term in our equations only begins to operate when the rate of change of prices rise above some threshold value (empirically estimated at 1.5 percent per year) and becomes fully operative only if $\dot{p}$ remains above this threshold for a substantial length of time (three years). It follows that our basic design consists in showing four different multipliers as follows: (a) full system with wealth effects; (b) same, without wealth effects; (c) full system without price expectational mechanism; and (d) same as (c) but without wealth. This enables us to examine not only the wealth effect but also its interaction with the price expectational mechanism.

(v) Because many of the policy variables in our system are functionally related to each other, the number of possible independent policy variables in any simulation is smaller than the set of policy variables. In carrying out a particular policy simulation one has to decide which other policy variables are taken as exogenous at their historical level, and this decision, in turn, determines which other potential policy variables are taken as endogenously determined. To illustrate, the set of our fiscal policy variables includes Federal expenditure, tax rates and government surplus; but only two of these variables can be chosen independently. Thus, in a simulation in which we change government expenditure we might take tax rates at their historical level. In this case, the receipts and the surplus will differ from their historical level and the expenditure effect will be partially offset by the fiscal drag (or built in stabilizers). Alternatively, we may take the surplus at its historical level, in which case, we cannot take tax rates as given. The same choices arise if the policy change were, say in money supply, except that now we would also have the choice of taking surplus and tax rates as exogenous and expenditure as endogenous. The multiplier will, of course, be quite different for the different possible choices. In the case of fiscal variables all this is well understood, and multipliers are generally defined on the assumption of given expenditure and tax rates and endogenous receipts and surplus. We shall here adhere to this convention; i.e. we will always take tax rates as given, and we also take Federal expenditure as given (in real terms) except when expenditure itself is the policy being changed. But when it comes to the monetary sector the situation is more complex and there are few clear precedents to go by. In particular, when we change a fiscal variable we could take as exogenous in the monetary sector any one of the following: (i) the money supply (currency plus demand deposits); (ii) the demand deposit component, (iii) the unborrowed base (bank reserves + net currency less borrowed reserves); (iv) unborrowed bank reserves.[7] Furthermore, if one takes unborrowed reserves as given, one also has the choice of taking as historically given the discount rate or instead the spread between the discount rate and the bill rate. Again, alternative choices can have significant effects on the size of the multiplier. For the present paper we have found it instructive to make different assumptions in different simulations and the choices made will be made explicit in each case.

III.2 The Expenditure Multiplier

We begin by presenting results for the multiplier response to an exogenous change in expenditure. This multiplier is of interest not merely because it measures the effect of a change in government expenditure on goods, but also because the response to any other policy variable is profoundly affected by "this multiplier". Indeed, this response can be looked upon as the superimposition of two effects: a direct effect of the policy variable on one or more component of aggregate demand plus the multiplier response to this direct effect.

Unfortunately, for the reasons explained in III.1, (v), "the multiplier" turns out to be an ill-defined concept, for it depends on what assumptions are made as to which monetary variable is exogenous. One possible assumption is that the exogenous monetary policy variable is the short-term interest rate, the Central bank supplying whatever amount of monetary base is required to maintain the short-term rate at the historical path. The multiplier under this assumption actually coincides approximately with the multiplier we have already presented in section II.1, figure 1b. We say "approximately" because there we took as given not just the short-term rates but all interest rates. Now, to a first approximation in our system all rates are determined by the history of the short-term rate (at least if we take as historically given the ceilings on all deposit rates). However, this approximation is really a good one only if the rate of change of prices does not differ significantly from the historical path,

[7] It is more questionable whether one could take as exogenous the total base or total bank reserves, at least in the short run, for borrowing initially responds to changes in the unborrowed component. In particular, under the present system in which required reserves are against *past* deposits, at least in the very short run, the asset decisions of (member) commercial banks largely determine (up to the very small level of excess reserves) the amount of reserves that the central bank *must* provide unless it wants to force banks to violate their reserve requirements; what the Fed can control is the volume of unborrowed reserves which in turn determines the extent of borrowing.

Figure III.1

EXPENDITURE MULTIPLIERS

Based on 10 Billion Change in Exports

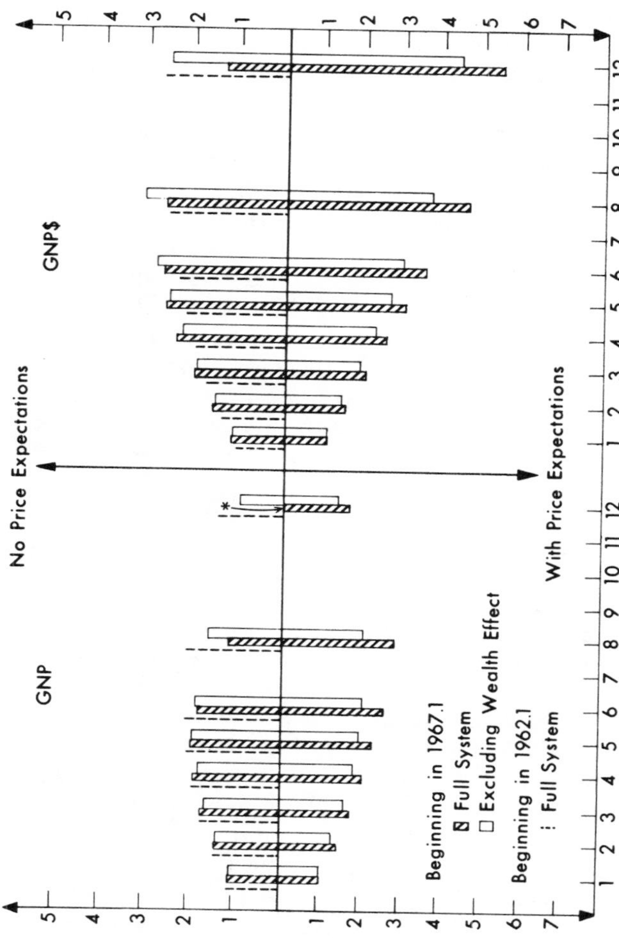

No Price Expectations

GNP

GNP$

Beginning in 1967.1

Full System

Excluding Wealth Effect

Beginning in 1962.1

Full System

With Price Expectations

quarters elapsed

quarters elapsed

* negative value -0.7 omitted

for otherwise, as already indicated under II.3, the long rate could move relative to the history of short rates.

Another possible assumption, which is frequently made, explicitly or implicitly, in speaking about *the* multiplier, is to take the money supply as given. This is the multiplier which we present in Figure III.1 but with one modification: what we take as historically given is not the total money supply but, more narrowly, the stock of demand deposits. This multiplier therefore assumes that the central bank provides all the base necessary to enforce the historical level of deposits and to accommodate the currency demand of the public. This particular choice for the exogenous monetary policy variable is perhaps a little unusual and indeed it was made more out of computational convenience and precedent than as a result of careful deliberation. However, it should be remembered that this definition will be roughly equivalent to taking the total money supply as exogenous as long as the policy experiment does not generate a significant discrepancy between the historical and the simulated ratio of demand deposits to currency, which is general can be taken as a good approximation. We shall therefore take the liberty of referring to this multiplier as "the multiplier-money-supply-given."

Our quantitative results are summarized in Figure III.1 in which we have tried to pack a good deal of information. First, the left portion of the figure deals with the real GNP multiplier while the right-hand side presents multipliers for GNP in current dollars, GNP$. In each half, the histograms appearing *above* the heavy horizontal line refer to multipliers computed *excluding* the price expectational mechanism for the quarter indicated at the bottom of the figure. The histograms appearing below the horizontal line are multipliers including the price expectation mechanism. Finally, for each quarter, we exhibit two columns: the black column shows the multiplier for the full system, while the white column shows the multiplier *excluding* the wealth effect. Both multipliers were obtained from a policy simulation in which real exports were increased by $10 billion beginning in the first quarter of 1967. Finally, the dashed vertical lines which appear for each quarter only on the upper left portion of the figure show the multiplier for a similar simulation beginning in the first quarter of 1962.

Examination of the black columns in the left top portion and comparison with Figure lb, which shows the "multiplier-interest-rate-given," brings out immediately some important facts. Taking money supply exogenous has very little effect on the multiplier M_y during the first year; in both cases, M_y begins just over one and reaches just below two by the end of the first year. Furthermore, excluding the wealth effect reduces the multiplier, but very marginally; in other words during the first year the wealth effect contributes but little to the size of the multiplier. But beginning with Q5 things look quite different. First, when M is given, M_y reaches its peak in Q5 as compared with three years when r is given, and the peak is very much lower, around two instead of three. Second, starting from Q6 the wealth effect actually *reduces* the multiplier and this unfavorable effect grows rapidly larger.

These results, are, at least qualitatively, very much in line with what one should expect. With M given, the increase in money GNP, shown in the right hand portion of the diagram, causes short-term interest rates to rise, which rise gradually communicates itself to long rates. The rise in long rates in turn tends to choke off some investment and also to reduce the value of corporate equity, choking off some consumption. This second effect, however, is absent when we exclude the wealth effect, and this explains why, with M given, the wealth link has eventually the effect of *reducing* the multiplier. On this ground, one would actually expect the multiplier cum-wealth to be lower than ex-wealth from the very first quarter rather than beginning with Q5 as in the graph. The reason why initially things work out the other way is that, while the higher interest rates do tend to increase the dividend price ratio, RDP, there is a small additional effect via the profit/dividend variable appearing in the RDP equation, which tends to lower RDP, and initially outweighs the interest effect.[8]

It is apparent from the graph in the right portion of the figure that the same general picture holds for the GNP$ multipliers, except that the increase in prices accompanying the increase in GNP leads to a higher multiplier, reaching a peak of 2.7 after six quarters (as compared with five for GNP). Of course, the very same price effect that bolsters the GNP$ multiplier contributes to reducing and turning around the GNP multiplier.

How sensitive are these multipliers to initial conditions? A rough qualitative answer can be obtained from the top left portion of the diagram by comparing the black histograms with the dashed line, showing the behavior of the multiplier in a relatively slack period, beginning in '62.1. It will be seen that the multipliers for the two

[8]As noted in I.3, the earning/dividend ratio enters with a negative sign; also, the increase in GNP through the multiplier increases corporate profits, while dividends are very sluggish; hence, the ratio rises, tending to reduce RDP and thereby having a favorable effect on wealth.

simulations are very close, indicating little effect of initial conditions. The earlier period multiplier is just a little higher and reaches a peak a little later because, through the curvilinearity of the Phillips curve, the multiplier effect on the rate of change of prices is a little lower in the early, slack period, which permits a little more growth in GNP. On the whole, this conclusion is qualitatively sensible; expenditure multipliers on real GNP are larger when there is more slack. Indeed, in the limit, if we started out with the labor force already at a very high rate of utilization, one would expect the real multiplier to dwindle toward zero as the government expenditure would have to crowd out rapidly other components of expenditure. The difference shown in the graph is perhaps smaller than one might expect; but, then it should be remembered that in 67.1 the rate of unemployment was still at 4.2, as compared with 5.5 in '62.

The fact that the GNP multiplier eventually decreases, both cum- and ex-wealth effects should not be regarded as surprising. Indeed, one can readily show that if our system is stable (as it seems to be at least with money supply given) then, in the longest run, the real multiplier, given M, must be zero. This is because as long as the multiplier is positive, prices must keep rising faster than in the base simulation (because of lower unemployment) and GNP$ must therefore be higher and so must interest rates. But the higher interest rate must tend to crowd out investment in any event, and consumption as well, if we allow for the wealth effect. In the longest run, therefore, the additional real exogenous increase in demand must displace an equal amount of other expenditure, leaving GNP unchanged. In this respect, our model should please the monetarists. But the relevant question is how long is the required run. It will be seen that for the simulation beginning in '67, the multiplier is negative by the twelfth quarter – crossing zero after about two and one-half years. For the earlier, slack period simulation, the zero crossing point is more like three and one-half years. Strictly speaking, of course, the zero crossing is not quite the end of the story, for, the response of the system to the shock is cyclical and, hence, the multiplier path will continue to oscillate around zero indefinitely. However, since the oscillations are quite damped, the first crossing point does provide a good fix as to the speed of the crowding-out effect. Using this criterion, the FMP model suggests that this effect occurs fairly fast, though much less so than the monetarists seem to hold.

What can we say about the longest run limiting value of the GNP$ multiplier? In contrast to the real multiplier we can be sure that in our model it will be positive. Indeed the limiting value of the interest effect must be positive in order for the exogenous increase to crowd out other components (and since, with GNP unchanged, real tax revenue must eventually also be unchanged if we assume real taxes to be a function only of real income, at least to a first approximation); but, with a higher r, there will be a higher velocity of circulation, which, with M constant, implies higher GNP$ through a higher price level.

Turning now to the lower half of the chart, we see that the price expectational mechanism considerably amplifies both multipliers, even with M given; the peak value of GNP is now around three and is reached after three years; the reason of course is that, at least for a while, the higher interest rates are offset by more bullish price expectations, which reduce pro tantum the "real" rate. Since this same expectation also tends to reduce RDP relative to the long rate, the wealth effect, at least initially, tends to amplify the multiplier. None the less, it is seen that eventually M_y reaches a peak and begins to decline rapidly, for with M given, eventually the increase in interest rates exceeds the increase in the expected rate of change of prices. In view of the low unemployment in the simulation period, the XOBE$ multiplier gets quite high; it reaches 6 by the end of our simulation and is still rising, though presumably it is not far from its peak.

Summarizing then, in the absence of price-expectational effects recognition of the wealth effect on consumption does not significantly affect our estimate of the real income multiplier in the first few quarters. But, eventually, it leads to a somewhat *lower* value, by contributing to the crowding out effect via consumption. With price expectations the wealth effect increases the multiplier somewhat over a period as long as three years, though again the effect is quantitatively modest.

III.3 Change in Money Supply (Demand Deposits)

Figure III.2 summarizes our results concerning the effect of an exogenous change in the stock of demand deposits. The results shown in part A were obtained from a simulation in which demand deposits (MD$) were reduced by $1 billion in 67.1 and another billion in 67.2. The choice of this particular pattern was dictated by two considerations. On the one hand, we wanted the change in M to be large enough so that our multipliers would not be distorted by rounding off errors. On the other hand, we wanted to avoid a large

Figure III.2A

RESPONSE OF GNP TO AN EXOGENOUS CHANGE IN THE STOCK OF DEMAND DEPOSITS

Effect, per Billion, of a 2 Billion Decrease Spread Evenly Over 2 Quarters

[sign reversed]

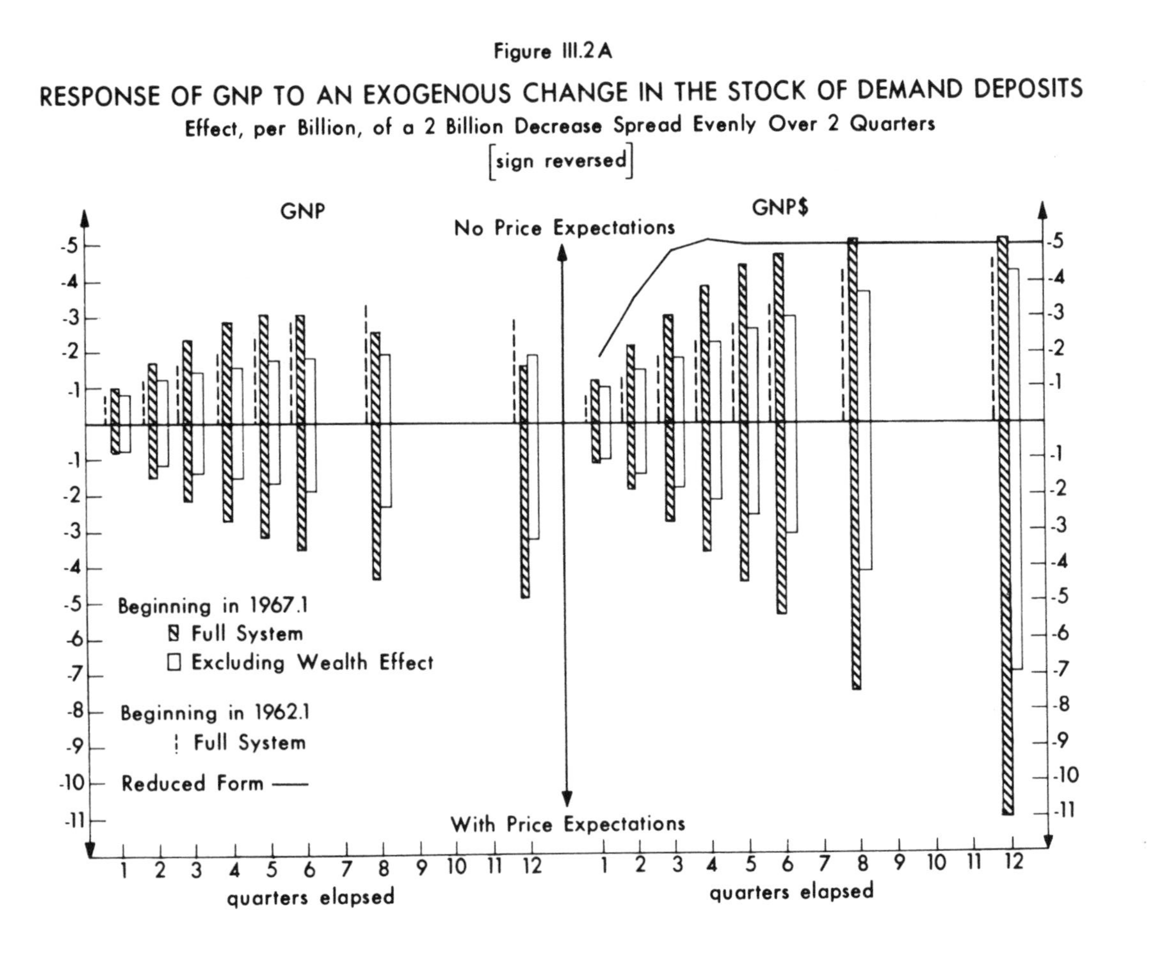

sudden jump in M which, for reasons discussed in I.3 would produce a sharp transient change in the short rate and hence increase the "risk premium" component of the long-rate equation. Since the stock of demand deposits in '67 was around $140 billion, an increase of $2 billion in a single quarter would have represented an annual rate of increase of some 6 percent over and above the historical growth which was already in the order of 4 percent. By smoothing the $2 billion increase over two quarters we halved the annual rate of increase in M over the period in which the additional M was injected. The histograms in Figure III.2 show the effect of the change in demand deposits on GNP beginning with the quarter of the second of the two increments, namely '67.2, per billion change in M.

In some respects the result of simulation of changes in M, discussed in this section, may be regarded as the most relevant ones for the purpose of this conference. We must warn, however, that in the light of the view of the monetary mechanism that underlies the construction and estimation of our model, we regard these results as somewhat less reliable than those resulting from a change in unborrowed reserves, reported in the next section.

Before looking at the results, it may be useful to observe that, from knowledge of the structure of the model, we can again deduce the limiting value of the multipliers in the longest run. By a reasoning analogous to that developed in III.2, one can readily show that, given time enough, our model has very classical properties: to a first approximation, money is neutral (though not "superneutral") and the quantity theory holds. Hence in the longest run, neither GNP, nor interest rates, can be affected by the change in M while GNP$ must change by dM times the velocity of circulation computed at the value of r prevailing for the undisturbed system. For the period covered by our simulation the velocity of circulation of demand deposits is of the order of five to six. But once again, we must stress that these results are of little more than academic interest; what is really important is what happens in the "short run", especially the first four to eight quarters, and, for an answer, we now turn to Figure III.2A.

The first impressive result here is the very large contribution of the wealth effect both to the size and the timing of the multiplier. In real terms, we see that, if we ignore the wealth effect, the multiplier, represented by the white columns, is modest and slow; it reaches a peak of just about two, after two years, and tends to remain at that level one year later. By contrast when we allow for the wealth effect – black columns – the peak effect is reached in the fifth quarter and that peak is just over three. By that quarter, the *wealth effect via consumption accounts for nearly half of the total.* Thereafter the multiplier decreases fairly rapidly; by the end of three years it is less than 1.5 and is appreciably smaller than the multiplier ex-wealth.

The results are equally striking when we turn to the XOBE$ multiplier. Ex-wealth the multiplier is rather sluggish, though it eventually rises to nearly five by the end of three years. But cum-wealth it rises rapidly; it reaches almost four by the end of one year, of which again, half is accounted for by the wealth effect; it is close to five by Q 6 and over five by Q 8 when it reaches a flat peak.

One significant feature of these GNP$ multipliers cum-wealth is that they bear at least a family resemblance to the kind of numbers that have come out of the Monetarist analysis a-la-Federal Reserve Bank of St. Louis. From the well known "reduced form" equations of Andersen et al (see e.g., Andersen and Carlson) in which the change in GNP$ is regressed on a distributed lag of past changes in the stock of money and other variables, one can readily compute the cumulated effect of GNP$ of a two-step change in money supply which was used in our simulation. The solid curve plotted above the histograms in the top right-hand side panel shows the effect implied by their latest regression available to us, estimated through the third quarter of 1970.[9]

Although somewhat different results would be obtained if one used the coefficients reported in some other estimates, the broad picture would not be appreciably different. It is apparent that their response still rises faster and turns around earlier than ours; however, the differences are not terribly large. In particular, both estimates agree that most of the effect is reached by the fifth quarter, and that effect is very similar in magnitude. By contrast, the multiplier ex-wealth bears much less resemblance to theirs.

While the broad similarity is in some sense encouraging and suggestive we should warn the reader against making too much of it. For a number of reasons, discussed below, the similarity is less than might appear, and furthermore, we are not at all sure that it should be very close. First, since our multiplier is computed for a change in demand deposits, it should be really larger than theirs, by something like one-fifth. Second, as we have observed, our lag is really somewhat longer than theirs. Third, and most important, our

[9]These estimates were kindly supplied by Andersen in a letter dated February 3, 1971.

multiplier is significantly affect by *initial conditions*, and is *not symmetrical* with respect to expansion or contraction in the stock of money.

The effect of initial conditions is illustrated by the vertical lines drawn next to each histogram, which show the multiplier for a policy simulation beginning in the slack period – 1962.1-2. Because of the greater slack in the economy we find, as in the case of the expenditure multiplier, that the GNP multiplier reaches a peak which is both higher and later; and, by the same token, the GNP$ response is also slower, reflecting the smaller rate of change of prices. Again, our multipliers are somewhat different if we allow for the price expectational mechanism, as can be seen from the lower panels of Figure III.1. Interestingly enough, the differences are actually rather minor for the first five-six quarters, because the price expectational mechanism is rather slow in getting going. However, once it gets going, toward the end of the second year, it carries the multipliers to much higher levels. The larger GNP multiplier reflects the lower *real* rates of interest while the larger GNP$ response results from the higher *money* rates which cause an increase in velocity. Needless to say, we are inclined to think that the significant dependence of the multipliers on initial conditions implied by our model is more intellectually satisfying and a-priori credible than the independence implied by the reduced form estimates.

The asymmetry of expansionary versus contractionary policy is brought out rather dramatically by contrasting Figure III.2A with III.2B, which gives the results of a policy simulation in which the stock of demand deposits was *increased* by $2 billion distributed over 1967.1 and 2. As a result of the various mechanisms discussed in Part II, the multipliers here are considerably slower; in particular, the GNP$ multiplier does not reach its peak of around five until the third year.

How reliable and credible is this marked asymmetry in the response of changes in money supply? The notion that monetary policy is more powerful and faster in *reducing* than in *expanding* activity is of course a very old one, though our model accounts for this by a mechanism somewhat different from that traditionally visualized ("You can lead a horse to water but you cannot make it drink"). On the whole, we feel that the mechanism in our model is credible; it is possible, however, that it may be quantitatively overestimated. This possibility arises in part from the fact that in constructing and estimating our model we have assumed that the exogenous policy variable is primarily unborrowed reserves (or

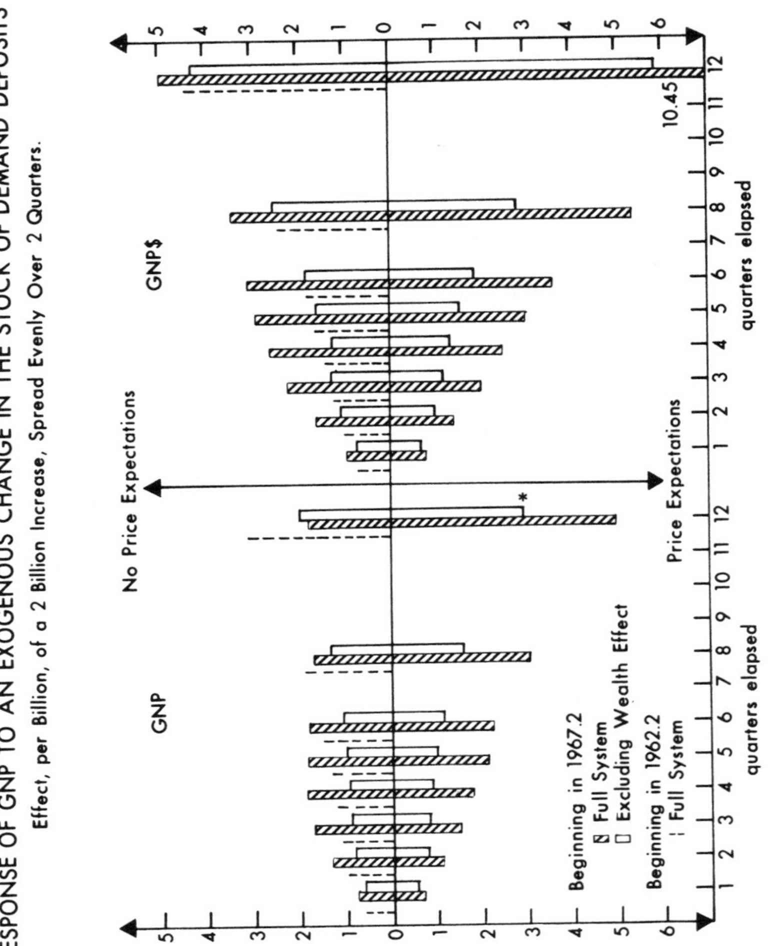

Figure III.2B

RESPONSE OF GNP TO AN EXOGENOUS CHANGE IN THE STOCK OF DEMAND DEPOSITS

Effect, per Billion, of a 2 Billion Increase, Spread Evenly Over 2 Quarters.

possibly short-term interest rates) but not the stock of money or demand deposits. For reasons noted in Part II, the asymmetry is especially marked when the policy variable is the stock of money. As will be shown in the next section, when the policy variable is for example, unborrowed reserves, the asymmetry is greatly reduced.

In the last paragraphs we have emphasized that the similarity between our money multipliers and those implied by St. Louis reduced form equations is really less close than might at first sight appear from the graphs in Figure III.2. Before moving on, we must, at least briefly, raise the other side of the question: should one really expect a close similarity? While this is not the place for us to engage in an extended criticism of the limitations of "reduced" form estimates, we must at least record here our serious misgivings about the reliability of the coefficients of St. Louis-type equations as a measure of response to exogenous changes in money supply. These misgivings are based on numerous considerations a few of which may be mentioned here.

i) In order for the reduced form to yield sensible estimates, it must be assumed that the response of the system to changes in money supply are reasonably stable in time. Yet both a priori considerations and the results of simulations presented above suggest that the response is instead significantly affected by such initial conditions as the slack in the economy, the general level of short-term rates, and the elasticity of price expectations.

ii) Of the other many exogenous variables that affect expenditure only some single measure of government expenditure is typically allowed for in the reduced form and the fiscal multiplier implied by the reduced form coefficients of these variables is patently absurd.

iii) There are ample grounds for doubting that as a rule and on the average the money supply can be regarded as exogenous over the period used in the tests. If, part of the time, the exogenous policy variable, at least in the short run, has been interest rates or unborrowed reserves, then one can expect the reduced forms to overestimate the size and speed of response of GNP to exogenous change in the money supply, and the bias will be compounded by failure to allow for the effect of other exogenous variables.

iv) Our grounds for doubt are also supported and reinforced by a number of empirical tests, a few of which are summarized in the epilogue to this paper. In particular, we provide there some empirical evidence that the reduced form coefficients can yield very unreliable and biased estimates of the response of the system to exogenous changes in money supply and, in particular, may tend to systematically overestimate the speed of response. We suggest, therefore, that, while the broad consistency between reduced form and simulation results is encouraging, the differences of detail do not deserve serious consideration, at least for the present.

We can now summarize the results of this section as follows.

(i) The multipliers generated by a contraction in the stock of demand deposits are quite substantial for the first two to three years both in real and in money terms; in particular, the GNP$ multiplier reaches a level of around five within 6 to 8 quarters; (ii) the wealth effect plays a major role in this result accounting for nearly half of the response in the first two to six quarters; (iii) if we sever the wealth effect the multiplier is much more sluggish and does not approach the steady state level until three years or so; (iv) the multiplier path depends non-negligibly on initial conditions; more slack in the economy leads to a larger response in real terms but the response is slower both in real and money terms; (v) the response to an *expansion* of the stock of money appears to be appreciably slower than the response to a *contraction,* but the difference may be overestimated by our model.

III.4 Effect of a Change in Unborrowed Reserves

The results of this experiment are reported in Figure III.3. The policy simulation consisted in increasing unborrowed reserves by $0.5 billion above the historical path, beginning in '67.1. In addition we aimed to prevent the initial fall in short-term rates, resulting from this action, from reducing the spread between market rates and the discount rate, which in turn would tend to reduce borrowing, offsetting in part the expansion of unborrowed reserves. In principle, this aim can be achieved by taking exogenous – that is, at the historical level – the spread between the discount and bill rate, thus making the discount rate endogenous. For purely technical reasons we have actually found it convenient to use an approximation which consists in making exogenous the spread between the discount rate and the average value of tthe bill rate in the previous two quarters.[10]

As background, we may note that a change in unborrowed reserves under these conditions should tend, in the longest run, to produce a change in the supply of demand deposits of roughly .5x7, or $3.5 billion. This change in turn should eventually lead to a change in GNP$ in the order of $20 billion. The longest run GNP multiplier, on the other hand, should still tend to zero.

We believe the picture emerging from Figure III.3 is self explanatory and, hence, shall limit ourselves to a few observations. (i) The response is clearly rather slow, as the money supply responds but gradually to the increase in reserves and in turn GNP responds gradually to the change in M. Still, by the end of the third year, the GNP$ multiplier seems to be close to its limiting value. (ii) The wealth effect again plays a major role in the response but only beginning with Q 4; between Q 4 and Q 8, it accounts for nearly half of the response. (iii) The price expectational mechanism makes again little difference for the first two years or so though it eventually becomes quite large. (iv) A *decrease* in unborrowed reserves has again a somewhat larger effect than an *increase* but the difference is now rather minor – the effect is very nearly symmetrical. This conclusion can be deduced from a comparison of the black columns shown on the upper right panel with the height of the vertical lines drawn next to each bar. These show the effect of a *decrease* in unborrowed reserves by .5 beginning again in '67.1 (with sign reversed). The reason for the far greater symmetry is that the response of short-term rates to a change in unborrowed reserves, in contrast to a change in M, is fairly smooth and, hence, does not significantly activate the variability effect in the term structure equation. To illustrate, for the simulation in which unborrowed reserves were increased in '67.1, one finds that the commercial paper rate declines fairly gradually throughout the first year to a maximum of some 60 basis points, and thereafter gradually moves back toward the original level. In the simulation cum-price-expectations, it actually eventually increases above the original level.

[10]The technical advantage of this procedure is that the discount rate in quarter t is then predetermined instead of simultaneous. There is nothing logically difficult about making the discount rate simultaneous, but it requires some changes in the simulation programs which have not as yet been readied.

Figure III.3

RESPONSE OF GNP TO A 0.5 BILLION CHANGE IN UNBORROWED RESERVES

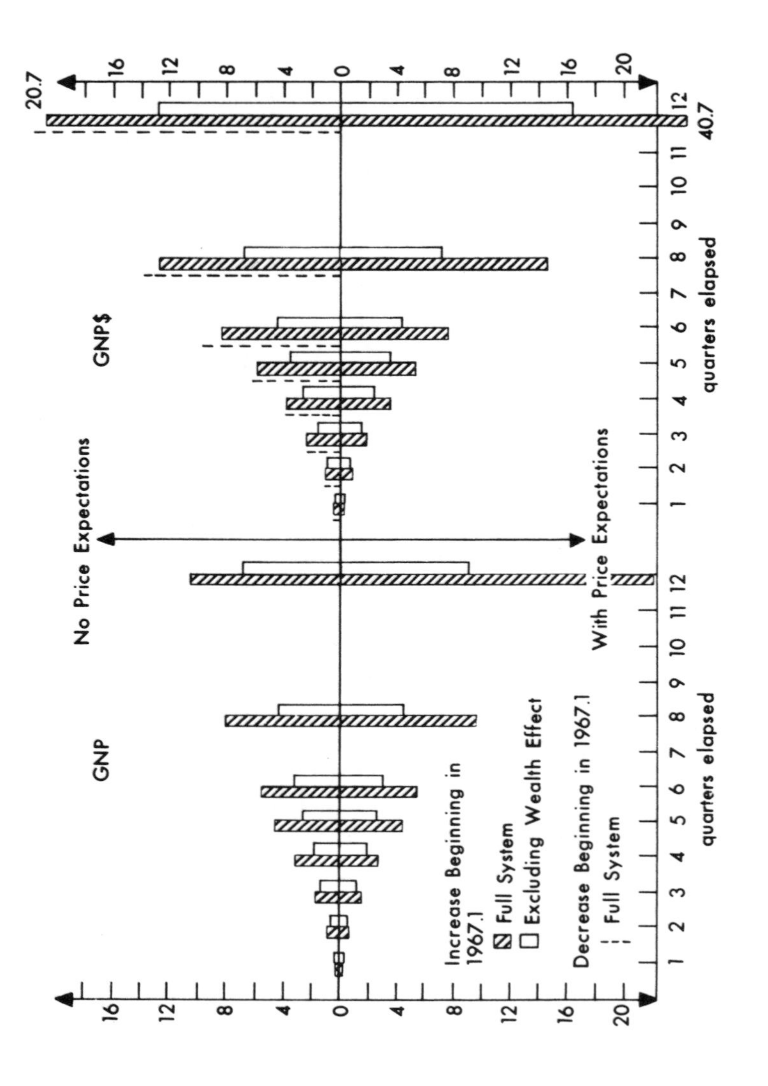

III.5 Response to Change in Short-term Rates

Figure III.4 reports the results of simulations in which the short-term rate – measured by the Treasury 3-month bill rate – was increased by 50 basis points beginning in '67.1. Again the figure should, by now, be self-explanatory. However, a few comments are appropriate about the reasonableness of the results and their implications.

In a sense, this simulation is of particular interest. Indeed, as we have pointed out repeatedly, in our model monetary policy works entirely through its impact on the short rate, – though the effects of the short rate on the system are to some extent different than is usually visualized. In particular, in our model these effects include the wealth effect through consumption and also a rather complex rationing effect on the housing market if, when market rates change, ceiling rates are kept unchanged and they are (or become) effective. Note here again a possible source of asymmetry, since a rise in market rates may produce effects (by making the ceiling effective) that a decline might not. However, interpretation of the results of this simulation is much more complicated because it is difficult to estimate the longest run multipliers as a guide to an understanding of the path and speed of response. Unfortunately, the causes of this difficulty can only be mentioned very briefly and superficially here.

The root of the problem lies in the fact that, in the longest run, our model tends to exhibit the characteristics of so-called "neo-classical" growth models. As in these models there exists also for our model – at least if we assume tax revenue approximately homogenous of first degree in money income and government expenditure proportional to income – a unique "natural real rate of interest" that is consistent with the model moving along a golden age growth path, with the natural rate of growth determined by technological progress and population growth. The natural real rate of interest is determined by the production function, the parameters of the consumption function, the natural rate of growth, and fiscal policy in the sense of the ratio of government deficit (or surplus) to GNP. Together with this real rate there is a "natural" money rate which equals the real rate plus the rate of change of prices, determined in turn by the rate of growth of the money supply (which must also be assumed constant on the golden age path). A policy of trying to force the interest rate away from this natural rate must eventually throw the system off the golden age path. In particular, holding the rate too low by an appropriate monetary

Figure III.4

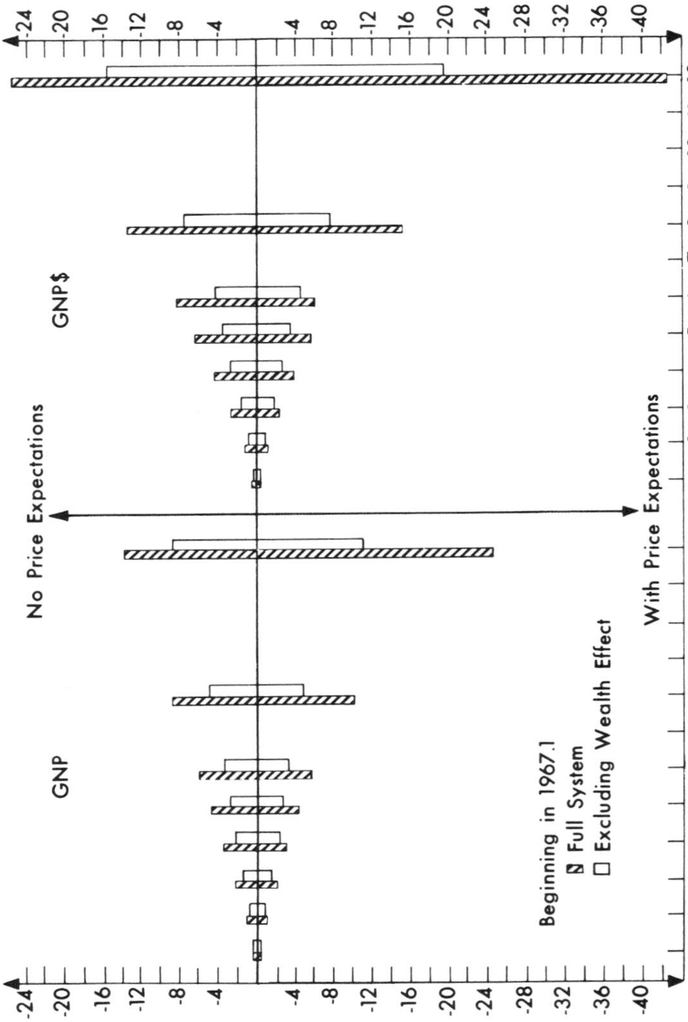

RESPONSE OF GNP TO A CHANGE OF 0.5 IN THE TREASURY BILLS RATE

policy, must tend to cause inflation at an accelerating rate. More generally, when the price expectational mechanism is working, a policy of holding the money rate constant tends to make the system unstable. To illustrate, an initial disturbance that raises output and employment and, hence, the rate of change of prices, p, will cause a fall in the *real* rate, thereby increasing investment and consumption, and thus raising output and p further and causing still further excess demand. It is this mechanism that accounts for the quite explosive behavior of GNP and especially GNP$ in the lower panels of the figure, in which the price expectational mechanism is allowed to operate.

In view of the complexities outlined above and limitations of space, we shall make no attempt at a detailed interpretation of figure III.4. We will merely note that the response builds up slowly, but eventually gets quite large, even if the price expectational mechanism is suppressed, and that the wealth effect makes again a very significant contribution beginning in the second or third quarter and building up to a peak of over one-half by the end of two years.

EPILOGUE

SOME EVIDENCE OF THE MODEL'S ABILITY TO CAPTURE MONETARY EFFECTS ON CONSUMPTION AND ON THE RELIABILITY OF THE REDUCED FORM APPROACH

1. *Review of Findings and Outline of Further Tests*

In this paper we have endeavored to show that the consumption sector of the FMP model plays a critical role in the mechanism that translates changes in monetary variables into changes in overall economic activity. In particular, we have shown that roughly one-half of the response to a change in either the money supply or unborrowed reserves or short-term rates is accounted for by the effect of these variables on wealth and of wealth on consumers expenditure. This holds for several quarters following the initial change. Some additional effects occur through the impact of interest rates on consumer durable expenditures. We have also shown that, if, and only if, account is taken of the wealth effect, one obtains a path of response to changes in money supply which bears some resemblance in both pattern and magnitude to results obtained by the so-called reduced form approach. On the other hand, the response to government expenditure implied by the model remains absolutely irreconcilable with the reduced form estimates.

How relevant and reliable are these results as a description of the true mechanisms that have been at work in the U.S. economy in recent decades and will be in the near future? There is, of course, no conclusive answer to this question. In the last analysis the reader must ask himself whether he is prepared to accept the modeling of the individual sectors of the FMP model and their interrelation. Measures of closeness of fit provided in the Appendices, and the results of simulations of sectors and of various partial mechanisms are relevant, though obviously not conclusive evidence in reaching a final assessment.

In order to provide further help to the reader in forming his judgment, we briefly report here the results of two further sets of tests which may be of some value in bolstering confidence in the relevance of our results. The first set is designed to provide evidence on whether our model has succeeded in capturing the major systematic mechanisms through which monetary variables, and, in particular, the money supply, affect consumption, and more generally GNP The second set deals with the problem created by apparent discrepancies between the implications of our model and those of reduced form estimates. Those discrepancies are of some magnitude even with respect to the response to monetary variables, but are drastic when it comes to the response of fiscal variables. Our tests are designed to show why these discrepancies should not, at this time, be a serious source for concern as they reflect more on the reliability of presently available reduced form estimates than on the validity of the model.

2. *"Reduced Form" Tests of the FMP Model Specifications of the Monetary Mechanism*

As is well known, the monetarists have successfully shown that there is a marked correlation between the money supply and consumption expenditure. In particular, recent work of the monetarists at the Federal Reserve Bank of St. Louis has shown fairly impressive correlation between *changes* in consumer expenditures in current dollars and current and lagged changes of some measure of the money supply. These findings are confirmed by the results reported in the paper prepared by Meiselman and Simpson for this conference – see especially Tables 8 and 9, and 13 to 16.

Suppose now that we use the FMP model to carry out a long dynamic simulation; that is, we start the model at some point of time t, and let it generate all the endogenous variables up to the present, by providing no additional information other than the actual course of all the exogenous variables. The output of this simulation will then include a time series of consumer expenditure both in constant and in current dollars. Let us denote by EPCE^c the computed value of consumption in current dollars, and by ΔEPCE^c the first difference of this series. Since our model does not track perfectly, especially in a simulation extending over a decade or more, there will be differences between ΔEPCE$ and ΔEPCE^c. If our model fails to capture some of the systematic effects which generate the observed association between ΔEPCE$ and ΔM, current and lagged, then one should expect that the simulation error, E $\equiv$ ΔEPCE$ – ΔEPCE^c, should itself be correlated with a distributed lag of ΔM. Thus, our basic test consists in regressing E on a distributed lag of ΔM, or in estimating the regression equation:

$$(1) \quad E(t) = \sum_{\tau=0}^{m} v_{\tau} \, \Delta M(t-\tau) + V$$

where V is the constant term. If we have failed to specify adequately all of the channels through which M, current and lagged, affects EPCE\$, then we should expect to find that the distributed lag explains a significant portion of the error E, or, equivalently, that the multiple correlation coefficient, R, of the above regression equation is significantly different from zero.

The test just described admits of an alternative enlightening interpretation. Consider first the St. Louis type equation obtained by regressing ΔEPCE\$ on ΔM current and lagged

$$(2) \quad \Delta EPCE\$(t) = \sum_{\tau=0}^{m} a_{\tau}\Delta M(t-\tau) + A .$$

Suppose next we run the same type of regression, but using as the dependent variable $\Delta EPCE\$^{c}$, or

$$(3) \quad \Delta EPCE\$^{c}(t) = \sum_{\tau=0}^{m} b_{\tau}\Delta M(t-\tau) + B .$$

It is then easy to establish, from well known properties of least squares estimates, that the coefficients of (2) and (3) are related to those of (1) by the equations

$$v_{\tau} = a_{\tau} - b_{\tau} , \tau = 0,\ldots,m, V = A-B .$$

It is apparent from the above that if, because of misspecification of the relevant channels, our model tended to *underestimate* the effect of ΔM on EPCE\$ than the individual coefficients v_{τ} or, at the very least, their sum, should be significantly positive. Conversely, a finding that the sum of weights is not significantly positive would enable us to reject the hypothesis that our formulation tended to underestimate systematically the cumulative effect of changes in M on consumption. More generally, if the multiple correlation R of Equation (1) is not significantly different from zero, then this would imply that the change in consumption generated by the model bears a relation to ΔM current and lagged which is not significantly *different* from the relation exhibited by the actual change in consumption. Put somewhat loosely, such a finding would imply that our model is able to account, up to insignificant differences, for the observed pattern of association between ΔEPCE\$ and current and lagged values of ΔM.

Since the structure of our model implies that the money supply can affect consumption, as well as every other component of demand, only through its effect on the short-term rate, it would appear that the most effective way of testing whether our formulation captures all of the monetary effects is to take as the exogeneous monetary variable in our long-run dynamic simulation, not the money supply directly, but rather the pivotal short-term rate, namely the three-months Treasury bill rate, RTB. This approach eliminates possible errors due to errors in the money demand equation in computing the bill rate from the money supply. (These errors are typically small but could still produce irrelevant disturbances, especially since they are somewhat serially correlated.) Furthermore, it sharpens the test of our central hypothesis that the money supply has no effect on the system except through its impact on short-term rates. Other exogenous variables for our simulation include Federal government expenditures, transfers, grants-in-aid, tax rates, population, productivity trends, and a host of other minor variables which are described in the list of exogenous variables obtainable from Wharton EFA, Inc.[1] In all tests reported below, "computed values" were obtainable from a dynamic simulation beginning in 1958.I, and terminating in 1969.IV, and all "reduced form" equations were estimated over the same period, unless otherwise noted.

In carrying out our test, we still need to specify the nature of the distributed lag to be used in Equation (1). Unfortunately, quite a variety of specifications has been used by the St. Louis school at different times, both in terms of the length of the lag---running typically between four and eight quarters---and in terms of the method of estimating it---unconstrained least squares or Almon polynomial of different order and with a variety of a priori constraints. To conserve space we present here only results using an eight quarter lag and two methods of estimation: unconstrained least squares and third degree Almon polynomial, constrained to zero at the ninth quarter. We chose to focus on eight-quarter lags because the policy simulations reported in the text suggest that lags are typically quite long. We have however made a number of tests with shorter lags and

[1]In addition, one important adjustment we made in the stock market equation: Because the dividend yield equation makes some occasional non-negligible short-term error, and because we see no reason to let our failure to account fully for this variable control the quality of our simulation, we have taken as exogenously given the single equation error of this equation. Note that this procedure is not equivalent to taking the dividend-price ratio as exogenous for we still allow errors in other endogenous variables to produce errors in the dividend yield.

consistently found that minor differences in this specification did not materially affect the conclusions reported below.

Before proceeding to an analysis of the results we must call attention to one likely bias of our proposed test. It can be shown that if, at least some of the time, the policy target of the monetary authority were not directly the money supply but rather some variable such as unborrowed reserves, or free reserves, or interest rates, then the actual money supply would tend to be *positively* correlated with the error E, of the model, even if the model's specification were completely correct, or at least unbiased. Thus a finding that the sum of the coefficients of equation (1) is moderately positive would not justify rejecting the hypothesis that our specifications were unbiased, whereas a finding that the sum is negative would correspondingly strengthen the conclusion that the model's specifications were not systematically underestimating the magnitude of the response of the system to changes in money supply.

The results of our test are reported in Part A of Table E.1. In the first three columns, the coefficients are estimated by unconstrained least squares. The pattern of coefficients in Column (1), where the dependent variable is the change in *observed* value of Consumers' Expenditure, looks rather puzzling, especially the sharp whipsaw shape at the tail end (though this shape is preserved even if the period of fit is extended back to the beginning of 1952.) In Column (2) the dependent variable is the change in *simulated* rather than actual expenditure. It is apparent that the pattern of coefficients is rather similar, except that the coefficient of current $\triangle M$ is rather larger and the whipsaw at the end is attenuated. As a result, when the difference between actual and simulated change (the model error, E) is regressed on current and past values of $\triangle M$ in Column (3) the individual coefficients are mostly small and entirely insignificant, as evidenced by the t-ratio given below each coefficient. The portion of the error explained by the distributed lag is also entirely insignificant, as evidenced by the very low R^2 and by an entirely insignificant value of the F statistics. Finally the sum of the coefficients is seen to be *negative* rather than positive, despite the bias of the test mentioned earlier. We must therefore conclude that the results of this test unequivocally reject the hypothesis that our model systematically underestimates the impact of the money supply on consumption; more generally the results reject the hypothesis of any systematic misspecification.

As a check on these conclusions we present in Columns (4) to (7) the results obtained when the coefficients of the distributed lag are

TABLE E.1

REDUCED FORM TESTS OF THE FMP MODEL SPECIFICATION OF THE MONETARY MECHANISM

Independent Variables \ Dependent Variable	A: Based on Consumers' Expenditure[2] (EPCE$)						B: Based on GNP$		
	$\Delta EPCE\$$	$\Delta EPCE\$^{c}$	$E \equiv \Delta EPCE\$ - \Delta EPCE\$^{c}$	$\Delta EPCE\$$	$\Delta EPCE\$^{c}$	E	$\Delta GNP\$$	$\Delta GNP\$^{c}$	$E \equiv \Delta GNP\$ - \Delta GNP\$^{c}$
	Unconstrained L.S.			3rd Degree Polynomial Zero at t-8			3rd Degree Polynomial		
	(1)	(2)	(3)	(4)	(5)	(6)	(7)	(8)	(9)
ΔM(t)	0.75	1.17	-0.42	0.32	0.73	-0.41	0.68	1.06	-0.37
	(1.3)[1]		(0.7)	(1.0)		(1.3)	(1.6)		(0.9)
ΔM(t-1)	0.24	0.20	+0.04	0.62	0.71	-0.09	1.30	1.27	0.03
	(0.3)		(0.1)	(4.0)		(0.6)	(6.4)		(0.1)
ΔM(t-2)	0.60	0.71	-0.11	0.70	0.65	0.05	1.39	1.27	0.12
	(0.8)		(0.2)	(3.8)		(0.3)	(6.0)		(0.5)
ΔM(t-3)	0.90	0.62	0.28	0.62	0.56	0.06	1.13	1.12	0.01
	(1.1)		(0.4)	(3.6)		(0.4)	(5.4)		(0.1)
ΔM(t-4)	0.58	0.78	-0.20	0.44	0.44	0.00	0.66	0.87	-0.20
	(0.7)		(0.3)	(3.5)		(0.0)	(4.3)		(1.3)
ΔM(t-5)	-0.14	-0.08	-0.06	0.23	0.31	-0.09	0.16	0.58	-0.41
	(0.2)		(0.1)	(1.6)		(0.6)	(0.9)		(2.4)
ΔM(t-6)	0.98	0.33	0.65	0.05	0.19	-0.15	-0.23	0.30	-0.52
	(1.24)		(0.8)	(0.3)		(0.9)	(1.0)		(2.3)
ΔM(t-7)	-1.22	-0.02	-1.20	-0.05	0.09	-0.14	-0.33	0.09	-0.42
	(1.81)		(1.0)	(0.3)		(0.9)	(1.7)		(2.1)
Constant	2.94	2.27	.67	2.75	2.33	0.42	4.39	3.18	1.21
	(3.12)		(.72)	(3.0)		(0.5)	(4.4)		(1.0)
Summed Weights	2.70	3.72	-1.02	2.95	3.73	-0.78	4.77	6.54	-1.77
				(5.0)		(1.4)	(6.6)		(2.4)
Measures of Fit									
R^2	.55		.14	.48		0.06	.58		0.09
D.W.	2.9		2.7	2.9		2.7	1.81		1.84
F			0.69			0.87			2.5
F* (.05 Significance)			2.3			2.9			2.8

[1] t-ratio.

[2] Period of Fit: 1959.4 – 1969.4.

estimated using a third degree Almon Polynomial, a procedure that smoothes out the improbable jagged pattern of coefficients of Column (1). It is readily apparent that the results of this second test confirm and reinforce in every respect our earlier conclusion.

In Part B of the Table we have applied the same technique to test for evidence of bias in the model as a whole, by taking as dependent variable total GNP rather than one specific component of it. The similarity of the pattern of coefficients of Column (7), where the dependent variable is the actual change in GNP$, with that of Column (8), where it is the change in simulated GNP$, is again apparent. We also note again a tendency for the coefficients of Column (8) to *exceed* those of Column (7), especially for the current quarter and at the tail end. Accordingly, the coefficients of Column (9) are prevailingly negative and not altogether insignificant, though the overall correlation remains quite low, and the F statistic is again insignificant.

On the basis of these tests, whose power is of course hard to assess, we must conclude that there is absolutely no evidence that the specifications of the FMP model tend to underestimate systematically the impact of money on consumption, or more generally on money GNP. Indeed, they suggest that, if there is a misspecification, it is in the direction of *overestimating* the impact of money, although even this indication is by no means conclusive.

3. The Power of Reduced Forms As a Method of Estimating Structural Properties

The conclusions of the last paragraph, while reassuring in a sense, present us with somewhat of a puzzle, for they seem hard to reconcile with the findings reported in Section III.3. In that section we pointed out that the response of GNP$ to a change in money supply implied by the FMP model was in fact rather smaller and slower than one could infer from the coefficients estimated by the reduced form approach. This concluding section is designated to shed some light on this puzzle. We propose to show that the likely answer to the puzzle must be found in the fact that the coefficients of reduced form as estimated by the St. Louis group, or in the Meiselman paper for this conference, tend to be seriously biased in the direction of overestimating the response of GNP$ (and its major components) to changes in money supply.

The evidence to be presented is basically in the spirit of a Monte Carlo experiment. Clearly we can think of the FMP model as a description of a possible economic system, regardless of whether it provides, in fact, an adequate operational description of the American economy in recent years. We can, therefore, regard the time series of GNP$ and its components generated by the dynamic simulation described in the previous section as representing the response of this economic system to the path of the exogenous variables used in the simulation. Furthermore, from the demand equation for demand deposits and the simulated value of other relevant variables, we can compute the time series of the money supply needed to produce the given path of the short-term rate. We can then ask the question: suppose an observer who did not know the structure of the FMP model tried to infer the response of GNP$ to changes in the money supply by the reduced form approach; how far and in what direction would his estimate differ from the true response implied by the structure of the model?

We begin by observing that if the model were linear there would be a true reduced form equation relating GNP (or any component thereof) to all the exogenous variables assumed in the simulation, including the money supply in place of the bill rate, since the bill rate could itself be expressed in terms of the money supply and all other exogenous variables. The coefficients of the money supply (current and lagged as far as necessary) in the last mentioned reduced form would measure the response of the system to an exogenous change in the money supply and would coincide with the response estimated by a policy simulation of the type underlying the results presented in Section III. But clearly the results could be quite different if the coefficients were estimated from a misspecified reduced form, e.g., using as independent variable only the money supply, with an arbitrarily chosen lag, and neglecting all other exogenous variables. Further difficulty would arise with a non-linear system, for then the true response to changes in M would vary with initial conditions.

One obvious and simple way to assess the size and direction of bias is to actually carry out the experiment. To this end we have estimated a reduced form by regressing the change in simulated GNP, $\Delta GNP\$^{c}$ on the simulated change in the stock of demand deposits $\Delta MD\$^{c}$. We use demand deposits rather than the total stock of money to make the results comparable with those of the policy simulations reported in Section III.2. The coefficients obtained using again a third degree Almon Polynomial are reported in Column (1), Table E.2. For comparison we report in Column (2) the coefficients estimated from a regression of actual changes in GNP$ on actual

TABLE E. 2

SIMULATION TEST OF REDUCED FORM ESTIMATES OF TRUE STRUCTURE

	A - Reduced Form Coefficients		B - Response of GNP$ to a 2 Billion Change in Demand Deposits, Spread Over Two Quarters			
					Based on Reduced Form Coefficients, Estimated on:	
Quarter	$\Delta GNP\$^c$ on $\Delta MD\$^c$	$\Delta GNP\$$ on $\Delta MD\$$	Quarters Elapsed from First Change	True Causal Effect from Policy Simulation	Simulated Values	Actual Values
	(1)	(2)		(1)	(2)	(3)
t	1.85	0.79	0	0.9	1.9	.8
	(3.5)	(1.6)				
t-1	1.45	1.51	1	2.4	5.2	3.1
	(7.0)	(6.1)				
t-2	1.20	1.68	2	4.3	7.8	6.3
	(4.5)	(6.2)				
t-3	1.05	1.45	3	6.1	10.1	9.4
	(4.1)	(5.9)				
t-4	0.95	0.99	4	7.7	12.1	11.9
	(5.3)	(5.1)				
t-5	0.86	0.45	5	8.8	13.9	13.3
	(4.6)	(2.0)				
t-6	0.70	-0.02	6	9.4	15.4	13.8
	(2.8)	(0.0)				
t-7	0.43	-0.21	7	10.0	16.5	13.5
	(2.0)	(0.9)	8	10.2	17.0	13.3
Sum	8.49	6.67	9	10.1		
Constant	3.47	4.07	10	10.1		
	(3.8)	(3.4)				
R^2	.73	.55				
D.W.	1.05	1.71				
S.E.	3.46	4.27				

changes in demand deposits. Once again the patterns of coefficients in Columns (1) and (2) are fairly close, but with the sum of weights again somewhat higher for the simulated values, largely because of the appreciably higher coefficient of current ΔM. It is also worth noting that, as expected, the sum of weights in Column (2) exceeds by some 25 percent the corresponding sum in Column (7) of Table E.1, in which the regressor was the total stock of money. Otherwise the pattern of coefficients is fairly similar and R^2 is only slightly lower. Note also that R^2 is larger in Column (1) than in Column (2); this is as one should expect since the computed values are not affected by the errors terms which attentuate the correlation of actual values. Indeed, reduced form estimated on computed values should tend to yield a perfect fit were it not for misspecifications in the reduced form used in the estimation.

We can now use the coefficients of Column (1) to derive an estimate of the response of GNP$ to a $2 billion change in demand deposits spread evenly over two successive quarters – the change which was used in our policy simulations. The result is shown in Part B of the Table, Column (2). For comparison, Column (3) shows the response implied by the reduced form coefficients estimated from the regression of *actual* values given in Part A, Column (2). The entries of the two columns can be compared with those of Column (1) which shows the true response of GNP$ to the stated exogenous change in demand deposits as obtained from the policy simulation. As we have seen, because of nonlinearities, this true response is somewhat dependent on initial conditions and the direction of the change in money supply; the figures we report are those corresponding to a *decrease* in M beginning in 1967.1, i.e., those corresponding to the policy simulation that produced the largest and fastest response among those tested. Even so, the response is strikingly smaller and slower than the response implied by the reduced form coefficients, shown in Column (2): in the first three quarters the latter response is larger than the true response by a factor of two, and eventually the overestimate settles down to about 70 percent.

The experiment of Table E.2 has also been repeated for individual components of GNP and while the results cannot be reported here in detail, it is worth noting that one finds a broad similarity between the *patterns* of response implied by reduced forms computed on actual and on simulated values, and the patterns obtained from policy simulation. In particular one finds, as in the Meiselman-Simpson paper, that for such components of GNP as consumers' expenditure, non-durable consumption, and state and local government expenditure the response continues to build up to the very end, while the peak response occurs quite early for housing expenditure and somewhat later for inventories and then plant and equipment. However, one finds large and varying differences in the *size* of the response.

In any event, insofar as GNP$ is concerned, the conclusion of our Monte Carlo experiment is unequivocal: the reduced form coefficients estimated on the time series generated by the model yield a severely upward biased estimate of the magnitude and speed of response of GNP$ to an exogenous change in the money supply.

It is unfortunately not possible to enter here into a detailed analysis of the causes of this bias. We can merely state that in our view the major source of bias lies in the fact that the computed money supply series is strongly positively associated with the movement of other variables which were taken as exogenously given in the simulation (including fiscal as well as other exogenous variables), and which, in terms of the model's specifications, account for a substantial portion of the simulated change in GNP$. The omission of these other variables in the reduced form gives rise to an error term which is positively correlated with the change in M, and hence produces an upward bias in the estimated coefficiencies of ΔM. To put the matter somewhat loosely, the reduced form attributes to ΔM part of the effect of changes in other omitted exogenous variables. Note also that the positive association with the omitted exogenous variables may be expected to hold not only for the computed, but also for the actual money supply, which is highly correlated with the computed one. And indeed if one regresses the simulated change in GNP on the actual rather than the computed change in demand deposits, one obtains coefficients which are quite close to those shown in Column (1) of Part A or Column (2) of Part B; in fact, the upward bias turns out to be even a little larger – the sum of weights being, for example, 9.3 instead of 8.5 as reported in Column (1).

Clearly this "Monte Carlo" experiment does not entitle us to conclude that the coefficients of the reduced form computed on actual values are a biased estimate of the true response of GNP$ to an exogenous change in the stock of money for the U.S. economy. Yet the fact that the figures of Columns (2) and (3) are fairly similar while both sets are quite different from the figures of Column (1) is quite suggestive; it provides at least a strong prima facie case for the hypothesis that the difference between the response as estimated from the FMP model and reported in Section III.3 and the response estimated from the standard reduced forms, reflects in good measure an upward bias of the latter. Note also that the size of this bias would depend on the specific circumstances of the period used in estimating the reduced form (i.e., on the degree of association between changes in the money supply and changes in the omitted exogenous variables over that period). This consideration might help to account for the instability of reduced form coefficients as evidenced, for example, by the result reported by Meiselman and Simpson for different periods (c.f. their Tables 3 and 9). Finally, the above mentioned biases could be further increased if and when the variable directly controlled by the monetary authority was, for example, unborrowed or free reserves or interest rates, a "crime" of which the Federal Reserve has been frequently accused by the monetarists.

There remains one significant puzzle to clear up. The argument developed in the previous paragraphs would imply that the major source of bias in the reduced form coefficients can be traced to failure to include in the regression other major exogenous variables beside a money measure. Yet in reduced form estimated by the St. Louis group, including such fiscal variables as government expenditure, deficit, or tax receipts, it is consistently found that the effect of these other variables is insignificant and/or extremely short-lived, while the coefficients of the monetary variable are hardly changed. These findings are confirmed by Table E.3 which reports the coefficients of a reduced form estimated by regressing the change in GNP$ on the change in money and in government expenditure on goods and services (ΔG$), over eight quarters, using again third degree polynomial. Column (1) reports the coefficients of ΔM and Column (2) those of ΔG$. It is apparent that the coefficients of ΔM are highly significant and almost identical with those reported in Table E.1 Column (7), estimated omitting the expenditure variable. On the other hand, the coefficients of the expenditure variable are small and insignificant, except possibly for the first, and turn quickly negative beginning with the third quarter. The implied expenditure multiplier, obtained by cumulating the coefficients of Column (2) and shown in Column (3), bears no resemblance to the multiplier implied by the FMP model and reported in Figure III.1.

In our view, however, these results as well as similar ones reported by other investigators are of very little relevance because of the serious misspecifications of the fiscal variable used, to which attention has been called by deLeeuw and Kalchbrenner, and especially by

Gramlich. In particular, Gramlich has pointed out the serious shortcomings of government expenditure, especially in a period in which changes in that variable are dominated by changes in defense procurements. As explicitly recognized in the FMP model, the stimulating effects of such procurement begin when the orders are placed and lasts while they are being processed, through their effect on inventory investment, while very little effect occurs in the quarter in which the goods are delivered and the expenditure is recorded, for the expenditure is then largely offset by a decline, or negative investment, in inventories.

The contention that, because of misspecifications, the coefficients of Columns (1) and (2) provide a totally distorted measure of the money supply and expenditure multiplier can again be at least indirectly supported by a "Monte Carlo" experiment. In Columns (4) and (5) of Table E.3 we report the coefficients of a reduced form estimated by regressing the simulated change in GNP$ on the simulated change in money supply and the simulated change in government expenditure – the latter variable being obtained as the product of the exogenously given real expenditure, used in the simulation, and the endogenously computed price index. In the absence of bias the coefficients of Column (4) should come close to those implied by the policy simulation of Figure III.2. Similarly, the expenditure multiplier of Column (6), obtained by cumulating the coefficients of Column (5), should come close to that reported in Figure III.1. What we find instead is that the coefficients of Column (4) are again hardly different from those obtained without the expenditure variable and reported in Column (7), and also very similar to those of Column (1), which we know appreciably overstates the magnitude and speed of response of GNP$ to change in M. Similarly, the expenditure coefficients of Column (5) and the implied multiplier of Column (6) closely resemble those of Columns (2) and (3), but bear no recognizable relation to the multiplier of Figure III.1.[2]

[2]It should be noted that Figure III.1 gives the response of GNP to a change in exports and therefore also to a change in government purchases of goods which do not go through the order process applying to defense procurement. The response to a change in real purchase of services is somewhat faster but not otherwise significantly different, as can be seen from the figures reported below, obtained from a simulation in which real expenditure on services was increased by $5 billion beginning in 1967.1. For reference the second row reproduces the multiplier underlying the black histograms in the upper right quadrant of Figure III.1.

MULTIPLIER RESPONSE OF GNP$
TO A CHANGE IN REAL GOVERNMENT EXPENDITURE

	Quarters Elapsed							
	1	2	3	4	5	6	8	12
On Services	1.47	1.92	2.20	2.43	2.67	2.80	2.57	1.57
On Goods (Based on Exports)	1.11	1.55	1.88	2.34	2.60	2.73	2.62	1.35

While this last experiment calls attention once more to the severe danger of bias in reduced form, it does not per se imply that reduced form could not possibly yield reasonable approximations to true response. What they rather imply is that one cannot expect to obtain reasonable estimates without painstaking attention to the specification of the variables to be used. It is at least suggestive in this context, that Gramlich (op. cit.), who gave careful consideration to the specification of both the monetary and fiscal variables, did obtain a set of estimates that appear *a priori* reasonable and are also roughly reconcilable with the results of the FMP policy simulations. This is especially true of the results reported in his Table 4, where the monetary variable is unborrowed reserves (which incidentally also yielded the lowest residual error variance.) In particular the sum of weights for unborrowed reserve, 25.7, which measures the cumulated effect of 1 billion change, after eight quarters, compares quite favorably with simulation results reported in Figure III.3 (12.6 per .5 billion implying 25.2 billions per billion for an increase, and -14, or -28 per billion, for a decrease). In the case of expenditure the agreement is not quite as good, though still reasonable (2.15 for Gramlich as compared with 2.62 for a simulation beginning in 1967.1 and 2.54 for one beginning in 1962.1).[3]

We thus feel entitled to close this epilogue on a somewhat cheerful note:

1. There is no evidence that the FMP model, according to which money affects economic activity only through the link of interest

[3] Although in the paper cited Gramlich reported only the sum of coefficients, the pattern of the individual coefficients, which he has kindly made available to us, also matches reasonably well the results of our simulation. For purpose of comparison with our Figure III.3 we give below the cumulated effect of a 0.5 change in unborrowed reserves implied by his coefficient for each of the eight quarters following the injection: -.8; -.1; 1.6; 4.0; 6.8; 9.4; 11.6; 12.8. Similarly the multiplier implied by his government expenditure coefficients are: 0.6; 1.1; 1.4; 1.7; 1.9; 2.0; 2.1; 2.2.

TABLE E. 3

SIMULATION TEST OF REDUCED FORM INCLUDING GOVERNMENT EXPENDITURE (G$) – DEPENDENT VARIABLE: CHANGE IN GNP$

	Estimated on Actual Values			Estimated on Simulated Values			
Lag	Coefficient of ΔM (1)	Coefficient of $\Delta G\$$ (2)	Expenditure Multiplier (Col. 2 Cumulated) – (3)	Coefficient of ΔM^c (4)	Coefficient of $\Delta G\$^c$ (5)	Expenditure Using Multiplier (6)	ΔM^c Only (7)
0	0.70	0.86	0.86	1.29	0.66	0.66	1.31
	(1.6)	(2.2)		(2.9)	(2.1)		(2.8)
-1	1.42	0.14	0.99	1.40	-0.25	0.41	1.18
	(6.2)	(0.8)		(7.4)	(1.7)		(6.5)
-2	1.54	-0.24	0.75	1.30	-0.60	-0.19	1.03
	(6.9)	(1.1)		(5.6)	(3.4)		(4.3)
-3	1.25	-0.37	0.38	1.05	-0.57	-0.76	0.85
	(5.8)	(1.7)		(4.8)	(3.4)		(3.7)
-4	0.74	-0.33	0.05	0.73	-0.30	-1.06	0.67
	(4.5)	(1.9)		(4.4)	(2.3)		(4.2)
-5	0.17	0.19	-0.13	0.39	0.05	-1.01	0.68
	(0.9)	(1.0)		(2.3)	(0.3)		(3.0)
-6	-0.26	-0.03	-0.16	0.12	0.32	-0.69	0.30
	(1.1)	(0.1)		(0.5)	(1.8)		(1.4)
-7	-0.37	0.06	-0.11	-0.04	0.35	-0.33	0.14
	(1.9)	(0.3)		(0.2)	(2.3)		(0.7)
Sum of Coefficients	5.2	-0.11		6.2	-0.33		5.9
Constant	3.95			3.62			3.73
	(3.7)			(4.9)			(4.6)
R^2	.61			.80			.75
DW	2.06			1.16			1.17

rates, significantly misspecifies the quantitative impact of money or its time path, though it may tend to *overstate* somewhat the long-run effect.

2. It may eventually be possible to reconcile the implications of a carefully specified structural model with those of carefully specified reduced forms, though much empirical, as well as theoretical, work remains to be done toward that highly desirable goal.

APPENDIX A

EQUATIONS OF THE CONSUMPTION SECTOR OF THE FMP MODEL

Key to symbols not explained elsewhere.

YD:	Real disposable personal income (billions of '58 dollars)
N:	Population (millions)
VCN$:	Consumers' net worth in current dollars ($, trillions)
PCON:	Consumption deflator (1958 = 100)
PCD:	Price index of consumers' durables (1958 = 100)
RCB:	Corporate bond yield
JIC:	Strike dummy
u:	Autocorrelated error term
e:	Residual error

The number in square brackets underneath each coefficient is the t-ratio. The number in parentheses above the coefficients is the identification number of that coefficient in the FMP model.

I.1 CONSUMPTION (CON, 4)

$$\frac{CON}{N} = +\sum_{i=o}^{11} b_i \left(\frac{YD}{N}\right)_{t-i} + \sum_{i=o}^{3} c_i \left(\frac{VCN\$_{-i}}{.01 * PCON_{-i-1} * N_{-i-1}}\right) + \overset{(480)}{.6098} u_{-1} + e$$

Coefficient	ID	Value	t-ratio
b_0	(1)	.1087	[4.72]
b_1	(2)	.0983	[6.10]
b_2	(3)	.0882	[8.68]
b_3	(4)	.0783	[14.41]
b_4	(5)	.0686	[23.04]
b_5	(6)	.0592	[14.19]
b_6	(7)	.0500	[8.28]
b_7	(8)	.0411	[5.65]
b_8	(9)	.0324	[4.23]
b_9	(10)	.0239	[3.35]
b_{10}	(11)	.0157	[2.76]
b_{11}	(12)	.0077	[2.33]
$\sum_i b_i$		.672	
$\sum_i c_i$		52.9032	
c_0	(476)	27.0447	[4.16]
c_1	(477)	15.8710	[7.94]
c_2	(478)	7.6389	[2.03]
c_3	(479)	2.3486	[.68]

$\bar{R}^2_e$ = .9982

S_e = .0074

$\bar{R}^2$ = .9973

S_u = .0090

d-w = 1.86

SAMPLE PERIOD: 1954.I - 1967.IV

CONSTRAINTS:

b_i: 2nd degree polynomial; constrained zero at t-12

c_i: 2nd degree polynomial; constrained zero at t-4

NOTES: Estimated on July, 1970 National Income Accounts revisions.

I.2 EXPENDITURES ON CONSUMER DURABLES (ECD,6)

$$\frac{ECD}{CON} = \underset{[1.51]}{\overset{(493)}{.2402}} + \underset{[3.50]}{\overset{(491)}{.3265}} \left[\frac{YD}{CON}\right] - \underset{[-3.66]}{\overset{(17)}{.2291}} \left[\frac{N}{CON}\right] - \underset{[-2.52]}{\overset{(494)}{.0034}}\ JIC$$

$$+\sum_{i=o}^{5} b_i \left[\frac{PCD}{PCON}\right] * [.22 + .01 * RCB - Q * \sum_{j=o}^{12} c^j \left\{ \frac{PCD_{-i-j+1} - PCD_{-i-j}}{PCD_{-i-j}} \right\}]$$

$$\underset{[-2.75]}{\overset{(492)}{-.2983}} \left[\frac{KCD_{-1}}{CON}\right] + \overset{(18)}{.6014} u_{-1} + e$$

$b_o = \underset{[-.87]}{\overset{(495)}{-.2164}}$

$b_1 = \underset{[-2.51]}{\overset{(496)}{-.1743}}$

$b_2 = \underset{[-1.10]}{\overset{(497)}{-.1316}}$

$b_3 = \underset{[-.55]}{\overset{(498)}{-.0883}}$

$b_4 = \underset{[-.36]}{\overset{(499)}{-.0445}}$

$b_5 = \overset{(500)}{.00}$

$\sum_{i=o}^{5} b_i = -.6551$

$c = .87$

$\bar{R}_e^2 = .9271$

$S_e = .0041$

$d\text{-}w = 1.75$

$\bar{R}_u^2 = .8877$

$S_u = .0051$

SAMPLE PERIOD: 1954.I - 1968.IV

$$Q = \begin{cases} 0.0 & 1954.I - 1966.IV \\ 4.0/\sum_{j=o}^{11} (.87)^j & 1967.I - 1968.IV \end{cases}$$

CONSTRAINTS: b_i: 2nd degree polynomial constrained to zero at t-5.

I.3 DEPRECIATION ON CONSUMER DURABLES (WCD, 7)

$$WCD = .05625*ECD + .225*KCD_{-1}$$

I.4 STOCK OF CONSUMER DURABLES (KCD, 8)

$$KCD = .25*(ECD-WCD) + KCD_{-1}$$

I.5 IMPUTED INCOME FROM CONSUMER DURABLES (YCD, 9)

$$YCD = .0379 \left\{ \left[\frac{ECD}{8.0}\right] + KCD_{-1} \right\}$$

I.6 PERSONAL CONSUMPTION EXPENDITURES (EPCE, 45)

$$EPCE = CON - WCD - YCD + ECD$$

FIGURE A. 1

DYNAMIC SIMULATION OF REAL CONSUMPTION (1958 DOLLARS)
1958.1 - 1969.4

Actual Value ($billions)	Computed Value ($billions)	Residual ($billions)	Period	
289.172	291.086	1.915	1958	1
292.255	292.075	0.180	1958	2
296.070	294.355	1.714	1958	3
298.450	297.479	0.971	1958	4
302.531	301.076	1.455	1959	1
305.636	305.190	0.446	1959	2
308.269	308.407	-0.138	1959	3
310.660	310.975	-0.315	1959	4
312.755	313.027	-0.272	1960	1
316.944	314.766	2.178	1960	2
316.670	316.721	-0.052	1960	3
318.478	317.979	0.499	1960	4
320.251	319.749	0.502	1961	1
323.199	322.727	0.472	1961	2
325.719	326.083	-0.364	1961	3
329.936	329.911	0.024	1961	4
332.447	333.044	-0.597	1962	1
335.338	335.658	-0.321	1962	2
338.699	337.508	1.191	1962	3
342.702	339.614	3.088	1962	4

FIGURE A.1 (cont'd)

345.863	342.790	3.073	1963	1
348.140	346.893	1.247	1963	2
352.669	351.324	1.345	1963	3
354.118	355.545	-1.427	1963	4
361.269	360.066	1.203	1964	1
364.886	364.803	0.083	1964	2
372.626	370.129	2.497	1964	3
375.814	375.213	0.601	1964	4
379.141	380.135	-0.994	1965	1
386.485	385.590	0.895	1965	2
391.736	391.693	0.042	1965	3
399.201	398.110	1.091	1965	4
403.783	403.805	-0.022	1966	1
407.811	407.771	0.040	1966	2
412.527	410.865	1.662	1966	3
413.086	413.519	-0.433	1966	4
419.746	417.539	2.207	1967	1
423.080	423.106	-0.026	1967	2
426.125	429.213	-3.088	1967	3
429.150	429.150	0.000	1967	4
436.971	435.669	1.302	1968	1
439.570	441.519	-1.949	1968	2
446.631	447.655	-1.024	1968	3
449.083	453.177	-4.094	1968	4
453.960	457.598	-3.638	1969	1
458.316	460.823	-2.507	1969	2
462.702	463.445	-0.743	1969	3
466.063	465.025	1.038	1969	4

APPENDIX B.1

XVII DIVIDEND-PRICE RATIO AND VALUE OF CORPORATE SHARES

Key to symbols: YPCT$: Net corporate profits after taxes, current dollars.
YDV$: Net corporate dividends, current dollars.

XVII.1 DIVIDEND PRICE RATIO (RDP, 126)

$$RDP = \underset{[-3.45]}{\overset{(796)}{-.5964}} \left[\frac{YPCT\$}{YDV\$}\right] + \underset{[6.98]}{\overset{(795)}{.1205}} \max [53.0 - TIME, 0] + \underset{[1.63]}{\overset{(794)}{1.3602}}$$

$$\underset{[-4.42]}{\overset{(801)}{-.5299}} \; Q * W * 400.0 * .13 \sum_{i=o}^{11} (.87)^i \left[\frac{PCON_{-i} - PCON_{-i-1}}{PCON_{-i-1}}\right] + \sum_{i=o}^{4} b_i RCB_{-i}$$

$$\overset{(800)}{+.6895} U_{-1} + e$$

$$b_o = \underset{[3.94]}{\overset{(802)}{.2350}}$$

$$b_1 = \underset{[3.94]}{\overset{(803)}{.1881}}$$

$$b_2 = \underset{[3.94]}{\overset{(804)}{.1410}}$$

$$b_3 = \underset{[3.94]}{\overset{(805)}{.0945}}$$

$$b_4 = \underset{[3.94]}{\overset{(806)}{.0471}}$$

$$\Sigma b_i = .7957$$

$R_e^2 = .946$

$S_e = .156$

$DW = 1.68$

$R_u^2 = .890$

$S_u = .223$

SAMPLE PERIOD: 1954.IV - 1969.II

$$Q = \begin{cases} 1.0 \text{ if } TIME > 80 \\ 0 \text{ if } TIME \leq 80 \end{cases}$$

$$W_t = \sum_{i=o}^{11} v_{t-i}, \qquad v_{t-i} = \begin{cases} (1/12) \text{ if } 400\left[\frac{PCON_{-i} - PCON_{-i-1}}{PCON_{-i-1}}\right] > 1.5 \\ 0 \text{ otherwise} \end{cases}$$

APPENDIX B.2

XVI.1 TERM STRUCTURE EQUATION FOR CORPORATE BOND RATE (RCB, 91)

$$RCB = \underset{[8.45]}{\overset{(890)}{.9004}} + \sum_{i=o}^{18} b_i RCP_{t-i} + \sum_{i=o}^{18} c_i \left(\frac{PCON_{-i}-PCON_{-i-1}}{PCON_{-i-1}}\right)$$

$$+ \underset{[3.80]}{\overset{(893)}{.2736}} \sqrt{\frac{8 * \sum_{i=1}^{8} (RCP)^2_{-i} - (\sum_{i=1}^{8} RCP_{-i})^2}{64.0}} + e$$

b_0 = (891) .2116 [8.82]	b_{10} = (906) .0637 [13.99]	c_o = (892) -1.3036 [-.21]	c_{10} = (924) -1.1480 [-.93]]
b_1 = (897) -.0086 [-.69]	b_{11} = (907) .0610 [13.10]	c_1 = (915) 12.4900 [2.79]	c_{11} = (925) -1.5020 [-1.35]
b_2 = (898) .0101 [1.18]	b_{12} = (908) .0568 [11.64]	c_2 = (916) 9.8210 [3.14]	c_{12} = (926) -1.6910 [-1.64]
b_3 = (899) .0257 [4.30]	b_{13} = (909) .0513 [9.98]	c_3 = (917) 7.4840 [3.45]	c_{13} = (927) -1.7360 [-1.74]
b_4 = (900) .0384 [8.10]	b_{14} = (910) .0446 [8.40]	c_4 = (918) 5.4600 [3.37]	c_{14} = (928) -1.6540 [-1.64]
b_5 = (901) .0484 [10.84]	b_{15} = (911) .0370 [7.04]	c_5 = (919) 3.7310 [2.61]	c_{15} = (929) -1.4640 [-1.45]
b_6 = (902) .0559 [12.27]	b_{16} = (912) .0285 [5.91]	c_6 = (920) 2.2780 [1.60]	c_{16} = (930) -1.1850 [-1.24]
b_7 = (903) .0610 [13.14]	b_{17} = (913) .0194 [5.00]	c_7 = (921) 1.0820 [.75]	c_{17} = (931) -.8353 [-1.05]
b_8 = (904) .0638 [13.80]	b^{18} = (914) .0098 [4.25]	c_8 = (922) .1250 [.09]	c_{18} = (932) -.4342 [-.89]
b_9 = (905) .0650 [14.17]	Σb_i = .94	c_9 = (923) -.6122 [-.46]	$\sum_{i=o}^{18} c_i$ = 28.91

$\bar{R}^2$ = .9850
S_e = .0782
DW = 1.20

SAMPLE PERIOD:
1954.IV - 1966.IV

CONSTRAINTS: RCP_{-1}: 3rd degree polynomial constrained to zero at t-19

$\left(\frac{PCON_{-1}-PCON_{-2}}{PCON_{-2}}\right)$: 3rd degree polynomial constrained to zero at t-19.

BIBLIOGRAPHY

Andersen, L. C., and Carson, K. M. "A Monetarist Model for Economic Stabilization," *Federal Reserve Bank of St. Louis Review,* Vol. 52, No. 4, April 1970.

Ando, A., and Modigliani, F. "The Life Cycle Hypothesis of Saving: Aggregate Implications and Tests," *American Economic Review,* Vol. 53, May 1963, pp. 55-84, and Vol. 54, Part I, March 1964, pp. 111-113.

deLeeuw, F., and Kalchbrenner, J. "Monetary and Fiscal Actions: A Test of Their Relative Importance in Economic Stabilization – Comment," *Federal Reserve Bank of St. Louis Review,* April 1969.

Fair, R. C. "Consumer Sentiment, The Stock Market, and Consumption Functions," Econometric Research Program Research Memorandum No. 119, Princeton University, January, 1971. (b)

Fair, R. C. *A Short-run Forecasting Model of the United States Economy,* D. C. Heath and Company, 1971. (a)

Friend, I., and Adams, G. "The Predictive Ability of Consumer Attitudes, Stock Prices and Non-attitudinal Variables," *Journal of the American Statistical Association,* LIX, December 1964.

Gramlich, E. M. "The Usefulness of Monetary and Fiscal Policies As Stabilization Tools," *Journal of Money Credit and Banking,* May 1971.

Houthakker, H. S. "On Some Determinants of Saving in Developed and Underdeveloped Countries," in *Problems in Economic Development,* edited by E. A. G. Robinson (London, MacMillan & Co., 1965), Chapter 10, pp. 212-224.

Hyman, S. H. "Consumer Durable Spending," *Brookings Papers on Economic Activity,* 1970.

Landsberg, M. "The Life Cycle Hypothesis: A Reinterpretation and Empirical Test," *American Economic Review,* LX, March 1970, pp. 175-183.

Leff, N. "Dependency Rates and Savings Rates," *American Economic Review,* Vol. LIX, No. 5, December 1969, pp. 886-896.

Lydal, H. F. "Saving and Wealth," *Australian Economic Papers,* December 1963, pp. 228-250.

Modigliani, F., and Brumberg, R. "Utility Analysis and Aggregate Consumption Functions: An Attempt at Integration," Unpublished.

Modigliani, F. "The Life Cycle Hypothesis of Saving, The Demand for Wealth and The Supply of Capital," *Social Research*, Vol. 33, No. 2, Summer 1966, pp. 160-217.

Modigliani, F. "The Life Cycle Hypothesis of Saving and Intercountry Differences in the Saving Ratio," in *Induction, Growth and Trade,* Essays in Honor of Sir Roy Harrod, Clarendon Press, Oxford, 1970.

Modigliani, F., and Sutch, R. "Innovations in Interest Rate Policy," *American Economic Review,* LVI, No. 2, May 1966, pp. 178-197.

Modigliani, F., Rasche, R., and Cooper, J. P., "Central Bank Policy, The Money Supply, and the Short-Term Rate of Interest," *Journal of Money, Credit and Banking,* Vol. 2 (May, 1970), pp. 166-218.

Singh, B., Drost, H., and Kumar, R. "The Postwar Theories of Consumption Function--An Empirical Evaluation," University of Toronto, Multilith.

Sprinkel, B. W. *Money and Stock Prices,* New York, Irwin, 1964.

Sutch, R. "Expectations, Risk and the Term Structure of Interest Rates," Ph.D. thesis, Department of Economics, MIT (1969).

Turnovsky, S. J. "Empirical Evidence on the Formation of Price Expectations," *Journal of the American Statistical Assoication,* Vol. 65, No. 332, December 1970.

Weber, W. R. "The Effect of Interest Rates on Aggregate Consumption," *American Economic Review,* LX, No. 4, September 1970, pp. 591-600.

Errata

Page 25, paragraph 2, line 7: "brough" should read "brought."

Page 26: equation (s.3) should read "$M_y(t) = \frac{1}{1 - c} = M_y$ for all t."

Page 26: equation (s.4) should read "$M_c(t) = \frac{c}{1 - c} = M_c$ for all t."

Page 26, equation (2′): add "$+ c_o$" at the end of the equation.

Page 32, paragraph 2, line 1: "dashed line e" should read "dotted line e."

Page 32, paragraph 3, line 4: "About 2/3 of the peal" should read "About 2/3 of the peak."

Page 34, line 8: "through this decline" should read "though this decline."

Page 49, paragraph 3, line 8: "cumulated effect of GNP$" should read "cumulated effect on GNP$."

Page 61, paragraph 3, line 3: "than the individual coefficients" should read "then the individual coefficients."

CONTENTS

Volume I Essays in Macroeconomics

Preface ix

Introduction xi

Part I. The Monetary Mechanism

1. "The Monetarist Controversy or, Should We Forsake Stabilization Policies?" *American Economic Review* 67 (March 1977): 1–19. 3
2. "Liquidity Preference and the Theory of Interest and Money," *Econometrica* 12 (January 1944): 45–88. Plus "Postscript" of the paper in *The Critics of Keynesian Economics,* edited by Henry Hazlitt, pp. 183–184. D. Van Nostrand Co., Inc., 1960. 23
3. "The Monetary Mechanism and Its Interaction with Real Phenomena," *Review of Economics and Statistics* 45 (February 1963):79–107. 69
4. "Liquidity Preference," *International Encyclopedia of the Social Sciences,"* edited by David L. Sills, vol. 9, pp. 394–409. Cromwell, Collier and McMillan, Inc., 1968. 98
5. "The Channels of Monetary Policy in the Federal Reserve-MIT-University of Pennsylvania Econometric Model of the United States," *Modelling the Economy,* based on papers presented at the Social Science Research Council's Conference on Economic Modelling, July 1972, edited by G. A. Renton, pp. 240–267. London: Heinemann Educational Books, 1975. 114
6. "Impacts of Fiscal Actions on Aggregate Income and the Monetarist Controversy: Theory and Evidence," (with Albert Ando, and with the assistance of J. Giangrande), *Monetarism,* edited by Jerome L. Stein, pp. 17–42. Studies in Monetary Economy, vol. 1. Amsterdam: North-Holland Pub. Co., 1976. 142

Part II. The Demand and Supply of Money and Other Deposits

7. "Central Bank Policy, the Money Supply, and the Short-Term Rate of Interest," (with Robert Rasche and J. Phillip Cooper), *Journal of Money, Credit, and Banking* 2 (1970): 166–218. 171

8. "The Dynamics of Portfolio Adjustment and the Flow of Savings Through Financial Intermediaries," *Savings Deposits, Mortgages, and Housing: Studies for the Federal Reserve-MIT-Penn Econometric Model,* edited by Edward M. Gramlich and Dwight M. Jaffee, pp. 63–102. Lexington Books, 1972. 224

Part III. The Term Structure of Interest Rates

9. "Innovations in Interest Rate Policy," (with Richard Sutch), *American Economic Review* 56 (May 1966): 178–197. Paper presented at the seventy-eighth annual meeting of the American Economics Association, Dec. 28–30, 1965. 267

10. "Debt Management and the Term Structure of Interest Rates: An Empirical Analysis," (with Richard Sutch), *Journal of Political Economy* 75, part 2 (August 1967): 569–589. Paper presented at the Conference of University Professors, The American Bankers Assoc., Sept. 19, 1966. 287

11. "Inflation, Rational Expectations and the Term Structure of Interest Rates," (with Robert J. Shiller), *Economica,* February 1973, pp. 12–43. 309

Part IV. The Determinants of Investment

12. "On the Role of Expectations of Price and Technological Change in an Investment Function," (with Albert K. Ando, Robert Rasche, and Stephen J. Turnovsky), *International Economic Review* 15 (June 1974): 384–414. 345

Part V. The Determinants of Wages and Prices

13. "A Generalization of the Phillips Curve for a Developing Country," (with Ezio Tarantelli), *Review of Economic Studies* 40 (April 1973): 203–223. 379

14. "New Development on the Oligopoly Front," *Journal of Political Economy* 66 (June 1958): 215–232. 400

15. "Targets for Monetary Policy in the Coming Year," (with Lucas Papademos), *Brookings Papers on Economic Activity* 1 (1975): 141–163. 419

Contents of Volumes 2 and 3 443

Acknowledgments 447

Name Index 449

CONTENTS

Volume 3 The Theory of Finance and Other Essays

Preface ix

Introduction xi

Part I. Essays in the Theory of Finance

1. "The Cost of Capital, Corporation Finance and the Theory of Investment," (with Merton H. Miller), *American Economic Review* 48 (June 1958): 261–297. 3
2. "Dividend Policy, Growth and the Valuation of Shares," (with Merton H. Miller), *Journal of Business* 34 (October 1961): 411–433. 40
3. "Corporate Income Taxes and the Cost of Capital: A Correction," (with Merton H. Miller), *American Economic Review* (June 1963): 433–443. 63
4. "A Theory and Test of Credit Rationing," (with Dwight M. Jaffee), *American Economic Review* 59 (December 1969): 850–872. 74
5. "Some Economic Implications of the Indexing of Financial Assets with Special Reference to Mortgages," *The New Inflation and Monetary Policy* by Mario Monti, pp. 90–116. London and Basingstoke: Macmillan, 1976. 97

Part II. Stabilization Policies

6. "Inflation, Balance of Payments Deficit and their Cure through Monetary Policy: The Italian Example," (with Giorgio La Malfa), *Banca Nazionale del Lavoro Quarterly Review*, no. 80 (March 1967): 3–47. 127
7. "The 1974 Report of the President's Council of Economic Advisers: A Critique of Past and Prospective Policies," *American Economic Review* 64 (September 1974): 544–557. 172
8. "Monetary Policy for the Coming Quarters: The Conflicting Views," (with Lucas Papademos), *New England Economic Review*, March/April 1976, pp. 2–35. 186

9. *The Management of an Open Economy with "100% Plus" Wage Indexation,* (with Tommaso Padoa-Schioppa), Essays in International Finance, no. 130. International Finance Section, Dept. of Economics, Princeton University, Dec. 1978. 220

Part III. Essays in International Finance

10. "A Suggestion for Solving the International Liquidity Problem," (with Peter Kenen), *Banca Nazionale del Lavoro Quarterly Review,* no. 76 (March 1966): 3–17. 263

11. *The Reform of the International Payments System,* (with Hossein Askari), Essays in International Finance, no. 89, pp. 3–28. International Finance Section, Dept. of Economics, Princeton University, Sept. 1971. 278

12. "International Capital Movements, Fixed Parities, and Monetary and Fiscal Policies," *Development and Planning: Essays in Honor of Paul Rosenstein-Rodan,* edited by Jagdish Bhagwati and Richard S. Eckaus, pp. 239–253. London: George Allen & Unwin, Ltd., 1972. 305

13. "The International Transfer of Capital and the Propagation of Domestic Disturbances Under Alternative Payment Systems," (with Hossein Askari), *Banca Nazionale del Lavoro Quarterly Review,* no. 107 (December 1973): 3–18. 321

14. "Balance of Payments Implications of the Oil Crisis and How to Handle Them through International Cooperation," *1974 Economic Report of the President,* pp. 650–655. Washington, D.C.: U.S. Government Printing Office, 1974. Prepared statement for Hearings before the Joint Economic Committee, Congress of the United States, Ninety-third Congress, Second Session, Part 2, Feb. 19–22, 1974. 338

Part IV. The Role of Expectations and Plans in Economic Behavior

15. "Production Planning over Time and the Nature of the Expectation and Planning Horizon," (with Franz E. Hohn), *Econometrica* 23 (January 1955): 46–66. 347

16. *The Role of Anticipations and Plans in Economic Behavior and Their Use in Economic Analysis and Forecasting,* (with Kalman J. Cohen), Studies in Business Expectations and Planning, no. 4. pp. 9–11, 14–42, 81–96, 158–166. Bureau of Economic and Business Research, University of Illinois, January 1961. 368

17. "Forecasting Uses of Anticipatory Data on Investment and Sales," (with H. M. Weingartner), *Quarterly Journal of Economics* 72 (February 1958): 23–54. 426

Part V. Miscellaneus

18. "The Predictability of Social Events," (with Emile Grunberg), *Journal of Political Economy* 62 (December 1954): 465–478. 461

Contents of Volumes 1 and 2 477

Acknowledgments 481

Name Index 485

ACKNOWLEDGMENTS

The author, editor, and The MIT Press wish to thank the publishers of the following essays for permission to reprint them here. The selections are arranged chronologically, with chapter numbers in brackets.

''Fluctuations in the Saving-Income Ratio: A Problem in Economic Forecasting,'' *Studies in Income and Wealth,* vol. 11, pp. 371–402, 427–431. New York: National Bureau of Economic Research, 1949. Paper presented at Conference on Research in Income and Wealth. Copyright 1949 by the National Bureau of Economic Research. [1]

''Utility Analysis and the Consumption Function: An Interpretation of Cross-Section Data,'' by Franco Modigliani and Richard Brumberg. In *Post Keynesian Economics,* edited by Kenneth K. Kurihara. Copyright 1954 by the Trustees of Rutgers College in New Jersey. Reprinted by permission of the Rutgers University Press. Pp. 388–436. [3]

''The 'Permanent Income' and the 'Life Cycle' Hypothesis of Saving Behavior: Comparison and Tests,'' (with Albert Ando), *Consumption and Saving,* vol. 2, pp. 74–108, 138–147. Wharton School of Finance and Commerce, University of Pennsylvania, 1960. Copyright 1960 by the University of Pennsylvania. [6]

''Long-run Implications of Alternative Fiscal Policies and the Burden of the National Debt,'' *Economic Journal* 71 (December 1961): 730–755. Copyright 1961 by the Cambridge University Press. [11]

''The 'Life Cycle' Hypothesis of Saving: Aggregate Implications and Tests,'' (with Albert Ando), *American Economic Review* 53, part 1 (March 1963): 55–84. Copyright 1963 by the American Economic Association. [7]

''The Life Cycle Hypothesis of Saving, the Demand for Wealth and the Supply of Capital,'' *Social Research* 33 (Summer 1966): 160–217. Copyright 1966 by the New School of Social Research. [9]

''The Life Cycle Hypothesis of Saving and Intercountry Differences in the Saving Ratio,'' *Induction, Growth and Trade: Essays in Honour of Sir Roy Harrod,* edited by W. A. Eltis, M. FG. Scott, and J. N. Wolfe (1970), pp. 197–225, by permission of Oxford University Press. [10]

''Monetary Policy and Consumption: Linkages via Interest Rate and Wealth Effects in the FMP Model,'' *Consumer Spending and Monetary Policy: The Linkages,* Conference Series No. 5, pp. 9–84. Copyright 1971 by the Federal Reserve Bank of Boston. [12]

''Consumption Decisions Under Uncertainty,'' (with Jacques Drèze), *Journal of Economic Theory* 5 (December 1972): 308–335. Copyright 1972 by the Academic Press. [5]

''The Life Cycle Hypothesis of Saving Twenty Years Later,'' *Contemporary Issues in Economics,* edited by Michael Parkin, pp. 2–35. Copyright 1975 by the Manchester University Press. [2]

''The Consumption Function in a Developing Economy and the Italian Experience,'' (with Ezio Tarantelli), *American Economic Review* 65 (December 1975): 825–842. Copyright 1975 by the American Economic Association. [8]

Name Index

Ackley, C., 52, 72, 321
Adams, G., 449, 515
Aitchison, J., 233n
Andersen, Leonall C., 482, 482n, 515, 575
Ando, Albert K., 47, 48, 56, 57, 61, 63, 65, 68, 74, 229–274, 243n, 247n, 275–302, 281n, 282n, 297n, 302, 303, 308, 316, 318, 319, 321, 350n, 370, 379n, 380n, 385n, 407n, 411, 427n, 428n, 435n, 442n, 446, 447, 448, 515, 516
Arrow, Kenneth J., 203, 217, 225n

Ball, R. J., 55, 72
Bannink, R., 74, 75, 316n, 322
Bans, R. B., 190n
Bassie, V. Lewis, 34, 34n, 35n, 190n, 196n
Bathia, K. B., 61, 72
Beals, Ralph, 198n, 277n, 415n, 435n
Bentzel, R., 49, 50, 72, 330n, 370
Bischoff, Charles W., 442n
Boddy, F., 192n
Bodkin, Ronald G., 261, 302
Boulding, Kenneth E., 84n, 120n
Bowen, W. G., 415n, 425, 425n
Brady, Dorothy S., 18–19, 18n, 19n, 42, 47, 72, 113–115, 120n, 129, 250n, 321
Brown, J. A. C., 233n
Brown, E. C., 282n, 302, 379n, 427n
Brown, R., 47, 73
Brown, T. M., 43, 55, 56, 72, 185, 190n, 193n, 196n, 197n, 321
Brumberg, Richard E., 41, 43, 44, 46, 49, 55, 72, 74, 79–127, 128–189, 191n, 193n, 195n, 197n, 230–274, 275–302, 276n, 302, 304, 314–321, 331, 370, 385, 386n, 427n, 435n, 516
Buchanan, James M., 415, 415n, 417n, 419, 431n

Carlucci, G., 321
Carlson, Keith M., 482, 575
Caron, M., 314n, 321
Cassel, Gustave, 117n
Chakravarty, Sukhamoy, 415n
Christ, Carl F., 79n
Clark, Colin, 4n
Cochrane, W. W., 98n
Cooper, J. Philip, 454, 516
Cotula, F., 314n, 321
Creamer, Daniel, 80n, 190n
Cyert, Richard, 79n

Davis, R. G., 415n, 425, 425n
Davis, Tom E., 196n, 321
Deaton, A. S., 59, 72
Debreu, G., 225n
De Leeuw, Frank, 442n, 503, 515
Denison, E. F. 406, 411
Di Fenizio, F., 310n, 321
Dolde, Walter C., 54, 62, 75, 190n, 317, 322

Drake, P., 55, 72
Drèze, J. H., 45, 73, 198–226, 225n
Drose, H., 448
Duesenberry, James S., 19n, 43, 55, 56, 73, 115n, 129, 190n, 196n, 302n, 321, 370
Durbin, J., 283, 285, 302

Eisner, Robert, 251, 302
Elliott, J. R., 415n
Enzler, Jared, 442n
Evans, M. K., 55, 73
Ezekiel, Mordecai, 190n

Fair, Ray C., 448–449, 450, 452, 515
Farrell, Michael J., 307, 321
Fazio, Antonio, 382n
Ferber, Robert, 196n, 197n, 275n
Fisher, Franklin M., 47, 73, 275n
Fisher, Irving, 41, 44, 73, 199, 225n, 321
Fisher, Janet A., 98n, 108n, 115, 117n, 120n, 194n, 195n
Fisher, M. R., 48, 73, 250n, 302
Florissi, C., 50n, 51n, 73
Frane, L., 303
Franklin, P., 197n
Friedman, Milton, 44–45, 47, 49–50, 55, 57, 58n, 62, 73, 95n, 230–274, 250n, 275, 303, 307, 308, 317, 321, 333n, 370
Friedman, Rose D., 18–19, 18n, 19n, 42, 47, 72, 113–115, 321
Friend, Irwin, 191n, 250n, 303, 449, 515

Gevers, Louis, 198n
Goldfeld, Stephen M., 275n
Goldsmith, Raymond W., 56, 73, 84n, 117n, 120n, 143, 191n, 192n, 196n, 296, 303, 321, 370, 379n, 380n, 382, 388, 411
Gramley, Edward, 442n
Gramlich, Edward M., 504, 505, 505n, 515
Graziani, A., 310n, 321
Griziotti, B., 417n
Gupta, K. L., 51, 73
Guthrie, H. W., 432n

Hakansson, N. H., 45, 46, 73
Hall, Margaret, 415n
Hamburger, William, 56, 73, 84n, 129, 178–181, 190n, 193n, 196n, 303
Hansen, Alvin H., 5, 5n, 6, 415n
Harris, Seymour, 190n
Harrod, Sir Roy F., 44, 73, 382, 404, 411, 435n
Hart, Albert G., 123
Hart, B. I., 4n, 15n
Heins,, Albert, 192n
Heller, Walter, 192n
Hicks, John R., 190n, 194n
Hirshleifer, Jack, 225n
Holter, William, 192n
Houthakker, Hendrik S., 251n, 303, 383, 384–389, 389n, 390, 390n, 405, 411, 448, 515
Hyman, S. H., 449, 452, 515

Kalchbrenner, John H., 503, 515
Kaldor, Nicholas, 73, 307, 321, 411
Kalecki, Michael, 19n
Kareken, J. H., 282n, 302, 379n, 427n
Katona, George, 98n, 105n, 190n, 262n–263n
Kendrick, M. S., 303
Keynes, John Maynard, 41, 73, 79, 79n, 82n, 120n, 121–122, 128, 129, 151, 190n, 191n, 193n, 197n, 303, 305, 321
Kilham, Lawrence, 323n
Klein, Lawrence R., 80n, 117n, 118n, 122–127, 126n, 190n, 303
Kopf, D. H., 415n, 425, 425n
Koyck, L. M., 321
Kravis, I., 250n, 303
Kreinen, M. E., 303
Kuh, Edwin, 303
Kumar, R. C., 59, 74, 448
Kurihara, Kenneth, 41, 191n, 427n
Kuznets, Simon, 7, 7n, 8, 9, 10, 11, 11n, 32n, 35n, 42, 73, 95n, 129, 143, 190n, 191n, 192n, 321

Landsberger, M., 48, 73, 448, 515
Lebergott, S., 303
Leff, N., 50, 51n, 73, 448, 515
Leland, H. E., 45, 73, 213, 214, 215, 225n
Lerner, A. P., 415n, 418
Lipsey, E., 379n
Livingston, Morris S., 190n
Lowe, Adolph, 3, 323n
Lydall, H. F., 57, 73, 335n, 340n, 370, 448, 516

Mack, Ruth P., 98n, 100n
Madansky, A., 256n, 257n
Marshack, Jacob, 120n, 202n, 225n
Marshall, Alfred, 12n
Marx, Karl, 310
Mayer, Thomas, 71n–72n, 73
Meade, J. E., 382n, 411, 415, 415n, 416n, 418n, 420, 420n, 436
Meiselman, D. I., 503
Mendelson, M., 379n
Menderhausen, Horst, 117n
Merton, R. C., 45, 46, 73
Meyer, J. R., 303
Miller, Merton H., 298n, 304, 348, 370, 415n, 424n
Mincer, J., 281n, 303
Mirman, L. J., 214, 225n
Modigliani, Franco, 41, 43, 44, 45, 46, 47, 48, 49, 49n, 50, 50n, 55, 56, 59, 60, 63, 64, 65, 67, 68, 73, 74, 79n, 128n, 190n,

191n, 193n, 195n, 196n, 197n, 243n, 247n, 298n, 303, 304, 308, 316, 317, 318, 319, 321, 322, 348, 370, 385, 385n, 386, 407n, 411, 415n, 424n, 427n, 435n, 445, 445n, 448, 454, 456, 516
Morgan, James N., 84n
Morgenstern, O., 199, 225n
Mosak, Jacob L., 5, 5n, 15, 16, 33, 34, 82n, 190n
Mueller, Eva L., 263n
Musgrave, Richard A., 415, 415n, 424n

Neisser, Hans P., 3, 193n, 323n, 329, 371
Nelson, C., 192n
Niccoli, A., 308, 321
Norman, Morris, 442n

Ohlin, Bertil, 193n
Orcutt, Guy H., 80n, 128, 190n

Pasinetti, L. L., 62, 74
Patinkin, Don, 193n
Pearson, K., 304
Pestican, P., 212, 225n
Pigou, A. C., 151–152, 193n
Polak, J. J., 191n
Pratt, J. W., 202–204, 205, 225n
Projector, D. S., 74

Rasche, Robert M., 48, 74, 442n, 454, 516
Reid, Margaret, 43, 74, 100n, 109, 109n, 110–113, 112n, 113n, 129, 190n, 250n, 266n
Rey, G. M., 321
Ricardo, David, 322, 431n
Ricci, Umberto, 81n, 191n
Rolph, E. R., 415n
Rothschild, M., 214, 225n
Roy, A. D., 80n, 128, 190n

Saad, Farid, 323n
Samuelson, Paul A., 45, 74, 190n
Sandmo, Agnar, 198n, 213, 214, 216, 225n
Sauerlender, O. H., 79n, 128n
Savage, L. J., 199, 225n
Scitovsky, Tibor, 129, 152, 190n, 193n, 415n
Seltzer, L. H., 304
Shapiro, Harold, 442n
Simpson, T. D., 503
Singh, B., 59, 74, 448
Sitzia, Bruno, 68n, 305n, 313n, 322
Smelker, Mary W., 84n
Smithies, Arthur, 5, 5n, 6–9, 7n, 8n, 9n, 10, 10n, 11, 14, 14n, 15, 15n, 16, 16n, 33, 34, 34n, 190n
Solow, Robert M., 282n, 302, 379n, 427n
Somermeyer, W. H., 74, 75, 316n, 322
Spiro, Alan, 55, 276n
Sprinkel, Beryl W., 516

Staab, Josephine H., 113n
Stiglitz, Joseph E., 198n, 214, 225
Stone, Richard, 57, 58, 58n, 70, 74–75, 320, 322
Suits, Daniel, 304, 427n
Sutch, Richard, 323n, 456, 516
Swamy, S., 50, 75
Sylos-Labini, P., 309n, 310n, 311, 322
Szwarc, Wlodzimierc, 221n

Tarantelli, Ezio, 59, 67, 69n, 74, 75, 305–321, 309n, 322
Terborgh, George, 35n
Ter Minassian, T., 322
Theil, H., 278n, 304
Tinbergen, Jan, 197n
Tobin, James, 49, 50, 54, 62, 75, 129, 190n, 317, 322, 382n, 386n, 411, 432n
Turnovsky, Stephen J., 517
Tyndall, David Gordon, 196n

Ulizzi, A., 308, 322

Vickrey, William, 100n, 113n, 415n, 426n, 429n
Vinci, S., 321, 322
Von Neumann, John, 15n, 199, 225n

Watson, G. S., 283, 285, 302
Watts, H. W., 251n
Weber, Warren R., 71, 75, 320, 322, 448, 450, 517
Weiss, G. S., 74
Westfield, Fred, 275n
Woytinsky, W. S., 5, 5n, 11–12, 34, 34n, 190n

Zellner, A., 304

LI